Leasehold Reform, Housing and Urban Development Act 1993

AUSTRALIA
The Law Book Company
Brisbane : Sydney : Melbourne : Perth

CANADA
Carswell
Ottawa : Toronto : Calgary : Montreal : Vancouver

Agents:
Steimatzky's Agency Ltd., Tel Aviv;
N. M. Tripathi (Private) Ltd., Bombay;
Eastern Law House (Private) Ltd., Calcutta;
M.P.P. House, Bangalore;
Universal Book Traders, Delhi;
Aditya Books, Delhi;
MacMillan Shuppan KK, Tokyo;
Pakistan Law House, Karachi

Leasehold Reform, Housing and Urban Development Act 1993

with annotations by

Professor Phillip Kenny

LL.B., Dip.Crim., LL.M., Solicitor, Head of Department of Law,
University of Northumbria, Consultant to
Messrs. Dickinson Dees, Solicitors, Newcastle Upon Tyne.

Additional material by Chris Himsworth, B.A., LL.B.,
Department of Public Law, University of Edinburgh
and Paul Finch, LL.B., Solicitor,
Messrs. Dickinson Dees, Solicitors,
Newcastle Upon Tyne.

LONDON
SWEET & MAXWELL
1993

Published in 1993 by
Sweet & Maxwell Limited of
South Quay Plaza,
183 Marsh Wall, London
Typeset by MFK Typesetting Ltd.,
Hitchin, Herts.
Printed and bound in Great Britain by
Butler & Tanner Ltd., Frome and London

A CIP catalogue record for this book is available
from The British Library

ISBN 0–421–49810–2

CONTENTS

Leasehold Reform, Housing and Urban Development Act 1993

References are to page numbers

TABLE OF CASES

References are to sections and Schedules

Where a section number appears followed by N, this refers to the notes for that particular section or subsection.

e.g. s.33N refers to the General Note following s.33
s.33(5)N refers to the notes for subs. (5) of s.33

TABLE OF CASES

TABLE OF STATUTES

References are to sections and Schedules

Where a section number appears followed by N, this refers to the notes for that particular section or subsection.

e.g. s.33N refers to the General Note following s.33
s.33(5)N refers to the notes for subs. (5) of s.33

TABLE OF STATUTORY INSTRUMENTS

References are to sections and Schedules

Where a section number appears followed by N, this refers to the notes for that particular section or subsection.

e.g. s.33N refers to the General Note following s.33
s.33(5)N refers to the notes for subs. (5) of s.33

LEASEHOLD REFORM, HOUSING AND URBAN DEVELOPMENT ACT 1993*

(1993 c. 28)

ARRANGEMENT OF SECTIONS

PART I

LANDLORD AND TENANT

CHAPTER I

COLLECTIVE ENFRANCHISEMENT IN CASE OF TENANTS OF FLATS

Preliminary

Preliminary inquiries by tenants

The initial notice

Participating tenants and nominee purchaser

Procedure following giving of initial notice

Applications to court or leasehold valuation tribunal

Termination of acquisition procedures

---

* Annotations by Professor Phillip H. Kenny, LL.B., Dip.Crim., LL.M., Solicitor, Head of Department of Law, University of Northumbria; Consultant to Messrs. Dickinson Dees, Solicitors, Newcastle-upon-Tyne; annotations on the Urban Regeneration Agency contributed by Paul Finch, LL.B., Solicitor of Messrs. Dickinson Dees, Solicitors, Newcastle-upon-Tyne; annotations on the Scottish provisions (Pt. II, Chap. II, by Chris Himsworth, B.A., LL.B., Department of Public Law, University of Edinburgh.

CHAPTER II

INDIVIDUAL RIGHT OF TENANT OF FLAT TO ACQUIRE NEW LEASE

PART II

PUBLIC SECTOR HOUSING

CHAPTER I

ENGLAND AND WALES

Right to buy

Abolition of certain ancillary rights

Right to acquire on rent to mortgage terms

Other rights of secure tenants

Housing welfare services

Delegation of housing management

Priority of charges securing repayment of discount

An Act to confer rights to collective enfranchisement and lease renewal on tenants of flats; to make further provision with respect to enfranchisement by tenants of houses; to make provision for auditing the management, by landlords or other persons, of residential property and for the approval of codes of practice relating thereto; to amend Parts III and IV of the Landlord and Tenant Act 1987; to confer jurisdiction on leasehold valuation tribunals as respects Crown land; to make provision for rendering void agreements preventing the occupation of leasehold property by persons with mental disorders; to amend Parts II, IV and V of the Housing Act 1985, Schedule 2 to the Housing Associations Act 1985, Parts I and III and sections 248 and 299 of the Housing (Scotland) Act 1987, Part III of the Housing Act 1988, and Part VI of the Local Government and Housing Act 1989; to make provision with respect to certain disposals requiring consent under Part II of the Housing Act 1985, including provision for the payment of a levy; to alter the basis of certain contributions by the Secretary of State under section 569 of that Act; to establish and confer functions on a body to replace the English Industrial Estates Corporation and to be known as the Urban Regeneration Agency; to provide for the designation of certain urban and other areas and to make provision as to the effect of such designation; to amend section 23 of the Land Compensation Act 1961, section 98 of the Local Government, Planning and Land Act 1980 and section 27 of the Housing and Planning Act 1986; to make further provision with respect to urban development corporations and urban development areas; and for connected purposes.

[20th July 1993]

PARLIAMENTARY DEBATES

Hansard, H.C. Vol. 213, cols. 152, 831, 842; Vol. 218, cols. 832, 937, 988; Vol. 226, col. 645; H.L. Vol. 543, cols. 85, 539, 930, 972, 1016, 1027, 1228, 1255, 1300; Vol. 544, cols. 9, 40, 79, 121, 598, 1244, 1271, 1349; Vol. 545, cols. 807, 1184, 1216, 1252, 1651, 1860, 1926; Vol. 546, col. 175; Vol. 547, col. 1522.

The Bill was discussed in Standing Committee B between November 10, 1992 and January 26, 1993.

INTRODUCTION AND GENERAL NOTE

The Leasehold Reform, Housing and Urban Development Act 1993 covers three quite distinct areas.

Part I—Landlord and Tenant

This part is really a "Landlord and Tenant Act". It fulfils the Government's manifesto promise to better the position of the long leaseholder of a flat. It is a radical piece of legislation. Since 1980 there has been a wealth of landlord and tenant legislation but none of this character. It gives most owners of long leases of flats a right either to *collective enfranchisement* or an *individual right* over a new lease.

Part I of the Act, which contains important and very complex new rights given to tenants of flats, has an unusual history. For some years the Lord Chancellor's Department through the Law Commission had been examining commonhold—a strata title alternative for flat-ownership. As the 1991 general election approached it became clear that the tenant flat lobby was vocal and potentially decisive. Thus, the present Bill (also known as the marginal London seats lifeboat measure) was born. A promise was made by the government to provide enfranchisement for tenants of long leases of flats. There was no usual green and white paper stage, the manifesto promise, as it were, came into the world fully clothed. After the election as it came to give effect to this rash promise a fairly complex Bill emerged. During the passage of the Bill, as will be seen, many concessions were made to different interest groups.

The present commentator has examined each state of landlord and tenant legislation over the last two decades and, though this is a hard prize to allocate, is convinced that the present is the most complex. There are many hurdles for tenants to overcome in achieving collective enfranchisement and the price and effort will, it is prophesised, both prove too great. The right to an individual extended lease will prove more attractive. The effect, however, of making the tenant's position attractive is not negative for the landlord. The Act requires full value to be paid and creates a population of tenants who will have a long-term incentive to pay this full value. Although the interests of those who have invested in the reversions of flat leases are affected in complex ways, the result on the whole is to create a market-place for those reversionary investments which will become very healthy indeed as the apparent threats of the Bill are transformed into the opportunities created by the Act. Does the Act really sound the death knell for the grander estates of Central London? As the Bill proceeded through Parliament this outcome was certainly feared. Chapter IV of Pt. I contains complex provisions permitting continuing estate management schemes and this and the complexity of the Act will assist in maintaining the status quo. However, the framework for collective enfranchisement now created can be simplified by a government of a different hue and will inevitably pave the way for commonhold.

The right to enfranchise given to flat-owners follows on several legislative attempts to improve their position. The imposition of unfair service charges has been attacked in the Landlord and Tenant Act 1985; the difficulties of discovering who is the landlord in some way solved by the same Act; the notorious problem of bad management grappled with in Pt. II of the Landlord and Tenant Act 1987 and a complex right of pre-emption conferred by Pt. I of that Act. To those involved in this area of practice many of the reforms have seemed to exist in a different sphere from "real life". The extraordinary vastness of the legislation in this area and its ever-increasing disjunction from practical reality are two very large factors. Where will the new legislation fit into this large and tangled tapestry?

First, it may be regarded as a staging post on the road to the introduction of *commonhold tenure*. This has become something of a "jam tomorrow" Government promise. For existing flats the logic of the position may be that they will at some future day first be able to use the new machinery of *collective enfranchisement* and then when future legislation permits convert to commonhold. In the meantime, though, three questions will be asked by the property industry—does the *risk* of enfranchisement affect the viability of new development; are existing flats affected as investment vehicles and in either case can the Act be avoided in its effect? The answer to the first is that the possibility of such enfranchisement increases the desirability of new leasehold flats. The developer will look to its reward from the sale and not the continued management. This will lead the adviser, as may have been the dictate of sensible practice for some time, to recommend that new flat developments are from the start established with a common-ownership management company as landlord and the developer "bows out". As to the second question it must have been clear for the last few years that the investment potential of blocks of flats was cast adrift on the uncertain shoals of imminent legislation. The valuation principles established by Sched. 5 will require careful examination. Clearly the potential for collective enfranchisement increases the value of each flat and by that token the value of the whole. Certainly it may be difficult to look upon such blocks as long-term income producing investments (but see below for possibilities of evading the Act) but, the upward pressure on values of the possibility of enfranchisement may provide opportunities to transform a block of flats in the relatively short-term. Pt. I was much amended in its passage through Parliament. Much of the attack on the Bill came from the Conservative side of both Houses. There were very significant amendments which alter the character of the final Act of Parliament: (a) the collective right of enfranchisement and the individual right to an extended lease became *alternatives* at a late stage in the Bill; (b) a residence qualification for the individual right to an extended lease was added to the Bill; (c) a complex residence qualification for the collective right to enfranchisement was introduced—in fact in the passage of the Bill the qualifying conditions for collective enfranchisement were changed in a number of ways which are in general to the disadvantage of tenants; (d) property which is designated as conditionally exempt from inheritance tax under Inheritance Tax Act 1984 is in effect excluded from the right to collective enfranchisement (s.31). This amendment made in the Lords is of some benefit in the preservation of historically important estates.

Pt. I of the Act also makes some amendments to Leasehold Reform Act 1967 and introduces a new tenants' right to a management audit.

Part II—Public Sector Housing

This part of the Act contains a large number of changes in the area of public sector housing.

The first group of sections deals with the right to buy under the Housing Act 1985. First of all certain tenants' rights are abolished. These are the right to a mortgage, the right to defer completion and the right to a shared ownership lease. The opposition made much of this ostensible removal of rights for tenants. But, in truth, they were of no significance, only crocodile tears were wept.

A considerable section of the Act (ss.104–116) introduces the new right to acquire on rent to mortgage terms. This allows the secure tenant to translate the amount of rent payments into the purchase of a proportion of the home together with a right to purchase the remaining proportion. Given the ready availability of mortgage finance to purchase the whole at a discounted price it is probably another unnecessary exercise in the parliamentary draftsman's skill.

The remainder of Chap. I deals with other aspects of public sector housing as follows. They continue the twin fork of conservative public sector housing policy—increasing tenant's rights and decreasing the importance of local authority housing. This is carried out by a strengthened tenant right to deal with disrepair, a right to compensation for improvements and complex provisions dealing further with the delegation of housing management, disposal of local authority housing and control of local authority housing finance. It will be for the social historian of the future to describe the benefits to British society achieved by the consistent approach begun in the 1980 Housing Act and nearing completion in the present Act. The process of removing housing from the huge mass ownership by local authorities of council housing—the legacy most frequently praised of the last lengthy conservative occupation of office and very often the proudest boast of the Macmillan years—will continue.

Part III—Development of Urban and Other Areas

Finally, 23 sections of and four Schedules to the Act are taken up with establishing the Urban Regeneration Agency. It may be that no historian will ever establish clearly the number of quangos established during the past 13 years of Conservative Government. The establishment of this last agency follows a very familiar pattern of Statutory Corporation. The powers of the Urban Regeneration Agency are very considerable and its objectives wide-ranging. The Agency takes over all the property rights and liabilities of English Industrial Estates. The shape of the residential parts of our large cities has been created by the huge waves of post-war housing public and private sector and the shopping construction that has gone with this. This Act adds most of all to the lack of coherence in housing law and policy. Its effects are unpredictable. The most optimistic outcome is that the Act will indeed be viewed in the future as paving legislation for a coherent reform of housing tenure.

PART I

LANDLORD AND TENANT

CHAPTER I

COLLECTIVE ENFRANCHISEMENT IN CASE OF TENANTS OF FLATS

DEFINITIONS
"appurtenant property": s.1(7).
"flat": s.101(1).
"freeholder": s.1(7).
"interest": s.101(1).
"lease": s.101(1).
"qualifying tenant": s.38(1).
"relevant date": s.38(1).

"relevant premises": s.1(7).
"right to collective enfranchisement": s.38(1).

GENERAL NOTE

Collective right to enfranchisement
Some general rules on how the parties are to reach agreement are found in the Leasehold Reform (Collective Enfranchisement and Lease Renewal) Regulations 1993 (S.I. 1993 No. 2407) found in Appendix 1. In particular they provide for (i) the reversioner to be able to require evidence of occupation; (ii) how title is to be defined; (iii) the raising and reply to requisitions; (iv) procedure when relevant landlords act independently; (v) how the actual sale contract is to be prepared; (vi) a deposit (up to five per cent.) to be paid; (vii) the cancellation of land charges in due course.

Preliminary

The right to collective enfranchisement

1.—(1) This Chapter has effect for the purpose of conferring on qualifying tenants of flats contained in premises to which this Chapter applies on the relevant date the right, exercisable subject to and in accordance with this Chapter, to have the freehold of those premises acquired on their behalf—
   (a) by a person or persons appointed by them for the purpose, and
   (b) at a price determined in accordance with this Chapter;
and that right is referred to in this Chapter as "the right to collective enfranchisement".

(2) Where the right to collective enfranchisement is exercised in relation to any such premises ("the relevant premises")—
   (a) the qualifying tenants by whom the right is exercised shall be entitled, subject to and in accordance with this Chapter, to have acquired, in like manner, the freehold of any property which is not comprised in the relevant premises but to which this paragraph applies by virtue of subsection (3); and
   (b) section 2 has effect with respect to the acquisition of leasehold interests to which paragraph (a) or (b) of subsection (1) of that section applies.

(3) Subsection (2)(a) applies to any property if the freehold of it is owned by the person who owns the freehold of the relevant premises and at the relevant date either—
   (a) it is appurtenant property which is demised by the lease held by a qualifying tenant of a flat contained in the relevant premises; or
   (b) it is property which any such tenant is entitled under the terms of the lease of his flat to use in common with the occupiers of other premises (whether those premises are contained in the relevant premises or not).

(4) The right of acquisition in respect of the freehold of any such property as is mentioned in subsection (3)(b) shall, however, be taken to be satisfied with respect to that property if, on the acquisition of the relevant premises in pursuance of this Chapter, either—
   (a) there are granted by the freeholder—
     (i) over that property, or
     (ii) over any other property,
   such permanent rights as will ensure that thereafter the occupier of the flat referred to in that provision has as nearly as may be the same rights as those enjoyed in relation to that property on the relevant date by the qualifying tenant under the terms of his lease; or
   (b) there is acquired from the freeholder the freehold of any other property over which any such permanent rights may be granted.

(5) A claim by qualifying tenants to exercise the right to collective enfranchisement may be made in relation to any premises to which this Chapter

applies despite the fact that those premises are less extensive than the entirety of the premises in relation to which those tenants are entitled to exercise that right.

(6) Any right or obligation under this Chapter to acquire any interest in property shall not extend to underlying minerals in which that interest subsists if—

(a) the owner of the interest requires the minerals to be excepted, and
(b) proper provision is made for the support of the property as it is enjoyed on the relevant date.

(7) In this section—

"appurtenant property", in relation to a flat, means any garage, out-house, garden, yard or appurtenances belonging to, or usually enjoyed with, the flat;

"the freeholder" means the person who owns the freehold of the relevant premises;

"the relevant premises" means any such premises as are referred to in subsection (2).

(8) In this Chapter "the relevant date", in relation to any claim to exercise the right to collective enfranchisement, means the date on which notice of the claim is given under section 13.

DEFINITIONS
"appurtenant property": subs. (7).
"freeholder": subs. (7).
"relevant premises": subs. (2).

GENERAL NOTE
This curious section is both introductory and deals with some of the minutiae of the right to collective enfranchisement. It is important, in particular, for identifying the extent of the property which will be the subject of collective enfranchisement.

Subs. (1)
This subsection exemplifies a modern drafting trend of explaining what is to follow. It defines the right to collective enfranchisement but adds little else. One important practical point is this: it is clear that the tenants seeking enfranchisement can choose whether to purchase in the name of one person or of more than one person, so, parts of the freehold acquired can be in the name of one company and parts in another. This might facilitate future management arrangements where the common parts include a range of facilities.

Subss. (2)–(4)
These provisions deal with an important detail of collective enfranchisement. There may be included in the enfranchisement appurtenant property let to any qualifying tenant in the premises. There may also be included in the enfranchisement common parts. There may be shared property not actually in the relevant premises such as a shared swimming-pool or squash courts. The landlord is proferred two alternatives under subs. (4): it may instead of transferring the freehold of such common parts offer permanent rights of continued user (subs. (4)(a)). These may be permanent rights over different property (subs. (4)(a)(ii)) such as a different swimming-pool owned by the same landlord. Alternatively, the landlord may offer the freehold of different property from that actually shared. Thus, the tenants may enjoy the right to share use of one tennis court but the landlord may offer instead the transfer freehold of a different tennis court. Ultimately it will be for the leasehold valuation tribunal to decide under s.24 if such arrangements are satisfactory.

Subs. (5)
This subsection states that tenants may if they choose claim to purchase only part of the relevant premises. Thus, if there are 60 tenants in a large six-storey Victorian building and 50 who live in, say, the bottom five storeys wish to enfranchise they may (if they choose) omit the top storey from their claim. Tenants may, then, omit unwanted parts or appurtenances from their claim. A near derelict swimming-pool could simply be left out of the claim. (But see s.21(3) and (4)—where the landlord may include such onerous property in its counter-notice— the issue will then be decided by negotiation or litigation).

Subs. (6)

This subsection fails to define "minerals". If, as is to be expected, the land-owner requires minerals to be excepted this poses a problem in drafting the necessary exception and reservation. The tenant might insist on the clause stating "excepting and recovering such underlying minerals as the transferor is permitted by s.1(6) of the Leasehold Reform, Housing and Urban Development Act 1993 to require to be excepted". This leaves it eventually to the court to decide what are minerals within this. (A starting point is found in *Earl of Lonsdale* v. *Att.-Gen.* [1982] 1 W.L.R. 887 and for further references see *Sweet & Maxwell's Conveyancing Practice*, 18–018). It should be noted that there does not appear to be any right for the landowner to reserve the right to work the minerals which it has the right to reserve. There is no reason why such a right should be implied and the straightforward effect of subs. (6) is that it is not. Under subs. (6)(b), if the landowner requires the minerals to be excepted, then it must comply with this paragraph. This requires not compensation for the removal of support but continuation of that support. The tenant seems under these words to be entitled to effective physical provision being made to provide support and to the freeholder being obliged by the conveyance to continue such support. Such a right of support is capable of being an easement (*Dalton* v. *Angus* (1881) 6 App.Cas. 740).

Subs. (7)

The following points may be noted:

Appurtenant property. This seems to have a narrow scope. If the property is a country property with a large estate attached it can be doubted if anything except the immediate garden can be termed "appurtenant".

Freeholder. The particular point is that where there is appurtenant or common property and rights are granted under subs. (4) instead of over *other* property then it must be the freeholder of the appurtenant or common property which grants the substitute rights under that subsection.

Acquisition of leasehold interests

2.—(1) Where the right to collective enfranchisement is exercised in relation to any premises to which this Chapter applies ("the relevant premises"), then, subject to and in accordance with this Chapter—

(a) there shall be acquired on behalf of the qualifying tenants by whom the right is exercised every interest to which this paragraph applies by virtue of subsection (2); and

(b) those tenants shall be entitled to have acquired on their behalf any interest to which this paragraph applies by virtue of subsection (3);

and any interest so acquired on behalf of those tenants shall be acquired in the manner mentioned in paragraphs (a) and (b) of section 1(1).

(2) Paragraph (a) of subsection (1) above applies to the interest of the tenant under any lease which is superior to the lease held by a qualifying tenant of a flat contained in the relevant premises.

(3) Paragraph (b) of subsection (1) above applies to the interest of the tenant under any lease (not falling within subsection (2) above) under which the demised premises consist of or include—

(a) any common parts of the relevant premises, or

(b) any property falling within section 1(2)(a) which is to be acquired by virtue of that provision,

where the acquisition of that interest is reasonably necessary for the proper management or maintenance of those common parts, or (as the case may be) that property, on behalf of the tenants by whom the right to collective enfranchisement is exercised.

(4) Where the demised premises under any lease falling within subsection (2) or (3) include any premises other than—

(a) a flat contained in the relevant premises which is held by a qualifying tenant,

(b) any common parts of those premises, or

(c) any such property as is mentioned in subsection (3)(b),

the obligation or (as the case may be) right under subsection (1) above to acquire the interest of the tenant under the lease shall not extend to his interest under the lease in any such other premises.

(5) Where the qualifying tenant of a flat is a public sector landlord and the flat is let under a secure tenancy, then if—

(a) the condition specified in subsection (6) is satisfied, and

(b) the lease of the qualifying tenant is directly derived out of a lease under which the tenant is a public sector landlord,

the interest of that public sector landlord as tenant under that lease shall not be liable to be acquired by virtue of subsection (1) to the extent that it is an interest in the flat or in any appurtenant property; and the interest of a public sector landlord as tenant under any lease out of which the qualifying tenant's lease is indirectly derived shall, to the like extent, not be liable to be so acquired (so long as the tenant under every lease intermediate between that lease and the qualifying tenant's lease is a public sector landlord).

(6) The condition referred to in subsection (5)(a) is that either—

(a) the qualifying tenant is the immediate landlord under the secure tenancy, or

(b) he is the landlord under a lease which is superior to the secure tenancy and the tenant under that lease, and the tenant under every lease (if any) intermediate between it and the secure tenancy, is also a public sector landlord;

and in subsection (5) "appurtenant property" has the same meaning as in section 1.

(7) In this section "the relevant premises" means any such premises as are referred to in subsection (1).

DEFINITIONS
"appurtenant property": subs. (6).
"flat": s.101(1).
"interest": s.101(1).
"lease": s.101(1).
"public sector landlord": s.38(1).
"qualifying tenant": s.38(1).
"relevant premises": subs. (6).
"right to collective enfranchisement": s.38(1).
"secure tenancy": s.38(1).

GENERAL NOTE
This section contains detailed provisions as to the interest and property to be acquired and begins to foreshadow the dense complexity of what is to come. It provides for the enfranchisement to include all leasehold interests superior to the leases of qualifying tenants (except for certain public sector leaseholds). It also provides for common parts and appurtenant property to be included in the enfranchisement.

Subs. (1)
This introduces the purpose of the section which is to specify the interests which are to be acquired and require them to be acquired in accordance with s.1.

Subs. (2)
This is intended to ensure qualifying tenants do enfranchise all the reversionary interests on their flats. This, of course, applies to the reversionary leases on the leases of all qualifying tenants not simply those which are participating in the enfranchisement.

Subs. (3)
Leases of the common parts of shared property or appurtenant property are to be included in enfranchisement only if they satisfy the test contained in this subsection. Is acquisition of that interest reasonably necessary for the proper management or maintenance of that property on behalf of the tenants by whom the right to collective enfranchisement is exercised? The qualification is important as there may be tenants not participating who enjoy other common parts or appurtenant property which will not fall to be the subject of enfranchisement.

Subs. (4)

Reversionary leases which the tenants are entitled to acquire may include property which is not relevant to the purchase. This subsection excludes such property from the right of enfranchisement. The kind of problem envisaged may be illustrated with the following example: Attlee Towers contains 100 flats. The tenants choose to claim enfranchisement. They have the right in their lease to use certain tennis courts. The freehold of these is owned by Eastminster Ltd. as part of a large parcel of land. The tennis courts together with other property are leased to Belflavour Ltd. Attlee Towers' tenants may be entitled to purchase the lease and the freehold to the tennis courts. The balance of the land in Belflavour Ltd.'s lease will still be held by it from Eastminster Ltd. There will, thus, have to be an apportionment of the rent under Belflavour's lease. If this cannot be agreed it will be resolved by the leasehold valuation tribunal under s.24.

Subss. (5) and (6)

The following example demonstrates the applicability of these subsections. The Gaitskell Building has 100 flats. In respect of flats 10 and 11, Norster Council has a long lease. It has let these two flats to secure tenants. Norster Council may be a qualifying tenant for each of these flats. (Note if it is holder of more than two flats then it will not be a qualifying tenant of any of the flats (s.6(6))). If Norster Council's lease is a head-lease then if the other tenants enfranchise Norster will remain as their tenant and its tenants will remain as secure tenants. If Norster Council's lease is a sub-lease then subs. (5)(b) is satisfied if it is granted by a public sector landlord. The effect is that in this case Norster Council's lease is not subject to enfranchisement providing that either condition of subs. (6) is met. That is either that Norster Council is the landlord of the secure tenant or that any intermediate tenancies between Norster and the secure tenant are also owned by a public sector landlord. Such intermediate public sector landlord leases are also not subject to enfranchisement.

Subs. (7)

The importance of this curiously circular definition is as follows: "relevant premises" may include shared property or appurtenant property falling within s.1(3) or substitute property within s.1(4). Public sector landlord's interests in all such property may fall to be dealt with under this section.

Premises to which this Chapter applies

3.—(1) Subject to section 4, this Chapter applies to any premises if—

(a) they consist of a self-contained building or part of a building and the freehold of the whole of the building or of that part of the building is owned by the same person;

(b) they contain two or more flats held by qualifying tenants; and

(c) the total number of flats held by such tenants is not less than two-thirds of the total number of flats contained in the premises.

(2) For the purposes of this section a building is a self-contained building if it is structurally detached, and a part of a building is a self-contained part of a building if—

(a) it constitutes a vertical division of the building and the structure of the building is such that that part could be redeveloped independently of the remainder of the building; and

(b) the relevant services provided for occupiers of that part either—

(i) are provided independently of the relevant services provided for occupiers of the remainder of the building, or

(ii) could be so provided without involving the carrying out of any works likely to result in a significant interruption in the provision of any such services for occupiers of the remainder of the building;

and for this purpose "relevant services" means services provided by means of pipes, cables or other fixed installations.

Definitions
  "flat": s.101(1).
  "qualifying tenant": s.38(1).
  "relevant services": subs. (2).

GENERAL NOTE

This section describes the blocks of flats to which the right of collective enfranchisement applies. It is intended to apply to self-contained premises consisting of more than one flat occupied by preponderantly qualifying tenants. But, the detail contained in the two subsections is crucial. This is one of the key sections for testing the applicability of the Act to a particular building. An important change was made in the passage of the Bill to the effect that two-thirds of the flats must be held by qualifying tenants as opposed to two-thirds of the units in the building.

Subss. (1) and (2)

These provisions contain a very simple method of avoidance. That is to ensure that the freehold of self-contained parts is held in separate parts by more than one person.

Subs. (1)

Note first that s.4 describes excluded premises and s.3 takes effect subject to those exclusions. Under subs. (1)(a) the building must be "self-contained" or a "self-contained" part of a building. Clearly the qualifier "self-contained" must apply to either whole buildings or part-buildings and this is made even clearer from s.3(2) which defines "self-contained". Under subs. (1)(c) the rule is not so straightforward to apply as it appears. It has to be read in the light of the very important rule in s.5(5) that if a tenant could be regarded as the qualifying tenant of three or more flats then all those flats are to be treated as having no qualifying tenant. The other major practical difficulty is discovering the nature of the tenancies of each flat in a building.

Subs. (2)

The concept of a "self-contained building" will cause few problems where the building is "structurally detached"—although problems may arise where one building is connected to another by bridges or similar passages. In cases where the building is not structurally detached then for there to be a self-contained building both subs. (2)(a) and (b) must be satisfied. In subs. (2)(a) the concept of being developed "independently of the remainder" is not an exact one. Subsection (2)(b) is also peppered with concepts which give ample scope for argument. There is some possible scope for arranging services so as to make enfranchisement difficult, impractical or even impossible.

Premises excluded from right

4.—(1) This Chapter does not apply to premises falling within section 3(1) if—

    (a) any part or parts of the premises is or are neither—

        (i) occupied, or intended to be occupied, for residential purposes, nor

        (ii) comprised in any common parts of the premises; and

    (b) the internal floor area of that part or of those parts (taken together) exceeds 10 per cent. of the internal floor area of the premises (taken as a whole).

(2) Where in the case of any such premises any part of the premises (such as, for example, a garage, parking space or storage area) is used, or intended for use, in conjunction with a particular dwelling contained in the premises (and accordingly is not comprised in any common parts of the premises), it shall be taken to be occupied, or intended to be occupied, for residential purposes.

(3) For the purpose of determining the internal floor area of a building or of any part of a building, the floor or floors of the building or part shall be taken to extend (without interruption) throughout the whole of the interior of the building or part, except that the area of any common parts of the building or part shall be disregarded.

(4) This Chapter does not apply to premises falling within section 3(1) if the premises are premises with a resident landlord and do not contain more than four units.

DEFINITIONS

  "common parts": s.101(1).
  "dwelling": s.101(1).

"premises with a resident landlord": s.38(1).
"unit": s.38(1).

GENERAL NOTE
This section contains two important exclusions from the right to enfranchisement and gives the so-desirous landlord some possibility of avoiding the effect of this legislation. Tenants excluded in this way from the right to collective enfranchisement may of course still have the individual right to an extended lease under Chap. II.

Subs. (1)
This is an important exclusion from the right to collective enfranchisement. It received much debate in the Bill's passage and was widely felt to be unnecessarily restrictive of the right to enfranchisement. Buildings are excluded if more than 10 per cent. of the whole is not occupied or intended to be occupied for residential purposes. Some marginal help in interpreting this may be obtained from cases on restrictive covenants restricting residential use (discussed in *Enderick's Conveyance, Re* [1978] 1 All E.R. 843); the definition of residential premises in the Landlord and Tenant Act 1954, s.18(2) as premises normally used or adapted for one or more dwellings; and the definition of "residential premises" formerly in the Town and Country Planning Act 1971, s.25(2)(b) as previously used or designed or constructed for use as one or more permanent residences. These, however, are uses in a different context with slightly different wording. The draftsman's clear intention here is to give a wide and inclusive meaning to "*occupied for residential purposes*". The test will be satisfied if it is occupied partly for residential purposes. Also residential purposes is wider than occupied as a residence and may include purposes ancillary to residence.

Subs. (2)
This subsection clarifies the point last made that the construction of occupied for residential purposes is meant to be liberal. Only examples of ancillary uses are given and the clearest sign-post is given that there is a legislative presumption in favour of residential purposes.

Subs. (3)
The effect of this subsection may not on one reading be so helpful to tenants as it first appears. The total internal floor area is calculated and then the area of all common parts is deducted. If more than 10 per cent. of the balance is not residential the building does not qualify. However, in the final calculation the common parts may be added back in (s.4(1)(a)(ii)). A calculation will illustrate this:
Gaitskell building has 90 flats and 10 offices.
The overall area internally is 405,000 sq.ft. of which
20,000 sq.ft. consis' of offices,
270,000 sq.ft. of flats
and 15,000 sq.ft. ' common parts.
Under s.4(3), the internal floor area is the offices and the flats, the common parts being ignored, resulting in a total of:
290,000 sq.ft.
Under s.4(1) one reading is that the building is excluded if the non-residential parts and the common parts exceed 10 per cent. of 290,000 sq.ft. which in the example they do. It is clear from s.4(2) which adds to premises occupied for residential purposes the parts used for ancillary purposes for "a particular dwelling" that other such parts used generally are common parts. Thus, the extent of a car-park or indoor sports hall which is shared is added to the excluded common parts.
An alternative reading of s.4(1)(a) is that property is included in the s.4(1)(b) figure of non-residential only if it satisfies the twin test of s.4(1)(b) of being neither residential nor common part as defined by s.4(2). Thus, in the example the 15,000 ft. of common part is excluded from both the overall area and the calculation of the 10 per cent. fraction. Only the 20,000 ft. of offices is included and this is far less than 10 per cent. of the 290,000 ft. overall area. Clearly the second of these is the intended reading but the section is ambiguous.

Subs. (4)
Note there is extensive case law on the interpretation of "resident landlord". This is discussed in the notes on s.10.

Qualifying tenants
5.—(1) Subject to the following provisions of this section, a person is a

qualifying tenant of a flat for the purposes of this Chapter if he is tenant of the flat under a long lease at a low rent.

(2) Subsection (1) does not apply where—

(a) the lease is a business lease; or

(b) the immediate landlord under the lease is a charitable housing trust and the flat forms part of the housing accommodation provided by it in the pursuit of its charitable purposes; or

(c) the lease was granted by sub-demise out of a superior lease other than a long lease at a low rent, the grant was made in breach of the terms of the superior lease, and there has been no waiver of the breach by the superior landlord;

and in paragraph (b) "charitable housing trust" means a housing trust within the meaning of the Housing Act 1985 which is a charity within the meaning of the Charities Act 1993.

(3) No flat shall have more than one qualifying tenant at any one time.

(4) Accordingly—

(a) where a flat is for the time being let under two or more leases to which subsection (1) applies, any tenant under any of those leases which is superior to that held by any other such tenant shall not be a qualifying tenant of the flat for the purposes of this Chapter; and

(b) where a flat is for the time being let to joint tenants under a lease to which subsection (1) applies, the joint tenants shall (subject to paragraph (a) and subsection (5)) be regarded for the purposes of this Chapter as jointly constituting the qualifying tenant of the flat.

(5) Where apart from this subsection—

(a) a person would be regarded for the purposes of this Chapter as being (or as being among those constituting) the qualifying tenant of a flat contained in any particular premises consisting of the whole or part of a building, but

(b) that person would also be regarded for those purposes as being (or as being among those constituting) the qualifying tenant of each of two or more other flats contained in those premises,

then, whether that person is tenant of the flats referred to in paragraphs (a) and (b) under a single lease or otherwise, there shall be taken for those purposes to be no qualifying tenant of any of those flats.

(6) For the purposes of subsection (5) in its application to a body corporate any flat let to an associated company (whether alone or jointly with any other person or persons) shall be treated as if it were so let to that body; and for this purpose "associated company" means another body corporate which is (within the meaning of section 736 of the Companies Act 1985) that body's holding company, a subsidiary of that body or another subsidiary of that body's holding company.

DEFINITIONS
"associated company": s.5(6).
"business lease": s.101(1).
"charitable housing trust": s.5(2).
"flat": s.101(1).
"lease": s.101(1).
"qualifying tenant": s.38(1).

GENERAL NOTE
This section introduces the two following sections which define "long lease" and "low rent". It also contains important exclusions from the definition of "qualifying tenant".

Subs. (1)
See the following two sections which deal *in extenso* with the definition of "long lease" and "low rent".

Subs. (2)(a)
A tenant of a business lease cannot be a qualifying tenant. A business lease is defined in s.97(1).

Subs. (2)(b)
The definition of a housing trust in the Housing Act 1985, s.6 reads:
"In this Act 'Housing Trust' means a corporation or body of persons which:
  (a) is required by the terms of its constituent instruments to use the whole of its funds, including any surplus which may arise from its operations, for the purpose of providing housing accommodation, or
  (b) is required by the terms of its constituent instrument to devote the whole, or substantially the whole, of its funds for charitable purposes and in fact uses the whole, or substantially the whole, of its funds for the purpose of providing housing accommodation."
(For case law see Sweet & Maxwell's Housing Encyclopaedia, 1–0013.)
Note: for the tenant not to be a qualifying tenant under subs. (2)(b) the *immediate* landlord must be a charitable housing trust. If the trust lets on a long lease to A who lets on a long lease to B who is in possession, then B may be a qualifying tenant but not A. This is also so if B has sub-let on a short lease to C (subject to the residence qualification).

Subs. (2)(c)
This seems to be a paragraph of limited application. The definition of a charity as contained in s.96(1) of the Charities Act 1993 reads: " 'Charity' means any institution, corporate or not, which is established for charitable purposes and is subject to the control of the High Court in the exercise of the court's jurisdiction with respect to charities". (Church of England ecclesiastical property is excluded from this definition by s.96(2)). Section 97(1) provides that *charitable purposes* means "purposes which are exclusively charitable according to the law of England and Wales". It will be apparent to the reader that this definition of charity still leaves the question essentially to the very extensive case law on the topic.

Subss. (3) and (4)
A head lessee cannot be a qualifying tenant if the under lessee holds a long lease. Where there are joint tenants of a flat then there can only be one qualifying tenant.

Subs. (4)(a)
This paragraph ensures that the relevant long lease is the one under which a tenant is entitled in possession. Tenants of leases which are reversionary on long leases are not tenants in possession.

Subs. (4)(b)
Whether co-owners of a flat are beneficial joint tenants or beneficial tenants in common they hold the legal estate as joint tenants. In either event they together constitute one qualifying tenant.

Subss. (5) and (6)
If a person appears to be the qualifying tenant of three flats then there is taken to be no qualifying tenant of these flats. Subsection (6) applies this rule to associated companies under s.736 Companies Act 1985.
These provisions are a considerable trap where a person is involved in ownership of more than one flat. For example, a person may buy three flats to be held on trust for his three children. If there is one set of trustees then all three flats are deemed to have no qualifying tenants. If there are three separate trusts then providing there is a single common trustee the effect of subs. (5) is that all three flats are treated as having no qualifying tenant.
The definition of "associated company" derived from s.736 of the Companies Act 1985 is as follows:

" **"Holding company", "subsidiary" and "wholly-owned subsidiary"**
  736.—(1) For the purposes of this Act, a company is deemed to be a subsidiary of another if (but only if)—
    (a) that other either—
      (i) is a member of it and controls the composition of its board of directors, or
      (ii) holds more than half in nominal value of its equity share capital, or
    (b) the first-mentioned company is a subsidiary of any company which is that other's subsidiary.
  The above is subject to subsection (4) below in this section.

(2) For purposes of subsection (1), the composition of a company's board of directors is deemed to be controlled by another company if (but only if) that other company by the exercise of some power exercisable by it without the consent or concurrence of any other person can appoint or remove the holders of all or a majority of the directorships.

(3) For purposes of this last provision, the other company is deemed to have power to appoint to a directorship with respect to which any of the following conditions is satisfied—

   (a) that a person cannot be appointed to it without the exercise in his favour by the other company of such a power as is mentioned above, or

   (b) that a person's appointment to the directorship follows necessarily from his appointment as director of the other company, or

   (c) that the directorship is held by the other company itself or by a subsidiary of it.

(4) In determining whether one company is a subsidiary of another—

   (a) any shares held or power exercisable by the other in a fiduciary capacity are to be treated as not held or exercisable by it,

   (b) subject to the two following paragraphs, any shares held or power exercisable—

     (i) by any person as nominee for the other (except where the other is concerned only in a fiduciary capacity), or

     (ii) by, or by a nominee for, a subsidiary of the other (not being a subsidiary which is concerned only in a fiduciary capacity),

    are to be treated as held or exercisable by the other,

   (c) any shares held or power exercisable by any person by virtue of the provisions of any debentures of the first-mentioned company or of a trust deed for securing any issue of such debentures are to be disregarded,

   (d) any shares held or power exercisable by, or by a nominee for, the other or its subsidiary (not being held or exercisable as mentioned in paragraph (c)) are to be treated as not held or exercisable by the other if the ordinary business of the other or its subsidiary (as the case may be) includes the lending of money and the shares are held or the power is exercisable as above mentioned by way of security only for the purposes of a transaction entered into in the ordinary course of that business.

(5) For purposes of this Act—

   (a) a company is deemed to be another's holding company if (but only if) the other is its subsidiary, and

   (b) a body corporate is deemed the wholly-owned subsidiary of another if it has no members except that other and that other's wholly-owned subsidiaries and its or their nominees.

(6) In this section "company" includes any body corporate."

Qualifying tenants satisfying residence condition

6.—(1) For the purposes of this Chapter a qualifying tenant of a flat satisfies the residence condition at any time when the condition specified in subsection (2) is satisfied with respect to him.

(2) That condition is that the tenant has occupied the flat as his only or principal home—

   (a) for the last twelve months, or

   (b) for periods amounting to three years in the last ten years,

whether or not he has used it also for other purposes.

(3) For the purposes of subsection (2)—

   (a) any reference to the tenant's flat includes a reference to part of it; and

   (b) it is immaterial whether at any particular time the tenant's occupation was in right of the lease by virtue of which he is a qualifying tenant or in right of some other lease or otherwise;

but any occupation by a company or other artificial person, or (where the tenant is a corporation sole) by the corporator, shall not be regarded as occupation for the purposes of that subsection.

(4) In the case of a lease held by joint tenants—

   (a) the condition specified in subsection (2) need only be satisfied with respect to one of the joint tenants; and

   (b) subsection (3) shall apply accordingly (the reference to the lease by virtue of which the tenant is a qualifying tenant being read for this purpose as a reference to the lease by virtue of which the joint tenants are a qualifying tenant).

DEFINITIONS
"flat": s.101(1).
"lease": s.101(1).
"qualifying tenant": s.38(1).

GENERAL NOTE
This section was introduced at a very late stage in the passage of the Bill. It was a major government concession to Conservative opposition to the effect of the Bill in permitting enfranchisement by absentee tenants. The section means nothing on its own but is given effect by the requirement in s.13(3) that "not less than one-half of the qualifying tenants by whom the *initial* notice is given must satisfy the residence condition". The residence qualification for collective enfranchisement was introduced as a result of pressure to tighten up the process of enfranchisement and prevent absentee tenants having too large a rôle. The condition in subs. (2) is taken from s.1(1)(b) of the Leasehold Reform Act 1967 except that occupation as "his only or principal home" is substituted for occupation as "his only or main residence" in the earlier act. The reversioner may require evidence of occupation to be given by statutory declaration, *see* the Leasehold Reform (Collective Enfranchisement and Lease Renewal) Regulations 1993 (S.I. 1993 No. 2407) reproduced in Appendix 1.

Subs. (1)
The time when the condition must be satisfied is the date of the initial notice under s.13. On occasions a group of tenants may need to delay the initial notice until this condition is satisfied.

Subs. (2)
The concept of occupation as the "only or principal" home occurs in other legislation. This is discussed in the note on s.39(2) where there is a residence condition for exercise of the individual right to an extended lease.

Subs. (3)
This subsection contains three very important points: the residence condition can be satisfied by occupying a part of the flat. It cannot be satisfied by occupying the flat as part of the tenant's only or principal home (subs. (3)(a)); the residence condition can be satisfied by occupying the flat for some of the time in any capacity such as licensee, freeholder or under a different lease from that under which the tenant is a qualifying tenant; no corporate body can satisfy the residence condition. This includes corporations sole such as rectors and bishops. This means that although a corporate tenant can be a qualifying tenant it can never be included among the number of those who satisfy the 50 per cent. residence rule under s.13(1).

Subs. (4)
In the case of joint tenants only one need satisfy the residence condition and the principles set out in subs. (3) are applied to each to see if any satisfies the test.

Meaning of "long lease"

7.—(1) In this Chapter "long lease" means (subject to the following provisions of this section)—
  (a) a lease granted for a term of years certain exceeding 21 years, whether or not it is (or may become) terminable before the end of that term by notice given by or to the tenant or by re-entry, forfeiture or otherwise;
  (b) a lease for a term fixed by law under a grant with a covenant or obligation for perpetual renewal (other than a lease by sub-demise from one which is not a long lease) or a lease taking effect under section 149(6) of the Law of Property Act 1925 (leases terminable after a death or marriage);
  (c) a lease granted in pursuance of the right to buy conferred by Part V of the Housing Act 1985 or in pursuance of the right to acquire on rent to mortgage terms conferred by that Part of that Act; or
  (d) a shared ownership lease, whether granted in pursuance of that Part of that Act or otherwise, where the tenant's total share is 100 per cent.
  (2) A lease terminable by notice after a death or marriage is not to be treated as a long lease for the purposes of this Chapter if—
  (a) the notice is capable of being given at any time after the death or marriage of the tenant;

   (b) the length of the notice is not more than three months; and

   (c) the terms of the lease preclude both—

        (i) its assignment otherwise than by virtue of section 92 of the Housing Act 1985 (assignments by way of exchange), and

        (ii) the sub-letting of the whole of the premises comprised in it.

(3) Where the tenant of any property under a long lease at a low rent, on the coming to an end of that lease, becomes or has become tenant of the property or part of it under any subsequent tenancy (whether by express grant or by implication of law), then that tenancy shall be deemed for the purposes of this Chapter (including any further application of this subsection) to be a long lease irrespective of its terms.

(4) Where—

   (a) a lease is or has been granted for a term of years certain not exceeding 21 years, but with a covenant or obligation for renewal without payment of a premium (but not for perpetual renewal), and

   (b) the lease is or has been renewed on one or more occasions so as to bring to more than 21 years the total of the terms granted (including any interval between the end of a lease and the grant of a renewal),

this Chapter shall apply as if the term originally granted had been one exceeding 21 years.

(5) References in this Chapter to a long lease include—

   (a) any period during which the lease is or was continued under Part I of the Landlord and Tenant Act 1954 or under Schedule 10 to the Local Government and Housing Act 1989;

   (b) any period during which the lease was continued under the Leasehold Property (Temporary Provisions) Act 1951.

(6) Where in the case of a flat there are at any time two or more separate leases, with the same landlord and the same tenant, and—

   (a) the property comprised in one of those leases consists of either the flat or a part of it (in either case with or without any appurtenant property), and

   (b) the property comprised in every other lease consists of either a part of the flat (with or without any appurtenant property) or appurtenant property only,

then in relation to the property comprised in such of those leases as are long leases, this Chapter shall apply as it would if at that time—

   (i) there were a single lease of that property, and

   (ii) that lease were a long lease;

but this subsection has effect subject to the operation of subsections (3) to (5) in relation to any of the separate leases.

(7) In this section—

"appurtenant property" has the same meaning as in section 1;

"shared ownership lease" means a lease—

        (a) granted on payment of a premium calculated by reference to a percentage of the value of the demised premises or the cost of providing them, or

        (b) under which the tenant (or his personal representatives) will or may be entitled to a sum calculated by reference, directly or indirectly, to the value of those premises; and

"total share", in relation to the interest of a tenant under a shared ownership lease, means his initial share plus any additional share or shares in the demised premises which he has acquired.

DEFINITIONS

"appurtenant property": subs. (7).

"flat": s.101(1).

"lease": s.101(1).

"long lease": subs. (1).

"shared ownership lease": subs. (7).
"tenancy": s.101(2).
"total share": subs. (7).

GENERAL NOTE
The definition of a qualifying tenant in terms of a tenant of a long lease at a low rent follows a well-travelled route in landlord and tenant law. This section follows the definition of a "long lease" in s.3 of the Leasehold Reform Act 1967. In parts the subsections have been re-arranged so as to be easier to follow and obsolete statutory references removed but otherwise the effect is the same. (See *Sweet & Maxwell's Encyclopaedia of Housing* 2–0379).

Subs. (1)(a)
There will be a long lease in cases where the tenant is at some point in time in a position to say that subject to options to determine, rights of entry and so forth, he is entitled to remain in possession for the next 21 years, whether at law or in equity—this principle was laid down in *Roberts* v. *Church Commissioners for England* [1972] 1 Q.B. 278. In that case the lease was expressed to be for 21 years from March 25, 1990. The lease was dated October 29, 1952. The fact that the lease was expressed to be for 21 years was not conclusive. This was not a long lease.

Subs. (1)(b)
Perpetually renewable leases are converted into terms of 2,000 years by Law of Property Act 1922, s.145 and Sched. 15. For recent discussions of the problem of perpetually renewable leases, see *Caerphilly Concrete Products* v. *Owen* [1972] 1 W.L.R. 372; *Marjorie Burnett* v. *Barclay* (1980) 125 S.J. 199. These cases illustrate an understandable judicial reluctance to construe a lease as perpetually renewable (where there is an option to renew on the same terms as the existing lease).

Subs. (2)
Compare with the Leasehold Reform Act 1967, s.3(1) proviso and note that it treats leases granted before April 18, 1980 differently—that is, if granted so as to become terminable by notice after death or marriage, they are excluded altogether from being long leases. This particular provision is absent from the present Act. This is to the same effect as the proviso to s.3 of the Leasehold Reform Act 1967 (as amended by the Housing (Consequential Provisions) Act 1985, s.4, Sched. 2, para. 12 and the Housing and Building Control Act 1984, s.64, Sched. 11, para. 3). The amended provision makes it clear that the notice must be one given after the death or marriage of the tenant. Such leases are subject to s.149(6) of the Law of Property Act 1925.

Subs. (3)
Compare with s.3(2) of the Leasehold Reform Act 1967. If the second lease is assigned then the assignee will be the holder of a long lease even though the second lease itself is less than 21 years (see *Austin* v. *Richards (Dick) Properties* [1975] 1 W.L.R. 1033). This is a very important principle—A has a 40-year lease and towards the end is granted a further 20-year lease to run from the term date of the first lease. That 20-year lease is a long lease and A should be so advised as this will very considerably affect the market-value of his interest when it is sold.

Subs. (4)
Compare with s.3(4) of the Leasehold Reform Act 1967. This is a provision that will have little practical application. There is no reported case law on the equivalent provision in s.3(4) of the Leasehold Reform Act 1967.

Subs. (6)
Compare with s.3(6) of the Leasehold Reform Act 1967. The reference to "occupied therewith" in s.3(6) of the 1967 Act has to be read in connection with the occupation requirement in s.1 of that Act and particularly s.1(2)(a) which provides that "references to a person occupying a house shall apply where he occupies it in part only". There is, of course, no occupation requirement for tenants to be able to enfranchise under that Act. In any event "occupied therewith" in the context of the 1967 Act almost certainly means "forming a part of the messuage of the house" rather than actually occupied in fact by the tenant seeking to enfranchise. The same meaning of "occupied therewith" probably applies here, so that land can be regarded as within this provision if it is in ordinary language a part of the flat notwithstanding that it is sub-let or otherwise in actual occupation of someone other than the tenant.

Subs. (8)

The consequence of this definition of "shared ownership" is that a shared ownership lease does not qualify for enfranchisement until the tenant's share is 100 per cent.

Leases at a low rent

8.—(1) For the purposes of this Chapter a lease of a flat is a lease at a low rent if either no rent was payable under it in respect of the flat during the initial year or the aggregate amount of rent so payable during that year did not exceed the following amount, namely—

(a) where the lease was entered into before 1st April 1963, two-thirds of the letting value of the flat (on the same terms) on the date of the commencement of the lease;

(b) where—

(i) the lease was entered into either on or after 1st April 1963 but before 1st April 1990, or on or after 1st April 1990 in pursuance of a contract made before that date, and

(ii) the flat had a rateable value at the date of the commencement of the lease or else at any time before 1st April 1990,

two-thirds of the rateable value of the flat on the appropriate date; or

(c) if any other case, £1,000 if the flat is in Greater London or £250 if elsewhere.

(2) For the purposes of subsection (1)—

(a) "the initial year", in relation to any lease, means the period of one year beginning with the date of the commencement of the lease;

(b) "the appropriate date" means the date of the commencement of the lease or, if the flat in question did not have a rateable value on that date, the date on which the flat first had a rateable value;

(c) section 25(1), (2) and (4) of the Rent Act 1977 (rateable value etc.) shall apply, with any necessary modifications, for the purpose of determining the amount of the rateable value of a flat on a particular date;

(d) "rent" means rent reserved as such, and there shall be disregarded any part of the rent expressed to be payable in consideration of services to be provided, or of repairs, maintenance or insurance to be effected by the landlord, or to be payable in respect of the cost thereof to the landlord under the lease or a superior landlord; and

(e) there shall be disregarded any term of the lease providing for suspension or reduction of rent in the event of damage to property demised, or for any penal addition to the rent in the event of a contravention of or non-compliance with the terms of the lease or an agreement collateral thereto.

(3) In subsection (1)(a) above the reference to letting value shall be construed in like manner as, under the law of England and Wales, the reference to letting value is to be construed where it appears in the proviso to section 4(1) of the Leasehold Reform Act 1967 (meaning of "low rent").

(4) Accordingly, in determining the letting value of a flat at any time for the purposes of subsection (1)(a) above, regard shall be had to whether, and (if so) in what amount, a premium might then have been lawfully demanded as the whole or part of the consideration for the letting.

(5) Where, by virtue of section 7(4), a lease which has been renewed on one or more occasions is to be treated as a long lease for the purposes of this Chapter, then for the purpose of determining under this section whether it is for those purposes a long lease at a low rent—

(a) the lease shall be deemed to have been entered into on the date of the last renewal of the lease; and

(b) that date shall be deemed to be the date of the commencement of the lease.

(6) Subsection (2)(a) above shall have effect in relation to any shared ownership lease falling within section 7(1)(d) as if the reference to the date of commencement of the lease were a reference to the date on which the tenant's total share became 100 per cent; and section 7(7) shall apply for the interpretation of this subsection.

(7) In this section any reference to a flat let under a lease includes a reference to any appurtenant property (within the meaning of section 1) which on the relevant date is let with the flat to the tenant under the lease.

DEFINITIONS

"appropriate date": subs. (2)(b).
"flat": s.101(1).
"initial year": subs. (2)(a).
"lease": s.101(1).
"rent": subs. (2)(d).

GENERAL NOTE

This contains the basic requirement that qualifying leases must be leases at a low rent. It is regarded as a controversial provision because of the obvious possibility that landlords will seek to fix the rent at a level slightly above the limit for a low rent.

Subss. (1)(a) and (3)

The concept of "letting value" is in fact not defined in the Leasehold Reform Act 1967. However, there has been some litigation (notably by the Duke of Westminster) on its meaning. The leading case is *Duke of Westminster* v. *Johnston*; *Same* v. *Voggenauer*; *Same* v. *Malnick*; *Same* v. *Williams* [1986] A.C. 839. A unanimous decision was delivered by Lord Griffiths who defined letting value concisely as "the best annual return obtainable in the open market for the grant of a long lease on the same terms whether this is achieved by letting at a rack rent or letting at a lower rent plus the payment of a rent". Thus, if the property was let a rent plus a premium in calculating the letting value the premium is expressed in annual terms. This construction of the term "letting value" assists tenants on such leases obtaining enfranchisement.

Subs. (2)(a)

In applying this subsection the definition of commencement of a lease in s.97(5) is important—the commencement of a lease means the commencement of the term. The purpose of this definition is presumably to prevent backdating the "initial year" to produce an artificial situation. *Shepherd's Touchstone* (272) suggests that a lease may begin in *in presenti* or *in futuro* that is from the present day or some future day. The authorities were discussed by Megarry V.-C. in *Bradshaw* v. *Pawley* [1980] 1 W.L.R. 10. The principle is neatly stated in *Woodfall* (1–0502)—"a lease may commence at one day in point of computation, and at another in point of interest, and it may commence from a day that is past". Thus, 100 years granted on January 1, 1994 and from January 1, 1954 is a grant of a term of which 50 years has already passed which commences in interest on January 1, 1994 and of which the initial year is 1994.

Subs. (2)(d)

This definition of rent as the "rent reserved as such" appears to cause a small problem in the case of leases granted before April 1, 1963. In *Gidlow-Jackson* v. *Middlegate Properties* [1974] Q.B. 361 it was held that the letting value could not exceed the amount recoverable under the Rent Acts. (A view accepted in *Mawson* v. *Duke of Westminster* [1981] Q.B. 323, 335). If that view is correct the rent reserved may well exceed two-thirds of this artificial figure.

Subs. (2)(e)

Suspension of rent in the case of severe damage by an insurable risk is common. Penal additions to the rent in the case of contravention are rare although the liability under s.145 of the Law of Property Act 1925 (for three years' rack rent for failure to give notice of a writ for recovery) may fall within this provision.

Subs. (4)

This makes it clear that the decision in *Duke of Westminster* v. *Johnston*; *Same* v. *Voggenauer*; *Same* v. *Malnick*; *Same* v. *Williams* (*supra*) is to be applied in calculating letting value.

Subs. (7)

If the rest of the flat and the appurtenant property are separately identified then they are added together to see if there is a lease at a low rent within this section.

The reversioner and other relevant landlords for the purposes of this Chapter

9.—(1) Where, in connection with any claim to exercise the right to collective enfranchisement in relation to any premises, it is not proposed to acquire any interests other than—

(a) the freehold of the premises, or

(b) any other interests of the person who owns the freehold of the premises,

that person shall be the reversioner in respect of the premises for the purposes of this Chapter.

(2) Where, in connection with any such claim, it is proposed to acquire interests of persons other than the person who owns the freehold of the premises to which the claim relates, then—

(a) the reversioner in respect of the premises shall for the purposes of this Chapter be the person identified as such by Part I of Schedule 1 to this Act; and

(b) the person who owns the freehold of the premises, and every person who owns any leasehold interest which it is proposed to acquire under or by virtue of section 2(1)(a) or (b), shall be a relevant landlord for those purposes.

(3) Subject to the provisions of Part II of Schedule 1, the reversioner in respect of any premises shall, in a case to which subsection (2) applies, conduct on behalf of all the relevant landlords all proceedings arising out of any notice given with respect to the premises under section 13 (whether the proceedings are for resisting or giving effect to the claim in question).

(4) Schedule 2 (which makes provision with respect to certain special categories of landlords) has effect for the purposes of this Chapter.

DEFINITIONS

"interest": s.101(1).
"relevant landlord": s.38(1).
"reversioner": s.38(1).
"right to collective enfranchisement": s.38(10).

GENERAL NOTE

The "reversioner" handles claims from the landlord's point of view. If the freeholder owns all the reversionary interests then the position is straightforward and is dealt with by subs. (1). If different persons own different interests then the "reversioner" is determined by applying Sched. 1 to the Act. All reversionary landlords retain certain rights in the transaction and they are also dealt with in Sched. 1. For this purpose every owner of a reversionary interest is known as a "relevant landlord".

Subs. (1)

If the freehold owns all the reversionary interests the freeholder is the reversioner.

Subs. (2)

This subsection introduces Sched. 1 and provides for it to decide who is the reversioner where there are reversionary interests owned by more than one person.

Subs. (3)

This subsection provides that generally the reversioner conducts proceedings on behalf of all those with a reversionary interest. However, other owners of a reversionary interest have rights to intervene in certain circumstances and these are contained in Sched. 1, Pt. II introduced by this subsection.

Subs. (4)

This subsection simply introduces Sched. 2 which provides for certain special kinds of landlord *viz.*: where there is a mortgagee in possession of the landlord's interest; where the landlord's interest is owned by a custodian trustee; landlords under disability; landlord's interest held on trust for sale; landlord's interest subject to a settlement; certain University or College landlords (those to whom the Universities and College Estates Act 1925) applies; ecclesiastical landlords.

Premises with a resident landlord

10.—(1) For the purposes of this Chapter any premises falling within section 3(1) are at any time premises with a resident landlord if—
  (a) the premises are not, and do not form part of, a purpose-built block of flats; and
  (b) the freeholder, or an adult member of the freeholder's family—
        (i) at that time occupies a flat contained in the premises as his only or principal home, and
        (ii) has so occupied such a flat throughout a period of not less than twelve months ending with that time.

(2) Where any premises falling within section 3(1) would at any time ("the relevant time") be premises with a resident landlord but for the fact that subsection (1)(b)(ii) above does not apply, the premises shall nevertheless be treated for the purposes of this Chapter as being at that time premises with a resident landlord if—
  (a) immediately before the date when the freeholder acquired his interest in the premises the premises were (or, had this Chapter then been in force, would have been) such premises for the purposes of this Chapter; and
  (b) the freeholder, or an adult member of the freeholder's family—
        (i) entered into occupation of a flat contained in the premises within the period of 28 days beginning with that date, and
        (ii) has occupied such a flat as his only or principal home throughout the period beginning with the time when he so entered into occupation and ending with the relevant time.

(3) In paragraph (b) of each of subsections (1) and (2) any reference to a flat includes a reference to a unit (other than a flat) which is used as a dwelling.

(4) Where the freehold interest in any premises is held on trust, subsections (1) and (2) shall apply as if, in paragraph (b) of each of those subsections, any reference to the freeholder were instead a reference to a person having an interest under the trust (whether or not also a trustee).

(5) For the purposes of this section a person is an adult member of another's family if that person is—
  (a) the other's wife or husband; or
  (b) a son or daughter or a son-in-law or daughter-in-law of the other, or of the other's wife or husband, who has attained the age of 18; or
  (c) the father or mother of the other, or of the other's wife or husband;
and in paragraph (b) any reference to a person's son or daughter includes a reference to any stepson or stepdaughter of that person, and "son-in-law" and "daughter-in-law" shall be construed accordingly.

(6) In this section—
  "the freeholder", in relation to any premises, means the person who owns the freehold of the premises;
  "purpose-built block of flats" means a building which as constructed contained two or more flats.

DEFINITIONS
  "flat": s.101(1).
  "freeholder": subs. (6).
  "interest": s.101(1).
  "premises with a relevant landlord": s.38(1).
  "purpose-built block of flats": subs. (6).

GENERAL NOTE
  The resident landlord provision follows closely in part the wording of s.12 of the Rent Act 1977 and relevant case law will doubtless be followed. In considering this section of the present

Act it must be remembered that if the premises are within the resident landlord exception (s.4(4)) then the tenants will have the right to an individual extended lease under Chap. II of Pt. I.

Subs. (1)

In considering the comparability of the Rent Act 1977, s.12 and Sched. 2 which deals with "purpose built blocks of flats" it should be recalled that the Rent Act definition of a flat (Rent Act 1977, Sched. 2, para. 4) is different and is similar to but again slightly different from the definition in the Landlord and Tenant Act 1987, s.60. There is some suggestion in case law that a building may constitute a purpose-built block of flats where it is substantially rebuilt inside. In *Barnes* v. *Gorsuch* (1982) 43 P. & C.R. 294 it appears that ordinarily the question will be answered as at the date of construction but a building may become a purpose-built block of flats even if not so originally if it has "sufficiently changed its character to become a different building" (but see subs. (6)).

"Only or principal home"—the expression used in other legislation usually is only or main residence, *e.g.* the Capital Gains Tax Act 1979, s.101. The particular phrase in this Act is used in s.81 of the Housing Act 1985 but is not defined. Its meaning was considered by the Court of Appeal in *Crawley Borough Council* v. *Sawyer* (1988) 20 H.L.R. 98, which is of some help. Parker L.J. stated "going through the whole thread of these matters is the common principle that in order to occupy premises as a home, first, there must be signs of occupation, that is to say, there must be furniture and so forth so that the home can be occupied as a home and, secondly, there must be an intention, if not physically present, to return to it . . . for example, the sea captain who is away for a while. His house is left fully furnished, ready for occupation, no doubt the rent paid in his absence, but he is not physically there and may not be for a very long period indeed."

A very recent illustration (in the context of compulsory purchase compensation) of the borderline between occupation as a private dwelling and not (under the Housing Act 1985, Sched. 24) is *Wilson's Estate* v. *Stockport Metropolitan Borough Council* (1993) 66 P. & C.R. 129. An old lady who died in hospital had not been in occupation of her home where void rate was claimed and the furniture removed for more than two years. Other relevant cases were referred to.

Subs. (2)

The purpose of this section is to permit purchaser or successor resident landlords to take advantage of the resident landlord exception. If one new resident landlord buys the premises from an existing resident landlord and has since then been in continuous occupation within subs. (2)(b), then, the full 12-month period of subs. (1)(b)(ii) does not have to be satisfied.

Subs. (3)

The resident landlord's part of a building may fail to satisfy the definition of a flat in s.97(1). This is most likely to be because it fails to "lie above or below some other part of the building". Thus, the resident landlord may have a vertical slice of the building and still take advantage of the resident landlord exception.

Subs. (4)

The resident landlord exception is satisfied if *any person* occupies a flat under a trust who comes within subs. (1)(b).

Subs. (5)

Definitions of members of the family occur elsewhere in Landlord and Tenant legislation, most notably the Housing Act 1985, s.113, the Leasehold Reform Act 1967, s.18(3) and the Mobile Homes Act 1983, s.5(3). Note that the 1985 and 1983 Acts include amongst members of the family persons living together as husband and wife. The Leasehold Reform Act 1967 and this Act do not. There is no such concept as a common-law spouse and the present definition contains an exclusive category of members of the family.

Subs. (6)

Note that if the freeholder is a company, even a trust company, the resident landlord exception can be met by any person who has an interest under the trust or any member of such a person's family.

The definition given of "purpose-built block of flats" suggests a very restrictive interpretation. The *Barnes* v. *Gorsuch* approach (*supra*) can be followed only if "as constructed" is taken to include "as reconstructed".

Preliminary inquiries by tenants

Right of qualifying tenant to obtain information about superior interests etc.

11.—(1) A qualifying tenant of a flat may give—

(a) to his immediate landlord, or

(b) to any person receiving rent on behalf of his immediate landlord,

a notice requiring the recipient to give the tenant (so far as known to the recipient) the name and address of the person who owns the freehold of the relevant premises and the name and address of every other person who has an interest to which subsection (2) applies.

(2) In relation to a qualifying tenant of a flat, this subsection applies to the following interests, namely—

(a) the freehold of any property not contained in the relevant premises—

(i) which is demised by the lease held by the tenant, or

(ii) which the tenant is entitled under the terms of his lease to use in common with other persons; and

(b) any leasehold interest in the relevant premises or in any such property which is superior to that of the tenant's immediate landlord.

(3) Any qualifying tenant of a flat may give to the person who owns the freehold of the relevant premises a notice requiring him to give the tenant (so far as known to him) the name and address of every person, apart from the tenant, who is—

(a) a tenant of the whole of the relevant premises, or

(b) a tenant or licensee of any separate set or sets of premises contained in the relevant premises, or

(c) a tenant or licensee of the whole or any part of any common parts so contained or of any property not so contained—

(i) which is demised by the lease held by a qualifying tenant of a flat contained in the relevant premises, or

(ii) which any such qualifying tenant is entitled under the terms of his lease to use in common with other persons.

(4) Any such qualifying tenant may also give—

(a) to the person who owns the freehold of the relevant premises, or

(b) to any person falling within subsection (3)(a), (b) or (c),

a notice requiring him to give the tenant—

(i) such information relating to his interest in the relevant premises or (as the case may be) in any such property as is mentioned in subsection (3)(c), or

(ii) (so far as known to him) such information relating to any interest derived (whether directly or indirectly) out of that interest,

as is specified in the notice, where the information is reasonably required by the tenant in connection with the making of a claim to exercise the right to collective enfranchisement in relation to the whole or part of the relevant premises.

(5) Where a notice is given by a qualifying tenant under subsection (4), the following rights shall be exercisable by him in relation to the recipient of the notice, namely—

(a) a right, on giving reasonable notice, to be provided with a list of documents to which subsection (6) applies;

(b) a right to inspect, at any reasonable time and on giving reasonable notice, any documents to which that subsection applies; and

(c) a right, on payment of a reasonable fee, to be provided with a copy of any documents which are contained in any list provided under paragraph (a) or have been inspected under paragraph (b).

(6) This subsection applies to any document in the custody or under the control of the recipient of the notice under subsection (4)—

(a) sight of which is reasonably required by the qualifying tenant in connection with the making of such a claim as is mentioned in that subsection; and

(b) which, on a proposed sale by a willing seller to a willing buyer of the recipient's interest in the relevant premises or (as the case may be) in any such property as is mentioned in subsection (3)(c), the seller would be expected to make available to the buyer (whether at or before contract or completion).

(7) Any person who—

(a) is required by a notice under any of subsections (1) to (4) to give any information to a qualifying tenant, or

(b) is required by a qualifying tenant under subsection (5) to supply any list of documents, to permit the inspection of any documents or to supply a copy of any documents,

shall comply with that requirement within the period of 28 days beginning with the date of the giving of the notice referred to in paragraph (a) or (as the case may be) with the date of the making of the requirement referred to in paragraph (b).

(8) Where—

(a) a person has received a notice under subsection (4), and

(b) within the period of six months beginning with the date of receipt of the notice, he—

(i) disposes of any interest (whether legal or equitable) in the relevant premises otherwise than by the creation of an interest by way of security for a loan, or

(ii) acquires any such interest (otherwise than by way of security for a loan),

then (unless that disposal or acquisition has already been notified to the qualifying tenant in accordance with subsection (7)) he shall notify the qualifying tenant of that disposal or acquisition within the period of 28 days beginning with the date when it occurred.

(9) In this section—

"document" has the same meaning as in Part I of the Civil Evidence Act 1968;

"the relevant premises", in relation to any qualifying tenant of a flat, means—

(a) if the person who owns the freehold interest in the flat owns the freehold of the whole of the building in which the flat is contained, that building, or

(b) if that person owns the freehold of part only of that building, that part of that building;

and any reference to an interest in the relevant premises includes an interest in part of those premises.

DEFINITIONS

"common parts": s.101(1).
"disposal": s.101(1).
"document": subs. (9).
"flat": s.101(1).
"interest": s.101(1).
"lease": s.101(1).
"qualifying tenant": s.38(1).
"relevant premises": subs. (9).

GENERAL NOTE

A very great difficulty for a tenant in a block of flats is exercising his now very numerous statutory rights in discovering information about the landlord and its title. Persons familiar with such flat titles will know that they are nearly always complex and confusing. Sometimes this is merely a result of chaotic conveyancing; sometimes it is the result of deliberate obfuscation. This section is aimed at assisting the tenant in his quest for the necessary information. The provision was much criticised in Parliament as lacking in "teeth". In particular the opposition wanted there to be a criminal sanction for non-compliance. Failure to comply with the section is dealt with by an application to the County Court under s.90. There is no prescribed form for a notice under this section.

Subs. (8)

Conveyancers need to note the requirement to notify tenants of disposals and acquisitions where a s.11 notice has been served in the previous six months.

Right of qualifying tenant to obtain information about other matters

12.—(1) Any notice given by a qualifying tenant under section 11(4) shall, in addition to any other requirement imposed in accordance with that provision, require the recipient to give the tenant—

(a) the information specified in subsection (2) below; and

(b) (so far as known to the recipient) the information specified in subsection (3) below.

(2) The information referred to in subsection (1)(a) is—

(a) whether the recipient has received in respect of any premises containing the tenant's flat—

(i) a notice under section 13 in the case of which the relevant claim is still current, or

(ii) a copy of such a notice; and

(b) if so, the date on which the notice under section 13 was given and the name and address of the nominee purchaser for the time being appointed for the purposes of section 15 in relation to that claim.

(3) The information referred to in subsection (1)(b) is—

(a) whether the tenant's flat is comprised in any property in the case of which any of paragraphs (a) to (d) of section 31(2) is applicable; and

(b) if paragraph (b) or (d) of that provision is applicable, the date of the application in question.

(4) Where—

(a) within the period of six months beginning with the date of receipt of a notice given by a tenant under section 11(4), the recipient of the notice receives in respect of any premises containing the tenant's flat—

(i) a notice under section 13, or

(ii) a copy of such a notice, and

(b) the tenant is not one of the qualifying tenants by whom the notice under section 13 is given,

the recipient shall, within the period of 28 days beginning with the date of receipt of the notice under section 13 or (as the case may be) the copy, notify the tenant of the date on which the notice was given and of the name and address of the nominee purchaser for the time being appointed for the purposes of section 15 in relation to the relevant claim.

(5) Where—

(a) the recipient of a notice given by a tenant under section 11(4) has, in accordance with subsection (1) above, informed the tenant of any such application as is referred to in subsection (3)(b) above; and

(b) within the period of six months beginning with the date of receipt of the notice, the application is either granted or refused by the Commissioners of Inland Revenue or is withdrawn by the applicant,

the recipient shall, within the period of 28 days beginning with the date of the granting, refusal or withdrawal of the application, notify the tenant that it has been granted, refused or withdrawn.

(6) In this section "the relevant claim", in relation to a notice under section 13, means the claim in respect of which that notice is given; and for the purposes of subsection (2) above any such claim is current if—

(a) that notice continues in force in accordance with section 13(11), or

(b) a binding contract entered into in pursuance of that notice remains in force, or

(c) where an order has been made under section 24(4)(a) or (b) or 25(6)(a) or (b) with respect to any such premises as are referred to in subsection (2)(a) above, any interests which by virtue of the order fall to be vested in the nominee purchaser have yet to be so vested.

DEFINITIONS
   "disposal": s.101(1).
   "document": s.11(9).
   "flat": s.101(1).
   "interest": s.101(1).
   "lease": s.101(1)(2).
   "qualifying tenant": s.38(1).
   "relevant premises": s.11(9).

GENERAL NOTE
   This forbidding looking section provides a further opportunity for the tenant to require information from the landlord. Under this section the recipient is required to provide information as to: whether any initial notice has been served in respect of the premises containing the tenant's flat (s.12(2)(a)(i)) and details of such notice; whether the property falls within the provisions of s.31 dealing with property which may be conditionally exempt for inheritance tax purposes.

The initial notice

Notice by qualifying tenants of claim to exercise right

13.—(1) A claim to exercise the right to collective enfranchisement with respect to any premises is made by the giving of notice of the claim under this section.

(2) A notice given under this section ("the initial notice")—
   (a) must be given to the reversioner in respect of those premises; and
   (b) must be given by a number of qualifying tenants of flats contained in the premises as at the relevant date which—
      (i) is not less than two-thirds of the total number of such tenants, and
      (ii) is not less than one-half of the total number of flats so contained;
and not less than one-half of the qualifying tenants by whom the notice is given must satisfy the residence condition.

(3) The initial notice must—
   (a) specify and be accompanied by a plan showing—
      (i) the premises of which the freehold is proposed to be acquired by virtue of section 1(1),
      (ii) any property of which the freehold is proposed to be acquired by virtue of section 1(2)(a), and
      (iii) any property of the person who owns the freehold of the specified premises over which it is proposed that rights (specified in the notice) should be granted by him in connection with the acquisition of the freehold of the specified premises or of any such property so far as falling within section 1(3)(a);
   (b) contain a statement of the grounds on which it is claimed that the specified premises are, on the relevant date, premises to which this Chapter applies;
   (c) specify—
      (i) any leasehold interest proposed to be acquired under or by virtue of section 2(1)(a) or (b), and
      (ii) any flats or other units contained in the specified premises in relation to which it is considered that any of the requirements in Part II of Schedule 9 to this Act are applicable;
   (d) specify the proposed purchase price for each of the following, namely—

(i) the freehold interest in the specified premises,

(ii) the freehold interest in any property specified under paragraph (a)(ii), and

(iii) any leasehold interest specified under paragraph (c)(i);

(e) state the full names of all the qualifying tenants of flats contained in the specified premises and the addresses of their flats, and contain the following particulars in relation to each of those tenants, namely—

(i) such particulars of his lease as are sufficient to identify it, including the date on which the lease was entered into, the term for which it was granted and the date of the commencement of the term,

(ii) such further particulars as are necessary to show that the lease is a lease at a low rent, and

(iii) if it is claimed that he satisfies the residence condition, particulars of the period or periods falling within the preceding ten years for which he has occupied the whole or part of his flat as his only or principal home;

(f) state the full name or names of the person or persons appointed as the nominee purchaser for the purposes of section 15, and an address in England and Wales at which notices may be given to that person or those persons under this Chapter; and

(g) specify the date by which the reversioner must respond to the notice by giving a counter-notice under section 21.

(4) In a case where the tenant's lease is held by joint tenants, subsection (3)(e)(iii) shall have effect as if any reference to the tenant were a reference to any joint tenant by virtue of whose occupation of the flat in question it is claimed that the residence condition is satisfied.

(5) The date specified in the initial notice in pursuance of subsection (3)(g) must be a date falling not less than two months after the relevant date.

(6) A notice shall not be given under this section with respect to any premises unless the qualifying tenants by whom it is given have obtained a valuation prepared by a qualified surveyor in respect of—

(a) the freehold interest in the specified premises,

(b) the freehold interest in any property specified under subsection (3)(a)(ii), and

(c) any leasehold interest specified under subsection (3)(c)(i),

and any such notice must contain a statement confirming that they have done so and state the name of the surveyor in question.

(7) For the purposes of subsection (6) a person is a qualified surveyor if—

(a) he is a fellow or professional associate of the Royal Institution of Chartered Surveyors or of the Incorporated Society of Valuers and Auctioneers or satisfies such other requirement or requirements as may be prescribed by regulations made by the Secretary of State; and

(b) he is reasonably believed by the qualifying tenants to have ability in, and experience of, the valuation of premises of the particular kind, and in the particular area, in question;

and any valuation prepared for the purposes of that subsection must be prepared in conformity with the provisions of Schedule 6 so far as relating to the determination of the price payable under this Chapter for the interest in question.

(8) Where any premises have been specified in a notice under this section, no subsequent notice which specifies the whole or part of those premises may be given under this section so long as the earlier notice continues in force.

(9) Where any premises have been specified in a notice under this section and—

(a) that notice has been withdrawn, or is deemed to have been withdrawn, under or by virtue of any provision of this Chapter or under section 74(3), or

(b) in response to that notice, an order has been applied for and obtained under section 23(1),

no subsequent notice which specifies the whole or part of those premises may be given under this section within the period of twelve months beginning with the date of the withdrawal or deemed withdrawal of the earlier notice or with the time when the order under section 23(1) becomes final (as the case may be).

(10) In subsections (8) and (9) any reference to a notice which specifies the whole or part of any premises includes a reference to a notice which specifies any premises which contain the whole or part of those premises; and in those subsections and this "specifies" means specifies under subsection (3)(a)(i).

(11) Where a notice is given in accordance with this section, then for the purposes of this Chapter the notice continues in force as from the relevant date—

(a) until a binding contract is entered into in pursuance of the notice, or an order is made under section 24(4)(a) or (b) or 25(6)(a) or (b) providing for the vesting of interests in the nominee purchaser;

(b) if the notice is withdrawn or deemed to have been withdrawn under or by virtue of any provision of this Chapter or under section 74(3), until the date of the withdrawal or deemed withdrawal, or

(c) until such other time as the notice ceases to have effect by virtue of any provision of this Chapter.

(12) In this Chapter "the specified premises", in relation to a claim made under this Chapter, means—

(a) the premises specified in the initial notice under subsection (3)(a)(i), or

(b) if it is subsequently agreed or determined under this Chapter that any less extensive premises should be acquired in pursuance of the notice in satisfaction of the claim, those premises;

and similarly references to any property or interest specified in the initial notice under subsection (3)(a)(ii) or (c)(i) shall, if it is subsequently agreed or determined under this Chapter that any less extensive property or interest should be acquired in pursuance of the notice, be read as references to that property or interest.

(13) Schedule 3 to this Act (which contains restrictions on participating in the exercise of the right to collective enfranchisement, and makes further provision in connection with the giving of notices under this section) shall have effect.

DEFINITIONS
"initial notice": s.38(1).
"interest": s.38(1).
"lease": s.101(1).
"qualifying tenant": s.38(1).
"relevant date": s.38(1).
"reversioner": s.38(1).
"right to collective enfranchisement": s.38(1).
"unit": s.101(1).

GENERAL NOTE
The initial notice is the formal beginning of the legal process which will end eventually in the tenants purchasing the freehold. In most cases it will be a complex document and will invariably require professional help from both a solicitor and a surveyor. The notice is registrable as a land charge under the Land Charges Act 1972 or as a notice or caution under the Land Registration Act 1925. This important step must not be omitted as the benefit of the notice may be lost if the freehold changes hands (see s.19). There is no prescribed form for an initial notice. A suitable form is reproduced here. It is likely that many landlords will challenge this notice. Particular effort is needed to make sure the details in Scheds. II, III and IV are accurate.

Subs. (3)
   A plan is obligatory.

Subs. (6)
   A professional valuation by a surveyor is obligatory before an initial notice is given.

Subs. (7)
   Note that this subsection imposes a rather odd standard of care on the tenants in the selection of their surveyor. If there are 100 tenants who has to have this reasonable belief?

Subs. (8)
   While the notice subsists no further notice can be given under s.13.

Subs. (13)
   Schedule 3 will need to be carefully checked to see which tenants are excluded.

LEASEHOLD REFORM, HOUSING AND URBAN DEVELOPMENT ACT 1993 INITIAL NOTICE UNDER S.13

Initial notice—example
   1. This Notice is given to [insert name and address of reversioner under s.9]
   2. The freehold is claimed of [address]
      — under s.1(1) of the land edged red on the plan annexed hereto
      — under s.1(2)(a) of the land edged blue on the said plans which together with the land edged red is the "specified premises".
   3. It is proposed that the freeholder should be granted the rights specified in Sched. I hereof over the property therein specified.
   4. The specified premises are premises to which Chap. I of the Leasehold Reform, Housing and Urban Development Act 1993 applies because they consist of a building which falls within s.3(1)(a) containing two or more flats held by qualifying tenants which are together at least two-thirds of the flats in the premises.
   5. The leasehold interests proposed to be acquired are specified in Sched. II hereof Column I.
   6. A mandatory leaseback under Sched. 9, Pt. 2 will be made of the property specified in Sched. III.
   7. The purchase price proposed is:
       (i) for the freehold of the land edged red   _____
      (ii) for the freehold of the land edged blue   _____
     (iii) in respect of each leasehold interest the sum specified in
           Sched. II Col. II of which the total is   _____
      This price is based on a valuation by [name] a qualified surveyor.
   8. Particulars of the qualifying tenants and their leases are stated in Sched. IV hereof.
   9. The nominee purchaser is [name and address for service]
  10. The reversioner is required to give a counter-notice under s.21 of the Act by [specify a date of at least two months after service of the notice].

Dated

Signed [by each of the tenants by whom it is given—see s.99(5)(a)]

SCHEDULES

Sched. IV must state:

(i) full names of qualifying purchaser	(ii) flat	(iii) date, term and commencement of lease	(iv) whether tenant satisfies the residence condition and if so for which periods

This can conveniently be done in four columns as indicated.

Participating tenants and nominee purchaser

The participating tenants

14.—(1) In relation to any claim to exercise the right to collective enfranchisement, the participating tenants are (subject to the provisions of this section and Part I of Schedule 3) the following persons, namely—
   (a) in relation to the relevant date, the qualifying tenants by whom the initial notice is given; and

(b) in relation to any time falling after that date, such of those qualifying tenants as for the time being remain qualifying tenants of flats contained in the specified premises.

(2) Where the lease by virtue of which a participating tenant is a qualifying tenant of his flat is assigned to another person, the assignee of the lease shall, within the period of 14 days beginning with the date of the assignment, notify the nominee purchaser—

(a) of the assignment, and

(b) as to whether or not the assignee is electing to participate in the proposed acquisition.

(3) Where a qualifying tenant of a flat contained in the specified premises—

(a) is not one of the persons by whom the initial notice was given, and

(b) is not such an assignee of the lease of a participating tenant as is mentioned in subsection (2),

then (subject to paragraph 8 of Schedule 3) he may elect to participate in the proposed acquisition, but only with the agreement of all the persons who are for the time being participating tenants; and, if he does so elect, he shall notify the nominee purchaser forthwith of his election.

(4) Where a person notifies the nominee purchaser under subsection (2) or (3) of his election to participate in the proposed acquisition, he shall be regarded as a participating tenant for the purposes of this Chapter—

(a) as from the date of the assignment or agreement referred to in that subsection; and

(b) so long as he remains a qualifying tenant of a flat contained in the specified premises.

(5) Where a participating tenant dies, his personal representatives shall, within the period of 56 days beginning with the date of death, notify the nominee purchaser—

(a) of the death of the tenant, and

(b) as to whether or not the personal representatives are electing to withdraw from participation in the proposed acquisition;

and, unless the personal representatives of a participating tenant so notify the nominee purchaser that they are electing to withdraw from participation in that acquisition, they shall be regarded as a participating tenant for the purpose of this Chapter—

(i) as from the date of the death of the tenant, and

(ii) so long as his lease remains vested in them.

(6) Where in accordance with subsection (4) or (5) any assignee or personal representatives of a participating tenant ("the tenant") is or are to be regarded as a participating tenant for the purposes of this Chapter, any arrangements made between the nominee purchaser and the participating tenants and having effect immediately before the date of the assignment or (as the case may be) the date of death shall have effect as from that date—

(a) with such modifications as are necessary for substituting the assignee or (as the case may be) the personal representatives as a party to the arrangements in the place of the tenant; or

(b) in the case of an assignment by a person who remains a qualifying tenant of a flat contained in the specified premises, with such modifications as are necessary for adding the assignee as a party to the arrangements.

(7) Where the nominee purchaser receives a notification under subsection (2), (3) or (5), he shall, within the period of 28 days beginning with the date of receipt of the notification—

(a) give a notice under subsection (8) to the reversioner in respect of the specified premises, and

(b) give a copy of that notice to every other relevant landlord.

(8) A notice under this subsection is a notice stating—

(a) in the case of a notification under subsection (2)—

(i) the date of the assignment and the name and address of the assignee,

(ii) that the assignee has or (as the case may be) has not become a participating tenant in accordance with subsection (4), and

(iii) if he has become a participating tenant (otherwise than in a case to which subsection (6)(b) applies), that he has become such a tenant in place of his assignor;

(b) in the case of a notification under subsection (3), the name and address of the person who has become a participating tenant in accordance with subsection (4); and

(c) in the case of a notification under subsection (5)—

(i) the date of death of the deceased tenant,

(ii) the names and addresses of the personal representatives of the tenant, and

(iii) that in accordance with that subsection those persons are or (as the case may be) are not to be regarded as a participating tenant.

(9) Every notice under subsection (8)—

(a) shall identify the flat with respect to which it is given; and

(b) if it states that any person or persons is or are to be regarded as a participating tenant, shall be signed by the person or persons in question.

(10) In this section references to assignment include an assent by personal representatives and assignment by operation of law, where the assignment is—

(a) to a trustee in bankruptcy, or

(b) to a mortgagee under section 89(2) of the Law of Property Act 1925 (foreclosure of leasehold mortgage),

and references to an assignee shall be construed accordingly.

(11) Nothing in this section has effect for requiring or authorising anything to be done at any time after a binding contract is entered into in pursuance of the initial notice.

DEFINITIONS
"flat": s.101(1).
"initial notice": s.38(1).
"lease": s.101(1).
"nominee purchaser": s.38(1).
"participating tenants": s.38(1).
"qualifying tenant": s.38(1).
"relevant date": s.38(1).
"reversioner": s.38(1).
"specified premises": s.38(1).

GENERAL NOTE
Between the date of the initial notice and completion of the enfranchisement process tenants will come and go. This section is intended to resolve questions of which of them is to be regarded as a qualifying tenant at which times. It is important to know who are qualifying tenants: (1) to test if the premises are premises to which the Act applies (s.3); (2) to test if a particular person is entitled to make preliminary enquiries (ss.11 and 12); and (3) at the time of the initial notice, to test its validity. Once the initial notice has been served a new concept arises by virtue of this section. That is the "participating tenants". It is these who are entitled to conduct the enfranchisement procedure and from this time it is necessary to test if a tenant is a qualifying tenant and a participating tenant. There are detailed provisions in Sched. 3, Pt. I preventing certain tenants from participating in cases such as notice to quit, forfeiture, compulsory purchase. These are considered in the note on that schedule.

One effect of this section seems to be this: if a person is the tenant of three or more flats then there is no qualifying tenant of any of those (s.6(6)). If that person assigns flats so as to remain the tenant of only two then each assignee could have been a qualifying tenant under subs. (3) above. The occupier may also become a qualifying tenant and be permitted to participate under subs. (3). But note that subs. (3) is subject to the provisions of Sched. 3, para. 8 annotated below.

Subs. (1)
This subsection provides that "participating tenants" at any time are firstly the qualifying tenants who give the initial notice and remain qualifying tenants. It is worth repeating that they are each required to sign the initial notice *personally* (s.99). This precise requirement will often be hard to achieve because of the mobility of many tenants. In practice the systematic collection from each tenant of special powers of attorney may be advisable.

Subs. (2)
If a participating tenant assigns his lease then the assignee has an election to become a participating tenant. This is not so if the assignee is prevented from being a qualifying tenant by virtue of s.5(5) because it now owns too many flats.

Subs. (3)
A qualifying tenant who has not joined in the initial notice may join in as a participating tenant with the agreement of all the persons who are participating tenants. There is no procedure stated for obtaining such agreement and no requirement that the other tenants behave reasonably in giving or withholding it. (Note the exclusion provided by para. 8 of Sched. 1 from such tenants joining in is dealt with in the note on that Schedule).

Subs. (5)
This is a small trap for personal representatives of a deceased tenant. Unless within 56 days of death they elect to withdraw, then the tenant's estate remains a participator in the enfranchisement. The personal representatives then become participating tenants from the date of death although, if they are administrators, it will not be known who they are until the grant. In the case of executors it is the proving executors who remain as participating tenants (subs. (5)(b)(ii)) because it is in them that the lease will be vested. However, they can clearly give the requisite notice under this subsection before the grant of probate as they are personal representatives from the date of death (see *Bilers* v. *Ceasar* [1957] 1 W.L.R. 156). An administrator cannot give such notice until the grant (see *Ingall* v. *Moran* [1944] K.B. 160).

Subs. (6)
This has the simple effect of making contractual arrangements continue between the nominee purchaser and the qualifying tenants where the identity of the qualifying tenants changes.

Subss. (7) and (8)
The obligation to notify the landlord of each change in the holding of a qualifying tenancy is potentially onerous. Where there are very many tenants in a building the overall paperwork generated by a Chap. I enfranchisement will in any case be enormous.

Subs. (9)
This subsection seems to require notices under this section to be signed by the tenant or personal representative themselves rather than on their behalf.

Subs. (10)
This subsection creates the important requirement that an assignee must notify the nominee purchaser if he wishes to participate in a collective enfranchisement. Such a notice must be given within 14 days of the assignment (subs. (3)). This includes an assent to a beneficiary under a will or intestacy and the vesting of property in a trustee in bankruptcy or to a mortgagee by a foreclosure order absolute (see s.89(2) of the Law of Property Act 1925).

Subs. (11)
Once a binding contract is entered into after service of the initial notice then the remaining provisions of this section are unnecessary. The assignee or other successor of a tenant who is a participating tenant at that time will simply stand in their shoes.

The nominee purchaser: appointment and replacement

15.—(1) The nominee purchaser shall conduct on behalf of the participating tenants all proceedings arising out of the initial notice, with a view to the eventual acquisition by him, on their behalf, of such freehold and other interests as fall to be so acquired under a contract entered into in pursuance of that notice.

(2) In relation to any claim to exercise the right to collective enfranchisement with respect to any premises, the nominee purchaser shall be such

person or persons as may for the time being be appointed for the purposes of this section by the participating tenants; and in the first instance the nominee purchaser shall be the person or persons specified in the initial notice in pursuance of section 13(3)(f).

(3) The appointment of any person as the nominee purchaser, or as one of the persons constituting the nominee purchaser, may be terminated by the participating tenants by the giving of a notice stating that that person's appointment is to terminate on the date on which the notice is given.

(4) Any such notice must be given—

(a) to the person whose appointment is being terminated, and

(b) to the reversioner in respect of the specified premises.

(5) Any such notice must in addition either—

(a) specify the name or names of the person or persons constituting the nominee purchaser as from the date of the giving of the notice, and an address in England and Wales at which notices may be given to that person or those persons under this Chapter; or

(b) state that the following particulars will be contained in a further notice given to the reversioner within the period of 28 days beginning with that date, namely—

(i) the name of the person or persons for the time being constituting the nominee purchaser,

(ii) if falling after that date, the date of appointment of that person or of each of those persons, and

(iii) an address in England and Wales at which notices may be given to that person or those persons under this Chapter;

and the appointment of any person by way of replacement for the person whose appointment is being terminated shall not be valid unless his name is specified, or is one of those specified, under paragraph (a) or (b).

(6) Where the appointment of any person is terminated in accordance with this section, anything done by or in relation to the nominee purchaser before the date of termination of that person's appointment shall be treated, so far as necessary for the purpose of continuing its effect, as having been done by or in relation to the nominee purchaser as constituted on or after that date.

(7) Where the appointment of any person is so terminated, he shall not be liable under section 33 for any costs incurred in connection with the proposed acquisition under this Chapter at any time after the date of termination of his appointment; but if—

(a) at any such time he is requested by the nominee purchaser for the time being to supply to the nominee purchaser, at an address in England and Wales specified in the request, all or any documents in his custody or under his control that relate to that acquisition, and

(b) he fails without reasonable cause to comply with any such request or is guilty of any unreasonable delay in complying with it,

he shall be liable for any costs which are incurred by the nominee purchaser, or for which the nominee purchaser is liable under section 33, in consequence of the failure.

(8) Where—

(a) two or more persons together constitute the nominee purchaser, and

(b) the appointment of any (but not both or all) of them is terminated in accordance with this section without any person being appointed by way of immediate replacement,

the person or persons remaining shall for the time being constitute the nominee purchaser.

(9) Where—

(a) a notice given under subsection (3) contains such a statement as is mentioned in subsection (5)(b), and

(b) as a result of the termination of the appointment in question there is no nominee purchaser for the time being,

the running of any period which—
    (i) is prescribed by or under this Part for the giving of any other notice or the making of any application, and
    (ii) would otherwise expire during the period beginning with the date of the giving of the notice under subsection (3) and ending with the date when the particulars specified in subsection (5)(b) are notified to the reversioner,

shall (subject to subsection (10)) be suspended throughout the period mentioned in paragraph (ii).

(10) If—
    (a) the circumstances are as mentioned in subsection (9)(a) and (b), but
    (b) the particulars specified in subsection (5)(b) are not notified to the reversioner within the period of 28 days specified in that provision,

the initial notice shall be deemed to have been withdrawn at the end of that period.

(11) A copy of any notice given under subsection (3) or (5)(b) shall be given by the participating tenants to every relevant landlord (other than the reversioner) to whom the initial notice or a copy of it was given in accordance with section 13 and Part II of Schedule 3; and, where a notice under subsection (3) terminates the appointment of a person who is one of two or more persons together constituting the nominee purchaser, a copy of the notice shall also be given to every other person included among those persons.

(12) Nothing in this section applies in relation to the termination of the appointment of the nominee purchaser (or of any of the persons constituting the nominee purchaser) at any time after a binding contract is entered into in pursuance of the initial notice; and in this Chapter references to the nominee purchaser, so far as referring to anything done by or in relation to the nominee purchaser at any time falling after such a contract is so entered into, are references to the person or persons constituting the nominee purchaser at the time when the contract is entered into or such other person as is for the time being the purchaser under the contract.

DEFINITIONS
    "initial notice": s.38(1).
    "nominee purchaser": s.38(1).
    "participating tenants": s.38(1).
    "relevant landlord": s.38(1).
    "reversioner": s.38(1).
    "right to collective enfranchisement": s.38(1).
    "specified premises": s.38(1).

GENERAL NOTE
    In most cases the tenants who exercise the right to collective enfranchisement will form a limited company as the vehicle for the purchase of the freehold. A scheme from which suitable provisions can be adapted is found in *Precedents for the Conveyancer* (Sweet & Maxwell), p. 2593, precedent 5–10 or for a part of a building, p. 2712, precedent 5–28; ready-made management companies are also readily available.
    The major problem in this legislation is that, detailed as it appears, it is a vacuum from the point of view of the tenants. There is no machinery or guidance as to how to establish the position between the tenants themselves and exactly how to arrive at the desired form of initial notice and structure for the nominee purchaser. The tenants have to reach an understanding between themselves as to the legal structure of their purchase. This will mean agreement on: (a) how each is to share the cost of purchase; (b) how each is to share the cost of management; (c) what the voting rights and share structure of the nominee purchaser will be and (d) what arrangements there will be for employing and paying professional advisers. It is clear that a formal legal agreement between the tenants is desirable at as early a stage as possible so that their "business" can proceed in an orderly fashion. The landlord has only his own interests to serve and may perceive that that is best done by delay—to counteract this the tenants will need their legal wits in good shape throughout.

Subs. (1)
    The nominee purchaser is named in the initial notice and it is then mandatory for it to conduct

the proceedings. There may be more than one nominee purchaser as appears in the next subsection. It is the nominee purchaser(s) who will enter into a contract with the reversioner for the purchase of the freehold and proceed to completion of this contract.

Subs. (2)
   This subsection makes it clear that the participating tenants may change the identity of the nominee purchaser as they choose. There may be more than one nominee purchaser. There is no machinery for the participating tenants to come to agreement on such a change. This may be dealt with in a contract between the tenants.

Subss. (3) to (12)
   These subsections deal in an elaborate way with a very simple procedure for changing the nominee purchaser and giving notice of this change to the reversioner and the former nominee purchaser.

Subs. (7)
   This subsection provides for a former nominee purchaser to provide information and documents relating to the transaction on pain of costs.

Subs. (9)
   This subsection provides for time to stop running while there is presently no nominee purchaser if that time period would expire during the 28 days specified in subs. (5)(b) to give notice of a new purchaser. This needs to be approached with some care. Time only stops running if a relevant period would expire during the 28 day period not if it would, for example, expire at the end of the period.

The nominee purchaser: retirement or death

16.—(1) The appointment of any person as the nominee purchaser, or as one of the persons constituting the nominee purchaser, may be terminated by that person by the giving of a notice stating that he is resigning his appointment with effect from 21 days after the date of the notice.
   (2) Any such notice must be given—
   (a) to each of the participating tenants; and
   (b) to the reversioner in respect of the specified premises.
   (3) Where the participating tenants have received any such notice, they shall, within the period of 56 days beginning with the date of the notice, give to the reversioner a notice informing him of the resignation and containing the following particulars, namely—
   (a) the name or names of the person or persons for the time being constituting the nominee purchaser,
   (b) if falling after that date, the date of appointment of that person or of each of those persons, and
   (c) an address in England and Wales at which notices may be given to that person or those persons under this Chapter;
and the appointment of any person by way of replacement for the person resigning his appointment shall not be valid unless his name is specified, or is one of those specified, under paragraph (a).
   (4) Subsections (6) to (8) of section 15 shall have effect in connection with a person's resignation of his appointment in accordance with this section as they have effect in connection with the termination of a person's appointment in accordance with that section.
   (5) Where the person, or one of the persons, constituting the nominee purchaser dies, the participating tenants shall, within the period of 56 days beginning with the date of death, give to the reversioner a notice informing him of the death and containing the following particulars, namely—
   (a) the name or names of the person or persons for the time being constituting the nominee purchaser,
   (b) if falling after that date, the date of appointment of that person or of each of those persons, and

    (c) an address in England and Wales at which notices may be given to that person or those persons under this Chapter;

and the appointment of any person by way of replacement for the person who has died shall not be valid unless his name is specified, or is one of those specified, under paragraph (a).

    (6) Subsections (6) and (8) of section 15 shall have effect in connection with the death of any such person as they have effect in connection with the termination of a person's appointment in accordance with that section.

    (7) If—

    (a) the participating tenants are required to give a notice under subsection (3) or (5), and

    (b) as a result of the resignation or death referred to in that subsection there is no nominee purchaser for the time being,

the running of any period which—

    (i) is prescribed by or under this Part for the giving of any other notice or the making of any application, and

    (ii) would otherwise expire during the period beginning with the relevant date and ending with the date when the particulars specified in that subsection are notified to the reversioner,

shall (subject to subsection (8)) be suspended throughout the period mentioned in paragraph (ii); and for this purpose "the relevant date" means the date of the notice of resignation under subsection (1) or the date of death (as the case may be).

    (8) If—

    (a) the circumstances are as mentioned in subsection (7)(a) and (b), but

    (b) the participating tenants fail to give a notice under subsection (3) or (as the case may be) subsection (5) within the period of 56 days specified in that subsection,

the initial notice shall be deemed to have been withdrawn at the end of that period.

    (9) Where a notice under subsection (1) is given by a person who is one of two or more persons together constituting the nominee purchaser, a copy of the notice shall be given by him to every other person included among those persons; and a copy of any notice given under subsection (3) or (5) shall be given by the participating tenants to every relevant landlord (other than the reversioner) to whom the initial notice or a copy of it was given in accordance with section 13 and Part II of Schedule 3.

    (10) Nothing in this section apples in relation to the resignation or death of the nominee purchaser (or any of the persons together constituting the nominee purchaser) at any time after a binding contract is entered into in pursuance of the initial notice.

DEFINITIONS
    "initial notice": s.38(1).
    "nominee purchaser": s.38(1).
    "participating tenants": s.38(1).
    "relevant landlord": s.38(1).
    "reversioner": s.38(1).
    "specified premises": s.38(1).

GENERAL NOTE
    This section contains provision for the nominee purchaser to retire and for the participating tenants to appoint a new nominee purchaser. Similarly it provides for the appointment of a new nominee purchaser where the nominee purchaser's partner dies. This applies when any one of a number of nominee purchasers dies.

    As with other provisions of this Act there is no indication as to how the participating tenants should arrive at a decision as to who the new nominee purchaser is or through whom they should communicate it to the reversioner. As suggested above, in any but the simplest cases the tenants are well advised to draw up a legally binding agreement regulating the position between themselves before they proceed.

Procedure following giving of initial notice

Access by relevant landlords for valuation purposes

17.—(1) Once the initial notice or a copy of it has been given in accordance with section 13 or Part II of Schedule 3 to the reversioner or to any other relevant landlord, that person and any person authorised to act on his behalf shall, in the case of—

(a) any part of the specified premises, or

(b) any part of any property specified in the notice under section 13(3)(a)(ii),

in which he has a freehold or leasehold interest which is included in the proposed acquisition by the nominee purchaser, have a right of access thereto for the purpose of enabling him to obtain a valuation of that interest in connection with the notice.

(2) Once the initial notice has been given in accordance with section 13, the nominee purchaser and any person authorised to act on his behalf shall have a right of access to—

(a) any part of the specified premises, or

(b) any part of any property specified in the notice under section 13(3)(a)(ii),

where such access is reasonably required by the nominee purchaser in connection with any matter arising out of the notice.

(3) A right of access conferred by this section shall be exercisable at any reasonable time and on giving not less than 10 days' notice to the occupier of any premises to which access is sought (or, if those premises are unoccupied, to the person entitled to occupy them).

DEFINITIONS
   "initial notice": s.38(1).
   "interest": s.101(1).
   "nominee purchaser": s.38(1).
   "relevant landlord": s.38(1).
   "reversioner": s.38(1).
   "specified premises": s.38(1).

GENERAL NOTE
   This gives the reversioner and each relevant landlord the right of access "to obtain a valuation" in connection with the initial notice. This clearly might involve several different "valuations" or stages in the valuation and the section obviously will permit more than one exercise of the right of access to achieve the required valuation, see Sched. 6.

Duty of nominee purchaser to disclose existence of agreements affecting specified premises etc.

18.—(1) If at any time during the period beginning with the relevant date and ending with the valuation date for the purposes of Schedule 6—

(a) there subsists between the nominee purchaser and a person other than a participating tenant any agreement (of whatever nature) providing for the disposal of a relevant interest, or

(b) if the nominee purchaser is a company, any person other than a participating tenant holds any share in that company by virtue of which a relevant interest may be acquired,

the existence of that agreement or shareholding shall be notified to the reversioner by the nominee purchaser as soon as possible after the agreement or shareholding is made or established or, if in existence on the relevant date, as soon as possible after that date.

(2) If—

(a) the nominee purchaser is required to give any notification under subsection (1) but fails to do so before the price payable to the reversioner or any other relevant landlord in respect of the acquisition of any interest of his by the nominee purchaser is determined for the purposes of Schedule 6, and

(b) it may reasonably be assumed that, had the nominee purchaser given the notification, it would have resulted in the price so determined being increased by an amount referable to the existence of any agreement or shareholding falling within subsection (1)(a) or (b),

the nominee purchaser and the participating tenants shall be jointly and severally liable to pay the amount to the reversioner or (as the case may be) the other relevant landlord.

(3) In subsection (1) "relevant interest" means any interest in, or in any part of, the specified premises or any property specified in the initial notice under section 13(3)(a)(ii).

(4) Paragraph (a) of subsection (1) does not, however, apply to an agreement if the only disposal of such an interest for which it provides is one consisting in the creation of an interest by way of security for a loan.

DEFINITIONS
   "disposal": s.101(1).
   "initial notice": s.38(1).
   "interest": s.101(1).
   "nominee purchaser": s.38(1).
   "participating tenants": s.38(1).
   "relevant date": s.38(1).
   "relevant interest": subs. (3).
   "relevant landlord": s.38(1).
   "reversioner": s.38(1).
   "specified premises": ss.13(12) and 38(1).

GENERAL NOTE
   This section is intended to ensure that the landlord is not deprived of any increase in value of the enfranchisement which results from a contract or other disposal entered into by the nominee purchaser between the relevant date and the valuation date.

Subs. (1)
   The "relevant date" simply means the date of the notice claiming enfranchisement, see s.1(8). The "valuation date" under Sched. 6, para. 1 is the date when the interest to be acquired is either agreed or determined by a leasehold valuation tribunal.
   The two circumstances defined, of which the nominee purchaser has to give notice to the reversioner, are described in paras. (a) and (b). The first is where there is "any agreement (of whatever nature) providing for the disposal of a relevant interest". Those of a cunning disposition will note that if the nominee purchaser has contracted to sell to a person who happens to be also a participating tenant then this paragraph does not apply.
   The second is where some persons, other than a participating tenant, owns share(s) in the nominee company. Again this is readily circumvented by the possibility of this shareholding being in the name of a participating tenant.

Subs. (2)
   The sanction for failure to give the notice required by subs. (1) is described in this subsection. It is that the nominee purchaser and the participating tenants are jointly and severally liable to make up any deficit in the purchase price resulting from the absence of this notification. The rather odd way of assessing this deficit is to consider whether "it may reasonably be assumed" that if the notification had been given the price would have "increased by an amount referable to the existence of any agreement or shareholding". Presumably this reasonable assumption is a task for the court when a dispute on this point arises and it will be assisted by expert evidence as to how such an agreement would have affected the valuation. However, the reversioner will have had the valuation according to the statutory formula in Sched. 6—why should he then have this very favourable hypothesis improved yet further by the interposition of reality?

Subs. (4)
   This subsection provides that the section has no application to arrangements made by the nominee purchaser solely to raise money on the security of the property.

Effect of initial notice as respects subsequent transactions by freeholder etc.

19.—(1) Where the initial notice has been registered in accordance with section 97(1), then so long as it continues in force—
  (a) the person who owns the freehold of the specified premises shall not—
        (i) make any disposal severing his interest in those premises or in any property specified in the notice under section 13(3)(a)(ii), or
        (ii) grant out of that interest any lease under which, if it had been granted before the relevant date, the interest of the tenant would to any extent have been liable on that date to acquisition by virtue of section 2(1)(a) or (b); and
  (b) no other relevant landlord shall grant out of his interest in the specified premises or in any property so specified any such lease as is mentioned in paragraph (a)(ii);
and any transaction shall be void to the extent that it purports to effect any such disposal or any such grant of a lease as is mentioned in paragraph (a) or (b).
  (2) Where the initial notice has been so registered and at any time when it continues in force—
  (a) the person who owns the freehold of the specified premises disposes of his interest in those premises or in any property specified in the notice under section 13(3)(a)(ii), or
  (b) any other relevant landlord disposes of any interest of his specified in the notice under section 13(3)(c)(i),
subsection (3) below shall apply in relation to that disposal.
  (3) Where this subsection applies in relation to any such disposal as is mentioned in subsection (2)(a) or (b), all parties shall for the purposes of this Chapter be in the same position as if the person acquiring the interest under the disposal—
  (a) had become its owner before the initial notice was given (and was accordingly a relevant landlord in place of the person making the disposal), and
  (b) had been given any notice or copy of a notice given under this Chapter to that person, and
  (c) had taken all steps which that person had taken;
and, if any subsequent disposal of that interest takes place at any time when the initial notice continues in force, this subsection shall apply in relation to that disposal as if any reference to the person making the disposal included any predecessor in title of his.
  (4) Where immediately before the relevant date there is in force a binding contract relating to the disposal to any extent—
  (a) by the person who owns the freehold of the specified premises, or
  (b) by any other relevant landlord,
of any interest of his falling within subsection (2)(a) or (b), then, so long as the initial notice continues in force, the operation of the contract shall be suspended so far as it relates to any such disposal.
  (5) Where—
  (a) the operation of a contract has been suspended under subsection (4) ("the suspended contract"), and
  (b) a binding contract is entered into in pursuance of the initial notice,
then (without prejudice to the general law as to the frustration of contracts) the person referred to in paragraph (a) or (b) of that subsection shall, together with all other persons, be discharged from the further performance of the suspended contract so far as it relates to any such disposal as is mentioned in subsection (4).
  (6) In subsections (4) and (5) any reference to a contract (except in the context of such a contract as is mentioned in subsection (5)(b)) includes a

contract made in pursuance of an order of any court; but those subsections do not apply to any contract providing for the eventuality of a notice being given under section 13 in relation to the whole or part of the property in which any such interest as is referred to in subsection (4) subsists.

DEFINITIONS
   "disposal": s.101(1).
   "initial notice": s.38(1).
   "interest": s.101(1).
   "lease": s.101(1).
   "relevant date": s.38(1).
   "relevant landlord": s.38(1).
   "specified premises": ss.13(12) and 38(1).

GENERAL NOTE
   This section contains various provisions to protect the leaseholders from the adverse consequences of disposals by the freeholder or other relevant landlords once an initial notice is served.

Subs. (1)
   This subsection applies only if the initial notice has been registered as a land charge, notice or caution. Paragraph (a)(i) protects the person who owns the freehold from making a disposal "severing his interest". This will apply to a division of different parts of the property among different owners or a transfer of all into several names or of a division into lesser interests. Paragraph (a)(ii) renders void the grant of a lease which would be reversionary upon the qualifying tenant's lease. Such a lease appears to be a disposal within para. (a)(i) in any event. Paragraph (b) renders void the grant by any other relevant landlord of a lease reversionary upon the lease of a qualifying tenant.

Subss. (2) and (3)
   These subsections also apply only when the initial notice has been registered as a land charge, notice or caution as is appropriate. The effect of subs. (3) is that a purchaser of the whole of a relevant landlord's interest is placed in the same position as if it had been the owner before the initial notice and any further successor is similarly so placed.

Subss. (4)–(6)
   These subsections contain very important provisions in their potential application to routine conveyancing. Before the date of the initial notice any of the relevant landlords may have entered into a contract to dispose of all or part of its interest. Service of the initial notice suspends that contract. If the initial notice results in a binding contract to effect the collective enfranchisement then the relevant landlord is discharged from the suspended contract, to the extent that it was a contract for a disposal within subs. (4). This very unsatisfactory position can be wholly avoided by taking advantage of subs. (6) which permits a contract not to be suspended in this way if it is made subject to the possibility of an initial notice being served. The provision need say no more, for example, than "this contract will continue notwithstanding the service of any initial notice under s.13 of the Leasehold Reform, Housing and Urban Development Act 1993" or "this contract will be rescinded by the service of any valid [or purported] initial notice under s.13 of the Leasehold Reform, Housing and Urban Development Act 1993."

Right of reversioner to require evidence of tenant's right to participate

   20.—(1) The reversioner in respect of the specified premises may, within the period of 21 days beginning with the relevant date, give the nominee purchaser a notice requiring him, in the case of any person by whom the initial notice was given, to deduce the title of that person to the lease by virtue of which it is claimed that he is a qualifying tenant of a flat contained in the specified premises.
   (2) The nominee purchaser shall comply with any such requirement within the period of 21 days beginning with the date of the giving of the notice.
   (3) Where—
   (a) the nominee purchaser fails to comply with a requirement under subsection (1) in the case of any person within the period mentioned in subsection (2), and

(b) the initial notice would not have been given in accordance with section 13(2)(b) if—

    (i) that person, and

    (ii) any other person in the case of whom a like failure by the nominee purchaser has occurred,

had been neither included among the persons who gave the notice nor included among the qualifying tenants of the flats referred to in that provision,

the initial notice shall be deemed to have been withdrawn at the end of that period.

DEFINITIONS
"flat": s.101(1).
"initial notice": s.38(1).
"lease": s.101(1).
"nominee purchaser": s.38(1).
"qualifying tenant": s.38(1).
"relevant date": s.38(1).
"reversioner": s.38(1).
"specified premises": ss.13(12) and 38(1).

GENERAL NOTE
This is an important provision, as it enables the reversioner to require the nominee purchaser to deduce the title of any qualifying tenant who joined in the initial notice. If the nominee purchaser fails to comply the initial notice is deemed to be withdrawn. Clearly the tenants collectively must ensure that the nominee purchaser is armed with this information before the initial notice is served. If not they are at the mercy of any individual tenant who fails to comply with this requisition, for example, one who in all innocence is spending a month on a lonely ramble through the Amazonian jungles. The task is considerably easier if the relevant titles have been registered as the open register enables office copies of each part of the title to be obtained readily. The manner in which title is to be deduced is governed by the regulations reproduced in Appendix I.

Reversioner's counter-notice

21.—(1) The reversioner in respect of the specified premises shall give a counter-notice under this section to the nominee purchaser by the date specified in the initial notice in pursuance of section 13(3)(g).

(2) The counter-notice must comply with one of the following requirements, namely—

(a) state that the reversioner admits that the participating tenants were on the relevant date entitled to exercise the right to collective enfranchisement in relation to the specified premises;

(b) state that, for such reasons as are specified in the counter-notice, the reversioner does not admit that the participating tenants were so entitled;

(c) contain such a statement as is mentioned in paragraph (a) or (b) above but state that an application for an order under subsection (1) of section 23 is to be made by such appropriate landlord (within the meaning of that section) as is specified in the counter-notice, on the grounds that he intends to redevelop the whole or a substantial part of the specified premises.

(3) If the counter-notice complies with the requirement set out in subsection (2)(a), it must in addition—

(a) state which (if any) of the proposals contained in the initial notice are accepted by the reversioner and which (if any) of those proposals are not so accepted, and specify—

    (i) in relation to any proposal which is not so accepted, the reversioner's counter-proposal, and

    (ii) any additional leaseback proposals by the reversioner;

(b) if (in a case where any property specified in the initial notice under section 13(3)(a)(ii) is property falling within section 1(3)(b)) any such counter-proposal relates to the grant of rights or the disposal of any freehold interest in pursuance of section 1(4), specify—

> (i) the nature of those rights and the property over which it is proposed to grant them, or
>
> (ii) the property in respect of which it is proposed to dispose of any such interest,

as the case may be;

(c) state which interests (if any) the nominee purchaser is to be required to acquire in accordance with subsection (4) below;

(d) state which rights (if any) the person who owns the freehold of the specified premises, or any other relevant landlord, desires to retain—

> (i) over any property in which he has any interest which is included in the proposed acquisition by the nominee purchaser, or
>
> (ii) over any property in which he has any interest which the nominee purchaser is to be required to acquire in accordance with subsection (4) below,

on the grounds that the rights are necessary for the proper management or maintenance of property in which he is to retain a freehold or leasehold interest; and

(e) include a description of any provisions which the reversioner or any other relevant landlord considers should be included in any conveyance to the nominee purchaser in accordance with section 34 and Schedule 7.

(4) The nominee purchaser may be required to acquire on behalf of the participating tenants the interest in any property of the person who owns the freehold of the specified premises or of any other relevant landlord, if the property—

(a) would for all practical purposes cease to be of use and benefit to him, or

(b) would cease to be capable of being reasonably managed or maintained by him,

in the event of his interest in the specified premises or (as the case may be) in any other property being acquired by the nominee purchaser under this Chapter.

(5) Where a counter-notice specifies any interest in pursuance of subsection (3)(c), the nominee purchaser or any person authorised to act on his behalf shall, in the case of any part of the property in which that interest subsists, have a right of access thereto for the purpose of enabling the nominee purchaser to obtain, in connection with the proposed acquisition by him, a valuation of that interest; and subsection (3) of section 17 shall apply in relation to the exercise of that right as it applies in relation to the exercise of a right of access conferred by that section.

(6) Every counter-notice must specify an address in England and Wales at which notices may be given to the reversioner under this Chapter.

(7) The reference in subsection (3)(a)(ii) to additional leaseback proposals is a reference to proposals which relate to the leasing back, in accordance with section 36 and Schedule 9, of flats or other units contained in the specified premises and which are made either—

(a) in respect of flats or other units in relation to which Part II of that Schedule is applicable but which were not specified in the initial notice under section 13(3)(c)(ii), or

(b) in respect of flats or other units in relation to which Part III of that Schedule is applicable.

(8) Schedule 4 (which imposes requirements as to the furnishing of information by the reversioner about the exercise of rights under Chapter II with respect to flats contained in the specified premises) shall have effect.

DEFINITIONS
"conveyance": s.38(1).
"flat": s.101(1).
"initial notice": s.38(1).
"interest": s.101(1).
"nominee purchaser": s.38(1).
"participating tenants": s.38(1).
"relevant date": s.38(1).
"relevant landlord": s.38(1).
"reversioner": s.38(1).
"right to collective enfranchisement": s.38(1).

GENERAL NOTE
The counter-notice to be given by the reversioner is a potentially complicated document. There is little mandatory content if the reversioner chooses to admit the claims put forward. A very difficult procedural problem will arise whenever the reversioner and some other relevant landlord disagree on the action to be taken. The opportunity for other relevant landlords to dispute the decisions of the reversioner are contained in Sched. 1, Pt. II and commented on in the notes to that Schedule. Note that the counter-notice may contain a requirement for the nominee purchaser to include in the purchase property which as a result of the enfranchisement is worthless in the hands of a relevant landlord (subss. (3) and (4)). There is no required form for the counter-notice.

Subs. (1)
The time-scale for the counter-notice is, thus, established by the tenants. This must be at least two months from the initial notice. The reversioner must give any s.17 notice requiring the tenants to deduce title promptly if they are to have sufficient time to consider the evidence supplied and respond correctly.

Subs. (2)
The counter-notice must contain an admission or rejection of the tenants' claim. If there is a rejection, reasons must be given and the reversioner will eventually be penalised in costs if those reasons are shown to be without foundation. The merits of obstruction will doubtless be carefully weighed against the gains that can be made from constructive negotiation by a well-represented landlord.

Subss. (3) and (4)
This is a most important provision which relates to property which after the enfranchisement would be of no practical use or benefit to a landlord or not be capable of reasonable management or maintenance by him. The counter-notice may specify any such property and require the nominee purchaser to purchase it. A dispute as to whether such property should be included is resolved either by agreement or under s.24.

Applications to court or leasehold valuation tribunal

Proceedings relating to validity of initial notice

22.—(1) Where—
(a) the reversioner in respect of the specified premises has given the nominee purchaser a counter-notice under section 21 which (whether it complies with the requirement set out in subsection (2)(b) or (c) of that section) contains such a statement as is mentioned in subsection (2)(b) of that section, but
(b) the court is satisfied, on an application made by the nominee purchaser, that the participating tenants were on the relevant date entitled to exercise the right to collective enfranchisement in relation to the specified premises,
the court shall by order make a declaration to that effect.

(2) Any application for an order under subsection (1) must be made not later than the end of the period of two months beginning with the date of the giving of the counter-notice to the nominee purchaser.

(3) If on any such application the court makes an order under subsection (1), then (subject to subsection (4)) the court shall make an order—

(a) declaring that the reversioner's counter-notice shall be of no effect, and
(b) requiring the reversioner to give a further counter-notice to the nominee purchaser by such date as is specified in the order.
(4) Subsection (3) shall not apply if—
(a) the counter-notice complies with the requirement set out in section 21(2)(c), and
(b) either—
    (i) an application for an order under section 23(1) is pending, or
    (ii) the period specified in section 23(3) as the period for the making of such an application has not expired.
(5) Subsections (3) to (5) of section 21 shall apply to any further counter-notice required to be given by the reversioner under subsection (3) above as if it were a counter-notice under that section complying with the requirement set out in subsection (2)(a) of that section.
(6) If an application by the nominee purchaser for an order under subsection (1) is dismissed by the court, the initial notice shall cease to have effect at the time when the order dismissing the application becomes final.

DEFINITIONS
"court": s.101(1).
"initial notice": s.38(1).
"nominee purchaser": s.38(1).
"participating tenants": s.38(1).
"relevant date": s.38(1).
"reversioner": s.38(1).
"right to collective enfranchisement": s.38(1).
"specified premises": ss.13(12) and 38(1).

GENERAL NOTE
This gives the tenants a very short period to challenge a landlord's counter-notice in the court. The court in question is the county court. It should be noted that the effect of the tenant "winning" is that the reversioner will have a period of time to serve another counter-notice and this need not be one which simply accepts the tenants' claim. A further court application can be made by the tenants in respect of such subsequent notice and so on *ad infinitum*.

Tenants' claim liable to be defeated where landlord intends to redevelop

23.—(1) Where the reversioner in respect of the specified premises has given a counter-notice under section 21 which complies with the requirement set out in subsection (2)(c) of that section, the court may, on the application of any appropriate landlord, by order declare that the right to collective enfranchisement shall not be exercisable in relation to those premises by reason of that landlord's intention to redevelop the whole or a substantial part of the premises.
(2) The court shall not make an order under subsection (1) unless it is satisfied—
(a) that not less than two-thirds of all the long leases on which flats contained in the specified premises are held are due to terminate within the period of five years beginning with the relevant date; and
(b) that for the purposes of redevelopment the applicant intends, once the leases in question have so terminated—
    (i) to demolish or reconstruct, or
    (ii) to carry out substantial works of construction on,
the whole or a substantial part of the specified premises; and
(c) that he could not reasonably do so without obtaining possession of the flats demised by those leases.
(3) Any application for an order under subsection (1) must be made within the period of two months beginning with the date of the giving of the counter-notice to the nominee purchaser; but, where the counter-notice is

one falling within section 22(1)(a), such an application shall not be proceeded with until such time (if any) as an order under section 22(1) becomes final.

(4) Where an order under subsection (1) is made by the court, the initial notice shall cease to have effect on the order becoming final.

(5) Where an application for an order under subsection (1) is dismissed by the court, the court shall make an order—

(a) declaring that the reversioner's counter-notice shall be of no effect, and

(b) requiring the reversioner to give a further counter-notice to the nominee purchaser by such date as is specified in the order.

(6) Where—

(a) the reversioner has given such a counter-notice as is mentioned in subsection (1), but

(b) either—

(i) no application for an order under that subsection is made within the period referred to in subsection (3), or

(ii) such an application is so made but is subsequently withdrawn,

then (subject to subsection (8)), the reversioner shall give a further counter-notice to the nominee purchaser within the period of two months beginning with the appropriate date.

(7) In subsection (6) "the appropriate date" means—

(a) if subsection (6)(b)(i) applies, the date immediately following the end of the period referred to in subsection (3); and

(b) if subsection (6)(b)(ii) applies, the date of withdrawal of the application.

(8) Subsection (6) shall not apply if any application has been made by the nominee purchaser under section 22(1).

(9) Subsections (3) to (5) of section 21 shall apply to any further counter-notice required to be given by the reversioner under subsection (5) or (6) above as if it were a counter-notice under that section complying with the requirement set out in subsection (2)(a) of that section.

(10) In this section "appropriate landlord", in relation to the specified premises, means—

(a) the reversioner or any other relevant landlord; or

(b) any two or more persons falling within paragraph (a) who are acting together.

DEFINITIONS

"appropriate date": subs. (7).
"appropriate landlord": subs. (10).
"court": s.101(1).
"flat": s.101(1).
"initial notice": s.38(1).
"lease": s.101(1).
"nominee purchaser": s.38(1).
"relevant date": s.38(1).
"relevant landlord": s.38(1).
"reversioner": s.38(1).
"right to collective enfranchisement": s.38(1).
"specified premises": ss.13(12) and 38(1).

GENERAL NOTE

This section gives the landlord an opportunity to resist collective enfranchisement where the landlord wishes to re-develop the premises. This requires an application to the county court and satisfaction of fairly stringent requirements. If the landlord admits that the tenants satisfy the qualifications to purchase, then the application to the court must be within two months of the counter-notice containing that admission. If the reversioner denies that the tenants satisfy the qualification to purchase then application to the court must still be made within two months of the counter-notice but will not be proceeded with until the court has determined the validity of the tenants' notice.

Subs. (1)
There is no definition given of "substantial" part of the premises. It is a reasonable supposition that this will be considered together with subs. (2)(c), that is, if possession is not necessary to carry out development can it be claimed to be a substantial part of the premises?

Subs. (2)
Paragraph (a) will scarcely ever be satisfied unless the landlord has made all leases in the block co-terminous. This has long been a desirable facet of good management and the opportunity to rectify any misalignment which could upset a future re-development should always be looked for. Note that the test here is two-thirds of *all* the long leases not two-thirds of the participating or qualifying leases. The provisions in paras. (b) and (c) are taken directly from s.30(1)(f) of the Landlord and Tenant Act 1954, Pt. II, on which there is now very extensive case law. (This is most accessible in *Woodfall* 22.1–5 *et seq.*). This case law will undoubtedly be applied to the new provisions.

Subs. (3)
This timescale has been referred to in the General Note above and it is worth stressing that it is mandatory and there is no relieving power granted to the court where a landlord fails to take advantage of the right within the two-month period.

Subs. (5)
Where the reversioner fails to make out a case for resisting enfranchisement under subs. (2), then another counter-notice may be served. There is no reason why that new counter-notice cannot dispute the tenants' claim. Neither does there seem to be any reason (save the risk of further costs) to prevent the landlord from putting forward its re-development claim again. This may be a worthwhile tactic if the landlord has lost on the ground of failure to show the necessary intention (perhaps the financial back-up or planning position was not convincing). On a second (or subsequent) run at the tilt the landlord may fare better.

Subss. (6) and (7)
These subsections introduce a curious halting procedure. The reversioner serves a counter-notice claiming the right under this section and then fails to apply to the court to prove that claim. The only consequence for the landlord is that it has to serve a further counter-notice within two months of the time available to it for applying to the court. If it applies to the court but withdraws the application then again the only consequence is that it has to serve a further counter-notice within two months of that withdrawal. There is no provision in the Act preventing any such further counter-notice also claiming the benefit of this section. Aside from pure obstruction this may conceivably be of benefit where the landlord is struggling to obtain the necessary time for subs. (2)(a) to be satisfied or to prove the necessary facts under subs. (2)(b).

Subs. (8)
If the landlord has served a counter-notice claiming a right under this section but also denying the tenants' right to qualify for enfranchisement then, in such a case, the nominee purchaser may have applied to the court under s.22 for it to declare that the participating tenants were so qualified. In such cases subs. (6) above does not apply to require the reversioner to serve a further counter-notice. This is because if the tenants are successful, the court order under s.22(3)(b) will require the reversioner to serve another notice.

Subs. (9)
This is a very unsatisfactorily drafted provision. Does it mean that such a counter-notice is deemed to contain an admission of the tenants' claim? This seems unfair to the landlord. The result is that if the new counter-notice denies the tenants' claim then it must contain the information (s.21(3) to (5)) that *would have been* in a notice admitting the claim. The purpose of this is presumably to try to hurry proceedings along. However, it can be doubted whether in a building of any size a well advised landlord (with a deep pocket) can ever be forced to the end of the procedural complexities of this Act.

Applications where terms in dispute or failure to enter contract

24.—(1) Where the reversioner in respect of the specified premises has given the nominee purchaser—

(a) a counter-notice under section 21 complying with the requirement set out in subsection (2)(a) of that section, or

(b) a further counter-notice required by or by virtue of section 22(3) or section 23(5) or (6),

but any of the terms of acquisition remain in dispute at the end of the period of two months beginning with the date on which the counter-notice or further counter-notice was so given, a leasehold valuation tribunal may, on the application of either the nominee purchaser or the reversioner, determine the matters in dispute.

(2) Any application under subsection (1) must be made not later than the end of the period of six months beginning with the date on which the counter-notice or further counter-notice was given to the nominee purchaser.

(3) Where—

(a) the reversioner has given the nominee purchaser such a counter-notice or further counter-notice as is mentioned in subsection (1)(a) or (b), and

(b) all of the terms of acquisition have been either agreed between the parties or determined by a leasehold valuation tribunal under subsection (1),

but a binding contract incorporating those terms has not been entered into by the end of the appropriate period specified in subsection (6), the court may, on the application of either the nominee purchaser or the reversioner, make such order under subsection (4) as it thinks fit.

(4) The court may under this subsection make an order—

(a) providing for the interests to be acquired by the nominee purchaser to be vested in him on the terms referred to in subsection (3);

(b) providing for those interests to be vested in him on those terms, but subject to such modifications as—

(i) may have been determined by a leasehold valuation tribunal, on the application of either the nominee purchaser or the reversioner, to be required by reason of any change in circumstances since the time when the terms were agreed or determined as mentioned in that subsection, and

(ii) are specified in the order; or

(c) providing for the initial notice to be deemed to have been withdrawn at the end of the appropriate period specified in subsection (6);

and Schedule 5 shall have effect in relation to any such order as is mentioned in paragraph (a) or (b) above.

(5) Any application for an order under subsection (4) must be made not later than the end of the period of two months beginning immediately after the end of the appropriate period specified in subsection (6).

(6) For the purposes of this section the appropriate period is—

(a) where all of the terms of acquisition have been agreed between the parties, the period of two months beginning with the date when those terms were finally so agreed;

(b) where all or any of those terms have been determined by a leasehold valuation tribunal under subsection (1)—

(i) the period of two months beginning with the date when the decision of the tribunal under that subsection becomes final, or

(ii) such other period as may have been fixed by the tribunal when making its determination.

(7) In this section "the parties" means the nominee purchaser and the reversioner and any relevant landlord who has given to those persons a notice for the purposes of paragraph 7(1)(a) of Schedule 1.

(8) In this Chapter "the terms of acquisition", in relation to a claim made under this Chapter, means the terms of the proposed acquisition by the nominee purchaser, whether relating to—

(a) the interests to be acquired,
(b) the extent of the property to which those interests relate or the rights to be granted over any property,
(c) the amounts payable as the purchase price for such interests,
(d) the apportionment of conditions or other matters in connection with the severance of any reversionary interest, or
(e) the provisions to be contained in any conveyance,

or otherwise, and includes any such terms in respect of any interest to be acquired in pursuance of section 1(4) or 21(4).

DEFINITIONS
    "conveyance": s.38(1).
    "initial notice": s.38(1).
    "interest": s.101(1).
    "nominee purchaser": s.38(1).
    "parties": subs. (7).
    "relevant landlord": s.38(1).
    "reversioner": s.38(1).
    "specified premises": ss.13(12) and 38(1).
    "terms of acquisition": subs. (8) and s.38(1).

GENERAL NOTE
    There are several routes by which the parties will arrive face to face with this section:
    (i) the reversioner may admit the tenants' qualifications to make a claim and the parties fail to negotiate agreeable terms;
    (ii) the reversioner may deny the tenants' claim but be ordered by the court to serve a counter-notice under s.21(3);
    (iii) the reversioner may claim the benefit of s.23 but be obliged (by virtue of s.23(5) and (6)) to serve a counter-notice when that claim fails.
It does not matter whether the counter-notices arising under (ii) and (iii) admit or deny the claim, the nominee purchaser may still apply to the leasehold valuation tribunal under this section.

Applications where reversioner fails to give counter-notice or further counter-notice

25.—(1) Where the initial notice has been given in accordance with section 13 but—
    (a) the reversioner has failed to give the nominee purchaser a counter-notice in accordance with section 21(1), or
    (b) if required to give the nominee purchaser a further counter-notice by or by virtue of section 22(3) or section 23(5) or (6), the reversioner has failed to comply with that requirement,
the court may, on the application of the nominee purchaser, make an order determining the terms on which he is to acquire, in accordance with the proposals contained in the initial notice, such interests and rights as are specified in it under section 13(3).

(2) The terms determined by the court under subsection (1) shall, if Part II of Schedule 9 is applicable, include terms which provide for the leasing back, in accordance with section 36 and that Part of that Schedule, of flats or other units contained in the specified premises.

(3) The court shall not make any order on an application made by virtue of paragraph (a) of subsection (1) unless it is satisfied—
    (a) that the participating tenants were on the relevant date entitled to exercise the right to collective enfranchisement in relation to the specified premises; and
    (b) if applicable, that the requirements of Part II of Schedule 3 were complied with as respects the giving of copies of the initial notice.

(4) Any application for an order under subsection (1) must be made not later than the end of the period of six months beginning with the date by

which the counter-notice or further counter-notice referred to in that sub-section was to be given to the nominee purchaser.

(5) Where—

(a) the terms of acquisition have been determined by an order of the court under subsection (1), but

(b) a binding contract incorporating those terms has not been entered into by the end of the appropriate period specified in subsection (8),

the court may, on the application of either the nominee purchaser or the reversioner, make such order under subsection (6) as it thinks fit.

(6) The court may under this subsection make an order—

(a) providing for the interests to be acquired by the nominee purchaser to be vested in him on the terms referred to in subsection (5);

(b) providing for those interests to be vested in him on those terms, but subject to such modifications as—

    (i) may have been determined by a leasehold valuation tribunal, on the application of either the nominee purchaser or the rever-sioner, to be required by reason of any change in circumstances since the time when the terms were determined as mentioned in that subsection, and

    (ii) are specified in the order; or

(c) providing for the initial notice to be deemed to have been withdrawn at the end of the appropriate period specified in subsection (8);

and Schedule 5 shall have effect in relation to any such order as is mentioned in paragraph (a) or (b) above.

(7) Any application for an order subsection (6) must be made not later than the end of the period of two months beginning immediately after the end of the appropriate period specified in subsection (8).

(8) For the purposes of this section the appropriate period is—

(a) the period of two months beginning with the date when the order of the court under subsection (1) becomes final, or

(b) such other period as may have been fixed by the court when making that order.

DEFINITIONS

"court": s.101(1).
"flat": s.101(1).
"initial notice": s.38(1).
"interest": s.101(1).
"nominee purchaser": s.38(1).
"participating tenants": s.38(1).
"relevant date": s.38(1).
"reversioner": s.38(1).
"right to collective enfranchisement": s.38(1).
"specified premises": ss.13(12) and 38(1).
"terms of acquisition": subs. (8) and s.38(1).
"unit": s.38(1).

GENERAL NOTE

This section enables the nominee purchaser to apply to the court for an order where the reversioner does not give the required counter-notice in response to the initial notice. The court in question is the county court. Where an application is made under this provision the court has to examine the question of whether the tenants' are entitled. It will then make an order stating the terms on which the acquisition is to proceed. It is clear that the purpose of the legislation is that this order will then be followed by the parties entering into a legal contract. If the reversioner is still obstructive at this stage the tenants will have to return to the court and the court can then order that the transaction proceed and order the preparation and execution of any necessary deed (C.C.R., Ord. 22, r. 7; R.S.C., Ord. 44, r. 3; Supreme Court Act 1981, s.39).

Subs. (3)

The court has to satisfy itself of these matters whether or not the reversioner raises them.

Further, the court must be satisfied that the facts supported the claim at the relevant date which is the time of the initial notice (s.1(8)).

Subs. (5)
    This subsection clearly indicates that the making of an order under this section is to be followed by the making of a legally binding agreement between the parties.

Subs. (6)
    Before this elaborate procedure is finished, either party may apply to a leasehold valuation tribunal for an order varying the terms of acquisition (subs. (6)(b)). Schedule 5 deals with the form of conveyance or vesting order and is annotated below.

Applications where relevant landlord cannot be found

26.—(1) Where not less than two-thirds of the qualifying tenants of flats contained in any premises to which this Chapter applies desire to make a claim to exercise the right to collective enfranchisement in relation to those premises but—

(a) (in a case to which section 9(1) applies) the person who owns the freehold of the premises cannot be found or his identity cannot be ascertained, or

(b) (in a case to which section 9(2) applies) each of the relevant landlords is someone who cannot be found or whose identity cannot be ascertained,

the court may, on the application of the qualifying tenants in question, make a vesting order under this subsection—

(i) with respect to any interests of that person (whether in those premises or in any other property) which are liable to acquisition on behalf of those tenants by virtue of section 1(1) or (2)(a) or section 2(1), or

(ii) with respect to any interests of those landlords which are so liable to acquisition by virtue of any of those provisions,

as the case may be.

(2) Where in a case to which section 9(2) applies—

(a) not less than two-thirds of the qualifying tenants of flats contained in any premises to which this Chapter applies desire to make a claim to exercise the right to collective enfranchisement in relation to those premises, and

(b) paragraph (b) of subsection (1) does not apply, but

(c) a notice of that claim or (as the case may be) a copy of such a notice cannot be given in accordance with section 13 or Part II of Schedule 3 to any person to whom it would otherwise be required to be so given because he cannot be found or his identity cannot be ascertained,

the court may, on the application of the qualifying tenants in question, make an order dispensing with the need to give such a notice or (as the case may be) a copy of such a notice to that person.

(3) If that person is the person who owns the freehold of the premises, then on the application of those tenants, the court may, in connection with an order under subsection (2), make an order appointing any other relevant landlord to be the reversioner in respect of the premises in place of that person; and if it does so references in this Chapter to the reversioner shall apply accordingly.

(4) The court shall not make an order on any application under subsection (1) or (2) unless it is satisfied—

(a) that on the date of the making of the application the premises to which the application relates were premises to which this Chapter applies; and

(b) that on that date the applicants would not have been precluded by any provision of this Chapter from giving a valid notice under section 13 with respect to those premises.

(5) Before making any such order the court may require the applicants to take such further steps by way of advertisement or otherwise as the court thinks proper for the purpose of tracing the person or persons in question; and if, after an application is made for a vesting order under subsection (1) and before any interest is vested in pursuance of the application, the person or (as the case may be) any of the persons referred to in paragraph (a) or (b) of that subsection is traced, then no further proceedings shall be taken with a view to any interest being so vested, but (subject to subsection (6))—

(a) the rights and obligations of all parties shall be determined as if the applicants had, at the date of the application, duly given notice under section 13 of their claim to exercise the right to collective enfranchisement in relation to the premises to which the application relates; and

(b) the court may give such directions as the court thinks fit as to the steps to be taken for giving effect to those rights and obligations, including directions modifying or dispensing with any of the requirements of this Chapter or of regulations made under this Part.

(6) An application for a vesting order under subsection (1) may be withdrawn at any time before execution of a conveyance under section 27(3) and, after it is withdrawn, subsection (5)(a) above shall not apply; but where any step is taken (whether by the applicants or otherwise) for the purpose of giving effect to subsection (5)(a) in the case of any application, the application shall not afterwards be withdrawn except—

(a) with the consent of every person who is the owner of any interest the vesting of which is sought by the applicants, or

(b) by leave of the court,

and the court shall not give leave unless it appears to the court just to do so by reason of matters coming to the knowledge of the applicants in consequence of the tracing of any such person.

(7) Where an order has been made under subsection (2) dispensing with the need to give a notice under section 13, or a copy of such a notice, to a particular person with respect to any particular premises, then if—

(a) a notice is subsequently given under that section with respect to those premises, and

(b) in reliance on the order, the notice or a copy of the notice is not to be given to that person,

the notice must contain a statement of the effect of the order.

(8) Where a notice under section 13 contains such a statement in accordance with subsection (7) above, then in determining for the purposes of any provision of this Chapter whether the requirements of section 13 of Part II of Schedule 3 have been complied with in relation to the notice, those requirements shall be deemed to have been complied with so far as relating to the giving of the notice or a copy of it to the person referred to in subsection (7) above.

(9) Rules of court shall make provision—

(a) for requiring notice of any application under subsection (3) to be served by the persons making the application on any person who the applicants know or have reason to believe is a relevant landlord; and

(b) for enabling persons served with any such notice to be joined as parties to the proceedings.

DEFINITIONS
"conveyance": s.38(1).
"court": s.101(1).
"flat": s.101(1).
"interest": s.101(1).
"qualifying tenant": s.38(1).
"relevant landlord": s.38(1).
"reversioner": s.38(1).
"right to collective enfranchisement": s.38(1).

GENERAL NOTE

The difficulties experienced by tenants in exercising their statutory rights due to the inability to discover the relevant landlord are notorious. This section and the following section are intended to allow collective enfranchisement to proceed in such cases.

Supplementary provisions relating to vesting orders under section 26(1)

27.—(1) A vesting order under section 26(1) is an order providing for the vesting of any such interests as are referred to in paragraph (i) or (ii) of that provision—

(a) in such person or persons as may be appointed for the purpose by the applicants for the order, and

(b) on such terms as may be determined by a leasehold valuation tribunal to be appropriate with a view to the interests being vested in that person or those persons in like manner (so far as the circumstances permit) as if the applicants had, at the date of their application, given notice under section 13 of their claim to exercise the right to collective enfranchisement in relation to the premises with respect to which the order is made.

(2) If a leasehold valuation tribunal so determines in the case of a vesting order under section 26(1), the order shall have effect in relation to interests which are less extensive than those specified in the application on which the order was made.

(3) Where any interests are to be vested in any person or persons by virtue of a vesting order under section 26(1), then on his or their paying into court the appropriate sum in respect of each of those interests there shall be executed by such person as the court may designate a conveyance which—

(a) is in a form approved by a leasehold valuation tribunal, and

(b) contains such provisions as may be so approved for the purpose of giving effect so far as possible to the requirements of section 34 and Schedule 7;

and that conveyance shall be effective to vest in the person or persons to whom the conveyance is made the interests expressed to be conveyed, subject to and in accordance with the terms of the conveyance.

(4) In connection with the determination by a leasehold valuation tribunal of any question as to the interests to be conveyed by any such conveyance, or as to the rights with or subject to which they are to be conveyed, it shall be assumed (unless the contrary is shown) that any person whose interests are to be conveyed ("the transferor") has no interest in property other than those interests and, for the purpose of excepting them from the conveyance, any minerals underlying the property in question.

(5) The appropriate sum which in accordance with subsection (3) is to be paid into court in respect of any interest is the aggregate of—

(a) such amount as may be determined by a leasehold valuation tribunal to be the price which would be payable in respect of that interest in accordance with Schedule 6 if the interest were being acquired in pursuance of such a notice as is mentioned in subsection (1)(b); and

(b) any amounts or estimated amounts determined by such a tribunal as being, at the time of execution of the conveyance, due to the transferor from any tenants of his of premises comprised in the premises in which that interest subsists (whether due under or in respect of their leases or under or in respect of agreements collateral thereto).

(6) Where any interest is vested in any person or persons in accordance with this section, the payment into court of the appropriate sum in respect of that interest shall be taken to have satisfied any claims against the applicants for the vesting order under section 26(1), their personal representatives or assigns in respect of the price payable under this Chapter for the acquisition of that interest.

(7) Where any interest is so vested in any person or persons, section 32(5) shall apply in relation to his or their acquisition of that interest as it applies in relation to the acquisition of any interest by a nominee purchaser.

DEFINITIONS
   "conveyance": s.38(1).
   "interest": s.101(1).
   "lease": s.101(1).
   "nominee purchaser": s.38(1).
   "right to collective enfranchisement": s.38(1).

GENERAL NOTE
   Where a vesting order is necessary to give effect to s.26 then it is dealt with in detail by this section.

Subs. (1)
   The vesting order may vest the property in question in any person that the applicants choose. This will not necessarily be the nominee purchaser. For example the ownership structure may be best served by vesting an intermediate leasehold interest in a different management company.

Subs. (2)
   The leasehold valuation tribunal may decide that the property to be enfranchised is less extensive than that which is claimed.

Subss. (3) and (4)
   The term of the conveyance is to be settled by a leasehold valuation tribunal as is any other dispute as to the interests or rights to be conveyed.

Subs. (4)
   Because the landlord is not available it is difficult to make any sensible conjecture as to what other property it owns. In consequence the leasehold valuation tribunal is required to assume that it has no other property interests except in underlying minerals. This presumption is subject to any contrary evidence.

Subs. (5)
   In order to obtain a vesting order, the applicants will have to make a payment into court of the amount due to the relevant landlord. This is made up of the price fixed under Sched. 6 and any sum due to the transferor from any tenants (subs. (5)(b)). This last sum obviously means any sum due from such tenant *qua tenant* and not a sum due in some other capacity despite the words in parentheses. This is fairly straightforward if the sums in question are outstanding rent or service charge. Does subs. (5)(b) include any estimate of sums due to the landlord for breach of covenant? The value of the freehold calculated under Sched. 6 must have been discounted by the value of such obligation under subs. (5)(b) otherwise there will be an element of double counting.

Termination of acquisition procedures

Withdrawal from acquisition by participating tenants

28.—(1) At any time before a binding contract is entered into in pursuance of the initial notice, the participating tenants may withdraw that notice by the giving of a notice to that effect under this section ("a notice of withdrawal").
   (2) A notice of withdrawal must be given—
   (a) to the nominee purchaser;
   (b) to the reversioner in respect of the specified premises; and
   (c) to every other relevant landlord who is known or believed by the participating tenants to have given to the nominee purchaser a notice under paragraph 7(1) or (4) of Schedule 1;
and, if by virtue of paragraph (c) a notice of withdrawal falls to be given to any person falling within that paragraph, it shall state that he is a recipient of the notice.

(3) The nominee purchaser shall, on receiving a notice of withdrawal, give a copy of it to every relevant landlord who—
  (a) has given to the nominee purchaser such a notice as is mentioned in subsection (2)(c); and
  (b) is not stated in the notice of withdrawal to be a recipient of it.

(4) Where a notice of withdrawal is given by the participating tenants under subsection (1)—
  (a) those persons, and
  (b) (subject to subsection (5)) every other person who is not a participating tenant for the time being but has at any time been such a tenant,
shall be liable—
  (i) to the reversioner, and
  (ii) to every other relevant landlord,
for all relevant costs incurred by him in pursuance of the initial notice down to the time when the notice of withdrawal or a copy of it is given to him in accordance with subsection (2) or (3).

(5) A person falling within paragraph (b) of subsection (4) shall not be liable for any costs by virtue of that subsection if—
  (a) the lease in respect of which he was a participating tenant has been assigned to another person; and
  (b) that other person has become a participating tenant in accordance with section 14(4);
and in paragraph (a) above the reference to an assignment shall be construed in accordance with section 14(10).

(6) Where any liability for costs arises under subsection (4)—
  (a) it shall be a joint and several liability of the persons concerned; and
  (b) the nominee purchaser shall not be liable for any costs under section 33.

(7) In subsection (4) "relevant costs", in relation to the reversioner or any other relevant landlord, means costs for which the nominee purchaser would (apart from subsection (6)) be liable to that person under section 33.

DEFINITIONS
  "initial notice": s.38(1).
  "lease": s.101(1).
  "nominee purchaser": s.38(1).
  "participating tenants": s.38(1).
  "relevant costs": subs. (7).
  "relevant landlord": s.38(1).
  "reversioner": s.38(1).
  "specified premises": ss.13(12) and 38(1).

GENERAL NOTE
  Should the tenants decide not to proceed they may make this decision at any time until a binding contract is entered into. The procedure for service of a notice of withdrawal must be used and it has the important effect of limiting the costs payable by the tenants to those incurred up to receipt of the withdrawal notice. There is no specified form of notice. What is required is an unambiguous communication to the persons specified in subs. (2) that the right is exercised. Note it must also state the information specified in s.25(2)(c). This section gives no help to the tenants so far as a mechanism for arriving at a decision to withdraw is concerned. This is one of the matters which the tenants should cover in their contract between themselves. It should specify a quorum or majority needed for this major decision.

Subs. (1)
  A satisfactory notice is simply one "to that effect", that is, indicating that the initial notice is withdrawn. It may be signed by or on behalf of the tenants (s.99).

Subs. (2)
  In order to be a valid notice of withdrawal the notice must be served upon the persons specified. Equally the withdrawal notice must state that it is served upon any relevant landlord

who has given notice of intention to act independently under para. 7 of Sched. 1. Such persons will be identified by name in the notice as having been served.

Subss. (4) and (5)(b)
 The costs payable to the relevant landlords are the joint and several liability of the participating tenants. They may have agreed amongst themselves how they are shared. If a tenant who joins in the initial notice assigns his lease then the assignee has a choice as to whether to become a participating tenant (s.14). From the assignor's point of view the contract between the assignor and the assignee should require the assignee to become such a participating tenant or to indemnify the assignor for the costs payable to the relevant landlords. The very wide definition of "assignment" in s.14(10) including by operation of law to a receiver in bankruptcy and on foreclosure to a mortgagee should not be overlooked.

Deemed withdrawal of initial notice

29.—(1) Where, in a case falling within paragraph (a) of subsection (1) of section 22—
  (a) no application for an order under that subsection is made within the period specified in subsection (2) of that section, or
  (b) such an application is so made but is subsequently withdrawn,
the initial notice shall be deemed to have been withdrawn—
    (i) (if paragraph (a) above applies) at the end of that period, or
    (ii) (if paragraph (b) above applies) on the date of the withdrawal of the application.
  (2) Where—
  (a) in a case to which subsection (1) of section 24 applies, no application under that subsection is made within the period specified in subsection (2) of that section, or
  (b) in a case to which subsection (3) of that section applies, no application for an order under subsection (4) of that section is made within the period specified in subsection (5) of that section,
the initial notice shall be deemed to have been withdrawn at the end of the period referred to in paragraph (a) or (b) above (as the case may be).
  (3) Where, in a case falling within paragraph (a) or (b) of subsection (1) of section 25, no application for an order under that subsection is made within the period specified in subsection (4) of that section, the initial notice shall be deemed to have been withdrawn at the end of that period.
  (4) Where, in a case to which subsection (5) of section 25 applies, no application for an order under subsection (6) of that section is made within the period specified in subsection (7) of that section, the initial notice shall be deemed to have been withdrawn at the end of that period.
  (5) The following provisions, namely—
  (a) section 15(10),
  (b) section 16(8),
  (c) section 20(3),
  (d) section 24(4)(c), and
  (e) section 25(6)(c),
also make provision for a notice under section 13 to be deemed to have been withdrawn at a particular time.
  (6) Where the initial notice is deemed to have been withdrawn at any time by virtue of any provision of this Chapter, subsections (4) and (5) of section 28 shall apply for the purposes of this section in like manner as they apply where a notice of withdrawal is given under that section, but as if the reference in subsection (4) of that section to the time when a notice or copy is given as there mentioned were a reference to the time when the initial notice is so deemed to have been withdrawn.
  (7) Where the initial notice is deemed to have been withdrawn by virtue of section 15(10) or 16(8)—
  (a) the liability for costs arising by virtue of subsection (6) above shall be a joint and several liability of the persons concerned; and

(b) the nominee purchaser shall not be liable for any costs under section 33.

(8) In the provisions applied by subsection (6), "relevant costs", in relation to the reversioner or any other relevant landlord, means costs for which the nominee purchaser is, or would (apart from subsection (7)) be, liable to that person under section 33.

DEFINITIONS
"initial notice": s.38(1).
"nominee purchaser": s.38(1).
"relevant costs": subs. (8).

GENERAL NOTE
If the landlord, by counter-notice, challenges the validity of the initial notice then the nominee purchaser may apply to the court to decide whether the tenants were entitled to exercise the right to collective enfranchisement. This section provides that if that right is not exercised the notice is deemed to be withdrawn. This also happens if the nominee purchaser applies to the court and the application is withdrawn. Deemed withdrawal thus occurs under this section: (1) where the nominee purchaser is entitled to challenge the counter-notice in court (s.22(1)) but does not within two months of that notice; (2) where the nominees' purchaser does challenge the counter-notice but withdraws the application (subs. (1)(b)); (3) where the terms of the acquisition are in dispute (s.22(1)) but there is no application to the leasehold valuation tribunal to settle the terms of the acquisition (subs. (2)); (4) where the terms have been agreed or determined by the leasehold valuation tribunal and a binding contract has not been made within the two month or other period specified s.24(6) (see subs. (2)(b)); (5) where the reversioner fails to give a counter-notice or further counter-notice and the nominee purchaser fails to apply to the court within the six-month period specified in s.25(4) (subs. (3)); (6) where the terms have been determined by the court but no binding contract has been made and no application is made for a vesting or other order within the period fixed by s.25(7) and (8) (see subs. (4)). Deemed withdrawal also occurs in the following cases listed by subs. (5): (a) under s.15(10) where there is no nominee purchaser appointed during a vacancy; (b) under s.16(8) where there is failure to give notice of retirement or death of nominee purchaser; (c) under s.20(3) where there is failure to supply evidence of a tenant's right to participate; (d) under s.24(4)(c) where there is failure to enter into a contract within a period specified by the court after an existing failure to enter a contract after terms settled by the leasehold valuation tribunal; (e) under s.25(b)(c) where there is failure to enter into a contract within a period specified by the court on an application made after the terms have been settled by the court following the landlord's failure to serve the appropriate counter-notice.

It has to be said that in this section as in so many others the skill of the draftsman has been extended on pure and needless obfuscation. There is no chance of the layperson or of most solicitor-conveyancers mastering the absurdly overlapping detail of these procedures. It all seems designed to hamper the usefulness of this Act. It would have been drafted this way if express Government instructions had been given to design an Act which gave to the tenant rights which the complexity of the procedure then removed.

Effect on initial notice or subsequent contract of institution of compulsory acquisition procedures

30.—(1) A notice given under section 13 shall be of no effect if on the relevant date—
(a) any acquiring authority has, with a view to the acquisition of the whole or part of the specified premises for any authorised purpose—
(i) served notice to treat on any relevant person, or
(ii) entered into a contract for the purchase of the interest of any such person in the premises or part of them, and
(b) the notice to treat or contract remains in force.
(2) In subsection (1) "relevant person", in relation to the specified premises, means—
(a) the person who owns the freehold of the premises; or
(b) any other person who owns any leasehold interest in the premises which is specified in the initial notice under section 13(3)(c)(i).

(3) A notice given under section 13 shall not specify under subsection (3)(a)(ii) or (c)(i) of that section any property or leasehold interest in property if on the relevant date—

(a) any acquiring authority has, with a view to the acquisition of the whole or part of the property for any authorised purpose—

(i) served notice to treat on the person who owns the freehold of, or any such leasehold interest in, the property, or

(ii) entered into a contract for the purchase of the interest of any such person in the property or part of it, and

(b) the notice to treat or contract remains in force.

(4) A notice given under section 13 shall cease to have effect if, before a binding contract is entered into in pursuance of the notice, any acquiring authority serves, with a view to the acquisition of the whole or part of the specified premises for any authorised purpose, notice to treat as mentioned in subsection (1)(a).

(5) Where any such authority so serves notice to treat at any time after a binding contract is entered into in pursuance of the notice given under section 13 but before completion of the acquisition by the nominee purchaser under this Chapter, then (without prejudice to the general law as to the frustration of contracts) the parties to the contract shall be discharged from the further performance of the contract.

(6) Where subsection (4) or (5) applies in relation to the initial notice or any contract entered into in pursuance of it, then on the occasion of the compulsory acquisition in question the compensation payable in respect of any interest in the specified premises (whether or not the one to which the relevant notice to treat relates) shall be determined on the basis of the value of the interest.

(a) (if subsection (4) applies) subject to and with the benefit of the rights and obligations arising from the initial notice and affecting that interest; or

(b) (if subsection (5) applies) subject to and with the benefit of the rights and obligations arising from the contract and affecting that interest.

(7) In this section—

(a) "acquiring authority", in relation to the specified premises or any other property, means any person or body of persons who has or have been, or could be, authorised to acquire the whole or part of those premises or that property compulsorily for any purpose; and

(b) "authorised purpose", in relation to any acquiring authority, means any such purpose.

<small>Definitions</small>

"acquiring authority": subs. (7)(a).
"authorised purpose": subs. (7)(b).
"initial notice": s.38(1).
"interest": s.101(1).
"nominee purchaser": s.38(1).
"relevant date": s.38(1).
"relevant person": subs. (2).
"specified premises": ss.13(12) and 38(1).

<small>General Note</small>

This section applies if on the "relevant date" (the date on which the initial notice is given under s.11) the property is subject to a notice to treat or has been contracted to be sold to an authority which could have been a compulsory purchase authority for that land. It also prevents land subject to such procedures being enfranchised under this Part of the Act.

Subs. (1)

This section which applies if a notice to treat is served or a contract entered into with an acquiring authority (subs. (7)) is so wide that it clearly includes a contract with such an authority in any capacity providing the purpose was one for which it could have used compulsory purchase.

Subs. (2)
   This definition of a relevant person has the effect that a notice to treat or contract negates the initial notice if it is in respect of any of the property contained in the initial notice however small that part may be, for example, a strip of garden land to be acquired as part of a road-widening scheme.

Subs. (3)
   An initial notice under s.11 must not include any land which is subject to a notice to treat or contract for purchase by an acquiring authority.

Subs. (4)
   Once an initial notice has been served then an acquiring authority may still serve a notice to treat. The effect of this will be to negate the initial notice.

Subs. (5)
   Once there is a binding contract between the relevant landlord and the nominee purchaser then an acquiring authority may still serve a notice to treat. The effect of this is to discharge the parties from further performance of the contract. This result is said to be "without prejudice to the general law as to the frustration of contracts". Compulsory purchase has long been treated as a frustrating event (see *Baily* v. *De Crespigny* (1869) L.R. 445, 189) in a contract for the occupation of land. It must certainly be a frustrating event of a contract to sell a freehold (see *Hillingdon Estates Co.* v. *Stonefield Estates* [1952] Ch. 627; *cf. Denny Mott and Dickinson* v. *James B. Fraser & Co.* [1944] A.C. 265 which was an option to purchase land). The effect of the common law of frustration applying is that the rights to recover money paid or to be compensated for partial performance created by the Law Reform (Frustrated Contracts) Act 1943 may apply. There seems to be little practical scope for this to have impact.

Subs. (6)
   In assessing the compensation on compulsory purchase it is assumed that the initial notice (subs. (4) cases) or contract (subs. (5) cases) are valid. Does this give the person whose interest is compulsory purchased higher compensation? The answer must be yes, because the price under enfranchisement includes elements that are not included in compulsory purchase compensation.

Effect on initial notice of designation for inheritance tax purposes and applications for designation

   31.—(1) A notice given under section 13 shall be of no effect if on the relevant date the whole or any part of—
   (a) the specified premises, or
   (b) any property specified in the notice under section 13(3)(a)(ii),
is qualifying property.
   (2) For the purposes of this section the whole or any part of the specified premises, or of any property specified as mentioned in subsection (1), is qualifying property if—
   (a) it has been designated under section 31(1)(b), (c) or (d) of the Inheritance Tax Act 1984 (designation and undertakings relating to conditionally exempt transfers), whether with or without any other property, and no chargeable event has subsequently occurred with respect to it; or
   (b) an application to the Board for it to be so designated is pending; or
   (c) it is the property of a body not established or conducted for profit and a direction has been given in relation to it under section 26 of that Act (gifts for public benefit), whether with or without any other property; or
   (d) an application to the Board for a direction to be so given in relation to it is pending.
   (3) For the purposes of subsection (2) an application is pending as from the time when it is made to the Board until such time as it is either granted or

refused by the Board or withdrawn by the applicant; and for this purpose an application shall not be regarded as made unless and until the applicant has submitted to the Board all such information in support of the application as is required by the Board.

(4) A notice given under section 13 shall cease to have effect if, before a binding contract is entered into in pursuance of the notice, the whole or any part of—

(a) the specified premises, or

(b) any property specified in the notice under section 13(3)(a)(ii), becomes qualifying property.

(5) Where a notice under section 13 ceases to have effect by virtue of subsection (4) above—

(a) the nominee purchaser shall not be liable for any costs under section 33; and

(b) the person who applied or is applying for designation or a direction shall be liable—

(i) to the qualifying tenants by whom the notice was given for all reasonable costs incurred by them in the preparation and giving of the notice; and

(ii) to the nominee purchaser for all reasonable costs incurred in pursuance of the notice by him or by any other person who has acted as the nominee purchaser.

(6) Where it is claimed that subsection (1) or (4) applies in relation to a notice under section 13, the person making the claim shall, at the time of making it, furnish the nominee purchaser with evidence in support of it; and if he fails to do so he shall be liable for any costs which are reasonably incurred by the nominee purchaser in consequence of the failure.

(7) In subsection (2)—

(a) paragraphs (a) and (b) apply to designation under section 34(1)(a), (b) or (c) of the Finance Act 1975 or section 77(1)(b), (c) or (d) of the Finance Act 1976 as they apply to designation under section 31(1)(b), (c) or (d) of the Inheritance Tax Act 1984; and

(b) paragraphs (c) and (d) apply to a direction under paragraph 13 of Schedule 6 to the Finance Act 1975 as they apply to a direction under section 26 of that Act of 1984.

(8) In this section—

"the Board" means the Commissioners of Inland Revenue;

"chargeable event" means—

(a) any event which in accordance with any provision of Chapter II of Part II of the Inheritance Tax Act 1984 (exempt transfers) is a chargeable event, including any such provision as applied by section 78(3) of that Act (conditionally exempt occasions); or

(b) any event which would have been a chargeable event in the circumstances mentioned in section 79(3) of that Act (exemption from ten-yearly charge).

DEFINITIONS

"Board": subs. (8).

"chargeable event": subs. (8).

"nominee purchaser": s.38(1).

"qualifying tenant": s.38(1).

"relevant date": s.38(1).

"specified premises": ss.13(12) and 38(1).

GENERAL NOTE

The Inheritance Tax Act 1984, s.26 exempts from inheritance tax certain gifts of property for national purposes and the public benefit. The Government was pressed during the passage of the Bill for such property to be excluded from the right to collective enfranchisement and this is the result. Under s.31 of the 1984 Act property can be designated as conditionally exempt. If there is a s.26 direction or a s.31 designation then an initial notice is of no effect. If an application under s.26 or s.31 is pending then an initial notice is of no effect. Once a valid s.13 notice has been served then it ceases to have effect if a s.26 direction or s.31 designation is made before a binding contract is entered into or a pending application for either is made.

Determination of price and costs of enfranchisement

Determination of price

32.—(1) Schedule 6 to this Act (which relates to the determination of the price payable by the nominee purchaser in respect of each of the freehold and other interests to be acquired by him in pursuance of this Chapter) shall have effect.

(2) The lien of the owner of any such interest (as vendor) on the specified premises, or (as the case may be) on any other property, for the price payable shall extend—

(a) to any amounts which, at the time of the conveyance of that interest, are due to him from any tenants of his of premises comprised in the premises in which that interest subsists (whether due under or in respect of their leases or under or in respect of agreements collateral thereto); and

(b) to any amount payable to him by virtue of section 18(2); and

(c) to any costs payable to him by virtue of section 33.

(3) Subsection (2)(a) does not apply in relation to amounts due to the owner of any such interest from tenants of any premises which are to be comprised in the premises demised by a lease granted in accordance with section 36 and Schedule 9.

(4) In subsection (2) the reference to the specified premises or any other property includes a reference to a part of those premises or that property.

(5) Despite the fact that in accordance with Schedule 6 no payment or only a nominal payment is payable by the nominee purchaser in respect of the acquisition by him of any interest he shall nevertheless be deemed for all purposes to be a purchaser of that interest for a valuable consideration in money or money's worth.

DEFINITIONS
"conveyance": s.38(1).
"interest": s.101(1).
"lease": s.101(1).
"nominee purchaser": s.38(1).
"specified premises": ss.13(12) and 38(1).

GENERAL NOTE
The price payable is calculated in accordance with Sched. 5 introduced by this section. The price is payable by the nominee purchaser which will be a company with no resources until the freehold interests are conveyed to it.

Subs. (2)
The unpaid vendor's lien arises by operation of law when the vendor completes without receiving the entire purchase price (*Mackreth* v. *Symmons* (1808) 15 Ves. 329). Note that if the contract is made subject to the Standard Conditions of Sale this provides for the vendor to have no lien after completion (7.4.2).

This subsection makes important extensions of that lien. In particular subs. (2)(a) extends it to sums due from any tenants and not just from tenants who are participating in the purchase. This can produce surprising results. The purchaser, *i.e.* the nominee purchaser is, after the purchase, entitled to recover any rent in arrears at the date of the conveyance without there being any express assignment of the benefit (see *London & County (A. & D.)* v. *Wilfred Sportsman*; *Greenwoods (Hosiers and Outfitters) Third Party* [1971] Ch. 764). The same principle applies in respect of any other outstanding breach see *King, Re, Robinson* v. *Gray* [1963] Ch. 459. Accordingly, this means that the valuation price should reflect the fact that the old landlord loses such outstanding sums which may be recovered by the new. There is little scope for operation of the lien in this area.

Subs. (3)

There may be a lease-back of secure tenancies and certain other premises under Sched. 8 and s.33. The extension of the unpaid vendor's lien provided for by subs. (2)(a) does not apply to any tenants of these premises.

Subs. (5)

It may be significant for the purchaser to be deemed to be a purchaser for valuable consideration in money or money's worth to apply for the following provisions: (a) implied covenants for title under s.76 of the Law of Property Act 1925 are different in a conveyance for valuable consideration; (b) a purchaser of a legal interest for money or money's worth takes free of unregistered land charges under s.4 of the Land Charges Act 1972.

Costs of enfranchisement

33.—(1) Where a notice is given under section 13, then (subject to the provisions of this section and sections 28(6), 29(7) and 31(5)) the nominee purchaser shall be liable, to the extent that they have been incurred in pursuance of the notice by the reversioner or by any other relevant landlord, for the reasonable costs of and incidental to any of the following matters, namely—

(a) any investigation reasonably undertaken—
(i) of the question whether any interest in the specified premises or other property is liable to acquisition in pursuance of the initial notice, or
(ii) of any other question arising out of that notice;
(b) deducing, evidencing and verifying the title to any such interest;
(c) making out and furnishing such abstracts and copies as the nominee purchaser may require;
(d) any valuation of any interest in the specified premises or other property;
(e) any conveyance of any such interest;

but this subsection shall not apply to any costs if on a sale made voluntarily a stipulation that they were to be borne by the purchaser would be void.

(2) For the purposes of subsection (1) any costs incurred by the reversioner or any other relevant landlord in respect of professional services rendered by any person shall only be regarded as reasonable if and to the extent that costs in respect of such services might reasonably be expected to have been incurred by him if the circumstances had been such that he was personally liable for all such costs.

(3) Where by virtue of any provision of this Chapter the initial notice ceases to have effect at any time, then (subject to subsection (4)) the nominee purchaser's liability under this section for costs incurred by any person shall be a liability for costs incurred by him down to that time.

(4) The nominee purchaser shall not be liable for any costs under this section if the initial notice ceases to have effect by virtue of section 23(4) or 30(4).

(5) The nominee purchaser shall not be liable under this section for any costs which a party to any proceedings under this Chapter before a leasehold valuation tribunal incurs in connection with the proceedings.

(6) In this section references to the nominee purchaser include references to any person whose appointment has terminated in accordance with section 15(3) or 16(1); but this section shall have effect in relation to such a person subject to section 15(7).

(7) Where by virtue of this section, or of this section and section 29(6) taken together, two or more persons are liable for any costs, they shall be jointly and severally liable for them.

DEFINITIONS
"conveyance": s.38(1).
"initial notice": s.38(1).

"interest": s.101(1).
"nominee purchaser": s.38(1).
"relevant landlord": s.38(1).
"reversioner": s.38(1).
"specified premises": ss.13(12) and 38(1).

GENERAL NOTE
This section deals with the detailed allocation of costs between the parties.

Subs. (1)
Costs of the reversioner and relevant landlord are generally payable by the nominee purchaser. This is not so if the initial notice is withdrawn or deemed to be withdrawn under ss.26(6) and 27(7). The overall test given is the reasonable and incidental costs of the particular items listed. The valuations (subs. (1)(d)) for which the purchaser must pay the cost will include the valuation reasonably undertaken of other property which the relevant landlords think may be devalued by the effect of enfranchisement (Sched. 5, Pt. II, para. 5). The proviso to this subsection refers to: (a) provisions that a purchaser will pay for a vesting order or appointment of new trustees (s.42(a) of the Law of Property Act 1925); (b) provisions for a purchaser to pay for stamping or execution of a trust for sale or vesting instrument (s.42(b) of the Law of Property Act 1925); (c) stipulations void under s.48 of the Law of Property Act 1925 which require the buyer to pay for the seller's legal work; (d) a condition requiring a purchaser to pay outstanding stamp duty on documents of title (Stamp Act 1891, s.117).

Completion of acquisition

Conveyance to nominee purchaser

34.—(1) Any conveyance executed for the purposes of this Chapter, being a conveyance to the nominee purchaser of the freehold of the specified premises or of any other property, shall grant to the nominee purchaser an estate in fee simple absolute in those premises or that property, subject only to such incumbrances as may have been agreed or determined under this Chapter to be incumbrances subject to which that estate should be granted, having regard to the following provisions of this Chapter.

(2) Any such conveyance shall, where the nominee purchaser is to acquire any leasehold interest in the specified premises or (as the case may be) in the other property to which the conveyance relates, provide for the disposal to the nominee purchaser of any such interest.

(3) Any conveyance executed for the purposes of this Chapter shall have effect under section 2(1) of the Law of Property Act 1925 (conveyances overreaching certain equitable interests etc.) to overreach any incumbrance capable of being overreached under section 2(1)—

(a) as if, where the interest conveyed is settled land for the purposes of the Settled Land Act 1925, the conveyance were made under the powers of that Act, and

(b) as if the requirements of section 2(1) as to payment of the capital money allowed any part of the purchase price paid or applied in accordance with section 35 below or Schedule 8 to this Act to be so paid or applied.

(4) For the purposes of this section "incumbrances" includes—
(a) rentcharges, and
(b) (subject to subsection (5)) personal liabilities attaching in respect of the ownership of land or an interest in land though not charged on that land or interest.

(5) Burdens originating in tenure, and burdens in respect of the upkeep or regulation for the benefit of any locality of any land, building, structure, works, ways or watercourse shall not be treated as incumbrances for the purposes of this section; but any conveyance executed for the purposes of this Chapter shall be made subject to any such burdens.

(6) A conveyance executed for the purposes of this Chapter shall not be made subject to any incumbrance capable of being overreached by the

conveyance, but shall be made subject (where they are not capable of being overreached) to—

   (a) rentcharges redeemable under sections 8 to 10 of the Rentcharges Act 1977, and

   (b) those falling within paragraphs (c) and (d) of section 2(3) of that Act (estate rentcharges and rentcharges imposed under certain enactments),

except as otherwise provided by subsections (7) and (8) below.

(7) Where any land is to be conveyed to the nominee purchaser by a conveyance executed for the purposes of this Chapter, subsection (6) shall not preclude the person who owns the freehold interest in the land from releasing, or procuring the release of, the land from any rentcharge.

(8) The conveyance of any such land ("the relevant land") may, with the agreement of the nominee purchaser (which shall not be unreasonably withheld), provide in accordance with section 190(1) of the Law of Property Act 1925 (charging of rentcharges on land without rent owner's consent) that a rentcharge—

   (a) shall be charged exclusively on other land affected by it in exoneration of the relevant land, or

   (b) shall be apportioned between other land affected by it and the relevant land.

(9) Except to the extent that any departure is agreed to by the nominee purchaser and the person whose interest is to be conveyed, any conveyance executed for the purposes of this Chapter shall—

   (a) as respects the conveyance of any freehold interest, conform with the provisions of Schedule 7, and

   (b) as respects the conveyance of any leasehold interest, conform with the provisions of paragraph 2 of that Schedule (any reference in that paragraph to the freeholder being read as a reference to the person whose leasehold interest is to be conveyed).

(10) Any such conveyance shall in addition contain a statement that it is a conveyance executed for the purposes of this Chapter; and any such statement shall comply with such requirements as may be prescribed by rules made in pursuance of section 144 of the Land Registration Act 1925 (power to make general rules).

DEFINITIONS
   "conveyance": s.38(1).
   "incumbrances": subs. (4).
   "interest": s.101(1).
   "nominee purchaser": s.38(1).
   "specified premises": ss.13(12) and 38(1).

GENERAL NOTE
   The detailed provisions of this section deal with the substance of the conveyance to the nominee purchaser. In accordance with usual practice this document can, if the land is unregistered, be in unregistered or registered form (*i.e.* a r. 72 transfer). Because of the complexity of the document it is immaterial in fact which is chosen.

Subs. (1)
   If the conveyance or transfer does not comply with this clear rule then rectification will be possible later.

Subs. (2)
   However many reversionary interests are acquired, there should be only one conveyance to the nominee purchaser and this will be executed by the freeholder (Sched. 1, para. 6(1)(b)(iii)). However, the parties may, if they feel the complexity of the case warrants this, use more than one conveyance to deal with different intermediate interests.

Subs. (3)
   The overreaching effect of the conveyance is of course to overreach such incumbrances on all

the interests conveyed by the single conveyance used. No recital of such interests is necessary or desirable. The conveyance thus should be expressed to be under Pt. I, Chap. I of this Act (see subs. (10)) and the purchase price paid in accordance with the Act (see s.35).

Subs. (5)
This subsection derives from the Leasehold Reform Act 1967, s.8(3). Few incidents of freehold tenure survive, and those that do are generally notorious and colourful. Formally copyhold land is subject to incidents reserved by s.128 of and Sched. 12 to the Law of Property Act 1922. Rights of the lord of the manor to a mine or mines may be important the remainder are of infrequent import. So far as burdens in respect of "upkeep", etc., are concerned, the most obvious is the duty to repair the chancel of a church which is attached to former tithe land. All tithe rent charges ceased to be payable as a result of the Finance Act 1977, s.56, but corn rents which are rentcharges resulting from the commutation of tithes under local Inclosure Acts may still occur and these may be redeemed under the Tithe Act 1918.

Discharge of existing mortgages on transfer to nominee purchaser

35.—(1) Subject to the provisions of Schedule 8, where any interest is acquired by the nominee purchaser in pursuance of this Chapter, the conveyance by virtue of which it is so acquired shall, as regards any mortgage to which this section applies, be effective by virtue of this section—
  (a) to discharge the interest from the mortgage, and from the operation of any order made by a court for the enforcement of the mortgage, and
  (b) to extinguish any term of years created for the purposes of the mortgage,
and shall do so without the persons entitled to or interested in the mortgage or in any such order or term of years becoming parties to or executing the conveyance.
  (2) Subject to subsections (3) and (4), this section applies to any mortgage of the interest so acquired (however created or arising) which—
  (a) is a mortgage to secure the payment of money or the performance of any other obligation by the person from whom the interest is so acquired or any other person; and
  (b) is not a mortgage which would be overreached apart from this section.
  (3) This section shall not apply to any such mortgage if it has been agreed between the nominee purchaser and the reversioner or (as the case may be) any other relevant landlord that the interest in question should be acquired subject to the mortgage.
  (4) In this section and Schedule 8 "mortgage" includes a charge or lien; but neither this section nor that Schedule applies to a rentcharge.

DEFINITIONS
  "conveyance": s.38(1).
  "interest": s.101(1).
  "mortgage": subs. (4).
  "nominee purchaser": s.38(1).
  "relevant landlord": s.38(1).
  "reversioner": s.38(1).

GENERAL NOTE
  Any of the interests to be acquired may be subject to a legal mortgage, charge or an equitable charge. The nominee purchaser automatically takes free from such interests. If the interests conveyed are registered then an entry protecting such a charge will be automatically removed from the register when the enfranchised title is registered. Subsection (3) permits the parties to agree if they wish that the nominee purchaser will take the land subject to a particular mortgage or mortgages. This section is made subject to Sched. 8 which provides for how the nominee purchaser is to discharge mortgages on the freehold. If the procedure in Sched. 8 is not followed the property remains subject to the mortgage.

Subs. (2)
  For mortgages which would be overreached, see s.72 of the Settled Land Act 1925 for

overreaching interests affecting settled land; s.2(1) of the Law of Property Act 1925 for overreaching interests affecting land held on trusts for sale; and s.104 of the Law of Property Act 1925 for overreaching of subsequent mortgages on a sale by a mortgagee.

Subs. (3)
This curiously hypothetical way of reaching a straightforward effect follows very closely (with inconsequential rearrangement and statutory references) the words of s.8(4) of the Leasehold Reform Act 1967. The straightforward result is achieved that a tenant for life or statutory owner selling property which is in fact settled land sells free of the equitable interests under the settlement.

Subs. (4)
Cf. with the first part of s.8(2) of the Leasehold Reform Act 1967.

Nominee purchaser required to grant leases back to former freeholder in certain circumstances

36.—(1) In connection with the acquisition by him of the freehold of the specified premises, the nominee purchaser shall grant to the person from whom the freehold is acquired such leases of flats or other units contained in those premises as are required to be so granted by virtue of Part II or III of Schedule 9.

(2) Any such lease shall be granted so as to take effect immediately after the acquisition by the nominee purchaser of the freehold of the specified premises.

(3) Where any flat or other unit demised under any such lease ("the relevant lease") is at the time of that acquisition subject to any existing lease, the relevant lease shall take effect as a lease of the freehold reversion in respect of the flat or other unit.

(4) Part IV of Schedule 9 has effect with respect to the terms of a lease granted in pursuance of Part II or III of that Schedule.

DEFINITIONS
"flat": s.101(1).
"lease": s.101(1).
"nominee purchaser": s.38(1).
"specified premises": ss.13(12) and 38(1).
"unit": s.38(1).

GENERAL NOTE
The mandatory grant of long leases back to the freeholder is dealt with in the note on Sched. 9. It must be noted that leasebacks are required: (a) where flats are let under secure tenancies (Sched. 9, Pt. II); (b) certain flats let by housing associations (Sched. 9, Pt. II). There are other cases also dealt with in Sched. 9 where the freeholder may choose to have a leaseback. These are: (a) any unit which is not a flat let to a qualifying tenant (Sched. 9, Pt. III, para. 5). This includes all non-residential units and all flats let to non-qualifying tenants; (b) any flat occupied by a residential landlord (Sched. 9, Pt. III, para. 6).

Acquisition of interests from local authorities etc.

37. Schedule 10 to this Act (which makes provision with respect to the acquisition of interests from local authorities etc. in pursuance of this Chapter) shall have effect.

DEFINITIONS
"interest": s.101(1).

GENERAL NOTE
The detailed provisions dealing with acquisitions from local authorities are dealt with in the note on Sched. 10.

Supplemental

Interpretation of Chapter I

38.—(1) In this Chapter (unless the context otherwise requires)—

"conveyance" includes assignment, transfer and surrender, and related expressions shall be construed accordingly;

"the initial notice" means the notice given under section 13;

"the nominee purchaser" shall be construed in accordance with section 15;

"the participating tenants" shall be construed in accordance with section 14;

"premises with a resident landlord" shall be construed in accordance with section 10;

"public sector landlord" means any of the persons listed in section 171(2) of the Housing Act 1985;

"qualifying tenant" shall be construed in accordance with section 5;

"the relevant date" has the meaning given by section 1(8);

"relevant landlord" and "the reversioner" shall be construed in accordance with section 9;

"the right to collective enfranchisement" means the right specified in section 1(1);

"secure tenancy" has the meaning given by section 79 of the Housing Act 1985;

"the specified premises" shall be construed in accordance with section 13(12);

"the terms of acquisition" has the meaning given by section 24(8);

"unit" means—

    (a) a flat;

    (b) any other separate set of premises which is constructed or adapted for use for the purposes of a dwelling; or

    (c) a separate set of premises let, or intended for letting, on a business lease.

(2) Any reference in this Chapter (however expressed) to the acquisition or proposed acquisition by the nominee purchaser is a reference to the acquisition or proposed acquisition by the nominee purchaser, on behalf of the participating tenants, of such freehold and other interests as fall to be so acquired under a contract entered into in pursuance of the initial notice.

(3) Any reference in this Chapter to the interest of a relevant landlord in the specified premises is a reference to the interest in those premises by virtue of which he is, in accordance with section 9(2)(b), a relevant landlord.

(4) Any reference in this Chapter to agreement in relation to all or any of the terms of acquisition is a reference to agreement subject to contract.

GENERAL NOTE

Subs. (1)

Public sector landlord. The list in s.171(2) of the Housing Act 1985 is as follows: (a) a local authority; (b) a new town corporation; (c) a housing action trust; (d) an urban development corporation; (e) the Development Board for Rural Wales; (f) the Corporation (this means either Scottish Homes, the Housing Corporation or Housing for Wales, see s.6A of the Housing Act 1985); (g) a registered housing association.

Secure tenancy. There is, of course, no definition in s.79 of the Housing Act 1985. Broadly it includes leases and licences of dwelling houses by certain landlords. These are now only local authorities, new town corporations, housing action trusts, urban development corporations, the Development Board for Rural Wales and certain Housing Co-operatives (ss.80 and 80(2)(b) of the Housing Act 1985). Housing Association tenancies granted on or after January 15, 1984 will normally not be secure tenancies. (See s.34 of the Housing Act 1988; Housing Association Law (Alder & Hardy) Sweet & Maxwell 1991, pp. 129 *et seq.*).

Unit. This definition means that there will be parts of a building which are not units as not falling within paras. (a), (b) or (c).

Subs. (4)
Presumably this is sloppy drafting and "agreement" also includes an agreement which is not subject to contract. For example under s.24(6) time for an application to the court starts running a specified time after the terms are agreed. Subsection (4) must be intended to make this mean agreed subject to contract **or** agreed not subject to contract. The concept of an agreement subject to contract is in itself a contradiction in terms and its application may be problematical.

CHAPTER II

INDIVIDUAL RIGHT OF TENANT OF FLAT TO ACQUIRE NEW LEASE

GENERAL NOTE
Chapter II gives individual tenants of flats who hold a long lease the right to a 90 year extension of that lease. When the Bill was first presented to Parliament this right was available only when the building did not qualify for collective enfranchisement. At a late stage the Government bowed to widespread pressure to make the individual right to a new lease available whether or not collective enfranchisement was also available. This was a hugely significant shift of direction. Those who have read Chap. I and the notes thereon will have discovered that the collective right to enfranchisement is so hedged round with procedural difficulties as to daunt all but the most organised and persistent bodies of tenants. The individual right will in practice prove a very welcome and popular alternative. It should be noted that the fact that some or all of the tenants have exercised the individual right does not present the collective right under Chap. I being employed. Clearly there may then be difficulties amongst the tenants in negotiating their respective contributions to a collective purchaser. It must also be noted that the right to an extended lease is a perpetual one. If exercised twice in quick succession then the second extended lease must be purchased at a very slight price.
Note that the Leasehold Reform (Collective Enfranchisement and Lease Renewal) Regulations 1993 (S.I. 1993 No. 2407), reproduced as Appendix 1, deal with certain aspects of procedure notably: (a) the deposit to be paid (up to 5 per cent.); (b) when the deposit is returnable; (c) the title to be produced by landlord and tenant; (d) the raising and reply to requisitions; (e) how the lease is to be prepared and amended; (f) cancellation in due course of land charges.

Preliminary

Right of qualifying tenant of flat to acquire new lease

39.—(1) This Chapter has effect for the purpose of conferring on a tenant of a flat, in the circumstances mentioned in subsection (2), the right, exercisable subject to and in accordance with this Chapter, to acquire a new lease of the flat on payment of a premium determined in accordance with this Chapter.
(2) Those circumstances are that on the relevant date for the purposes of this Chapter—
(a) the tenant is a qualifying tenant of the flat; and
(b) the tenant has occupied the flat as his only or principal home—
(i) for the last three years, or
(ii) for periods amounting to three years in the last ten years,
whether or not he has used it also for other purposes.
(3) The following provisions, namely—
(a) section 5 (with the omission of subsections (5) and (6)),
(b) section 7, and
(c) section 8,
shall apply for the purposes of this Chapter as they apply for the purposes of Chapter I; and references in this Chapter to a qualifying tenant of a flat shall accordingly be construed by reference to those provisions.
(4) For the purposes of this Chapter a person can be (or be among those constituting) the qualifying tenant of each of two or more flats at the same time, whether he is tenant of those flats under one lease or under two or more separate leases.
(5) For the purposes of subsection (2)(b) above—

(a) any reference to the tenant's flat includes a reference to part of it; and
(b) it is immaterial whether at any particular time the tenant's occupation was in right of the lease by virtue of which he is a qualifying tenant or in right of some other lease or otherwise;

but any occupation by a company or other artificial person, or (where the tenant is a corporation sole) by the corporator, shall not be regarded as occupation for the purposes of that provision.

(6) In the case of a lease held by joint tenants—
(a) the condition in subsection (2)(b) need only be satisfied with respect to one of the joint tenants; and
(b) subsection (5) shall apply accordingly (the reference to the lease by virtue of which the tenant is a qualifying tenant being read for this purpose as a reference to the lease by virtue of which the joint tenants are a qualifying tenant).

(7) The right conferred by this Chapter on a tenant to acquire a new lease shall not extend to underlying minerals comprised in his existing lease if—
(a) the landlord requires the minerals to be excepted, and
(b) proper provision is made for the support of the premises demised by that existing lease as they are enjoyed on the relevant date.

(8) In this Chapter "the relevant date", in relation to a claim by a tenant under this Chapter, means the date on which notice of the claim is given to the landlord under section 42.

DEFINITIONS
"flat": s.101(1).
"lease": s.101(1).
"qualifying tenant": s.62(1).
"relevant date": subs. (8) and s.62(1).

GENERAL NOTE
This section describes the basic circumstances in which the right to an individual extended lease exists.

Subs. (1)
This subsection does nothing and simply has the purpose of introducing what is to follow.

Subs. (2)(b)
The occupation test is taken directly from the Leasehold Reform Act 1967, s.1 with one very significant change. The test under s.1 of the 1967 Act is that the tenant has been "occupying it as his residence". The test under this Act is that the tenant "has occupied the flat as his only or principal home". A person may have more than one residence but only one principal home. The expression used in this Act is taken from the "tenant condition" for secure tenancies now found in s.81 of the Housing Act 1985 (formerly s.28(3) of the Housing Act 1980). See also the notes on s.6 of this Act above.

Subs. (3)
The omission of subss. (5) and (6) of s.5 from the definition of a qualifying tenant in Chap. II has one very important consequence. It means that a person can have the individual right to an extended lease however many flats he owns in the block. However, he will not ordinarily at one time have this right in respect of more than one of these flats because of the "only or principal home" test in subs. (2). It is conceivable that cases will arise where a tenant claims he owns two (or even more) flats in one building which together constitute his only or principal home. In this case it seems that the tenants must fail to satisfy, literally, the wording of subs. (2)(b) of occupying the flat as his only or principal home.

Subs. (4)
The tenant of a flat may have sub-let part but still satisfy the occupation test in subs. (2)(b). In calculating the three year occupation period the tenant's occupation in any right may be included—this may be as lessee under a different lease, licence or even as a former freehold owner. The reference to occupation by a corporator of a corporation sole means occupation *qua corporator*—a Bishop who occupies in his right as Bishop does not occupy within this section. A Bishop who occupies a flat in his personal capacity *qua* Mr. Morgan does occupy within this

section. If the nominal tenant is a company or other artificial person then the actual occupation by a real person appears not to come within the section.

Subs. (5)

One of the joint tenants must satisfy the three year occupation test; the wording appears to exclude the possibility of them adding periods of occupation together to make up the three years.

Subs. (6)

A positive stipulation is required by the landlord who requires the minerals to be excepted. This will ordinarily be irrelevant if the parcels clause is drawn in a normal way. Equally it will be in rare cases when proper provisions can be made for support to the premises and still retain any sensible possibility of under-mining. (See also s.1(6) *supra*).

The landlord for the purposes of this Chapter

40.—(1) In this Chapter "the landlord", in relation to the lease held by a qualifying tenant of a flat, means the person who is the owner of that interest in the flat which for the time being fulfils the following conditions, namely—

   (a) it is an interest in reversion expectant (whether immediately or not) on the termination of the tenant's lease, and

   (b) it is either a freehold interest or a leasehold interest whose duration is such as to enable that person to grant a new lease of that flat in accordance with this Chapter,

and is not itself expectant (whether immediately or not) on an interest which fulfils those conditions.

(2) Where in accordance with subsection (1) the immediate landlord under the lease of a qualifying tenant of a flat is not the landlord in relation to that lease for the purposes of this Chapter, the person who for those purposes is the landlord in relation to it shall conduct on behalf of all the other landlords all proceedings arising out of any notice given by the tenant with respect to the flat under section 42 (whether the proceedings are for resisting or giving effect to the claim in question).

(3) Subsection (2) has effect subject to the provisions of Schedule 11 to this Act (which makes provision in relation to the operation of this Chapter in cases to which that subsection applies).

(4) In this section and that Schedule—

   (a) "the tenant" means any such qualifying tenant as is referred to in subsection (2) and "the tenant's lease" means the lease by virtue of which he is a qualifying tenant;

   (b) "the competent landlord" means the person who, in relation to the tenant's lease, is the landlord (as defined by subsection (1)) for the purposes of this Chapter;

   (c) "other landlord" means any person (other than the tenant or a trustee for him) in whom there is vested a concurrent tenancy intermediate between the interest of the competent landlord and the tenant's lease.

(5) Schedule 2 (which makes provision with respect to certain special categories of landlords) has effect for the purposes of this Chapter.

DEFINITIONS

"competent landlord": subss. (4) and (6).

"flat": s.101(1).

"interest": s.101(1).

"landlord": subs. (1) and s.62(1).

"lease": s.101(1).

"other landlord": subs. (4)(c).

"qualifying tenant": s.62(1).

"tenant": subs. (4)(a).

"tenant's lease": subs. (4)(a).

GENERAL NOTE

The landlord is the owner of the reversionary interest, sufficient to grant a lease expiring 90 years after the current lease, which is most proximate to the tenants. Thus, assume the tenant has a lease expiring in 40 years from now, then a lease expiring at least 130 years from now will be the landlord's lease providing it is not reversionary to another lease ending at least 130 years from now. If there is an intermediate lease ending less than 130 years from now then these leases will be dealt with under this section and Sched. 11. Once that landlord is identified then it conducts the proceedings on behalf of all intermediate landlords. Further detailed provisions on the rôle of the landlord are contained in Sched. 11; see the notes on that Schedule.

Subs. (2)
This subsection should be compared with the similar provision in s.9 of this Act dealing with the collective right to enfranchisement.

Subs. (3)
Schedule 11 which deals with the complex implementation of the right to an extended lease where there is more than one landlord is annotated below.

Subs. (4)(c)
It will be appreciated that landlords of leases reversionary on the lease held by the immediate landlord are irrelevant when considering the right to an extended lease under this Chapter.

Preliminary inquiries by qualifying tenant

Right of qualifying tenant to obtain information about superior interests etc.

41.—(1) A qualifying tenant of a flat may give—
(a) to his immediate landlord, or
(b) to any person receiving rent on behalf of his immediate landlord,
a notice requiring the recipient to state whether the immediate landlord is the owner of the freehold interest in the flat and, if not, to give the tenant such information as is mentioned in subsection (2) (so far as known to the recipient).
(2) That information is—
(a) the name and address of the person who owns the freehold interest in the flat;
(b) the duration of the leasehold interest in the flat of the tenant's immediate landlord and the extent of the premises in which it subsists; and
(c) the name and address of every person who has a leasehold interest in the flat which is superior to that of the tenant's immediate landlord, the duration of any such interest and the extent of the premises in which it subsists.
(3) If the immediate landlord of any such qualifying tenant is not the owner of the freehold interest in the flat, the tenant may also—
(a) give to the person who is the owner of that interest a notice requiring him to give the tenant such information as is mentioned in paragraph (c) of subsection (2) (so far as known to that person);
(b) give to any person falling within that paragraph a notice requiring him to give the tenant—
(i) particulars of the duration of his leasehold interest in the flat and the extent of the premises in which it subsists, and
(ii) (so far as known to him) such information as is mentioned in paragraph (a) of that subsection and, as regards any other person falling within paragraph (c) of that subsection, such information as is mentioned in that paragraph.
(4) Any notice given by a qualifying tenant under this section shall, in addition to any other requirement imposed in accordance with subsections (1) to (3), require the recipient to state—
(a) whether he has received in respect of any premises containing the tenant's flat—
(i) a notice under section 13 in the case of which the relevant claim under Chapter I is still current, or

(ii) a copy of such a notice; and

(b) if so, the date on which the notice under section 13 was given and the name and address of the nominee purchaser for the time being appointed for the purposes of section 15 in relation to that claim.

(5) For the purposes of subsection (4)—

(a) "the relevant claim under Chapter I", in relation to a notice under section 13, means the claim in respect of which that notice is given; and

(b) any such claim is current if—

(i) that notice continues in force in accordance with section 13(11), or

(ii) a binding contract entered into in pursuance of that notice remains in force, or

(iii) where an order has been made under section 24(4)(a) or (b) or 25(6)(a) or (b) with respect to any such premises as are referred to in subsection (4)(a) above, any interests which by virtue of the order fall to be vested in the nominee purchaser for the purposes of Chapter I have yet to be so vested.

(6) Any person who is required to give any information by virtue of a notice under this section shall give that information to the qualifying tenant within the period of 28 days beginning with the date of the giving of the notice.

DEFINITIONS
   "flat": s.101(1).
   "interest": s.101(1).
   "landlord": s.101(1).
   "qualifying tenant": s.62(1).
   "tenant": s.40(4)(a).

GENERAL NOTE
   Compare with s.11 which is a similar provision dealing with the collective right to enfranchisement. As with s.11 the obvious lacuna is a genuine sanction for non-compliance. The opposition during the passage of the Bill argued forcibly that there should be a criminal sanction for non-compliance. Without such a sanction a section such as this and s.11 reinforce the cynic's view that the Government have on paper fulfilled their manifesto promise on leasehold reform but tenants will find it quite a different matter translating this into reality. Forms of notice under this section do not have to be in a prescribed form and may be given by letter. The notice should make it expressly clear that it is a notice under this section. The following form may be followed:

   "Notice under Section 41 of the Leasehold Reform, Housing and Urban Development Act 1993
   This notice is given by AB of Flat [address] to CD and require the recipient:
   To state if [he] is the owner of the freehold interest in the flat AND IF NOT TO GIVE SO FAR AS IS KNOWN to the recipient the following information: (a) the name and address of the person who owns the freehold interest in the flat; (b) the duration of the leasehold interest in the flat of the tenant's immediate landlord and the extent of the premises in which it subsists; and (c) the name and address of every person who has a leasehold interest in the flat which is superior to that of the tenant's immediate landlord, the duration of any such interest and the extent of the premises in which it subsists."

Subs. (2)
   The landlord is discovered by applying s.40. There is no definition of third parties to the tenant's lease. There may be a guarantor or surety. Persons who may have joined in to confirm the landlord's grant such as trustees of a settlement or mortgagees cannot be regarded as third parties for this purpose as their position is clearly dealt with under other provisions of the Act. See Sched. 13 and s.58.

The tenant's notice

Notice by qualifying tenant of claim to exercise right

42.—(1) A claim by a qualifying tenant of a flat to exercise the right to acquire a new lease of the flat is made by the giving of notice of the claim under this section.

(2) A notice given by a tenant under this section ("the tenant's notice") must be given—

(a) to the landlord, and

(b) to any third party to the tenant's lease.

(3) The tenant's notice must—

(a) state the full name of the tenant and the address of the flat in respect of which he claims a new lease under this Chapter;

(b) contain the following particulars, namely—

(i) sufficient particulars of that flat to identify the property to which the claim extends,

(ii) such particulars of the tenant's lease as are sufficient to identify it, including the date on which the lease was entered into, the term for which it was granted and the date of the commencement of the term,

(iii) such further particulars as are necessary to show that the tenant's lease is, in accordance with section 8 (as that section applies in accordance with section 39(3)), a lease at a low rent, and

(iv) particulars of the period or periods falling within the preceding ten years for which the tenant has occupied the whole or part of the flat as his only or principal home;

(c) specify the premium which the tenant proposes to pay in respect of the grant of a new lease under this Chapter and, where any other amount will be payable by him in accordance with any provision of Schedule 13, the amount which he proposes to pay in accordance with that provision;

(d) specify the terms which the tenant proposes should be contained in any such lease;

(e) state the name of the person (if any) appointed by the tenant to act for him in connection with his claim, and an address in England and Wales at which notices may be given to any such person under this Chapter; and

(f) specify the date by which the landlord must respond to the notice by giving a counter-notice under section 45.

(4) If the tenant's lease is held by joint tenants, the reference to the tenant in subsection (3)(b)(iv) shall be read as a reference to any joint tenant with respect to whom it is claimed that the condition in section 39(2)(b) is satisfied.

(5) The date specified in the tenant's notice in pursuance of subsection (3)(f) must be a date falling not less than two months after the date of the giving of the notice.

(6) Where a notice under this section has been given with respect to any flat, no subsequent notice may be given under this section with respect to the flat so long as the earlier notice continues in force.

(7) Where a notice under this section has been given with respect to a flat and—

(a) that notice has been withdrawn, or is deemed to have been withdrawn, under or by virtue of any provision of this Chapter, or

(b) in response to that notice, an order has been applied for and obtained under section 47(1),

no subsequent notice may be given under this section with respect to the flat within the period of twelve months beginning with the date of the withdrawal or deemed withdrawal of the earlier notice or with the time when the order under section 47(1) becomes final (as the case may be).

(8) Where a notice is given in accordance with this section, then for the purposes of this Chapter the notice continues in force as from the relevant date—

(a) until a new lease is granted in pursuance of the notice;
(b) if the notice is withdrawn, or is deemed to have been withdrawn, under or by virtue of any provision of this Chapter, until the date of the withdrawal or deemed withdrawal; or
(c) until such other time as the notice ceases to have effect by virtue of any provision of this Chapter;
but this subsection has effect subject to section 54.

(9) Schedule 12 (which contains restrictions on terminating a tenant's lease where he has given a notice under this section and makes other provision in connection with the giving of notices under this section) shall have effect.

DEFINITIONS
"flat": s.101(1).
"landlord": ss.40(1) and 62(1).
"lease": s.101(1).
"qualifying tenant": s.62(1).
"tenant": s.40(4)(a).
"tenant's lease": s.40(4)(a).
"tenant's notice": s.62(1).
"third party": s.62(1).

GENERAL NOTE
As with the collective right to enfranchisement the formal procedure commences with a tenant's notice. None of the procedural problems of obtaining agreement from other tenants exist and the individual right to a new lease will be substantially easier to operate in practice than the collective right to enfranchisement. It is not the Government's intention to provide for specified forms for notices and counter-notices. Consequently a draft is reproduced below.

"NOTICE UNDER S.42 OF THE LEASEHOLD REFORM, HOUSING AND URBAN DEVELOPMENT ACT 1993
1. This notice is given by [*tenant's full name and address*].
2. The tenant claims an extended lease of the flat identified in Sched. I of which it holds the lease therein identified for the term stated at the low rent therein mentioned.
3. The tenant has occupied the flat as [h:~] only or principal home during the following periods [set these out].
4. (i)   the premium which the tenant proposes to pay is [   ];
   [(ii) the sum which the tenant proposes to pay for the landlord's share of marriage value is   ];
   [(iii) the sum which the tenant proposes to pay the landlord for compensation under para. 5 of Sched. 13 is   ];
   [(iv) the sum[s] which the tenant proposes to pay in respect of [an] intermediate interest[s] [is][are]   ].
5. The terms which the tenant proposes for the new lease are set out in Sched. II.
6. The landlord is required to respond thereto by [state a date at least two months after the date of giving of the notice].
7. The tenant is represented by [himself] [————] and the address for service of notices is [   ].

SCHEDULE I

SCHEDULE II

Subs. (8)
Chapter I (the right to collective enfranchisement) takes priority after Chap. II (the right to an individual extended lease). This very important principle is explained further in the note on s.54(2) and (3).

General provisions as respects effect of tenant's notice

43.—(1) Where a notice has been given under section 42 with respect to any flat, the rights and obligations of the landlord and the tenant arising from the notice shall ensure for the benefit of and be enforceable against them, their personal representatives and assigns to the like extent (but no further) as rights and obligations arising under a contract for leasing freely entered into between the landlord and the tenant.

(2) Accordingly, in relation to matters arising out of any such notice, references in this Chapter to the landlord and the tenant shall, in so far as the context permits, include their respective personal representatives and assigns.

(3) Notwithstanding anything in subsection (1), the rights and obligations of the tenant shall be assignable with, but shall not be capable of subsisting apart from, the lease of the entire flat; and, if the tenant's lease is assigned without the benefit of the notice, the notice shall accordingly be deemed to have been withdrawn by the tenant as at the date of the assignment.

(4) In the event of any default by the landlord or the tenant in carrying out the obligations arising from the tenant's notice, the other of them shall have the like rights and remedies as in the case of a contract freely entered into.

(5) In a case to which section 40(2) applies, the rights and obligations of the landlord arising out of the tenant's notice shall, so far as their interests are affected, be rights and obligations respectively of the competent landlord and of each of the other landlords, and references to the landlord in subsections (1) and (2) above shall apply accordingly.

(6) In subsection (5) "competent landlord" and "other landlord" have the meaning given by section 40(4); and subsection (5) has effect without prejudice to the operation of section 40(2) or Schedule 11.

DEFINITIONS
"competent landlord": s.40(4)(b).
"flat": s.101(1).
"landlord": ss.40(1) and 62(1).
"lease": s.101(1).
"other landlord": s.40(4)(c).
"tenant": s.40(4)(a).
"tenant's lease": s.40(4)(a).
"tenant's notice": ss.40(4)(b) and 62(1).

GENERAL NOTE
The effect of a notice is to create a contract between the landlord and the tenant. This contract must be registered against the freeholder and other landlords whom it is intended to bind (see s.97 *infra*). Since it is an estate contract it will be void against a purchaser of a legal estate for money or money's worth unless registered (s.4(6) of the Land Charges Act 1972 for unregistered land). In registered land a transferee for valuable consideration when registered will take free of an unregistered contract (s.20(1) of the Land Registration Act 1925); a transferee not for valuable consideration will take subject to the contract (s.20(4) of the Land Registration Act 1925).

Subs. (3)
If the tenant assigns the lease of the whole flat then the benefit of the notice must be expressly assigned or it is deemed to be withdrawn. If part of the lease is assigned (as opposed to sub-let) then the notice is again automatically deemed to be withdrawn as it can have no effect except in relation to the entire flat. If any issue arises as to the date of the assignment it will be taken as the date the deed or transfer is executed and not the date it is registered, notwithstanding that the latter is the effective date of passing the legal estate where the land is already registered.

Subs. (4)
Given the clear wording of subs. (3) that the notice takes effect to the like extent as a contract this subsection seems otiose.

Subs. (5)
Section 40(2) applies to cases where the immediate landlord is not the landlord who has to grant the long lease. Each of the reversionary landlords is, thus, subject to this deemed contract with the tenant and possible liability for its breach. Registration must be effected against each such landlord and, if desired, by each against the tenant.

Subs. (6)
This restatement of the previous definitions is symptomatic of considerable anxiety in the drafting as to the nature of leasehold titles and the practical operation of these provisions. The

apparent need to define landlord in s.40(1) and s.62 and again in this subsection appears to have the same practical effect as if the draftsperson had specified that the competent landlord is the holder of the reversionary interest which handles the procedure and the other landlords whose interests have to be purchased to effect the new lease and "landlord", wherever used in this chapter, means "competent landlord" unless the context requires a different meaning.

Procedure following giving of tenant's notice

Access by landlords for valuation purposes

44.—(1) Once the tenant's notice or a copy of it has been given in accordance with section 42 or Part I of Schedule 11—

(a) to the landlord for the purposes of this Chapter, or

(b) to any other landlord (as defined by section 40(4)),

that landlord and any person authorised to act on his behalf shall have a right of access to the flat to which the notice relates for the purpose of enabling that landlord to obtain, in connection with the notice, a valuation of his interest in the flat.

(2) That right shall be exercisable at any reasonable time and on giving not less than three days' notice to the tenant.

DEFINITIONS
"flat": s.101(1).
"interest": s.101(1).
"landlord": ss.40(1) and 62(1).
"tenant": s.40(4)(a).
"tenant's notice": s.62(1).

GENERAL NOTE
The relevant landlords are given a right of access for the purpose of valuation. That is clearly a several right of access independently exercisable (see s.17 for equivalent right in case of collective enfranchisement).

Landlord's counter-notice

45.—(1) The landlord shall give a counter-notice under this section to the tenant by the date specified in the tenant's notice in pursuance of section 42(3)(f).

(2) The counter-notice must comply with one of the following requirements—

(a) state that the landlord admits that the tenant had on the relevant date the right to acquire a new lease of his flat;

(b) state that, for such reasons as are specified in the counter-notice, the landlord does not admit that the tenant had such a right on that date;

(c) contain such a statement as is mentioned in paragraph (a) or (b) above but state that the landlord intends to make an application for an order under section 47(1) on the grounds that he intends to redevelop any premises in which the flat is contained.

(3) If the counter-notice complies with the requirement set out in subsection (2)(a), it must in addition—

(a) state which (if any) of the proposals contained in the tenant's notice are accepted by the landlord and which (if any) of those proposals are not so accepted; and

(b) specify, in relation to each proposal which is not accepted, the landlord's counter-proposal.

(4) The counter-notice must specify an address in England and Wales at which notices may be given to the landlord under this Chapter.

(5) Where the counter-notice admits the tenant's right to acquire a new lease of his flat, the admission shall be binding on the landlord as to the matters mentioned in section 39(2)(a) and (b), unless the landlord shows that he was induced to make the admission by misrepresentation or the

concealment of material facts; but the admission shall not conclude any question whether the particulars of the flat stated in the tenant's notice in pursuance of section 42(3)(b)(i) are correct.

DEFINITIONS
"flat": s.101(1).
"landlord": ss.40(1) and 62(1).
"lease": s.101(1).
"relevant date": s.62(1).
"tenant": s.40(4)(a).
"tenant's notice": s.62(1).

GENERAL NOTE
There is to be no specified form of counter-notice and accordingly a draft is produced here. A procedural table follows this showing the effect of various steps and counter-steps that may be taken.

"**COUNTER-NOTICE FORM—DRAFT EXAMPLE**

COUNTER NOTICE UNDER S.45 LEASEHOLD REFORM, HOUSING AND URBAN DEVELOPMENT ACT 1993 BY LANDLORD TO TENANT'S NOTICE REQUIRING NEW LEASE

To AB

Tenant of

Counter-notice under s.45 of the Leasehold Reform, Housing and Urban Development Act 1993:

ALTERNATIVE ONE

The landlord admits the tenant had on the relevant date the right to acquire a new lease of the flat and in respect of the tenant's proposals as to the new lease accepts those listed in Pt. A of the Schedule hereto and does not accept those listed in the first column of Pt. B of the Schedule hereto and makes in respect of each of those the counter-proposal listed in Col. II thereof.

ALTERNATIVE TWO

1. The landlord does not admit for the reasons stated in the Schedule hereto that the tenant had the right on the relevant date to acquire a new lease of the flat.

DELETE IF NOT RELEVANT

1.1 The landlord intends to make an application under s.47(1) on the grounds that (he) intends to redevelop any premises in which the flat is contained.
2. The address at which notices may be given to the landlord is

This   day of   19

Signed for or on
behalf of landlord   ''

PROCEDURAL TABLE

The landlord fails to serve a counter-notice.	Section 49—the tenant may apply to the court to determine whether it has the right to a new lease and on what terms.
The landlord serves a counter-notice admitting the claim in full.	Section 48—the grant proceeds by negotiation until dispute is reached then an application is made to leasehold valuation tribunal to decide terms.
The landlord admits the claim but contests the terms.	Section 48—The areas of dispute may be resolved by negotiation or failing that by application to the leasehold valuation tribunal.
The landlord serves a counter-notice denying the claim.	Section 46—(i) the tenant may concede OR (ii) the landlord may apply to the court

	which will declare whether the claim is made out. Sections 40(2) and 49—the tenant may (where the landlord does not) apply to the court for it to determine whether the claim is made out and the terms of the application.
The landlord claims the right to redevelop under s.45(2)(c).	(i) The tenant may concede this claim. (ii) The landlord may apply to the court for a declaration that the tenant has no right to a new lease. If this fails then the landlord may proceed to (a) concede the claim OR (b) apply to the court to show that it is entitled to object on the right to redevelop ground (s.47) AND will be required to serve a new counter-notice unless an application as in (iii) is pending. (iii) The landlord may after giving the counter-notice apply to the court to show it is entitled to object on the right to redevelop ground. If this fails the landlord will be required to serve a new counter-notice (s.47(4)).

Subs. (5)
The significance of making these admissions must be carefully noted. In admitting that the tenant had a right to a new lease the landlord is taken to admit that: (a) the tenant is a qualifying tenant; and (b) the occupation condition is satisfied.

Applications to court or leasehold valuation tribunal

Proceedings relating to validity of tenant's notice

46.—(1) Where—
(a) the landlord has given the tenant a counter-notice under section 45 which (whether it complies with the requirement set out in subsection (2)(b) or (c) of that section) contains such a statement as is mentioned in subsection (2)(b) of that section, and
(b) the court is satisfied, on an application made by the landlord, that on the relevant date the tenant had no right under this Chapter to acquire a new lease of his flat,
the court shall by order make a declaration to that effect.

(2) Any application for an order under subsection (1) must be made not later than the end of the period of two months beginning with the date of the giving of the counter-notice to the tenant; and if, in a case falling within paragraph (a) of that subsection, either—
(a) no application for such an order is made by the landlord within that period, or
(b) such an application is so made but is subsequently withdrawn,
section 49 shall apply as if the landlord had not given the counter-notice.

(3) If on any such application the court makes such a declaration as is mentioned in subsection (1), the tenant's notice shall cease to have effect on the order becoming final.

(4) If, however, any such application is dismissed by the court, then (subject to subsection (5)) the court shall make an order—
(a) declaring that the landlord's counter-notice shall be of no effect, and
(b) requiring the landlord to give a further counter-notice to the tenant by such date as is specified in the order.

(5) Subsection (4) shall not apply if—

(a) the counter-notice complies with the requirement set out in section 45(2)(c), and
(b) either—
(i) an application for an order under section 47(1) is pending, or
(ii) the period specified in section 47(3) as the period for the making of such an application has not expired.

(6) Subsection (3) of section 45 shall apply to any further counter-notice required to be given by the landlord under subsection (4) above as if it were a counter-notice under that section complying with the requirement set out in subsection (2)(a) of that section.

DEFINITIONS
"court": s.101(1).
"flat": s.101(1).
"landlord": ss.40(1) and 62(1).
"lease": s.101(1).
"relevant date": s.62(1).
"tenant": s.40(4)(a).
"tenant's notice": s.62(1).

GENERAL NOTE
Disputes as to the validity of the tenant's notice are decided by the county court. There are precise time-scales for making such applications and they must be adhered to. The provisions in ss.46 to 49 seem quite unnecessarily complicated and the table following the note on s.45 gives a picture of the effect of the different provisions. If the landlord takes no action at all, the tenant will eventually have to apply to the court to prosecute the claim. The court cannot make an order at any stage allowing the tenant to proceed to a new lease unless either the landlord has conceded the claim or the court is satisfied that the claim is made out.

Subs. (1)
This envisages the landlord making an application seeking a declaration by the court that the tenant has no right to a new lease. The onus will be on the landlord to show this and there appears to be little advantage in making such an application. However, it may be advantageous for the status of a particular building to be settled.

Subs. (2)
This time-scale is one from which the court can give no relief. But the consequence of the landlord failing to apply to the court is simply that the tenant must do so (under s.49). The s.49 application will then be a tenant's application on which the court must be satisfied that the claim is made out. The two-month period will be calculated: (i) from actual service of the notice or if relevant; (ii) from the date of deemed service under s.196(4) of the Law of Property Act 1925 if served by registered post or recorded delivery. That is from the day after posting by first class post or the second day after posting by second class post. Two months will mean two calendar months and the corresponding-day rule will be applied. Thus, if a notice is served or deemed to be served on April 3, 1994 the two-month period will end at the end of May 2, 1994. The application must be made to the court during that period and thereafter served in accordance with the County Court Rules.

Subs. (4)
The further counter-notice will follow the same general form. There seems to be no reason why the landlord cannot produce a new reason for claiming that the tenant's claim is not made out.

Subs. (5)
No new counter-notice will be required where the landlord's counter-notice claims the right to redevelop and either the landlord has applied to the court to make out this claim or the two-month period after the counter-notice is still running (s.44(3)).

Subs. (6)
A further counter-notice is required to state which of the tenant's proposals are accepted and the landlord's counter proposal in respect of any which are not.

Application to defeat tenant's claim where landlord intends to redevelop

47.—(1) Where the landlord has given the tenant a counter-notice under section 45 which complies with the requirement set out in subsection (2)(c) of that section, the court may, on the application of the landlord, by order declare that the right to acquire a new lease shall not be exercisable by the tenant by reason of the landlord's intention to redevelop any premises in which the tenant's flat is contained; and on such an order becoming final the tenant's notice shall cease to have effect.

(2) The court shall not make an order under subsection (1) unless it is satisfied—

(a) that the tenant's lease of his flat is due to terminate within the period of five years beginning with the relevant date; and

(b) that for the purposes of redevelopment the landlord intends, once the lease has so terminated—

(i) to demolish or reconstruct, or

(ii) to carry out substantial works of construction on,

the whole or a substantial part of any premises in which the flat is contained; and

(c) that he could not reasonably do so without obtaining possession of the flat.

(3) Any application for an order under subsection (1) must be made within the period of two months beginning with the date of the giving of the counter-notice to the tenant; but, where the counter-notice is one falling within section 46(1)(a), such an application shall not be proceeded with until such time (if any) as any order dismissing an application under section 46(1) becomes final.

(4) Where an application for an order under subsection (1) is dismissed by the court, the court shall make an order—

(a) declaring that the landlord's counter-notice shall be of no effect, and

(b) requiring the landlord to give a further counter-notice to the tenant by such date as is specified in the order.

(5) Where—

(a) the landlord has given such a counter-notice as is mentioned in subsection (1), but

(b) either—

(i) no application for an order under that subsection is made within the period referred to in subsection (3), or

(ii) such an application is so made but is subsequently withdrawn,

then (subject to subsection (7)), the landlord shall give a further counter-notice to the tenant within the period of two months beginning with the appropriate date.

(6) In subsection (5) "the appropriate date" means—

(a) if subsection (5)(b)(i) applies, the date immediately following the end of the period referred to in subsection (3); and

(b) if subsection (5)(b)(ii) applies, the date of withdrawal of the application.

(7) Subsection (5) shall not apply if any application has been made by the landlord for an order under section 46(1).

(8) Subsection (3) of section 45 shall apply to any further counter-notice required to be given by the landlord under subsection (4) or (5) above as if it were a counter-notice under that section complying with the requirement set out in subsection (2)(a) of that section.

DEFINITIONS
"appropriate date": subs. (6).
"court": s.101(1).
"flat": s.101(1).
"landlord": ss.40(1) and 62(1).
"lease": s.101(1).
"relevant date": s.62(1).
"tenant": s.40(4)(a).

"tenant's lease": s.40(4)(a).
"tenant's notice": s.62(1).

GENERAL NOTE

Although this provision is at first sight the mirror of the landlord's right to object to collective enfranchisement on the ground of intention to redevelop it must operate quite differently in its application to a single flat. Tenants should be specifically warned against leaving the operation of their rights under this Act until the last five years of the lease, which is when this section bites. Equally landlords faced with a notice outside the five-year period but close to it may attempt to obstruct that notice until it is possible to bring the lease within this section.

Subs. (1)

The counter-notice given by the landlord will claim that the landlord intends to redevelop. The landlord then, if it wishes to sustain its objection on this ground, must apply to the court to show it makes out the necessary conditions of s.47. If it does then the tenant's notice fails. If it does not then the landlord has to give a further counter-notice.

Subs. (2)(a)

Does "due to terminate" include termination as a result of a break clause? Literally the paragraph appears not to have this effect.

Subs. (2)(b)

The very many decided cases under s.30(1)(f) of the Landlord and Tenant Act 1954, Pt. II must be relevant. The court will, thus, look for evidence of the practicality of the landlord's intention in terms of planning permissions obtained, building plans and financial wherewithal. The work must be carried out "on the whole or a substantial part of any premises in which the flat is contained". For this purpose s.62(2) and its interpretation of what is meant by a "flat" appear to be relevant and occasionally provide a surprisingly helpful result for the landlord— will the court hold that subs. (2)(b) is satisfied if the landlord wishes to demolish premises which contain an outhouse which is part of the flat? Unfortunately for the landlord s.62(3) makes it clear that a restrictive definition of a flat applies for the purposes of this section. Clearly demolition of the appurtenant outhouse will not satisfy s.47.

Subss. (3)–(5)

An example of the working of this time-scale would be as follows:
January 2: the tenant gives an initial notice.
February 1: the landlord gives a counter-notice claiming the right to redevelop. The landlord has until the end of March to apply to the court to make out the right to develop.
(i) If the tenant fails to make an application then the landlord has until the end of May to serve a further counter-notice.
(ii) If the tenant withdraws its application then the landlord has two months from withdrawal to serve a further counter-notice.
(iii) If the tenant fails in court then the landlord has to serve a further counter-notice by such date as the court lays down.
(iv) If the landlord applies to the court under s.46(1) to contest the validity of the initial notice then if that application is dismissed a further counter-notice is required under s.46(4) and, accordingly, s.47(7) makes s.47(5) and its further counter-notice procedure inapplicable to that circumstance.

Subss. (6) and (7)

If there is landlord A and another landlord B who cannot be found then the court may grant an order that landlord B need not be served. Any initial notice later served must state "The court by an order dated [   ] ordered that this notice need not be served upon landlord B". This will ensure that the notice complies with the provisions for service on landlord B which take effect under Sched. 11, Pt. I.

Applications where terms in dispute or failure to enter into new lease

48.—(1) Where the landlord has given the tenant—
(a) a counter-notice under section 45 which complies with the requirement set out in subsection (2)(a) of that section, or
(b) a further counter-notice required by or by virtue of section 46(4) or section 47(4) or (5),
but any of the terms of acquisition remain in dispute at the end of the period of two months beginning with the date when the counter-notice or further

counter-notice was so given, a leasehold valuation tribunal may, on the application of either the tenant or the landlord, determine the matters in dispute.

(2) Any application under subsection (1) must be made not later than the end of the period of six months beginning with the date on which the counter-notice or further counter-notice was given to the tenant.

(3) Where—

(a) the landlord has given the tenant such a counter-notice or further counter-notice as is mentioned in subsection (1)(a) or (b), and

(b) all the terms of acquisition have been either agreed between those persons or determined by a leasehold valuation tribunal under subsection (1),

but a new lease has not been entered into in pursuance of the tenant's notice by the end of the appropriate period specified in subsection (6), the court may, on the application of either the tenant or the landlord, make such order as it thinks fit with respect to the performance or discharge of any obligations arising out of that notice.

(4) Any such order may provide for the tenant's notice to be deemed to have been withdrawn at the end of the appropriate period specified in subsection (6).

(5) Any application for an order under subsection (3) must be made not later than the end of the period of two months beginning immediately after the end of the appropriate period specified in subsection (6).

(6) For the purposes of this section the appropriate period is—

(a) where all of the terms of acquisition have been agreed between the tenant and the landlord, the period of two months beginning with the date when those terms were finally so agreed; or

(b) where all or any of those terms have been determined by a leasehold valuation tribunal under subsection (1)—

(i) the period of two months beginning with the date when the decision of the tribunal under subsection (1) becomes final, or

(ii) such other period as may have been fixed by the tribunal when making its determination.

(7) In this Chapter "the terms of acquisition", in relation to a claim by a tenant under this Chapter, means the terms on which the tenant is to acquire a new lease of his flat, whether they relate to the terms to be contained in the lease or to the premium or any other amount payable by virtue of Schedule 13 in connection with the grant of the lease, or otherwise.

DEFINITIONS

"court": s.101(1).
"flat": s.101(1).
"landlord": ss.40(1) and 62(1).
"lease": s.101(1).
"tenant": s.40(4)(a).
"tenant's notice": s.62(1).
"terms of acquisition": subs. (7) and s.62(1).

GENERAL NOTE

Despite its extraordinary-seeming complexity the Act does little to guide the tenant towards successful completion of a claim. Eventually negotiations will break down and the terms of the acquisition fall to be determined by a leasehold valuation tribunal. This tribunal is one in which each party pays its own legal costs. This is important when considering the tactics of a claim under the Act. This aspect of a leasehold valuation tribunal application signifies there is nothing to detract from a landlord bargaining very hard indeed in the negotiations.

Subs. (1)

The counter-notice procedure is intended to lead to a negotiation as to the terms of the proposed new lease. The subsection envisages at least two months of negotiation followed by an application to a leasehold valuation tribunal to settle the term of the lease.

Subs. (2)

This period of time for applying to the leasehold valuation tribunal must be observed because at its end there will, if there is no such application, be no agreement to enforce and no further steps under the Act to take to arrive at an enforceable agreement.

Subss. (3)–(6)

Once the terms of the new lease have been arrived at either by agreement or by the leasehold valuation tribunal then difficulties may still arise in achieving the completion of the grant. The time-scale for any application to the court to resolve such a dispute is as follows: (i) the parties are expected to deal with each other during the appropriate period (subs. (6)) of two months from the determination of the terms or a different period if the leasehold valuation tribunal has decreed a different period; (ii) once the appropriate period has ended then an application to the court may be made within two months after the end of that period. It will not have escaped the reader's attention that it will not always be easy to be certain of the date on which "all of the terms of acquisition have been agreed". It will be more satisfactory if there is a formal exchange of terms at an agreed date. They might well also agree a completion date in the usual way for conveyancing contracts. It will be noted that Chap. II does not contain an equivalent to s.38(4) in Chap. I, which defines agreement of the terms as "agreement subject to contract".

Subs. (7)

There are many provisions in this Act which appear to make no meaningful addition and this is one of them. "Or otherwise" presumably covers two areas in which there may be terms: (i) the normal conveyancing mechanics such as completion provisions; (ii) collateral terms dealing with fittings, fixtures or apportionments of outgoings.

NOTE: See Appendix 1 for the draft regulations dealing with some conveyancing details.

Applications where landlord fails to give counter-notice or further counter-notice

49.—(1) Where the tenant's notice has been given in accordance with section 42 but—

  (a) the landlord has failed to give the tenant a counter-notice in accordance with section 45(1), or

  (b) if required to give a further counter-notice to the tenant by or by virtue of section 46(4) or section 47(4) or (5), the landlord has failed to comply with that requirement,

the court may, on the application of the tenant, make an order determining, in accordance with the proposals contained in the tenant's notice, the terms of acquisition.

(2) The court shall not make such an order on an application made by virtue of paragraph (a) of subsection (1) unless it is satisfied—

  (a) that on the relevant date the tenant had the right to acquire a new lease of his flat; and

  (b) if applicable, that the requirements of Part I of Schedule 11 were complied with as respects the giving of copies of the tenant's notice.

(3) Any application for an order under subsection (1) must be made not later than the end of the period of six months beginning with the date by which the counter-notice or further counter-notice referred to in that subsection was required to be given.

(4) Where—

  (a) the terms of acquisition have been determined by an order of the court under this section, but

  (b) a new lease has not been entered into in pursuance of the tenant's notice by the end of the appropriate period specified in subsection (7),

the court may, on the application of either the tenant or the landlord, make such order as it thinks fit with respect to the performance or discharge of any obligations arising out of that notice.

(5) Any such order may provide for the tenant's notice to be deemed to have been withdrawn at the end of the appropriate period specified in subsection (7).

(6) Any application for an order under subsection (4) must be made not later than the end of the period of two months beginning immediately after the end of the appropriate period specified in subsection (7).

(7) For the purposes of this section the appropriate period is—

(a) the period of two months beginning with the date when the order of the court under subsection (1) becomes final, or

(b) such other period as may have been fixed by the court when making that order.

DEFINITIONS

"court": s.101(1).
"flat": s.101(1).
"landlord": ss.40(1) and 62(1).
"lease": s.101(1).
"relevant date": s.62(1).
"tenant": s.40(4)(a).
"tenant's notice": s.62(1).
"terms of acquisition": ss.48(7) and 62(1).

GENERAL NOTE

This section is intended to deal with the landlord who obstructs by inactivity. The landlord may fail in its duty to give a counter-notice in response to the initial notice (s.45(1)) or a further counter-notice where it has unsuccessfully challenged the validity of the tenant's notice (s.46(4)); may fail in its application to the court to establish the right to redevelop (s.47(4)); or may fail to make or withdraw such an application (s.47(5)). The tenant may then apply under this provision for the terms of the acquisition to be determined. The deterrent to the landlord from letting things take this course is that the proceedings will be subject to the normal county court rules as to costs. The leasehold valuation tribunal is not subject to these rules and may in some cases prove a better forum for challenging and obstructing a tenant's claim (if that is desired).

Subs. (1)

The court order is one determining "in accordance with the proposals contained in the tenant's notice, the term of acquisition". Does this mean that the terms must be in accordance with the tenant's proposals. If so, this is a very considerable pitfall for the indolent, obstructive or absentee landlord.

Subs. (2)

On an application under this section the tenant still has to ensure that it was entitled to a new lease and served the initial notice properly. The onus of proof of these matters is on the tenant.

Subs. (3)

Failure to comply with this time-scale means that the tenant's application under its initial notice is deemed to be withdrawn (see s.53(2)). A tenant who wishes to proceed must wait 12 months from the deemed withdrawal and serve a new initial notice (s.42(7)).

Subss. (4) to (7)

The time-scale under these provisions operates as follows: on January 2 the court makes a final order under subs. (1) determining the term of the lease then the parties have the "appropriate period" to try to bring the matter to completion. This is until March 2 or such other day as may be determined by the court in its order on January 2. Either party may by May 2 apply to the court for an order enforcing or discharging the tenant's notice. If no application is made within this period can the right to a new lease still be enforced as a matter of contract? The answer to this is no it cannot because the tenant's notice will be deemed to be withdrawn under s.53(3).

Applications where landlord cannot be found

50.—(1) Where—

(a) a qualifying tenant of a flat desires to make a claim to exercise the right to acquire a new lease of his flat, but

(b) the landlord cannot be found or his identity cannot be ascertained, the court may, on the application of the tenant, make a vesting order under this subsection.

(2) Where—

(a) a qualifying tenant of a flat desires to make such a claim as is mentioned in subsection (1), and

(b) paragraph (b) of that subsection does not apply, but

(c) a copy of a notice of that claim cannot be given in accordance with Part I of Schedule 11 to any person to whom it would otherwise be required to be so given because that person cannot be found or his identity cannot be ascertained,

the court may, on the application of the tenant, make an order dispensing with the need to give a copy of such a notice to that person.

(3) The court shall not make an order on any application under subsection (1) or (2) unless it is satisfied—

(a) that on the date of the making of the application the tenant had the right to acquire a new lease of his flat; and

(b) that on that date he would not have been precluded by any provision of this Chapter from giving a valid notice under section 42 with respect to his flat.

(4) Before making any such order the court may require the tenant to take such further steps by way of advertisement or otherwise as the court thinks proper for the purpose of tracing the person in question; and if, after an application is made for a vesting order under subsection (1) and before any lease is executed in pursuance of the application, the landlord is traced, then no further proceedings shall be taken with a view to a lease being so executed, but (subject to subsection (5))—

(a) the rights and obligations of all parties shall be determined as if the tenant had, at the date of the application, duly given notice under section 42 of his claim to exercise the right to acquire a new lease of his flat; and

(b) the court may give such directions as the court thinks fit as to the steps to be taken for giving effect to those rights and obligations, including directions modifying or dispensing with any of the requirements of this Chapter or of regulations made under this Part.

(5) An application for a vesting order under subsection (1) may be withdrawn at any time before execution of a lease under section 51(3) and, after it is withdrawn, subsection (4)(a) above shall not apply; but where any step is taken (whether by the landlord or the tenant) for the purpose of giving effect to subsection (4)(a) in the case of any application, the application shall not afterwards be withdrawn except—

(a) with the consent of the landlord, or

(b) by leave of the court,

and the court shall not give leave unless it appears to the court just to do so by reason of matters coming to the knowledge of the tenant in consequence of the tracing of the landlord.

(6) Where an order has been made under subsection (2) dispensing with the need to give a copy of a notice under section 42 to a particular person with respect to any flat, then if—

(a) a notice is subsequently given under that section with respect to that flat, and

(b) in reliance on the order, a copy of the notice is not to be given to that person,

the notice must contain a statement of the effect of the order.

(7) Where a notice under section 42 contains such a statement in accordance with subsection (6) above, then in determining for the purposes of any provision of this Chapter whether the requirements of Part I of Schedule 11 have been complied with in relation to the notice, those requirements shall

be deemed to have been complied with so far as relating to the giving of a copy of the notice to the person referred to in subsection (6) above.

DEFINITIONS
"court": s.101(1).
"flat": s.101(1).
"landlord": ss.40(1) and 62(1).
"lease": s.101(1).
"qualifying tenant": s.62(1).
"tenant": s.40(4)(a).

GENERAL NOTE
This section enables the right to an extended lease to be enforced where the landlord cannot be found or service cannot be effected on a person on whom the initial notice must otherwise be served.

Subs. (1)
No guidance is given as to when a tenant is justified in assuming that the landlord cannot be found.

Subs. (2)
Part I of Sched. 11 requires service of the initial notice on the competent landlord and all the "other landlords", that is, all the mesne landlords whose interests are to be affected by the grant of lease.

Subs. (3)
The onus is on the tenant to prove that he is entitled to the grant of a new lease.

Subs. (4)
It is far from obvious what is meant by "the landlord is traced". It is clear that if this happens no vesting order can be made under subs. (1). To make sense of this it means "the landlord comes forward in response to the further steps the court orders to identify it". Clearly subs. (4) will apply if the landlord enters an appearance in the application. If its identity becomes known to the tenant (or some other party) then does that mean the landlord "is traced"?

Subs. (5)
This opaque provision has the following effect. The tenant is allowed to withdraw an application for a vesting order and if he does so and the landlord is traced under subs. (4) then the proceedings are not continued under subs. (4)(a). Once, however, the landlord is traced before a withdrawal and the parties continue the proceedings at all under subs. (4)(a) then there can be no withdrawal unless either the landlord consents or the court gives leave. The ground on which the court can give this leave is found in the last paragraph of the subsection. Such matters may include knowledge of injurious affectation of other property of the landlord which would increase the purchase price.

Supplementary provisions relating to vesting orders under section 50(1)

51.—(1) A vesting order under section 50(1) is an order providing for the surrender of the tenant's lease of his flat and for the granting to him of a new lease of it on such terms as may be determined by a leasehold valuation tribunal to be appropriate with a view to the lease being granted to him in like manner (so far as the circumstances permit) as if he had, at the date of his application, given notice under section 42 of his claim to exercise the right to acquire a new lease of his flat.

(2) If a leasehold valuation tribunal so determines in the case of a vesting order under section 50(1), the order shall have effect in relation to property which is less extensive than that specified in the application on which the order was made.

(3) Where any lease is to be granted to a tenant by virtue of a vesting order under section 50(1), then on his paying into court the appropriate sum there shall be executed by such person as the court may designate a lease which—

(a) is in a form approved by a leasehold valuation tribunal, and

(b) contains such provisions as may be so approved for the purpose of giving effect so far as possible to section 56(1) and section 57 (as that section applies in accordance with subsections (7) and (8) below);

and that lease shall be effective to vest in the person to whom it is granted the property expressed to be demised by it, subject to and in accordance with the terms of the lease.

(4) In connection with the determination by a leasehold valuation tribunal of any question as to the property to be demised by any such lease, or as to the rights with or subject to which it is to be demised, it shall be assumed (unless the contrary is shown) that the landlord has no interest in property other than the property to be demised and, for the purpose of excepting them from the lease, any minerals underlying that property.

(5) The appropriate sum to be paid into court in accordance with sub-section (3) is the aggregate of—

(a) such amount as may be determined by a leasehold valuation tribunal to be the premium which is payable under Schedule 13 in respect of the grant of the new lease;

(b) such other amount or amounts (if any) as may be determined by such a tribunal to be payable by virtue of that Schedule in connection with the grant of that lease; and

(c) any amounts or estimated amounts determined by such a tribunal as being, at the time of execution of that lease, due to the landlord from the tenant (whether due under or in respect of the tenant's lease of his flat or under or in respect of any agreement collateral thereto).

(6) Where any lease is granted to a person in accordance with this section, the payment into court of the appropriate sum shall be taken to have satisfied any claims against the tenant, his personal representatives or assigns in respect of the premium and any other amounts payable as mentioned in subsection (5)(a) and (b).

(7) Subject to subsection (8), the following provisions, namely—

(a) sections 57 to 59, and

(b) section 61 and Schedule 14,

shall, so far as capable of applying to a lease granted in accordance with this section, apply to such a lease as they apply to a lease granted under section 56; and subsections (6) and (7) of that section shall apply in relation to a lease granted in accordance with this section as they apply in relation to a lease granted under that section.

(8) In its application to a lease granted in accordance with this section—

(a) section 57 shall have effect as if—

(i) any reference to the relevant date were a reference to the date of the application under section 50(1) in pursuance of which the vesting order under that provision was made, and

(ii) in subsection (5) the reference to section 56(3)(a) were a reference to subsection (5)(c) above; and

(b) section 58 shall have effect as if—

(i) in subsection (3) the second reference to the landlord were a reference to the person designated under subsection (3) above, and

(ii) subsections (6)(a) and (7) were omitted.

DEFINITIONS

"court": s.101(1).
"flat": s.101(1).
"landlord": ss.40(1) and 62(1).
"lease": s.101(1).
"relevant date": s.62(1).
"tenant": s.40(4)(a).
"tenant's lease": s.40(4)(a).

GENERAL NOTE

This section contains detailed provisions as to vesting orders under s.50 in cases where the landlord cannot be found or his identity ascertained.

Subs. (1)

The order provides for the surrender of the existing lease and the grant of a new lease. Thus, if the lease is registered the register of the old lease is closed and a new register opened. If the old lease is subject to a registered charge then s.58(4) applies to the registered charge but see the note on s.58(4).

Subs. (2)

This subsection gives the court a very wide discretion to omit property from the new lease. The effect will be that that property is lost to the tenant because the old lease is surrendered. It will also be lost insofar as it was a part of the tenant's mortgagee's security.

Subs. (3)

This subsection requires the terms of the lease to be approved by a leasehold valuation tribunal. This necessitates an application to such a tribunal in every case where a vesting order is sought.

Subs. (4)

This is a very odd provision. The assumption that the landlord has no interest "in property other than the property to be demised" will virtually always be untrue. It may actually be true if the reversion has been severed so that the landlord is only landlord of this flat. The original lease will make it clear in almost every case that exceptions and reservations are required and it will rarely be in the interests of the tenant to proceed on the basis that the assumption stated in this subsection is true, in order to achieve a sensible form of lease the tenant will ensure that "the contrary is shown". The closing words of the subsection seem to assume that minerals will be excepted.

Termination or suspension of acquisition procedures

Withdrawal by tenant from acquisition of new lease

52.—(1) At any time before a new lease is entered into in pursuance of the tenant's notice, the tenant may withdraw that notice by the giving of a notice to that effect under this section ("a notice of withdrawal").

(2) A notice of withdrawal must be given—

(a) to the landlord for the purposes of this Chapter;

(b) to every other landlord (as defined by section 40(4)); and

(c) to any third party to the tenant's lease.

(3) Where a notice of withdrawal is given by the tenant to any person in accordance with subsection (2), the tenant's liability under section 60 for costs incurred by that person shall be a liability for costs incurred by him down to the time when the notice is given to him.

DEFINITIONS

"landlord": ss.40(1) and 62(1).
"lease": s.101(1).
"tenant": s.40(4)(a).
"tenant's lease": s.40(4)(a).
"tenant's notice": s.62(1).
"third party": s.62(1).

GENERAL NOTE

So far as withdrawal is concerned no lengthy form of notice is required. A simple notice referring to the lease and the property and stating that the notice given under s.42 is withdrawn will suffice.

Subs. (2)

The notice is only effective if served on the competent landlord and the other mesne landlords and on any surety or guarantor of the tenant's lease.

Subs. (3)

See the notes on s.60 for liability for costs.

Deemed withdrawal of tenant's notice

53.—(1) Where—
(a) in a case to which subsection (1) of section 48 applies, no application under that subsection is made within the period specified in subsection (2) of that section, or
(b) in a case to which subsection (3) of that section applies, no application for an order under that subsection is made within the period specified in subsection (5) of that section,

the tenant's notice shall be deemed to have been withdrawn at the end of the period referred to in paragraph (a) or (b) above (as the case may be).

(2) Where, in a case falling within paragraph (a) or (b) of subsection (1) of section 49, no application for an order under that subsection is made within the period specified in subsection (3) of that section, the tenant's notice shall be deemed to have been withdrawn at the end of that period.

(3) Where, in a case to which subsection (4) of section 49 applies, no application for an order under that subsection is made within the period specified in subsection (6) of that section, the tenant's notice shall be deemed to have been withdrawn at the end of that period.

(4) The following provisions, namely—
(a) section 43(3),
(b) section 48(4), and
(c) section 49(5),

also make provision for a notice under section 42 to be deemed to have been withdrawn at a particular time.

DEFINITIONS
"tenant's notice": s.62(1).

GENERAL NOTE
This section deals with circumstances where the tenant's notice is deemed to be withdrawn because the tenant has not pursued the statutory procedures sufficiently timeously. The timescales for each procedural step pose an alarming degree of complexity. The penalty for deemed withdrawal is that a new initial notice cannot be given for 12 months (s.42(7)). The price may also increase significantly in later years of the tenancy and, even worse, the landlord's right to defeat the claim where it intends to redevelop may become available (s.47).

Subs. (1)(a)
Under s.48(1) the following may occur. The landlord will serve a counter-notice or further counter-notice but the terms of the acquisition will remain in dispute. The tenant may then, within the six month period specified, apply to the leasehold valuation tribunal to have the terms of the new lease decided. If the tenant does not do so the initial notice is deemed to be withdrawn.

Subs. (1)(b)
Where the terms have been agreed or decided by a leasehold valuation tribunal then there may still be delay or dispute in achieving completion of the grant of a new lease. In this case the tenant may apply to the court under s.48(3) within the period set out in s.48(5) and if it does not then the tenant's initial notice is deemed to be withdrawn.

Subs. (2)
Where the landlord fails to give a counter-notice or further counter-notice under s.49(1) then the tenant may apply to the court within the six month period set out in s.49(3) and if he does not then the initial advice is deemed to be withdrawn.

Subs. (3)
Where the landlord has failed to serve a counter-notice or further counter-notice and the terms of acquisition have been determined by the court then there may still be delay or dispute in completing the grant of a new lease. The tenant or the landlord may apply to the court under s.49(4) to resolve this but if no application is made within the period of two months specified in s.49(6) then the initial notice is deemed to be withdrawn.

Subs. (4)

An initial notice is deemed to be withdrawn: (a) if the lease is assigned and there is no assignment of the benefit of an initial notice given before the assignment (s.43(3)); (b) where a court order provides for the notice to be deemed to be withdrawn at the end of specified period. This will arise where there has been an application to the court following delay in completing a grant and that delay is due to the tenant's dilatoriness not the landlord's (s.48(4)); (c) this is to the same effect as (b). Paragraph (b) applies when the court order is made in a case where the landlord has served a counter-notice or further counter-notice and para. (c) when it has not (s.49(5)).

SUMMARY OF EVENTS WHERE TENANT'S NOTICE IS DEEMED WITHDRAWN

Event	Provision	Time-scale
Failure to apply to the leasehold valuation tribunal to settle terms of acquisition.	s.48(2)	Within six months of landlord's counter-notice or further counter-notice.
Failure to apply to court to compel performance or discharge of obligation to grant lease.	s.48(3)	Within two months of end of appropriate period which is itself either: (i) two months from agreement of terms; (ii) two months from final determination of terms by leasehold valuation tribunal; or (iii) other period fixed by the leasehold valuation tribunal in its determination.
Failure to apply to court where landlord fails to give notice or counter-notice.	s.49	Six months from the date when the notice or counter-notice was required to be served.
Failure when terms decided by court but new lease not granted to apply to court to order performance or discharge.	s.49(4)	Within two months after the appropriate period which is either two months after the final order of the court or such other period as fixed by the court.
If the tenant assigns the lease without express assignment of the tenant's notice.	s.43(3)	The date of the assignment.
After a landlord's counter-notice or further counter-notice where there is an application to the court requiring performance or discharge of the obligation to grant a new lease.	s.48(4)	At the end of the appropriate period if the court so orders which is: (i) two months from agreement of terms; (ii) two months from final determination of terms by the leasehold valuation tribunal; or (iii) other period fixed by the leasehold valuation tribunal in its determination.
After the terms of the acquisition have been settled by a court order but no new lease granted and tenant or landlord applies requiring performance or discharge of the obligation to grant a new lease.	s.49(5)	At the end of the appropriate period if the court so orders: (i) two months after the final court order; or (ii) other period fixed by the court in its order.

Suspension of tenant's notice during currency of claim under Chapter I

54.—(1) If, at the time when the tenant's notice is given—
(a) a notice has been given under section 13 with respect to any premises containing the tenant's flat, and

(b) the relevant claim under Chapter I is still current,
the operation of the tenant's notice shall be suspended during the currency
of that claim; and so long as it is so suspended no further notice shall be
given, and no application shall be made, under this Chapter with a view to
resisting or giving effect to the tenant's claim.

(2) If, at any time when the tenant's notice continues in force, a notice is
given under section 13 with respect to any premises containing the tenant's
flat, then, as from the date which is the relevant date for the purposes of
Chapter I in relation to that notice under section 13, the operation of the
tenant's notice shall be suspended during the currency of the relevant claim
under Chapter I; and so long as it is so suspended no further notice shall be
given, and no application shall be made or proceeded with, under this
Chapter with a view to resisting or giving effect to the tenant's claim.

(3) Where the operation of the tenant's notice is suspended by virtue of
subsection (1) or (2), the landlord shall give the tenant a notice informing
him of its suspension—

(a) (if it is suspended by virtue of subsection (1)) not later than the date
specified in the tenant's notice in pursuance of section 42(3)(f); or

(b) (if it is suspended by virtue of subsection (2)) as soon as possible after
the date referred to in that subsection;

and any such notice shall in addition inform the tenant of the date on which
the notice under section 13 was given and of the name and address of the
nominee purchaser for the time being appointed for the purposes of section
15 in relation to the relevant claim under Chapter I.

(4) Where—

(a) the operation of the tenant's notice is suspended by virtue of subsection (1), and

(b) as a result of the relevant claim under Chapter I ceasing to be current,
the operation of the tenant's notice subsequently ceases to be so
suspended and the tenant's notice thereupon continues in force in
accordance with section 42(8),

then, as from the date when that claim ceases to be current ("the termination
date"), this Chapter shall apply as if there were substituted for the date
specified in the tenant's notice in pursuance of section 42(3)(f) such date as
results in the period of time intervening between the termination date and
that date being equal to the period of time intervening between the relevant
date and the date originally so specified.

(5) Where—

(a) the operation of the tenant's notice is suspended by virtue of subsection (2), and

(b) its suspension began in circumstances falling within subsection (6),
and

(c) as a result of the relevant claim under Chapter I ceasing to be current,
the operation of the tenant's notice subsequently ceases to be so
suspended and the tenant's notice thereupon continues in force in
accordance with section 42(8),

any relevant period shall be deemed to have begun on the date when that
claim ceases to be current.

(6) The circumstances referred to in subsection (5)(b) are that the suspension of the operation of the tenant's notice began—

(a) before the date specified in the tenant's notice in pursuance of section
42(3)(f) and before the landlord had given the tenant a counter-notice
under section 45; or

(b) after the landlord had given the tenant a counter-notice under section
45 complying with the requirement set out in subsection 2(b) or (c) of
that section but—

(i) before any application had been made for an order under
section 46(1) or 47(1), and

(ii) before the period for making any such application had expired; or

(c) after an order had been made under section 46(4) or 47(4) but—

(i) before the landlord had given the tenant a further counter-notice in accordance with the order, and

(ii) before the period for giving any such counter-notice had expired.

(7) Where—

(a) the operation of the tenant's notice is suspended by virtue of sub-section (2), and

(b) its suspension began otherwise than in circumstances falling within subsection (6), and

(c) as a result of the relevant claim under Chapter I ceasing to be current, the operation of the tenant's notice subsequently ceases to be so suspended and the tenant's notice thereupon continues in force in accordance with section 42(8),

any relevant period shall be deemed to have begun on the date on which the tenant is given a notice under subsection (8) below or, if earlier, the date on which the tenant gives the landlord a notice informing him of the circumstances by virtue of which the operation of the tenant's notice has ceased to be suspended.

(8) Where subsection (4), (5) or (7) applies, the landlord shall, as soon as possible after becoming aware of the circumstances by virtue of which the operation of the tenant's notice has ceased to be suspended as mentioned in that subsection, give the tenant a notice informing him that, as from the date when the relevant claim under Chapter I ceased to be current, the operation of his notice is no longer suspended.

(9) Subsection (8) shall not, however, require the landlord to give any such notice if he has received a notice from the tenant under subsection (7).

(10) In subsections (5) and (7) "relevant period" means any period which—

(a) is prescribed by or under this Part for the giving of any notice, or the making of any application, in connection with the tenant's notice; and

(b) was current at the time when the suspension of the operation of the tenant's notice began.

(11) For the purposes of this section—

(a) "the relevant claim under Chapter I", in relation to a notice under section 13, means the claim in respect of which that notice is given; and

(b) any such claim is current if—

(i) that notice continues in force in accordance with section 13(11), or

(ii) a binding contract entered into in pursuance of that notice remains in force, or

(iii) where an order has been made under section 24(4)(a) or (b) or 25(6)(a) or (b) with respect to any such premises as are referred to in subsection (1) or (2) above (as the case may be), any interests which by virtue of the order fall to be vested in the nominee purchaser for the purposes of Chapter I have yet to be so vested.

DEFINITIONS
"court": s.101(1).
"flat": s.101(1).
"landlord": ss.40(1) and 62(1).
"relevant claim under Chap. I": subs. (11)(a).
"relevant date": s.62(1).
"relevant period": subs. (10).
"tenant": s.40(4)(a).
"tenant's notice": s.62(1).

GENERAL NOTE

This deals with two possibilities. There may be an initial notice claiming the collective right to enfranchisement served under Chap. I at a time when an initial notice claiming the individual right to an extended lease is served. The individual right initial notice will, in such a case, be of no effect. In the contrary case an initial notice claiming the individual extended lease may have been served and then an initial notice claiming collective enfranchisement is served. In this case the initial notice under s.42 claiming an extended long lease is suspended until the position under the s.13 notice claiming the collective right to enfranchisement is clarified.

Subs. (3)

Where a notice claiming an extended lease becomes suspended because of an initial notice claiming enfranchisement (subss. (1) and (2)) then the landlord is obliged to give the tenant notice of this fact.

Subs. (4)

A tenant's claim to an extended lease will cease to be suspended when the s.13 notice ceases to be effective. The landlord is by this subsection given the same period of time from then as it had from the original tenant's claim to provide a counter-notice.

Effect on tenant's notice of institution of compulsory acquisition procedures

55.—(1) A notice given by a tenant under section 42 shall be of no effect if on the relevant date—

(a) any person or body of persons who has or have been, or could be, authorised to acquire the whole or part of the tenant's flat compulsorily for any purpose has or have, with a view to its acquisition for that purpose—
    (i) served notice to treat on the landlord or the tenant, or
    (ii) entered into a contract for the purchase of the interest of either of them in the flat or part of it, and

(b) the notice to treat or contract remains in force.

(2) A notice given by a tenant under section 42 shall cease to have effect if, before a new lease is entered into in pursuance of it, any such person or body of persons as is mentioned in subsection (1) serves or serve notice to treat as mentioned in that subsection.

(3) Where subsection (2) applies in relation to a notice given by a tenant under section 42, then on the occasion of the compulsory acquisition in question the compensation payable in respect of any interest in the tenant's flat (whether or not the one to which the relevant notice to treat relates) shall be determined on the basis of the value of the interest subject to and with the benefit of the rights and obligations arising from the tenant's notice and affecting that interest.

DEFINITIONS

"flat": s.101(1).
"interest": s.101(1).
"landlord": ss.40(1) and 62(1).
"lease": s.101(1).
"relevant date": s.62(1).
"tenant": s.40(4)(a).
"tenant's notice": s.62(1).

GENERAL NOTE

This is in the same words and to the same effect as s.30 which deals with the effect of compulsory purchase orders on initial notices claiming the collective right to enforcement. Compulsory purchase prevents the giving of an effective initial notice and if a tenant's initial notice has been given renders it ineffective. Further points applicable to this section are made in the note on s.30. The restrictive definition of a flat under this section must be particularly noted (s.62(3)).

Grant of new lease

Obligation to grant new lease

56.—(1) Where a qualifying tenant of a flat has under this Chapter a right to acquire a new lease of the flat and gives notice of his claim in accordance with section 42, then except as provided by this Chapter the landlord shall be bound to grant to the tenant, and the tenant shall be bound to accept—

(a) in substitution for the existing lease, and

(b) on payment of the premium payable under Schedule 13 in respect of the grant,

a new lease of the flat at a peppercorn rent for a term expiring 90 years after the term date of the existing lease.

(2) In addition to any such premium there shall be payable by the tenant in connection with the grant of any such new lease such amounts to the owners of any intermediate leasehold interests (within the meaning of Schedule 13) as are so payable by virtue of that Schedule.

(3) A tenant shall not be entitled to require the execution of any such new lease otherwise than on tendering to the landlord, in addition to the amount of any such premium and any other amounts payable by virtue of Schedule 13, the amount so far as ascertained—

(a) of any sums payable by him by way of rent or recoverable from him as rent in respect of the flat up to the date of tender;

(b) of any sums for which at that date the tenant is liable under section 60 in respect of costs incurred by any relevant person (within the meaning of that section); and

(c) of any other sums due and payable to him to any such person under or in respect of the existing lease;

and, if the amount of any such sums is not or may not be fully ascertained, on offering reasonable security for the payment of such amount as may afterwards be found to be payable in respect of them.

(4) To the extent that any amount tendered to the landlord in accordance with subsection (3) is an amount due to a person other than the landlord, that amount shall be payable to that person by the landlord; and that subsection has effect subject to paragraph 7(2) of Schedule 11.

(5) No provision of any lease prohibiting, restricting or otherwise relating to a sub-demise by the tenant under the lease shall have effect with reference to the granting of any lease under this section.

(6) It is hereby declared that nothing in any of the provisions specified in paragraph 1(2) of Schedule 10 (which impose requirements as to consent or consultation or other restrictions in relation to disposals falling within those provisions) applies to the granting of any lease under this section.

(7) For the purposes of subsection (6), paragraph 1(2) of Schedule 10 has effect as if the reference to section 79(2) of the Housing Act 1988 (which is not relevant in the context of subsection (6)) were omitted.

DEFINITIONS

"disposal": s.101(1).
"existing lease": s.62(1).
"flat": s.101(1).
"interest": s.101(1).
"landlord": ss.40(1) and 62(1).
"lease": s.101(1).
"qualifying tenant": s.62(1).
"tenant": s.40(4)(a).
"term date": s.101(1).

GENERAL NOTE

This section states the obligation to grant a new lease to the tenant. Its detailed provisions deal with the sums to be paid by the tenant. It also provides (subs. (5)) that any provision in a lease preventing the grant is of no effect. The detailed terms of the lease are contained in the next section.

Subss. (1) and (2)
The new extended lease replaces the existing lease. The only rent that is to be reserved is "a peppercorn". The peppercorn rent is the rent for the entire term of the new substitute lease notwithstanding the fact that a rent of several hundred pounds may have been payable under the existing lease. The method of calculating the premium is discussed in the notes on Sched. 13.

Subs. (3)
This curious subsection provides that the tenant is not entitled to the grant of an extended lease unless he tenders the money due to the landlord. However, if these sums are not fully ascertained then he is entitled to completion if he offers reasonable security in respect of them. If the sums are small but unclear then a solicitor may undertake for their payment. It is hard to see how in other cases security will be arranged for unascertained liabilities. What in any event is "reasonable security" and why should the landlord be put in the position of a secured lender?

Subs. (4)
Schedule 11, para. 7(2) enables any of the "other" or mesne landlords to require any sums due to it to be paid directly to it.

Subs. (5)
The new lease may be granted by a landlord which is itself a tenant under another lease. That lease may in terms forbid the grant of the lease by the landlord. Such a provision is of no effect however phrased. Nor is a clause requiring notice to be given to a superior landlord or a registration fee to be paid or containing stipulations as to the terms of the lease of any effect.

Subs. (6)
The provisions mentioned are discussed in the note on Sched. 10.

Terms on which new lease is to be granted

57.—(1) Subject to the provisions of this Chapter (and in particular to the provisions as to rent and duration contained in section 56(1)), the new lease to be granted to a tenant under section 56 shall be a lease on the same terms as those of the existing lease, as they apply on the relevant date, but with such modifications as may be required or appropriate to take account—

(a) of the omission from the new lease of property included in the existing lease but not comprised in the flat;

(b) of alterations made to the property demised since the grant of the existing lease; or

(c) in a case where the existing lease derives (in accordance with section 7(6) as it applies in accordance with section 39(3)) from more than one separate leases, of their combined effect and of the differences (if any) in their terms.

(2) Where during the continuance of the new lease the landlord will be under any obligation for the provision of services or for repairs, maintenance or insurance—

(a) the new lease may require payments to be made by the tenant (whether as rent or otherwise) in consideration of those matters or in respect of the cost thereof to the landlord; and

(b) (if the terms of the existing lease do not include any provision for the making of any such payments by the tenant or include provision only for the payment of a fixed amount) the terms of the new lease shall make, as from the term date of the existing lease, such provision as may be just—

(i) for the making by the tenant of payments related to the cost from time to time to the landlord, and

(ii) for the tenant's liability to make those payments to be enforceable by distress, re-entry or otherwise in like manner as if it were a liability for payment of rent.

(3) Subject to subsection (4), provision shall be made by the terms of the new lease or by an agreement collateral thereto for the continuance, with any suitable adaptations, of any agreement collateral to the existing lease.

(4) For the purposes of subsections (1) and (3) there shall be excluded from the new lease any term of the existing lease or of any agreement collateral thereto in so far as that term—

(a) provides for or relates to the renewal of the lease,

(b) confers any option to purchase or right of pre-emption in relation to the flat demised by the existing lease, or

(c) provides for the termination of the existing lease before its term date otherwise than in the event of a breach of its terms;

and there shall be made in the terms of the new lease or any agreement collateral thereto such modifications as may be required or appropriate to take account of the exclusion of any such term.

(5) Where the new lease is granted after the term date of the existing lease, then on the grant of the new lease there shall be payable by the tenant to the landlord, as an addition to the rent payable under the existing lease, any amount by which, for the period since the term date or the relevant date (whichever is the later), the sums payable to the landlord in respect of the flat (after making any necessary apportionment (for the matters referred to in subsection (2) fall short in total of the sums that would have been payable for such matters under the new lease if it had been granted on that date; and section 56(3)(a) shall apply accordingly.

(6) Subsections (1) to (5) shall have effect subject to any agreement between the landlord and tenant as to the terms of the new lease or any agreement collateral thereto; and either of them may require that for the purposes of the new lease any term of the existing lease shall be excluded or modified in so far as—

(a) it is necessary to do so in order to remedy a defect in the existing lease; or

(b) it would be unreasonable in the circumstances to include, or include without modification, the term in question in view of changes occurring since the date of commencement of the existing lease which affect the suitability on the relevant date of the provisions of that lease.

(7) The terms of the new lease shall—

(a) make provision in accordance with section 59(3); and

(b) reserve to the person who is for the time being the tenant's immediate landlord the right to obtain possession of the flat in question in accordance with section 61.

(8) In granting the new lease the landlord shall not be bound to enter into any covenant for title beyond that implied from the grant, and a person entering into any covenant required of him as landlord shall be entitled to limit his personal liability to breaches of that covenant for which he is responsible.

(9) Where any person—

(a) is a third party to the existing lease, or

(b) (not being the landlord or tenant) is a party to any agreement collateral thereto,

then (subject to any agreement between him and the landlord and the tenant) he shall be made a party to the new lease or (as the case may be) to an agreement collateral thereto, and shall accordingly join in its execution; but nothing in this section has effect so as to require the new lease or (as the case may be) any such collateral agreement to provide for him to discharge any function at any time after the term date of the existing lease.

(10) Where—

(a) any such person ("the third party") is in accordance with subsection (9) to discharge any function down to the term date of the existing lease, but

(b) it is necessary or expedient in connection with the proper enjoyment by the tenant of the property demised by the new lease for provision to be made for the continued discharge of that function after that date,

the new lease or an agreement collateral thereto shall make provision for that function to be discharged after that date (whether by the third party or by some other person).

(11) The new lease shall contain a statement that it is a lease granted under section 56; and any such statement shall comply with such requirements as may be prescribed by rules made in pursuance of section 144 of the Land Registration Act 1925 (power to make general rules).

DEFINITIONS
  "existing lease": s.62(1).
  "flat": s.101(1).
  "landlord": ss.40(1) and 62(1).
  "lease": s.101(1).
  "relevant date": s.62(1).
  "tenant": s.40(4)(a).
  "term date": s.101(1).
  "third party": s.62(1).

GENERAL NOTE
  The detailed provisions of this section deal with the contents of the lease to be granted.

Subs. (1)
  This subsection states that the starting point is the existing lease. This gives a very important presumption in favour of the terms of that lease even if they are out of fashion or indeed unsuitable in a modern context (*cf.* the approach of the House of Lords to ascertaining the terms of new leases under the Landlord and Tenant Act 1954, Pt. IV in *O'May* v. *City of London Real Property Co.* [1983] 2 A.C. 726). This case is more of use in pointing out by contrast how closely the present Act directs towards following the existing lease. The 1954 Act is much less prescriptive, simply requiring that "the court shall have regard to the terms of the current tenancy and to all relevant circumstances" (s.35). In contrast this section says that the new lease "shall be a lease on the same terms as those of the existing lease". It then continues to say precisely what modifications are permitted.

Subs. (2)
  This provides that the new lease may contain service charge provisions both in cases where such provisions are present and in cases where they are absent from the original lease. It also allows existing service charge provisions to be varied. The provision is confusingly drafted and in some respects quite restrictive. If there are no service charge provisions in the old lease then the court has a wide discretion (subs. (2)(b)). If there are existing provisions it appears they can be varied only if they are for payment of a fixed amount which is quite unlikely. Similarly, only if there are no provisions or provisions for a fixed amount can the new lease vary the old to make the payments enforceable as if they were rent (but see the power given in subs. (6) to remedy defects in the existing lease).

Subss. (3) and (4)
  These two subsections cause problems in implementation. Subsection (3) provides that all agreements collateral to the existing lease shall be carried over into or collaterally to the existing lease. This will include agreements which are in the nature of general arrangements between the landlord and tenant and do not touch and concern the subject matter of the lease. These will be carried forward to the same terms and effect. Subsection (4) excludes from the new lease certain matters: subs. (4)(a)—the exclusion of rights to renewals is unproblematic because the extended lease can be renewed; subs. (4)(b)—rights of pre-emption or options in relation to property other than the flat are not excluded from the new arrangement but obviously their operational length will not be extended; subs. (4)(c)—this may be a surprise to the landlord. Forfeiture clauses do commonly provide for termination for reasons other than a breach of the terms of the lease, they often provide for forfeiture on a range of insolvency events. This provision should not be found in leases of flats (because of the difficulty it poses in raising money on mortgage) but where it is it must be omitted from a replacement lease.

Subs. (5)

The initial notice will usually be served before the end of the original lease. Sometimes the new lease will be granted after the end of that original lease. The tenant, on completion, must pay a sum to make up for any shortfall in the rent payable up to the date of the grant.

Subs. (6)

This provision must be carefully noted. The parties may agree any terms they wish in the new lease. This may include, for example, provision for the termination of the new lease before its term date.

Subs. (6)(a)

There is no definition of "defect in the existing lease". The paragraph does require it to be necessary to make the change requested and this does strongly suggest a restrictive interpretation.

Subs. (6)(b)

This very important paragraph takes a different approach from that followed under the Landlord and Tenant Act 1954, Pt. II as a result of the decision in *O'May* referred to above. But, note, it is directed at excluding existing provisions in the lease and not at including wholly new but suitable terms.

Subs. (7)(a)

The effect of s.59(3) is to prevent sub-tenants of the tenant under an extended lease claiming an extended lease themselves under this chapter. The present subsection requires the lease to state this. Presumably this is a statement that "no long lease created immediately or derivatively by way of sub-demise under this lease shall confer on the sub-tenant as against the landlord a right under Chap. II of the Leasehold Reform, Housing and Urban Development Act 1993 to acquire a new lease".

Subs. (7)(b)

Section 61 gives the landlord a right to terminate the extended lease in certain circumstances. This right is also required to be stated in the extended lease. It will state: "the right to obtain possession in accordance with s.61 of the Leasehold Reform, Housing and Urban Development Act 1993 is reserved to the landlord".

Subs. (9)

If there is an existing lease with a surety (or other third party) then he can be required to be a surety to the new lease until the term date of the existing lease is reached. He cannot be required to undertake any obligation lasting beyond this time.

Subs. (10)

What kind of "third party" does this subsection have in mind? It cannot be a surety or guarantor for such is never necessary or expedient for "the proper enjoyment by the tenant". An example would be a management company which is a party to the existing lease or has functions under an agreement collateral thereto.

Subs. (11)

The necessary statement is "this lease is granted under s.56 of the Leasehold Reform, Housing and Urban Development Act 1993". It indicates that the lease is one the value of which must be in serious doubt (see note on s.61).

Grant of new lease where interest of landlord or tenant is subject to a mortgage

58.—(1) Subject to subsection (2), a qualifying tenant shall be entitled to be granted a new lease under section 56 despite the fact that the grant of the existing lease was subsequent to the creation of a mortgage on the landlord's interest and not authorised as against the persons interested in the mortgage; and a lease granted under that section—

(a) shall be deemed to be authorised as against the persons interested in any mortgage on the landlord's interest (however created or arising), and

(b) shall be binding on those persons.

(2) A lease granted under section 56 shall not, by virtue of subsection (1) above, be binding on the persons interested in any such mortgage if the existing lease—

(a) is granted after the commencement of this Chapter, and

(b) being granted subsequent to the creation of the mortgage, would not, apart from that subsection, be binding on the persons interested in the mortgage.

(3) Where—

(a) a lease is granted under section 56, and

(b) any person having a mortgage on the landlord's interest is thereby entitled to possession of the documents of title relating to that interest,

the landlord shall, within one month of the execution of the lease, deliver to that person a counterpart of it duly executed by the tenant.

(4) Where the existing lease is, immediately before its surrender on the grant of a lease under section 56, subject to any mortgage, the new lease shall take effect subject to the mortgage in substitution for the existing lease; and the terms of the mortgage, as set out in the instrument creating or evidencing it, shall accordingly apply in relation to the new lease in like manner as they applied in relation to the existing lease.

(5) Where—

(a) a lease granted under section 56 takes effect subject to any such subsisting mortgage on the existing lease, and

(b) at the time of execution of the new lease the person having the mortgage is thereby entitled to possession of the documents of title relating to the existing lease,

he shall be similarly entitled to possession of the documents of title relating to the new lease; and the tenant shall deliver the new lease to him within one month of the date on which the lease is received from Her Majesty's Land Registry following its registration.

(6) Where—

(a) the landlord fails to deliver a counterpart of the new lease in accordance with subsection (3), or

(b) the tenant fails to deliver the new lease in accordance with subsection (5),

the instrument creating or evidencing the mortgage in question shall apply as if the obligation to deliver a counterpart or (as the case may be) deliver the lease were included in the terms of the mortgage as set out in that instrument.

(7) A landlord granting a lease under section 56 shall be bound to take such steps as may be necessary to secure that the lease is not liable in accordance with subsection (2) to be defeated by persons interested in a mortgage on his interest; but a landlord is not obliged, in order to grant a lease for the purposes of that section, to acquire a better title than he has or could require to be vested in him.

DEFINITIONS

"existing lease": s.62(1).

"interest": s.101(1).

"landlord": ss.40(1) and 62(1).

"lease": s.101(1).

"mortgage": s.62(1).

"qualifying tenant": s.62(1).

"tenant": s.40(4)(a).

GENERAL NOTE

A number of possibilities arise of the landlord or the tenant's existing interest being encumbered by a mortgage and this section deals with them.

Subss. (1) and (2)

The landlord may have granted the existing lease without the permission of the landlord's then existing mortgagee. A mortgagor in possession does have an implied statutory right to grant leases (s.99 of the Law of Property Act 1925). This statutory right is, however, invariably excluded by institutional mortgages. A mortgagor will, thus, require the consent of the mortgagee in order to grant leases. A lease which is granted without consent is binding upon the landlord but not upon the mortgagee (see *Britannia Building Society* v. *Earl and Amin* [1990] 2 All E.R. 469).

Subsection (1) has the effect that the new extended lease granted by a landlord who has previously granted a lease not binding upon its mortgagee will be binding upon that mortgagee (or other persons interested in the mortgage). But, if the lease rendered invalid against the mortgagee was granted after the commencement of this part of the Act then in that case the new lease is not binding on the mortgagee either (subs. (2)).

Subs. (3)

This requires the landlord to send to the mortgagee of its interest who is entitled to possession of the landlord's title deeds *a* counterpart of the new lease. Presumably it means *the* counterpart and does not envisage the landlord requiring two counterparts and keeping one apart from the security. Where the landlord's interest is registered the new lease will be noted on the charges register of its title and the old removed. Such a charge would ordinarily require the charge certificate (held by the mortgagee) to be produced to the Land Registry.

Subss. (4) and (5)

Where the tenant's interest is subject to a mortgage, the mortgage simply transfers to the new lease. Subsection (5) provides for the new lease to be forwarded to the mortgagee. More usual in practice will be for the existing lease to be obtained from the mortgagee subject to an undertaking and the new lease returned directly to the mortgagee's solicitor (who may, of course, also be the mortgagee's solicitor).

Subs. (6)

Failure to deliver the new counterpart lease to the landlord's mortgagee or the new lease to the tenant's mortgagee is treated as a breach of a term in the mortgage and this may lead to the lender taking enforcement action.

Subs. (7)

The landlord is not obliged to obtain a mortgagee's consent before granting the new lease, nor is the landlord obliged to pay off the existing mortgage. Both of these steps would be requiring the landlord to obtain "a better title". The steps short of this which are necessary to secure that the lease is not defeated appear to be continuing to comply with the remaining conditions on the mortgage; paying sums due as they arise and if the lender takes enforcement action then taking steps to ensure the lease is not forfeited. At this stage it may become necessary for the landlord to redeem the mortgage.

Further renewal, but no security of tenure, after grant of new lease

59.—(1) The right to acquire a new lease under this Chapter may be exercised in relation to a lease of a flat despite the fact that the lease is itself a lease granted under section 56; and the provisions of this Chapter shall, with any necessary modifications, apply for the purposes of or in connection with any claim to exercise that right in relation to a lease so granted as they apply for the purposes of or in connection with any claim to exercise that right in relation to a lease which has not been so granted.

(2) Where a lease has been granted under section 56—

(a) none of the statutory provisions relating to security of tenure for tenants shall apply to the lease;

(b) after the term date of the lease none of the following provisions, namely—

    (i) section 1 of the Landlord and Tenant Act 1954 or Schedule 10 to the Local Government and Housing Act 1989 (which make provision for security of tenure on the ending of long residential tenancies), or

    (ii) Part II of that Act of 1954 (business tenancies),

shall apply to any sub-lease directly or indirectly derived out of the lease; and

(c) after that date no person shall be entitled by virtue of any such sub-lease to retain possession under—

(i) Part VII of the Rent Act 1977 (security of tenure for protected tenancies etc.) or any enactment applying or extending that Part of that Act,

(ii) the Rent (Agriculture) Act 1976, or

(iii) Part I of the Housing Act 1988 (assured tenancies etc.).

(3) Where a lease has been granted under section 56, no long lease created immediately or derivatively by way of sub-demise under the lease shall confer on the sub-tenant, as against the tenant's landlord, any right under this Chapter to acquire a new lease (and for this purpose "long lease" shall be construed in accordance with section 7).

(4) Any person who—

(a) grants a sub-lease to which subsection (2)(b) and (c) will apply, or

(b) negotiates with a view to the grant of such a sub-lease by him or by a person for whom he is acting as agent,

shall inform the other party that the sub-lease is to be derived out of a lease granted under section 56, unless either he knows that the other party is aware of it or he himself is unaware of it.

(5) Where any lease contains a statement to the effect that it is a lease granted under section 56, the statement shall be conclusive for the purposes of subsections (2) to (4) in favour of any person who is not a party to the lease, unless the statement appears from the lease to be untrue.

DEFINITIONS
"flat": s.101(1).
"landlord": ss.40(1) and 62(1).
"lease": s.101(1).
"tenant": s.40(4)(a).
"term date": s.101(1).

GENERAL NOTE
The provisions of this section deal with a variety of ways in which the rights under Chap. II interrelate with other landlord and tenant legislation and are given effect.

Subs. (1)
The right to an extended lease applies to an extended lease and can be repeated in perpetuity. Should new legislation ever be promised to replace this over-complicated Act a person advising tenants must consider seriously whether this opportunity to grasp a further 90 years should be grasped. Successive extensions obviously become regressively cheaper if made early on during the previous extended lease.

Subs. (2)(a)
What are the statutory provisions relating to security of tenure? This is not a term of art. For example, if the flat is used for business and is otherwise within the Landlord and Tenant Act 1954, Pt. II, do those provisions apply? They do not create security of tenure strictly but the right to another lease. Does the Protection from Eviction Act 1977 in any part apply? Strictly the effect of this paragraph is to exclude (should they ever appear relevant) the security of tenure provision of the Rent Act 1977—the application of which is impossible; the Housing Act 1985—the application of which is virtually impossible; the Housing Act 1988—which can apply to tenancies of any length but excludes tenancies at a low rent (Sched. 1, para. 3 to 3(c)); the Landlord and Tenant Act 1954, Pt. I and the Local Government and Housing Act 1989, Sched. 10—these do apply to long tenancies at a low rent but are excluded by this provision; the Landlord and Tenant Act 1954, Pt. II—could come to apply if the premises were used for business purposes but is excluded by this provision if it is a statutory provision which provides security of tenure.

Subs. (2)(b)
Where a sub-lease is granted or has been granted out of an original lease or an extended lease

then the statutory provisions mentioned cease to apply to that sub-lease on the term date of the extended lease.

Subs. (2)(c)
This applies in the same way as subs. (3)(c) immediately above. As soon as the term date of the extended tenancy arises sub-tenancies have no statutory security. The sub-tenants will have the protection of the Protection from Eviction Act 1977 but that is all.

Subs. (3)
Once there is a tenant of an extended lease then no long lease having rights within Chap. II as against the landlord if that extended lease can be created. But it seems from the wording such a sub-tenant can have rights against any other person. These may be of little practical value while the landlord of the extended lease remains. If that landlord holds under a lease which is terminated, surrendered or expired it is not clear whether the words "as against the tenant's landlord" means the tenant's landlord for the time being.

Subs. (4)
This subsection contains an obligation to inform persons that leases derived out of an extended lease will be deprived of certain valuable areas of statutory protection. The statement should be "this lease will be a sub-lease derived out of a lease granted under s.53 of the Leasehold Reform, Housing and Urban Development Act 1993". In conveyancing the seller should not be drawn into enlarging or explaining this statement but should refer the buyer to the Act. No consequence is stated for failure to make this statement, however, clearly the facts it refers to are a matter of title and the subsection creates a duty of disclosure. The usual position for breach of a duty to disclose a defect of title will therefore follow (see Sweet & Maxwell's *Conveyancing Practice*, 2–042 *et seq.*).

Subs. (5)
Since it is inconceivable that any lease will include such a statement unless it is granted under s.56 this statutory presumption is likely to lead to little litigation.

Costs incurred in connection with new lease

Costs incurred in connection with new lease to be paid by tenant

60.—(1) Where a notice is given under section 42, then (subject to the provisions of this section) the tenant by whom it is given shall be liable, to the extent that they have been incurred by any relevant person in pursuance of the notice, for the reasonable costs of and incidental to any of the following matters, namely—

(a) any investigation reasonably undertaken of the tenant's right to a new lease;

(b) any valuation of the tenant's flat obtained for the purposes of fixing the premium or any other amount payable by virtue of Schedule 13 in connection with the grant of a new lease under section 56;

(c) the grant of a new lease under that section;

but this subsection shall not apply to any costs if on a sale made voluntarily a stipulation that they were to be borne by the purchaser would be void.

(2) For the purposes of section (1) any costs incurred by a relevant person in respect of professional services rendered by any person shall only be regarded as reasonable if and to the extent that costs in respect of such services might reasonably be expected to have been incurred by him if the circumstances had been such that he was personally liable for all such costs.

(3) Where by virtue of any provision of this Chapter the tenant's notice ceases to have effect, or is deemed to have been withdrawn, at any time, then (subject to subsection (4)) the tenant's liability under this section for costs incurred by any person shall be a liability for costs incurred by him down to that time.

(4) A tenant shall not be liable for any costs under this section if the tenant's notice ceases to have effect by virtue of section 47(1) or 55(2).

(5) A tenant shall not be liable under this section for any costs which a party to any proceedings under this Chapter before a leasehold valuation tribunal incurs in connection with the proceedings.

(6) In this section "relevant person", in relation to a claim by a tenant under this Chapter, means the landlord for the purposes of this Chapter, any other landlord (as defined by section 40(4)) or any third party to the tenant's lease.

Definitions
"flat": s.101(1).
"landlord": ss.40(1) and 62(1).
"lease": s.101(1).
"relevant person": subs. (6).
"tenant": s.40(4)(a).
"tenant's lease": s.40(4)(a).
"tenant's notice": s.62(1).
"third party": s.62(1).

General Note
    Some comments on costs generally are made on the very similar section found in Chap. I (s.32). The above note also deals with the void terms as to costs which are referred to in subs. (1).

Landlord's right to terminate new lease

Landlord's right to terminate new lease on grounds of redevelopment

61.—(1) Where a lease of a flat ("the new lease") has been granted under section 56 but the court is satisfied, on an application made by the landlord—
(a) that for the purposes of redevelopment the landlord intends—
(i) to demolish or reconstruct, or
(ii) to carry out substantial works of construction on,
the whole or a substantial part of any premises in which the flat is contained, and
(b) that he could not reasonably do so without obtaining possession of the flat,
the court shall by order declare that the landlord is entitled as against the tenant to obtain possession of the flat and the tenant is entitled to be paid compensation by the landlord for the loss of the flat.

(2) An application for an order under this section may be made—
(a) at any time during the period of 12 months ending with the term date of the lease in relation to which the right to acquire a new lease was exercised; and
(b) at any time during the period of five years ending with the term date of the new lease.

(3) Where the new lease is not the first lease to be granted under section 56 in respect of a flat, subsection (2) shall apply as if paragraph (b) included a reference to the term date of any previous lease granted under that section in respect of the flat, but paragraph (a) shall be taken to be referring to the term date of the lease in relation to which the right to acquire a new lease was first exercised.

(4) Where an order is made under this section, the new lease shall determine, and compensation shall become payable, in accordance with Schedule 14 to this Act; and the provisions of that Schedule shall have effect as regards the measure of compensation payable by virtue of any such order and the effects of any such order where there are sub-leases, and as regards other matters relating to orders and applications under this section.

(5) Except in subsection (1)(a) or (b), any reference in this section to the flat held by the tenant under the new lease includes any premises let with the flat under that lease.

DEFINITIONS
   "court": s.101(1).
   "flat": s.101(1).
   "landlord": ss.40(1) and 62(1).
   "lease": s.101(1).
   "tenant": s.40(4)(a).
   "term date": s.101(1).

GENERAL NOTE
   This is a crucial section of the Act. It is possible that this right to terminate the extended lease prematurely will have a serious effect on the attractiveness of such leases. One of the main reasons put forward for introducing this legislation has been the difficulty of mortgaging existing depreciating terms of flat leases. Mortgagees will, though, consider carefully whether the "s.61 break clause" is in itself a defect which affects their view of whether the lease is a valuable security.

Subs. (1)
   The right to terminate the lease depends on proof of facts which have been discussed in the notes to s.57 which is an almost identical provision.

Subs. (2)
   This subsection gives the landlord two "windows of opportunity" for proving the right to terminate for redevelopment. The last year of the original term and the last five years of the new term.

Subs. (3)
   Where the lease is a second or subsequent extended lease then the effect is that the right to terminate for redevelopment can be determined in the last 12 months of the original lease and in the last five years of each extended lease.

Subs. (4)
   The measure of compensation is crucial in considering the effect of s.61 and is considered in the note on Sched. 14. Here it may be noted that the compensation is payable directly to the tenant (Sched. 14, para. 7) and not to a mortgagee.

Subs. (5)
   Note, if the landlord can gain possession because of his activities on some outlying part of the tenant's holding this may be very satisfactory for the landlord. However, he needs to show that to carry out the proposed redevelopment possession of the flat itself is required.

Supplemental

Interpretation of Chapter II

   62.—(1) In this Chapter—
   "the existing lease", in relation to a claim by a tenant under this Chapter, means the lease in relation to which the claim is made;
   "the landlord", in relation to such a claim, has the meaning given by section 40(1);
   "mortgage" includes a charge or lien;
   "qualifying tenant" shall be construed in accordance with section 39(3);
   "the relevant date" (unless the context otherwise requires) has the meaning given by section 39(8);
   "the tenant's notice" means the notice given under section 42;
   "the terms of acquisition" shall be construed in accordance with section 48(7);
   "third party", in relation to a lease, means any person who is a party to the lease apart from the tenant under the lease and his immediate landlord.
   (2) Subject to subsection (3), references in this Chapter to a flat, in relation to a claim by a tenant under this Chapter, include any garage, outhouse, garden, yard and appurtenances belonging to, or usually enjoyed

with, the flat and let to the tenant with the flat on the relevant date (or, in a case where an application is made under section 50(1), on the date of the making of the application).

(3) Subsection (2) does not apply—

(a) to any reference to a flat in section 47 or 55(1); or

(b) to any reference to a flat (not falling within paragraph (a) above) which occurs in the context of a reference to any premises containing the flat.

(4) In the application of section 8 for the purposes of this Chapter (in accordance with section 39(3)) references to a flat shall be construed in accordance with subsection (2) above, instead of in accordance with sub-section (7) of section 8.

GENERAL NOTE
Notes on the various definitions appear in the sections to which they apply.

Subss. (2) and (3)
The definition of flat is liberal but it must be noted that under s.47 (landlord's right to redevelop) and s.55 (effect of compulsory purchase) a restrictive definition of flat is applied. Thus, garages and so on are excluded in applying these provisions.

CHAPTER III

ENFRANCHISEMENT UNDER LEASEHOLD REFORM ACT 1967

GENERAL NOTE
Reforms to the Leasehold Reform Act 1967 can be summarised as follows:

Present Rule	New Rule
Right to purchase freehold confined to houses below certain rateable values (or by applying formula in References to Rating in Housing Regulations 1990).	No such limit on right to purchase freehold [this change doesn't apply to rights to an extended lease]. Thus, right to enfranchisement applies irrespective of the rateable value. (See ss.63 and 65).
Right to freehold or extended lease confined to houses at low rent (i) below two thirds of rateable value for pre-April 1, 1990 tenancies; (ii) for tenancies from April 1, 1990 with rent exceeding £1,000 p.a. in Greater London or £250 elsewhere.	Test altered to apply at commencement of lease instead of at time of application for enfranchisement as at present [this change does not apply to right to an extended lease]. (See s.65). In the cases brought within the categories above the basis of valuation is the special basis for high value houses in s.9(1A) of the Leasehold Reform Act 1967—reprinted as amended in Sched. 15 to this Act.
Long tenancies include certain tenancies terminable by notice after a death or marriage (s.3(1) of the Leasehold Reform Act 1967).	Section 3 amended to include tenancies granted before April 18, 1980 or in pursuance of a contract entered into before that date—but in such a case only the right to enfranchisement is available. The Leasehold Reform Act 1967 amended to exclude certain leases by Charitable Housing Trusts (s.67). The Leasehold Reform Act 1967 amended to exclude certain property transferred for public benefit or designated as conditionally exempt from inheritance tax (s.68).

Extension of right to enfranchise

Extension of right to enfranchise to houses whose value or rent exceeds applicable limit

63. After section 1 of the Leasehold Reform Act 1967 there shall be inserted—

> **"Right to enfranchisement only in case of houses whose value or rent exceeds limit under s.1 or 4**
>
> 1A.—(1) Where subsection (1) of section 1 above would apply in the case of the tenant of a house but for the fact that the applicable financial limited specified in subsection (1)(a)(i) or (ii) or (as the case may be) subsection (5) or (6) of that section is exceeded, this Part of this Act shall have effect to confer on the tenant the same right to acquire the freehold of the house and premises as would be conferred by subsection (1) of that section if that limit were not exceeded.
>
> (2) Where a tenancy of any property is not a tenancy at a low rent in accordance with section 4(1) below but is a tenancy falling within section 4A(1) below, the tenancy shall nevertheless be treated as a tenancy at a low rent for the purposes of this Part of this Act so far as it has effect for conferring on any person a right to acquire the freehold of a house and premises."

DEFINITIONS
  "tenancy": s.101(2).

GENERAL NOTE
  This introduces a new section into the Leasehold Reform Act 1967. Its effect is to remove the financial limits for enfranchisement but leave the financial limits to apply to the right to an extended lease. The new s.1A(1) removes the rateable value limit from applying to the right to acquire the freehold. The new s.1A(2) amends the low rent limit in its application to the right to buy the freehold. This is explained in the note on s.65.

Tenancies terminable after death or marriage

64.—(1) The following section shall be inserted in the Leasehold Reform Act 1967 after the section 1A inserted by section 63 above—

> **"Right to enfranchisement only in case of certain tenancies terminable after death or marriage**
>
> 1B. Where a tenancy granted so as to become terminable by notice after a death or marriage—
> - (a) is (apart from this section) a long tenancy in accordance with section 3(1) below, but
> - (b) was granted before 18th April 1980 or in pursuance of a contract entered into before that date,
>
> then (notwithstanding section 3(1)) the tenancy shall be a long tenancy for the purposes of this Part of this Act only so far as this Part has effect for conferring on any person a right to acquire the freehold of a house and premises."

(2) In section 3(1) of that Act (meaning of "long tenancy")—
- (a) after "and includes" there shall be inserted "both a tenancy taking effect under section 149(6) of the Law of Property Act 1925 (leases terminable after a death or marriage) and"; and
- (b) in the proviso (which prevents certain categories of tenancies termin-

able after death or marriage being long tenancies), for the words from "if either" onwards there shall be substituted "if—

    (a) the notice is capable of being given at any time after the death or marriage of the tenant;

    (b) the length of the notice is not more than three months; and

    (c) the terms of the tenancy preclude both—

        (i) its assignment otherwise than by virtue of section 92 of the Housing Act 1985 (assignments by way of exchange), and

        (ii) the sub-letting of the whole of the premises comprised in it."

GENERAL NOTE

The effect of these amendments to the Leasehold Reform Act 1967 is more straightforward than appears. The definition of long lease (s.3) is amended to include leases determinable after a death or marriage granted before April 18, 1980 or in pursuance of a contract made before that date. But, then, the new s.1B introduced into the 1967 Act confines tenants of such leases to the right to enfranchisement (purchase of the freehold reversion) and excludes the right to an extended lease.

Additional "low rent" test

65. After section 4 of the Leasehold Reform Act 1967 there shall be inserted—

"Alternative rent limits for purposes of section 1A(2)

4A.—(1) For the purposes of section 1A(2) above a tenancy of any property falls within this subsection if either no rent was payable under it in respect of the property during the initial year or the aggregate amount of rent so payable during that year did not exceed the following amount, namely—

    (a) where the tenancy was entered into before 1st April 1963, two-thirds of the letting value of the property (on the same terms) on the date of the commencement of the tenancy;

    (b) where—

        (i) the tenancy was entered into either on or after 1st April 1963 but before 1st April 1990, or on or after 1st April 1990 in pursuance of a contract made before that date, and

        (ii) the property had a rateable value at the date of the commencement of the tenancy or else at any time before 1st April 1990,

    two-thirds of the rateable value of the property on the relevant date; or

    (c) in any other case, £1,000 if the property is in Greater London or £250 if elsewhere.

(2) For the purposes of subsection (1) above—

    (a) "the initial year", in relation to any tenancy, means the period of one year beginning with the date of the commencement of the tenancy;

    (b) "the relevant date" means the date of the commencement of the tenancy or, if the property did not have a rateable value on that date, the date on which it first had a rateable value; and

    (c) paragraphs (b) and (c) of section 4(1) above shall apply as they apply for the purposes of section 4(1);

and it is hereby declared that in subsection (1) above the reference to the letting value of any property is to be construed in like manner as the reference in similar terms which appears in the proviso to section 4(1) above.

(3) Section 1(7) above applies to any amount referred to in sub-section (1)(c) above as it applies to the amount referred to in sub-section (1)(a)(ii) of that section."

<small>DEFINITIONS</small>
"initial year": subs. (2)(a).
"relevant date": subs. (2)(b).
"tenancy": s.101(2).

<small>GENERAL NOTE</small>
This introduces a new s.4A to the Leasehold Reform Act 1967. It introduces an additional low rent test. If a property does not come within the Leasehold Reform Act 1967 because of the application of the low rent test then an additional low rent test can be applied to confer the right to acquire the freehold. This applies the low rent test set out in the new s.4A for the initial year of the tenancy. Comment on the term "commencement of the tenancy" is made in the note on s.101(5).

Price payable by tenant on enfranchisement by virtue of section 63 or 64

66.—(1) In section 9 of the Leasehold Reform Act 1967 (purchase price and costs of enfranchisement, etc.), after subsection (1B) there shall be inserted—

"(1C) Notwithstanding subsection (1) above, the price payable for a house and premises where the right to acquire the freehold arises by virtue of any one or more of the provisions of sections 1A and 1B above shall be determined in accordance with subsection (1A) above, but in any such case—

(a) if in determining the price so payable there falls to be taken into account any marriage value arising by virtue of the coa-lescence of the freehold and leasehold interests, the share of the marriage value to which the tenant is to be regarded as being entitled shall not exceed one-half of it; and

(b) section 9A below has effect for determining whether any additional amount is payable by way of compensation under that section;

and in a case where the provision (or one of the provisions) by virtue of which the right to acquire the freehold arises is section 1A(1) above, subsection (1A) above shall apply with the omission of the assumption set out in paragraph (b) of that subsection."

(2) Section 9 of that Act, as amended by this section and with the omission of repealed provisions, is set out in Schedule 15 to this Act.

(3) After section 9 of that Act there shall be inserted—

"Compensation payable in cases where right to enfranchisement arises by virtue of section 1A or 1B

9A.—(1) If, in a case where the right to acquire the freehold of a house and premises arises by virtue of any one or more of the provisions of sections 1A and 1B above, the landlord will suffer any loss or damage to which this section applies, there shall be payable to him such amount as is reasonable to compensate him for that loss or damage.

(2) This section applies to—

(a) any diminution in value of any interest of the landlord in other property resulting from the acquisition of his interest in the house and premises; and

(b) any other loss or damage which results therefrom to the extent that it is referable to his ownership of any interest in other property.

(3) Without prejudice to the generality of paragraph (b) of sub-section (2) above, the kinds of loss falling within that paragraph

include loss of development value in relation to the house and premises to the extent that it is referable as mentioned in that paragraph.

(4) In subsection (3) above "development value", in relation to the house and premises, means any increase in the value of the landlord's interest in the house and premises which is attributable to the possibility of demolishing, reconstructing, or carrying out substantial works of construction on, the whole or a substantial part of the house and premises.

(5) In relation to any case falling within subsection (1) above—

(a) any reference (however expressed)—
    (i) in section 8 or 9(3) or (5) above, or
    (ii) in any of the following provisions of this Act,
to the price payable under section 9 above shall be construed as including a reference to any amount payable to the landlord under this section; and

(b) for the purpose of determining any such separate price as is mentioned in paragraph 7(1)(b) of Schedule 1 to this Act, this section shall accordingly apply (with any necessary modifications) to each of the superior interests in question."

DEFINITIONS
"development value": subss. (3) and (4).
"interest": s.101(1).

GENERAL NOTE
The purpose of this section is to introduce a new valuation provision in s.9 of the Leasehold Reform Act 1967. It applies to cases brought within the right to enfranchisement by the amendments to that Act made by the previous sections of this Act. It provides in such cases for the special basis of valuation applicable to higher value homes to apply. To assist the new s.9 is set out as amended in Sched. 15 to this Act.

Exceptions to right to enfranchise

Exclusion of right to enfranchise in case of houses let by charitable housing trusts

67.—(1) Section 1 of the Leasehold Reform Act 1967 (tenants entitled to enfranchisement or extension) shall be amended as follows.

(2) In subsection (3) (excepted cases) there shall be added at the end—
"or, in the case of any right to which subsection (3A) below applies, at any time when the tenant's immediate landlord is a charitable housing trust and the house forms part of the housing accommodation provided by the trust in the pursuit of its charitable purposes."

(3) After subsection (3) there shall be inserted—
"(3A) For the purposes of subsection (3) above this subsection applies as follows—

(a) where the tenancy was created after the commencement of Chapter III of Part I of the Leasehold Reform, Housing and Urban Development Act 1993, this subsection applies to any right to acquire the freehold of the house and premises, but

(b) where the tenancy was created before that commencement, this subsection applies only to any such right exercisable by virtue of any one or more of the provisions of sections 1A and 1B below;

and in that subsection "charitable housing trust" means a housing trust within the meaning of the Housing Act 1985 which is a charity within the meaning of the Charities Act 1993."

DEFINITIONS
"tenancy": s.101(2).

GENERAL NOTE

This subsection amends s.1 of the Leasehold Reform Act 1967 so that it does not apply to certain tenancies of charitable housing trusts which are provided in pursuit of its charitable purposes. It operates as follow: (i) if the tenancy is created after the commencement of this part of the Act then the right to purchase the freehold is excluded but the right to an extended lease remains; (ii) if the tenancy was created before the commencement of this part of the Act then the rights conferred by ss.63 and 64 of this Act (inserting the new ss.1A and 1B in the Leasehold Reform Act 1967) are excluded.

Exclusion of right in case of property transferred for public benefit etc.

68. After section 32 of the Leasehold Reform Act 1967 there shall be inserted—

> **"Property transferred for public benefit etc.**
> 32A.—(1) A notice of a person's desire to have the freehold of a house and premises under this Part shall be of no effect if at the relevant time the whole or any part of the house and premises is qualifying property and either—
> (a) the tenancy was created after the commencement of Chapter III of Part I of the Leasehold Reform, Housing and Urban Development Act 1993; or
> (b) (where the tenancy was created before that commencement) the tenant would not be entitled to have the freehold if either or both of sections 1A and 1B above were not in force.
> (2) For the purposes of this section the whole or any part of the house and premises is qualifying property if—
> (a) it has been designated under section 31(1)(b), (c) or (d) of the Inheritance Tax Act 1984 (designation and undertakings relating to conditionally exempt transfers), whether with or without any other property, and no chargeable event has subsequently occurred with respect to it; or
> (b) an application to the Board for it to be so designated is pending; or
> (c) it is the property of a body not established or conducted for profit and a direction has been given in relation to it under section 26 of that Act (gifts for public benefit), whether with or without any other property; or
> (d) an application to the Board for a direction to be so given in relation to it is pending.
> (3) For the purposes of subsection (2) above an application is pending as from the time when it is made to the Board until such time as it is either granted or refused by the Board or withdrawn by the applicant; and for this purpose an application shall not be regarded as made unless and until the applicant has submitted to the Board all such information in support of the application as is required by the Board.
> (4) A notice of a person's desire to have the freehold of a house and premises under this Part shall cease to have effect if—
> (a) before completion of the conveyance in pursuance of the tenant's notice, the whole or any part of the house and premises becomes qualifying property; and
> (b) the condition set out in subsection (1)(a) (as the case may be) subsection (1)(b) above is satisfied.
> (5) Where a tenant's notice ceases to have effect by virtue of subsection (4) above—
> (a) section 9(4) above shall not apply to require the tenant to make any payment to the landlord in respect of costs incurred by reason of the notice; and

(b) the person who applied or is applying for designation or a direction shall be liable to the tenant for all reasonable costs incurred by the tenant in connection with his claim to acquire the freehold of the house and premises.

(6) Where it is claimed that subsection (1) or (4) above applies in relation to a tenant's notice, the person making the claim shall, at the time of making it, furnish the tenant with evidence in support of it; and if he fails to do so he shall be liable for any costs which are reasonably incurred by the tenant in consequence of the failure.

(7) In subsection (2) above—

(a) paragraphs (a) and (b) apply to designation under section 34(1)(a), (b) or (c) of the Finance Act 1975 or section 77(1)(b), (c) or (d) of the Finance Act 1976 as they apply to designation under section 31(1)(b), (c) or (d) of the Inheritance Tax Act 1984; and

(b) paragraphs (c) and (d) apply to a direction under paragraph 13 of Schedule 6 to the Finance Act 1975 as they apply to a direction under section 26 of that Act of 1984.

(8) In this section—

"the Board" means the Commissioners of Inland Revenue;

"chargeable event" means—

(a) any event which in accordance with any provision of Chapter II of Part II of the Inheritance Tax Act 1984 (exempt transfers) is a chargeable event, including any such provision as applied by section 78(3) of that Act (conditionally exempt occasions); or

(b) any event which would have been a chargeable event in the circumstances mentioned in section 79(3) of that Act (exemption from ten-yearly charge)."

DEFINITIONS

"Board": subs. (8).
"chargeable event": subs. (8).
"tenancy": s.101(2).

GENERAL NOTE

This section excludes in part from the Leasehold Reform Act 1967 property transferred for public benefit or under s.26 of the Inheritance Tax Act 1984 or conditionally exempt under s.31 of that Act. It also excludes property where there is a pending application under these provisions. These provisions are to the same effect as s.31 which excludes such property from the right to collective enfranchisement under the present Act. (See notes on that section.) Note the property is excluded only from the right to enfranchise (purchase the freehold) and not from the right to an extended lease.

CHAPTER IV

ESTATE MANAGEMENT SCHEMES IN CONNECTION WITH ENFRANCHISEMENT

GENERAL NOTE

The purpose of this chapter is very similar to that of s.19 of the Leasehold Reform Act 1967. It is intended to permit landlords to make an attempt to establish a legally binding scheme which will preserve the quality and appearance of an area where they are landlords. As with the Leasehold Reform Act 1967 the precise political pressure has come from the large inherited London estates. But the provision for management schemes is not, by any means, limited to such estates. *Sweet & Maxwell's Handbook on Leasehold Reform* (p. 607) lists applicants under s.19 of the Leasehold Reform Act 1967 and they are a surprisingly wide variety of landlords. The provisions were said by the Government to be an improvement on the 1967 Act provisions in three ways: (i) by giving a clearer rôle to public bodies to take over schemes in danger of lapsing; (ii) by providing if the property is a conservation area for notification of English Heritage and the Local Planning Authority; and (iii) for allowing interested persons to make representations on a wider range of matters.

Estate management schemes

69.—(1) For the purposes of this Chapter an estate management scheme is a scheme which (subject to sections 71 and 73) is approved by a leasehold valuation tribunal under section 70 for an area occupied directly or indirectly under leases held from one landlord (apart from property occupied by him or his licensees or for the time being unoccupied) and which is designed to secure that in the event of tenants—

(a) acquiring the landlord's interest in their house and premises ("the house") under Part I of the Leasehold Reform Act 1967 by virtue of any one or more of the provisions of sections 1A and 1B of that Act (as inserted by sections 63 and 64 above), or

(b) acquiring the landlord's interest in any premises ("the premises") in accordance with Chapter I of this Part of this Act,

the landlord will—

(i) retain powers of management in respect of the house or premises, and

(ii) have rights against the house or premises in respect of the benefits arising from the exercise elsewhere of his powers of management.

(2) An estate management scheme may make different provision for different parts of the area of the scheme, and shall include provision for terminating or varying all or any of the provisions of the scheme, or excluding part of the area, if a change of circumstances makes it appropriate, or for enabling it to be done by or with the approval of a leasehold valuation tribunal.

(3) Without prejudice to any other provision of this section, an estate management scheme may provide for all or any of the following matters—

(a) for regulating the redevelopment, use or appearance of property in which tenants have acquired the landlord's interest as mentioned in subsection (1)(a) or (b);

(b) for empowering the landlord for the time being to carry out works of maintenance, repair, renewal or replacement in relation to any such property or carry out work to remedy a failure in respect of any such property to comply with the scheme, or for making the operation of any provisions of the scheme conditional on his doing so or on the provision or maintenance by him of services, facilities or amenities of any description;

(c) for imposing on persons from time to time occupying or interested in any such property obligations in respect of the carrying out of works of maintenance, repair, renewal or replacement in relation to the property or property used or enjoyed by them in common with others, or in respect of costs incurred by the landlord for the time being on any matter referred to in this paragraph or in paragraph (b) above;

(d) for the inspection from time to time of any such property on behalf of the landlord for the time being, and for the recovery by him of sums due to him under the scheme in respect of any such property by means of a charge on the property;

and the landlord for the time being shall have, for the enforcement of any charge imposed under the scheme, the same powers and remedies under the Law of Property Act 1925 and otherwise as if he were a mortgagee by deed having powers of sale and leasing and of appointing a receiver.

(4) Except as provided by the scheme, the operation of an estate management scheme shall not be affected by any disposition or devolution of the landlord's interest in the property within the area of the scheme or in parts of that property; but the scheme—

(a) shall include provision for identifying the person who is for the purposes of the scheme to be treated as the landlord for the time being; and

(b) shall also include provision for transferring, or allowing the landlord for the time being to transfer, all or any of the powers and rights conferred by the scheme on the landlord for the time being to a local authority or other body, including a body constituted for the purpose.

(5) Without prejudice to the generality of paragraph (b) of subsection (4), an estate management scheme may provide for the operation of any provision for transfer included in the scheme in accordance with that paragraph to be dependent—

(a) on a determination of a leasehold valuation tribunal effecting or approving the transfer;

(b) on such other circumstances as the scheme may provide.

(6) An estate management scheme may extend to property in which the landlord's interest is disposed of otherwise than as mentioned in subsection (1)(a) or (b) (whether residential property or not), so as to make that property, or allow it to be made, subject to any such provision as is or might be made by the scheme for property in which tenants acquire the landlord's interest as mentioned in either of those provisions.

(7) In this Chapter references to the landlord for the time being shall have effect, in relation to powers and rights transferred to a local authority or other body as contemplated by subsection (4)(b) above, as references to that authority or body.

DEFINITIONS
"interest": s.101(1).
"lease": s.101(1).

GENERAL NOTE
This section describes estate management schemes. Unlike the procedure under s.19 of the Leasehold Reform Act 1967 the schemes are to be approved by the leasehold valuation tribunal. This is a marked change from the former procedure which required first the consent of the Secretary of State and then the approval of the High Court. It can be expected that applications will be looked at in more variable ways and approval be even more easily obtained. Appeals from the leasehold valuation tribunal are to the Lands Tribunal (s.91(10) applying paras. 1–3 and 7 of Sched. 22 to the Housing Act 1980 and the Lands Tribunal Rules).

Subs. (1)
A scheme under this section can be made only if the whole area of the scheme is occupied by one landlord or directly or indirectly under leases from that landlord. For joint applications see s.71.

Subs. (2)
This subsection follows exactly the wording of s.19(6) of the Leasehold Reform Act 1967 except that the former provision requires consent of the High Court and this requires consent of the leasehold valuation tribunal.

Subs. (3)
This subsection follows the wording of the Leasehold Reform Act 1967, s.19(8). A charge imposed under this section is protected by registration of the scheme as a local land charge (s.70(11)) and is not otherwise registrable (Land Charges Act 1972, s.2(4)). As to the effect of registration and priority of charges see further (s.70).

Subss. (4) and (5)
Subsection (4) derives from s.19(7) of the Leasehold Reform Act 1967. The provisions have, however, been strengthened with a view to "ensure that existing schemes are not allowed to lapse, particularly where that is likely to affect our historic heritage" (Lord Strathclyde, *Hansard*, H.L. Vol. 546, col. 214). In subs. (4)(b) this is done by replacing "may" with "shall" at the commencement of the paragraph so that provisions for transfer of the power to a public body are mandatory. Subsection (5) envisages that the public body may be able to take over the powers on conditions set out in the scheme.

Subs. (6)
This subsection is derived from s.19(9) of the Leasehold Reform Act 1967. The area of land

within a scheme may include property which is enfranchised under this Act and other property which the landlord sells outside the framework of this Act. Such latter property may remain within the scheme if the scheme is so worded.

Subs. (7)
This subsection is derived from the proviso to s.19(7) of the Leasehold Reform Act 1967.

Approval by leasehold valuation tribunal of estate management scheme

70.—(1) A leasehold valuation tribunal may, on an application made by a landlord for the approval of a scheme submitted by him to the tribunal, approve the scheme as an estate management scheme for such area falling within section 69(1) as is specified in the scheme; but any such application must (subject to section 72) be made within the period of two years beginning with the date of the coming into force of this section.

(2) A leasehold valuation tribunal shall not approve a scheme as an estate management scheme for any area unless it is satisfied that, in order to maintain adequate standards of appearance and amenity and regulate redevelopment within the area in the event of tenants acquiring the interest of the landlord in any property as mentioned in section 69(1)(a) or (b), it is in the general interest that the landlord should retain such powers of management and have such rights falling within section 69(1)(i) and (ii) as are conferred by the scheme.

(3) In considering whether to approve a scheme as an estate management scheme for any area, a leasehold valuation tribunal shall have regard primarily to—

(a) the benefit likely to result from the scheme to the area as a whole (including houses or premises likely to be acquired from the landlord as mentioned in section 69(1)(a) or (b)); and

(b) the extent to which it is reasonable to impose, for the benefit of the area, obligations on tenants so acquiring the interest of their landlord;

but the tribunal shall also have regard to the past development and present character of the area and to architectural or historical considerations, to neighbouring areas and to the circumstances generally.

(4) A leasehold valuation tribunal shall not consider any application for it to approve a scheme unless it is satisfied that the applicant has, by advertisement or otherwise, given adequate notice to persons interested—

(a) informing them of the application for approval of the scheme and the provision intended to be made by the scheme, and

(b) inviting them to make representations to the tribunal about the application within a time which appears to the tribunal to be reasonable.

(5) In subsection (4) "persons interested" includes, in particular, in relation to any application for the approval of a scheme for any area ("the scheme area") within a conservation area—

(a) each local planning authority within whose area any part of the scheme area falls, and

(b) if the whole of the scheme area is in England, the Historic Buildings and Monuments Commission for England.

(6) Where representations about an application are made under subsection (4)(b), the tribunal shall afford to the persons making those representations an opportunity to appear and be heard by the tribunal at the time when the application is considered by it.

(7) Subject to the preceding provisions of this section, a leasehold valuation tribunal shall, after considering the application, approve the scheme in question either—

(a) as originally submitted, or

(b) with any relevant modifications proposed or agreed to by the applicant,

if the scheme (with those modifications if any) appears to the tribunal—

(i) to be fair and practicable, and

(ii) not to give the landlord a degree of control out of proportion to that previously exercised by him or to that required for the purposes of the scheme.

(8) In subsection (7) "relevant modifications" means modifications relating to the extent of the area to which the scheme is to apply or to the provisions contained in it.

(9) If, having regard to—

(a) the matters mentioned in subsection (3), and

(b) the provision which it is practicable to make by a scheme,

the tribunal thinks it proper to do so, the tribunal may declare that no scheme can be approved for the area in question in pursuance of the application.

(10) A leasehold valuation tribunal shall not dismiss an application for the approval of a scheme unless—

(a) it makes such a declaration as is mentioned in subsection (9); or

(b) in the opinion of the tribunal the applicant is unwilling to agree to a suitable scheme or is not proceeding in the matter with due despatch.

(11) A scheme approved under this section as an estate management scheme for an area shall be a local land charge, notwithstanding section 2(a) or (b) of the Local Land Charges Act 1975 (matters which are not local land charges), and for the purposes of that Act the landlord for that area shall be treated as the originating authority as respects any such charge.

(12) Where such a scheme is registered in the appropriate local land charges register—

(a) the provisions of the scheme relating to property of any description shall so far as they respectively affect the persons from time to time occupying or interested in that property be enforceable by the landlord for the time being against them, as if each of them had covenanted with the landlord for the time being to be bound by the scheme; and

(b) in relation to any acquisition such as is mentioned in section 69(1)(a) above, section 10 of the Leasehold Reform Act 1967 (rights to be conveyed on enfranchisement) shall have effect subject to the provisions of the scheme, and the price payable under section 9 of that Act shall be adjusted so far as is appropriate (if at all); and

(c) in relation to any acquisition such as is mentioned in section 69(1)(b) above, section 34 of, and Schedule 7 to, this Act shall have effect subject to the provisions of the scheme, and any price payable under Schedule 6 to this Act shall be adjusted so far as is appropriate (if at all).

(13) Section 10 of the Local Land Charges Act 1975 (compensation for non-registration etc.) shall not apply to schemes which, by virtue of subsection (11) above, are local land charges.

(14) In this section and in section 73 "conservation area" and "local planning authority" have the same meaning as in the Planning (Listed Buildings and Conservation Areas) Act 1990; and in connection with the latter expression—

(a) the expression "the planning Acts" in the Town and Country Planning Act 1990 shall be treated as including this Act; and

(b) paragraphs 4 and 5 of Schedule 4 to the Planning (Listed Buildings and Conservation Areas) Act 1990 (further provisions as to exercise of functions by different authorities) shall apply in relation to functions under or by virtue of this section or section 73 of this Act as they apply in relation to functions under section 69 of that Act.

DEFINITIONS
    "conservation area": subs. (14).
    "interest": s.101(1).
    "local planning authority": subs. (14).
    "persons interested": subs. (5).
    "relevant modifications": subs. (8).

GENERAL NOTE
    This section deals with applications to a leasehold valuation tribunal for an estate manage-
ment scheme. Generally an application must be made within two years of this section coming
into force (but see s.72). The task of the leasehold valuation tribunal is to decide whether it is in
the general interest (subs. (2)) to approve a scheme. The matters to which it should have regard
primarily in coming to this view are contained in subs. (3). Note the leasehold valuation tribunal
has no power to vary the scheme put forward unless the landlord agrees (subs. (7)).

Subs. (2)
    "General interest" is not defined. It literally goes wider than the common interest of landlord
and occupiers and looks at the wider local or public interest which is involved in preserving,
maintaining or improving the character of a particular area. Landlords should be encouraged to
look upon this not merely as an opportunity for the preservation of fine historic areas but for
producing sensible schemes for the improvement of rundown or blighted areas which are as
common in inner cities as the areas near Belgravia which featured so much in the Parliamentary
debate and doubtless the legislative thinking behind these provisions.

Subs. (3)
    This subsection seems a well-phrased exhortation giving the leasehold valuation tribunal a
first charge of considering the locality and its amenities but widening the focus also should there
be other important or aesthetic considerations.

Subs. (4)
    The advertisements or other forms of communication must be exhibited with the application
to the leasehold valuation tribunal (see Rent Assessment Committee (England & Wales)
(Leasehold Valuation Tribunal) Regulations 1993, Sched. 12 (S.I. 1993 No. 2408) reproduced
as Appendix 2 to these annotations). The regulations require the applicant to "show compliance" with this subsection. It is not absolutely clear how that should be done or what is a
reasonable time to allow for making representations. It would appear more adequate to write to
each tenant than advertise alone.

Subs. (5)
    This subsection adds to the persons who can made representations to the leasehold valuation
tribunal where property is in a conservation area.

Subs. (7)
    If the scheme satisfies the requirement of subs. (2), as explained in subs. (3), then the
leasehold valuation tribunal has a duty to approve it if the requirements of subs. (7)(i) and (ii)
are also met. If these conditions are met then the leasehold valuation tribunal has no overriding
discretion and failure to realise this will lead to judicial review but, see further subss. (9) and
(10).

Subss. (9) and (10)
    These two subsections together take the only grounds on which a leasehold valuation tribunal
can refuse to approve a scheme. The combined effect of this and the previous subsections is to
place an onus on the leasehold valuation tribunal to assist the applicant in finding suitable
modifications to permit approval of a scheme.

Subs. (11)
    The scheme should be registered as a local land charge. This precludes registration as a land
charge (s.2(4) of the Land Charges Act 1972). If the charge is registered as a local land charge
then a purchaser has notice of it by virtue of s.198(1) of the Law of Property Act 1925 if it is
unregistered land. If it is registered land it takes effect as an overriding interest by virtue of
s.70(1)(i) of the Land Registration Act 1925.

Subs. (12)
    The straightforward effects of this subsection are: (a) the scheme is enforceable against every

person occupying or with an interest in the affected property as if they had covenanted directly with the landlord; (b) and (c) the existence of the scheme is a factor in assessing any price payable by the tenant.

Applications by two or more landlords or by representative bodies

71.—(1) Where, on a joint application made by two or more persons as landlords of neighbouring areas, it appears to a leasehold valuation tribunal—

  (a) that a scheme could in accordance with subsections (1) and (2) of section 70 be approved as an estate management scheme for those areas, treated as a unit, if the interests of those persons were held by a single person, and

  (b) that the applicants are willing to be bound by the scheme to co-operate in the management of their property in those areas and in the administration of the scheme,

the tribunal may (subject to the provisions of section 70 and subsection (2) below) approve the scheme under that section as an estate management scheme for those areas as a whole.

(2) Any such scheme shall be made subject to conditions (enforceable in such manner as may be provided by the scheme) for securing that the landlords and their successors co-operate as mentioned in subsection (1)(b) above.

(3) Where it appears to a leasehold valuation tribunal—

  (a) that a scheme could, on the application of any landlord or landlords, be approved under section 70 as an estate management scheme for any area or areas, and

  (b) that any body of persons—

      (i) is so constituted as to be capable of representing for the purposes of the scheme the persons occupying or interested in property in the area or areas (other than the landlord or landlords or his or their licensees), or such of them as are or may become entitled to acquire their landlord's interest as mentioned in section 69(1)(a) or (b), and

      (ii) is otherwise suitable,

an application for the approval of the scheme under section 70 may be made to the tribunal by the representative body alone or by the landlord or landlords alone or by both jointly and, by leave of the tribunal, may be proceeded with by the representative body or by the landlord or landlords despite the fact that the body or landlord or landlords in question did not make the application.

(4) Without prejudice to section 69(4)(b), any such scheme may with the consent of the landlord or landlords, or on such terms as to compensation or otherwise as appear to the tribunal to be just—

  (a) confer on the representative body any such rights or powers under the scheme as might be conferred on the landlord or landlords for the time being, or

  (b) enable the representative body to participate in the administration of the scheme or in the management by the landlord or landlords of his or their property in the area or areas.

(5) Where any such scheme confers any rights or powers on the representative body in accordance with subsection (4) above, section 70(11) and (12)(a) shall have effect with such modifications (if any) as are provided for in the scheme.

DEFINITIONS
  "interest": s.101(1).

GENERAL NOTE
  Two or more landlords with neighbouring estates may apply for a joint scheme. They may

apply together or by forming a representative body, such as a registered company, to be the applicant.

Applications after expiry of two-year period

72.—(1) An application for the approval of a scheme for an area under section 70 (including an application in accordance with section 71(1) or (3)) may be made after the expiry of the period mentioned in subsection (1) of that section if the Secretary of State has, not more than six months previously, consented to the making of such an application for that area or for an area within which that area falls.

(2) The Secretary of State may give consent under subsection (1) to the making of an application ("the proposed application") only where he is satisfied—

(a) that either or both of the conditions mentioned in subsection (3) apply; and

(b) that adequate notice has been given to persons interested informing them of the request for consent and the purpose of the request.

(3) The conditions referred to in subsection (2)(a) are—

(a) that the proposed application could not have been made before the expiry of the period mentioned in section 70(1); and

(b) that—

(i) any application for the approval under section 70 of a scheme for the area, or part of the area, to which the proposed application relates would probably have been dismissed under section 70(10) (a) had it been made before the expiry of that period; but

(ii) because of a change in any of the circumstances required to be considered under section 70(3) the proposed application would, if made following the giving of consent by the Secretary of State, probably be granted.

(4) A request for consent under subsection (1) must be in writing and must comply with such requirements (if any) as to the form of, or the particulars to be contained in, any such request as the Secretary of State may by regulations prescribe.

(5) The procedure for considering a request for consent under subsection (1) shall be such as may be prescribed by regulations made by the Secretary of State.

GENERAL NOTE

The basic rule is that applications for a scheme must be made within two years of coming into force of this part of the Act. This section makes provision for late applications. First, the applicant has to give adequate notice of this application to interested persons, it is suggested that this be done by letter to the tenants and by prominent advertisements displayed in the area. Then the applicant has to apply to the Secretary of State for consent to make a late application to the leasehold valuation tribunal. The conditions to satisfy to obtain the Secretary of State's consent are either of subs. (3)(a) or subs. (3)(b). These are very stringent conditions requiring it to be shown that an application could not have been made in the prescribed period or would have failed but because of a change of circumstances would probably be granted. If either of these conditions is made out the Secretary of State still has a discretion as to whether or not to give consent (see subs. (2) "the Secretary of State may give consent"). Having obtained consent the landlord then applies to the leasehold valuation tribunal in the same way as described above. This application must be within six months of the Secretary of State's consent.

Applications by certain public bodies

73.—(1) Where it appears to a leasehold valuation tribunal after the expiry of the period mentioned in section 70(1) that a scheme could, on the application of any landlord or landlords within that period, have been approved under section 70 as an estate management scheme for any area or areas within a conservation area, an application for the approval of the scheme under that section may, subject to subsections (2) and (3) below, be made to the tribunal by one or more bodies constituting the relevant authority for the purposes of this section.

(2) An application under subsection (1) may only be made if—

(a) no scheme has been approved under section 70 for the whole or any part of the area or areas to which the application relates ("the scheme area"); and

(b) any application which has been made in accordance with section 70(1), 71(1) or 71(3) for the approval of a scheme for the whole or any part of the scheme area has been withdrawn or dismissed; and

(c) no request for consent under section 72(1) which relates to the whole or any part of the scheme area is pending or has been granted within the last six months.

(3) An application under subsection (1) above must be made within the period of six months beginning—

(a) with the date on which the period mentioned in section 70(1) expires, or

(b) if any application has been made as mentioned in subsection (2)(b) above, with the date (or, as the case may be, the latest date) on which any such application is withdrawn or dismissed,

whichever is the later; but if at any time during that period of six months a request of a kind mentioned in subsection (2)(c) above is pending or granted, an application under subsection (1) above may, subject to subsection (2) above, be made within the period of—

(i) six months beginning with the date on which the request is withdrawn or refused, or

(ii) twelve months beginning with the date on which the request is granted,

as the case may be.

(4) A scheme approved on an application under subsection (1) may confer on the applicant or applicants any such rights or powers under the scheme as might have been conferred on the landlord or landlords for the time being.

(5) For the purposes of this section the relevant authority for the scheme area is—

(a) where that area falls wholly within the area of a local planning authority—

(i) that authority; or

(ii) subject to subsection (6), that authority acting jointly with the Historic Buildings and Monuments Commission for England ("the Commission"); or

(iii) subject to subsection (6), the Commission; or

(b) in any other case—

(i) all of the local planning authorities within each of whose areas any part of the scheme area falls, acting jointly; or

(ii) subject to subsection (6), one or more of those authorities acting jointly with the Commission; or

(iii) subject to subsection (6), the Commission.

(6) The Commission may make, or join in the making of, an application under subsection (1) only if—

(a) the whole of the scheme area is in England; and

(b) they have consulted any local planning authority within whose area the whole or any part of the scheme area falls.

(7) Where a scheme is approved on an application under subsection (1) by two or more bodies acting jointly, the scheme shall, if the tribunal considers it appropriate, be made subject to conditions (enforceable in such manner as may be provided by the scheme) for securing that those bodies co-operate in the administration of the scheme.

(8) Where a scheme is approved on an application under subsection (1)—

(a) section 70(11) and (12)(a) shall (subject to subsection (9) below) have effect as if any reference to the landlord, or the landlord for the time being, for the area for which an estate management scheme has been approved were a reference to the applicant or applicants; and

(b) section 70(12)(b) and (c) shall each have effect with the omission of so much of that provision as relates to the adjustment of any such price as is there mentioned.

(9) A scheme so approved shall not be enforceable by a local planning authority in relation to any property falling outside the authority's area; and in the case of a scheme approved on a joint application made by one or more local planning authorities and the Commission, the scheme may provide for any of its provisions to be enforceable in relation to property falling within the area of a local planning authority either by the authority alone, or by the Commission alone, or by the authority and the Commission acting jointly, as the scheme may provide.

(10) For the purposes of—

(a) section 9(1A) of the Leasehold Reform Act 1967 (purchase price on enfranchisement) as it applies in relation to any acquisition such as is mentioned in section 69(1)(a) above, and

(b) paragraph 3 of Schedule 6 to this Act as it applies in relation to any acquisition such as is mentioned in section 69(1)(b) above (including that paragraph as it applies by virtue of paragraph 7 or 11 of that Schedule),

it shall be assumed that any scheme approved under subsection (1) and relating to the property in question had not been so approved, and accordingly any application for such a scheme to be approved, and the possibility of such an application being made, shall be disregarded.

(11) Section 70(14) applies for the purposes of this section.

GENERAL NOTE
  This section permits local planning authorities or the Historic Buildings and Monuments Commission in certain circumstances to apply for a scheme. This can be done only after the two-year period has expired within which landlords should normally apply (s.72) and no request for "late consent" has been made to the Secretary of State within the last six months. The relevant authority will be able to enforce the scheme as if it were a landlord.

Effect of application for approval on claim to acquire freehold

74.—(1) Subject to subsections (5) and (6), this subsection applies where—

(a) an application ("the scheme application") is made for the approval of a scheme as an estate management scheme for any area or a request ("the request for consent") is made for consent under section 72(1) in relation to any area, and

(b) whether before or after the making of the application or request—
  (i) the tenant of a house in that area gives notice of his desire to have the freehold under Part I of the Leasehold Reform Act 1967, being entitled to do so by virtue only of either or both of the sections of that Act referred to in section 69(1)(a) above, or
  (ii) a notice is given under section 13 above in respect of any premises in the area.

(2) Where subsection (1) applies by virtue of paragraph (b)(i) of that subsection, then—

(a) no further steps need be taken towards the execution of a conveyance to give effect to section 10 of the 1967 Act beyond those which appear to the landlord to be reasonable in the circumstances; and

(b) if the notice referred to in subsection (1)(b)(i) ("the tenant's notice") was given before the making of the scheme application or the request for consent, that notice may be withdrawn by a further notice given by the tenant to the landlord.

(3) Where subsection (1) applies by virtue of paragraph (b)(ii) of that subsection, then—

(a) if the notice referred to in that provision ("the initial notice") was given before the making of the scheme application or the request for consent, the notice may be withdrawn by a further notice given by the nominee purchaser to the reversioner;

(b) unless the initial notice is so withdrawn, the reversioner shall, if he has not already given the nominee purchaser a counter-notice under section 21, give him by the date referred to in subsection (1) of that section a counter-notice which complies with one of the requirements set out in subsection (2) of that section (but in relation to which subsection (3) of that section need not be complied with); and

(c) no proceedings shall be brought under Chapter I in pursuance of the initial notice otherwise than under section 22 or 23, and, if the court under either of those sections makes an order requiring the reversioner to give a further counter-notice to the nominee purchaser, the date by which it is to be given shall be such date as falls two months after subsection (1) above ceases to apply;

but no other counter-notice need be given under Chapter I, and (subject to the preceding provisions of this subsection) no further steps need be taken towards the final determination (whether by agreement or otherwise) of the terms of the proposed acquisition by the nominee purchaser beyond those which appear to the reversioner to be reasonable in the circumstances.

(4) If the tenant's notice or the initial notice is withdrawn in accordance with subsection (2) or (3) above, section 9(4) of the 1967 Act or (as the case may be) section 33 above shall not have effect to require the payment of any costs incurred in pursuance of that notice.

(5) Where the scheme application is withdrawn or dismissed, subsection (1) does not apply at any time falling after—

(a) the date of the withdrawal of the application, or

(b) the date when the decision of the tribunal dismissing the application becomes final,

as the case may be; and subsection (1) does not apply at any time falling after the date on which a scheme is approved for the area referred to in that subsection, or for any part of it, in pursuance of the scheme application.

(6) Where the request for consent is withdrawn or refused, subsection (1) does not apply at any time falling after the date on which the request is withdrawn or refused, as the case may be; and where the request is granted, subsection (1) does not apply at any time falling more than six months after the date on which it is granted (unless that subsection applies by virtue of an application made in reliance on the consent).

(7) Where, in accordance with subsection (5) or (6), subsection (1) ceases to apply as from a particular date, it shall do so without prejudice to—

(a) the effect of anything done before that date in pursuance of subsection (2) or (3); or

(b) the operation of any provision of this Part, or of regulations made under it, in relation to anything so done.

(8) If, however, no notice of withdrawal has been given in accordance with subsection (3) before the date when subsection (1) so ceases to apply and before that date either—

(a) the reversioner has given the nominee purchaser a counter-notice under section 21 complying with the requirement set out in subsection (2)(a) of that section, or

(b) section 23(6) would (but for subsection (3) above) have applied to require the reversioner to give a further counter-notice to the nominee purchaser, the reversioner shall give a further counter-notice to the nominee purchaser within the period of two months beginning with the date when subsection (1) ceases to apply.

(9) Subsections (3) to (5) of section 21 shall apply to any further counter-notice required to be given by the reversioner under subsection (8) above as if it were a counter-notice under that section complying with the requirement set out in subsection (2)(a) of that section; and sections 24 and 25 shall apply in relation to any such counter-notice as they apply in relation to one required by section 22(3).

(10) In this section—
> "the 1967 Act" means the Leasehold Reform Act 1967; and
> "the nominee purchaser" and "the reversioner" have the same meaning as in Chapter I of this Part of this Act;

and references to the approval of a scheme for any area include references to the approval of a scheme for two or more areas in accordance with section 71 or 73 above.

DEFINITIONS
"1967 Act": subs. (10).
"nominee purchaser": subs. (10).
"reversioner": subs. (10).

GENERAL NOTE
The effect of an application for a scheme on claims for enfranchisement may be summarised as follows:

Claims under the Leasehold Reform Act 1967
  (i) if a scheme has been approved the enfranchisement proceeds subject to the scheme;
 (ii) if an application for approval is pending then: (a) the landlord does not have to proceed except so far as it considers it reasonable (subs. (2)(a)); (b) if the tenant's notice was given before the application to the leasehold valuation tribunal or in the case of a "late consent" application the application to the Secretary of State for consent then the tenant may withdraw by notice to the landlord;
(iii) once a scheme application is withdrawn, dismissed or approved then the enfranchisement proceeds in the usual way unless the application has been withdrawn (subs. (5));
 (iv) once the application for the Secretary of State's consent is withdrawn or refused then the enfranchisement can proceed. If it is granted the enfranchisement is still frozen for six months pending an application to the leasehold valuation tribunal in which case the above rules apply.

Claims under Chapter I of the Leasehold Reform, Housing and Urban Development Act 1993
  (i) if a scheme has been approved then the application proceeds subject to the scheme;
 (ii) if the tenants' initial notice was given before the application to the leasehold valuation tribunal for a scheme or in the case of a "late consent" application before the application to the Secretary of State then (a) the nominee purchaser may withdraw the notice; (b) the reversioner's counter-notice should be given but in a curtailed form in some cases (subs. (3)(b)); (c) the reversioner need take no other steps except those which appear to it to be reasonable; (d) the only proceedings that can be taken are in relation to the validity of the initial notice (s.22) and the landlord's right to redevelopment (s.23);
(iii) once a scheme application is withdrawn, dismissed or approved then the collective enfranchisement proceeds in the usual way unless the initial notice has been withdrawn (subs. (5));
 (iv) see point (iv) under the Leasehold Reform Act 1967 above, the position is the same in regard to applications under the 1993 Act.

Variation of existing schemes

75.—(1) Where a scheme under section 19 of the Leasehold Reform Act 1967 (estate management schemes in connection with enfranchisement under that Act) includes, in pursuance of subsection (6) of that section, provision for enabling the termination or variation of the scheme, or the exclusion of part of the area of the scheme, by or with the approval of the High Court, that provision shall have effect—

(a) as if any reference to the High Court were a reference to a leasehold valuation tribunal, and

(b) with such modifications (if any) as are necessary in consequence of paragraph (a).

(2) A scheme under that section may be varied by or with the approval of a leasehold valuation tribunal for the purpose of, or in connection with, extending the scheme to property within the area of the scheme in which the landlord's interest may be acquired as mentioned in section 69(1)(a) above.

(3) Where any such scheme has been varied in accordance with subsection (2) above, section 19 of that Act shall apply as if the variation had been effected under provisions included in the scheme in pursuance of subsection (6) of that section (and accordingly the scheme may be further varied under provisions so included).

(4) Any application made under or by virtue of this section to a leasehold valuation tribunal shall comply with such requirements (if any) as to the form of, or the particulars to be contained in, any such application as the Secretary of State may by regulations prescribe.

(5) In this section any reference to a leasehold valuation tribunal is a reference to such a rent assessment committee as is mentioned in section 142(2) of the Housing Act 1980 (leasehold valuation tribunals).

DEFINITIONS
"interest": s.101(1).
"rent assessment committee": s.101(1).

GENERAL NOTE
Many existing schemes have been made under the Leasehold Reform Act 1967. These may now be terminated or varied by application to the leasehold valuation tribunal instead of as before by application to the High Court.

CHAPTER V

TENANTS' RIGHT TO MANAGEMENT AUDIT

GENERAL NOTE
This chapter consists of a group of sections concerned solely with conferring a new right on tenants. Its assumption is that tenants have difficulty obtaining reliable information about the financial management of the premises they occupy. Accordingly, it provides for tenants to appoint an accountant or a surveyor as an auditor who will then be entitled to carry out an audit of them. The provisions were amended at a very late stage (Third Reading in the House of Lords, *Hansard*, H.L. Vol. 546, col. 175) to permit chartered surveyors to be auditors. The very sensible reason is "because most of the hands-on management of property, and indeed the verification of expenses and matters related to the supervision of contract work in residential properties, are dealt with by qualified surveyors" (Earl of Lytton, *Hansard*, H.L. Vol. 546, col. 216).

There is very much concern amongst tenants of flats, about the cost and quality of the landlord's managements. This chapter is one of many legislative attempts to remedy this perceived problem. Previous legislative forays into this area have led to:

(a) Landlord and Tenant Act 1985 which contains extensive provisions relating to service charges, insurance and the rôle of managing agents;

(b) Landlord and Tenant Act 1987 which enabled tenants to take action to replace "bad management" by court-appointed managers or by compulsory acquisition of the Landlord's interest.

It is generally accepted that these previous pieces of legislation have not been as successful in assisting tenants as anticipated. The new provisions enabling a tenant to obtain an audit of management are even more likely to fall into the same legislative limbo. Tenants do not need more legal rights they need cheaper, quicker and more effective access to justice. These provisions for tenants struggling against the bad, the incompetent, the absent and the obstructive will be more or less an irrelevance.

Right to audit management by landlord

76.—(1) This Chapter has effect to confer on two or more qualifying tenants of dwellings held on leases from the same landlord the right, exercisable subject to and in accordance with this Chapter, to have an audit carried out on their behalf which relates to the management of the relevant premises and any appurtenant property by or on behalf of the landlord.

(2) That right shall be exercisable—

(a) where the relevant premises consist of or include two dwellings let to qualifying tenants of the same landlord, by either or both of those tenants; and

(b) where the relevant premises consist of or include three or more dwellings let to qualifying tenants of the same landlord, by not less than two-thirds of those tenants;

and in this Chapter the dwellings let to those qualifying tenants are referred to as "the constituent dwellings".

(3) In relation to an audit on behalf of two or more qualifying tenants—

(a) "the relevant premises" means so much of—

(i) the building or buildings containing the dwellings let to those tenants, and

(ii) any other building or buildings,

as constitutes premises in relation to which management functions are discharged in respect of the costs of which common service charge contributions are payable under the leases of those qualifying tenants; and

(b) "appurtenant property" means so much of any property not contained in the relevant premises as constitutes property in relation to which any such management functions are discharged.

(4) This Chapter also has effect to confer on a single qualifying tenant of a dwelling the right, exercisable subject to and in accordance with this Chapter, to have an audit carried out on his behalf which relates to the management of the relevant premises and any appurtenant property by or on behalf of the landlord.

(5) That right shall be exercisable by a single qualifying tenant of a dwelling where the relevant premises contain no other dwelling let to a qualifying tenant apart from that let to him.

(6) In relation to an audit on behalf of a single qualifying tenant—

(a) "the relevant premises" means so much of—

(i) the building containing the dwelling let to him, and

(ii) any other building or buildings,

as constitutes premises in relation to which management functions are discharged in respect of the costs of which a service charge is payable under his lease (whether as a common service charge contribution or otherwise); and

(b) "appurtenant property" means so much of any property not contained in the relevant premises as constitutes property in relation to which any such management functions are discharged.

(7) The provisions of sections 78 to 83 shall, with any necessary modifications, have effect in relation to an audit on behalf of a single qualifying tenant as they have effect in relation to an audit on behalf of two or more qualifying tenants.

(8) For the purposes of this section common service charge contributions are payable by two or more persons under their leases if they may be required under the terms of those leases to contribute to the same costs by the payment of service charges.

DEFINITIONS

"appurtenant property": subss. (3)(6) and s.84.

"constituent dwellings": s.84.

"dwelling": s.101(1).

"landlord": subs. (6)(a) and s.84.

"lease": s.101(1).
"management audit": s.84.
"management functions": s.84.
"relevant premises": subs. (3)(a) and s.84.
"service charge": s.84.

GENERAL NOTE
This section is essentially introductory and descriptive. The right to a management audit is conferred by it separately on two or more qualifying tenants and on a single qualifying tenant.

Subs. (1)
This subsection continues the curiously platitudinous style of legislation by introducing what is to follow by a prefatory statement. It is necessary to look at subs. (4) to see that the right is also in certain circumstances conferred on a single tenant, the introductory statement being then both unnecessary and misleading.

Subs. (2)
If there are only two qualifying tenants either or both can claim an audit. If there are more than two qualifying tenants then at least two-thirds are required to mount a successful claim.

Subs. (3)
The effect of this subsection is to allow the audit to include any management costs which contribute to the pool of costs from which each person's service charge is calculated. Thus, "appurtenant property" can be anywhere at all—the adjective appurtenant is quite misleading.

Subss. (4) to (7)
These subsections deal with requests for an audit by a single tenant. If the building contains any other qualifying tenant, then a single tenant has no right to a management audit. If there are other qualifying tenants of different landlords but with shared management costs then it appears, in this rather unlikely event, that there will be no right to a management audit by the single qualifying tenant of one of these landlords. If there are different landlords who do not pool their management costs then the single tenant of one of them will have the right to a management audit. This distinction comes from the definition of "relevant premises" in subs. (6)(a) and (b), as including all property in respect of which the management costs are pooled.

Qualifying tenants

77.—(1) Subject to the following provisions of this section, a tenant is a qualifying tenant of a dwelling for the purposes of this Chapter if—
  (a) he is a tenant of the dwelling under a long lease other than a business lease; and
  (b) any service charge is payable under the lease.
(2) For the purposes of subsection (1) a lease is a long lease if—
  (a) it is a lease falling within any of paragraphs (a) to (c) of subsection (1) of section 7; or
  (b) it is a shared ownership lease (within the meaning of that section), whether granted in pursuance of Part V of the Housing Act 1985 or otherwise and whatever the share of the tenant under it.
(3) No dwelling shall have more than one qualifying tenant at any one time.
(4) Accordingly—
  (a) where a dwelling is for the time being let under two or more leases falling within subsection (1), any tenant under any of those leases which is superior to that held by any other such tenant shall not be a qualifying tenant of the dwelling for the purposes of this Chapter; and
  (b) where a dwelling is for the time being let to joint tenants under a lease falling within subsection (1), the joint tenants shall (subject to paragraph (a)) be regarded for the purposes of this Chapter as jointly constituting the qualifying tenant of the dwelling.
(5) A person can, however, be (or be among those constituting) the qualifying tenant of each of two or more dwellings at the same time, whether he is tenant of those dwellings under one lease or under two or more separate leases.

(6) Where two or more persons constitute the qualifying tenant of a dwelling in accordance with subsection (4)(b), any one or more of those persons may sign a notice under section 80 on behalf of both or all of them.

DEFINITIONS
  "business lease": s.101(1).
  "dwelling": s.101(1).
  "lease": s.101(1).
  "service charge": s.84.

GENERAL NOTE
  The definition of qualifying tenant incorporates the definition in s.76 above.

Subs. (1)
  "Business lease" defined in s.101(1) is the subject of considerable case law. If the lease contains an express prohibition from use for business purposes altogether then it can never be a business lease (s.23(4) of the Landlord and Tenant Act 1954). Otherwise the definition of business in s.23 of that Act is very wide and on the facts a lease of a flat may turn out to be a business lease. The exceptions to the Landlord and Tenant Act 1954 contained in s.43 are unlikely to apply (agricultural holdings, mining leases) except for s.43(2) which excludes certain service tenancies from the business code.

Subs. (2)
  This subsection applies the definition of long lease in s.7, except that s.7 applies to a narrower range of shared ownership leases.

Subs. (3)
  If there are joint tenants then they count as one qualifying tenant.

Subs. (4)(a)
  If there is more than one long lease then the tenant entitled to possession is the qualifying tenant.

Subs. (4)(b)
  Subsection (3) seems to have the same effect as this subsection.

Subs. (5)
  This subsection is unnecessary (or for the avoidance of doubt). A person who owns several flats can for this purpose be a qualifying tenant of each.

Subs. (6)
  This provision is at first sight helpful in clarifying the ability of one of the joint tenants to act singly. However, a problem does arise in that "may sign . . . on behalf of" is ambiguous. Does this mean may if he has the authority of the other or may whether he has the authority of the others or not. Inclusion of the words "on behalf" indicate that the latter is the correct reading.

Management audits

78.—(1) The audit referred to in section 76(1) is an audit carried out for the purpose of ascertaining—
  (a) the extent to which the obligations of the landlord which—
        (i) are owed to the qualifying tenants of the constituent dwellings, and
        (ii) involve the discharge of management functions in relation to the relevant premises or any appurtenant property,
      are being discharged in an efficient and effective manner; and
  (b) the extent to which sums payable by those tenants by way of service charges are being applied in an efficient and effective manner;
and in this Chapter any such audit is referred to as a "management audit".
  (2) In determining whether any such obligations as are mentioned in subsection (1)(a) are being discharged in an efficient and effective manner, regard shall be had to any applicable provisions of any code of practice for the time being approved by the Secretary of State under section 87.

(3) A management audit shall be carried out by a person who—

(a) is qualified for appointment by virtue of subsection (4); and

(b) is appointed—

(i) in the circumstances mentioned in section 76(2)(a), by either or both of the qualifying tenants of the constituent dwellings, or

(ii) in the circumstances mentioned in section 76(2)(b), by not less than two-thirds of the qualifying tenants of the constituent dwellings;

and in this Chapter any such person is referred to as "the auditor".

(4) A person is qualified for appointment for the purposes of subsection (3) above if—

(a) he has the necessary qualification (within the meaning of subsection (1) of section 28 of the 1985 Act (meaning of "qualified accountant")) or is a qualified surveyor;

(b) he is not disqualified from acting (within the meaning of that subsection); and

(c) he is not a tenant of any premises contained in the relevant premises.

(5) For the purposes of subsection (4)(a) above a person is a qualified surveyor if he is a fellow or professional associate of the Royal Institution of Chartered Surveyors or of the Incorporated Society of Valuers and Auctioneers or satisfies such other requirement or requirements as may be prescribed by regulations made by the Secretary of State.

(6) The auditor may appoint such persons to assist him in carrying out the audit as he thinks fit.

DEFINITIONS

"appurtenant property": s.84.
"auditor": s.84.
"constituent dwellings": s.84.
"landlord": s.84.
"management audit": s.84.
"management functions": s.84.
"relevant premises": s.84.
"service charge": s.84.

GENERAL NOTE

The audit is to be carried out principally by an accountant. However, to fulfil the objectives of this section in judging the efficiency and effectiveness of management, a surveyor, building engineer, architect, quantity surveyor or other professional is likely to be essential. Instead of an accountant the tenants may choose a qualified surveyor as the auditor. Because of surveyors' close involvement this will often prove the more sensible alternative.

Subs. (3)

An appointment by "two-thirds" of the qualifying tenants must be taken literally—see s.73(2). However, in the same way as with exercising the collective right to enfranchisement the tenants must find their own way of co-operating with each other. This will sensibly mean a legally binding agreement dealing with who acts on their behalf and responsibility for any costs involved.

Subs. (4)

Under s.28 of the Landlord and Tenant Act 1985 qualified accountants are persons who are qualified to act as company auditors under s.25 of the Companies Act 1989. Section 28 of the 1985 Act disqualifies accountants who are associated in various ways with the landlord. The same disqualifications apply to qualified surveyors who are associated in those ways with the landlord.

Subs. (6)

Presumably the tenants may limit this by their terms of appointment of the auditor and in view of the cost implications such a limitation is highly to be recommended.

Rights exercisable in connection with management audits

79.—(1) Where the qualifying tenants of any dwellings exercise under section 80 their right to have a management audit carried out on their behalf, the rights conferred on the auditor by subsection (2) below shall be exercisable by him in connection with the audit.

(2) The rights conferred on the auditor by this subsection are—

(a) a right to require the landlord—

    (i) to supply him with such a summary as is referred to in section 21(1) of the 1985 Act (request for summary of relevant costs) in connection with any service charges payable by the qualifying tenants of the constituent dwellings, and

    (ii) to afford him reasonable facilities for inspecting, or taking copies of or extracts from, the accounts, receipts and other documents supporting any such summary;

(b) a right to require the landlord or any relevant person to afford him reasonable facilities for inspecting any other documents sight of which is reasonably required by him for the purpose of carrying out the audit; and

(c) a right to require the landlord or any relevant person to afford him reasonable facilities for taking copies of or extracts from any documents falling within paragraph (b).

(3) The rights conferred on the auditor by subsection (2) shall be exercisable by him—

(a) in relation to the landlord, by means of a notice under section 80; and

(b) in relation to any relevant person, by means of a notice given to that person at (so far as is reasonably practicable) the same time as a notice under section 80 is given to the landlord;

and, where a notice is given to any relevant person in accordance with paragraph (b) above, a copy of that notice shall be given to the landlord by the auditor.

(4) The auditor shall also be entitled, on giving notice in accordance with section 80, to carry out an inspection of any common parts comprised in the relevant premises or any appurtenant property.

(5) The landlord or (as the case may be) any relevant person shall—

(a) where facilities for the inspection of any documents are required under subsection (2)(a)(ii) or (b), make those facilities available free of charge;

(b) where any documents are required to be supplied under subsection (2)(a)(i) or facilities for the taking of copies or extracts are required under subsection (2)(a)(ii) or (c), be entitled to supply those documents or (as the case may be) make those facilities available on payment of such reasonable charge as he may determine.

(6) The requirement imposed on the landlord by subsection (5)(a) to make any facilities available free of charge shall not be construed as precluding the landlord from treating as part of his costs of management any costs incurred by him in connection with making those facilities so available.

(7) In this Chapter "relevant person" means a person (other than the landlord) who—

(a) is charged with responsibility—

    (i) for the discharge of any such obligations as are mentioned in section 78(1)(a), or

    (ii) for the application of any such service charges as are mentioned in section 78(1)(b); or

(b) has a right to enforce payment of any such service charges.

(8) In this Chapter references to the auditor in the context of—

(a) being afforded any such facilities as are mentioned in subsection (2), or

(b) the carrying out of any inspection under subsection (4),

shall be read as including a person appointed by the auditor under section 78(6).

"1985 Act": s.84.
"appurtenant property": s.84.
"auditor": s.84.
"common parts": s.101(1).
"constituent dwellings": s.84.
"dwelling": s.101(1).
"landlord": s.84.
"management audit": s.84.
"relevant person": subs. (7) and s.84.
"relevant premises": s.84.
"service charge": s.84.

GENERAL NOTE

This section describes a range of activities which the auditor can carry out or insist on the landlord carrying out for him. The landlord is required to provide facilities for inspection of documents free of charge under subs. (5)(a) but the sting in the tail is found in subs. (6) which provides that the cost of making these facilities available may be added to the "costs of management" (subs. (6)). It will seem ironic to the tenant having gone through the laborious process of a management audit to eventually pay an increased management charge including the costs of the audit.

Exercise of right to have a management audit

80.—(1) The right of any qualifying tenants to have a management audit carried out on their behalf shall be exercisable by the giving of a notice under this section.

(2) A notice given under this section—

(a) must be given to the landlord by the auditor, and

(b) must be signed by each of the tenants on whose behalf it is given.

(3) Any such notice must—

(a) state the full name of each of those tenants and the address of the dwelling of which he is a qualifying tenant;

(b) state the name and address of the auditor;

(c) specify any documents or description of documents—

(i) which the landlord is required to supply to the auditor under section 79(2)(a)(i), or

(ii) in respect of which he is required to afford the auditor facilities for inspection or for taking copies or extracts under any other provision of section 79(2); and

(d) if the auditor proposes to carry out an inspection under section 79(4), state the date on which he proposes to carry out the inspection.

(4) The date specified under subsection (3)(d) must be a date falling not less than one month nor more than two months after the date of the giving of the notice.

(5) A notice is duly given under this section to the landlord of any qualifying tenants if it is given to a person who receives on behalf of the landlord the rent payable by any such tenants; and a person to whom such a notice is so given shall forward it as soon as may be to the landlord.

DEFINITIONS
"auditor": s.84.
"dwelling": s.101(1).
"landlord": s.84.
"management audit": s.84.

GENERAL NOTE

This section deals with the manner of exercising the right to a management audit. It is exercised by a formal notice given by the auditor and signed by all the tenants who are demanding the audit. The form of the notice is not prescribed and a draft version follows:

NOTICE UNDER S.80 OF THE LEASEHOLD REFORM, HOUSING AND URBAN DEVELOPMENT ACT 1993

To [name and address of landlord]
1. The tenants whose details are specified in Sched. 1 hereto require an audit under Chap. V of the Leasehold Reform, Housing and Urban Development Act 1993.
2. The Auditor is [   ].
3. The landlord is required to supply to or make available to the auditor the documents [and descriptions of documents] specified in Sched. 2 hereto.
[4. The auditor proposes to carry out an inspection under s.79(4) on [specify a date not less than one month nor more than two months after the date of giving the notice]].

Signed [by each of the qualifying tenants requiring the audit]

Sched. 1
Tenant's Name: Address of Dwelling:

Sched. 2
List of documents or descriptions of documents.

Procedure following giving of notice under section 80

81.—(1) Where the landlord is given a notice under section 80, then within the period of one month beginning with the date of the giving of the notice, he shall—
(a) supply the auditor with any document specified under subsection (3)(c)(i) of that section, and afford him, in respect of any document falling within section 79(2)(a)(ii), any facilities specified in relation to it under subsection (3)(c)(ii) of section 80;
(b) in the case of every other document or description of documents specified in the notice under subsection (3)(c)(ii) of that section, either—
(i) afford the auditor facilities for inspection or (as the case may be) taking copies or extracts in respect of that document or those documents, or
(ii) give the auditor a notice stating that he objects to doing so for such reasons as are specified in the notice; and
(c) if a date is specified in the notice under subsection (3)(d) of that section, either approve the date or propose another date for the carrying out of an inspection under section 79(4).
(2) Any date proposed by the landlord under subsection (1)(c) must be a date falling not later than the end of the period of two months beginning with the date of the giving of the notice under section 80.
(3) Where a relevant person is given a notice under section 79 requiring him to afford the auditor facilities for inspection or taking copies or extracts in respect of any documents or description of documents specified in the notice, then within a period of one month beginning with the date of the giving of the notice, he shall, in the case of every such document or description of documents, either—
(a) afford the auditor the facilities required by him; or
(b) give the auditor a notice stating that he objects to doing so for such reasons as are specified in the notice.
(4) If by the end of the period of two months beginning with—
(a) the date of the giving of the notice under section 80, or
(b) the date of the giving of such a notice under section 79 as is mentioned in subsection (3) above,
the landlord or (as the case may be) a relevant person has failed to comply with any requirement of the notice, the court may, on the application of the auditor, make an order requiring the landlord or (as the case may be) the relevant person to comply with that requirement within such period as is specified in the order.

(5) The court shall not make an order under subsection (4) in respect of any document or documents unless it is satisfied that the document or documents falls or fall within paragraph (a) or (b) of section 79(2).

(6) If by the end of the period of two months specified in subsection (2) no inspection under section 79(4) has been carried out by the auditor, the court may, on the application of the auditor, make an order providing for such an inspection to be carried out on such date as is specified in the order.

(7) Any application for an order under subsection (4) or (6) must be made before the end of the period of four months beginning with—
  (a) in the case of an application made in connection with a notice given under section 80, the date of the giving of that notice; or
  (b) in the case of an application made in connection with such a notice under section 79 as is mentioned in subsection (3) above, the date of the giving of that notice.

DEFINITIONS
  "auditor": s.84.
  "court": s.101(1).
  "landlord": s.84.
  "relevant person": s.101(1).

GENERAL NOTE
  This section deals with the carrying out and the enforcement of the carrying out of the management audit. After the notice is given the landlord has a very short time to make the required documents or facilities available (one month). The landlord may propose an alternative date for the carrying out of any inspection required by the s.80 notice providing that date is within two months of the notice. If the landlord or other relevant person fails to comply with all or part of a s.80 notice then the auditor may apply to the county court for an order requiring compliance.

Requirement relating to information etc. held by superior landlord

82.—(1) Where the landlord is required by a notice under section 80 to supply any summary falling within section 79(2)(a), and any information necessary for complying with the notice so far as relating to any such summary is in the possession of a superior landlord—
  (a) the landlord shall make a written request for the relevant information to the person who is his landlord (and so on, if that person is himself not the superior landlord);
  (b) the superior landlord shall comply with that request within the period of one month beginning with the date of the making of the request; and
  (c) the landlord who received the notice shall then comply with it so far as relating to any such summary within the time allowed by section 81(1) or such further time, if any, as is reasonable.

(2) Where—
  (a) the landlord is required by a notice under section 80 to afford the auditor facilities for inspection or taking copies or extracts in respect of any documents or description of documents specified in the notice, and
  (b) any of the documents in question is in the custody or under the control of a superior landlord,

the landlord shall on receiving the notice inform the auditor as soon as may be of that fact and of the name and address of the superior landlord, and the auditor may then give the superior landlord a notice requiring him to afford the facilities in question in respect of the document.

(3) Subsections (3) to (5) and (7) of section 81 shall, with any necessary modifications, have effect in relation to a notice given to a superior landlord under subsection (2) above as they have effect in relation to any such notice given to a relevant person as is mentioned in subsection (3) of that section.

GENERAL NOTE
   This provides for a landlord to pass on requirements of a s.80 notice to a superior landlord who is able to comply therewith. If the superior landlord fails to comply then legal action can be taken against the superior landlord under s.81.

Supplementary provisions

83.—(1) Where—
(a) a notice has been given to a landlord under section 80, and
(b) at a time when any obligations arising out of the notice remain to be discharged by him—
>   (i) he disposes of the whole or part of his interest as landlord of the qualifying tenants of the constituent dwellings, and
>   (ii) the person acquiring any such interest of the landlord is in a position to discharge any of those obligations to any extent,

that person shall be responsible for discharging those obligations to that extent, as if he had been given the notice under that section.

(2) If the landlord is, despite any such disposal, still in a position to discharge those obligations to the extent referred to in subsection (1), he shall remain responsible for so discharging them; but otherwise the person referred to in that subsection shall be responsible for so discharging them to the exclusion of the landlord.

(3) Where a person is so responsible for discharging any such obligations (whether with the landlord or otherwise)—
(a) references to the landlord in section 81 shall be read as including, or as, references to that person to such extent as is appropriate to reflect his responsibility for discharging those obligations; but
(b) in connection with the discharge of any such obligations by that person, that section shall apply as if any reference to the date of the giving of the notice under section 80 were a reference to the date of the disposal referred to in subsection (1).

(4) Where—
(a) a notice has been given to a relevant person under section 79, and
(b) at a time when any obligations arising out of the notice remain to be discharged by him, he ceases to be a relevant person, but
(c) he is, despite ceasing to be a relevant person, still in a position to discharge those obligations to any extent,

he shall nevertheless remain responsible for discharging those obligations to that extent; and section 81 shall accordingly continue to apply to him as if he were still a relevant person.

(5) Where—
(a) a notice has been given to a landlord under section 80, or
(b) a notice has been given to a relevant person under section 79,

then during the period of twelve months beginning with the date of that notice, no subsequent such notice may be given to the landlord or (as the case may be) that person on behalf of any persons who, in relation to the earlier notice, were qualifying tenants of the constituent dwellings.

GENERAL NOTE

This section deals with a change of landlord or relevant person after a s.80 notice and before it has been wholly complied with. It also deals with situations when a fresh s.80 notice can be served.

Subs. (1)

A landlord subject to a s.80 notice who sells the property will be obliged to disclose this notice under S.C.S. (Standard Conditions of Sale) 3.2.2 and 3.1.4 and it may surprisingly fall within the definition of a "public requirement" within S.C.S. 1.1.1.

Subs. (2)

If the seller is put to any cost after completion in complying with a s.80 notice it seems that he is entitled to an indemnity from the buyer under S.C.S. 3.2.2(d).

Subs. (5)

A fresh notice cannot be given by the same qualifying tenants for a further 12 months.

Interpretation of Chapter V

84. In this Chapter—

"the 1985 Act" means the Landlord and Tenant Act 1985;

"appurtenant property" shall be construed in accordance with section 76(3) or (6);

"the auditor", in relation to a management audit, means such a person as is mentioned in section 78(3);

"the constituent dwellings" means the dwellings referred to in section 76(2)(a) or (b) (as the case may be);

"landlord" means immediate landlord;

"management audit" means such an audit as is mentioned in section 78(1);

"management functions" includes functions with respect to the provision of services or the repair, maintenance or insurance of property;

"relevant person" has the meaning given by section 79(7);

"the relevant premises" shall be construed in accordance with section 76(3) or (6);

"service charge" has the meaning given by section 18(1) of the 1985 Act.

GENERAL NOTE

The definition of "service charge" in the Housing Act 1985, s.18 is as follows:

"(1) In the following provisions of this Act "service charge" means an amount payable by a tenant of a [dwelling] as part of or in addition to the rent (a) which is payable, directly or indirectly, for services, repairs, maintenance or insurance or the landlord's costs of management, and (b) the whole or part of which varies or may vary according to the relevant costs.

(2) The relevant costs are the costs, or estimated costs, incurred or to be incurred by or on behalf of the landlord, or a superior landlord, in connection with the matters for which the service charge is payable.

(3) For this purpose (a) "costs" includes overheads, and (b) costs are relevant costs in relation to a service charge whether they are incurred, or to be incurred, in the period for which the service charge is payable or in an earlier or later period."

CHAPTER VI

MISCELLANEOUS

Compulsory acquisition of landlord's interest

Amendment of Part III of Landlord and Tenant Act 1987

85.—(1) Part III of the Landlord and Tenant Act 1987 (compulsory acquisition by tenants of their landlord's interest) shall be amended as follows.

(2) In section 25 (compulsory acquisition of landlord's interest by qualifying tenants)—

(a) for subsection (2)(c) there shall be substituted—

  "(c) the total number of flats held by such tenants is not less than two-thirds of the total number of flats contained in the premises."; and

(b) subsection (3) shall be omitted.

(3) In section 27(4) (meaning of requisite majority in relation to qualifying tenants), for "more than 50 per cent." there shall be substituted "not less than two-thirds".

(4) In section 29(2) (conditions for making acquisition orders), the words from "and (c)" onwards shall be omitted.

DEFINITIONS
"flat": s.101(1).
"interest": s.101(1).

GENERAL NOTE
This section contains a series of small amendments to Pt. III of the Landlord and Tenant Act 1987. That provision allows tenants of badly managed blocks of flats, occupied on long leases, to apply to the court for an order that the tenants be allowed to acquire the landlord's interest. The right to compulsory acquisition by tenants under the Landlord and Tenant Act 1987 was introduced as part of a battery of measures in that Act aimed at bad management. This section makes three significant amendments. Two of those make it easier to obtain an acquisition order (subss. (2) and (4)) and one (subs. (3)) sets a more difficult requirement. It is notorious that this part of the 1987 Act is largely a dead letter and it will probably remain so.

The effect of the amendments is as follows:

(i) new subs. (2)(c) has the effect that the provision applies to premises where at least two-thirds of the total flats in the building are held on qualifying leases. The previous requirement was at least 90 per cent. of the flats which excluded very many badly managed blocks;

(ii) the amendment to s.27(4) requires at least two-thirds of the qualifying tenants to join in the preliminary notice to the landlord claiming the benefit of this provision;

(iii) the amendment to s.29(2) is important. It removes the requirement that before an order is made under Pt. III of the 1987 Act there should either have been a manager appointed under Pt. II of the Act for a three-year period or that the appointment of a manager would not be an adequate remedy. The tenants may, thus, consider applying for an acquisition order under Pt. III without the preliminary stage of considering asking for a manager to be appointed under Pt. II.

Subs. (2)
This amends the Landlord and Tenant Act 1987, s.25(2)(c) to provide that in buildings containing 10 or more flats then at least two-thirds must be qualifying tenants. The previous requirement was 90 per cent. and made the provision largely a dead letter. Qualifying tenants are defined in s.26 of the 1987 Act and are tenants of long residential leases as there defined.

Subs. (3)
All qualifying tenants in a block have a vote but each flat has only one vote. The previous s.27 required a notice commencing the exercise of this right to be subscribed to by 50 per cent. of the qualifying tenants. The amendment requires at least two-thirds.

Subs. (4)
The provision of s.29(2) which is repealed stated as a pre-requisite of an acquisition order "that the appointment of a manager under Pt. II to act in relation to those premises would not be an adequate remedy". Removing this requirement should make it easier to obtain an acquisition order.

Variation of leases

Variation of leases under Part IV of Landlord and Tenant Act 1987

86. In section 35(4) of the Landlord and Tenant Act 1987 (variation of lease on grounds that it fails to make satisfactory provision with respect to the computation of a service charge), in paragraph (c), for "exceed" there shall be substituted "either exceed or be less than".

DEFINITIONS
    "lease": s.101(1).

GENERAL NOTE
    Section 35 of the Landlord and Tenant Act 1987 gives the court power to vary defective long leases of flats for a variety of reasons. Section 35(4)(c) includes among those reasons service charge provisions which produce an aggregate amount exceeding the required expenditure. This amendment extends that to service charge provisions which fail to produce sufficient money to meet the required expenditure.

Codes of practice

Approval by Secretary of State of codes of management practice

87.—(1) The Secretary of State may, if he considers it appropriate to do so, by order—
    (a) approve any code of practice—
        (i) which appears to him to be designed to promote desirable practices in relation to any matter or matters directly or indirectly concerned with the management of residential property by relevant persons; and
        (ii) which has been submitted to him for his approval;
    (b) approve any modifications of any such code which have been so submitted; or
    (c) withdraw his approval for any such code or modifications.
    (2) The Secretary of State shall not approve any such code or any modifications of any such code unless he is satisfied that arrangements have been made for the text of the code or the modifications to be published in such manner as he considers appropriate for bringing the provisions of the code or the modifications to the notice of those likely to be affected by them (which, in the case of modifications of a code, may include publication of a text of the code incorporating the modifications).
    (3) The power of the Secretary of State under this section to approve a code of practice which has been submitted to him for his approval includes power to approve a part of any such code; and references in this section to a code of practice may accordingly be read as including a reference to a part of a code of practice.
    (4) At any one time there may be two or more codes of practice for the time being approved under this section.
    (5) A code of practice approved under this section may make different provision with respect to different cases or descriptions of cases, including different provision for different areas.
    (6) Without prejudice to the generality of subsections (1) and (5)—
    (a) a code of practice approved under this section may, in relation to any such matter as is referred to in subsection (1), make provision in respect of relevant persons who are under an obligation to discharge any function in connection with that matter as well as in respect of relevant persons who are not under such an obligation; and
    (b) any such code may make provision with respect to—
        (i) the resolution of disputes with respect to residential property between relevant persons and the tenants of such property;
        (ii) competitive tendering for works in connection with such property; and
        (iii) the administration of trusts in respect of amounts paid by tenants by way of service charges.
    (7) A failure on the part of any person to comply with any provision of a code of practice for the time being approved under this section shall not of itself render him liable to any proceedings; but in any proceedings before a court or tribunal—

(a) any code of practice approved under this section shall be admissible in evidence; and

(b) any provision of any such code which appears to the court or tribunal to be relevant to any question arising in the proceedings shall be taken into account in determining that question.

(8) For the purposes of this section—

(a) "relevant person" means any landlord of residential property or any person who discharges management functions in respect of such property, and for this purpose "management functions" includes functions with respect to the provision of services or the repair, maintenance or insurance of such property;

(b) "residential property" means any building or part of a building which consists of one or more dwellings let on leases, but references to residential property include—

(i) any garage, outhouse, garden, yard and appurtenances belonging to or usually enjoyed with such dwellings,

(ii) any common parts of any such building or part, and

(iii) any common facilities which are not within any such building or part; and

(c) "service charge" means an amount payable by a tenant of a dwelling as part of or in addition to the rent—

(i) which is payable, directly or indirectly, for services, repairs, maintenance or insurance or any relevant person's costs of management, and

(ii) the whole or part of which varies or may vary according to the costs or estimated costs incurred or to be incurred by any relevant person in connection with the matters mentioned in sub-paragraph (i).

(9) This section applies in relation to dwellings let on licences to occupy as it applies in relation to dwellings let on leases, and references in this section to landlords and tenants of residential property accordingly include references to licensors and licensees of such property.

DEFINITIONS
"common parts": s.101(1).
"court": s.101(1).
"dwelling": s.101(1).
"lease": s.101(1).
"management functions": subs. (8)(a).
"relevant person": subs. (8)(a).
"residential property": subs. (8)(b).
"service charge": subs. (8)(c).

GENERAL NOTE
This section is in the spirit of the many citizens' charters that have emerged in the last few years. Codes of practice published under this provision will not have direct legal effect. However, they will be very important in practice because there are so many areas where the court has to make a judgment as to the "reasonableness" of a landlord's actions and the code of practice may provide an important benchmark of the standard to be attained. It should be noted (subs. (9)) that unlike the great bulk of landlord and tenant legislation this section applies to dwellings let on licences.

Subs. (6)(b)
It is very hard to see the legislative sense in including these three very important areas in a mere code of practice. A system of arbitration of residential landlord and tenant disputes which is cheap and accessible would be a very great step forward and of more value to tenants than all the hundreds of pages of palliative legislation produced in the past decade. However, a non-binding recommendation of such a system will pose little worry to the "bad" landlord.

Subs. (7)
This subsection produces the "bite" which codes of practice will have. They may be relevant

in deciding questions on landlord's speed and standard of carrying out repairs and in provision of and charging for services.

Subs. (9)
  This subsection extends the potential scope very considerably but still probably excludes hotels and boarding houses as these are not "dwellings let on licences".

Jurisdiction of leasehold valuation tribunals in relation to enfranchisement etc. of Crown land

Jurisdiction of leasehold valuation tribunals in relation to enfranchisement etc. of Crown land

  88.—(1) This section applies where any tenant under a lease from the Crown is proceeding with a view to acquiring the freehold or an extended lease of a house and premises in circumstances in which, but for the existence of any Crown interest in the land subject to the lease, he would be entitled to acquire the freehold or such an extended lease under Part I of the Leasehold Reform Act 1967.
  (2) Where—
  (a) this section applies in accordance with subsection (1), and
  (b) any question arises in connection with the acquisition of the freehold or an extended lease of the house and premises which is such that, if the tenant were proceeding as mentioned in that subsection in pursuance of a claim made under Part I of that Act, a leasehold valuation tribunal constituted for the purposes of that Part of that Act would have jurisdiction to determine it in proceedings under that Part, and
  (c) it is agreed between—
      (i) the appropriate authority and the tenant, and
      (ii) all other persons (if any) whose interests would fall to be represented in proceedings brought under that Part for the determination of that question by such a tribunal,
    that that question should be determined by such a tribunal,
a rent assessment committee constituted for the purposes of this section shall have jurisdiction to determine that question.
  (3) A rent assessment committee shall, when constituted for the purposes of this section, be known as a leasehold valuation tribunal.
  (4) Paragraphs 1 to 3 of Schedule 22 to the Housing Act 1980 (provisions relating to leasehold valuation tribunals constituted for the purposes of Part I of the Leasehold Reform Act 1967) shall apply to a leasehold valuation tribunal constituted for the purposes of this section.
  (5) Any application made to such a leasehold valuation tribunal must comply with such requirements (if any) as to the form of, or the particulars to be contained in, any such application as the Secretary of State may by regulations prescribe.
  (6) For the purposes of this section "lease from the Crown" means a lease of land in which there is, or has during the subsistence of the lease been, a Crown interest superior to the lease; and "Crown interest" and "the appropriate authority" in relation to a Crown interest mean respectively.
  (a) an interest comprised in the Crown Estate, and the Crown Estate Commissioners;
  (b) an interest belonging to Her Majesty in right of the Duchy of Lancaster, and the Chancellor of the Duchy;
  (c) an interest belonging to the Duchy of Cornwall, and such person as the Duke of Cornwall or the possessor for the time being of the Duchy appoints;
  (d) any other interest belonging to a government department or held on behalf of Her Majesty for the purposes of a government department, and the Minister in charge of that department.

(7) In this section any reference to a leasehold valuation tribunal constituted for the purposes of Part I of the Leasehold Reform Act 1967 is a reference to such a rent assessment committee as is mentioned in section 142(2) of the Housing Act 1980 (leasehold valuation tribunals).

DEFINITIONS
"appropriate authority": subs. (6).
"Crown interest": subs. (6).
"interest": s.101(1).
"lease": s.101(1).
"lease from the Crown": subs. (6).
"rent assessment committee": s.101(1).

GENERAL NOTE
This section applies so that leasehold valuation tribunals have the same jurisdiction in respect of claims under the Leasehold Reform Act 1967 where a Crown interest in land is involved as in other claims, providing that the Crown agrees.

Subs. (4)
Paragraphs 1–3 of Sched. 22 to the Housing Act 1980 are as follows:

"Constitution of tribunals:
(1) the president of a panel drawn up under Sched. 10 to the 1977 Act shall, when constituting a leasehold valuation tribunal, ensure that at least one of its members is a person who has experience in the valuation of land.

Appeals:
(2) no appeal shall lie from a decision of a leasehold valuation tribunal to the High Court by virtue of s.13(1) of the Tribunals and Inquiries Act 1971 and no case may be stated for the opinion of the High Court in respect of such a decision, but any person who (a) appeared before a tribunal in proceedings to which he was a party; and (b) is dissatisfied with its decision, may within such time as rules under s.3(6) of the Lands Tribunal Act 1949 may specify, appeal to the Lands Tribunal.
(3) a leasehold valuation tribunal shall not be treated as a person aggrieved for the purposes of s.3(4) of the Lands Tribunal Act 1949 (which enables a person aggrieved by a decision of the Tribunal on a point of law to require the Tribunal to state a case for decision of the Court of Appeal)".

Provision of accommodation for persons with mental disorders

Avoidance of provisions preventing occupation of leasehold property by persons with mental disorders

89.—(1) Any agreement relating to a lease of any property which comprises or includes a dwelling (whether contained in the instrument creating the lease or not and whether made before the creation of the lease or not) shall be void in so far as it would otherwise have the effect of prohibiting or imposing any restriction on—
  (a) the occupation of the dwelling, or of any part of the dwelling, by persons with mental disorders (within the meaning of the Mental Health Act 1983), or
  (b) the provision of accommodation within the dwelling for such persons.
  (2) Subsection (1) applies to any agreement made after the coming into force of this section.

DEFINITIONS
"dwelling": s.101(1).
"lease": s.101(1).

GENERAL NOTE
This section does not prevent anyone who chooses to do so refusing to let their property to mentally disordered persons. It does render void provisions in or collateral to leases which have

that effect. The section (subs. (2)) applies only to agreements made after the section is brought into force. It seems to apply to agreements which have the forbidden effect whether or not they contained a dwelling at the time of the lease. This condition is reached from the clear words rendering void an agreement which would have the effect of enforcing such a forbidden restriction. Thus, you must see if an agreement restricts occupation of a dwelling, etc., by a mentally disordered person. If it does and there is then a dwelling included in that lease then the provision is void. Suppose a restrictive covenant prevents occupation as a dwelling altogether. That is literally a covenant which prevents occupation by a person with a mental disorder and the covenant is to that extent void. The bizarre and presumably accidental effect is that the covenant prevents occupation as a dwelling by anyone except the mentally disordered. The courts can avoid this literal meaning only by a contrived purposive construction of the section. The court may now consider parliamentary materials in interpreting this clause (see *Pepper* (*Inspector of Taxes*) v. *Hart* [1992] 3 W.L.R. 1032). However, the clause in its present form was introduced only in the Third Reading debate in the House of Lords (*Hansard*, H.L. Vol. 546, cols. 216 and 217) and received no debate or helpful explanation except that it was intended to prevent discrimination against the mentally ill and mentally handicapped in relation to housing.

CHAPTER VII

GENERAL

Jurisdiction of county courts

90.—(1) Any jurisdiction expressed to be conferred on the court by this Part shall be exercised by a county court.

(2) There shall also be brought in a county court any proceedings for determining any question arising under or by virtue of any provision of Chapter I or II or this Chapter which is not a question falling within its jurisdiction by virtue of subsection (1) or one falling within the jurisdiction of a leasehold valuation tribunal by virtue of section 91.

(3) Where, however, there are brought in the High Court any proceedings which, apart from this subsection, are proceedings within the jurisdiction of the High Court, the High Court shall have jurisdiction to hear and determine any proceedings joined with those proceedings which are proceedings within the jurisdiction of a county court by virtue of subsection (1) or (2).

(4) Where any proceedings are brought in a county court by virtue of subsection (1) or (2), the court shall have jurisdiction to hear and determine any other proceedings joined with those proceedings, despite the fact that, apart from this subsection, those other proceedings would be outside the court's jurisdiction.

DEFINITIONS
"court": s.101(1).

GENERAL NOTE
Disputes under this part of the Act are to be resolved in the county court unless the leasehold valuation tribunal is specifically mentioned as the tribunal with jurisdiction. Where a question under this part of the Act is incidental to a case properly brought in the High Court, then the High Court can deal with these issues which would otherwise have come within the jurisdiction of the county court.

Jurisdiction of leasehold valuation tribunals

91.—(1) Any jurisdiction expressed to be conferred on a leasehold valuation tribunal by the provisions of this Part (except section 75 or 88) shall be exercised by a rent assessment committee constituted for the purposes of this section; and any question arising in relation to any of the matters specified in subsection (2) shall, in default of agreement, be determined by such a rent assessment committee.

(2) Those matters are—
(a) the terms of acquisition relating to—
(i) any interest which is to be acquired by a nominee purchaser in pursuance of Chapter I, or

      (ii) any new lease which is to be granted to a tenant in pursuance
      of Chapter II,
including in particular any matter which needs to be determined for
the purposes of any provision of Schedule 6 or 13;
  (b) the terms of any lease which is to be granted in accordance with
      section 36 and Schedule 9;
  (c) the amount of any payment falling to be made by virtue of section
      18(2);
  (d) the amount of any costs payable by any person or persons by virtue of
      any provision of Chapter I or II and, in the case of costs to which
      section 33(1) or 60(1) applies, the liability of any person or persons by
      virtue of any such provision to pay any such costs; and
  (e) the apportionment between two or more persons of any amount
      (whether of costs or otherwise) payable by virtue of any such
      provision.
  (3) A rent assessment committee shall, when constituted for the purposes
of this section, be known as a leasehold valuation tribunal; and in the
following provisions of this section references to a leasehold valuation
tribunal are (unless the context otherwise requires) references to such a
committee.
  (4) Where in any proceedings before a court there falls for determination
any question falling within the jurisdiction of a leasehold valuation tribunal
by virtue of Chapter I or II or this section, the court—
  (a) shall by order transfer to such a tribunal so much of the proceedings as
      relate to the determination of that question; and
  (b) may then dispose of all or any remaining proceedings, or adjourn the
      disposal of all or any such proceedings pending the determination of
      that question by the tribunal, as it thinks fit;
and accordingly once that question has been so determined the court shall, if
it is a question relating to any matter falling to be determined by the court,
give effect to the determination in an order of the court.
  (5) Without prejudice to the generality of any other statutory provision—
  (a) the power to make regulations under section 74(1)(b) of the Rent Act
      1977 (procedure of rent assessment committees) shall extend to pre-
      scribing the procedure to be followed consequent on a transfer under
      subsection (4) above; and
  (b) rules of court may prescribe the procedure to be followed in connec-
      tion with such a transfer.
  (6) Any application made to a leasehold valuation tribunal under or by
virtue of this Part must comply with such requirements (if any) as to the form
of, or the particulars to be contained in, any such application as the Secretary of State may by regulations prescribe.
  (7) In any proceedings before a leasehold valuation tribunal which relate
to any claim made under Chapter I, the interests of the participating tenants
shall be represented by the nominee purchaser, and accordingly the parties
to any such proceedings shall not include those tenants.
  (8) No costs which a party to any proceedings under or by virtue of this
Part before a leasehold valuation tribunal incurs in connection with the
proceedings shall be recoverable by order of any court (whether in consequence of a transfer under subsection (4) or otherwise).
  (9) A leasehold valuation tribunal may, when determining the property in
which any interest is to be acquired in pursuance of a notice under section 13
or 42, specify in its determination property which is less extensive than that
specified in that notice.
  (10) Paragraphs 1 to 3 and 7 of Schedule 22 to the Housing Act 1980
(provisions relating to leasehold valuation tribunals constituted for the
purposes of Part I of the Leasehold Reform Act 1967) shall apply to a
leasehold valuation tribunal constituted for the purposes of this section;
but—

(a) in relation to any proceedings which relate to a claim made under Chapter I of this Part of this Act, paragraph 7 of that Schedule shall apply as if the nominee purchaser were included among the persons on whom a notice is authorised to be served under that paragraph; and

(b) in relation to any proceedings on an application for a scheme to be approved by a tribunal under section 70, paragraph 2(a) of that Schedule shall apply as if any person appearing before the tribunal in accordance with subsection (6) of that section were a party to the proceedings.

(11) In this section—

"the nominee purchaser" and "the participating tenants" have the same meaning as in Chapter I;

"the terms of acquisition" shall be construed in accordance with section 24(8) or section 48(7), as appropriate;

and the reference in subsection (10) to a leasehold valuation tribunal constituted for the purposes of Part I of the Leasehold Reform Act 1967 shall be construed in accordance with section 88(7) above.

DEFINITIONS
"disposal": s.101(1).
"interest": s.101(1).
"lease": s.101(1).
"nominee purchaser": subs. (11).
"participating tenants": subs. (11).
"rent assessment committee": s.101(1).
"terms of acquisition": subs. (11).

GENERAL NOTE
Leasehold valuation tribunals (which are rent assessment committees by another name) are given a further lease of life by this section. The costs before a leasehold valuation tribunal are borne by each party (subs. (8)) and there is no exception to this. The relevant rules under subs. (3) are the Rent Assessment Committee (England and Wales) (Leasehold Valuation Tribunal) Rules 1993 (S.I. 1993 No. 2408) reproduced as Appendix 2 below.

Subs. (7)
This subsection is particularly important when considering the right to appeal (Housing Act 1980, Sched. 22, para. 2). On the "tenants' side" in collective enfranchisement proceedings only the nominee purchaser has the right to appeal.

Subs. (10)
The provisions of the Housing Act 1980, Sched. 22, paras. (1)–(3) and (7) are as follows:

"Constitution of tribunals:
(1) the president of a panel drawn up under Schedule 10 to the 1977 Act shall, when constituting a leasehold valuation tribunal, ensure that at least one of its members is a person who has experience in the valuation of land.

Appeals:
(2) no appeal shall lie from a decision of a leasehold valuation tribunal to the High Court by virtue of section 13(1) of the Tribunals and Inquiries Act 1971 and no case may be stated for the opinion of the High Court in respect of such a decision, but any person who (a) appeared before a tribunal in proceedings to which he was a party; and (b) is dissatisfied with its decision, may, within such time as rules under section 3(6) of the Lands Tribunal Act 1949 may specify, appeal to the Lands Tribunal.

(3) a leasehold valuation tribunal shall not be treated as a person aggrieved for the purposes of section 3(4) of the Lands Tribunal Act 1949 (which enables a person aggrieved by a decision of the Tribunal on a point of law to require the Tribunal to state a case for decision of the Court of Appeal).

Provision of information:
(7) (1) where a matter is referred to a leasehold valuation tribunal for determination, the

tribunal may by notice in writing served on the tenant or landlord or on a superior landlord require him to give to the tribunal, within such period but not less than 14 days from the service of the notice as may be specified in the notice, such information as the tribunal may reasonably require. (2) If any person fails without reasonable cause to comply with any notice served on him under this paragraph he shall be liable, on summary conviction, to a fine not exceeding [level 3 on the standard scale]."

Enforcement of obligations under Chapters I and II

92.—(1) The court may, on the application of any person interested, make an order requiring any person who has failed to comply with any requirement imposed on him under or by virtue of any provision of Chapter I to II to make good the default within such time as is specified in the order.

(2) An application shall not be made under subsection (1) unless—

(a) a notice has been previously given to the person in question requiring him to make good the default, and

(b) more than 14 days have elapsed since the date of the giving of that notice without his having done so.

DEFINITIONS
"court": s.101(1).

GENERAL NOTE
The generality of this provision should be noted. Obligations arise directly under many provisions of Chaps. I and II. Further obligation will arise during court proceedings as directions are given by the court. The important point in s.92 is that any of these obligations may be the subject of an application to the court by "any person interested". There is no definition of this but it will include any of the qualifying tenants, probably any other tenant, any person interested in the reversion and in each case any mortgagee.

Subs. (2)
The notice to be given under s.92(2) is not in a prescribed form. An example as to the form of such notice is as follows:

NOTICE UNDER S.92 OF THE LEASEHOLD REFORM, HOUSING AND URBAN DEVELOPMENT ACT 1993

1. Under or by virtue of s.[   ] Leasehold Reform, Housing and Urban Development Act 1993 you are obliged to
[   ].
2. You have not performed this obligation and are hereby required so to do.
3. This notice is given on behalf of [of
                          ] who may apply to the court for an order requiring you to perform the above stated obligation once 14 days have elapsed from the giving of this notice.

Agreements excluding or modifying rights of tenant under Chapter I or II

93.—(1) Except as provided by this section, any agreement relating to a lease (whether contained in the instrument creating the lease or not and whether made before the creation of the lease or not) shall be void in so far as it—

(a) purports to exclude or modify—

(i) any entitlement to participate in the making of a claim to exercise the right to collective enfranchisement under Chapter I,

(ii) any right to acquire a new lease under Chapter II, or

(iii) any right to compensation under section 61; or

(b) provides for the termination or surrender of the lease in the event of the tenant becoming a participating tenant for the purposes of Chapter I or giving a notice under section 42; or

(c) provides for the imposition of any penalty or disability on the tenant in that event.

(2) Subsection (1) shall not be taken to preclude a tenant from surrendering his lease, and shall not—

(a) invalidate any agreement for the acquisition on behalf of a tenant of an interest superior to his lease, or for the acquisition by a tenant of a new lease, on terms different from those provided by Chapters I and II; or

(b) where a tenant has become a participating tenant for the purposes of Chapter I or has given a notice under section 42, invalidate—

(i) any agreement that the notice given under section 13 or (as the case may be) section 42 shall cease to have effect, or

(ii) any provision of such an agreement excluding or restricting for a period not exceeding three years any such entitlement or right as is mentioned in subsection (1)(a)(i) or (ii); or

(c) where a tenant's right to compensation under section 61 has accrued, invalidate any agreement as to the amount of the compensation.

(3) Where—

(a) a tenant having the right to acquire a new lease under Chapter II—

(i) has entered into an agreement for the surrender of his lease without the prior approval of the court, or

(ii) has entered into an agreement for the grant of a new lease without any of the terms of acquisition (within the meaning of that Chapter) having been determined by a leasehold valuation tribunal under that Chapter, or

(b) a tenant has been granted a new lease under Chapter II or by virtue of subsection (4) below and, on his landlord claiming possession for the purposes of redevelopment, enters into an agreement without the prior approval of the court for the surrender of the lease,

then on the application of the tenant a county court, or any court in which proceedings are brought on the agreement, may, if in its opinion the tenant is not adequately recompensed under the agreement for his rights under Chapter II, set aside or vary the agreement and give such other relief as appears to it to be just having regard to the situation and conduct of the parties.

(4) Where a tenant has the right to acquire a new lease under Chapter II, there may with the approval of the court be granted to him in satisfaction of that right a new lease on such terms as may be approved by the court, which may include terms excluding or modifying—

(a) any entitlement to participate in the making of a claim to exercise the right to collective enfranchisement under Chapter I, or

(b) any right to acquire a further lease under Chapter II.

(5) Subject to the provisions specified in subsection (6) and to subsection (7), a lease may be granted by virtue of subsection (4), and shall if so granted be binding on persons entitled to any interest in or charge on the landlord's estate—

(a) despite the fact that, apart from this subsection, it would not be authorised against any such person, and

(b) despite any statutory or other restrictions on the landlord's powers of leasing.

(6) The provisions referred to in subsection (5) are—

(a) section 36 of the Charities Act 1993 (restrictions on disposition of charity land); and

(b) paragraph 8(2)(c) of Schedule 2 to this Act.

(7) Where the existing lease of the tenant is granted after the commencement of Chapter II and, the grant being subsequent to the creation of a charge on the landlord's estate, the existing lease is not binding on the persons interested in the charge, a lease granted by virtue of subsection (4) shall not be binding on those persons.

(8) Where a lease is granted by virtue of subsection (4), then except in so far as provision is made to the contrary by the terms of the lease, the following provisions shall apply in relation to the lease as they apply in relation to a lease granted under section 56, namely—

 (a) section 58(3), (5) and (6);
 (b) section 59(2) to (5); and
 (c) section 61 and Schedule 14;
and subsections (5) to (7) of section 56 shall apply in relation to the lease as
they apply in relation to a lease granted under that section.

DEFINITIONS
 "court": s.101(1).
 "lease": s.101(1).

GENERAL NOTE
  This section vitiates agreements excluding or modifying the rights granted by Chap. I and
Chap. II. The provisions are complex and will inevitably lead to litigation as landlords attempt
to pick their way through them to their advantage. The question arises whether this section
applies to agreements made before the Act comes into force. The retrospective effect of
housing legislation has been before the court a number of times. In *Harrison* v. *Hammersmith
and Fulham London Borough*; *Haringey London Borough* v. *Mosner*; *Watson* v. *Hackney
London Borough*; *sub nom. Hammersmith and Fulham London Borough* [1981] 1 W.L.R. 650
the authorities were considered although no principle of general application can be found in it
or the cases referred to. So far as the present Act is concerned it undoubtedly applies to lessees
whenever granted. The plain meaning of s.93 is that its provisions apply to any lease to which
the Act applies. This straightforward view is re-inforced by subs. (7) which clearly envisages the
section applying in different ways to leases granted before and after the commencement of the
Act, *ipso facto* the section applies to tenancies granted before the Act.

Subs. (1)
  Difficult issues will arise here, first is the application of this subsection to agreements
between the tenants themselves. They may make an agreement excluding or limiting the right
of one tenant to participate. That appears clearly void under subs. (1)(a)(i). They may (for
example where two tenants are divorcing) make an agreement sharing compensation under
s.61. That appears clearly not void as it distributes the right to compensation but does not
modify it. Suppose there are perquisites attached to being a tenant of Lord "A" or the Duke of
"O", such as the right to shoot in his coverts or join his sports and recreation club—is losing
these on enfranchisement a "disability" within subs. (1)(c)?

Subs. (2)(a)
  The purpose of this is to permit the landlord and tenants to come to any reasonable bargain
they wish as to the terms of an acquisition or a new lease. Despite the clear wording of subs.
(2)(1)(a), it must be subject to the general purpose of subs. (1) invalidating agreements which
substantially take away the tenants' rights. Thus, an agreement that if the tenant commences
the Chap. I or Chap. II process it will instead purchase an interest superior to the existing lease
is void under subs. (1) and not valid under subs. (2)(a).

Subs. (2)(c)
  The right to compensation under s.61 accrues when an order is made under that section
because it is then that compensation becomes payable (see s.61(4)).

Subs. (3)
  This subsection gives a tenant who had the right to an individual extended lease the right to
have a bargain made with the landlord reopened in the court in certain circumstances. The
concept of the tenant being "adequately recompensed" is not explained. If the case is one where
compensation under s.61 would have been paid, then, it will prima facie be the compensation so
payable. In other cases it will be the market value of the rights forgone.

Subs. (4)
  It is hard to see any justification for the inclusion of this subsection or for a tenant agreeing to
the concessions it involves. Where it is applied, the new lease may exclude the right to join in a
future collective enfranchisement or the right to a further individual extended lease. The
tenant's agreement is not in fact needed to an order under this subsection.

Subss. (5)–(7)
  Where a lease is granted under subs. (4), it will bind the landlord's estate and interests therein
if the existing lease was granted before the date of commencement of this Chapter.

Crown land

94.—(1) Subject to subsection (2), Chapters I and II shall apply to a lease from the Crown if (and only if) there has ceased to be a Crown interest in the land subject to it.

(2) Where a tenant under a lease from the Crown would, but for the existence of any Crown interest, be entitled to acquire a new lease under Chapter II, then if—

(a) that Crown interest is superior to the interest of the person who for the purposes of Chapter II is the landlord in relation to the lease, and

(b) either—

(i) that landlord is entitled to grant such a new lease without the concurrence of the appropriate authority, or

(ii) the appropriate authority notifies that landlord that, as regards any Crown interest affected, the authority will concur in granting such a new lease,

subsection (1) shall apply as if there had ceased to be any Crown interest in the land subject to the lease, and Chapter II shall apply accordingly.

(3) The restriction imposed by section 3(2) of the Crown Estate Act 1961 (general provisions as to management) on the term for which a lease may be granted by the Crown Estate Commissioners shall not apply where—

(a) the lease is granted by way of renewal of a long lease at a low rent, and

(b) it appears to the Crown Estate Commissioners that, but for the existence of any Crown interest, there would be a right to acquire a new lease under Chapter II of this Part of this Act.

(4) Where, in the case of land belonging—

(a) to Her Majesty in right of the Duchy of Lancaster, or

(b) to the Duchy of Cornwall,

it appears to the appropriate authority that a tenant under a long lease at a low rent would, but for the existence of any Crown interest, be entitled to acquire a new lease under Chapter II, then a lease corresponding to that to which the tenant would be so entitled may be granted to take effect wholly or partly out of the Crown interest by the same person and with the same formalities as in the case of any other lease of such land.

(5) In the case of land belonging to the Duchy of Cornwall, the purposes authorised by section 8 of the Duchy of Cornwall Management Act 1863 for the advancement of parts of such gross sums as are there mentioned shall include the payment to tenants under leases from the Crown of sums corresponding to those which, but for the existence of any Crown interest, would be payable by way of compensation under section 61 above.

(6) The appropriate authority in relation to any area occupied under leases from the Crown may make an application for the approval under section 70 of a scheme for that area which is designed to secure that, in the event of tenants under those leases acquiring freehold interests in such circumstances as are mentioned in subsection (7) below, the authority will—

(a) retain powers of management in respect of the premises in which any such freehold interests are acquired, and

(b) have rights against any such premises in respect of the benefits arising from the exercise elsewhere of the authority's powers of management.

(7) The circumstances mentioned in subsection (6) are circumstances in which, but for the existence of any Crown interest, the tenants acquiring any such freehold interests would be entitled to acquire them as mentioned in section 69(1)(a) or (b).

(8) Subject to any necessary modifications—

(a) subsections (2) to (7) of section 69 shall apply in relation to any such scheme as is mentioned in subsection (6) above as they apply in relation to an estate management scheme; and

(b) section 70 shall apply in relation to the approval of such a scheme as it applies in relation to the approval of a scheme as an estate management scheme.

(9) Subsection (10) applies where—

(a) any tenants under leases from the Crown are proceeding with a view to acquiring the freehold of any premises in circumstances in which, but for the existence of any Crown interest, they would be entitled to acquire the freehold under Chapter I, or

(b) any tenant under a lease from the Crown is proceeding with a view to acquiring a new lease of his flat in circumstances in which, but for the existence of any Crown interest, he would be entitled to acquire such a lease under Chapter II.

(10) Where—

(a) this subsection applies in accordance with subsection (9), and

(b) any question arises in connection with the acquisition of the freehold of those premises or any such new lease which is such that, if the tenants or tenant were proceeding as mentioned in that subsection in pursuance of a claim made under Chapter I or (as the case may be) Chapter II, a leasehold valuation tribunal would have jurisdiction to determine it in proceedings under that Chapter, and

(c) it is agreed between—

(i) the appropriate authority and the tenants or tenant, and

(ii) all other persons (if any) whose interests would fall to be represented in proceedings brought under that Chapter for the determination of that question by a leasehold valuation tribunal,

that that question should be determined by such a tribunal,

a leasehold valuation tribunal shall have jurisdiction to determine that question; and references in this subsection to a leasehold valuation tribunal are to such a tribunal constituted for the purposes of section 91.

(11) For the purposes of this section "lease from the Crown" means a lease of land in which there is, or has during the subsistence of the lease been, a Crown interest superior to the lease; and "Crown interest" and "the appropriate authority" in relation to a Crown interest mean respectively—

(a) an interest comprised in the Crown Estate, and the Crown Estate Commissioners;

(b) an interest belonging to Her Majesty in right of the Duchy of Lancaster, and the Chancellor of the Duchy;

(c) an interest belonging to the Duchy of Cornwall, and such person as the Duke of Cornwall or the possessor for the time being of the Duchy appoints;

(d) any other interest belonging to a government department or held on behalf of Her Majesty for the purposes of a government department, and the Minister in charge of that department.

(12) For the purposes of this section "long lease at a low rent" shall be construed in accordance with sections 7 and 8.

DEFINITIONS

"appropriate authority": subs. (11).
"Crown interest": subs. (11).
"interest": s.101(1).
"lease": s.101(1).
"lease from the Crown": subs. (11).
"long lease at low rent": subs. (11).

GENERAL NOTE

The provisions in Chap. I and Chap. II apply to Crown land as follows: (i) if there is currently a reversionary interest which is vested in the Crown then there is no right to compulsory enfranchisement under Chap. I; (ii) if the lease was granted by the Crown but there is no longer any lease vested in the Crown then both Chaps. I and II may apply if the other conditions are satisfied; (iii) if there is presently a superior interest held by the Crown then the individual right to an extended lease may be exercised if the Crown's concurrence is not necessary, that is, because the extended lease can be granted out of a superior interest not held by the Crown. Alternatively, the individual right to an extended lease can be exercised with the concurrence of the Crown. The extended definition of Crown interest given in subs. (11) should be noted.

Saving for National Trust

95. Chapters I and II shall not prejudice the operation of section 21 of the National Trust Act 1907, and accordingly there shall be no right under Chapter I or II to acquire any interest in or new lease of any property if an interest in the property is under that section vested inalienably in the National Trust for Places of Historic Interest or Natural Beauty.

DEFINITIONS
  "interest": s.101(1).
  "lease": s.101(1).

GENERAL NOTE
  This section applies if any interest in the property or any part of it is vested in the National Trust under s.21 of the National Trust Act 1907. This may not always be obvious to a tenant and is not revealed by any of the standard conveyancing searches and enquiries. Accordingly, in very rare cases, money may be wasted preparing a claim before this obstacle becomes clear.

Property within cathedral precinct

96. There shall be no right under Chapter I or II to acquire any interest in or lease of any property which for the purposes of the Care of Cathedrals Measure 1990 is within the precinct of a cathedral church.

DEFINITIONS
  "interest": s.101(1).
  "lease": s.101(1).

GENERAL NOTE
  Land within the precinct of a cathedral is excluded both from the collective right to enfranchisement and the individual right to an excluded lease. The Care of Cathedrals Measure defines the precinct of a cathedral by reference to the plan kept by the Cathedrals Fabric Commission for England (see ss.20 and 13). Its address is 83 London Wall, London EC2M 5NA. Tel: 071-638 0971.

Registration of notices, applications and orders under Chapters I and II

97.—(1) No lease shall be registrable under the Land Charges Act 1972 or be taken to be an estate contract within the meaning of that Act by reason of any rights or obligations of the tenant or landlord which may arise under Chapter I or II, and any right of a tenant arising from a notice given under section 13 or 42 shall not be an overriding interest within the meaning of the Land Registration Act 1925; but a notice given under section 13 or 42 shall be registrable under the Land Charges Act 1972, or may be the subject of a notice or caution under the Land Registration Act 1925, as if it were an estate contract.

(2) The Land Charges Act 1972 and the Land Registration Act 1925—

(a) shall apply in relation to an order made under section 26(1) or 50(1) as they apply in relation to an order affecting land which is made by the court for the purpose of enforcing a judgment or recognisance; and

(b) shall apply in relation to an application for such an order as they apply in relation to other pending land actions.

(3) The persons applying for such an order in respect of any premises shall be treated for the purposes of section 57 of the Land Registration Act 1925 (inhibitions) as persons interested in relation to any registered land containing the whole or part of those premises.

DEFINITIONS
    "court": s.101(1).
    "interest": s.101(1).
    "lease": s.101(1).

GENERAL NOTE
    The provisions of this section deal with the application of the Land Charges Act 1972 and the Land Registration Act 1925. Though it is not stated in the Act, both collective enfranchisement and the grant of an extended lease will lead to compulsory registration if the land is unregistered land.

Subs. (1)
    This provides that the initial notice is to be registered as if it were an estate contract. That is as a Class C IV land charge under the Land Charges Act 1972 or a notice or caution under the Land Registration Act 1925. The consequence of stating that the tenant's rights under a notice under Chaps. I or II are not overriding interests under s.70 of the Land Registration Act 1925 must be carefully noted. This means they must be protected by an appropriate entry on the register and there is no "fall-back" position of protection by virtue of the fact of occupation (under s.70(1)(g) of the Land Registration Act 1925).

Subs. (2)
    Sections 26 and 50 deal with applications for enfranchisement or an extended lease where the landlord cannot be found or his identity ascertained. The open land register will make this a receding problem but in unregistered land cases registration in the Land Charges Register may be impossible because registration must be against the name of the estate owner.

Subs. (3)
    The power to register an inhibition under s.57 of the Land Registration Act 1925 is exercised by the court or the registrar. An applicant may apply to the registrar or the court. In this case the application will be made to the court as part of the proceedings under s.26 or s.50. Although applications for an inhibition have been formerly in the High Court they will be made to the county court (s.90).

Power to prescribe procedure under Chapters I and II

98.—(1) Where a claim to exercise the right to collective enfranchisement under Chapter I is made by the giving of a notice under section 13, or a claim to exercise the right to acquire a new lease under Chapter II is made by the giving of a notice under section 42, then except as otherwise provided by Chapter I or (as the case may be) Chapter II—
(a) the procedure for giving effect to the notice, and
(b) the rights and obligations of all parties in relation to the investigation of title and other matters arising in giving effect to the notice,
shall be such as may be prescribed by regulations made by the Secretary of State and, subject to or in the absence of provision made by any such regulations, shall be as nearly as may be the same as in the case of a contract of sale or leasing freely negotiated between the parties.
(2) Regulations under this section may, in particular, make provision—
(a) for a person to be discharged from performing any obligations arising out of a notice under section 13 or 42 by reason of the default or delay of some other person;
(b) for the payment of a deposit—
        (i) by a nominee purchaser (within the meaning of Chapter I) on exchange of contracts, or
        (ii) by a tenant who has given a notice under section 42; and
(c) with respect to following matters, namely—
        (i) the person with whom any such deposit is to be lodged and the capacity in which any such person is to hold it, and
        (ii) the circumstances in which the whole or part of any such deposit is to be returned or forfeited.

DEFINITIONS
    "lease": s.101(1).

This section authorises the Secretary of State to prescribe appropriate conveyancing procedures by Statutory Instrument. The lacunae in these are to be filled in by the parties following routine conveyancing procedures. See the Leasehold Reform (Collective Enfranchisement and Lease Renewal) Regulations. These regulations are set out as Appendix 1 below.

Notices

99.—(1) Any notice required or authorised to be given under this Part—

(a) shall be in writing; and

(b) may be sent by post.

(2) Where in accordance with Chapter I or II an address in England and Wales is specified as an address at which notices may be given to any person or persons under that Chapter—

(a) any notice required or authorised to be given to that person or those persons under that Chapter may (without prejudice to the operation of subsection (3)) be given to him or them at the address so specified; but

(b) if a new address in England and Wales is so specified in substitution for that address by the giving of a notice to that effect, any notice so required or authorised to be given may be given to him or them at that new address instead.

(3) Where a tenant is required or authorised to give any notice under Chapter I or II to a person who—

(a) is the tenant's immediate landlord, and

(b) is such a landlord in respect of premises to which Part VI of the Landlord and Tenant Act 1987 (information to be furnished to tenants) applies,

the tenant may, unless he has been subsequently notified by the landlord of a different address in England and Wales for the purposes of this section, give the notice to the landlord—

(i) at the address last furnished to the tenant as the landlord's address for service in accordance with section 48 of that Act (notification of address for service of notices on landlord); or

(ii) if no such address has been furnished, at the address last furnished to the tenant as the landlord's address in accordance with section 47 of that Act (landlord's name and address to be contained in demands for rent).

(4) Subsections (2) and (3) apply to notices in proceedings under Chapter I or II as they apply to notices required or authorised to be given under that Chapter.

(5) Any notice which is given under Chapter I or II by any tenants or tenant must—

(a) if it is a notice given under section 13 or 42, be signed by each of the tenants, or (as the case may be) by the tenant, by whom it is given; and

(b) in any other case, be signed by or on behalf of each of the tenants, or (as the case may be) by or on behalf of the tenant, by whom it is given.

(6) The Secretary of State may by regulations prescribe—

(a) the form of any notice required or authorised to be given under this Part; and

(b) the particulars which any such notice must contain (whether in addition to, or in substitution for, any particulars required by virtue of any provision of this Part).

Subs. (5)

The provisions for signature by tenants are unduly burdensome. Sections 13 and 42 notices are to be signed by all the tenants who give the notice and this must be in person. Other notices can be signed by or on behalf of each tenant and one or a small number of persons can be given a general authority to do that.

Subs. (6)

It is not planned by the Department of the Environment for there to be a multiplicity of prescribed notices, although the Act itself is complex the sections stating the contents of different notices are clear and can be easily followed.

Orders and regulations

100.—(1) Any power of the Secretary of State to make orders or regulations under this Part—

(a) may be so exercised as to make different provision for different cases or descriptions of cases, including different provision for different areas; and

(b) includes power to make such procedural, incidental, supplementary and transitional provision as may appear to the Secretary of State necessary or expedient.

(2) Any power of the Secretary of State to make orders or regulations under this Part shall be exercisable by statutory instrument which (except in the case of regulations making only such provision as is mentioned in section 99(6) shall be subject to annulment in pursuance of a resolution of either House of Parliament.

General interpretation of Part I

101.—(1) In this Part—

"business lease" means a tenancy to which Part II of the Landlord and Tenant Act 1954 applies;

"common parts", in relation to any building or part of a building, includes the structure and exterior of that building or part and any common facilities within it;

"the court" (unless the context otherwise requires) means, by virtue of section 90(1), a county court;

"disposal" means a disposal whether by the creation or the transfer of an interest, and includes the surrender of a lease and the grant of an option or right of pre-emption, and "acquisition" shall be construed accordingly (as shall expressions related to either of these expressions);

"dwelling" means any building or part of a building occupied or intended to be occupied as a separate dwelling;

"flat" means a separate set of premises (whether or not on the same floor)—

(a) which forms part of a building, and

(b) which is constructed or adapted for use for the purposes of a dwelling, and

(c) either the whole or a material part of which lies above or below some other part of the building;

"interest" includes estate;

"lease" and "tenancy", and related expressions, shall be construed in accordance with subsection (2);

"rent assessment committee" means a rent assessment committee constituted under Schedule 10 to the Rent Act 1977;

"the term date", in relation to a lease granted for a term of years certain, means (subject to subsection (6)) the date of expiry of that term, and, in relation to a tenancy to which any of the provisions of section 102 applies, shall be construed in accordance with those provisions.

(2) In this Part "lease" and "tenancy" have the same meaning, and both expressions include (where the context so permits)—

(a) a sub-lease or sub-tenancy, and

(b) an agreement for a lease or tenancy (or for a sub-lease or sub-tenancy),

but do not include a tenancy at will or at sufferance; and the expressions "landlord" and "tenant", and references to letting, to the grant of a lease or to covenants or the terms of a lease, shall be construed accordingly.

(3) In this Part any reference (however expressed) to the lease held by a qualifying tenant of a flat is a reference to a lease held by him under which the demised premises consist of or include the flat (whether with or without one or more other flats).

(4) Where two or more persons jointly constitute either the landlord or the tenant or qualifying tenant in relation to a lease of a flat, any reference in this Part to the landlord or to the tenant or qualifying tenant is (unless the context otherwise requires) a reference to both or all of the persons who jointly constitute the landlord or the tenant or qualifying tenant, as the case may require.

(5) Any reference in this Part to the date of the commencement of a lease is a reference to the date of the commencement of the term of the lease.

(6) In the case of a lease which derives (in accordance with section 7(6)) from more than one separate leases, references in this Part to the date of the commencement of the lease or to the term date shall, if the terms of the separate leases commenced at different dates or those leases have different term dates, have effect as references to the date of the commencement, or (as the case may be) to the term date, of the lease comprising the flat in question (or the earliest date of commencement or earliest term date of the leases comprising it).

(7) For the purposes of this Part property is let with other property if the properties are let either under the same lease or under leases which, in accordance with section 7(6), are treated as a single lease.

(8) For the purposes of this Part any lease which is reversionary on another lease shall be treated as if it were a concurrent lease intermediate between that other lease and any interest superior to that other lease.

(9) For the purposes of this Part an order of a court or a decision of a leasehold valuation tribunal is to be treated as becoming final—

(a) if not appealed against, on the expiry of the time for bringing an appeal; or

(b) if appealed against and not set aside in consequence of the appeal, at the time when the appeal and any further appeal is disposed of—

(i) by the determination of it and the expiry of the time for bringing a further appeal (if any), or

(ii) by its being abandoned or otherwise ceasing to have effect.

GENERAL NOTE

Subs. (5)

Comment is made on this in the note on s.8(2).

Subs. (8)

Woodfall, 1–0611 defines a concurrent lease as one granted for a term which is to commence before the expiration or other determination of a previous lease of the same premises to another person. The purpose of subs. (8), thus, appears simply to be to state that any reversionary lease, in calculating its term, is regarded as a concurrent lease so that its term starts from the time limited for its commencement and not from the expiry date of the lease on which it is expectant. This is important for ascertaining its value.

Term date and other matters relating to periodical tenancies

102.—(1) Where either of the following provisions (which relate to continuation tenancies) applies to a tenancy, namely—

(a) section 19(2) of the Landlord and Tenant Act 1954 ("the 1954 Act"), or

(b) paragraph 16(2) of Schedule 10 to the Local Government and Housing Act 1989 ("the 1989 Act"),

the tenancy shall be treated for the relevant purposes of this Part as granted to expire—

(i) on the date which is the term date for the purposes of the 1954 Act (namely, the first date after the commencement of the 1954 Act on which, apart from the 1954 Act, the tenancy could have been brought to an end by a notice to quit given by the landlord under the tenancy), or

(ii) on the date which is the term date for the purposes of Schedule 10 to the 1989 Act (namely, the first date after the commencement of Schedule 10 to the 1989 Act on which, apart from that Schedule, the tenancy could have been brought to an end by such a notice to quit),

as the case may be.

(2) Subject to subsection (1), where under section 7(3) a tenancy created or arising as a tenancy from year to year or other periodical tenancy is to be treated as a long lease, then for the relevant purposes of this Part, the term date of that tenancy shall be taken to be the date (if any) on which the tenancy is to terminate by virtue of a notice to quit given by the landlord under the tenancy before the relevant date for those purposes, or else the earliest date on which it could as at that date (in accordance with its terms and apart from any enactment) be brought to an end by such a notice to quit.

(3) Subject to subsection (1), in the case of a tenancy granted to continue as a periodical tenancy after the expiry of a term of years certain, or to continue as a periodical tenancy if not terminated at the expiry of such a term, any question whether the tenancy is at any time to be treated for the relevant purposes of this Part as a long lease, and (if so) with what term date, shall be determined as it would be if there had been two tenancies, as follows—

(a) one granted to expire at the earliest time (at or after the expiry of that term of years certain) at which the tenancy could (in accordance with its terms and apart from any enactment) be brought to an end by a notice to quit given by the landlord under the tenancy; and

(b) the other granted to commence at the expiry of the first (and not being one to which subsection (1) applies).

(4) In this section "the relevant purposes of this Part" means the purposes of Chapter I or, to the extent that section 7 has effect for the purposes of Chapter II in accordance with section 39(3), the purposes of that Chapter.

DEFINITIONS
  "lease": s.101(1).
  "relevant purpose of this Part": subs. (4).
  "tenancy": s.101(1).
  "term date": s.101(1).

GENERAL NOTE

Subs. (1)
  The relevance of this assumption of a term date for leases which continue under either the Landlord and Tenant Act 1954 or the Local Government and Housing Act 1989 is for valuation purposes. Section 19(2) of the 1954 Act and para. 16(2) of Sched. 10 of the 1989 Act both apply to tenancies from year-to-year; ordinarily such a tenancy may be determined by notice at the end of any year of the tenancy (*Doe & Clarke* v. *Smaridge* (1845) 7 Q.B. 957). The length of the notice will be six months. This may be varied by express agreement between the parties in the tenancy agreement.

Subs. (2)
This is similar in its effect to subs. (1) producing a definite hypothetical term date for periodic tenancies treated as long leases.

Subs. (3)
Subsection (1) will apply only if the tenancy is a tenancy from year-to-year. The effect is, thus first see if subs. (1) applies, if it does not, apply the test in s.7 to see if there is a long lease separately during the subsistence of the initial long lease and then during the periodic term. It is likely that during the periodic tenancy there will not be a long lease under s.7.

Application of Part I to Isles of Scilly

103. This Part applies to the Isles of Scilly subject to such exceptions, adaptations and modifications as the Secretary of State may by order direct.

PART II

PUBLIC SECTOR HOUSING

CHAPTER I

ENGLAND AND WALES

Right to buy

GENERAL NOTE
The provisions amending the right to buy (public sector housing) generated considerable heat in Parliament. Despite both this and their complexity they will be of very little impact practically in housing terms, providing probably the clearest illustration (though this is an area of strong competition) of housing policy in the last decade being one of "much legislation, little progress".

Landlord's notice of purchase price and other matters

104. For subsection (5) of section 125 (landlord's notice of purchase price and other matters) of the Housing Act 1985 (in this Chapter referred to as "the 1985 Act") there shall be substituted the following subsection—
     "(5) The notice shall also inform the tenant of—
     (a) the effect of sections 125D and 125E(1) and (4) (tenant's notice of intention, landlord's notice in default and effect of failure to comply),
     (b) his right under section 128 to have the value of the dwelling-house at the relevant time determined or re-determined by the district valuer,
     (c) the effect of section 136(2) (change of tenant after service of notice under section 125),
     (d) the effect of sections 140 and 141(1), (2) and (4) (landlord's notices to complete and effect of failure to comply),
     (e) the effect of the provisions of this Part relating to the right to acquire on rent to mortgage terms, and
     (f) the relevant amount and multipliers for the time being declared by the Secretary of State for the purposes of section 143B."

GENERAL NOTE
This section amends s.125(5) of the Housing Act 1985 so that the landlord's reply to a right to buy notice reflects the amendments of the right to buy made by the following sections.

Tenant's notice of intention etc.

105.—(1) After section 125C of the 1985 Act there shall be inserted the following sections—

"Tenant's notice of intention
     125D.—(1) Where a notice under section 125 has been served on a

secure tenant, he shall within the period specified in subsection (2) either—

(a) serve a written notice on the landlord stating either that he intends to pursue his claim to exercise the right to buy or that he withdraws that claim, or

(b) serve a notice under section 144 claiming to exercise the right to acquire on rent to mortgage terms.

(2) The period for serving a notice under subsection (1) is the period of twelve weeks beginning with whichever of the following is the later—

(a) the service of the notice under section 125, and

(b) where the tenant exercises his right to have the value of the dwelling-house determined or re-determined by the district valuer, the service of the notice under section 128(5) stating the effect of the determination or re-determination.

Landlord's notice in default

125E.—(1) The landlord may, at any time after the end of the period specified in section 125D(2) or, as the case may require, section 136(2), serve on the tenant a written notice—

(a) requiring him, if he has failed to serve the notice required by section 125D(1), to serve that notice within 28 days, and

(b) informing him of the effect of this subsection and subsection (4).

(2) At any time before the end of the period mentioned in subsection (1)(a) (or that period as previously extended) the landlord may by written notice served on the tenant extend it (or further extend it).

(3) If at any time before the end of that period (or that period as extended under subsection (2)) the circumstances are such that it would not be reasonable to expect the tenant to comply with a notice under this section, that period (or that period as so extended) shall by virtue of this subsection be extended (or further extended) until 28 days after the time when those circumstances no longer obtain.

(4) If the tenant does not comply with a notice under this section, the notice claiming to exercise the right to buy shall be deemed to be withdrawn at the end of that period (or, as the case may require, that period as extended under subsection (2) or (3))."

(2) For subsections (2) to (5) of section 136 of the 1985 Act (change of tenant after notice claiming to exercise the right to buy) there shall be substituted the following subsection—

"(2) If a notice under section 125 (landlord's notice of purchase price and other matters) has been served on the former tenant, then, whether or not the former tenant has served a notice under subsection (1) of section 125D (tenant's notice of intention), the new tenant shall serve a notice under that subsection within the period of twelve weeks beginning with whichever of the following is the later—

(a) his becoming the secure tenant, and

(b) where the right to have the value of the dwelling-house determined or re-determined by the district valuer is or has been exercised by him or the former tenant, the service of the notice under section 128(5) stating the effect of the determination or re-determination."

GENERAL NOTE

This section is consequential on the changes made to the right to buy in the sections which follow. It amends the content of the tenant's notice and the landlord's notice in default to reflect the abolition of existing rights contained in s.96 and the creation of the new right to acquire on rent or mortgage terms contained in s.97.

Exceptions to the right to buy

106.—(1) In paragraph 10(1) (groups of dwelling-houses for persons of pensionable age) of Schedule 5 to the 1985 Act (exceptions to the right to buy)—

(a) for the words "persons of pensionable age", in the first place where they occur, there shall be substituted the words "elderly persons"; and

(b) for those words, in the second place where they occur, there shall be substituted the words "persons aged 60 or more".

(2) For paragraph 11 (individual dwelling-houses for persons of pensionable age) of that Schedule there shall be substituted the following paragraph—

"11.—(1) The right to buy does not arise if the dwelling-house—

(a) is particularly suitable, having regard to its location, size, design, heating system and other features, for occupation by elderly persons, and

(b) was let to the tenant or a predecessor in title of his for occupation by a person who was aged 60 or more (whether the tenant or predecessor or another person).

(2) In determining whether a dwelling is particularly suitable, no regard shall be had to the presence of any feature provided by the tenant or a predecessor in title of his.

(3) Notwithstanding anything in section 181 (jurisdiction of county court), any question arising under this paragraph shall be determined as follows.

(4) If an application for the purpose is made by the tenant to the Secretary of State before the end of the period of 56 days beginning with the service of the landlord's notice under section 124, the question shall be determined by the Secretary of State.

(5) If no such application is so made, the question shall be deemed to have been determined in favour of the landlord.

(6) This paragraph does not apply unless the dwelling-house concerned was first let before 1st January 1990."

(3) Subsections (1) and (2) do not apply in any case where the tenant's notice claiming to exercise the right to buy was served before the day on which this section comes into force.

(4) For the purposes of subsection (3), no account shall be taken of any steps taken under section 177 of the 1985 Act (amendment or withdrawal and re-service of notice to correct mistakes).

GENERAL NOTE

Subs. (1)

This amendment to Sched. 5 of the Housing Act 1985 removes discrimination between sexes in this exception to the right to buy. The exception now applies to accommodation for elderly persons provided for persons aged 60 or more.

Subs. (2)

This has the same purpose as subs. (1) in dealing with the exception for individual dwelling houses for elderly persons from the right to buy.

Abolition of certain ancillary rights

Abolition of right to a mortgage, right to defer completion and right to be granted a shared ownership lease

107. The following rights ancillary to the right to buy are hereby abolished, namely—

(a) the right to a mortgage conferred by sections 132 to 135 of the 1985 Act;

(b) the right to defer completion conferred by section 142 of that Act; and
(c) the right to be granted a shared ownership lease conferred by sections 143 to 151 of that Act.

GENERAL NOTE
This section removes the right to a mortgage, the right to defer completion and the right to a shared ownership lease. There was much discussion in the passage of the Bill of the significance of these rights but in truth they have been little used and will be little mourned. The relevant consequential repeals are found in Sched. 21. Sections 143 to 147 remain unrepealed because of their relevance to the few existing shared ownership leases.

Right to acquire on rent to mortgage terms

Right to acquire on rent to mortgage terms

108. For section 143 of the 1985 Act there shall be substituted the following sections—

"Right to acquire on rent to mortgage terms

Right to acquire on rent to mortgage terms

143.—(1) Subject to subsection (2) and sections 143A and 143B, where—
(a) a secure tenant has claimed to exercise the right to buy, and
(b) his right to buy has been established and his notice claiming to exercise it remains in force,
he also has the right to acquire on rent to mortgage terms in accordance with the following provisions of this Part.

(2) The right to acquire on rent to mortgage terms cannot be exercised if the exercise of the right to buy is precluded by section 121 (circumstances in which right to buy cannot be exercised).

(3) Where the right to buy belongs to two or more persons jointly, the right to acquire on rent to mortgage terms also belongs to them jointly.

Right excluded by entitlement to housing benefit

143A.—(1) The right to acquire on rent to mortgage terms cannot be exercised if—
(a) it has been determined that the tenant is or was entitled to housing benefit in respect of any part of the relevant period, or
(b) a claim for housing benefit in respect of any part of that period has been made (or is treated as having been made) by or on behalf of the tenant and has not been determined or withdrawn.

(2) In this section 'the relevant period' means the period—
(a) beginning twelve months before the day on which the tenant claims to exercise the right to acquire on rent to mortgage terms, and
(b) ending with the day on which the conveyance or grant is executed in pursuance of that right.

Right excluded if minimum initial payment exceeds maximum initial payment

143B.—(1) The right to acquire on rent to mortgage terms cannot be exercised if the minimum initial payment in respect of the dwelling-house exceeds the maximum initial payment in respect of it.

(2) The maximum initial payment in respect of a dwelling-house is 80 per cent. of the price which would be payable if the tenant were exercising the right to buy.

(3) Where, in the case of a dwelling-house which is a house, the

weekly rent at the relevant time did not exceed the relevant amount, the minimum initial payment shall be determined by the formula—

$$P = R \times M$$

where—

 P = the minimum initial payment;

 R = the amount of the weekly rent at the relevant time;

 M = the multiplier which at that time was for the time being declared by the Secretary of State for the purposes of this subsection.

(4) Where, in the case of a dwelling-house which is a house, the weekly rent at the relevant time exceeded the relevant amount, the minimum initial payment shall be determined by the formula—

$$P = Q + (E \times M)$$

where—

 P = the minimum initial payment;

 Q = the qualifying maximum for the year of assessment which included the relevant time;

 E = the amount by which the weekly rent at that time exceeded the relevant amount;

 M = the multiplier which at that time was for the time being declared by the Secretary of State for the purposes of this subsection.

(5) The minimum initial payment in respect of a dwelling-house which is a flat 80 per cent. of the amount which would be the minimum initial payment in respect of the dwelling-house if it were a house.

(6) The relevant amount and multipliers for the time being declared for the purposes of this section shall be such that, in the case of a dwelling-house which is a house, they will produce a minimum initial payment equal to the capital sum which, in the opinion of the Secretary of State, could be raised on a 25 year repayment mortgage in the case of which the net amount of the monthly mortgage payments was equal to the rent at the relevant time calculated on a monthly basis.

(7) For the purposes of subsection (6) the Secretary of State shall assume—

(a) that the interest rate applicable throughout the 25 year term were the standard national rate for the time being declared by the Secretary of State under paragraph 2 of Schedule 16 (local authority mortgage interest rates); and

(b) that the monthly mortgage payments represented payments of capital and interest only.

(8) In this section—

'net amount', in relation to monthly mortgage payments, means the amount of such payments after deduction of tax under section 369 of the Income and Corporation Taxes Act 1988 (mortgage interest payable under deduction of tax);

'qualifying maximum' means the qualifying maximum defined in section 367(5) of that Act (limit on relief for interest on certain loans);

'relevant amount' means the amount which at the relevant time was for the time being declared by the Secretary of State for the purposes of this section;

'relevant time' means the time of the service of the landlord's notice under section 146 (landlord's notice admitting or denying right);

'rent' means rent payable under the secure tenancy, but excluding any element which is expressed to be payable for services, repairs, maintenance or insurance or the landlord's costs of management."

DEFINITIONS

"net amount": subs. (8).
"qualifying maximum": subs. (8).
"relevant amount": subs. (8).
"relevant period": subs. (2).
"relevant time": subs. (8).
"rent": subs. (8).

GENERAL NOTE

The right to buy on rent to mortgage terms is given to tenants who have the right to buy and are able to exercise it. Tenants on housing benefit are not entitled to the right to buy on rent to mortgage terms. The essence of the scheme is that a tenant may calculate the share it is able to buy at present rent levels. The tenant may choose to buy this or a larger share. The share it is buying is then raised on mortgage and the landlord's share redeemed on a sale or earlier at the tenant's choice.

Tenant's notice claiming right

109. For sections 144 and 145 of the 1985 Act there shall be substituted the following section—

"Tenant's notice claiming right

144.—(1) A secure tenant claims to exercise the right to acquire on rent to mortgage terms by written notice to that effect served on the landlord.

(2) The notice may be withdrawn at any time by notice in writing served on the landlord.

(3) On the service of a notice under this section, any notice served by the landlord under section 140 or 141 (landlord's notices to complete purchase in pursuance of right to buy) shall be deemed to have been withdrawn; and no such notice may be served by the landlord whilst a notice under this section remains in force.

(4) Where a notice under this section is withdrawn, the tenant may complete the transaction in accordance with the provisions of this Part relating to the right to buy."

GENERAL NOTE

This section provides for the tenant who is claiming the right to acquire on rent to mortgage terms to serve written notice to that effect. A tenant has the right to withdraw such a notice and continue with the right to buy in the normal way but forgoing the right to buy on rent to mortgage terms.

Landlord's notice admitting or denying right

110. For section 146 of the 1985 Act there shall be substituted the following section—

"Landlord's notice admitting or denying right

146.—(1) Where a notice under section 144 (notice claiming to exercise the right to acquire on rent to mortgage terms) has been served by the tenant, the landlord shall, unless the notice is withdrawn, serve on the tenant as soon as practicable a written notice either—

(a) admitting the tenant's right and informing him of the matters mentioned in subsection (2), or

(b) denying it and stating the reasons why, in the opinion of the landlord, the tenant does not have the right to acquire on rent to mortgage terms.

(2) The matters are—

(a) the relevant amount and multipliers for the time being declared by the Secretary of State for the purposes of section 143B;

(b) the amount of the minimum initial payment;

(c) the proportion which that amount bears to the price which would be payable if the tenant exercised the right to buy;

(d) the landlord's share on the assumption that the tenant makes the minimum initial payment;

(e) the amount of the initial discount on that assumption; and

(f) the provisions which, in the landlord's opinion, should be contained in the conveyance or grant and the mortgage required by section 151B (mortgage for securing redemption of landlord's share)."

GENERAL NOTE

Where a tenant serves a notice under the new s.144 of the Housing Act 1985 the landlord under the new s.146 must serve a notice either admitting or denying the tenant's claim. This landlord's notice sets out the terms and consequences of the tenant's exercise of the right to buy on rent to mortgage terms. Tenants would benefit from financial advice before deciding whether to take up this option or not. Since genuinely independent financial advice is unlikely to be available one must wonder how the tenant is going to decide sensibly between the different options.

Tenant's notice of intention etc.

111. After section 146 of the 1985 Act there shall be inserted the following sections—

"Tenant's notice of intention

146A.—(1) Where a notice under section 146 has been served on a secure tenant, he shall within the period specified in subsection (2) serve a written notice on the landlord stating either—

(a) that he intends to pursue his claim to exercise the right to acquire on rent to mortgage terms and the amount of the initial payment which he proposes to make, or

(b) that he withdraws that claim and intends to pursue his claim to exercise the right to buy, or

(c) that he withdraws both of those claims.

(2) The period for serving a notice under subsection (1) is the period of twelve weeks beginning with the service of the notice under section 146.

(3) The amount stated in a notice under subsection (1)(a)—

(a) shall not be less than the minimum initial payment and not more than the maximum initial payment, and

(b) may be varied at any time by notice in writing served on the landlord.

Landlord's notice in default

146B.—(1) The landlord may, at any time after the end of the period specified in section 146A(2), serve on the tenant a written notice—

(a) requiring him, if he has failed to serve the notice required by section 146A(1), to serve that notice within 28 days, and

(b) informing him of the effect of this subsection and subsection (4).

(2) At any time before the end of the period mentioned in subsection (1)(a) (or that period as previously extended) the landlord

may by written notice served on the tenant extend it (or further extend it).

(3) If at any time before the end of that period (or that period as extended under subsection (2)) the circumstances are such that it would not be reasonable to expect the tenant to comply with a notice under this section, that period (or that period as so extended) shall by virtue of this subsection be extended (or further extended) until 28 days after the time when those circumstances no longer obtain.

(4) If the tenant does not comply with a notice under this section the notice claiming to exercise the right to acquire on rent to mortgage terms shall be deemed to be withdrawn at the end of that period (or, as the case may require, that period as extended under subsection (2) or (3))."

GENERAL NOTE
   This section introduces a notice procedure requiring the tenant to make up his mind whether or not he requires the right to acquire on rent to mortgage terms. The new s.146A requires the tenant to inform the landlord of his decision and the new s.146B expects the landlord to chase up the tenant who is slow in making up his mind. Eventually the tenant's right to acquire in rent for mortgage term will be deemed to be withdrawn if the tenant does not serve the required notice (s.146B(4)).

Notice of landlord's share and initial discount

112.—(1) For section 147 of the 1985 Act there shall be substituted the following section—

   "Notice of landlord's share and initial discount
      147.—(1) Where a secure tenant has served—
      (a) a notice under section 146A(1)(a) stating that he intends to pursue his claim to exercise the right to acquire on rent on mortgage terms, and the amount of the initial payment which he proposes to make, or
      (b) a notice under section 146A(3)(b) varying the amount stated in a notice under section 146A(1)(a),
   the landlord shall, as soon as practicable, serve on the tenant a written notice complying with this section.
      (2) The notice shall state—
      (a) the landlord's share on the assumption that the amount of the tenant's initial payment is that stated in the notice under section 146A(1)(a) or, as the case may be, section 146A(3)(b), and
      (b) the amount of the initial discount on that assumption,
   determined in each case in accordance with section 148."

GENERAL NOTE
   This section introduces a new s.147 to the 1985 Housing Act. It requires the landlord to inform the tenant by a further notice of the amount of the landlord's share and initial discount. This is calculated under the new s.148 inserted by s.102 following.

Determination of landlord's share, initial discount etc.

113. For section 148 of the 1985 Act there shall be substituted the following section—

   "Determination of landlord's share initial discount etc.
      148. The landlord's share shall be determined by the formula—

$$S = \frac{P - IP}{P} \times 100$$

the amount of the initial discount shall be determined by the formula—

$$ID = \frac{IP}{P} \times D$$

and the amount of any previous discount which will be recovered by virtue of the transaction shall be determined by the formula—

$$RD = \frac{IP}{P} \times PD$$

where—
    S = the landlord's share expressed as a percentage;
    P = the price which would be payable if the tenant were exercising the right to buy;
   IP = the amount of the tenant's initial payment (but disregarding any reduction in pursuance of section 153B(3));
  ID = the amount of the initial discount;
    D = the amount of the discount which would be applicable if the tenant were exercising the right to buy;
  RD = the amount of any previous discount which will be recovered by virtue of the transaction;
  PD = the amount of any previous discount which would be recovered if the tenant were exercising the right to buy."

GENERAL NOTE
  Despite the formidable looking formula, the new s. 148 of the Housing Act 1985 introduces a straightforward calculation of the landlord's share. The landlord's share is the balance of the full purchase price of the house left after deducting the initial payment and expressed as a percentage of the whole value. The initial discount is the fraction of the discount on the whole price which the initial payment bears to the whole price. The recoverable discount is the same fraction of any previous discount which would be made repayable if tenant exercised the right to buy without exercising the right to acquire on rent to mortgage terms.

Change of landlord after notice claiming right

114. For section 149 of the 1984 Act there shall be substituted the following section—

"Change of landlord after notice claiming right
149.—(1) Where the interest of the landlord in the dwelling-house passes from the landlord to another body after a secure tenant has given a notice claiming to exercise the right to acquire on rent to mortgage terms, all parties shall subject to subsection (2) be in the same position as if the other body—
  (a) had become the landlord before the notice was given, and
  (b) had been given that notice and any further notice given by the tenant to the landlord, and
  (c) had taken all steps which the landlord had taken.
  (2) If the circumstances after the disposal differ in any material respect, as for example, where—
  (a) the interest of the disponee in the dwelling-house after the disposal differs from that of the disponor before the disposal, or
  (b) any of the provisions of Schedule 5 (exceptions to the right to buy) becomes or ceases to be applicable,
all those concerned shall, as soon as practicable after the disposal, take all such steps (whether by way of amending or withdrawing and re-serving any notice or extending any period or otherwise) as may be requisite for the purpose of securing that all parties are, as nearly as

may be, in the same position as they would have been if those
circumstances had obtained before the disposal."

GENERAL NOTE
Local authorities are currently encouraged by the government to disembarrass themselves of
council housing. This section introduces a replacement for s.149 of the Housing Act 1985 which
deals with dispositions by landlords after the right to buy process has begun. The effect where a
tenant has given a notice claiming exercise of the right to buy on rent to mortgage terms is that
the right is within the provisions of Sched. 5 to the 1985 Act—exception to the right to buy. This
does not, however, affect the protected right to buy provisions under the 1985 Act.

Duty of landlord to convey freehold or grant lease

115. For section 150 of the 1985 Act there shall be substituted the following section—

"Duty of landlord to convey freehold or grant lease
150.—(1) Where a secure tenant has claimed to exercise the right
to acquire on rent to mortgage terms and that right has been established, then, as soon as all matters relating to the grant and to
securing the redemption of the landlord's share have been agreed or
determined, the landlord shall make to the tenant—
(a) if the dwelling-house is a house and the landlord owns the
    freehold, a grant of the dwelling-house for an estate in fee
    simple absolute, or
(b) if the landlord does not own the freehold or if the dwelling-
    house is a flat (whether or not the landlord owns the freehold),
    a grant of a lease of the dwelling house,
in accordance with the following provisions of this Part.
(2) If the tenant has failed to pay the rent or any other payment due
from him as a tenant for a period of four weeks after it has been
lawfully demanded from him, the landlord is not bound to comply
with subsection (1) while the whole or part of that payment remains
outstanding.
(3) The duty imposed on the landlord by subsection (1) is enforceable by injunction."

GENERAL NOTE
This section replaces s.150 of the Housing Act 1985 with an obligation to grant the required
freehold or leasehold interest in the right to acquire on rent to mortgage cases.

Terms and effect of conveyance or grant: general

116.—(1) For section 151 of the 1985 Act there shall be substituted the
following section—

"Terms and effect of conveyance or grant: general
151.—(1) A conveyance of the freehold executed in pursuance of
the right to acquire on rent to mortgage terms shall conform with
Parts I and II of Schedule 6; a grant of a lease so executed shall
conform with Parts I and III of that Schedule; and Part IV of that
Schedule applies to such a conveyance or lease as it applies to a
conveyance or lease executed in pursuance of the right to buy.
(2) The secure tenancy comes to an end on the grant to the tenant
of an estate in fee simple, or of a lease, in pursuance of the right to
acquire on rent to mortgage terms; and if there is then a sub-tenancy
section 139 of the Law of Property Act 1925 (effect of extinguishment
of reversion) applies as on a merger or surrender."
(2) In Part III of Schedule 6 to the 1985 Act (terms of lease granted in
pursuance of right to buy or right to acquire on rent to mortgage terms),
after paragraph 16D there shall be inserted the following paragraph—

"16E.—(1) Where a lease of a flat granted in pursuance of the right to acquire on rent to mortgage terms requires the tenant to pay—

(a) service charges in respect of repairs (including works for the making good of structural defects), or

(b) improvement contributions,

his liability in respect of costs incurred at any time before the final payment is made is restricted as follows.

(2) He is not required to pay any more than the amount determined by the formula—

$$M = P \times \frac{100 - S}{100}$$

where—

M = the maximum amount which he is required to pay;

P = the amount which, but for this paragraph, he would be required to pay;

S = the landlord's share at the time expressed as a percentage."

GENERAL NOTE
The forms of a conveyance or lease in right to buy cases are negotiated in accordance with Sched. 6 to the 1985 Act. This section makes amendments appropriate to right to acquire on rent to mortgage cases. A new para. 16 is introduced into Sched. 6. The effect of this is that in such cases the tenant pays a reduced share of the service charge. The amount paid is the same proportion of the service charge as the tenant's share of the house or flat. This simple proposition is again expressed in a daunting looking legislative formula.

Redemption of landlord's share

117.—(1) After section 151 of the 1985 Act there shall be inserted the following section—

"Redemption of landlord's share

151A. Schedule 6A (which makes provision for the redemption of the landlord's share) shall have effect; and a conveyance of the freehold or a grant of a lease executed in pursuance of the right to acquire on rent to mortgage terms shall conform with that Schedule."

(2) After Schedule 6 to the 1985 Act there shall be inserted as Schedule 6A the Schedule set out in Schedule 16 to this Act.

GENERAL NOTE
This section introduces a new s. 151A to the Housing Act 1985. It introduces a new Sched. 6A to that Act which contains the provisions dealing with the redemption of the landlord's share. These contain financial pitfalls for the tenant which are dealt with in the notes on Sched. 16 to this Act (which contains the new Sched. 6A).

Mortgage for securing redemption of landlord's share

118. After section 151A of the 1985 Act there shall be inserted the following section—

"Mortgage for securing redemption of landlord's share

151B.—(1) The liability that may arise under the covenant required by paragraph 1 of Schedule 6A (covenant for the redemption of the landlord's share in the circumstances there mentioned) shall be secured by a mortgage.

(2) Subject to subsections (3) and (4), the mortgage shall have priority immediately after any legal charge securing an amount advanced to the secure tenant by an approved lending institution for the purpose of enabling him to exercise the right to acquire on rent-to mortgage terms.

(3) The following, namely—

(a) any advance which is made otherwise than for the purpose mentioned in subsection (2) and is secured by a legal charge having priority to the mortgage, and

(b) any further advance which is so secured,

shall rank in priority to the mortgage if, and only if, the landlord by written notice served on the institution concerned gives its consent; and the landlord shall so give its consent if the purpose of the advance or further advance is an approved purpose.

(4) The landlord may at any time by written notice served on an approved lending institution postpone the mortgage to any advance or further advance which—

(a) is made to the tenant by that institution, and

(b) is secured by a legal charge not having priority to the mortgage;

and the landlord shall serve such a notice if the purpose of the advance or further advance is an approved purpose.

(5) The approved lending institutions for the purposes of this section are—

the Corporation,

a building society,

a bank,

a trustee savings bank,

an insurance company,

a friendly society,

and any body specified, or of a class or description specified, in an order made under section 156.

(6) The approved purposes for the purposes of this section are—

(a) to enable the tenant to make an interim or final payment,

(b) to enable the tenant to defray, or to defray on his behalf, any of the following—

(i) the cost of any works to the dwelling-house,

(ii) any service charge payable in respect of the dwelling-house for works, whether or not to the dwelling-house, and

(iii) any service charge or other amount payable in respect of the dwelling-house for insurance, whether or not of the dwelling-house, and

(c) to enable the tenant to discharge, or to discharge on his behalf, any of the following—

(i) so much as is still outstanding of any advance or further advance which ranks in priority to the mortgage,

(ii) any arrears of interest on such an advance or further advance, and

(iii) any costs and expenses incurred in enforcing payment of any such interest, or repayment (in whole or in part) of any such advance or further advance.

(7) Where different parts of an advance or further advance are made for different purposes, each of those parts shall be regarded as a separate advance or further advance for the purposes of this section.

(8) The Secretary of State may by order prescribe—

(a) matters for which the deed by which the mortgage is effected must make provision, and

(b) terms which must, or must not, be contained in that deed,

but only in relation to deeds executed after the order comes into force.

(9) The deed by which the mortgage is effected may contain such other provisions as may be—

(a) agreed between the mortgagor and the mortgagee, or

(b) determined by the county court to be reasonably required by the mortgagor or the mortgagee.

(10) An order under this section—

(a) may make different provision with respect to different cases or descriptions of case, including different provision for different areas, and

(b) shall be made by statutory instrument which shall be subject to annulment in pursuance of a resolution of either House of Parliament."

GENERAL NOTE

This section introduces a new s.151B to the Housing Act 1985. Its purpose is to deal with various aspects of the mortgage which secures the redemption of the landlord's share. The tenant may have paid £30,000 for "the tenant's share" secured by a Building Society mortgage. The landlord's share of 40 per cent. must be redeemed on certain events and this is secured by another mortgage. The new s.151B ensures that the Building Society mortgage has priority over the landlord's mortgage providing it is granted by an approved lending institution (subs. (5)) and for the purpose of the right to acquire on rent to mortgage terms. Further advances by the Building Society (or another approved lending institution) will also have priority if the procedures set out in s.151B are followed. These procedures specify the purpose of the further advance (subs. (6)) and how the landlord's consent is to be obtained (subs. (4)). If the advance or further advance is for the purchase or for approved purposes and also for other purposes, then in order to deal with priority it will be treated as more than one loan (subs. (7)). Lending institutions will probably choose to confine secured loans on these properties to loans which qualify for priority over the landlord's mortgage. Section 151B(9) provides for the court to decide the terms of a mortgage in case of dispute.

Landlord's notices to complete

119.—(1) For subsection (3) of section 152 of the 1985 Act (landlord's first notice to complete) there shall be substituted the following section—

"(3) A notice under this section shall not be served earlier than twelve months after the service of the notice under section 146 (landlord's notice admitting or denying right)."

(2) In subsection (5) of that section, for the words "the amount to be left outstanding or advanced on the security of the dwelling-house" there shall be substituted the words "securing the redemption of the landlord's share".

(3) In subsection (4) of section 153 of the 1985 Act (landlord's second notice to complete), for the words "the right to be granted a shared owner-ship lease" there shall be substituted the words "the right to acquire on rent to mortgage terms".

GENERAL NOTE

This section amends ss.152 and 153 of the Housing Act 1985. It amends the process for landlords to "hurry up" lethargic tenants so that they relate to acquisition on rent to mortgage cases.

Repayment of discount on early disposal

120.—(1) For subsection (3) of section 155 of the 1985 Act (repayment of discount on early disposal) there shall be substituted the following subsection—

"(3) In the case of a conveyance or grant in pursuance of the right to acquire on rent to mortgage terms, the covenant shall be to pay to the landlord on demand, if within the period of three years commencing with the making of the initial payment there is a relevant disposal which is not an exempted disposal (but if there is more than one such disposal, then only on the first of them), the discount (if any) to which the tenant was entitled on the making of—

(a) the initial payment,

(b) any interim payment made before the disposal, or

(c) the final payment if so made,
reduced, in each case, by one-third for each complete year which has
elapsed after the making of the initial payment and before the
disposal."
(2) In subsection (3A) of that section, for paragraph (b) there shall be
substituted the following paragraph—
"(b) any reference in subsection (3) (other than paragraph (a) thereof) to the making of the initial payment shall be construed as a
reference to the date which precedes that payment by the period
referred to in paragraph (a) of this subsection."
(3) For subsection (2) of section 156 of the 1985 Act (liability to repay
discount is a charge on the premises) there shall be substituted the following
subsections—
"(2) Subject to subsections (2A) and (2B), the charge has priority as
follows—
(a) if it secures the liability that may arise under the covenant
required by section 155(2), immediately after any legal charge
securing an amount advanced to the secure tenant by an
approved lending institution for the purpose of enabling him to
exercise the right to buy;
(b) if it secures the liability that may arise under the covenant
required by section 155(3), immediately after the mortgage—
(i) which is required by section 151B (mortgage for securing
redemption of landlord's share), and
(ii) which, by virtue of subsection (2) of that section, has
priority immediately after any legal charge securing an amount
advanced to the secure tenant by an approved lending institution
for the purpose of enabling him to exercise the right to acquire on
rent to mortgage terms.
(2A) The following, namely—
(a) any advance which is made otherwise than for the purpose mentioned in paragraph (a) or (b) of subsection (2) and is secured by
a legal charge having priority to the charge taking effect by virtue
of this section, and
(b) any further advance which is so secured,
shall rank in priority to that charge if, and only if, the landlord by
written notice served on the institution concerned gives its consent; and
the landlord shall so give its consent if the purpose of the advance or
further advance is an approved purpose.
(2B) The landlord may at any time by written notice served on an
approved lending institution postpone the charge taking effect by virtue
of this section to any advance or further advance which—
(a) is made to the tenant by that institution, and
(b) is secured by a legal charge not having priority to that charge;
and the landlord shall serve such a notice if the purpose of the advance
or further advance is an approved purpose."
(4) After subsection (4) of that section there shall be inserted the following subsections—
"(4A) The approved purposes for the purposes of this section are—
(a) to enable the tenant to make an interim or final payment,
(b) to enable the tenant to defray, or to defray on his behalf, any of
the following—
(i) the cost of any works to the dwelling-house,
(ii) any service charge payable in respect of the dwelling-
house for works, whether or not to the dwelling-house, and

(iii) any service charge or other amount payable in respect of the dwelling-house for insurance, whether or not of the dwelling-house, and

(c) to enable the tenant to discharge, or to discharge on his behalf, any of the following—

(i) so much as is still outstanding of any advance or further advance which ranks in priority to the charge taking effect by virtue of this section,

(ii) any arrears of interest on such an advance or further advance, and

(iii) any costs and expenses incurred in enforcing payment of any such interest, or repayment (in whole or in part) of any such advance or further advance.

(4B) Where different parts of an advance or further advance are made for different purposes, each of those parts shall be regarded as a separate advance or further advance for the purposes of this section."

GENERAL NOTE

This section amends ss.155 and 156 of the Housing Act 1985 to apply those sections to repayment of discount on early disposal in cases where the tenant has exercised the right to acquire on rent to mortgage terms. It applies the existing provision for repayment of discount so that it applies to the discount of which the tenant has actually received the benefit in these cases.

Other rights of secure tenants

Right to have repairs carried out

121. For section 96 of the 1985 Act there shall be substituted the following section—

"Right to have repairs carried out

96.—(1) The Secretary of State may make regulations for entitling secure tenants whose landlords are local housing authorities, subject to and in accordance with the regulations, to have qualifying repairs carried out, at their landlords' expense, to the dwelling-houses of which they are such tenants.

(2) The regulations may make all or any of the following provisions, namely—

(a) provision that, where a secure tenant makes an application to his landlord for a qualifying repair to be carried out, the landlord shall issue a repair notice—

(i) specifying the nature of the repair, the listed contractor by whom the repair is to be carried out and the last day of any prescribed period; and

(ii) containing such other particulars as may be prescribed;

(b) provision that, if the contractor specified in a repair notice fails to carry out the repair within a prescribed period, the landlord shall issue a further repair notice specifying such other listed contractor as the tenant may require; and

(c) provision that, if the contractor specified in a repair notice fails to carry out the repair within a prescribed period, the landlord shall pay to the tenant such sum by way of compensation as may be determined by or under the regulations.

(3) The regulations may also make such procedural, incidental, supplementary and transitional provisions as may appear to the Secretary of State necessary or expedient, and may in particular—

(a) require a landlord to take such steps as may be prescribed to make its secure tenants aware of the provisions of the regulations;

    (b) require a landlord to maintain a list of contractors who are prepared to carry out repairs for which it is responsible under the regulations;

    (c) provide that, where a landlord issues a repair notice, it shall give to the tenant a copy of the notice and the prescribed particulars of at least two other listed contractors who are competent to carry out the repair;

    (d) provide for questions arising under the regulations to be determined by the county court; and

    (e) enable the landlord to set off against any compensation payable under the regulations any sums owed to it by the tenant.

(4) Nothing in subsection (2) or (3) shall be taken as prejudicing the generality of subsection (1).

(5) Regulations under this section—

    (a) may make different provision with respect to different cases or descriptions of case, including different provision for different areas, and

    (b) shall be made by statutory instrument which shall be subject to annulment in pursuance of a resolution of either House of Parliament.

(6) In this section—

    'listed contractor', in relation to a landlord, means any contractor (which may include the landlord) who is specified in the landlord's list of contractors;

    'qualifying repair', in relation to a dwelling-house, means any repair of a prescribed description which the landlord is obliged by a repairing covenant to carry out;

    'repairing covenant', in relation to a dwelling-house, means a covenant, whether express or implied, obliging the landlord to keep in repair the dwelling-house or any part of the dwelling-house;

and for the purposes of this subsection a prescribed description may be framed by reference to any circumstances whatever."

DEFINITIONS
  "listed contractor": subs. (6).
  "qualifying repair": subs. (6).
  "repairing covenant": subs. (6).

GENERAL NOTE
  A right to repair scheme for secure tenants was introduced by s.41A of the Housing Act 1980 consolidated as s.96 of the Housing Act 1985. Regulations under that scheme are the Secure Tenancies (Right to Repair Scheme) Regulations 1985 (S.I. 1985 No. 1493). The detail of the replacement scheme will be contained in new regulations which have been the subject of consultation. The existing scheme has had little practical effect. The new regulations are intended to give tenants more effective rights. The thrust of the new scheme is that the tenant will be provided with compensation automatically if the landlord's contractor fails to carry out repairs in a prescribed period. The new scheme applies only to local housing authority tenants.

Right to compensation for improvements

122. After section 99 of the 1985 Act there shall be inserted the following sections—

"Right to compensation for improvements

99A.—(1) The powers conferred by this section shall be exercisable as respects cases where a secure tenant has made an improvement and—

(a) the work on the improvement was begun not earlier than the commencement of section 122 of the Leasehold Reform, Housing and Urban Development Act 1993,

(b) the landlord, or a predecessor in title of the landlord (being a local authority), has given its written consent to the improvement or is to be treated as having given its consent, and

(c) at the time when the tenancy comes to an end the landlord is a local authority and the tenancy is a secure tenancy.

(2) The Secretary of State may make regulations for entitling the qualifying person or persons (within the meaning given by section 99B)—

(a) at the time when the tenancy comes to an end, and

(b) subject to and in accordance with the regulations,

to be paid compensation by the landlord in respect of the improvement.

(3) The regulations may provide that compensation shall be not payable if—

(a) the improvement is not of a prescribed description,

(b) the tenancy comes to an end in prescribed circumstances,

(c) compensation has been paid under section 100 in respect of the improvement, or

(d) the amount of any compensation which would otherwise be payable in less than a prescribed amount;

and for the purposes of this subsection a prescribed description may be framed by reference to any circumstances whatever.

(4) The regulations may provide that the amount of any compensation payable shall not exceed a prescribed amount but, subject to that, shall be determined by the landlord, or calculated, in such manner, and taking into account such matters, as may be prescribed.

(5) The regulations may also make such procedural, incidental, supplementary and transitional provisions as may appear to the Secretary of State necessary or expedient, and may in particular—

(a) provide for the manner in which and the period within which claims for compensation under the regulations are to be made, and for the procedure to be followed in determining such claims,

(b) prescribe the form of any document required to be used for the purposes of or in connection with such claims,

(c) provide for questions arising under the regulations to be determined by the district valuer or the county court, and

(d) enable the landlord to set off against any compensation payable under the regulations any sums owed to it by the qualifying person or persons.

(6) Nothing in subsections (3) to (5) shall be taken as prejudicing the generality of subsection (2).

(7) Regulations under this section—

(a) may make different provision with respect to different cases or descriptions of case, including different provision for different areas, and

(b) shall be made by statutory instrument which (except in the case of regulations making only such provision as is mentioned in subsection (5)(b)) shall be subject to annulment in pursuance of a resolution of either House of Parliament.

(8) For the purposes of this section and section 99B, a tenancy shall be treated as coming to an end if—

(a) it ceases to be a secure tenancy by reason of the landlord condition no longer being satisfied, or

(b) it is assigned, with the consent of the landlord—

> (i) to another secure tenant who satisfies the condition in subsection (2) of section 92 (assignments by way of exchange), or
> (ii) to an assured tenant who satisfies the conditions in subsection (2A) of that section.

Persons qualifying for compensation
99B.—(1) A person is a qualifying person for the purposes of section 99A(2) if—
  (a) he is, at the time when the tenancy comes to an end, the tenant or, in the case of a joint tenancy at that time, one of the tenants, and
  (b) he is a person to whom subsection (2) applies.
(2) This subsection applies to—
  (a) the improving tenant;
  (b) a person who became a tenant jointly with the improving tenant;
  (c) a person in whom the tenancy was vested, or to whom the tenancy was disposed of, under section 89 (succession to periodic tenancy) or section 90 (devolution of term certain) on the death of the improving tenant or in the course of the administration of his estate;
  (d) a person to whom the tenancy was assigned by the improving tenant and who would have been qualified to succeed him if he had died immediately before the assignment;
  (e) a person to whom the tenancy was assigned by the improving tenant in pursuance of an order made under section 24 of the Matrimonial Causes Act 1973 (property adjustment orders in connection with matrimonial proceedings);
  (f) a spouse or former spouse of the improving tenant to whom the tenancy has been transferred by an order under paragraph 2 of Schedule 1 to the Matrimonial Homes Act 1983.
(3) Subsection (2)(c) does not apply in any case where the tenancy ceased to be a secure tenancy by virtue of section 89(3) or, as the case may be, section 90(3).
(4) Where, in the case of two or more qualifying persons, one of them ('the missing person') cannot be found—
  (a) a claim under regulations made under section 99A may be made by, and compensation under those regulations may be paid to, the other qualifying person or persons; but
  (b) the missing person shall be entitled to recover his share of any compensation so paid from that person or those persons.
(5) In this section 'the improving tenant' means—
  (a) the tenant by whom the improvement mentioned in section 99A(1) was made, or
  (b) in the case of a joint tenancy at the time when the improvement was made, any of the tenants at that time."

DEFINITIONS
  "improving tenant": subs. (5).

GENERAL NOTE
  Under s.100 of the Housing Act 1985, housing authorities have the power to pay compensation for improvements carried out by secure tenants. Section 99A inserted in that Act by this section gives a right in certain circumstances to compensation for improvement and the new s.99B deals with the practical implementation of that right. As with the new right to repair the proposed regulations have been the subject of consultation.

Right to information

123. After subsection (2) of section 104 of the 1985 Act (provision of information about tenancies) there shall be inserted the following subsection—

"(3) A local authority which is the landlord under a secure tenancy shall supply the tenant, at least once in every relevant year, with a copy of such information relating to the provisions mentioned in subsection (1)(b) and (c) as was last published by it; and in this subsection 'relevant year' means any period of twelve months beginning with an anniversary of the date of such publication."

Existing rights with respect to disposals by housing action trusts

124.—(1) In subsection (2)(b) of section 79 of the Housing Act 1988 (disposals by housing action trusts), the words "in accordance with section 84 below" shall be omitted.

(2) For subsection (1) of section 84 of that Act (provisions applicable to disposals of dwelling-houses let on secure tenancies) there shall be substituted the following subsection—

"(1) The provisions of this section apply in any case where—
(a) a housing action trust proposes to make a disposal of one or more houses let on secure tenancies which would result in a person who, before the disposal, is a secure tenant of the trust becoming, after the disposal, the tenant of another person, and
(b) that other person is not a local housing authority or other local authority."

(3) In subsection (7) of that section—
(a) after the words "a disposal to which this section applies," there shall be inserted the words "or a disposal which would be such a disposal if subsection (1)(b) above were omitted,"; and
(b) after the words "such further consultation" there shall be inserted the words "or, as the case may be, such consultation".

(4) Where—
(a) a house held by a housing action trust is specified in a notice served by the trust under section 84(2) of the Housing Act 1988, and
(b) the building containing the house is specified in an application subsequently made to the trust under section 96 of that Act (application to exercise right conferred by Part IV),
that Part shall apply as if the building containing the house, and any other property reasonably required for occupation with that building, had not been specified in the application.

(5) Where—
(a) a building containing a house held by a housing action trust is specified in an application made to the trust under section 96 of the Housing Act 1988, and
(b) the house is specified in a notice subsequently served by the trust under subsection (2) of section 84 of that Act,
that section shall apply as if the house had not been specified in the notice.

(6) In this section "house" has the same meaning as in Part III of the Housing Act 1988.

DEFINITIONS
   "house": subs. (6).

GENERAL NOTE
   Housing Action Trusts were introduced by the Housing Act 1988. Section 84 of that Act deals
with the protection of existing rights of secure tenants where a Housing Action Trust disposes of
houses. This section amends s.84. This section limits the application of s.84 to cases where the
property transferee is not a local authority (new s.88(1)). It also provides that houses included
in a notice under s.84(2) are excluded from any application under Pt. IV of the Housing Act
1988 for removing property from the public sector (subs. (4)) and provides that houses included
in an application under s.96 of the Housing Act 1988 cannot be included in a subsequent notice
under s.84(2) of that Act (subs. (5)).

New rights with respect to such disposals

   125.—(1) For subsections (2) and (3) of section 84 of the Housing Act
1988 (disposal by housing action trusts of dwelling-houses let on secure
tenancies) there shall be substituted the following subsections—
       "(2) Before applying to the Secretary of State for consent to the
   proposed disposal or serving notice under subsection (4) below, the
   housing action trust shall serve notice in writing on any local housing
   authority in whose area any houses falling within subsection (1)
   above are situated—
           (a) informing the authority of the proposed disposal and specify-
               ing the houses concerned, and
           (b) requiring the authority within such period, being not less than
               28 days, as may be specified in the notice, to serve on the trust a
               notice under subsection (3) below.
       (3) A notice by a local housing authority under this subsection shall
   inform the housing action trust, with respect to each of the houses
   specified in the notice under subsection (2) above which is in the
   authority's area, of the likely consequences for the tenant if the house
   were to be acquired by the authority."
   (2) In subsection (4) of that section, for paragraphs (d) and (e) there shall
be substituted the following paragraphs—
       "(d) if the local housing authority in whose area the house of which
            he is tenant is situated has served notice under subsection (3)
            above, informing him (in accordance with the information
            given in the notice) of the likely consequences for him if the
            house were to be acquired by that authority;
       (e) informing him, if he wishes to become a tenant of that
            authority, of his right to make representations to that effect
            under paragraph (f) below and of the rights conferred by
            section 84A below;".
   (3) For subsection (5) of that section there shall be substituted the following subsections—
       "(5) If, by virtue of any representations made to the housing action
   trust in accordance with subsection (4)(f) above, section 84A below
   applies in relation to any house or block of flats, the trust shall—
           (a) serve notice of that fact on the Secretary of State, on the local
               housing authority and on the tenant of the house or each of the
               tenants of the block, and
           (b) so amend its proposals with respect to the disposal as to
               exclude the house or block;
   and in this subsection 'house' and 'block of flats' have the same meanings as in that section.
       (5A) The housing action trust shall consider any other representa-
   tions so made and, if it considers it appropriate to do so having regard to
   any of those representations—

(a) may amend (or further amend) its proposals with respect to the disposal, and

(b) in such a case, shall serve a further notice under subsection (4) above (in relation to which this subsection will again apply)."

(4) In subsection (6) of that section, after the words "subsection (5)" there shall be inserted the words "or subsection (5A)".

(5) After that section there shall be inserted the following section—

"Transfer by order of certain dwelling-houses let on secure tenancies
84A.—(1) This section applies in relation to any house or block of flats specified in a notice under subsection (2) of section 84 above if—

(a) in the case of a house, the tenant makes representations in accordance with paragraph (f) of subsection (4) of that section to the effect that he wishes to become a tenant of the local housing authority in whose area the house is situated; or

(b) in the case of a block of flats, the majority of the tenants who make representations in accordance with that paragraph make representations to the effect that they wish to become tenants of the local housing authority in whose area the block is situated.

(2) The Secretary of State shall by order provide for the transfer of the house or block of flats from the housing action trust to the local housing authority.

(3) The Secretary of State may also by order transfer from the housing action trust to the local housing authority so much as appears to the Secretary of State to be appropriate of any property belonging to or usually enjoyed with the house or, as the case may be, the block or any flat contained in it; and for this purpose 'property' includes chattels of any description and rights and liabilities, whether arising by contract or otherwise.

(4) A transfer of any house, block of flats or other property under this section shall be on such terms, including financial terms, as the Secretary of State thinks fit; and an order under this section may provide that, notwithstanding anything in section 141 of the Law of Property Act 1925 (rent and benefit of lessee's covenants to run with the reversion), any rent or other sum which—

(a) arises under the tenant's tenancy or any of the tenants' tenancies, and

(b) falls due before the date of the transfer,

shall continue to be recoverable by the housing action trust to the exclusion of the authority.

(5) Without prejudice to the generality of subsection (4) above, the financial terms referred to in that subsection may include provision for payments to a local housing authority (as well as or instead of payments by a local housing authority); and the transfer from a housing action trust of any house, block of flats or other property by virtue of this section shall not be taken to give rise to any right to compensation.

(6) In this section—

'block of flats' means a building containing two or more flats;

'common parts', in relation to a building containing two or more flats, means any parts of the building which the tenants of the flats are entitled under the terms of their tenancies to use in common with each other;

'flat' and 'house' have the meanings given by section 183 of the Housing Act 1985;

and any reference to a block of flats specified in a notice under section 84(2) above is a reference to a block in the case of which each flat which is let on a secure tenancy is so specified.

(7) For the purposes of subsection (6) above, a building which contains—

(a) one or more flats which are let, or available for letting, on secure tenancies by the housing action trust concerned, and

(b) one or more flats which are not so let or so available,

shall be treated as if it were two separate buildings, the one containing the flat or flats mentioned in paragraph (a) above and the other containing the flat or flats mentioned in paragraph (b) above and any common parts."

DEFINITIONS
"block of flats": subs. (6).
"common parts": subs. (6).
"flat": subs. (6).
"house": subs. (6).

GENERAL NOTE
This section amends s.84 of the Housing Act 1988. This provides for the tenant to have certain rights where property of which he is a tenant is disposed of by a Housing Action Trust. The local housing authority has to inform such a tenant of the consequences of the property being acquired by the authority. Tenants may then inform the Housing Action Trust that they would like to become tenants of the authority. The Housing Action Trust may then amend its proposals in the light of the tenant's views and if it does give further notice to the tenants. A new s.84A is introduced into the Housing Act 1988. This provides for houses the tenants of which wish to transfer as tenants to the local housing authority (and blocks of flats the majority of whose tenants so wish) to transfer to the local authority by order of the Secretary of State. For tenants there may be valuable advantages in transferring to a local authority. Firstly because local authorities are good and fair landlords and secondly to retain or gain the advantage of the right to buy provision of the Housing Act 1985. The effect of a transfer to the local authority or to another landlord in relation to the preserved right to buy (Housing Act 1985, ss.171A–171H) should be made clear as a result of the operation of the amended s.84 and new s.84A.

Housing welfare services

Provision of housing welfare services

126. Part II of the 1985 Act (provision of housing accommodation) shall have effect, and be deemed at all times on and after 1st April 1990 to have had effect, as if after section 11 there were inserted the following section—

"Provision of welfare services

11A.—(1) A local housing authority may provide in connection with the provision of housing accommodation by them (whether or not under this Part) such welfare services, that is to say, services for promoting the welfare of the persons for whom the accommodation is so provided, as accord with the needs of those persons.

(2) The authority may make reasonable charges for welfare services provided by virtue of this section.

(3) In this section 'welfare services' does not include the repair, maintenance, supervision or management of houses or other property.

(4) The powers conferred by this section shall not be regarded as restricting those conferred by section 137 of the Local Government Act 1972 (powers to incur expenditure for purposes not authorised by any other enactment) and accordingly the reference to any other enactment in subsection (1)(a) of that section shall not include a reference to this section."

GENERAL NOTE
This section inserts a new s.11A into the Housing Act 1985. It permits local housing authorities to provide housing welfare services for persons for whom it provides accommodation. This may include legal and financial advice.

Accounting for housing welfare services

127. Schedule 4 to the Local Government and Housing Act 1989 (the keeping of the Housing Revenue Account) shall have effect, and be deemed always to have had effect, as if—
  (a) at the end of paragraph (b) of item 2 of Part I (credits to the account) there were inserted the words "or income in respect of services provided under section 11A of that Act (power to provide welfare services)"; and
  (b) after paragraph 3 of Part III (special cases) there were inserted the following paragraph—

"Provision of welfare services

3A.—(1) This paragraph applies where in any year a local housing authority provide welfare services (within the meaning of section 11A of the Housing Act 1985) for persons housed by them in houses or other property within their Housing Revenue Account.
  (2) The authority may carry to the credit of the account—
  (a) an amount equal to the whole or any part of the income of the authority for the year from charges in respect of the provision of those services;
  (b) any sum from some other revenue account of theirs which represents the whole or any part of that income.
  (3) The authority may carry to the debit of the account—
  (a) an amount equal to the whole or any part of the expenditure of the authority for the year in respect of the provision of those services;
  (b) any sum from some other revenue account of theirs which represents the whole or any part of that expenditure."

GENERAL NOTE
In successive measures since 1980 the government has controlled and restricted local authority expenditure in housing. This small addition to the régime amends the schedule to the Local Government and Housing Act 1989. It permits it to add to its Housing Revenue Account sums charged for welfare services and debit to it the cost of such services.

Power to repeal provisions made by sections 126 and 127

128.—(1) The Secretary of State may at any time by order made by statutory instrument provide that, on such day or in relation to such periods as may be appointed by the order, the provisions made by sections 126 and 127—
  (a) shall cease to have effect; or
  (b) shall cease to apply for such purposes as may be specified in the order.
  (2) An order under this section—
  (a) may appoint different days or periods for different provisions or purposes or for different authorities or descriptions of authority, and
  (b) may contain such incidental, supplementary or transitional provisions as appear to the Secretary of State to be necessary or expedient.

GENERAL NOTE
This section allows the Secretary of State to repeal or vary ss.126 and 127 by statutory instrument. This can be done differently in respect of different authorities and gives an extraordinary degree of legislative control over the provision of welfare services for tenants by local authorities. There is little point in having primary legislation which gives such unfettered

and arbitrary power to the executive. The spectre it is obviously aimed at is local authorities giving welfare services (advice) which is politically unacceptable to the government. This expression of a phobia of divergence of users expressed through democratic local authorities must be an unwelcome trend in legislation in a liberal democracy. The Government's plans in this area are explained in the following Department of Environment statement of July 23, 1993: "Housing Minister Sir George Young has today announced a secure and long-term framework for the provision by local authorities of housing welfare services for their tenants. In answer to a written Parliamentary Question from Dr Liam Fox MP (Woodspring), Sir George said: 'when the provision of welfare services to elderly people in local authority sheltered housing was put in doubt following the judgment of the Court of Appeal in the Ealing case, the Government acted immediately to provide protection. New powers were taken in the Leasehold Reform, Housing and Urban Development Act 1993, and my Department and the Welsh Office issued a consultation paper about the long-term arrangements for local authority housing welfare services. We have now decided how to proceed, taking careful account of the information and views expressed by local authorities and others. First, we have decided to leave in place indefinitely the powers for local authorities to provide housing welfare services to their tenants. This will give housing authorities the long-term certainty that they need, and will be widely welcomed. Second, we have decided that some of the welfare services which may be provided by wardens in sheltered accommodation, and which are concerned with the provision of *essential care*, should no longer be charged to the Housing Revenue Account. These services are those of the kind which involve: helping tenants into and out of bed; toileting, dressing, feeding and bathing; administering medication; and nursing care. Instead, these services should be funded from the General Funds of local authorities, and the appropriate public resource transfer will be considered. The exclusion of these services from the Housing Revenue Account, will be subject to the making of an Order, on which consultation will be conducted in the normal way. It will not affect authorities powers to provide these services. Remaining housing welfare services provided by wardens should be able to be charged to the Housing Revenue Account, but local authorities will need to consider this carefully in each individual case. We are satisfied that these decisions and proposals will produce no disruption to the services provided to elderly people in sheltered housing schemes, consistent with the commitment that the Government has given. There should be no implications for tenants' existing entitlements to housing benefit. During the consultation on wardens' welfare services in sheltered housing schemes, a broader range of issues has been drawn out, which concern the rôle of all social housing managers. These issues again fall into two groups. First, those which concern the powers given to housing management; and second, the source of the funds to pay for management activities. Housing managers do need the ability to use broad powers. The primary rôle of professional council housing management is to ensure that housing is properly utilised, is kept in good repair and that rents are collected. But in cases of special needs, and in the most difficult and challenging housing estates, the responsibility of managers covers a wide range of functions, alongside the efficient and effective delivery of the normal estate management duties. The Government has worked with local authorities, through a range of policies and programmes, to encourage and support a better life for tenants on estates. Additional services are required by these programmes. In some instances, managers may need to provide these services themselves. Often they can better act as co-ordinators and facilitators of services provided by other agencies. It does not follow that all the costs of these additional services should be paid for from rents or from the subsidy provided by central government to Housing Revenue Accounts. Rents are paid by tenants essentially towards housing costs, and the Housing Revenue Account is primarily an account for the costs of meeting landlord functions. Local authorities therefore need to consider carefully, within the requirements of Sched. 4 to the Local Government and Housing Act 1989, which costs should be charged to their Housing Revenue Accounts, and which should be funded from elsewhere. There has been much debate on these issues during consultation on the proposals for welfare services. It may be that some further discussion of the wider rôle of social housing managers would be helpful to provide a greater degree of understanding and clarity. The Government wants to ensure that its policies of working with local housing authorities to assist tenants and for better housing estates remain strong. My Department and the Welsh Office will shortly consult local authority associations about how best to approach this, including whether it would be helpful to issue a Departmental circular.'"

Delegation of housing management

Management agreements

129.—(1) At the end of subsection (3) of section 27 of the 1985 Act (management agreements), there shall be inserted the words "and shall contain such provisions as may be prescribed by regulations made by the Secretary of State".

(2) For subsection (5) of that section there shall be substituted the following subsection—

"(5) The Secretary of State's approval may be given—

(a) either generally to all local housing authorities or to a particular authority or description of authority, and

(b) either in relation to a particular case or in relation to a particular description of case,

and may be given unconditionally or subject to conditions."

(3) For subsection (6) of that section there shall be substituted the following subsections—

"(6) References in this section to the management functions of a local housing authority in relation to houses or land—

(a) do not include such functions as may be prescribed by regulations made by the Secretary of State, but

(b) subject to that, include functions conferred by any statutory provision and the powers and duties of the authority as holder of an estate or interest in the houses or land in question.

(7) Regulations under this section—

(a) may make different provision with respect to different cases or descriptions of case, including different provision for different areas,

(b) may contain such incidental, supplementary or transitional provisions as appear to the Secretary of State to be necessary or expedient, and

(c) shall be made by statutory instrument which shall be subject to annulment in pursuance of a resolution of either House of Parliament."

GENERAL NOTE

Local authorities are encouraged to delegate management of their housing (in cases where they have not been encouraged to dispose of it altogether). This section amends the relevant provisions of s.27 of the 1985 Housing Act. The purpose of these amendments is to give central government higher control over management agreements. If the expressed purpose of the various legislative attacks on local authority autonomy was "to turn the provision of housing into a central executive body operating through a range of local agents" then this section would be a prime example of a step on the way to achieving that objective. This seems to be typical of a central government's approach to dictate, belittle and destabilize at local government level. A draft Statutory Instrument relating to this section is included as Appendix 3 to these annotations.

Consultation with respect to management agreements

130. For section 27A of the 1985 Act there shall be substituted the following section—

"Consultation with respect to management agreements

27A.—(1) A local housing authority who propose to enter into a management agreement shall make such arrangements as they consider appropriate to enable the tenants of the houses to which the proposal relates—

(a) to be informed of the following details of the proposal, namely—

(i) the terms of the agreement (including in particular the standards of service to be required under the agreement),

(ii) the identity of the person who is to be manager under the agreement, and

(iii) such other details (if any) as may be prescribed by regulations made by the Secretary of State, and

(b) to make known to the authority within a specified period their views as to the proposal;

and the authority shall, before making any decision with respect to the proposal, consider any representations made to them in accordance with those arrangements.

(2) A local housing authority who have made a management agreement shall—

(a) during the continuance of the agreement, maintain such arrangements as they consider appropriate to enable the tenants of the houses to which the agreement relates to make known to the authority their views as to the standards of service for the time being achieved by the manager, and

(b) before making any decision with respect to the enforcement of the standards of service required by the agreement, consider any representations made to them in accordance with those arrangements.

(3) Arrangements made or maintained under subsection (1) or (2) above shall—

(a) include provision for securing that the authority's responses to any representations made to them in accordance with the arrangements are made known to the tenants concerned, and

(b) comply with such requirements as may be prescribed by regulations made by the Secretary of State.

(4) Regulations under this section—

(a) may make different provision with respect to different cases or descriptions of case, including different provision for different areas,

(b) may contain such incidental, supplementary or transitional provisions as appear to the Secretary of State to be necessary or expedient, and

(c) shall be made by statutory instrument which shall be subject to annulment in pursuance of a resolution of either House of Parliament.

(5) In the case of secure tenants the provisions of this section apply in place of the provisions of section 105 (consultation on matters of housing management) in relation to the making of a management agreement."

GENERAL NOTE
   This section introduces a replacement s.27A to the Housing Act 1985. It strengthens the requirement for consultation with tenants in respect of management agreements.

Management agreements and compulsory competitive tendering

131. After section 27A of the 1985 Act there shall be inserted the following section—

"Management agreements and compulsory competitive tendering
   27AA.—(1) This section shall apply if the Secretary of State makes an order under section 2(3) of the Local Government Act 1988 ('the 1988 Act') providing for the exercise of any management functions to be a defined activity for the purposes of Part I of that Act (compulsory competitive tendering).

   (2) The Secretary of State may by regulations provide that in any case where—

(a) a local housing authority propose to make an invitation to carry out any functional work in accordance with the rules set out in subsection (4) of section 7 of the 1988 Act (functional work: conditions), and

(b) the proposal is such that any decision by the authority that the work should be carried out by the person or one of the persons proposed to be invited would necessarily involve their entering into a management agreement with that person,

the provisions of section 27A shall have effect with such modifications as appear to the Secretary of State to be necessary or expedient.

(3) Nothing in section 6 of the 1988 Act (functional work: restrictions) shall apply in relation to any functional work which, in pursuance of a management agreement, is carried out by the manager as agent of the local housing authority.

(4) In this section 'functional work' has the same meaning as in Part I of the 1988 Act.

(5) Regulations under this section shall be made by statutory instrument which shall be subject to annulment in pursuance of a resolution of either House of Parliament."

DEFINITIONS
"functional work": subs. (4).

GENERAL NOTE
This section inserts a new s.27AA into the Housing Act 1985. It applies when housing management functions become subject to compulsory competitive tendering under s.2 of the Local Government Act 1988. Management agreements envisaged by this process would be subject to the cancellation arrangements contained in the new s.27A.

Management agreements with tenant management organisations

132.—(1) After section 27AA of the 1985 Act there shall be inserted the following section—

"Management agreements with tenant management organisations
27AB.—(1) The Secretary of State may make regulations for imposing requirements on a local housing authority in any case where a tenant management organisation serves written notice on the authority proposing that the authority should enter into a management agreement with that organisation.

(2) The regulations may make provisions requiring the authority—

(a) to provide or finance the provision of such office accommodation and facilities, and such training, as the organisation reasonably requires for the purpose of pursuing the proposal;

(b) to arrange for such feasibility studies with respect to the proposal as may be determined by or under the regulations to be conducted by such persons as may be so determined;

(c) to arrange for such ballots or polls with respect to the proposal as may be determined by or under the regulations to be conducted of such persons as may be so determined; and

(d) in such circumstances as may be prescribed by the regulations (which shall include the organisation becoming registered if it has not already done so), to enter into a management agreement with the organisation.

(3) The regulations may make provision with respect to any management agreement which is to be entered into in pursuance of the regulations—

(a) for determining the houses and land to which the agreement should relate, and the amounts which should be paid under the agreement to the organisation;

(b) requiring the agreement to be in such form as may be approved by the Secretary of State and to contain such provisions as may be prescribed by the regulations;

(c) requiring the agreement to take effect immediately after the expiry or other determination of any previous agreement; and

(d) where any previous agreement contains provisions for its determination by the authority, requiring the authority to determine it as soon as may be after the agreement is entered into.

(4) The regulations may also make such procedural, incidental, supplementary and transitional provisions as may appear to the Secretary of State necessary or expedient, and may in particular make provision—

(a) for particular questions arising under the regulations to be determined by the authority;

(b) for other questions so arising to be determined by an arbitrator agreed to by the parties or, in default of agreement, appointed by the Secretary of State;

(c) requiring any person exercising functions under the regulations to act in accordance with any guidance given by the Secretary of State; and

(d) for enabling the authority, if invited to do so by the organisation concerned, to nominate one or more persons to be directors or other officers of any tenant management organisation with whom the authority have entered into, or propose to enter into, a management agreement.

(5) Nothing in subsections (2) to (4) above shall be taken as prejudicing the generality of subsection (1).

(6) Regulations under this section—

(a) may make different provision with respect to different cases or descriptions of case, including different provision for different areas, and

(b) shall be made by statutory instrument which shall be subject to annulment in pursuance of a resolution of either House of Parliament.

(7) Except as otherwise provided by regulations under this section—

(a) a local housing authority shall not enter into a management agreement with a tenant management organisation otherwise than in pursuance of the regulations; and

(b) the provisions of the regulations shall apply in relation to the entering into of such an agreement with such an organisation in place of—

(i) the provisions of section 27A (consultation with respect to management agreements),

(ii) in the case of secure tenants, the provisions of section 105 (consultation on matters of housing management), and

(iii) in the case of an organisation which is associated with the authority, the provisions of section 33 of the Local Government Act 1988 (restrictions on contracts with local authority companies).

(8) In this section—

'arbitrator' means a member of a panel approved for the purposes of the regulations by the Secretary of State;

'associated' shall be construed in accordance with section 33 of the Local Government Act 1988;

'previous agreement', in relation to an agreement entered into in pursuance of the regulations, means a management agreement previously entered into in relation to the same houses and land;

'registered' means registered under the Industrial and Provident Societies Act 1965 or the Companies Act 1985;

'tenant management organisation' means a body which satisfies such conditions as may be determined by or under the regulations."

(2) Section 27C of the 1985 Act (which is superseded by this section) shall cease to have effect.

DEFINITIONS
"arbitrator": subs. (8).
"associated": subs. (8).
"previous agreement": subs. (8).
"registered": subs. (8).
"tenant management organisation": subs. (8).

GENERAL NOTE
This section introduces a new s.27AB to the Housing Act 1985. Its purpose is to enable tenant management organisations to be in a better position to negotiate management agreements. This is done by allowing the Secretary of State to make regulations facilitating the work of tenant management organisations at local authority expense. This provision replaces the former s.27(c) of the 1985 Act.

Priority of charges securing repayment of discount

Voluntary disposals by local authorities

133.—(1) For subsection (2) of section 36 of the 1985 Act (liability to repay discount is a charge on the premises) there shall be substituted the following subsections—

"(2) Subject to subsections (2A) and (2B), the charge has priority immediately after any legal charge securing an amount—
(a) left outstanding by the purchaser, or
(b) advanced to him by an approved lending institution for the purpose of enabling him to acquire the interest disposed of on the first disposal.

(2A) The following, namely—
(a) any advance which is made otherwise than for the purpose mentioned in subsection (2)(b) and is secured by a legal charge having priority to the charge taking effect by virtue of this section, and
(b) any further advance which is so secured,
shall rank in priority to that charge if, and only if, the local authority by written notice served on the institution concerned gives their consent; and the local authority shall so give their consent if the purpose of the advance or further advance is an approved purpose.

(2B) The local authority may at any time by written notice served on an approved lending institution postpone the charge taking effect by virtue of this section to any advance or further advance which—
(a) is made to the purchaser by that institution, and
(b) is secured by a legal charge not having priority to that charge;
and the local authority shall serve such a notice if the purpose of the advance or further advance is an approved purpose."

(2) After subsection (4) of that section there shall be inserted the following subsections—

"(5) The approved purposes for the purposes of this section are—
(a) to enable the purchaser to defray, or to defray on his behalf, any of the following—
(i) the cost of any works to the house,
(ii) any service charge payable in respect of the house for works, whether or not to the house, and

(iii) any service charge or other amount payable in respect of the house for insurance, whether or not of the house, and

(b) to enable the purchaser to discharge, or to discharge on his behalf, any of the following—

(i) so much as is still outstanding of any advance or further advance which ranks in priority to the charge taking effect by virtue of this section,

(ii) any arrears of interest on such an advance or further advance, and

(iii) any costs and expenses incurred in enforcing payment of any such interest, or repayment (in whole or in part) of any such advance or further advance.

(6) Where different parts of an advance or further advance are made for different purposes, each of those parts shall be regarded as a separate advance or further advance for the purposes of this section."

GENERAL NOTE
    Section 36 of the Housing Act 1985 provides for the liability to repay discount to be a charge on the premises. That provision is postponed to legal charges made by approved lending institutions. The local authority may permit further advances to have priority over the charge to secure repayment discount (s.36(2B) of the 1985 Act). The new subs. (5) of s.36 enlarges the approved purposes for which loans can be given priority by the local authority. Thus, further advances for improving the house or paying service charges can be given priority. Under the new subs. (5)(b) a charge may be given priority over the charge to repay discount where it is used to pay off a prior charge.

Voluntary disposals by housing associations

134.—(1) For sub-paragraph (2) of paragraph 2 of Schedule 2 to the Housing Associations Act 1985 (liability to repay discount is a charge on the premises) there shall be substituted the following sub-paragraphs—

"(2) Subject to sub-paragraphs (2A) and (2B), the charge has priority immediately after any legal charge securing an amount—

(a) left outstanding by the purchaser, or

(b) advanced to him by an approved lending institution for the purpose of enabling him to acquire the interest disposed of on the first disposal.

(2A) The following, namely—

(a) any advance which is made otherwise than for the purpose mentioned in sub-paragraph (2)(b) and is secured by a legal charge having priority to the charge taking effect by virtue of this paragraph, and

(b) any further advance which is so secured,

shall rank in priority to that charge if, and only if, the housing association by written notice served on the institution concerned gives its consent; and the housing association shall so give its consent if the purpose of the advance or further advance is an approved purpose.

(2B) The housing association may at any time by written notice served on an approved lending institution postpone the charge taking effect by virtue of this paragraph to any advance or further advance which—

(a) is made to the purchaser by that institution, and

(b) is secured by a legal charge not having priority to that charge;

and the housing association shall serve such a notice if the purpose of the advance or further advance is an approved purpose."

(2) After sub-paragraph (4) of that paragraph there shall be inserted the following sub-paragraphs—

"(5) The approved purposes for the purposes of this paragraph are—
  (a) to enable the purchaser to defray, or to defray on his behalf, any of the following—
    (i) the cost of any works to the house,
    (ii) any service charge payable in respect of the house for works, whether or not to the house, and
    (iii) any service charge or other amount payable in respect of the house for insurance, whether or not of the house, and
  (b) to enable the purchaser to discharge, or to discharge on his behalf, any of the following—
    (i) so much as is still outstanding of any advance or further advance which ranks in priority to the charge taking effect by virtue of this paragraph,
    (ii) any arrears of interest on such an advance or further advance, and
    (iii) any costs and expenses incurred in enforcing payment of any such interest, or repayment (in whole or in part) of any such advance or further advance;
and in this sub-paragraph 'service charge' has the meaning given by section 621A of the Housing Act 1985.
  (6) Where different parts of an advance or further advance are made for different purposes, each of those parts shall be regarded as a separate advance or further advance for the purposes of this paragraph."

DEFINITIONS
"service charge": subss. (2) and (5)(b)(iii).

GENERAL NOTE
  The amendment to Sched. 2 to the Housing Association Act 1985 made by this section is very similar to the amendment to s.36 of the Housing Act 1985 made by s.133—see the note above. It deals in the same way with priority of the charge to repay discount and other charges made by approved lending authorities.

Disposals of dwelling-houses by local authorities

Programmes for disposals

135.—(1) For the purposes of this section a disposal of one or more dwelling-houses by a local authority to any person (in this section referred to as a "disposal") is a qualifying disposal if—
  (a) it requires the consent of the Secretary of State under section 32 of the 1985 Act (power to dispose of land held for the purposes of Part II), or section 43 of that Act (consent required for certain disposals not within section 32); and
  (b) the aggregate of the following, namely—
    (i) the number of dwelling-houses included in the disposal; and
    (ii) the number of dwelling-houses which, within the relevant period, have been previously disposed of by the authority to that person, or that person and any associates of his taken together,
  exceeds 499 or, if the Secretary of State by order so provides, such other number as may be specified in the order.
  (2) In subsection (1) "the relevant period" means—
  (a) the period of five years ending with the date of the disposal or, if that period begins before the commencement of this section, so much of it as falls after that commencement; or
  (b) if the Secretary of State by order so provides, such other period

ending with that date and beginning after that commencement as may be specified in the order.

(3) A local authority shall not make a qualifying disposal in any financial year unless the Secretary of State has included the disposal in a disposals programme prepared by him for that year.

(4) A disposal may be included in a disposals programme for a financial year either—

(a) by specifically including the disposal in the programme; or

(b) by including in the programme a description of disposal which includes the disposal.

(5) An application by a local authority for the inclusion of a disposal in a disposals programme for a financial year—

(a) shall be made in such manner and contain such information; and

(b) shall be made before such date,

as the Secretary of State may from time to time direct.

(6) In preparing a disposals programme for any financial year, the Secretary of State shall secure that the aggregate amount of his estimate of the exchequer costs of each of the disposals included in the programme does not exceed such amount as he may, with the approval of the Treasury, determine.

(7) In deciding whether to include a disposal in a disposals programme for a financial year or, having regard to subsection (6), which disposals to include in such a programme, the Secretary of State may, in relation to the disposal or (as the case may be) each disposal, have regard in particular to—

(a) his estimate of the exchequer costs of the disposal;

(b) whether or not a majority of the secure tenants who would be affected by the disposal are (in his opinion) likely to oppose it; and

(c) the matters mentioned in section 34(4A) or 43(4A) (as the case may be) of the 1985 Act;

and in this subsection "secure tenant" has the same meaning as in Part IV of that Act.

(8) In subsections (6) and (7) "the exchequer costs", in relation to a disposal, means any increase which is or may be attributable to the disposal in the aggregate of any subsidies payable under—

(a) section 135(1) of the Social Security Administration Act 1992 (housing benefit finance); or

(b) section 79 of the 1989 Act (Housing Revenue Account subsidy);

and the Secretary of State's estimate of any such increase shall be based on such assumptions (including assumptions as to the period during which such subsidies may be payable) as he may, with the approval of the Treasury, from time to time determine, regardless of whether those assumptions are or are likely to be borne out by events.

(9) The inclusion of a disposal in a disposals programme for a financial year shall not prejudice the operation of section 32 or 43 of the 1985 Act in relation to the disposal.

(10) The Secretary of State may prepare different disposals programmes under this section for different descriptions of authority; and any disposals programme may be varied or revoked by a subsequent programme.

(11) An order under this section—

(a) shall be made by statutory instrument which shall be subject to annulment in pursuance of a resolution of either House of Parliament;

(b) may make different provision for different cases or descriptions of case, or for different authorities or descriptions of authority; and

(c) may contain such transitional and supplementary provisions as the Secretary of State considers necessary or expedient.

(12) Any direction or determination under this section—

(a) may make different provision for different cases or descriptions of case, or for different authorities or descriptions of authority; and

(b) may be varied or revoked by a subsequent direction or determination.

(13) In this section—

"the 1989 Act" means the Local Government and Housing Act 1989;

"dwelling-house" has the same meaning as in Part V of the 1985 Act except that it does not include a hostel (as defined in section 622 of that Act) or any part of a hostel;

"local authority" has the meaning given by section 4 of that Act;

"long lease" means a lease for a term of years certain exceeding 21 years other than a lease which is terminable before the end of that term by notice given by or to the landlord;

"subsidiary" has the same meaning as in section 28(8) of the Housing Associations Act 1985.

(14) For the purposes of this section—

(a) a disposal of any dwelling-house shall be disregarded if at the time of the disposal the local authority's interest in the dwelling-house is or was subject to a long lease;

(b) two persons are associates of each other if—

(i) one of them is a subsidiary of the other;

(ii) they are both subsidiaries of some other person; or

(iii) there exists between them such relationship or other connection as may be specified in a determination made by the Secretary of State; and

(c) a description of authority may be framed by reference to any circumstances whatever.

DEFINITIONS

"1989 Act": subs. (13).
"dwelling-house": subs. (13).
"exchequer costs": subs. (8).
"local authority": subs. (13).
"long lease": subs. (13).
"relevant period": subs. (2).
"secure tenant": subs. (7).
"subsidiary": subs. (13).

GENERAL NOTE

Local authorities are encouraged to undertake large scale disposals of housing. This is, however, subject to the overall control of the Secretary of State in an annual "disposals programme".

Levy on disposals

136.—(1) For the purposes of this section a disposal of one or more dwelling-houses by a local authority to any person is a qualifying disposal if—

(a) it requires the consent of the Secretary of State under section 32 of the 1985 Act (power to dispose of land held for the purposes of Part II), or section 43 of that Act (consent required for certain disposals not within section 32); and

(b) the aggregate of the following, namely—

(i) the number of dwelling-houses included in the disposal; and

(ii) the number of dwelling-houses which, within any relevant period, have been previously or are subsequently disposed of by the authority to that person, or that person and any associates of his taken together,

exceeds 499 or, if the Secretary of State by order so provides, such other number as may be specified in the order.

(2) In subsection (1) "relevant period" means—

(a) any period of five years beginning after the commencement of this section and including the date of the disposal; or

(b) if the Secretary of State by order so provides, any such other period beginning after that commencement and including that date as may be specified in the order.

(3) A local authority which after the commencement of this section makes a disposal which is or includes, or which subsequently becomes or includes, a qualifying disposal shall be liable to pay to the Secretary of State a levy of an amount calculated in accordance with the formula—

$$L = (CR - D) \times P$$

where—

    L = the amount of the levy;

    CR = the aggregate of—

        (i) any sums received by the authority in respect of the disposal which are, by virtue of section 58 of the 1989 Act (capital receipts), capital receipts for the purposes of Part IV of that Act and do not fall within a description determined by the Secretary of State; and

        (ii) where paragraph (a) or (c) of subsection (1) of section 61 of that Act (capital receipts not wholly in money paid to the authority) applies in relation to the disposal, any notional capital receipts determined in accordance with subsections (2) and (3) of that section;

    D = such amount as may be calculated in accordance with such formula as the Secretary of State may determine;

    P = 20 per cent. or, if the Secretary of State by order so provides, such other percentage as may be specified in the order.

(4) A formula determined for the purposes of item D in subsection (3) may include any variable which is included in a determination made for the purposes of section 80 of the 1989 Act (calculation of Housing Revenue Account subsidy).

(5) The administrative arrangements for the payment of any levy under this section shall be such as may be specified in a determination made by the Secretary of State, and such a determination may in particular make provision as to—

(a) the information to be supplied by authorities;

(b) the form and manner in which, and the time within which, the information is to be supplied;

(c) the payment of the levy in stages in such circumstances as may be provided in the determination;

(d) the date on which payment of the levy (or any stage payment of the levy) is to be made;

(e) the adjustment of any levy which has been paid in such circumstances as may be provided in the determination;

(f) the payment of interest in such circumstances as may be provided in the determination; and

(g) the rate or rates (whether fixed or variable, and whether or not calculated by reference to some other rate) at which such interest is to be payable;

and any such administrative arrangements shall be binding on local authorities.

(6) Any amounts by way of levy or interest which are not paid to the Secretary of State as required by the arrangements mentioned in subsection (5) shall be recoverable in a court of competent jurisdiction.

(7) For the purposes of Part IV of the 1989 Act (revenue accounts and capital finance of local authorities) any payment of levy by a local authority under this section shall be treated as expenditure for capital purposes.

(8) Notwithstanding the provisions of section 64 of the 1989 Act (use of amounts set aside to meet credit liabilities) but subject to subsection (9), amounts for the time being set aside by a local authority (whether volunta-

rily or pursuant to a requirement under Part IV of that Act) as provision to meet credit liabilities may be applied to meet any liability of the authority in respect of any levy payable under this section, other than a liability in respect of interest.

(9) The Secretary of State may by regulations provide that the amounts which may by virtue of subsection (8) be applied as mentioned in that subsection shall not exceed so much of the levy concerned as may be determined in accordance with the regulations.

(10) Any sums received by the Secretary of State under this section shall be paid into the Consolidated Fund; and any sums paid by the Secretary of State by way of adjustment of levies paid under this section shall be paid out of money provided by Parliament.

(11) Before making an order or determination under this section, the Secretary of State shall consult such representatives of local government as appear to him to be appropriate.

(12) An order or regulations under this section—

(a) shall be made by statutory instrument which shall be subject to annulment in pursuance of a resolution of either House of Parliament;

(b) may make different provision for different cases or descriptions of case, or for different authorities or descriptions of authority; and

(c) may contain such transitional and supplementary provisions as the Secretary of State considers necessary or expedient.

(13) Any determination under this section—

(a) may make different provision for different cases or descriptions of case, or for different authorities or descriptions of authority; and

(b) may be varied or revoked by a subsequent determination.

(14) Subsections (13) and (14) of section 135 shall apply for the purposes of this section as they apply for the purposes of that section.

Disposals: transitional provisions

137.—(1) The period beginning with the commencement of section 135 and ending with 31st March 1994 (in this section referred to as "the first financial year") shall be treated as a financial year for the purposes of that section; but in relation to that period subsection (5) of that section shall not apply.

(2) If before the commencement of section 135 any statement was made by or on behalf of the Secretary of State—

(a) that, if that section were then in force, he would prepare under that section such disposals programmes for the first financial year as are set out in the statement, and

(b) that, when that section comes into force, he is to be regarded as having prepared under that section the programmes so set out,

those programmes shall have effect as if they had been validly made under that section at the time of the statement.

(3) Any determination or estimate made, or any approval given—

(a) before the commencement of section 135,

(b) before the making of such a statement as is mentioned in subsection (2), and

(c) in connection with the disposals programmes proposed to be set out in the statement, shall be as effective, in relation to those programmes, as if that section had been in force at the time the determination or estimate was made, or the approval was given.

(4) If before the commencement of section 136 any statement was made by or on behalf of the Secretary of State—

(a) that, if that section were then in force, he would make under that section such determinations as are set out in the statement, and

(b) that, when that section comes into force, he is to be regarded as having made under that section the determinations set out in the statement,

those determinations shall have effect as if they had been validly made under that section at the time of the statement.

(5) Any consultation undertaken—

(a) before the commencement of section 136,

(b) before the making of such a statement as is mentioned in subsection (4), and

(c) in connection with determinations proposed to be set out in the statement,

shall be as effective, in relation to those determinations, as if that section had been in force at the time the consultation was undertaken.

GENERAL NOTE

The aim of this section is to allow the Secretary of State to announce and deal with disposal programmes before the Act is brought into force. They will be validated retrospectively when ss.123 and 124 are brought into effect. Where consultation is required if it is to take place it will have taken place under the Act.

Expenses on defective housing

Contributions in respect of certain post-March 1989 expenses

138.—(1) In section 157 of the Local Government and Housing Act 1989 (commutation of and interest on periodic payments of grants etc.), in subsection (8) (which changes certain contributions under section 569 of the 1985 Act from annual payments to lump sums), for paragraph (b) there shall be substituted the following paragraph—

"(b) so much of any contributions in respect of an expense incurred on or after 1st April 1989 and before 1st April 1990 as have not been made before 1st April 1990".

(2) This section shall be deemed to have come into force on 1st January 1993.

Contributions in respect of certain pre-April 1989 expenses

139.—(1) Where—

(a) before 1st April 1989 a local housing authority incurred any such expense as is referred to in subsection (1) of section 569 of the 1985 Act (assistance by way of reinstatement grant, repurchase or payments for owners of defective housing); and

(b) before 1st January 1993, the Secretary of State has not made in respect of that expense any contribution of such a description as is referred to in subsection (2) of that section, as amended by section 157(8) of the Local Government and Housing Act 1989 (single commuted contributions),

any contributions in respect of that expense which are made under section 569 on or after 1st January 1993 shall be annual payments calculated and payable in accordance with the following provisions of this section.

(2) The amount of the annual payment in respect of any relevant financial year shall be a sum equal to the relevant percentage of the annual loan charges referable to the amount of the expense incurred.

(3) Notwithstanding that annual loan charges are calculated by reference to a 20 year period, annual payments made by virtue of this section shall be made only in respect of relevant financial years ending at or before the end of the period of 20 years beginning with the financial year in which, as the case may be—

(a) the work in respect of which the reinstatement grant was payable was completed;

(b) the acquisition of the interest concerned was completed; or

(c) the payment referred to in subsection (1)(c) of section 569 was made.

(4) Subsections (3) and (4) of section 569 (which determine the relevant percentage and the amount of the expense incurred) apply for the purposes of the preceding provisions of this section as they apply for the purposes of that section.

(5) Nothing in this section affects the operation of subsection (6) of section 569 (terms etc. for payment of contributions).

(6) In this section—

"the annual loan charges referable to the amount of the expense incurred" means the annual sum which, in the opinion of the Secretary of State, would fall to be provided by a local housing authority for the payment of interest on, and the repayment of, a loan of that amount repayable over a period of 20 years;

"relevant financial year" means the financial year beginning on 1st April 1991 and each successive financial year.

(7) This section shall be deemed to have come into force on 1st January 1993.

Housing Revenue Account subsidy

Calculation of Housing Revenue Account subsidy

140. In subsection (1) of section 80 of the Local Government and Housing Act 1989 (determination of formulae for calculating Housing Revenue Account subsidy), the words "and for any year the first such determination shall be made before the 25th December immediately preceding that year" shall cease to have effect.

GENERAL NOTE

This makes a small change to the formula for calculating Housing Revenue Account subsidy. The change is to remove the fixed time by which the government must calculate the subsidy. Instead it may be done as the Secretary of State "may from time to time determine" (s.80 of the Local Government and Housing Act 1989).

CHAPTER II

SCOTLAND

GENERAL NOTE

Although Pt. IV of the Act (supplemental), ss.174, 179, 180 and para. 8 of Sched. 17 all extend to Scotland, Chapter II of Part II contains the substantive Scottish provisions. They all amend, replace or supplement sections in the Housing (Scotland) Act 1987 and extend solely to Scotland. Minor repeals are contained in Sched. 22.

In brief, this Chapter introduces a new "rent to loan scheme" for the purchase of public sector housing (ss.141 to 143); new rules for the abatement of the purchase price under the existing right-to-buy scheme where the landlord is in default (ss.144 to 145); a revised right for secure tenants to have repairs carried out (s.146); a new right to compensation for improvements (s.147); a new right to information (s.148); new powers for local authorities to provide housing welfare services (ss.149 to 151); new provision for management agreements between local authorities and housing co-operatives (s.152); and new duties for local authorities to publish information on standards and performance in housing management (s.153). In addition, minor changes are made to existing provisions on housing allocation (ss.154 to 155), on defective dwellings (s.156) and other sections in the 1987 Act (s.157).

Parliamentary Debates on the Scottish provisions
One consequence of the immersion of Scottish clauses in a predominantly English Bill is that they received only intermittent treatment in Parliament. Principal references to Pt. II, Chap. II appear at *Hansard*, H.C. Vol. 213, cols. 159–160, 166 and 247–250 (Second Reading); Vol. 218, cols. 932–935, 951–952 and 1023–1026 (Report); H.L. Vol. 543, cols. 88–89, 103–107 and 170 (Second Reading); Vol. 544, cols. 635–638 and 682–684 (Committee); Vol. 545, cols. 1912–1915, 1927–1929 and 1935–1938 (Report) and Vol. 546, col. 241 (Third Reading). In Standing Committee B, principal references were at cols. 9–10, 450–474, 530–537, 552–562, 579–581, 716–740, 897–903 and 916–920. At some points there was criticism from Scottish MPs and peers of the way in which the Scottish provisions were handled. See, for instance, reference to Scottish provisions being "tagged on" (*Hansard*, H.C. Vol. 217, col. 159) and the attempt to have the Bill committed to a Committee of the whole House (col. 247). See also criticism of the "off-hand way" in which the "tartan element" in the Bill was handled (*Hansard*, H.L. Vol. 543, cols. 103–104).

Commencement
In accordance with s.188(2)(b), ss.149 to 151 (Housing Welfare Services) came into force on the day on which the Act received the Royal Assent on July 20, 1993. The same section provides that the other Scottish sections come into force on dates to be prescribed. The Leasehold Reform, Housing and Urban Development Act 1993 (Commencement No. 2) (Scotland) Order 1993, S.I. 1993 No. 2163 provides that the Scottish provisions be brought into force as follows: September 27, 1993—ss.141 to 145, 148, 154 to 157 and 187(2) and Sched. 22 (repeals). April 1, 1994—ss.146, 147, 152, 153.

ABBREVIATIONS
The following abbreviation is used in the annotations to Pt. II, Chap. II:
The 1987 Act: The Housing (Scotland) Act 1987.

Rent to loan scheme

Eligibility for rent to loan scheme

141. After section 62 of the Housing (Scotland) Act 1987 (in this Chapter referred to as "the 1987 Act") there shall be inserted the following section—

> **"Eligibility for rent to loan scheme**
> 62A.—(1) Subject to subsection (2), a tenant who has the right under section 61 to purchase a house may exercise the right by way of the rent to loan scheme.
> (2) Subsection (1) does not apply—
> (a) to the tenant of a house which is designated as defective under Part XIV; or
> (b) to a tenant—
> > (i) in respect of whom a determination has been made that he is entitled to housing benefit in respect of any part of the relevant period; or
> > (ii) by or on behalf of whom a claim for housing benefit has been made (or is treated as having been made) and has not been determined or withdrawn.
> (3) In subsection (2), 'the relevant period' means the period—
> (a) beginning twelve months before the date of the application to purchase the house; and
> (b) ending on the day when the contract of sale of the house is constituted under section 66(2)."

DEFINITIONS
"application to purchase": s.82 of the 1987 Act.
"defective dwelling": s.303 of the 1987 Act.
"house": ss.302 and 338 of the 1987 Act.
"relevant period": s.62A(3) below.
"rent to loan scheme": s.82 of the 1987 Act (as inserted by s.143 below).

GENERAL NOTE
In the *Tenant's Charter for Scotland*, the government undertook to extend to all public sector

tenants the right to acquire their houses under a rent to mortgage scheme (in preference to exercising their existing right to buy)—a facility previously available only to tenants of Scottish Homes and the new town development corporations. The *Charter* explained: "Not all tenants are able to use their right to buy. If you cannot quite afford the right to buy payments, the rent to mortgage scheme enables you to buy your house for a monthly cost close to your present rent. The results of the pilot scheme have been encouraging, but under present arrangements the scheme is complicated to operate and is not as quick as it should be". For debate on the different lessons to be learned about advantages and disadvantages of rent to mortgage and the probable future rate of take-up from research conducted by the Scottish Office, see Standing Committee B, cols. 450–469. The research referred to is H. Kay and J. Hardin *The Rent to Mortgage Scheme in Scotland*, Scottish Office 1992. The new s.62A inserted into the 1987 Act defines the eligibility of tenants for the rent to loan scheme, details of which are contained in the new ss.73A to 73D inserted by s.142 below. The parallel scheme for England and Wales is introduced by ss.108 to 120 above.

S.62A(1)
Subject to the exceptions set out in subs. (2), all tenants with the rights to purchase their houses under the ordinary rules may do so instead by way of the rent to loan scheme.

S.62A(2) and (3)
There are two statutory exceptions. The first relates to the condition of the house and excludes tenants of houses designated as "defective" under Pt. XIV of the 1987 Act (originally contained in the Housing Defects Act 1984). Such designation was introduced to provide some relief for tenants who bought their houses in the early years of the right to buy, only to find that the houses had severe hidden defects. Designation does not, however, preclude purchase (or repurchase) but subs. (2) denies access to the rent to loan scheme. The other exception relates to the means of the tenant and excludes those tenants who have made an as yet undetermined (and not withdrawn) claim for housing benefit or who have been held to be entitled to housing benefit in respect of any part of the period ("relevant period" s.62A(3)) beginning 12 months before the date of the application to purchase and ending when the contract of sale is constituted (notice of acceptance served in response to offer to sell).

The rent to loan scheme

142. After section 73 of the 1987 Act there shall be inserted the following sections—

"Rent to loan scheme

The rent to loan scheme
73A.—(1) Under the rent to loan scheme, the price fixed for a house under section 62 shall be payable in two elements, viz—
(a) the initial capital payment; and
(b) the deferred financial commitment.
(2) In the application of subsection (3) of section 62 to the price of a house being purchased by way of the rent to loan scheme, each of the percentage figures specified in that subsection shall be reduced by 15 or such other number as may, with the consent of the Treasury, be prescribed.
(3) The conditions which are, under section 64, to be contained in an offer to sell under section 63(2) shall, in the case of a house which is to be purchased by way of the rent to loan scheme, include a condition providing that the tenant will be entitled to ownership of the house in exchange for the initial capital payment.
(4) The deferred financial commitment shall be secured by a standard security over the house.

The initial capital payment
73B.—(1) The initial capital payment in respect of a house is a sum determined by the tenant, being of an amount not less than the maximum amount of loan which could be repaid at the statutory rate of interest over the loan period by weekly payments each equal to the adjusted weekly rent for the house.

(2) In this section—
(a) the 'statutory rate of interest' is the rate of interest which would be charged under section 219(4) on the application date by the local authority for the area in which the house is situated;
(b) the 'loan period' is the period beginning on the application date and ending on whichever of the following is the earlier—
   (i) the expiry of a period of 25 years starting on that date; and
   (ii) the date when the applicant will (if he survives) reach pensionable age within the meaning of the Social Security Act 1975 or, in the case of joint applicants, the date when the one who will (if they both or all survive) reach pensionable age later than the other or the others reaches that age, but if the period arrived at under sub-paragraph (ii) is less than 10 years, then the loan period shall be a period of 10 years beginning on the application date;
(c) the 'adjusted weekly rent' is an amount equal to 90 per cent. of the weekly rent for the house payable as at the application date; and
(d) the 'application date' is the date of the application to purchase the house.

The deferred financial commitment

73C.—(1) The deferred financial commitment in respect of a house is the sum arrived at by—
(a) finding the difference between—
   (i) the price which was fixed for the purchase of the house under section 62(1); and
   (ii) the initial capital payment;
(b) expressing that difference as a percentage of the market value which was determined under section 62(2) for the purpose of fixing the price of the house;
(c) reducing that percentage figure by—
   (i) 7 or such other number as may, with the consent of the Treasury, be prescribed; and
   (ii) in a case where payment has been made under subsection (4), the percentage figure which the amount so paid represents in relation to the market value mentioned in paragraph (b);
(d) finding the sum which is equal to that resultant percentage of the resale value of the house; and
(e) in a case to which subsection (5) of section 73D applies, adding to that sum the amount which falls to be added under subsection (6) of that section.
(2) No interest shall accrue on the deferred financial commitment.
(3) Payment of the deferred financial commitment—
(a) shall, subject to section 73D, be made to the original seller of the house—
   (i) on the sale or other disposal of the house by the rent to loan purchaser; or
   (ii) if the rent to loan purchaser does not sell or dispose of it, on his death; and
(b) may be so made in whole at any earlier time.
(4) Subject to section 73D(3), payment may be made at any time for the purpose of reducing the deferred financial commitment in accordance with subsection (1)(c)(ii).
(5) Subject to subsection (6), payment of the deferred financial commitment shall be made as soon as may be after the destruction of

or damage to the house by fire, tempest, flood or any other cause against the risk of which it is normal practice to insure.

(6) Subsection (5) does not apply where, following the destruction of or damage to a house, it is rebuilt or reinstated.

(7) A standard security granted in security of the deferred financial commitment shall, notwithstanding section 13 of the Conveyancing and Feudal Reform (Scotland) Act 1970, have priority before any standard security securing the liability to make a repayment under section 72(1) but immediately after—

    (a) any standard security granted in security of any amount advanced by a recognised lending institution—

        (i) to enable payment of the initial capital payment or payment under subsection (4);

        (ii) for the improvement of the house; or

        (iii) for any combination of those purposes,

    (together with any interest, expenses and outlays payable thereunder); and

    (b) with the consent of the original seller, a standard security over the house granted in security of any other loan (together with any such interest, expenses and outlays).

In this subsection—

    a 'recognised lending institution' is one which is recognised for the purposes of section 222;

    references to interest payable under a standard security are references both to present and future interest payable thereunder including interest which has accrued or may accrue; and

    references to expenses and outlays include interest thereon.

(8) In this section—

    (a) the 'resale value' of a house is, subject to subsections (9) and (10)—

        (i) where it is being sold by the rent to loan purchaser on the open market with vacant possession and a good and marketable title, the price at which it is being so sold;

        (ii) where the rent to loan purchaser has died not having sold or disposed of it, its value for the purpose of confirmation to his estate;

        (iii) in any other case, such amount as is agreed for the purposes of this sub-paragraph between the rent to loan purchaser and the original seller or, failing such agreement, such amount as is determined for those purposes by an independent valuer as the value of the house, assuming it to be available for sale in the circumstances specified in sub-paragraph (i) on a date as near as may be to the date when payment of the deferred financial commitment is to be made; and

    (b) the 'original seller' of a house is the body which, as the landlord of the house, sold it in pursuance of this Part to the rent to loan purchaser or, where another body has succeeded to the rights and duties of that body in relation to the house, that other body.

(9) In arriving at the resale value of a house no account shall be taken of—

    (a) anything done by the rent to loan purchaser (or any predecessor of his as secure tenant of the house) which has added to the value of the house; or

    (b) any failure by him (but not by any such predecessor) to keep the house in good repair (including decorative repair).

(10) For the purposes of agreeing or determining the amount of the resale value of a house under subsection (8)(a)(iii) in a case where it has been destroyed or damaged by a cause referred to in subsection (5), that value shall be taken as including the value of any sums paid or falling to be paid to the rent to loan purchaser under a policy insuring against the risk of the cause of destruction of or damage to the house except to the extent that they have been or fall to be applied in meeting the cost of any rebuilding or reinstatement which has been carried out.

Deferred financial commitment: further provisions
73D.—(1) This subsection applies where—
  (a) the person who has purchased a house by way of the rent to loan scheme sells or otherwise disposes of it to his spouse or any other person with whom he is living as if they were husband and wife and the house is, at the time of the sale or disposal, the spouse's or other person's only or principal home;
  (b) the person who has so purchased the house dies and there succeeds to the house, by operation of the law of succession, a person for whom or persons for whom or for one or more of whom the house was, for the period of 12 months immediately preceding the death, his or their only or principal home; or
  (c) in the case of a house which was so purchased jointly, one of the joint purchasers dies and, at the time of the death, the house was the only or principal home of the survivor or the survivors or one or more of them.
(2) Where subsection (1) applies—
  (a) the deferred financial commitment shall not be payable on the sale, disposal or death referred to in paragraph (a) of subsection (3) of section 73C but on the sale or other disposal of the house by the person or persons acquiring it, succeeding to it or surviving in the circumstances whereby subsection (1) applies or on the death of such person or of the last of them for whom the house was, both at the time of such acquisition, succession or survival and at the time of his death, his only or principal home; and
  (b) paragraph (b) of the said subsection (3) shall have effect accordingly.
(3) A payment made under section 73C(4) shall not—
  (a) be less than £1500 or such other sum as may, with the consent of the Treasury, be prescribed;
  (b) exceed the statutory maximum; or
  (c) be made within the period of one year after any previous such payment in respect of the same transaction.
(4) In subsection (3)(b), the 'statutory maximum' is the amount by which the initial capital payment would be required to be augmented so as to produce, by operation of the calculations specified in paragraphs (a) to (c) of section 73C(1), a resultant percentage of 7.5 per cent. or such other percentage as may, with the consent of the Treasury, be prescribed.
(5) This subsection applies where—
  (a) the subtraction of discount for the purposes of section 62(1) falls to be limited or excluded by operation of subsection (6A) of that section; and
  (b) any part of those costs which, in accordance with that subsection, are to be represented by an amount arrived at under that subsection, was incurred in the period commencing with the beginning of the financial year of the landlord which was

current 5 years prior to the date of payment in whole of the deferred financial commitment.

(6) Where subsection (5) applies, the amount which is, under section 73C(1)(e), to be added is an amount equal to the difference between the aggregate of the amounts mentioned in paragraph (a) and the amount mentioned in paragraph (b)—

    (a) the initial capital payment and the deferred financial commitment (including any payment under section 73C(4)) which would be payable apart from this subsection;

    (b) the price which would have been payable under section 62 had the purchase of the house proceeded otherwise than by way of the rent to loan scheme."

DEFINITIONS

"adjusted weekly rent": s.73B(2)(c) of the 1987 Act.
"application date": s.73B(2)(d) of the 1987 Act.
"deferred financial commitment": s.73C of the 1987 Act.
"financial year": s.338 of the 1987 Act.
"house": s.338 of the 1987 Act.
"initial capital payment": s.73B of the 1987 Act.
"loan period": s.73B(2)(b) of the 1987 Act.
"local authority": s.338 of the 1987 Act.
"original seller": s.73C(8)(b) of the 1987 Act.
"recognised lending institution": ss.73C(7) and 222 of the 1987 Act.
"rent to loan scheme": s.82 of the 1987 Act (as inserted by s.143 below).
"resale value": s.73C(8)(a) of the 1987 Act.
"secure tenant": ss.44 and 82 of the 1987 Act.
"statutory rate of interest": s.73B(2)(a) of the 1987 Act.
"tenant": s.82 of the 1987 Act.

GENERAL NOTE

Eligibility for the rent to loan scheme is established by the new s.62A inserted into the 1987 Act by s.141 above. Now s.142 inserts new ss.73A to 73D which contain the scheme's principal rules. Section 73A defines the scheme as one which divides the price payable into two elements: an "initial capital payment" (whose rules are elaborated in s.73B) and a "deferred financial commitment" (the main rules of which are set out in s.73C, with further provisions supplied by s.73D). Section 143 below makes consequential amendments to provisions in the 1987 Act affected by the introduction of the rent to loan scheme.

S.73A(1) of the 1987 Act

This distinguishes the two elements in the price payable under scheme: the initial capital payment (on payment of which the tenant becomes entitled to ownership of the house—subs. (3)) and the deferred financial commitment (the rules on the honouring of which are contained in s.73C).

S.73A(2) of the 1987 Act

Under s.62 of the 1987 Act the price of a house to be bought under the standard right to buy scheme is calculated by deducting a discount from the market value of the house. Section 62(3) provides that the percentage discount is 32 per cent. (44 per cent. in the case of a flat) rising by one per cent. (two per cent. in the case of a flat) per year (beyond two) of continuous occupation by the tenant of the house (or other relevant houses) up to a maximum discount of 60 per cent. (70 per cent. in the case of a flat). Under the rent to loan scheme the same principles apply but with the level of discount reduced across the board by 15 per cent. (subject to adjustment by order). Thus, in the case of a house (as opposed to a flat) the normal minimum discount is 17 per cent. rising by one per cent. per year (a figure which is presumably but not absolutely unambiguously left unaffected by the adjustment) to a maximum discount of 45 per cent.

S.73A(3) of the 1987 Act

Sections 63(2)(d) and 64 of the 1987 Act require the seller to include in the offer to sell reasonable conditions including, *e.g.* "such terms as are necessary to entitle the tenant to receive a good and marketable title to the house". Now s.73A(3) requires that, under the rent to loan scheme, the offer must include "a condition providing that the tenant will be entitled to ownership of the house in exchange for the initial capital payment".

S.73A(4) of the 1987 Act
Further provisions relating to the standard security are contained in s.73C(7) of the 1987 Act.

S.73B(1) of the 1987 Act
The actual amount to be paid by the rent to loan purchaser as his or her initial capital payment is left to the rent to loan purchaser to decide (see also s.63(2)(cc) of the 1987 Act inserted by s.143(2)(b) below)—the greater the initial capital payment, the smaller will be the deferred financial commitment but subject to the minimum payment defined by this subsection. It is the probable size of this minimum payment which commentators have said will be a deterrent for some potential users of the scheme. The minimum initial capital payment is calculated by treating it as the (maximum) amount of loan which could be repaid at the statutory rate of interest (s.73B(2)(a)) over a notional loan period (s.73B(2)(b)) by weekly payments equal to the adjusted weekly rent for the house (s.73B(2)(c)).

S.73B(2) of the 1987 Act
Section 219 of the 1987 Act makes provision for determining home loan interest rates used for various purposes under the Act and it is the "statutory rate of interest" determined under s.219(4) as at the "application date" (the date of the application to purchase the house) which is used in the calculation of an initial capital payment. The notional "loan period" is normally a period of 25 years from the date of the application to purchase but will be a shorter period (subject to a minimum of 10 years) where the applicant is approaching pensionable age (currently 60 for women, 65 for men) in which case the period from application to that date is the "loan period". In the case of joint applicants, it is the period to the date when the last of the applicants will reach pensionable age. The "adjusted weekly rent" (reduced from the actual level of rent for the reasons explained above) is 90 per cent. of that actual weekly rent.

S.73C(1) of the 1987 Act
Simply put, the deferred financial commitment is, as already explained, the difference between the price of the house and the initial capital payment but, since it is a *deferred* commitment, it has to be expressed as a percentage of the market value of the house carried forward as the same percentage of the (usually inflating) resale value of the house and always translatable, therefore, into a particular sum of money at the time when actual payment of the deferred financial commitment is required.

What this subsection does, therefore, is to set out the stages according to which the required calculations are to be carried out, calculations which are a little more complicated than the above outline because of the need to accommodate certain statutory adjustments required by the subsection itself and other provisions in ss.73C and 73D. Thus, incorporating those additional adjustments, the stages in the calculation of the deferred financial commitment are:

Stage 1
Finding the difference between the purchase price of the house (*i.e.* market value minus discount) and the initial capital payment.

Stage 2
Expressing that difference as a percentage of the *market value*.

Stage 3
Reducing that percentage figure by seven (or other figure prescribed).

Stage 4
Where appropriate, further reducing that percentage figure where a payment is made by the rent to loan purchaser for the purpose of reducing his or her deferred financial commitment. Such a payment may, in terms of s.73C(4), be made at any time (prior to the eventual *requirement* to pay the deferred financial commitment itself, see s.73C(3)). However, in terms of s.73D(4), such payment may not be of less than £1,500 or other prescribed figure; nor may it exceed the "statutory maximum" which, in s.73D(5), is defined as the amount which would reduce the percentage figure calculated under stages 1 to 3 above to seven-and-a-half (after any earlier payments under s.73C(4) have been taken into account) *i.e.* the rent to loan purchaser should pay either the statutory maximum or the *whole* amount. It is further provided that no payment to reduce the deferred financial commitment may be made with a period of one year from a previous one. There is no restriction on making a payment within a year of the original purchase.

Stage 5
Applying the percentage figure to the "resale value" of the house to produce the actual

amount, at that (later) time, of the deferred financial commitment. That "resale value" is defined in s.73C(8) to (10). Where the house is being sold "on the open market with vacant possession and a good and marketable title" the resale value is the price at which the house is being sold. Alternatively, if the rent to loan purchaser dies, the resale value is the value for the purpose of confirmation of the estate. These two alternatives represent the two situations in which, in terms of s.73C(3), the deferred financial commitment will normally become payable. If, however, the deferred financial commitment is being paid voluntarily or under other circumstances or, for some other reason, has to be calculated, it is an amount agreed between the rent to loan purchaser and the "original seller", the landlord body (or a successor body) which originally sold the house and to which payment of the deferred financial commitment is (normally) to be made. Failing such agreement, the resale value is to be determined by an independent valuer (no definition supplied), assuming the house to be for sale (on the open market etc) on a date as near as may be to the date when the deferred financial commitment is to be paid. In all of these circumstances, no account is to be taken of: (a) anything done by the rent to loan purchaser (or by a predecessor secure tenant) which has added to the value of the house (*cf.*, in relation to calculation of the original market value, s.62(1)), or of (b) any failure by the rent to loan purchaser (but not by a predecessor) to keep the house in good repair (including decorative repair). (Special valuation rules apply in the case of destruction or severe damage to the house. See s.73C(5)).

Stage 6

In some circumstances, the amount of the deferred financial commitment calculated at stage 5 may have to be increased. This occurs (under s.73C(1)(c) and s.73D(5) to (6)) where, at the time of the sale to the rent to loan purchaser, the amount of the discount on the price fell to be limited or excluded by the "cost floor" provisions in s.62(A) of the 1987 Act. Normally, as already mentioned, the rent to loan purchaser is entitled to a discount (though at a reduced level) like other purchasers and is, incidentally, obliged like them to repay discount in the event of an early sale, a commitment to be borne in mind (while it subsists) alongside the deferred financial commitment. Where the "cost floor" provisions have been applied to reduce or exclude discount on the grounds that the price should not fall below the level of costs incurred on the house during the preceding five-year period *and* any part of those costs was incurred during the five-year period up to the payment in whole of the deferred financial commitment then s.73D(7) ensures that the total of the initial capital payment and the final deferred financial commitment should not fall below the level of the price which would have been payable by a "normal purchaser". If necessary, an additional sum, equal to the difference between those two amounts is added to the deferred financial commitment—thus maintaining, for a maximum of five years the "cost floor".

S.73C(2) of the 1987 Act

No interest accrues on the deferred financial commitment.

S.73C(3) of the 1987 Act

This subsection has to be read with s.73(C)(5)(6) and s.73D(1)(2). Although, under s.73(C)(4) (and 73D(3)), interim payments may be made with a view to reducing its level, the deferred financial commitment normally becomes fully payable when one or other of two events occurs: the sale or other disposal of the house by the rent to loan purchaser; or the death of such a person. However, the subsection provides that the deferred financial commitment *may* be paid at any earlier time. Payment is made to the "original seller" (see s.73C(8)(b) and note on s.73C(1), Stage 5 above).

There are two exceptions to these general rules. First, in terms of s.73C(5)(6), payment of the deferred financial commitment is required as soon as may be after the destruction of the house or of damage to it by fire, tempest or flood or "any other cause against the risk of which it is normal practice to insure" *except* where, following such destruction or damage, the house is in fact rebuilt or reinstated. When the deferred financial commitment does fall to be paid in these circumstances the "resale value" (see s.73C(8) and note on s.73C(1) Stage 5 above) is to be taken to include the value of sums paid or payable to the rent to loan purchaser under an insurance policy, *except* to the extent that they are to be applied in meeting the cost of any rebuilding or reinstatement (s.73C(10)).

Secondly, the obligation to pay the deferred financial commitment, whether on sale/disposal or death, is deferred if the house passes by sale/disposal from the rent to loan purchaser to his or her spouse (or person with whom he or she was living as husband and wife) and the house was that person's only or principal home; or the house passes "by operation of the law of succession" (for discussion of this phrase and its capacity to include both testate and intestate succession, see *Hansard*, H.L.Vol. 544, col. 636) to a person (or persons) for whom the house was, for the 12 months up to the death, his or her (or their) only or principal home; or, where the house was purchased jointly one of the joint purchasers dies and the house was, at the death, the only or principal home of the survivor or survivors. In all these cases, the deferred financial commitment becomes payable on a sale/disposal by or on the death of the later owner (s.73D(1)(2)). Where there has been a succession to the house by more than one person or there is more than one survivor, this rule applies on the death of the last of them for whom the house was, both at acquisition by succession or survival and at the time of his or her death, his or her only or principal home.

S.73C(4) of the 1987 Act
See also s.73D(4) and the notes on s.73C(1), Stage 5.

S.73C(5)–(6) of the 1987 Act
See also s.73C(10) and the notes on s.73C(3).

S.73C(7) of the 1987 Act
It is, of course, necessary that the original seller's interest in the eventual payment of the deferred financial commitment should be secured and this is achieved by requiring a standard security over the house, see s.73A(4). This subsection establishes that such a standard security has priority *before* a standard security protecting a repayment of discount on early resale of the house (s.72 of the 1987 Act) but immediately (inserted at Committee stage in the House of Lords) *after* a standard security granted by a recognised lending institution (ss.222 and 224 of the 1987 Act—building societies, *etc.*) to secure the initial capital payment or interim payment of the deferred financial commitment; or to secure a loan for the improvement of the house; or (as inserted at Committee stage in the House of Lords) for any combination of these purposes. With the consent of the original seller, the standard security may rank after standard securities protecting other loans. In all cases, priority of ranking attaches to not only the amount of the advance but also interest (present and future, accrued and yet to accrue) and "expenses and outlays" (again including interest). These protections were tightened at Committee stage in the House of Lords.

S.73C(8)–(9) of the 1987 Act
See the notes on s.73C(1), Stage 5.

S.73C(10) of the 1987 Act
See s.73C(5).

S.73D(1)–(2) of the 1987 Act
See the notes on s.73C(3). In earlier versions of the Bill, these subsections were cast in a rather different form and supplemented by a (now deleted subs. (3)) until amendments were made at the Committee stage in the House of Commons.

S.73D(3)–(4) of the 1987 Act
See s.73C(4) and the notes on s.73C(1), Stage 5.

S.73D(5)–(6) of the 1987 Act
See the notes on s.73C(1), Stage 6.

Rent to loan scheme: related amendments

143.—(1) The 1987 Act shall have effect subject to the following amendments (being amendments related to the rent to loan scheme).
(2) In section 63—
(a) in subsection (1), after paragraph (c) there shall be inserted the following "; and
　(d) in the case of a tenant who is entitled to purchase the house by way of the rent to loan scheme, a statement whether he wishes to proceed so to purchase the house.";
(b) in subsection (2), after paragraph (c), there shall be inserted the following paragraph—
　"(cc) where the application to purchase contains a statement under subsection (1)(d) that the applicant wishes to proceed by way of the rent to loan scheme and the statement has not been withdrawn, the minimum amount of the initial capital payment, a statement that the applicant, if so minded, may make

an initial capital payment greater than the minimum and a description of the deferred financial commitment including—
　　(i) the amount of the deferred financial commitment calculated as if due to be paid as at the date of the offer to sell;
　　(ii) an explanation of why and how the amount of the deferred financial commitment when payable under section 73C(3)(a) can vary from its amount as calculated under sub-paragraph (i); and
　　(iii) the procedure for paying the deferred financial commitment."

(c) at the end there shall be inserted the following subsection—
　　"(3) Where, in response to an offer to sell containing the matters referred to in paragraph (cc) of subsection (2), an applicant has informed a landlord in writing of his intention to make an initial capital payment of an amount greater than the minimum, the landlord shall, before the end of the period specified in subsection (2) or, if later, the expiry of one month from the date when the landlord was so informed of the tenant's intention, serve an amended offer to sell in which the calculation of the deferred financial commitment is revised accordingly."

(3) In section 67, there shall be inserted at the end the following subsection—
　　"(4) This section does not apply where the tenant is exercising his right to purchase under section 61 by way of the rent to loan scheme."

(4) In section 71—
(a) in subsection (1)—
　　(i) in paragraph (a), after "offer", in both places where it occurs, there shall be inserted "or amended offer";
　　(ii) in paragraph (d), after "offer" there shall be inserted "or amended offer" and there shall be added at the end "and, in the case of an amended offer, they do not conform with the requirements of section 63(3)"; and

(b) in subsection (2)—
　　(i) in paragraph (b), after "offer" there shall be inserted "or amended offer"; and
　　(ii) after "63(2)" there shall be inserted "and, in the case of an amended offer, under section 63(3)".

(5) In section 82—
(a) after "20" there shall be inserted "214"; and
(b) the following definitions shall be inserted at the appropriate places—
　　"the 'rent to loan purchaser' of a house is the person who exercised his right to purchase it under section 61 by way of the rent to loan scheme or, where section 73D(1) applies, the person whose selling or otherwise disposing of the house or whose death is, by virtue of subsection (2) of that section, the occasion for payment of the deferred financial commitment, that person;
　　'rent to loan scheme' means the provisions of sections 62A and 73A to 73D."

(6) In section 214, there shall be inserted at the end the following subsection—
　　"(9) This section applies to the deferred financial commitment as it applies to an advance and references in it and in section 215 to the making of advances shall be construed as references to such functions of a local authority under the rent to loan scheme as relate to the creation of the deferred financial commitment, but Schedule 17 shall not so apply."

(7) In section 216, there shall be inserted at the end the following subsection—

"(10) This section does not apply in the case of the purchase of a house by way of the rent to loan scheme."

DEFINITIONS
"application to purchase": s.82 of the 1987 Act.
"house": s.338 of the 1987 Act.
"landlord": s.82 of the 1987 Act.
"offer to sell": s.82 of the 1987 Act.
"rent to loan purchaser": s.82 of the 1987 Act, as amended by this section.
"rent to loan scheme": s.82 of the 1987 Act, as amended by this section.
"tenant": s.82 of the 1987 Act.

GENERAL NOTE
This section makes a number of small amendments to the 1987 Act related to the introduction of the rent to loan scheme contained in ss.141 and 142.

Subs. (2)
These amendments make necessary adjustments to the content of the statutory application to purchase (subs. (2)(a)) and offer to sell (subs. (2)(b)). Also added is a new requirement of an amended offer to sell where, having been made one offer based on the minimum initial capital payment, the tenant in response offers a larger payment, thus affecting the calculation of the deferred financial commitment. See also consequential amendment in subs. (4).

Subs. (3)
This subsection disapplies the "fixed price option" in the case of the rent to loan scheme.

Subs. (4)
Section 71(1) of the 1987 Act sets out the circumstances in which a purchasing tenant may complain to the Lands Tribunal for Scotland. This amendment adds the service of an offer or amended offer to sell which fails to comply with the new subs. (3) of s.63 (see subs. (2) above).

Subs. (5)
This makes consequential adjustments to s.82 (Interpretation of Part III) of the 1987 Act.

Subss. (6) and (7)
These make consequential adjustments to ss.214 and 216 of the 1987 Act whilst also ensuring that Sched. 17 (Conditions attaching to house loans) does not apply to the deferred financial commitment and that s.216 itself (loans to assist purchase under the right to buy) does not apply to the rent to loan scheme.

Right to purchase

Abatement of purchase price

144. After section 66 of the 1987 Act there shall be inserted the following sections—

"**Abatement of purchase price on landlord's failure before contract of sale**
66A.—(1) Where a tenant who seeks to exercise a right to purchase a house under section 61 has served an application to purchase on the landlord and the landlord—
(a) not having served a notice of refusal, has failed to serve an offer to sell on the tenant within 2 months of the application or, where an amended offer to sell falls to be served on the tenant under subsection (3) of section 63, has failed to do so within the time limit specified in that subsection;
(b) having agreed to serve an amended offer to sell on the tenant in response to a request under section 65(1), has failed to do so within one month of the request;
(c) following an order by the Lands Tribunal to serve an amended offer to sell on the tenant under section 65(3), has failed to do so within 2 months of the date of the order;

(d) following a finding by the Lands Tribunal under section 68(4), has failed to serve an offer to sell within 2 months of the date of the finding; or

(e) following an order by the Lands Tribunal under section 71(2)(b), has failed to serve an offer or amended offer to sell within the time specified in the order,

the tenant may serve on the landlord a notice in writing requiring the landlord to serve on him, within one month of the date of the notice, the offer to sell or (as the case may be) the amended offer to sell which the landlord has failed to serve.

(2) Where the landlord fails to serve the offer to sell or the amended offer to sell within one month of the date of the notice in writing under subsection (1), the price fixed under section 62 shall be reduced by the amount of rent paid by the tenant during the period commencing with the date on which the one month period expired and ending with the date on which the offer is served.

Abatement of purchase price on landlord's failure after contract of sale

66B.—(1) Where the landlord has failed and continues to fail to deliver a good and marketable title to the tenant in accordance with the contract of sale, the tenant may at any time serve on the landlord a notice (the 'initial notice of delay') setting out the landlord's failure and specifying—

(a) the most recent action of which the tenant is aware which has been taken by the landlord in fulfilment of his duties under this Part;

(b) a period (the 'response period'), of not less than one month beginning on the date of service of the notice, within which the service by the landlord of a counter notice under subsection (2) will have the effect of cancelling the initial notice of delay.

(2) If there is no action under this Part which, at the beginning of the response period it was for the landlord to take in order to grant a good and marketable title to the tenant in implementation of the contract of sale, the landlord may serve on the tenant a counter notice either during or after the response period.

(3) At any time when—

(a) the response period specified in the initial notice of delay has expired; and

(b) the landlord has not served a counter notice under subsection (2),

the tenant may serve on the landlord a notice (the 'operative notice of delay') that this subsection shall apply to the price fixed under section 62; and thereupon the price fixed under section 62 shall be reduced by the amount of rent paid by the tenant during the period commencing with the date of service of the operative notice of delay and ending with whichever is the earlier of the following dates—

(i) the date of service by the landlord of a counter notice; or

(ii) the date of delivery by the landlord of a good and marketable title in implementation of the contract of sale.

(4) Where the landlord has served a counter notice under subsection (2) the tenant (together with any joint purchaser) may, by serving on the clerk to the Lands Tribunal a copy of the initial notice of delay and of the landlord's counter notice together with a request for the matter to be so referred, refer the matter to the Tribunal for its consideration under subsection (5).

(5) Where the matter has been so referred to the Lands Tribunal it shall consider whether or not in its opinion action which would have

enabled a good and marketable title to be delivered in implementation of the contract of sale could have been taken by the landlord and shall find accordingly.

(6) Where the Lands Tribunal finds that action could have been taken by the landlord the tenant shall be entitled to serve an operative notice of delay as if the landlord had not served a counter notice and in that event the commencement date for the purposes of subsection (3) shall be the date on which an operative notice of delay could first have been served if no counter notice had been served.

Provisions relating to sections 66A and 66B
66C.—(1) Where there is more than one period in respect of which the price fixed under section 62 can be reduced under section 66A(2) or 66B(3), the periods may be aggregated and the price reduced by the total amount of the rent.

(2) If the period in respect of which the price fixed can be so reduced is, or if the periods aggregated under subsection (1) together amount to, more than twelve months, the amount by which the price fixed under section 62 would, apart from this subsection, fall to be reduced shall be increased by 50 per cent. or such other percentage as the Secretary of State may by order made by statutory instrument and subject to annulment in pursuance of a resolution of either House of Parliament provide."

DEFINITIONS
"application to purchase": s.82 of the 1987 Act.
"house": s.338 of the 1987 Act.
"landlord": s.82 of the 1987 Act.
"Lands Tribunal": s.338 of the 1987 Act.
"notice of refusal": s.68(1) of the 1987 Act.
"offer to sell": s.82 of the 1987 Act.
"tenant": s.82 of the 1987 Act.

GENERAL NOTE
One of the complaints made in the *Tenant's Charter* was that, although many sales under the right to buy were completed in six months or less, "too many tenants are faced with lengthy delays when they want to buy their home. The Government will change the law so that rent paid can count towards the Right to Buy price, when the Landlord delays a sale". The way in which this change is implemented is by the insertion of three new sections into the 1987 Act. Section 66A deals with the abatement of the purchase price because of the landlord's failure to take action required at the stage *before* a contract of sale is made. Section 66B deals with the stage after a contract of sale. Section 66C makes brief further provision dealing with the aggregation of periods of landlord delay and additional penalties for delay of over a year. See also s.145 for the effect of abatement on recovery of discount on early resale. For debate on whether there is a need in Scotland for these abatement provisions; on the impact on the public purse; and unfair gains to tenants on housing benefit (who would not, therefore, have to pay the full amount of the rent from which they subsequently benefit) see Standing Committee B, cols. 717–720.

S.66A(1) of the 1987 Act
This subsection defines the situations in which the tenant, following delay on the part of the landlord, may serve the notice which gives the landlord a "last chance" to serve, within one month, the required offer to sell, failing which the tenant's rent falls, under subs. (2), to be reduced. Unsurprisingly, the situations listed in (a) to (e) closely match those listed in s.71(1) of the 1987 Act which deal with delays (and other failures on the part of the landlord) on the grounds of which the tenant may apply for relief to the Lands Tribunal: (a) this is the "standard" situation. The normal obligation on the landlord is to serve an offer to sell within two months of an application to purchase (s.63(2)). The paragraph applies where it fails to do so (or fails to serve an amended offer in time under the new s.63(3)—see s.143(2) above). The reference in the paragraph to the absence of a "notice of refusal" is a little more complex. The standard form of refusal (because the landlord disputes the tenant's right to purchase) must be served within one month (s.68(1)). The same applies to a refusal under s.70 (house needed for educational purposes). A refusal to sell a house with special facilities for persons of pensionable age does

not under the terms of s.69 itself require to be served within one month of the application to purchase although s.63(2) *does* require an offer to sell within two months if no notice of refusal is issued; (b) this applies where, under s.65(1), the landlord agrees (failing which the tenant must refer the matter to the Lands Tribunal) to serve an offer amended, *e.g.* to contain different conditions or to name a new joint purchaser, as requested by the tenant, but fails to do so within a month of the request; (c) following a request, as in (b), which is refused by the landlord, the Lands Tribunal may, on the application of the tenant, order that an amended offer be served within two months; (d) similarly, where the Lands Tribunal has adjudicated upon a disputed refusal to sell it may, under s.68(4), make a finding that the tenant has the right to purchase. There is no direct statutory requirement that an offer to sell must follow within two months but this paragraph nevertheless triggers the abatement process after that period; (e) the final circumstance arises where the tenant complains to the Lands Tribunal under s.72(1)(d) that an offer made is defective (*e.g.* as to the calculation of the price) and the Lands Tribunal orders service of an offer in proper form within the period specified in the order (which may not exceed two months). Any of these failures gives the tenant the right to serve the notice requiring an offer or amended offer within a month.

S.66A(2) of the 1987 Act

The penalty for non compliance with the notice under s.66A(1) is that, when the landlord does finally serve the offer to sell the price, calculated initially under the ordinary rules in s.62, must, subject to the further rules in s.66C below, be reduced by the amount of rent paid by the tenant between expiry of the period of a month and the date of the offer. Failure to adjust the price in accordance with this section would produce an offer challengeable by complaint to the Lands Tribunal under s.71(1)(d).

S.66B(1) of the 1987 Act

Section 66(2) provides that after an offer to sell followed by a notice of acceptance served on the landlord, a contract of sale of the house is constituted on the terms contained in the offer. At this point, there are no further statutory obligations on the landlord imposed by the 1987 Act; there is no further recourse to the Lands Tribunal by the tenant; normal conveyancing procedures with their attendant obligations on both parties take over. It is, above all, the duty of the selling landlord to deliver a good and marketable title (for discussion of which, especially in relation to land register transactions, see *Hansard*, H.L. Vol. 544, cols. 637–8) to the tenant and it is the failure to do this which gives the tenant the opportunity to take the first step towards reducing the price eventually to be paid from the figure named in the offer to sell by the amount of rent paid during the period attributable to the landlord's delay at this stage. The tenant must first formally bring to the notice of the landlord what he regards as the landlord's failure to deliver and specifying the most recent action taken by the landlord, of which the tenant is aware. This is done in the tenant's "initial notice of delay". What this notice must offer, however, is a "response period" of not less than a month. During or after this response period, the landlord may serve a counter-notice under subs. (2). Such a counter-notice, unless success-fully challenged by the tenant by reference to the Lands Tribunal under subs. (4), has the effect of cancelling the initial notice of delay. In the absence, however, of such a counter-notice within the response period or after rejection by the Lands Tribunal of the counter-notice under subss. (5) and (6), the tenant is entitled to serve an "operative notice of delay" under subs. (3).

S.66B(2) of the 1987 Act

For the general function of the landlord's counter-notice, see the note on subs. (1). The precise meaning of subs. (2) may, however, be a little unclear. The meaning of the phrase "no action under this Part . . . it was for the landlord to take" is something which may cause difficulty for the Lands Tribunal if a counter-notice is challenged before it. The specific reference to "the beginning of the response period" is especially odd since it is provided that a counter-notice may be served "during or after" the response period and may surely, therefore, need to be based in some cases on circumstances which have arisen substantially later than "the beginning of the response period"? The origins of the phrase are in an earlier version of the Bill which explicitly confined any counter-notice to the response period itself. The words "either during or after" were inserted (to make better sense of the operation of subs. (3)) at Report stage in the House of Lords.

S.66B(3) of the 1987 Act

This subsection has to be read subject to the Lands Tribunal reference procedure in subs. (4) to (6). That procedure apart, the tenant may trigger the price abatement by service, after expiry of the "response period", of an "operative notice of delay". This has the effect of reducing the contract price by the amount of rent paid by the tenant during the period from the date of the operative notice up to the earlier of (i) service of a counter-notice; (ii) the date of delivery of a good and marketable title.

S.66B(4)–(6) of the 1987 Act

These subsections provide the Lands Tribunal reference procedure already referred to. The Tribunal is provided with copies of the "initial notice of delay" and the counter-notice and must decide whether, in its opinion, action should have been taken by the landlord, and find accordingly.

S.66C(1) of the 1987 Act

This subsection provides for the aggregation of periods of delay in the calculation of the overall reduction of the purchase price.

S.66C(2) of the 1987 Act

This subsection imposes an additional penalty on landlords who are in delay for long periods. If the period or periods in respect of which the price is abated total more than 12 months, the amount of the reduction is increased by 50 per cent. (or other prescribed percentage).

Effect of abatement of purchase price on recovery of discount

145. In section 72 of the 1987 Act (recovery of discount on early resale), after subsection (1) there shall be inserted the following subsection—

"(1A) Where a tenant has served on the landlord a notice under section 66A(1), the commencement of the period of 3 years referred to in subsection (1) shall be backdated by a period equal to the time (or, where section 66C(1) applies, the aggregate of the times) during which, by virtue of section 66A(2), any payment of rent falls to be taken into account."

DEFINITIONS

"landlord": s.82 of the 1987 Act.
"tenant": s.82 of the 1987 Act.

GENERAL NOTE

This section makes a further amendment to the 1987 Act consequential upon the insertion of ss.66A to C by s.144. Section 72 of the 1987 Act provides, subject to s.73, for the repayment of a proportion of the discount permitted at the time of a "right to buy" sale if the tenant sells the house within three years of the tenant's notice of acceptance. Now, the new subs. (1A) inserted by this section provides that, if the tenant has obtained an abatement of the price under s.66A(1) on the basis of a delayed offer to sell, then the commencement of the three-year period will be back-dated (from the eventual notice of acceptance) by a period equal to the period or periods (s.66C(1)) counted for price abatement purposes. This gives the tenant a greater opportunity to sell earlier without penalty if he or she wishes.

Other rights of secure tenants

Right to have repairs carried out

146. For section 60 of the 1987 Act there shall be substituted the following section—

"Right to have repairs carried out
   60.—(1) The Secretary of State may make regulations for entitling a secure tenant of a landlord prescribed by the Secretary of State, subject to and in accordance with the regulations, to have qualifying repairs carried out to the house which is the subject of the secure tenancy.
   (2) Those regulations shall prescribe—
   (a) the maximum amount which will be paid in respect of any single qualifying repair;
   (b) the maximum time within which a qualifying repair is to be completed.

(3) The regulations may also provide that—

(a) a landlord which has been prescribed under subsection (1) shall—

    (i) maintain a list of contractors who are prepared to carry out qualifying repairs;

    (ii) take such steps as may be prescribed to make its secure tenants aware of the provisions of the regulations and of the list of contractors;

    (iii) where the tenant makes an application to him for a qualifying repair to be carried out, issue a works order to the usual contractor specifying the nature of the repair and the last day of the maximum time prescribed under subsection (2)(b);

(b) where the usual contractor has not started the repair work by the last day specified in the works order, the tenant shall have the right to instruct one of the other listed contractors to carry out the repair;

(c) where the repair work is carried out by that other listed contractor, the landlord shall be liable to pay for the work carried out;

(d) a listed contractor who is instructed by a tenant shall notify the landlord that he has been so instructed as soon as he receives the instruction;

(e) if the usual contractor fails to carry out the repair within the specified maximum time, the landlord shall pay to the tenant such sum by way of compensation as may be determined by or under the regulations;

(f) the landlord may set off against any compensation payable under the regulations any sums owed to it by the tenant.

(4) The regulations may—

(a) make different provision with respect to different cases or descriptions of case, including different provision for different areas;

(b) make such procedural, incidental, supplementary and transitional provision as appears to the Secretary of State necessary or expedient.

(5) Nothing in subsections (2) to (4) above shall be taken as prejudicing the generality of subsection (1).

(6) Regulations under this section shall be made by statutory instrument.

(7) In this section—

'listed contractor' means any contractor (including the usual contractor) specified the landlord's list of contractors;

'qualifying repair' means a repair prescribed as such in the regulations;

'usual contractor' means the direct services organisation of the landlord or the contractor to whom the landlord has contracted its repairs."

DEFINITIONS

"house": s.338 of the 1987 Act.
"landlord": s.82 of the 1987 Act.
"listed contractor": s.60(7) of the 1987 Act.
"prescribed": s.338 of the 1987 Act.
"qualifying repair": s.60(7) of the 1987 Act.
"secure tenancy": s.82 of the 1987 Act.
"tenant": s.82 of the 1987 Act.
"usual contractor": s.60(7) of the 1987 Act.

GENERAL NOTE

Section 60 of the 1987 Act was, prior to consolidation, originally s.17A of the Tenants' Rights, Etc. (Scotland) Act 1980 as inserted by the Tenants' Rights, Etc. (Scotland) Amendment Act 1984. It contained powers for the Secretary of State to set up, by regulations, a scheme entitling secure tenants to carry out repairs (which the landlord was under an obligation to carry out) and recover the costs from the landlord. The necessary regulations were never made. As explained by the junior minister in Committee, this was because experience south of the border suggested that a rather different scheme would be required in Scotland. (For this and debate on the right to repair in general see Standing Committee B, cols. 530–537). In the *Tenant's Charter* the government undertook to introduce a new right to repair which "will be easy to understand, simple to use, and take account of your views . . . will give you a right to get urgent minor repairs done when your landlord has not done them promptly". The new s.60 is intended to honour that undertaking. Once again, it relies completely for its implementation, upon the making of regulations by the Secretary of State.

S.60(1) of the 1987 Act

This subsection provides the Secretary of State with the initial power to make regulations under which the repairs scheme is to operate. It is confined to secure tenancies and does not extend, for instance, to assured tenancies (*e.g.* of housing associations if made after January 2, 1989). A key component in the regulations will be the definition of a "qualifying repair". It is expected to be confined to small repairs. Further specification of what may or must be contained in the regulation (subject to subs. (5)) appears in subss. (2) to (4). At the time the Bill was being enacted, the proposed scheme was subject to consultation on the basis of a paper issued by the Scottish Office Environment Department in December 1991 which listed, *inter alia*, the suggested categories of repair work.

S.60(2)–(6) of the 1987 Act

Once the "qualifying repair" has been defined the essence of the scheme will be contained in the procedures referred to in subs. (3) read subject to the maximum amount (of money) and the maximum time prescribed under subs. (2). The consultation paper has suggested a maximum amount of £250 and two maximum periods of time of 24 hours and seven days, depending on the nature of the repair.

Right to compensation for improvements

147. After section 58 of the 1987 Act there shall be inserted the following section—

> **"Right to compensation for improvements**
> 58A.—(1) For the purposes of this section—
> (a) 'qualifying improvement work' is improvement work which is prescribed as such by the Secretary of State and which is begun not earlier than the commencement of section 147 of the Leasehold Reform, Housing and Urban Development Act 1993;
> (b) 'qualifying person' is a person who is, at the time the tenancy comes to an end, the tenant of a landlord named in sub-paragraphs (i) to (iv) of section 61(2)(a); and—
> > (i) is the tenant by whom the qualifying work was carried out; or
> > (ii) is a tenant of a joint tenancy which existed at the time the improvement work was carried out; or
> > (iii) succeeded to the tenancy under section 52 of the death of the tenant who carried out the work and the tenancy did not cease to be a secure tenancy on his succession;
> (c) a tenancy is terminated when—
> > (i) any of the circumstances of subsection (1) of section 46 apply and, in a case where the termination is under paragraph (c) or (f) of that subsection, the house which is the subject of the secure tenancy is vacated;

(ii) there is a change of landlord;
(iii) it is assigned to a new tenant.

(2) Where the tenant of a landlord specified in sub-paragraphs (i) to (iv) of section 61(2)(a) has carried out qualifying improvement work with the consent of that landlord under section 57, the qualifying person or persons shall on the termination of the tenancy be entitled to be paid compensation by the landlord in respect of the improvement work.

(3) Compensation shall not be payable if—
(a) the improvement is not of a prescribed description; or
(b) the tenancy comes to an end in prescribed circumstances; or
(c) compensation has been paid under section 58 in respect of the improvement; or
(d) the amount of any compensation which would otherwise be payable is less than such amount as may be prescribed,
and for the purposes of this subsection a prescribed description may be framed by reference to any circumstances whatever.

(4) Regulations under this section may provide that—
(a) any compensation payable shall be—
(i) determined by the landlord in such manner and taking into account such matters as may be prescribed; or
(ii) calculated in such manner and taking into account such matters as may be prescribed,
and shall not exceed such amount, if any, as may be prescribed; and
(b) the landlord may set off against any compensation payable under this section any sums owed to it by the qualifying person or persons.

(5) Where, in the case of two or more qualifying persons, one of them ('the missing person') cannot be found—
(a) a claim for compensation under this section may be made by, and compensation may be paid to, the other qualifying person or persons; but
(b) the missing person shall be entitled to recover his share of any compensation so paid from that person or those persons.

(6) The Secretary of State may by regulations made under this section make such procedural, incidental, supplementary and transitional provisions as appear to him to be necessary or expedient, and may in particular—
(a) provide for the manner in which and the period within which claims for compensation under this section are to be made, and for the procedure to be followed in determining such claims;
(b) prescribe the form of any document required to be used for the purposes of or in connection with such claims; and
(c) provide for the determination of questions arising under the regulations.

(7) Regulations under this section—
(a) may make different provision with respect to different cases or descriptions of case, including different provision for different areas;
(b) shall be made by statutory instrument which (except in the case of regulations which are made only under subsection (6)(b)) shall be subject to annulment in pursuance of a resolution of either House of Parliament."

DEFINITIONS
"house": s.338 of the 1987 Act.
"landlord": s.82 of the 1987 Act.

"prescribed": s.338 of the 1987 Act.
"secure tenancy": ss.44 and 82 of the 1987 Act.
"tenancy": s.82 of the 1987 Act.
"tenant": s.82 of the 1987 Act.

GENERAL NOTE
This section makes a further amendment to the 1987 Act by inserting a new s.58A. Like the new s.60 substituted by s.146 it falls within a group of sections which deal with the landlord's consent to work on a house (s.57), the landlord's power to reimburse the cost of work carried out (s.58) and the effect of works on rent (s.59). Now this new s.58A establishes the framework for a scheme under which tenants will qualify for direct compensation for works of improvement. Like the right to repair scheme under s.60, it depends heavily upon regulations to be made by the Secretary of State and which will contain all the important details. At the time the Bill was proceeding through Parliament, the proposed scheme was the subject of consultation in terms of a paper issued by the Scottish Office Environment Department in December 1992.

S.58A(1) of the 1987 Act
This subsection puts in place some necessary definitions: (a) "qualifying improvement work". The meaning of this depends on regulations to be made by the Secretary of State (see also subs. (7)) but cannot include work begun prior to the commencement of s.147. According to the consultation paper, the question of whether the qualifying work should be confined to the categories listed in s.57 (the discretionary scheme) or extended to embrace a new list of "works such as kitchen, bathroom or window replacements, insulation, central heating, rewiring, etc." was still to be decided; (b) "qualifying person". This definition is *not* subject to further expansion by regulations. Compensation is payable not only to the tenant who may have carried out the improvements but also in an appropriate case to a joint tenant (presumably, but this is not stated, of the improved house?) of a tenancy existing at the time of the improvement; or to a person who succeeded to the tenancy on the death of the tenant who did the work (under s.52). In all cases the qualifying person is the person who is "at the time the tenancy comes to an end" (why not "terminated" as defined in subs. (1)(c)?) the tenant of a local authority (including joint committee etc.), a development corporation or Scottish Homes (s.61(2)(a)(i) to (iv)) but not, *e.g.* of a housing association. The paragraph does not define the qualifying person as a secure tenant, although it may perhaps be argued that this was Parliament's intention, given the references to a "secure tenancy" in (iii) (and in (c)(i) below); (c) the termination of the tenancy is what triggers the obligation to compensate and this is defined as: (i) the circumstances listed in s.46(1) of the 1987 Act: (a) death of tenant where no qualified person (within the meaning of s.52) as successor; (b) a successor tenant declines tenancy/dies; (c) written agreement between landlord and tenant; (d) repossession of an abandoned house; (e) court order for recovery of possession; (f) four weeks' notice by tenant. In the case of (c) and (f) the termination is stated to occur when the house has been vacated; (ii) a change of landlord; (iii) tenancy assigned to a new tenant (assignation is permitted under s.55 of the 1987 Act).

S.58A(2) of the 1987 Act
This subsection defines the right to compensation by reference to the tenant's carrying out of the "qualifying improvement work" (see subs. (1)(a)) and the entitlement of the "qualifying person" or "qualifying persons" (subs. (1)(b)) to compensation (see subss. (3) and (4)) on the termination of the tenancy (see subs. (1)(c)). For the problem of "missing" qualifying persons, see subs. (5). The reference to s.57 is presumably intended to incorporate the requirements that the landlord's consent be in writing and that it be not unreasonably withheld. There is no express reference in this subsection to payment (in the case of termination of the tenancy by death) to personal representatives (*cf.* s.58(3)).

S.58A(3) of the 1987 Act
This subsection defines the circumstances in which compensation shall not be payable. All depend on regulations yet to be made to prescribe the exact conditions except (c) which refers to the situation in which, by s.58, compensation has been paid under the landlord's discretionary powers. The final three lines of the subsection, conferring very broad discretionary powers on the minister, were added at Standing Committee stage in the House of Commons (Standing Committee B, col. 553). Possible exclusions of eligibility may be where the tenancy is terminated either by application to purchase or by court order following breach of tenancy conditions.

S.58A(4) of the 1987 Act
This subsection was substituted for an earlier version at Committee stage in the House of Commons. The new formulation introduced the reference to the landlord's power to set off

against compensation payable any sums owed by the "qualifying person". The consultation paper suggested principles (especially an increase in the value of the property) and mechanisms (whether based on increased capital or rental value) for assessment of compensation. It seems likely that a maximum amount of £500 per item of qualifying work may be prescribed.

S.58A(5) of the 1987 Act
This subsection provides that the payment of compensation may proceed, notwithstanding the fact that a qualifying person cannot be found, but subject to the entitlement of that missing person to recover a "share" from the other person or persons.

S.58A(6) and (7) of the 1987 Act
The power to make regulations. It is not completely clear what the exception in subs. 7(b) achieves in relation to regulations under subs. (6)(b). Section 331 of the 1987 Act provides: "subject to the provisions of this Act, regulations made by a statutory instrument under this Act shall be subject to annulment in pursuance of a resolution of either House of Parliament". At the time of the consultation paper, it was unclear whether disputes arising from claims for compensation would go to the sheriff or to *e.g.* the district valuer or the regional assessor.

Right to information

148. After section 75 of the 1987 Act there shall be inserted the following section—

> **"Duty of local authority landlord to provide information about right to buy**
> 75A.—(1) A landlord which is one of those mentioned in section 61(2)(a)(i) or (ii) shall supply each of its secure tenants at least once every year with information about his right to purchase his house under this Part.
>
> (2) The information supplied under subsection (1) shall be in such form as the landlord considers best suited to explain in simple terms and so far as it considers appropriate the right referred to in that subsection."

DEFINITIONS
"house": s.338 of the 1987 Act.
"landlord": s.82 of the 1987 Act.
"secure tenant": ss.44 and 82 of the 1987 Act.

GENERAL NOTE
This section was added to the Bill as a new clause at House of Lords Report stage. The minister (Lord Fraser) explained that it was designed to have the same effect for Scotland as s.123 will for England and Wales (*Hansard*, H.L. Vol. 545, col. 1927). The new s.75A of the 1987 Act simply requires local authorities to provide their secure tenants with information about the right to buy.

Housing welfare services

Provision of housing welfare services

149. Part I of the 1987 Act shall have effect, and be deemed always to have had effect, as if after section 5 there were inserted the following section—

> **"Power of local authority to provide welfare services**
> 5A.—(1) A local authority may provide in connection with housing accommodation provided by them (whether or not under this Part) such welfare services, that is to say services for promoting the welfare of the persons for whom the accommodation is so provided, as accord with the needs of those persons.
>
> (2) The local authority may make reasonable charges for welfare services provided by virtue of this section.
>
> (3) Notwithstanding the provisions of section 203, a local authority may attribute the income from and the expenditure on the welfare

services provided under subsection (1) to a revenue account other than their housing revenue account.

(4) In this section 'welfare services' does not include the repair, maintenance, supervision or management of houses or other property.

(5) The powers conferred by this section shall not be regarded as restricting those conferred by section 83 of the Local Government (Scotland) Act 1973 (power to incur expenditure for purposes not otherwise authorised) and accordingly the references in subsection (1) of that section to any other enactment shall not include a reference to this section."

DEFINITIONS
  "house": s.338 of the 1987 Act.
  "local authority": s.338 of the 1987 Act.

GENERAL NOTE
  This section is designed to reverse the presumed effect in Scotland of the English Court of Appeal in *R.* v. *Ealing London Borough*, ex p. *Lewis* (*Jennifer*) 90 L.G.R. 571 and inserts retrospectively a new s.5A into the 1987 Act to enable housing authorities to provide in connection with their housing accommodation "services for promoting the welfare of the persons for whom the accommodation is so provided, as accord with the needs of those persons" but not including "the repair, maintenance, supervision or management of houses or other property". The point is to permit (though perhaps only temporarily—see s.151) authorities to provide, *e.g.* a warden in sheltered house together with other personal services and to charge for this provision if they wish. Net costs may be charged either to the housing revenue account or to another account in the general fund (and financed out of council tax). For the housing revenue account, see also s.150. For the power to repeal s.5A, see s.151.

S.5A(5) of the 1987 Act
  This subsection was inserted at House of Lords Report stage. In relation to the equivalent amendment for England and Wales, it was explained that the provision of the specific power to provide welfare services for their own tenants might have inadvertently narrowed the powers of authorities to provide services (*e.g.* community alarm schemes) for people in the private sector using s.137 of the Local Government Act 1972 (s.83 of the 1973 Act in Scotland) (*Hansard*, H.L. Vol. 545, cols. 1928 and 1929).

Accounting for housing welfare services

150. Schedule 15 to the 1987 Act (the housing revenue account) shall have effect, and be deemed always to have had effect, as if after paragraph 4 there were inserted the following paragraph—

"Provision of welfare services

4A. Where in any year a local authority provide welfare services under section 5A, they may—
  (a) carry to the credit of the housing revenue account an amount equal to the whole or any part of the income of the authority for the year from charges in respect of the provision of those services;
  (b) carry to the debit of the account an amount equal to the whole or any part of the expenditure of the authority for the year in respect of the provision of those services."

DEFINITIONS
  "local authority": s.338 of the 1987 Act.

GENERAL NOTE
  This section should be read in conjunction with s.149 (and s.151); this section is a consequential (and retrospective) amendment to Sched. 15 to the 1987 Act relating to the housing revenue account (s.203).

Power to repeal provisions relating to housing welfare services

151. After section 5A of the 1987 Act there shall be inserted the following section—

> **"Power to repeal provisions relating to welfare services**
>
> 5B.—(1) The Secretary of State may at any time by order made by statutory instrument provide that, on such day or in relation to such periods as may be appointed by the order, section 5A, this section and paragraph 4A of Schedule 15 shall—
>
> (a) cease to have effect; or
> (b) cease to apply for such purposes as may be specified in the order.
>
> (2) An order under this section may—
>
> (a) appoint different days or periods for different provisions or purposes or for different authorities or descriptions of authority; and
> (b) contain such incidental, supplementary or transitional provisions as appear to the Secretary of State to be necessary or expedient."

GENERAL NOTE

This section inserts (without need of retrospectivity) a new s.5B into the 1987 Act giving power to the Secretary of State to repeal ss.5A and 5B and para. 4A of Sched. 15 by order (subject only to the negative resolution procedure—s.331). The point is that the provision of welfare services by local authorities is not intended by the Government to be a permanent arrangement. Their view is that local government reorganisation to combine housing with social work services will remove the need for the powers in the new s.5A. It will not be repealed before reorganisation (see, *e.g. Hansard*, H.L. Vol. 544, col. 683).

Miscellaneous

Management agreements with housing co-operatives

152. After section 22 of the 1987 Act there shall be inserted the following section—

> **"Management agreements with housing co-operatives**
>
> 22A.—(1) In this section 'housing co-operative' has the meaning given in subsection (1) of section 22 except that the reference in that subsection to the Secretary of State's approval shall be construed as a reference to his approval in relation to the purposes of this section.
>
> (2) On an application by a housing co-operative a local authority shall make an agreement with them for the performance by that housing co-operative, on such terms as may be provided in the agreement, of the local authority's functions under section 17(1) relating to the management of houses which are subject to the agreement.
>
> (3) Before making such an agreement the local authority shall satisfy themselves that the housing co-operative—
>
> (a) have the approval of the Secretary of State;
> (b) are able to perform the functions competently and efficiently;
> (c) are representative of the tenants of the houses.
>
> (4) Where the local authority refuse to enter into an agreement on the grounds that the housing co-operative do not satisfy paragraph (b) or (c) of subsection (3), the housing co-operative may appeal to the Secretary of State who may confirm or reverse the decision of the local authority.
>
> (5) Where the Secretary of State reverses the decision of the local authority, the authority and the housing co-operative shall make the agreement.

(6) Where the local authority and the housing co-operative are unable to agree on the terms of the agreement, the housing co-operative may appeal to the Secretary of State who may determine the terms of the agreement.

(7) An agreement to which this section applies shall be made only with the approval of the Secretary of State, which may be given either generally or to any local authority or description or local authority or in any particular case, and may be given unconditionally or subject to any conditions."

DEFINITIONS
   "house": s.338 of the 1987 Act.
   "housing co-operative": s.22A(1) of the 1987 Act (as inserted by this section).
   "local authority": s.338 of the 1987 Act.
   "tenant": s.82 of the 1987 Act.

GENERAL NOTE
   This section was inserted as a new clause at House of Commons Report stage (*Hansard*, H.C. Vol. 218, cols. 932–935). Under s.22 of the 1987 Act there is provision for an agreement to be made between a local authority and a "society, company or body of trustees for the time being approved by the Secretary of State for the purposes of this section (in this section called a 'housing co-operative')" under which the housing co-operative is to exercise, on terms agreed, any of the authority's powers and duties relating to land held under Pt. I of the Act (general duties and powers). Although not widely used, this provision has enabled co-operatives established under the section to assume powers as landlord. Their tenants are secure tenants with the right to buy (ss.44 and 61). Now this new s.22A incorporates the idea of the "housing co-operative" and uses it as the means of delegating to the co-operative not the authority's general function as landlord but only the authority's powers under s.17(1) relating to the management of houses under the agreement. The section provides that the co-operative must, among other things, be "representative of the tenants of the houses" under the agreement and also that an authority is required to enter into an agreement on application by a co-operative unless, subject to appeal to the Secretary of State, the authority refuses under subss. (4) or (6). For debate on ensuring the representation of tenants see House of Commons Report stage above.

S.22A(1) of the 1987 Act
   For the meaning of "housing co-operative" under s.22(1), see the General Note. The Secretary of State's "approval" takes two forms under the section. He must "approve" the co-operative (see also subs. 3(a)) but also, whether in a particular case or generally, the agreement (subs. (7)). He is also involved in any appeal under subss. (4) to (6).

S.22A(2) of the 1987 Act
   This requires the authority to enter into the management agreement on application by a co-operative but see the possibility of refusal under subs. (4) and disagreement on terms under subs. (6).

S.22A(3) of the 1987 Act
   The section does not itself give further guidance on how an authority is to satisfy itself under paras. (b) and (c) but it is, on both matters, open to appeal to the Secretary of State.

S.22A(4) and (5) of the 1987 Act
   These sections provide the appeal mechanism in the event of local authority refusal of agreement by reference to subs. (3)(b) or (c). Although, under subs. (5) the two parties must make an agreement if the Secretary of State reverses the authority's refusal, there is still scope for continued disagreement on terms subject to further appeal.

S.22A(6) of the 1987 Act
   The co-operative's further right of appeal to the Secretary of State in the event of disagreement on terms.

S.22A(7) of the 1987 Act
   The Secretary of State's approval of the agreement is required (although this may be given in general terms) as well as his approval of the co-operative itself.

Standards and performance in housing management

153. After section 17 of the 1987 Act there shall be inserted the following sections—

"Standards and performance in housing management

Publication of information

17A.—(1) A local authority shall, in relation to their management of the houses which they hold for housing purposes, publish each year such information as—

  (a) may be prescribed by the Secretary of State about—

    (i) the standard of service of management which the authority undertake to provide;

    (ii) the authority's performance in the past in the achievement of that standard;

    (iii) the authority's intentions for the future in relation to the achievement of that standard;

    (iv) any other matter which he thinks should be included in the information to be published;

  (b) the authority consider it appropriate to publish in relation to the matters mentioned in paragraph (a) above, either as a result of having consulted tenants or otherwise;

  (c) the authority consider it appropriate to publish in relation to any other matter, either as a result of consulting tenants or otherwise.

(2) Before publishing such information, a local authority shall consult their tenants as to the information to be published under subsection (1) and shall take account of the characteristics of the different parts of their districts or areas and of the difference in information which may be appropriate in relation to these parts.

(3) The Secretary of State may direct a local authority to consult tenants or groups of tenants representing less than the whole of their district or area.

Power of Secretary of State to direct local authority

17B. At the same time as the information is published, the local authority shall send a copy of the document in which it is published to the Secretary of State who may, if he considers that the publication is unsatisfactory, direct the local authority to publish the information in such manner as he specifies in the direction.

Management plan

17C. A local authority shall, if the Secretary of State gives them notice to do so, prepare and submit to him within three months after such notice, a plan for the management of the houses which they hold for housing purposes."

DEFINITIONS
  "house": s.338 of the 1987 Act.
  "local authority": s.338 of the 1987 Act.
  "prescribed": s.338 of the 1987 Act.
  "tenant": s.82 of the 1987 Act.

GENERAL NOTE
  This section is another which derives from the *Tenant's Charter for Scotland*. The Government's intention (*Charter*, p. 12) was that, following upon similar developments in relation to housing associations, local authority tenants and tenants' organisations should be able to have information about an authority's standards, *i.e.* what it proposes to achieve on, *e.g.* repair times, letter response times and speed of processing right to buy sales. There should also be information on actual performance on such matters and, *e.g.* the number of tenants allocated

houses and the number of homeless people housed. The government would insist on full consultation with tenants and on the production of a "housing management plan" including details of how the authority would involve tenants. There would also be a rôle for the Accounts Commission which would, *inter alia*, be able to publish "league tables of local authority standards of performance and costs". This section inserts new ss.17A to 17C into the 1987 Act which are intended to achieve many of these objectives. A Scottish Office consultation paper on "Standards and Performance in Housing Management" was issued in December 1991.

S.17A(1) of the 1987 Act
The Secretary of State is to prescribe the main categories of information as to both standards and performance which each authority must publish annually.

S.17A(2) and (3) of the 1987 Act
It was part of the argument in the *Charter* that tenants needed information at the level of their own estate/village. The Secretary of State has an apparently very wide power to "direct" forms of local consultation.

S.17B of the 1987 Act
There is nothing in these new sections about the mode of publication or the cost of access to the published information except that, in this section, there is reference to a "document". The power to direct republication in this section does seem to be exceptionally broadly drawn.

S.17C of the 1987 Act
This implements the idea of the "housing management plan" although it seems, on the one hand, to be a less comprehensively imposed requirement than that which was promised but, on the other, to be an extraordinarily open-ended obligation once imposed by notice from the Secretary of State. There is nothing to define what a plan for the management of houses consists of.

Further provision as to allocation of housing

154. In section 20 of the 1987 Act (persons to have priority on housing list and allocation of housing) at the end there shall be added the following subsection—

> "(3) A member of a local authority shall be excluded from a decision on the allocation of local authority housing, or of housing in respect of which the local authority may nominate the tenant, where—
> (a) the house in question is situated; or
> (b) the applicant for the house in question resides,
> in the electoral division or ward for which that member is elected."

DEFINITIONS
"house": s.338 of the 1987 Act.
"local authority": s.338 of the 1987 Act.

GENERAL NOTE
This section makes an extraordinary addition to local government legislation. There are, in the Local Government (Scotland) Act 1973, ss.38–42, rules designed to prevent the direct involvement in local authority decisions of members (of councils, committees, sub-committees) in matters in which they have a direct or indirect interest, pecuniary or otherwise. By adding to s.20 of the 1987 Act this section produces a new restriction on decision-making by councillors. A member is "excluded from a decision", a phrase not further defined, on the allocation of "local authority housing" where the house to be allocated is situated (or the applicant for it resides) in the member's own division or ward. In debate the principle underlying this innovation was generally welcomed (see Standing Committee B, cols. 726–735, but, for a passionately opposing view, in part because the provision affects Scotland only, see *Hansard*, H.L. Vol. 543, cols. 106–107) although, on the one hand, it was also suggested that the clause should go further and exclude all elected members from allocation decisions and, on the other hand, it was observed that exclusion of a member might cause administrative difficulties (*e.g.* as to a quorum for a particular decision). The question of involvement in a "decision on appeal" was also raised. What happens if an excluded councillor does, inadvertently, vote? The extension to include houses to which a local authority nominates tenants was made at House of Commons Report stage (*Hansard*, H.C. Vol. 218, col. 951).

Rules relating to housing list

155.—(1) For subsection (1) of section 21 of the 1987 Act (publication of rules relating to the housing list) there shall be substituted the following subsection—

"(1) It shall be the duty—

(a) of every local authority to make and to publish in accordance with subsection (4), and again within six months of any alteration thereof, rules governing—

(i) the admission of applicants to any housing list;
(ii) the priority of allocation of houses;
(iii) the transfer of tenants from houses owned by the landlord to houses owned by other bodies;
(iv) exchange of houses;

(b) of Scottish Homes and development corporations (including urban development corporations) to publish in accordance with subsection (4), and again within six months of any alteration thereof, any rules they may have governing the matters set out in sub-paragraphs (i) to (iv) of paragraph (a) above."

(2) In subsection (3) of section 19 of that Act (admission to housing list) for the words "Where a local authority has rules which" there shall be substituted the words "Where the rules made by a local authority under section 21(1)".

DEFINITIONS
"development corporation": s.338 of the 1987 Act.
"house": s.338 of the 1987 Act.
"housing list": s.19(4) of the 1987 Act.
"local authority": s.338 of the 1987 Act.
"tenant": s.82 of the 1987 Act.

GENERAL NOTE
Prior to the amendments made by this section, s.21 of the 1987 Act imposed a duty upon local authorities, Scottish Homes and development corporations to publish any house allocation rules they may have. In contrast with housing associations, it was not specified in statute what rules they should actually have, although the content of some rules was effectively prescribed by s.20. As a result of these amendments, local authorities (but still not Scottish Homes or the development corporations—for debate on that issue, see Standing Committee B, cols. 735–736) join housing associations in being obliged to have rules on the matters listed in the new subs. (1)(a) of s.21.

Defective dwellings: damages for landlord's failure to notify

156. After subsection (3) of section 299 of the 1987 Act (jurisdiction of sheriff) there shall be added the following subsections—

"(4) Where damages are awarded in proceedings commenced before December 1, 1994, which arise out of a failure on the part of the public sector authority to give a person acquiring a relevant interest in a dwelling notice in writing under section 291, the amount of damages for the purposes of this subsection shall be equal to the difference between—

(a) the market value of the dwelling assessed as if it were not a defective dwelling and were available for sale on the open market with vacant possession; and

(b) the market value of the dwelling assessed as a defective dwelling and as if available for sale on the open market with vacant possession.

(5) Subsection (4) applies in relation to proceedings which arise out of a failure by the authority before the coming into force of section 156 of the Leasehold Reform, Housing and Urban Development Act

28–219

1993 as it does to proceedings which arise out of a failure by the authority after that date."

DEFINITIONS
"defective dwelling": s.303 of the 1987 Act.
"interest in a dwelling": s.303 of the 1987 Act.
"public sector authority": ss.300 and 303 of the 1987 Act.
"relevant interest": s.303 of the 1987 Act.

GENERAL NOTE
This section was added at House of Lords Report stage (*Hansard*, H.L. Vol. 545, cols. 1935–8) after an earlier version had been proposed by Archy Kirkwood M.P. at House of Commons Report stage (*Hansard*, H.C. Vol. 218, cols. 1023–1026). As explained by the Lord Advocate, the section is intended to assist the purchasers of certain "defective dwellings". The Housing Defects Act 1984, subsequently consolidated for Scotland as Pt. XIV of the 1987 Act, provided substantial remedies (including repurchase by the landlord) to secure tenants who had exercised their right to buy a house, only to discover subsequently that it was defective in ways which were formally designated. Such remedies were available only in relation to sales up to April 26, 1984. Thereafter, it was the duty of landlords to give written notice to purchasing tenants to warn them of the defect (s.291). If no such notice is given and a tenant buys a defective house thinking it to be sound, he or she is entitled to claim damages under s.299. Problems had, however, arisen as to the measure of damages payable as these were being assessed as the difference between the low (defective) value and the purchase price actually paid, *i.e.* after deduction of discount. The government wishes, by means of this addition to s.299, to establish that, so long as any proceedings for compensation are commenced before December 1, 1994, damages will be calculated as the difference between the defective value and the *full market value*.

Other amendments of 1987 Act

157.—(1) In section 17 of the 1987 Act (management of local authority houses), in subsection (1), the words "and exercised by" shall cease to have effect.

(2) In section 61 of that Act (secure tenant's right to purchase), in subsection (10), subparagraphs (i) and (ii) of paragraph (b) shall cease to have effect.

(3) In section 62 of that Act (price)—
(a) in subsection (3)(b), the words "continuous" and "immediately" shall cease to have effect;
(b) after subsection (3) there shall be inserted—
"(3A) there shall be deducted from the discount an amount equal to any previous discount, or the aggregate of any previous discounts, received by the appropriate person on any previous purchase of a house by any of these persons from a landlord who is a person specified in subsection (11) of section 61 or prescribed in an order made under that subsection, reduced by any amount of such previous discount recovered by such a landlord.";
(c) in subsection (4)—
(i) for paragraph (a) there shall be substituted—
"(a) the "appropriate person" is whoever of—
(i) the tenant; or
(ii) the tenant's spouse if living with him at the date of service of the application to purchase; or
(iii) a deceased spouse if living with the tenant at the time of death; or
(iv) any joint tenant who is a joint purchaser of the house,
has the longer or longest such occupation;" and
(ii) at the end there shall be inserted—
"and, for the purposes of subsection (3A), the "appropriate person" is any of the persons mentioned in sub-paragraphs (i) to (iv) of paragraph (a)."

(4) In section 248 of that Act (repairs grants), the proviso to subsection (5) shall be amended as follows—

(a) after the words "shall not apply" there shall be inserted "(a)"; and

(b) at the end there shall be added—

"(b) in relation to an application for a repairs grant in respect of works intended to reduce exposure to radon gas."

"house": s.338 of the 1987 Act.
"local authority": s.338 of the 1987 Act.
"repairs grant": s.338 of the 1987 Act.
"secure tenant": ss.82 and 44 of the 1987 Act.

GENERAL NOTE
This section makes a number of miscellaneous but, especially in subss. (2) and (3), important amendments to the 1987 Act.

Subs. (1)
This subsection was inserted at House of Commons Report stage (*Hansard*, H.C. Vol. 218, col. 933). As it stood prior to this amendment, s.17(1) of the 1987 Act provided that the management of houses held (for housing purposes) by a local authority is to be "vested in and exercised by the authority". This amendment removes the need for the duties actually to be exercised by the authority itself—to remove any impediment for their being contracted out/privatised.

Subs. (2)
This subsection removes from s.61(10)(b) the two paragraphs which concern the treatment of interruptions in tenant occupation of public sector housing compatible with the "continuity" of occupation required for the purposes of establishing the level of discount allowed under the right to buy. Because of the further amendment made by subs. (3)(a), such continuity of occupation is no longer required.

Subs. (3)(a) See subs. (2) above.

Subs. (3)(b) and (c). Paragraph (b) was inserted at House of Commons Report stage (*Hansard*, H.C. Vol. 218, col. 952) but then a new version (adding para. (c)) was substituted at House of Lords Report stage (*Hansard*, H.L. Vol. 545, col. 1938). The insertion of the new subs. (3A) in s.62 of the Act is intended to reduce the amount of discount otherwise allowable under the right to buy by the amount of any discount previously paid (under the 1987 Act or the equivalent provisions in the Housing Act 1985) to any of the persons listed in subs. (4) as revised by para. (c) *less* any discount recovered on early resale. The point is to exclude the benefit of a second discount within the same "family" which was thought to be unfair. The reference to "these persons" in subs. (3A) seems inelegant and possibly misleading.

Subs. (4)
Section 248 of the 1987 Act on repairs grants incorporates and applies to repairs grants some of the content of s.240 which imposes certain restrictions on access to improvement grants. One of these (s.240(2)(c)) imposes a "rateable value" limit but there is an exception, as this is related to repairs grants, in respect of grants for the replacement of lead pipes. This exception is now extended to works reducing exposure to radon gas.

PART III

DEVELOPMENT OF URBAN AND OTHER AREAS

The Urban Regeneration Agency

The Agency

158.—(1) There shall be a body corporate to be known as the Urban Regeneration Agency ("the Agency") for the purpose of exercising the functions conferred on it by the following provisions of this Part.

(2) Schedule 17 to this Act shall have effect with respect to the constitution of the Agency and Schedule 18 to this Act shall have effect with respect to the finances of the Agency.

(3) It is hereby declared that, except as provided by section 175, the Agency is not to be regarded as the servant or agent of the Crown or as enjoying any status, immunity or privilege of the Crown and that its property is not to be regarded as the property of, or property held on behalf of, the Crown.

GENERAL NOTE
This section establishes the Urban Regeneration Agency.

Subs. (2)
Schedule 17 to the Act sets out the constitution of the Agency, its membership, staffing, *etc.* Schedule 18 outlines the Agency's financial duties, methods of achieving them and various controls with regard to accounting and finance.

Subs. (3)
See note to s.175.

Objects of Agency

159.—(1) The main object of the Agency shall be to secure the regeneration of land in England—
  (a) which is land of one or more of the descriptions mentioned in subsection (2); and
  (b) which the Agency (having regard to guidance, and acting in accordance with directions, given by the Secretary of State under section 167) determines to be suitable for regeneration under this Part.
(2) The descriptions of land referred to in subsection (1)(a) are—
  (a) land which is vacant or unused;
  (b) land which is situated in an urban area and which is under-used or ineffectively used;
  (c) land which is contaminated, derelict, neglected or unsightly; and
  (d) land which is likely to become derelict, neglected or unsightly by reason of actual or apprehended collapse of the surface as the result of the carrying out of relevant operations which have ceased to be carried out;
and in this subsection "relevant operations" has the same meaning as in section 1 of the Derelict Land Act 1982.
(3) The Agency shall also have the object of securing the development of land in England which the Agency—
  (a) having regard to guidance given by the Secretary of State under section 167;
  (b) acting in accordance with directions given by the Secretary of State under that section; and
  (c) with the consent of the Secretary of State,
determines to be suitable for development under this Part.
(4) The objects of the Agency are to be achieved in particular by the following means (or by such of them as seem to the Agency to be appropriate in any particular case), namely—
  (a) by securing that land and buildings are brought into effective use;
  (b) by developing, or encouraging the development of, existing and new industry and commerce;
  (c) by creating an attractive and safe environment;
  (d) by facilitating the provision of housing and providing, or facilitating the provision of, social and recreational facilities.

DEFINITIONS
"Agency": ss.158 and 185.

GENERAL NOTE
This section details the objects of the Agency and the means by which they are to be achieved. These are further amplified in draft guidance from the Department of Environment set out as Appendix 5 below.

Subs. (2)

In this subsection "relevant operations" means: "underground mining operations other than operations for the purpose of the working and getting of coal, or of coal and other minerals worked with coal, or for the purpose of getting any product from coal in the course of working and getting coal", the Derelict Land Act 1982, s.1.

General powers of Agency

160.—(1) Subject to the following provisions of this Part, for the purpose of achieving its objects the Agency may—

(a) acquire, hold, manage, reclaim, improve and dispose of land, plant, machinery, equipment and other property;

(b) carry out the development or redevelopment of land, including the conversion or demolition of existing buildings;

(c) carry out building and other operations;

(d) provide means of access, services or other facilities for land;

(e) seek to ensure the provision of water, electricity, gas, sewerage and other services;

(f) carry on any business or undertaking for the purposes of its objects;

(g) with the consent of the Secretary of State, form, or acquire interests in, bodies corporate;

(h) act with other persons, whether in partnership or otherwise;

(i) give financial assistance to other persons;

(j) act as agent for other persons;

(k) provide advisory or other services and facilities; and

(l) generally do anything necessary or expedient for the purposes of its objects or for purposes incidental to those purposes.

(2) Nothing in section 159 or this section shall empower the Agency—

(a) to provide housing otherwise than by acquiring existing housing accommodation and making it available on a temporary basis for purposes incidental to the purposes of its objects;

(b) to acquire an interest in a body corporate which at the time of the acquisition is carrying on a trade or business, if the effect of the acquisition would be to make the body corporate a subsidiary of the Agency; or

(c) except with the consent of the Secretary of State, to dispose of any land otherwise than for the best consideration which can reasonably be obtained.

(3) For the avoidance of doubt it is hereby declared that subsection (1) relates only to the capacity of the Agency as a statutory corporation and nothing in section 159 or this section authorises it to disregard any enactment or rule of law.

(4) In this section—

"improve", in relation to land, includes refurbish, equip and fit out;

"subsidiary" has the meaning given by section 736 of the Companies Act 1985;

and in this section and the following provisions of this Part references to land include land not falling within subsection (1) or (3) of section 159.

DEFINITIONS

"Agency": ss.158 and 185.

GENERAL NOTE

This section outlines the general powers of the Agency. It may only provide housing on a temporary basis and then only where that is existing housing which it has acquired (separate powers exist in the Housing Act 1988 to create other bodies for housing regeneration purposes). It may not acquire interests in a body corporate such as to make that body corporate a subsidiary of the Agency, and it must sell land at the best prices reasonably obtainable unless it has the express consent of the Secretary of State to do otherwise.

"Subsidiary"—a company is a subsidiary of another for the purposes of s.736 of the Companies Act 1985 if the other is a member of it and controls the composition of its board of directors or holds more than half the nominal value of its equity share capital, or is the subsidiary of any company which is that other's subsidiary, subject to certain qualifications within the section.

Vesting of land by order

161.—(1) Subject to subsections (2) and (3), the Secretary of State may by order provide that land specified in the order which is vested in a local authority, statutory undertakers or other public body, or in a wholly-owned subsidiary of a public body, shall vest in the Agency.

(2) An order under subsection (1) may not specify land vested in statutory undertakers which is used for the purpose of carrying on their statutory undertakings or which is held for that purpose.

(3) In the case of land vested in statutory undertakers, the power to make an order under subsection (1) shall be exercisable by the Secretary of State and the appropriate Minister.

(4) An order under subsection (1) shall have the same effect as a declaration under the Compulsory Purchase (Vesting Declarations) Act 1981 except that, in relation to such an order, the enactments mentioned in Schedule 19 to this Act shall have effect with the modifications specified in that Schedule.

(5) Compensation under the Land Compensation Act 1961, as applied by subsection (4) and Schedule 19 to this Act, shall be assessed by reference to values current on the date the order under subsection (1) comes into force.

(6) No compensation is payable, by virtue of an order under subsection (1), under Part IV of the Land Compensation Act 1961.

(7) In this section—

"the appropriate Minister"—

    (a) in relation to statutory undertakers who are or are deemed to be statutory undertakers for the purposes of any provision of Part XI of the Town and Country Planning Act 1990, shall be construed as if contained in that Part;

    (b) in relation to any other statutory undertakers, shall be construed in accordance with an order made by the Secretary of State;

and the reference to the Secretary of State and the appropriate Minister shall be similarly construed;

"local authority" means a county council, a district council, a London borough council or the Common Council of the City of London;

"statutory undertakers", except where the context otherwise requires, means—

    (a) persons authorised by any enactment to carry on any railway, light railway, tramway, road transport, water transport, canal, inland navigation, dock, harbour, pier or lighthouse undertaking, or any undertaking for the supply of hydraulic power;

    (b) British Shipbuilders, the Civil Aviation Authority, the British Coal Corporation and the Post Office;

    (c) any other authority, body or undertakers specified in an order made by the Secretary of State;

    (d) any wholly-owned subsidiary of any person, authority or body mentioned in paragraphs (a) and (b) or of any authority, body or undertakers specified in an order made under paragraph (c);

and "statutory undertaking" shall be construed accordingly;

"wholly-owned subsidiary" has the meaning given by section 736 of the Companies Act 1985.

(8) If any question arises as to which Minister is the appropriate Minister in relation to any statutory undertakers, that question shall be determined by the Treasury.

(9) An order under subsection (1) shall be made by statutory instrument but no such order shall be made unless a draft of the order has been laid before and approved by resolution of each House of Parliament.

(10) An order under subsection (7) shall be made by statutory instrument which shall be subject to annulment in pursuance of a resolution of either House of Parliament.

DEFINITIONS
  "Agency": ss.158 and 185.

GENERAL NOTE
  This section creates the power to vest land in the Agency which is currently vested in other public bodies. It excludes land vested in statutory undertakers used or held for the purposes of carrying on their statutory undertakings (subs. (2)) (compare the definition of "operational land" in s.263 of the Town and Country Planning Act 1990).

Subs. (4)
  A vesting order has the same effect as a declaration under the Compulsory Purchase (Vesting Declarations) Act 1981, *i.e.* on the vesting date the land specified together with the right to enter on it and take possession of it vests in the Agency. Compensation is calculated on the basis of the value on the date of the order, not the date when possession is taken.

Subs. (7)
  The appropriate minister. See s.265 of the Town and Country Planning Act 1990. It is generally the minister with general supervisory responsibility for the activities carried on by the particular statutory undertaker. A body corporate is a "wholly owned subsidiary" of another if it has no members except that other and that other's wholly owned subsidiaries and its or their nominees.

Acquisition of land

162.—(1) The Agency may, for the purpose of achieving its objects or for purposes incidental to that purpose, acquire land by agreement or, on being authorised to do so by the Secretary of State, compulsorily.

(2) The Agency may, for those purposes, be authorised by the Secretary of State, by means of a compulsory purchase order, to acquire compulsorily such new rights over land as are specified in the order.

(3) Where the land referred to in subsection (1) or (2) forms part of a common, open space or fuel or field garden allotment, the Agency may acquire (by agreement or, on being authorised to do so by the Secretary of State, compulsorily) land for giving in exchange for the land or, as the case may be, rights acquired.

(4) Subject to section 169, the Acquisition of Land Act 1981 shall apply to the compulsory acquisition of land by virtue of subsection (1) or (3).

(5) Schedule 3 to that Act shall apply to the compulsory acquisition of a right by virtue of subsection (2) but with the modification that the reference in paragraph 4(3) to statutory undertakers includes a reference to the Agency.

(6) The provisions of Part I of the Compulsory Purchase Act 1965 (so far as applicable), other than section 31, shall apply to the acquisition by the Agency of land by agreement; and in that Part as so applied "land" has the meaning given by the Interpretation Act 1978.

(7) In subsection (2)—
  "new rights over land" means rights over land which are not in existence when the order specifying them is made;

"compulsory purchase order" has the same meaning as in the Acquisition of Land Act 1981.

DEFINITIONS
"Agency": ss.158 and 185.

GENERAL NOTE

This section lays down the powers of the Agency to acquire land. This may be done either voluntarily or compulsorily in order to achieve its objects under Pt. III of the Act. The section also provides for the compulsory acquisition of rights so that where only the taking of rights is necessary to achieve the Agency's objects this in itself may be done by means of a compulsory purchase order (subs. (2)).

Subs. (4)

The Acquisition of Land Act 1986 consolidates the statutory provisions regulating the procedures for compulsory acquisition of land.

Subs. (6)

The Compulsory Purchase Act 1965 governs compensation and the taking of lands compulsorily acquired. This allows for the acquisition of land either voluntarily or compulsorily (but in the latter case only with the authorisation of the Secretary of State). The standard statutory provisions relating to such acquisition apply, but subject to certain amendments or substitutions detailed later in this Act (see s.169 and Sched. 20).

Power to enter and survey land

163.—(1) Any person who is duly authorised in writing by the Agency may at any reasonable time enter any land for the purpose of surveying it, or estimating its value, in connection with—

(a) any proposal to acquire that land or any other land; or

(b) any claim for compensation in respect of any such acquisition.

(2) The power to survey land shall be construed as including power to search and bore for the purpose of ascertaining the nature of the subsoil or the presence of minerals in it.

(3) A person authorised under this section to enter any land—

(a) shall, if so required, produce evidence of his authority before entry, and

(b) shall not demand admission as of right to any land which is occupied unless 28 days' notice of the intended entry has been given to the occupier by the Agency.

(4) Any person who wilfully obstructs a person acting in exercise of his powers under this section shall be guilty of an offence and liable on summary conviction to a fine not exceeding level 2 on the standard scale.

(5) If any person who, in compliance with the provisions of this section, is admitted into a factory, workshop or workplace discloses to any person any information obtained by him in it as to any manufacturing process or trade secret, he shall be guilty of an offence.

(6) Subsection (5) does not apply if the disclosure is made by a person in the course of performing his duty in connection with the purpose for which he was authorised to enter the premises.

(7) A person who is guilty of an offence under subsection (5) shall be liable on summary conviction to a fine not exceeding the statutory maximum or on conviction on indictment to imprisonment for a term not exceeding two years or a fine or both.

(8) Where any land is damaged—

(a) in the exercise of a right of entry under this section, or

(b) in the making of any survey under this section,

compensation in respect of that damage may be recovered by any person interested in the land from the Agency.

(9) The provisions of section 118 of the Town and Country Planning Act 1990 (determination of claims for compensation) shall apply in relation to

compensation under subsection (8) as they apply in relation to compensation under Part IV of that Act.

(10) No person shall carry out under this section any works authorised by virtue of subsection (2) unless notice of his intention to do so was included in the notice required by subsection (3).

(11) The authority of the appropriate Minister shall be required for the carrying out of any such works if—

(a) the land in question is held by statutory undertakers; and

(b) they object to the proposed works on the ground that the execution of the works would be seriously detrimental to the carrying on of their undertaking;

and expressions used in this subsection have the same meanings as they have in section 325(9) of the Town and Country Planning Act 1990 (supplementary provisions as to rights of entry).

DEFINITIONS
    "Agency": ss.158 and 185.
    "appropriate minister": ss.265 and 336(i) of the Town and Country Planning Act 1990.
    "statutory undertakers": s.262 of the Town and Country Planning Act 1990.

GENERAL NOTE
    This section makes similar provisions to other statutes for persons authorised by the Authority to enter and survey land, subject to the giving of proper notice (subs. 3), but only limited to proposals to acquire the land or in relation to any compensation claim, and not for any other purpose. It is an offence to prevent a person acting in exercise of his powers under this section but subject to the formalities required by the section having been observed. This is enforceable by issuing a summons before the magistrates, but the exercise of the power would also properly be enforceable by injunction issued by the High Court.

Subs. (4)
    Level 2 on the Standard Scale. The current maximum fine is £100.

Subs. (7)
    Statutory maximum. The current level is £2,000.

Subs. (9)
    Section 118 of the Town and Country Planning Act 1990 provides for disputed claims for compensation to be referred to the Lands Tribunal.

Financial assistance

164.—(1) The consent of the Secretary of State is required for the exercise of the Agency's power to give financial assistance; and such assistance—

(a) may be given by the Agency only in respect of qualifying expenditure; and

(b) may be so given on such terms and conditions as the Agency, with the consent of the Secretary of State, considers appropriate.

(2) Expenditure incurred in connection with any of the following matters is qualifying expenditure—

(a) the acquisition of land;

(b) the reclamation, improvement or refurbishment of land;

(c) the development or redevelopment of land, including the conversion or demolition of existing buildings;

(d) the equipment or fitting out of land;

(e) the provision of means of access, services or other facilities for land;

(f) environmental improvements.

(3) Financial assistance may be given in any form and may, in particular, be given by way of—

(a) grants;

(b) loans;

(c) guarantees; or

(d) incurring expenditure for the benefit of the person assisted;
but the Agency shall not in giving financial assistance purchase loan or share capital in a company.

(4) A consent under subsection (1) may be given only with the approval of the Treasury.

(5) The terms and conditions on which financial assistance is given may, in particular, include provision as to—

(a) the circumstances in which the assistance must be repaid, or otherwise made good, to the Agency, and the manner in which that is to be done;

(b) the circumstances in which the Agency is entitled to recover the proceeds or part of the proceeds of any disposal of land in respect of which the assistance was provided.

(6) Any person receiving financial assistance shall comply with the terms and conditions on which it is given and compliance may be enforced by the Agency.

DEFINITIONS
"Agency": ss.158 and 185.

GENERAL NOTE
This section provides for the Agency to give financial assistance. Financial assistance may be given in a variety of forms but may only be given in respect of qualifying expenditure as defined in subs. (2) and only with the Secretary of State's consent. The Authority may make provision to recover any financial assistance so provided and in particular can make provision to recover the proceeds or part of the proceeds of any disposal of the land in respect of which the assistance was given (subs. (5)) (see also s.178 for Urban Development Corporation powers). Subject to the Secretary of State's consent the Agency has discretion as to the terms of any assistance and it need not, for example, be secured, or may be in the form of guarantees rather than actual finance.

Connection of private streets to highway

165.—(1) For the purpose of achieving its objects or for purposes incidental to that purpose, the Agency may serve a notice (a "connection notice") on the local highway authority requiring the authority to connect a private street to an existing highway (whether or not it is a highway which for the purposes of the Highways Act 1980 is a highway maintainable at the public expense).

(2) A connection notice must specify—

(a) the private street and the existing highway;

(b) the works which appear to the Agency to be necessary to make the connection; and

(c) the period within which those works should be carried out.

(3) Before serving a connection notice the Agency shall consult the local highway authority about the proposed contents of the notice.

(4) Within the period of two months beginning with the date on which the connection notice was served, the local highway authority may appeal against the notice to the Secretary of State.

(5) After considering any representations made to him by the Agency and the local highway authority, the Secretary of State shall determine an appeal under subsection (4) by setting aside or confirming the connection notice (with or without modifications).

(6) A connection notice becomes effective—

(a) where no appeal is made within the period of two months referred to in subsection (4), upon the expiry of that period;

(b) where an appeal is made within that period but is withdrawn before it has been determined by the Secretary of State, on the date following the expiry of the period of 21 days beginning with the date on which the Secretary of State is notified of the withdrawal;

(c) where an appeal is made and the connection notice is confirmed by a determination under subsection (5), on such date as the Secretary of State may specify in the determination.

(7) Where a connection notice becomes effective, the local highway authority shall carry out the works specified in the notice within such period as may be so specified and may recover from the Agency the expenses reasonably incurred by them in doing so.

(8) If the local highway authority do not carry out the works specified in the notice within such period as may be so specified, the Agency may itself carry out or complete those works or arrange for another person to do so.

(9) In this section "local highway authority" has the same meaning as in the Highways Act 1980.

DEFINITIONS
"Agency": ss.158 and 185.
"highway": s.328(1) of the Highways Act 1980.
"local highways authority": s.1 of the Highways Act 1980.
"private streets": Highways Act 1980, Pt. XI.

GENERAL NOTE
The Agency can serve a connection notice requiring the highways authority to connect a private street to a highway. The highways authority has a right to appeal against such a notice to the Secretary of State within two months of its service. There are not specified here the grounds on which appeal may be made but presumably in the absence of specific guidance, objection could be on technical or financial grounds. Where a notice becomes effective the highways authority must carry out the works of connection and recover the costs from the Agency.

The Agency: supplemental

Consents of Secretary of State

166. A consent of the Secretary of State under the foregoing provisions of this Part—
(a) may be given unconditionally or subject to conditions;
(b) may be given in relation to a particular case or in relation to such descriptions of case as may be specified in the consent; and
(c) except in relation to anything already done or agreed to be done on the authority of the consent, may be varied or revoked by a notice given by the Secretary of State to the Agency.

DEFINITIONS
"Agency": ss.158 and 185.

GENERAL NOTE
This section provides that if consent is given under s.164(1) for the Agency to give financial assistance it may only be given with the approval of the Treasury.

Guidance and directions by Secretary of State

167.—(1) The Agency shall have regard to guidance from time to time given by the Secretary of State in deciding—
(a) which land is suitable for regeneration or development under this Part; and
(b) which of its functions under this Part it is to exercise for securing the regeneration or development of any particular land and how it is to exercise those functions.

(2) Without prejudice to any of the foregoing provisions of this Part requiring the consent of the Secretary of State to be obtained for anything to be done by the Agency, he may give directions to the Agency—
(a) for restricting the exercise by it of any of its functions under this Part; or

(b) for requiring it to exercise those functions in any manner specified in the directions.

(3) Directions under subsection (2) may be of a general or particular nature and may be varied or revoked by subsequent directions.

DEFINITIONS
"Agency": ss.158 and 185.

GENERAL NOTE
This section gives extensive advisory powers to the Secretary of State with regard to the manner, extent and location of performance of the Agency's functions to which the Agency must have regard. In particular the Secretary has specific directive powers in relation to the exercise of functions in subs. (2) over and above the consents required from him elsewhere (see for example compulsory acquisition of land (s.162), financial aid (s.164).

Validity of transactions

168.—(1) A transaction between a person and the Agency shall not be invalidated by reason only of any failure by the Agency to observe its objects or the requirement in subsection (1) of section 160 that the Agency shall exercise the powers conferred by that subsection for the purpose of achieving its objects, and such a person shall not be concerned to see or enquire whether there has been any such failure.

(2) A transaction between a person and the Agency acting in purported exercise of its functions under this Part shall not be invalidated by reason only that it was carried out in contravention of any direction given under subsection (2) of section 167, and such a person shall not be concerned to see or enquire whether any directions under that subsection have been given or complied with.

DEFINITIONS
"Agency": ss.158 and 185.

GENERAL NOTE
This section seeks to avoid the *ultra vires* rule for Agency transactions. A person entering into a transaction with the Agency need not look behind the transaction to ensure the Agency is obeying its objects, or that it is not acting in contravention of guidance or directions given by the Secretary of State. (For the basic position on *ultra vires* in relation to statutory corporations powers see *Associated Provincial Picture Houses* v. *Wednesbury Corporation* [1948] 1 K.B. 223).

Supplementary provisions as to vesting and acquisition of land

169.—(1) Schedule 20 to this Act shall have effect.

(2) Part I of that Schedule modifies the Acquisition of Land Act 1981 as applied by section 162.

(3) Part II of that Schedule contains supplementary provisions about land vested in or acquired by the Agency under this Part.

(4) Part III of that Schedule contains supplementary provisions about the acquisition by the Agency of rights over land by virtue of section 162(2).

DEFINITIONS
"Agency": ss.158 and 185.

GENERAL NOTE
This section brings into effect Sched. 20 to the Act. See the notes to that schedule for the specific changes to normal procedures in relation to compulsory acquisition, *etc.*

Designation orders and their effect

Power to make designation orders

170.—(1) Where, as respects any area in England which is an urban area or which, in the opinion of the Secretary of State, is suitable for urban development, it appears to the Secretary of State—

  (a) that all or any of the provisions authorised by section 171 should be made in relation to the whole or any part of it; or

  (b) that either or both of sections 172 and 173 should apply in relation to it,

the Secretary of State may by order designate that area and either so make the provision or provisions, or direct that the section or sections shall so apply, or (as the case may require) do both of those things.

(2) In this Part "designation order" means an order under this section and "designated area" means, subject to subsection (5), an area designated by a designation order.

(3) Before making a designation order the Secretary of State shall consult every local authority any part of whose area is intended to be included in the proposed designated area.

(4) A designation order—

  (a) shall be made by statutory instrument which shall be subject to annulment in pursuance of a resolution of either House of Parliament; and

  (b) may contain such savings and transitional and supplementary provisions as may be specified in the order.

(5) The power to amend a designation order conferred by section 14 of the Interpretation Act 1978 includes power to amend the boundaries of the designated area; and where any such amendment is made, any reference in this Part to a designated area is a reference to the designated area as so amended.

(6) In this section "local authority" means a county council, a district council, a London borough council or the Common Council of the City of London.

GENERAL NOTE

This section creates the power to designate areas by order where the Agency becomes the local planning authority (s.171) or should have powers to require adoption of private streets (s.172) or request traffic regulation orders (s.173).

Agency as local planning authority

171.—(1) If a designation order so provides, the Agency shall be the local planning authority for the whole or any part of the designated area—

  (a) for such purposes of Part III of the Town and Country Planning Act 1990 and sections 67 and 73 of the Planning (Listed Buildings and Conservation Areas) Act 1990 as may be specified in the order; and

  (b) in relation to such kinds of development as may be so specified.

(2) A designation order making such provision as is mentioned in subsection (1) may also provide—

  (a) that any enactment relating to local planning authorities shall not apply to the Agency; and

  (b) that any such enactment which applies to the Agency shall apply to it subject to such modifications as may be specified in the order.

(3) If a designation order so provides—

  (a) subject to any modifications specified in the order, the Agency shall have, in the whole or any part of the designated area, such of the functions conferred by the provisions mentioned in subsection (4) as may be so specified; and

  (b) such of the provisions of Part VI and sections 249 to 251 and 258 of the Town and Country Planning Act 1990 and sections 32 to 37 of the Planning (Listed Buildings and Conservation Areas) Act 1990 as are mentioned in the order shall have effect, in relation to the Agency and to land in the designated area, subject to the modifications there specified.

(4) The provisions referred to in subsection (3)(a) are—

(a) sections 171C, 171D, 172 to 185, 187 to 202, 206 to 222, 224, 225, 231 and 320 to 336 of, and paragraph 11 of Schedule 9 to, the Town and Country Planning Act 1990;

(b) Chapters I, II and IV of Part I and sections 54 to 56, 59 to 61, 66, 68 to 72, 74 to 76 and 88 of the Planning (Listed Buildings and Conservation Areas) Act 1990; and

(c) sections 4 to 15, 17 to 21, 23 to 26AA, 36 and 36A of the Planning (Hazardous Substances) Act 1990.

(5) A designation order making such provision as is mentioned in subsection (3) may also provide that, for the purposes of any of the provisions specified in the order, any enactment relating to local planning authorities shall apply to the Agency subject to such modifications as may be so specified.

DEFINITIONS
"Agency": ss.158 and 185.
"designated area": s.170.
"designation order": s.170.

GENERAL NOTE
This section provides for the Agency to be designated the local planning authority for the whole or any part of the designated area for the purposes of Pt. III of the Town and Country Planning Act 1990 and ss.67 and 73 of the Planning (Listed Buildings and Conservation Areas) Act 1990. Part III of the Town and Country Planning Act 1990 deals with control over development and is the part of the Act principally concerned with the consideration of planning applications and grants of consent. Sections 67 and 73 of the Planning (Listed Buildings and Conservation Areas) Act 1990 govern, respectively, publicity for applications affecting the setting of listed buildings, and applications affecting conservation areas. If the designation order so provides the Agency becomes the local planning authority for all these functions and may also become local planning authority if the designation order specifically so provides for other matters, including enforcement of planning control, advertisement control, trees, and preservation of listed buildings. It may provide that the Agency becomes the local planning authority only for specific kinds of development. In addition the Agency may similarly assume control of the issue of consents and contravention notices in respect of hazardous substances.

Adoption of private streets

172.—(1) Where—

(a) this section applies in relation to a designated area; and

(b) any street works have been executed on any land in the designated area which was then or has since become a private street (or part of a private street),

the Agency may serve a notice (an "adoption notice") on the street works authority requiring the authority to declare the street (or part) to be a highway which for the purposes of the Highways Act 1980 is a highway maintainable at the public expense.

(2) Within the period of two months beginning with the date on which the adoption notice was served, the street works authority may appeal against the notice to the Secretary of State.

(3) After considering any representations made to him by the Agency and the street works authority, the Secretary of State shall determine an appeal under subsection (2) by setting aside or confirming the adoption notice (with or without modifications).

(4) Where, under subsection (3), the Secretary of State confirms the adoption notice—

(a) he may at the same time impose conditions (including financial conditions) upon the Agency with which it must comply in order for the notice to take effect; and

(b) with effect from such date as the Secretary of State may specify, the street (or part) shall become a highway which for the purposes of the Highways Act 1980 is a highway maintainable at the public expense.

(5) Where a street works authority neither complies with the adoption notice, nor appeals under subsection (2), the street (or part) shall become, upon the expiry of the period of two months referred to in subsection (2), a highway which for the purposes of the Highways Act 1980 is a highway maintainable at the public expense.

(6) In this section "street works" and "street works authority" have the same meanings as in Part XI of the Highways Act 1980.

DEFINITIONS
"Agency": ss.158 and 185.
"designated area": s.170.
"highway": s.328(i) of the Highways Act 1980.

GENERAL NOTE
This section parallels the power of Urban Development Corporations in s.157 of the 1980 Act to serve notices requiring a street works authority to adopt a private street but with the reservation of power of appeal to Secretary of State for the environment rather than to a magistrates' court, as in the 1980 Act.

Traffic regulation orders for private streets

173.—(1) Where—
(a) this section applies in relation to a designated area;
(b) the Agency submits to the Secretary of State that an order under this section should be made in relation to any road in the designated area which is a private street; and
(c) it appears to the Secretary of State that the traffic authority do not intend to make an order under section 1 or, as the case may be, section 6 of the Road Traffic Regulation Act 1984 (orders concerning traffic regulation) in relation to the road,
the Secretary of State may by order under this section make in relation to the road any such provision as he might have made by order under that section if he had been the traffic authority.

(2) The Road Traffic Regulation Act 1984 applies to an order under this section as it applies to an order made by the Secretary of State under section 1 or, as the case may be, section 6 of that Act in relation to a road for which he is the traffic authority.

(3) In this section "road" and "traffic authority" have the same meanings as in the Road Traffic Regulation Act 1984.

DEFINITIONS
"Agency": ss.158 and 185.
"designated area": s.170.
"private streets": Highways Act 1980 Pt. XI.

GENERAL NOTE
This section gives the Secretary of State, in default of any action on the part of the traffic authority, and on request by the Agency, the power to make road traffic regulation orders. Under the Road Traffic Regulation Act 1984, s.1 covers orders for avoiding danger on roads or preventing damage to them, for facilitating or preventing the passage of roads, or for preserving the character and amenities of roads or improving them and s.6 covers similar orders for controlling or regulating traffic in Greater London.

Other functions of Secretary of State

Financial assistance for urban regeneration

174. For section 27 of the Housing and Planning Act 1986 (power to give financial assistance) there shall be substituted the following section—

"Power to give assistance
    27.—(1) The Secretary of State may, with the consent of the
Treasury, give financial assistance to any person in respect of expenditure incurred in connection with activities contributing to the
regeneration of an urban area.
    (2) Activities contributing to the regeneration of an urban area
include in particular—
    (a) securing that land and buildings are brought into effective use;
    (b) developing, or encouraging the development of, existing and
         new industry and commerce;
    (c) creating an attractive and safe environment;
    (d) providing housing or social and recreational facilities so as to
         encourage people to live or work in the area;
    (e) providing employment for people who live in the area;
    (f) providing training, educational facilities or health services for
         people who live in the area."

GENERAL NOTE
  This section creates broader powers of financial assistance in relation to regeneration than
existed hitherto, and allows for financial assistance to any person in connection with regeneration activities in an urban area.

Power to appoint Agency as agent

175.—(1) The Secretary of State may, on such terms as he may with the
approval of the Treasury specify, appoint the Agency to act as his agent in
connection with such of the functions mentioned in subsection (2) as he may
specify; and where such an appointment is made, the Agency shall act as
such an agent in accordance with the terms of its appointment.
    (2) The functions referred to in subsection (1) are—
    (a) functions under section 1 of the Derelict Land Act 1982 or any
         enactment superseded by that section (grants for reclaiming or
         improving land or bringing land into use), other than the powers to
         make orders under subsections (5) and (7) of that section, and
    (b) so far as exercisable in relation to England, functions under sections
         27 to 29 of the Housing and Planning Act 1986 (financial assistance for
         urban regeneration).
    (3) In so far as an appointment under subsection (1) relates to functions
mentioned in subsection (2)(b), the terms of the appointment shall preclude
the Agency from giving financial assistance in respect of expenditure which
is not qualifying expenditure within the meaning of section 164.

DEFINITIONS
  "Agency": ss.158 and 185.

GENERAL NOTE
  This section allows the Secretary of State to appoint the Agency to act as his agent for specific
functions, in subs. (2), subject to Treasury approval.

Subs. (2)
  Section 1 of the Derelict Land Act 1982. Where land is derelict, neglected or unsightly or
where there is a risk of collapse where underground mining operations have ceased the
Secretary of State has power to make finance available with Treasury consent for reclaiming,
improving, or bringing into use such land. The Agency can be agents of the Secretary of State
for these purposes under the provisions of this section. Similarly it can be agents for the
purposes of ss.27 to 29 of the Housing and Planning Act 1986 relating to financial assistance (see
s.174) of this Act.

Power to direct disposal of unused etc. land held by public bodies

    176.—(1) In subsection (1) of section 98 (disposal of land by public bodies at direction of Secretary of State) of the Local Government, Planning and Land Act 1980 ("the 1980 Act")—

    (a) in paragraph (a), for the words "is for the time being entered on a register maintained by him under section 95 above" there shall be substituted the words "for the time being satisfies the conditions specified in section 95(2) above"; and

    (b) in paragraph (b), for the words "is for the time being entered on such a register" there shall be substituted the words "for the time being satisfies those conditions".

(2) In section 99A of that Act (powers of entry), subsection (2) (which precludes entry on land which is not for the time being entered on a register maintained under section 95) shall cease to have effect.

GENERAL NOTE

    This section amends ss.98 and 99A of the Local Government Planning and Land Act 1980. Part X of the Local Government Planning and Land Act 1980 related to land held by public bodies and required registers to be kept of such land. Under s.98 of the 1980 Act the Secretary of State can direct such bodies to dispose of such land subject to certain qualifications. Section 176 amends this so that the Secretary of State can require disposal whether or not the land is registered provided in broad terms that: (i) the freehold or leasehold is held by a body to which the relevant part of the Act applies; (ii) it is situated in or adjoining an area where the relevant part of the Act applies; and (iii) the Secretary of State does not consider it is being used or adequately used for the purposes of the body's functions or undertaking. There are rights to the relevant public bodies to make representations regarding such a direction but the Secretary of State can make a direction unless it would be prejudicial to their functions or undertaking. Section 99A of the 1980 Act gives powers to enter to discover if land is suitable for a direction. Subsection (2) of this section extends these powers to include powers to enter land not for the time being on the s.95 register.

Urban development corporations

Power to act as agents of Agency

    177.—(1) The Agency may, with the consent of the Secretary of State, appoint an urban development corporation, on such terms as may be agreed, to act as its agent in connection with such of its functions (other than its power to give financial assistance) as may be specified in the appointment; and where such an appointment is made, the urban development corporation shall act as such an agent in accordance with the terms of its appointment.

    (2) For the purpose of assisting the Agency to carry out any of its functions, an urban development corporation, on being so requested by the Agency, may arrange for any of its property or staff to be made available to the Agency for such period and on such other terms as it thinks fit.

    (3) In this section "urban development corporation" means a corporation established by an order under section 135 of the 1980 Act.

DEFINITIONS

    "Agency": ss.158 and 185.

    "urban development corporation": s.171 of the Local Government Planning and Land Act 1980.

GENERAL NOTE

    This section gives the Agency the power to appoint an urban development corporation to act as its agent. The urban development corporation does not appear to have any discretion as to whether it accepts such an appointment.

Powers with respect to private streets

    178. For section 157 of the 1980 Act (highways) there shall be substituted the following sections—

"Private streets

Adoption of private streets
157.—(1) Where any street works have been executed on any land in an urban development area which was then or has since become a private street (or part of a private street), the urban development corporation may serve a notice (an 'adoption notice') on the street works authority requiring the authority to declare the street (or part) to a highway which for the purposes of the Highways Act 1980 is a highway maintainable at the public expense.

(2) Within the period of two months beginning with the date on which the adoption notice was served, the street works authority may appeal against the notice to the Secretary of State.

(3) After considering any representations made to him by the corporation and the street works authority, the Secretary of State shall determine an appeal under subsection (2) above by setting aside or confirming the adoption notice (with or without modifications).

(4) Where, under subsection (3) above, the Secretary of State confirms the adoption notice—

(a) he may at the same time impose conditions (including financial conditions) upon the corporation with which it must comply in order for the notice to take effect; and

(b) with effect from such date as the Secretary of State may specify, the street (or part) shall become a highway which for the purposes of the Highways Act 1980 is a highway maintainable at the public expense.

(5) Where a street works authority neither complies with the adoption notice, nor appeals under subsection (2) above, the street (or part) shall become, upon the expiry of the period of two months referred to in subsection (2) above, a highway which for the purposes of the Highways Act 1980 is a highway maintainable at the public expense.

(6) In this section—

'highway' has the same meaning as in the Highways Act 1980;

'private street', 'street works' and 'street works authority' have the same meanings as in Part XI of that Act.

(7) This section does not extend to Scotland.

Connection of private streets to highway
157A.—(1) An urban development corporation may serve a notice (a 'connection notice') on the local highway authority requiring the authority to connect a private street in the urban development area to an existing highway (whether or not it is a highway which for the purposes of the Highways Act 1980 is a highway maintainable at the public expense).

(2) A connection notice must specify—

(a) the private street and the existing highway;

(b) the works which appear to the corporation to be necessary to make the connection; and

(c) the period within which those works should be carried out.

(3) Before serving a connection notice an urban development corporation shall consult the local highway authority about the proposed contents of the notice.

(4) Within the period of two months beginning with the date on which the connection notice was served, the local highway authority may appeal against the notice to the Secretary of State.

(5) After considering any representations made to him by the corporation and the local highway authority, the Secretary of State

shall determine an appeal under subsection (4) above by setting aside or confirming the connection notice (with or without modifications).

(6) A connection notice becomes effective—

(a) where no appeal is made within the period of two months referred to in subsection (4) above, upon the expiry of that period;

(b) where an appeal is made within that period but is withdrawn before it has been determined by the Secretary of State, on the date following the expiry of the period of 21 days beginning with the date on which the Secretary of State is notified of the withdrawal;

(c) where an appeal is made and the connection notice is confirmed by a determination under subsection (5) above, on such date as the Secretary of State may specify in the determination.

(7) Where a connection notice becomes effective, the local highway authority shall carry out the works specified in the notice within such period as may be so specified and may recover from the corporation the expenses reasonably incurred by them in doing so.

(8) If the local highway authority do not carry out the works specified in the notice within such period as may be so specified, the corporation may themselves carry out or complete those works or arrange for another person to do so.

(9) In this section—

'highway' and 'local highway authority' have the same meanings as in the Highways Act 1980;

'private street' has the same meaning as in Part XI of that Act.

(10) This section does not extend to Scotland.

Traffic regulation orders for private streets

157B.—(1) Where—

(a) an urban development corporation submits to the Secretary of State that an order under this section should be made in relation to any road in the urban development area which is a private street; and

(b) it appears to the Secretary of State that the traffic authority do not intend to make an order under section 1 or, as the case may be, section 6 of the Road Traffic Regulation Act 1984 (orders concerning traffic regulation) in relation to the road,

the Secretary of State may by order under this section make in relation to the road any such provision as he might have made by order under that section if he had been the traffic authority.

(2) The Road Traffic Regulation Act 1984 applies to an order under this section as it applies to an order made by the Secretary of State under section 1 or, as the case may be, section 6 of that Act in relation to a road for which he is the traffic authority.

(3) In this section—

'private street' has the same meaning as in Part XI of the Highways Act 1980;

'road' and 'traffic authority' have the same meanings as in the Road Traffic Regulation Act 1984.

(4) This section does not extend to Scotland."

DEFINITIONS

"1980 Act": s.185.
"local highway authority": s.1 of the Highways Act 1980.
"private street": Highways Act 1980, Pt. XI.
"street works": Highways Act 1980, Pt. XI.
"street works authority": Highways Act 1980, Pt. XI.
"urban development area": s.171 of the Local Government Planning and Land Act 1980.

"urban development corporation": s.171 of the Local Government Planning and Land Act 1980.

GENERAL NOTE
Under s.157 of the Local Government Planning and Land Act 1980, urban development corporations could serve a notice requiring adoption of a private street. If the street works authority declined to do so it could apply to the magistrates' court for an order setting aside the notice. If no such order was made the street became maintainable at public expense after two months. Section 178 substitutes a similar power for the urban development corporation in a revised s.157 to the 1980 Act but with the street works authority having its right to challenge the notice by way of appeal to the Secretary of State for the Environment (see also s.172 which gives similar powers to the Agency). Section 178 also creates a new power in substituted s.157A of the 1980 Act for urban development corporations to require local highways authorities to connect private streets within an urban development area to the public highway with a similar power of appeal to the Secretary of State. Where the notice becomes effective, the highways authority must carry out the works specified in it and recover the expenses from the urban development corporation. Substituted s.157B in the 1980 Act allows an urban development corporation to submit that a traffic regulation order under ss.1 or 6 of the Road Traffic Regulation Act 1984 should be made (see note to s.173). Where the Secretary of State considers that the traffic authority do not intend to make such an order, he may make it in their stead.

Adjustment of areas

179.—(1) After subsection (3) of section 134 (urban development areas) of the 1980 Act there shall be inserted the following subsections—

"(3A) The Secretary of State may by order alter the boundaries of any urban development area so as to exclude any area of land.

(3B) Before making an order under subsection (3A) above, the Secretary of State shall consult any local authority the whole or any part of whose area is included in the area of land to be excluded by the order."

(2) In subsection (4) of that section, for the words "this section" there shall be substituted the words "subsection (1) above".

(3) After that subsection there shall be inserted the following subsection—

"(5) The power to make an order under subsection (3A) above—
(a) shall be exercisable by statutory instrument subject to annulment in pursuance of a resolution of either House of Parliament; and
(b) shall include power to make such incidental, consequential, transitional or supplementary provision as the Secretary of State thinks fit."

(4) In section 135(2) of that Act (establishment of urban development corporations), for the words "section 134" there shall be substituted the words "section 134(1)".

(5) In section 171 of that Act (interpretation of Part XVI: general), for the definition of "urban development area" there shall be substituted the following definition—

" 'urban development area' means so much of an area designated by an order under subsection (1) of section 134 above as is not excluded from it by an order under subsection (3A) of that section;".

DEFINITIONS
"1980 Act": s.185.
"urban development area": s.171 of the Local Government Planning and Land Act 1980.
"urban development corporation": s.171 of the Local Government Planning and Land Act 1980.

GENERAL NOTE
Section 134 of the 1980 Act allowed the Secretary of State to designate the areas of urban development corporations. Orders designating such areas have to be approved by resolution of

each House of Parliament. Orders under substituted subs. (3A) of s.134 of the 1980 Act do not, but if made may be annulled by resolution of either House of Parliament.

Transfers of property, rights and liabilities

180.—(1) In subsection (1) of section 165 of the 1980 Act (power to transfer undertaking of urban development corporation), after the words "local authority", in both places where they occur, there shall be inserted the words "or other body".

(2) Subsection (3) of that section (transfer of liabilities by order) shall cease to have effect; and after that section there shall be inserted the following section—

"Transfer of property, rights and liabilities by order

165A.—(1) Subject to this section, the Secretary of State may at any time by order transfer to himself, upon such terms as he thinks fit, any property, rights or liabilities which—

(a) are for the time being vested in an urban development corporation, and

(b) are not proposed to be transferred under an agreement made under section 165 above and approved by the Secretary of State with the Treasury's concurrence.

(2) An order under this section may terminate—

(a) any appointment of the corporation under subsection (1) of section 177 of the Leasehold Reform, Housing and Urban Development Act 1993 (power of corporations to act as agents of the Urban Regeneration Agency); and

(b) any arrangements made by the corporation under subsection (2) of that section.

(3) Before making an order under this section, the Secretary of State shall consult each local authority in whose area all or part of the urban development area is situated.

(4) An order under this section shall be made by statutory instrument which shall be subject to annulment in pursuance of a resolution of either House of Parliament."

(3) In subsection (9) of that section—

(a) after the words "this section" there shall be inserted the words "and sections 165A and 166 below";

(b) for the words "the section", in both places where they occur, there shall be substituted the words "the sections".

(4) For subsection (1) of section 166 of that Act (dissolution of urban development corporations) there shall be substituted the following subsection—

"(1) Where all property, rights and liabilities of an urban development corporation have been transferred under or by one or more relevant instruments, the Secretary of State may make an order by statutory instrument under this section."

(5) For subsection (5) of that section there shall be substituted the following subsection—

"(5) In this section 'relevant instrument' means an agreement made under section 165 above or an order made under section 165A above."

DEFINITIONS
    "local authority": s.165(9) of the Local Government Planning and Land Act 1980.
    "urban development area": s.171 of the Local Government Planning and Land Act 1980.
    "urban development corporation": s.171 of the Local Government Planning and Land Act 1980.

Section 165 of the 1980 Act gives an urban development corporation power to transfer the whole or a part of its undertaking by agreement to a local authority or statutory undertaker provided it has approval of the Secretary of State and concurrence of the Treasury. Section 180(1) of this Act extends the power to allow such transfer to any other body. Section 180 also creates a new s.165A in the 1980 Act which allows the Secretary of State similarly to transfer to himself any property, rights or liabilities of urban development corporations by order. Subsections (4) and (5) of s.166 of the 1980 Act dealt with the dissolution of urban development corporations after all their property and undertakings had been transferred under s.165 of that Act. It also now includes a similar provision for dissolution where the Secretary of State has made a transfer to himself under s.165A as inserted into the 1980 Act by this Act.

Miscellaneous

No compensation where planning decision made after certain acquisitions

181.—(1) Section 23(3) of the Land Compensation Act 1961 (no compensation where planning decision made after certain acquisitions) shall be amended as follows.

(2) After paragraph (a) there shall be inserted the following paragraph—
"(aa) under section 104 of that Act (acquisition by the Land Authority for Wales);".

(3) After paragraph (c) there shall be inserted the words "or

(d) under Part III of the Leasehold Reform, Housing and Urban Development Act 1993 (acquisition by the Urban Regeneration Agency)."

(4) Subsection (2) above shall apply to an acquisition or sale of an interest in land if the date of completion (within the meaning of Part IV of that Act) falls on or after the day on which this Act is passed.

Section 23(3) of the Land Compensation Act 1961 provides that no compensation is payable where a planning decision is made after acquisition of land under compulsory purchase powers if it is acquired under certain statutory provisions, *e.g.* s.142 of the 1980 Act. This section tidies up an anomaly by extending the exception to land acquired by the land authority for Wales (subs. (2)) and provides that the Agency shall enjoy similar exemption to that of urban development corporations (subs. (3)).

Powers of housing action trusts with respect to private streets

182.—(1) In subsection (1) of section 69 of the Housing Act 1988 (powers of housing action trusts with respect to private streets), for the words "in a private street (or part of a private street) in a designated area" there shall be substituted the words "on any land in a designated area which was then or has since become a private street (or part of a private street)".

(2) In subsection (2) of that section, the words from "on grounds" onwards shall be omitted.

"private streets": Highways Act 1980, Pt. XI.

The 1988 Act gave the Secretary of State power to designate areas of land which required a housing action trust, the objects being to secure the repair or improvement of housing stock held by the trust and to improve the environment within their areas. Where works were executed in a private street the housing action trusts had power to require adoption of the highway similar to that of urban development corporations. Subsection (1) extends this power to situations where the land has become a private street since the works were carried out. Section 69(2) of the 1988 Act gave a limited number of grounds on which the street works authority could appeal to the Secretary of State against the notice. Subsection (2) removes these, presumably leaving an absolute right of appeal.

Supplemental

Notices

183.—(1) This section has effect in relation to any notice required or authorised by this Part to be given to or served on any person.

(2) Any such notice may be given to or served on the person in question either by delivering it to him, or by leaving it at his proper address, or by sending it by post to him at that address.

(3) Any such notice may—

(a) in the case of a body corporate, be given to or served on the secretary or clerk of that body; and

(b) in the case of a partnership, be given to or served on a partner or a person having the control or management of the partnership business.

(4) For the purposes of this section and of section 7 of the Interpretation Act 1978 (service of documents by post) in its application to this section, the proper address of any person to or on whom a notice is to be given or served shall be his last known address, except that—

(a) in the case of a body corporate or its secretary or clerk, it shall be the address of the registered or principal office of that body; and

(b) in the case of a partnership, a partner or a person having the control or management of the partnership business, it shall be that of the principal office of the partnership;

and for the purposes of this subsection the principal office of a company registered outside the United Kingdom or of a partnership carrying on business outside the United Kingdom shall be its principal office within the United Kingdom.

(5) If the person to be given or served with any notice mentioned in subsection (1) has specified an address within the United Kingdom other than his proper address within the meaning of subsection (4) as the one at which he or someone on his behalf will accept documents of the same description as that notice, that address shall also be treated for the purposes of this section and section 7 of the Interpretation Act 1978 as his proper address.

(6) If the name or address of any owner, lessee or occupier of land to or on whom any notice mentioned in subsection (1) is to be served cannot after reasonable inquiry be ascertained, the document may be served either by leaving it in the hands of a person who is or appears to be resident or employed on the land or by leaving it conspicuously affixed to some building or object on the land.

Dissolution of English Industrial Estates Corporation

184.—(1) The English Industrial Estates Corporation shall cease to exist on the commencement of this section.

(2) All the property, rights and liabilities to which that Corporation was entitled or subject immediately before that commencement shall become by virtue of this section property, rights and liabilities of the Agency.

DEFINITIONS
"Agency": ss.158 and 185.

GENERAL NOTE
This section transfers the property rights and liabilities of the English Industrial Estates Corporation to the Agency. The corporation was set up by the Local Employment Act 1960 and continued by subsequent statutes with a view to providing and managing sites and premises for occupation by industrial or commercial operations as a means of supporting employment and industry. Its absorption into the Agency is intended to prevent duplication and overlap of functions.

Interpretation of Part III

185. In this Part—
"the 1980 Act" means the Local Government, Planning and Land Act
1980;
"the Agency" means the Urban Regeneration Agency;
"designation order" and "designated area" have the meanings given by
section 170;
"highway" has the same meaning as in the Highways Act 1980;
"private street" has the same meaning as in Part XI of that Act.

DEFINITIONS
"highway": s.328(1) of the Highways Act 1980.
"private street": s.203(2) of the Highways Act 1980.

GENERAL NOTE
Highway. This means the whole or part of a highway other than a ferry or waterway.
Private street. This means a street which is not a highway maintainable at the public expense
(and includes certain other categories of land defined in s.203(2)(a)(b) of the Highways Act
1980.

PART IV

SUPPLEMENTAL

Financial provisions

186.—(1) There shall be paid out of money provided by Parliament—
(a) any expenses of the Secretary of State incurred in consequence of this
Act; and
(b) any increase attributable to this Act in the sums payable out of money
so provided under any other enactment.
(2) There shall be paid into the Consolidated Fund any increase attributable to this Act in the sums payable into that Fund under any other
enactment.

Amendments and repeals

187.—(1) The enactments mentioned ion Schedule 21 to this Act shall
have effect subject to the amendments there specified (being minor amendments and amendments consequential on the provisions of this Act).
(2) The enactments mentioned in Schedule 22 to this Act (which include
some that are spent or no longer of practical utility) are hereby repealed to
the extent specified in the third column of that Schedule.

Short title, commencement and extent

188.—(1) This Act may be cited as the Leasehold Reform, Housing and
Urban Development Act 1993.
(2) This Act, except—
(a) this section;
(b) sections 126 and 127, 135 to 140, 149 to 151, 181(1), (2) and (4) and
186; and
(c) the repeal in section 80(1) of the Local Government and Housing Act
1989,
shall come into force on such day as the Secretary of State may by order
made by statutory instrument appoint; and different days may be so
appointed for different provisions or for different purposes.
(3) An order under subsection (2) may contain such transitional provisions and savings (whether or not involving the modification of any statutory
provision) as appear to the Secretary of State necessary or expedient in
connection with the provisions thereby brought into force by the order.

(4) The following, namely—

(a) Part I of this Act;

(b) Chapter I of Part II of this Act; and

(c) subject to subsection (6), Part III of this Act,

extend to England and Wales only.

(5) Chapter II of Part II of this Act extends to Scotland only.

(6) In Part III of this Act—

(a) sections 174, 179 and 180 also extend to Scotland; and

(b) paragraph 8 of Schedule 17 also extends to Scotland and Northern Ireland.

(7) This Part, except this section, paragraph 3 of Schedule 21 and the repeals in the House of Commons Disqualification Act 1975 and the Northern Ireland Assembly Disqualification Act 1975, does not extend to Northern Ireland.

GENERAL NOTE

For commencement provisions and transitional provisions see also Appendix 6.

SCHEDULES

Section 9   SCHEDULE 1

CONDUCT OF PROCEEDINGS BY REVERSIONER ON BEHALF OF OTHER LANDLORDS

PART I

THE REVERSIONER

Freeholder to be reversioner

1. Subject to paragraphs 2 to 4, the reversioner in respect of any premises is the person who owns the freehold of those premises.

Replacement of freeholder by other relevant landlord

2. The court may, on the application of all the relevant landlords of any premises, appoint to be the reversioner in respect of those premises (in place of the person designated by paragraph (1) such person as may have been determined by agreement between them.

3. If it appears to the court, on the application of a relevant landlord of any premises—

(a) that the respective interests of the relevant landlords of those premises, the absence or incapacity of the person referred to in paragraph 1 or other special circumstances require that some person other than the person there referred to should act as the reversioner in respect of the premises, or

(b) that the person referred to in that paragraph is unwilling to act as the reversioner,

the court may appoint to be the reversioner in respect of those premises (in place of the person designated by paragraph 1) such person as it thinks fit.

4. The court may also, on the application of any of the relevant landlords or of the nominee purchaser, remove the reversioner in respect of any premises and appoint another person in his place, if it appears to the court proper to do so by reason of any delay or default, actual or apprehended, on the part of the reversioner.

5. A person appointed by the court under any of paragraphs 2 to 4—

(a) must be a relevant landlord; but

(b) may be so appointed on such terms and conditions as the court thinks fit.

PART II

CONDUCT OF PROCEEDINGS ON BEHALF OF OTHER LANDLORDS

Acts of reversioner binding on other landlords

6.—(1) Without prejudice to the generality of section 9(3)—

(a) any notice given by or to the reversioner under this Chapter or section 74(3) following the giving of the initial notice shall be given or received by him on behalf of all the relevant landlords; and

(b) the reversioner may on behalf and in the name of all or (as the case may be) any of those landlords—

(i) deduce, evidence or verify the title to any property;

(ii) negotiate and agree with the nominee purchaser the terms of acquisition;

(iii) execute any conveyance for the purpose of transferring any interest to the nominee purchaser;

(iv) receive the price payable for the acquisition of any interest;

(v) take or defend any legal proceedings under this Chapter in respect of matters arising out of the initial notice.

(2) Subject to paragraph 7—

(a) the reversioner's acts in relation to matters within the authority conferred on him by section 9(3), and

(b) any determination of the court or a leasehold valuation tribunal under this Chapter in proceedings between the reversioner and the nominee purchaser,

shall be binding on the other relevant landlords and on their interests in the specified premises or any other property; but in the event of dispute the reversioner or any of the other relevant landlords may apply to the court for directions as to the manner in which the reversioner should act in the dispute.

(3) If any of the other relevant landlords cannot be found, or his identity cannot be ascertained, the reversioner shall apply to the court for directions and the court may make such order as it thinks proper with a view to giving effect to the rights of the participating tenants and protecting the interests of other persons, but subject to any such directions—

(a) the reversioner shall proceed as in other cases;

(b) any conveyance executed by the reversioner on behalf of that relevant landlord which identifies the interest to be conveyed shall have the same effect as if executed in his name; and

(c) any sum paid as the price for the acquisition of that relevant landlord's interest, and any other sum payable to him by virtue of Schedule 6, shall be paid into court.

(4) The reversioner, if he acts in good faith and with reasonable care and diligence, shall not be liable to any of the other relevant landlords for any loss or damage caused by any act or omission in the exercise or intended exercise of the authority conferred on him by section 9(3).

Other landlords acting independently

7.—(1) Notwithstanding anything in section 9(3) or paragraph 6, any of the other relevant landlords shall, at any time after the giving by the reversioner of a counter-notice under section 21 and on giving notice of his intention to do so to both the reversioner and the nominee purchaser, be entitled—

(a) to deal directly with the nominee purchaser in connection with any of the matters mentioned in sub-paragraphs (i) to (iii) of paragraph 6(1)(b) so far as relating to the acquisition of any interest of his;

(b) to be separately represented in any legal proceedings in which his title to any property comes in question, or in any legal proceedings relating to the terms of acquisition so far as relating to the acquisition of any interest of his.

(2) If the nominee purchaser so requires by notice given to the reversioner and any of the other relevant landlords, that landlord shall deal directly with the nominee purchaser for the purpose of deducing, evidencing or verifying the landlord's title to any property.

(3) Any of the other relevant landlords may by notice given to the reversioner require him to apply to a leasehold valuation tribunal for the determination by the tribunal of any of the terms of acquisition so far as resulting to the acquisition of any interest of the landlord.

(4) Any of the other relevant landlords may also, on giving notice to the reversioner and the nominee purchaser, require that the price payable for the acquisition of his interest shall be paid by the nominee purchaser to him, or to a person authorised by him to receive it, instead of to the reversioner; but if, after being given proper notice of the time and method of completion with the nominee purchaser, either—

(a) he fails to notify the reversioner of the arrangements made with the nominee purchaser to receive payment, or

(b) having notified the reversioner of those arrangements, the arrangements are not duly implemented,

the reversioner shall be authorised to receive the payment for him, and the reversioner's written receipt for the amount payable shall be a complete discharge to the nominee purchaser.

Obligations of other landlords to reversioner

8.—(1) It shall be the duty of each of the other relevant landlords—

(a) (subject to paragraph 7) to give the reversioner all such information and assistance as he may reasonably require; and

(b) after being given proper notice of the time and method of completion with the nominee purchaser, to ensure that all deeds and other documents that ought on his part to be delivered to the nominee purchaser on completion are available for the purpose, including in the case of registered land the land certificate and any other documents necessary to perfect the nominee purchaser's title;

and, if any of the other relevant landlords fails to comply with this sub-paragraph, that relevant landlord shall indemnify the reversioner against any liability incurred by the reversioner in consequence of the failure.

(2) Each of the other relevant landlords shall make such contribution as shall be just to the costs and expenses properly incurred by the reversioner in pursuance of section 9(3) which are not recoverable or not recovered from the nominee purchaser or any other person.

Applications made by other landlords under section 23(1)

9. The authority given to the reversioner by section 9(3) shall not extend to the bringing of proceedings under section 23(1) on behalf of any of the other relevant landlords, or preclude any of those landlords from bringing proceedings under that provision on his own behalf.

GENERAL NOTE
This schedule explains who is to conduct proceedings on behalf of the landlord and how they are to be conducted. It provides the framework for handling the "landlord's side" of the procedures in collective enfranchisement cases. Ordinarily the freeholder will act on behalf of all tenants and have power to bind them. Subject to this the reversioners or the court may appoint some other person, in the latter case, one of the reversioners. Any reversioner may choose to act independently and in very many cases will choose so to do. The Leasehold Reform (Collective Enfranchisement and Lease Renewal) Regulations 1993 (S.I. 1993 No. 2407), reproduced as Appendix 1 below give further guidance in cases where landlords choose to act independently.

Para. 1
Note, in applying this it must be remembered that if the premises are a building with freehold ownership split between two or more persons then the collective right of enfranchisement does not apply (see s.(1)(a)). However, the individual right to a new lease under Pt. I, Chap. II will still apply to each qualifying tenant.

Para. 2
The relevant landlords together may have any person at all appointed as reversioner. If they do not agree any of them can apply to the court who may appoint one of the relevant landlords as reversioners. For an explanation of "relevant landlord" see s.10(2). It means the freeholder and every intermediate leasehold which falls to be acquired. The appointed person need not be one of these estate owners but may be any person they choose to act on their behalf. The court has a discretion as to whether to appoint under this paragraph.

Para. 3
Any relevant landlord can apply under this paragraph for a replacement of the reversioner. On such an application the discretion as to whom to appoint rests in the court.

Para. 4
This paragraph allows either a relevant landlord or the nominee purchaser to apply to have the reversioner replaced in case of delay or default by the reversioner. For example, the landlord may be an overseas landlord who has persistently neglected management of the building. In such a case the court may appoint any person (not necessarily another relevant landlord) to act in his place.

Para. 6
The power of the reversioner to bind other relevant landlords is wide and for many this will make imperative the opportunity given by para. 7 to act independently. Paragraph 6(2) is not entirely clear—assume the reversioner agrees a price for all of the purchaseable interests, this can be challenged by any of the other relevant landlords in court. Does the court have power in giving "directions as to the manner in which the reversioner should act in the dispute" to re-open bargains which the reversioner has made? It appears on a literal interpretation that the court does not. This paragraph seems to envisage that there will be a process of negotiation. If there is a dispute it may be resolved in court. Paragraph 6(4) is ambiguous. It is clear from it when a reversioner is not liable. It gives no clue as to when the reversioner is liable. The wording of para. 6(4) gives a defence to any action brought whatever the cause of action. Assuming the reversioner does not commit an intentional wrong the only apparent course of action is breach of duty of care. This requires the usual ingredients of duty, breach and damage.

Para. 9
It is important to note that any of the relevant landlords may resist collective enfranchisement on the "intention to redevelop" grounds. In this each landlord acts independently.

Sections 9 and 40   SCHEDULE 2

<small>SPECIAL CATEGORIES OF LANDLORDS</small>

Interpretation

1.—(1) In this Schedule—
"Chapter I landlord" means a person who is, in relation to a claim made under Chapter I, the reversioner or any other relevant landlord within the meaning of that Chapter;
"Chapter II landlord" means a person who is, in relation to a claim made under Chapter II, the landlord within the meaning of that Chapter or any of the other landlords (as defined by section 40(4));
"debenture holders' charge" means a charge (whether a floating charge or not) in favour of the holders of a series of debentures issued by a company or other body of persons, or in favour of trustees for such debenture holders;
"mortgage" includes a charge or lien, and related expressions shall be construed accordingly;
"the relevant notice" means—
   (a) in relation to a Chapter I landlord, the notice given under section 13, and
   (b) in relation to a Chapter II landlord, the notice given under section 42.
(2) In paragraphs 5 to 8 any reference to a premium payable on the grant of a lease includes a reference to any other amount payable by virtue of Schedule 13 in connection with its grant.

Mortgagee in possession of landlord's interest

2.—(1) Where—
(a) the interest of a Chapter I or Chapter II landlord is subject to a mortgage, and
(b) the mortgagee is in possession,
all such proceedings arising out of the relevant notice as would apart from this sub-paragraph be taken by or in relation to that landlord ("the mortgagor") shall, as regards his interest, be conducted by and through the mortgagee as if he were that landlord; but this sub-paragraph shall not, in its application to a Chapter I landlord, affect the operation in relation to the mortgagee of section 35 or Schedule 8.
(2) Where sub-paragraph (1) above applies to a Chapter I landlord, then (without prejudice to the generality of that sub-paragraph) any application under section 23(1) that would otherwise be made by the mortgagor (whether alone or together with any other person or persons) shall be made by the mortgagee as if he were the mortgagor.
(3) Where—
(a) the interest of a Chapter I landlord is subject to a mortgage, and
(b) a receiver appointed by the mortgagee or by order of any court is in receipt of the rents and profits,
the person referred to in paragraph (a) shall not make any application under section 23(1) without the consent of the mortgagee, and the mortgagee may by notice given to that person require that, as regards his interest, this paragraph shall apply, either generally or so far as it relates to section 23, as if the mortgagee were a mortgagee in possession.
(4) Where—
(a) the interest of a Chapter I or Chapter II landlord is subject to a mortgage, and
(b) the mortgagee is in possession or a receiver appointed by the mortgagee or by order of any court is in receipt of the rents and profits,
the relevant notice or a copy of it shall be regarded as duly given to that landlord if it is given to the mortgagee or to any such receiver; but whichever of the landlord, the mortgagee and any such receiver are not the recipient of the notice shall be given a copy of it by the recipient.
(5) Sub-paragraph (4) has effect in relation to a debenture holders' charge as if any reference to the mortgagee were a reference to the trustees for the debenture holders; but, where the relevant notice is given to a Chapter I or Chapter II landlord whose interest is subject to any such charge and there is no trustee for the debenture holders, the landlord shall forthwith send it or a copy of it to any receiver appointed by virtue of the charge.
(6) Where—
(a) a Chapter I or Chapter II landlord is given the relevant notice or a copy of it, and
(b) his interest is subject to a mortgage to secure the payment of money,
then (subject to sub-paragraph (7)), the landlord shall forthwith inform the mortgagee (unless the notice was given to him or a receiver appointed by virtue of the mortgage) that the notice has

been given, and shall give him such further information as may from time to time be reasonably required from the landlord by the mortgagee.

(7) Sub-paragraph (6) does not apply to a debenture holders' charge.

Landlord's interest vested in custodian trustee

3. Where the interest of a Chapter I or Chapter II landlord is vested in a person as custodian trustee, then for the purposes of Chapter I or (as the case may be) Chapter II the interest shall be deemed to be vested in the managing trustees or committee of management as owners of that interest, except as regards the execution of any instrument disposing of or otherwise affecting that interest.

Landlord under a disability

4. Where a Chapter I or Chapter II landlord is incapable by reason of mental disorder (within the meaning of the Mental Health Act 1983) of managing and administering his property and affairs, then for the purposes of Chapter I or (as the case may be) Chapter II—

(a) the landlord's receiver appointed under Part VII of that Act or Part VIII of the Mental Health Act 1959, or

(b) (if no such receiver is acting for him) any person authorised in that behalf,

shall, under an order of the authority having jurisdiction under Part VII of the Mental Health Act 1983, take the place of the landlord.

Landlord's interest held on trust for sale

5.—(1) Where the interest of a Chapter I landlord is held on trust for sale, any sum payable to the landlord by way of the price payable for the interest on its acquisition in pursuance of Chapter I shall be dealt with as if it were proceeds of sale arising under the trust.

(2) Where the interest of a Chapter II landlord is held on trust for sale—

(a) any sum payable to the landlord by way of a premium on the grant of a new lease under Chapter II or section 93(4) shall be dealt with as if it were proceeds of sale arising under the trust; and

(b) the purposes authorised—

(i) by section 73 of the Settled Land Act 1925, as applied by section 28 of the Law of Property Act 1925, for the application of capital money, and

(ii) by section 71 of the Settled Land Act 1925, as applied as aforesaid, as purposes for which money may be raised by mortgage,

shall include the payment of compensation by the landlord on the termination of a new lease granted under Chapter II or section 93(4) (whether the payment is made in pursuance of an order under section 61 or in pursuance of an agreement made in conformity with paragraph 5 of Schedule 14 without an application having been made under that section).

Landlord's interest subject to a settlement

6. Where the interest of a Chapter II landlord is subject to a settlement (within the meaning of the Settled Land Act 1925), the purposes authorised—

(a) by section 73 of that Act for the application of capital money, and

(b) by section 71 of that Act as purposes for which money may be raised by mortgage,

shall include the payment of compensation as mentioned in paragraph 5(2)(b) above.

University or college landlords

7.—(1) Where a Chapter I landlord is a university or college to which the Universities and College Estates Act 1925 applies, any sum payable to the landlord by way of the price payable for any interest on its acquisition in pursuance of Chapter I shall be dealt with as if it were an amount payable by way of consideration on a sale effected under that Act.

(2) Where a Chapter II landlord is a university or college to which that Act applies—

(a) any sum payable to the landlord by way of a premium on the grant of a new lease under Chapter II or section 93(4) shall be dealt with as if it were an amount payable by way of consideration on a sale effected under that Act; and

(b) the purposes authorised—

(i) by section 26 of that Act for the application of capital money, and

(ii) by section 31 of that Act as purposes for which money may be raised by mortgage,

shall include the payment of compensation as mentioned in paragraph 5(2)(b) above.

Ecclesiastical landlords

8.—(1) The provisions of this paragraph shall have effect as regards Chapter I or Chapter II landlords who are ecclesiastical landlords; and in this paragraph "ecclesiastical landlord" means—

(a) a capitular body within the meaning of the Cathedrals Measure 1963 having an interest as landlord in property, or

(b) a diocesan board of finance having an interest as landlord in property belonging to the board as diocesan glebe land.

(2) In relation to an interest of an ecclesiastical landlord, the consent of the Church Commissioners shall be required to sanction—

(a) the provisions to be contained in a conveyance in accordance with section 34 and Schedule 7, or in any lease granted under section 56, and the price or premium payable, except as regards matters determined by the court or a leasehold valuation tribunal;

(b) any exercise of the ecclesiastical landlord's rights under section 61, except as aforesaid, and any agreement for the payment of compensation to a tenant in conformity with paragraph 5 of Schedule 14 without an application having been made under that section; and

(c) any grant of a lease in pursuance of section 93(4);

and the Church Commissioners shall be entitled to appear and be heard in any proceedings under this Part to which an ecclesiastical landlord is a party or in which he is entitled to appear and be heard.

(3) Where a capitular body has an interest in property which forms part of the endowment of a cathedral church—

(a) any sum payable to that body by way of—

(i) the price payable for any interest in the property on its acquisition in pursuance of Chapter I, or

(ii) a premium on the grant of a new lease under Chapter II or section 93(4), shall be treated as part of that endowment; and

(b) the powers conferred by sections 21 and 23 of the Cathedrals Measure 1963 in relation to the investment in the acquisition of land of money forming part of the endowment of a cathedral church shall extend to the application of any such money in the payment of compensation as mentioned in paragraph 5(2)(b) above.

(4) In the case of a diocesan board of finance—

(a) no consent or concurrence other than that of the Church Commissioners under subparagraph (2) above shall be required to a disposition under this Part of the interest of the diocesan board of finance in property (including a grant of a new lease in pursuance of section 93(4));

(b) any sum payable to the diocesan board of finance by way of—

(i) the price payable for any interest in property on its acquisition in pursuance of Chapter I, or

(ii) a premium on the grant of a new lease of property under Chapter II or section 93(4),

shall be paid to the Church Commissioners to be applied for purposes for which the proceeds of any such disposition of property by agreement would be applicable under any enactment or Measure authorising such a disposition or disposing of the proceeds of such a disposition; and

(c) any sum required for the payment of compensation as mentioned in paragraph 5(2)(b) above may be paid by the Church Commissioners on behalf of the diocesan board of finance out of any money held by them.

(5) In this paragraph "diocesan board of finance" and "diocesan glebe land" have the same meaning as in the Endowments and Glebe Measure 1976.

GENERAL NOTE

Schedule 2 applies to both collective enfranchisement and the individual right to an extended lease. Its purpose is to deal with the technicalities of conveyancing in a wide variety of different circumstances. It is vital in applying this schedule to note the wide definition of landlord.

Para. 1

The important point is that "landlord" means all relevant landlords.

Para. 2

Where a landlord's interest is subject to a mortgage, the mortgagee in possession will stand in the landlord's shoes. Note that the discharge of mortgages following enfranchisement is dealt with in the notes on Sched. 8. Paragraph 2(3) has effect in collective enfranchisement cases.

Where a receiver has been appointed by a mortgagee the receiver's consent is necessary before the landlord can exercise its right to resist enfranchisement on the "intention to redevelop" ground. Where the procedure under Chaps. I or II has been commenced and the mortgagee takes possession or appoints a receiver then the further proceedings are dealt with by the mortgagee or receiver in the way indicated by this paragraph.

Section 13   SCHEDULE 3

THE INITIAL NOTICE: SUPPLEMENTARY PROVISIONS

PART I

RESTRICTIONS ON PARTICIPATION BY INDIVIDUAL TENANTS, EFFECT OF CLAIMS ON OTHER NOTICES, FORFEITURES ETC.

Prior notice by tenant terminating lease

1. A qualifying tenant of a flat shall not participate in the giving of a relevant notice of claim if the notice is given—
    (a) after the tenant has given notice terminating the lease of the flat (other than a notice that has been superseded by the grant, express or implied, of a new tenancy); or
    (b) during the subsistence of an agreement for the grant to the tenant of a future tenancy of the flat, where the agreement is one to which paragraph 17 of Schedule 10 to the Local Government and Housing Act 1989 applies.

Prior notice by landlord terminating lease

2.—(1) A qualifying tenant of a flat shall not participate in the giving of a relevant notice of claim if the notice is given more than four months after a landlord's notice terminating the tenant's lease of the flat has been given under section 4 of the Landlord and Tenant Act 1954 or served under paragraph 4(1) of Schedule 10 to the Local Government and Housing Act 1989 (whether or not the notice has effect to terminate the lease).
    (2) Where in the case of any qualifying tenant of a flat—
    (a) any such landlord's notice is given or served as mentioned in sub-paragraph (1), but
    (b) that notice was not given or served more than four months before the date when a relevant notice of claim is given,
the landlord's notice shall cease to have effect on that date.
    (3) If—
    (a) any such landlord's notice ceases to have effect by virtue of sub-paragraph (2), but
    (b) the claim made in pursuance of the relevant notice of claim is not effective,
then sub-paragraph (4) shall apply to any landlord's notice terminating the tenant's lease of the flat which—
        (i) is given under section 4 of the Landlord and Tenant Act 1954 or served under paragraph 4(1) of Schedule 10 to the Local Government and Housing Act 1989, and
        (ii) is so given or served within one month after the expiry of the period of currency of that claim.
    (4) Where this sub-paragraph applies to a landlord's notice, the earliest date which may be specified in the notice as the date of termination shall be—
    (a) in the case of a notice given under section 4 of that Act of 1954—
        (i) the date of termination specified in the previous notice, or
        (ii) the date of expiry of the period of three months beginning with the date of the giving of the new notice,
        whichever is the later; or
    (b) in the case of a notice served under paragraph 4(1) of Schedule 10 to that Act of 1989—
        (i) the date of termination specified in the previous notice, or
        (ii) the date of expiry of the period of four months beginning with the date of service of the new notice,
        whichever is the later.
    (5) Where—
    (a) by virtue of sub-paragraph (4) a landlord's notice specifies as the date of termination of a lease a date earlier than six months after the date of the giving of the notice, and
    (b) the notice proposes a statutory tenancy,
section 7(2) of the Landlord and Tenant Act 1954 shall apply in relation to the notice with the substitution, for references to the period of two months ending with the date of termination specified in the notice and the beginning of that period, of references to the period of three months beginning with the date of the giving of the notice and the end of that period.

Orders for possession and pending proceedings for forfeiture etc.

3.—(1) A qualifying tenant of a flat shall not participate in the giving of a relevant notice of claim if at the time when it is given he is obliged to give up possession of his flat in pursuance of an order of a court or will be so obliged at a date specified in such an order.

(2) Except with the leave of the court, a qualifying tenant of a flat shall not participate in the giving of a relevant notice of claim at a time when any proceedings are ending to enforce a right of re-entry of forfeiture terminating his lease of the flat.

(3) Leave shall only be granted under sub-paragraph (2) if the court is satisfied that the tenant does not wish to participate in the giving of such a notice of claim solely or mainly for the purpose of avoiding the consequences of the breach of the terms of his lease in respect of which proceedings are pending.

(4) If—

(a) leave is so granted, and

(b) a relevant notice of claim is given,

the tenant's lease shall be deemed for the purposes of the claim to be a subsisting lease despite the existence of those proceedings and any order made afterwards in those proceedings; and, if the claim is effective, the court in which those proceedings were brought may set aside or vary any such order to such extent and on such terms as appear to that court to be appropriate.

Institution of compulsory purchase procedures

4.—(1) A qualifying tenant of a flat shall not participate in the giving of a relevant notice of claim if on the date when the notice is given—

(a) any person or body of persons who has or have been, or could be, authorised to acquire the whole or part of the flat compulsorily for any purpose has or have, with a view to its acquisition for that purpose—

(i) served a notice to treat on that tenant, or

(ii) entered into a contract for the purchase of his interest in the whole or part of the flat; and

(b) the notice to treat or contract remains in force.

(2) Where—

(a) a relevant notice of claim is given, and

(b) during the currency of the claim any such person or body of persons as is mentioned in sub-paragraph (1)(a) serves or serve, in relation to the flat held by a participating tenant, notice to treat as mentioned in that provision,

the tenant shall cease to be entitled to participate in the making of the claim by virtue of being a qualifying tenant of the flat, and shall accordingly cease to be a participating tenant in respect of the flat.

Notice terminating lease given by tenant or landlord during currency of claim

5. Where a relevant notice of claim is given, any notice terminating the lease of any flat held by a participating tenant, whether it is—

(a) a notice given by the tenant, or

(b) a landlord's notice given under section 4 of the Landlord and Tenant Act 1954 or served under paragraph 4(1) of Schedule 10 to the Local Government and Housing Act 1989,

shall be of no effect if it is given or served during the currency of the claim.

Initial notice operates to prevent termination of tenant's lease by other means

6.—(1) Where a relevant notice of claim is given, then during the currency of the claim and for three months thereafter the lease of any flat held by a participating tenant shall not terminate—

(a) by effluxion of time, or

(b) in pursuance of a notice to quit given by the landlord, or

(c) by the termination of a superior lease;

but if the claim is not effective, and but for this sub-paragraph the lease would have so terminated before the end of those three months, the lease shall so terminate at the end of those three months.

(2) Sub-paragraph (1) shall not be taken to prevent an earlier termination of the lease in any manner not mentioned in that sub-paragraph, and shall not affect—

(a) the power under section 146(4) of the Law of Property Act 1925 (relief against forfeiture of leases) to grant a tenant relief against the termination of a superior lease, or

(b) any right of the tenant to relief under section 16(2) of the Landlord and Tenant Act 1954 (relief where landlord proceeding to enforce covenants) or under paragraph 9 of Schedule 5 to that Act (relief in proceedings brought by superior landlord).

(3) The reference to sub-paragraph (2) to section 16(2) of, and paragraph 9 of Schedule 5 to, the Landlord and Tenant Act 1954 includes a reference to those provisions as they apply in relation to Schedule 10 to the Local Government and Housing Act 1989.

Restriction on proceedings against participating tenant to enforce right of re-entry or forfeiture

7.—(1) Where a relevant notice of claim is given, then during the currency of the claim—

(a) no proceedings to enforce any right of re-entry or forfeiture terminating the lease of any flat held by a participating tenant shall be brought in any court without the leave of that court; and

(b) leave shall only be granted if the court is satisfied that the tenant is participating in the making of the claim solely or mainly for the purpose of avoiding the consequences of the breach of the terms of his lease in respect of which proceedings are proposed to be brought.

(2) If leave is granted under sub-paragraph (1), the tenant shall cease to be entitled to participate in the making of the claim by virtue of being a qualifying tenant of the flat referred to in that sub-paragraph, and shall accordingly cease to be a participating tenant in respect of the flat.

Restrictions for purposes of s.14(3) on tenant electing to become participating tenant during currency of claim

8.—(1) Where a relevant notice of claim is given, a qualifying tenant of a flat may not subsequently make an election under section 14(3)—

(a) if he was prohibited from participating in the giving of the notice by virtue of paragraph 1, 2(1), 3(1) or 4(1) above; or

(b) at a time when he would be so prohibited from participating in the giving of a relevant notice of claim, if such a notice were to be given then.

(2) Where a relevant notice of claim is given, then except with the leave of the court, a qualifying tenant of a flat may not subsequently make an election under section 14(3) at a time when any proceedings are pending to enforce a right of re-entry or forfeiture terminating his lease of the flat.

(3) Leave shall only be granted under sub-paragraph (2) if the court is satisfied that the tenant does not wish to make such an election solely or mainly for the purpose of avoiding the consequences of the breach of the terms of his lease in respect of which proceedings are pending.

(4) If—

(a) leave is so granted, and

(b) the tenant makes such an election,

the tenant's lease shall be deemed for the purposes of the claim to be a subsisting lease despite the existence of those proceedings and any order made afterwards in those proceedings; and, and if the claim is effective, the court in which those proceedings were brought may set aside or vary any such order to such extent and on such terms as appear to that court to be appropriate.

(5) References in this paragraph and paragraph 9 below to making an election under section 14(3) are references to making such an election to participate in the making of the claim in respect of which the relevant notice of claim is given.

Effect of tenant's election on certain notices given by landlord

9.—(1) This paragraph applies to a qualifying tenant of a flat who, following the giving of a relevant notice of claim, makes an election under section 14(3).

(2) Where in the case of any such tenant—

(a) a landlord's notice terminating the tenant's lease of the flat has been given or served as mentioned in paragraph 2(1) above (whether or not the notice has effect to terminate the lease), but

(b) that notice was not given or served more than four months before the date when the tenant makes his election under section 14(3),

the landlord's notice shall cease to have effect on that date.

(3) If—

(a) any such landlord's notice ceases to have effect by virtue of sub-paragraph (2) above, but

(b) the claim made in pursuance of the relevant notice of claim is not effective,

then paragraph 2(4) above shall apply to any landlord's notice terminating the tenant's lease of the flat which—

(i) is given under section 4 of the Landlord and Tenant Act 1954 or served under paragraph 4(1) of Schedule 10 to the Local Government and Housing Act 1989, and

(ii) is so given or served within one month after the expiry of the period of currency of that claim;

and paragraph 2(5) above shall apply accordingly.

(4) Paragraph 8(5) above applies for the purposes of this paragraph.

Interpretation

10.—(1) For the purposes of this Part of this Schedule—

(a) "relevant notice of claim", in relation to any flat, means a notice under section 13 in the case of which the specified premises contain that flat, and references to participating in the giving of such a notice are references to being one of the persons by whom the notice is given;

(b) references to a notice under section 13 include, in so far as the context permits, references to a notice purporting to be given under that section (whether by persons who are qualifying tenants or not);

(c) references to a claim being effective are references to a binding contract being entered into for the acquisition of the freehold and other interests falling to be acquired in pursuance of the claim or to the making of an order under section 24(4)(a) or (b) or 25(6)(a) or (b) which provides for the vesting of those interests; and

(d) references to the currency of a claim are—

(i) where the claim is made by a valid notice under section 13, references to the period during which the notice continues in force in accordance with subsection (11) of that section, or

(ii) where the claim is made by a notice which is not a valid notice under section 13, references to the period beginning with the giving of the notice and ending with the time when the notice is set aside by the court or is withdrawn or when it would (if valid) cease to have effect or be deemed to have been withdrawn.

(2) For the purposes of sub-paragraph (1)(d) the date when a notice is set aside, or would (if valid) (cease to have effect, in consequence of an order of a court shall be taken to be the date when the order becomes final.

PART II

PROCEDURE FOR GIVING COPIES TO RELEVANT LANDLORDS

Application of Part II

11. This Part of this Schedule has effect where a notice under section 13 is given in a case to which section 9(2) applies.

Qualifying tenants to give copies of initial notice

12.—(1) The qualifying tenants by whom the initial notice is given shall, in addition to giving the initial notice to the reversioner in respect of the specified premises, give a copy of the notice to every other person known or believed by them to be a relevant landlord of those premises.

(2) The initial notice shall state whether copies are being given in accordance with sub-paragraph (1) to anyone other than the recipient and, if so, to whom.

Recipient of notice or copy to give further copies

13.—(1) Subject to sub-paragraph (2), a recipient of the initial notice or of a copy of it (including a person receiving a copy under this sub-paragraph) shall forthwith give a copy to any person who—

(a) is known or believed by him to be a relevant landlord, and

(b) is not stated in the recipient's copy of the notice, or known by him, to have received a copy.

(2) Sub-paragraph (1) does not apply where the recipient is neither the reversioner nor another relevant landlord.

(3) Where a person gives any copies of the initial notice in accordance with sub-paragraph (1), he shall—

(a) supplement the statement under paragraph 12(2) by adding any further persons to whom he is giving copies or who are known to him to have received one; and

(b) notify the qualifying tenants by whom the initial notice is given of the persons added by him to that statement.

Consequences of failure to comply with paragraph 12 or 13

14.—(1) Where—

(a) a relevant landlord of the specified premises does not receive a copy of the initial notice before the end of the period specified in it in pursuance of section 13(3)(g), but

(b) he was given a notice under section 11 by any of the qualifying tenants by whom the initial notice was given and, in response to the notice under that section, notified the tenant in question of his interest in the specified premises,

the initial notice shall cease to have effect at the end of that period.

(2) Where—

(a) sub-paragraph (1) does not apply, but

(b) any person fails without reasonable cause to comply with paragraph 12 or 13 above, or is guilty of any unreasonable delay in complying with either of those paragraphs,

he shall be liable for any loss thereby occasioned to the qualifying tenants by whom the initial notice was given or to the reversioner or any other relevant landlord.

PART III

OTHER PROVISIONS

Inaccuracies or misdescription in initial notice

15.—(1) The initial notice shall not be invalidated by any inaccuracy in any of the particulars required by section 13(3) or by any misdescription of any of the property to which the claim extends.

(2) Where the initial notice—

(a) specifies any property or interest which was not liable to acquisition under or by virtue of section 1 or 2, or

(b) fails to specify any property or interest which is so liable to acquisition,

the notice may, with the leave of the court and on such terms as the court may think fit, be amended so as to exclude or include the property or interest in question.

(3) Where the initial notice is so amended as to exclude any property or interest, references to the property or interests specified in the notice under any provision of section 13(3) shall be construed accordingly; and, where it is so amended as to include any property or interest, the property or interest shall be treated as if it had been specified under the provision of that section under which it would have fallen to be specified if its acquisition had been proposed at the relevant date.

Effect on initial notice of tenant's lack of qualification to participate

16.—(1) It is hereby declared that, where at the relevant date any of the persons by whom the initial notice is given—

(a) is not a qualifying tenant of a flat contained in the specified premises, or

(b) is such a qualifying tenant but is prohibited from participating in the giving of the notice by virtue of Part I of this Schedule, or

(c) (if it is claimed in the notice that he satisfies the residence condition) does not satisfy that condition,

the notice shall not be invalidated on that account, so long as the notice was in fact properly given by a sufficient number of qualifying tenants of flats contained in the premises as at the relevant date, and not less than one-half of the qualifying tenants by whom it was so given then satisfied the residence condition.

(2) For the purposes of sub-paragraph (1) a sufficient number is a number which—

(a) is not less than two-thirds of the total number of qualifying tenants of flats contained in the specified premises as at the relevant date, and

(b) is not less than one-half of the total number of flats so contained.

GENERAL NOTE

Para. 1

(a) a tenant cannot join in an initial notice under s.11 if he has given a notice to quit and has not been granted a new tenancy.

(b) para. 17 of Sched. 10 to the Local Government and Housing Act 1989 permits a landlord and tenant of a long residential tenancy to agree a new tenancy at a rent which is not a low rent to which the limited protection afforded by that Act will then no longer apply. If there is a contract to grant such a tenancy then the tenant cannot join in an initial notice under s.11. This is a possible (if recondite) route for avoiding the collective enfranchisement provisions. Such an agreement need not, for example, become effective until shortly before the term date of the existing tenancy.

Para. 2

Where the Landlord and Tenant Act 1954, Pt. I applies or Sched. 10 to the Local Government and Housing Act 1989, the landlord may by notice terminate the tenancy.

SCHEDULE 4

INFORMATION TO BE FURNISHED BY REVERSIONER ABOUT EXERCISE OF RIGHTS UNDER CHAPTER II

Information to accompany counter-notice

1.—(1) This paragraph applies where before the date of the giving of a counter-notice under section 21 the reversioner or any other relevant landlord—

(a) has received—

(i) a notice given under section 42 with respect to any flat contained in the specified premises (being a notice to which section 54(1) or (2) applies on that date), or

(ii) a copy of such a notice, or

(b) has given any counter-notice under section 45 in response to any such notice.

(2) A copy of every notice which, or a copy of which, has been received as mentioned in sub-paragraph (1)(a), and a copy of every counter-notice which has been given as mentioned in sub-paragraph (1)(b), shall either—

(a) accompany any counter-notice given under section 21, or

(b) be given to the nominee purchaser by the reversioner as soon as possible after the date of the giving of any such counter-notice.

Continuing duty to furnish information

2.—(1) Subject to sub-paragraph (3), this paragraph applies where on or after the date of the giving of a counter-notice under section 21 the reversioner or any other relevant landlord receives—

(a) a notice given under section 42 with respect to any flat contained in the specified premises or a copy of such a notice, or

(b) any notice of withdrawal given under section 52 and relating to any notice under section 42 of which a copy has already been furnished to the nominee purchaser under this Schedule.

(2) A copy of every notice which, or a copy of which, is received as mentioned in sub-paragraph (1)(a) or (b) shall be given to the nominee purchaser by the reversioner as soon as possible after the time when the notice or copy is received by the reversioner or (as the case may be) the other relevant landlord.

(3) This paragraph does not apply if the notice or copy is received by the reversioner or (as the case may be) the other relevant landlord otherwise than at a time when—

(a) the initial notice continues in force, or

(b) a binding contract entered into in pursuance of that notice remains in force, or

(c) where an order has been made under section 24(4)(a) or (b) or 25(6)(a) or (b) with respect to the specified premises, any interests which by virtue of the order fall to be vested in the nominee purchaser have yet to be so vested.

Duty of other landlords to furnish copies to reversioner

3.—(1) Without prejudice to the generality of paragraph 8(1)(a) of Schedule 1, the duty imposed by that provision shall extend to requiring any relevant landlord (other than the reversioner) who—

(a) receives a relevant notice or a copy of such a notice, or

(b) gives a relevant counter-notice,

to furnish a copy of the notice or counter-notice to the reversioner as soon as possible after the time when the notice or copy is received or (as the case may be) the counter-notice is given by the relevant landlord.

(2) In this paragraph "relevant notice" and "relevant counter-notice" mean respectively any notice of which a copy is required to be given to the nominee purchaser by the reversioner in accordance with this Schedule and any counter-notice of which a copy is required to be so given.

GENERAL NOTE

Considerable complexity may arise where individual tenants are seeking to exercise their rights under Chap. II (individual extended lease) and other tenants are seeking to exercise the collective right to enfranchisement under Chap. II. This schedule is intended to help reduce this by ensuring that the landlord keeps the tenants exercising the Chap. II rights informed of any Chap. II notices.

Para. 1

The reversioner when serving a s.21 counter-notice should also send any Chap. II notices or counter-notices to the nominee purchaser together with the counter-notice or as soon as possible after.

Para. 2

Where the reversioner has served a s.21 counter-notice in response to an initial notice seeking collective enfranchisement it may receive individual notices claiming the individual right to an extended lease under s.42. Copies of this and any withdrawal under s.42 have to be supplied to the nominee purchaser. This obligation ceases if the initial notice ceases to have effect, a binding contract is made or a court determines the interests to be acquired under ss.24(4)(a) or 25(6)(a).

Para. 3

It may be that individual tenants will serve notices under s.42 or be given counter-notices by other relevant landlords. These landlords are obliged to give copies to the reversioner which must then comply with paras. 1 or 2 above.

Sections 24 and 25 SCHEDULE 5

VESTING ORDERS UNDER SECTIONS 24 AND 25

Interpretation

1.—(1) In this Schedule "a vesting order" means an order made by the court under section 24(4)(a) or (b) or section 25(6)(a) or (b).

(2) In this Schedule "the relevant terms of acquisition", in relation to any such order, means the terms of acquisition referred to in section 24(4)(a) or (b) or section 25(6)(a) or (b), as the case may be.

Execution of conveyance

2.—(1) Where any interests are to be vested in the nominee purchaser by virtue of a vesting order, then on his paying into court the appropriate sum in respect of each of those interests there shall be executed by such person as the court may designate a conveyance which—

(a) is in a form approved by a leasehold valuation tribunal, and

(b) contains such provisions as may be so approved for the purpose of giving effect to the relevant terms of acquisition.

(2) The conveyance shall be effective to vest in the nominee purchaser the interests expressed to be conveyed, subject to and in accordance with the terms of the conveyance.

The appropriate sum

3.—(1) In the case of any vesting order, the appropriate sum which in accordance with paragraph 2(1) is to be paid into court in respect of any interest is the aggregate of—

(a) such amount as is fixed by the relevant terms of acquisition as the price which is payable in accordance with Schedule 6 in respect of that interest; and

(b) any amounts or estimated amounts determined by a leasehold valuation tribunal as being, at the time of execution of the conveyance, due to the transferor from any tenants of his of premises comprised in the premises in which that interest subsists (whether due under or in respect of their leases or under or in respect of agreements collateral thereto).

(2) In this paragraph "the transferor", in relation to any interest, means the person from whom the interest is to be acquired by the nominee purchaser.

Effect of payment of appropriate sum into court

4. Where any interest is vested in the nominee purchaser in accordance with this Schedule, the payment into court of the appropriate sum in respect of that interest shall be taken to have satisfied any claims against the nominee purchaser or the participating tenants, or the personal representatives or assigns of any of them, in respect of the price payable under this Chapter for the acquisition of that interest.

Supplemental

5.—(1) In the provisions specified in sub-paragraph (2) references to a binding contract being entered into in pursuance of the initial notice shall be read as including references to the making of a vesting order.

(2) Those provisions are—

(a) section 14(11);

(b) section 15(12) (except so far as it provides for the interpretation of references to the nominee purchaser);

(c) section 16(10);

(d) section 19(5)(b);

(e) section 28(1);

(f) section 30(4); and

(g) section 31(4).

(3) Where, at any time after a vesting order is made but before the interests falling to be vested in the nominee purchaser by virtue of the order have been so vested, any acquiring authority (within the meaning of section 30) serves notice to treat as mentioned in subsection (1)(a) of that section, the vesting order shall cease to have effect.

(4) Where sub-paragraph (3) applies to any vesting order, then on the occasion of the compulsory acquisition in question the compensation payable in respect of any interest in the specified premises (whether or not the one to which the notice to treat relates) shall be determined on the basis of the value of the interest subject to and with the benefit of the rights and obligations arising from the initial notice and affecting the interest.

(5) In section 38(2) (except so far as it provides for the interpretation of references to the proposed acquisition by the nominee purchaser) the reference to a contract entered into in pursuance of the initial notice shall be read as including a reference to a vesting order.

GENERAL NOTE

Vesting orders under ss.24 or 25 are made when the landlord has proved so uncooperative that the tenants have had to proceed through the court.

Para. 2

The court will have determined the term of the acquisition. However, in every case the form of the conveyance has to be approved by a leasehold valuation tribunal which will require a separate application to the tribunal.

Para. 3

The leasehold valuation tribunal has also to determine or estimate any amounts due to the landlord from its tenants.

Para. 4

The payment into court discharges any outstanding mortgages on the interest transferred.

Paras. 5(3) and (4)

These paragraphs should be noted as dealing with the effect of a compulsory purchase after a vesting order but before the interests have actually vested in the nominee purchaser by means of a conveyance. When this happens the vesting order is discharged but the compensation is assessed as if the initial notice was effective.

Section 32

SCHEDULE 6

PURCHASE PRICE PAYABLE BY NOMINEE PURCHASER

PART I

GENERAL

Interpretation and operation of Schedule

1.—(1) In this Schedule—

"the freeholder" means the person who owns the freehold of the specified premises;

"intermediate leasehold interest" means the interest of the tenant under a lease which is superior to the lease held by a qualifying tenant of a flat contained in the specified premises, to the extent that—

(a) any such interest is to be acquired by the nominee purchaser by virtue of section 2(1)(a), and

(b) it is an interest in the specified premises;

"the valuation date" means the date when the interest in the specified premises which is to be acquired by the nominee purchaser from the freeholder is determined either by agreement or by a leasehold valuation tribunal under this Chapter.

(2) Parts II to IV of this Schedule have effect subject to the provisions of Parts V and VI (which relate to interests with negative values).

PART II

FREEHOLD OF SPECIFIED PREMISES

Price payable for freehold of specified premises

2.—(1) Subject to the provisions of this paragraph, the price payable by the nominee purchaser for the freehold of the specified premises shall be the aggregate of—

(a) the value of the freeholder's interest in the premises as determined in accordance with paragraph 3,

(b) the freeholder's share of the marriage value as determined in accordance with paragraph 4, and

(c) any amount of compensation payable to the freeholder under paragraph 5.

(2) Where the amount arrived at in accordance with sub-paragraph (1) is a negative amount, the price payable by the nominee purchaser for the freehold shall be nil.

Value of freeholder's interest

3.—(1) Subject to the provisions of this paragraph, the value of the freeholder's interest in the specified premises is the amount which at the valuation date that interest might be expected to realise if sold on the open market by a willing seller (with neither the nominee purchaser nor any participating tenant buying or seeking to buy) on the following assumptions—

(a) on the assumption that the vendor is selling for an estate in fee simple—

(i) subject to any leases subject to which the freeholder's interest in the premises is to be acquired by the nominee purchaser, but

(ii) subject also to any intermediate or other leasehold interests in the premises which are to be acquired by the nominee purchaser;

(b) on the assumption that this Chapter and Chapter II confer no right to acquire any interest in the specified premises or to acquire any new lease (except that this shall not preclude the taking into account of a notice given under section 42 with respect to a flat contained in the specified premises where it is given by a person other than a participating tenant);

(c) on the assumption that any increase in the value of any flat held by a participating tenant which is attributable to an improvement carried out at his own expense by the tenant or by any predecessor in title is to be disregarded; and

(d) on the assumption that (subject to paragraphs (a) and (b)) the vendor is selling with and subject to the rights and burdens with and subject to which the conveyance to the nominee purchaser of the freeholder's interest is to be made, and in particular with and subject to such permanent or extended rights and burdens as are to be created in order to give effect to Schedule 7.

(2) It is hereby declared that the fact that sub-paragraph (1) requires assumptions to be made as to the matters specified in paragraphs (a) to (d) of that sub-paragraph does not preclude the making of assumptions as to other matters where those assumptions are appropriate for determining the amount which at the valuation date the freeholder's interest in the specified premises might be expected to realise if sold as mentioned in that sub-paragraph.

(3) In determining that amount there shall be made such deduction (if any) in respect of any defect in title as on a sale of the interest on the open market might be expected to be allowed between a willing seller and a willing buyer.

(4) Where a lease of any flat or other unit contained in the specified premises is to be granted to the freeholder in accordance with section 36 and Schedule 9, the value of his interest in those premises at the valuation date so far as relating to that flat or other unit shall be taken to be the difference as at that date between—

(a) the value of his freehold interest in it, and

(b) the value of his interest in it under that lease, assuming it to have been granted to him at that date;

and each of those values shall, so far as is appropriate, be determined in like manner as the value of the freeholder's interest in the whole of the specified premises is determined for the purposes of paragraph 2(1)(a).

(5) The value of the freeholder's interest in the specified premises shall not be increased by reason of—

(a) any transaction which—

(i) is entered into on or after the date of the passing of this Act (otherwise than in pursuance of a contract entered into before that date), and

(ii) involves the creation or transfer of an interest superior to (whether or not preceding) any interest held by a qualifying tenant of a flat contained in the specified premises; or

(b) any alteration on or after that date of the terms on which any such superior interest is held.

(6) Sub-paragraph (5) shall not have the effect of preventing an increase in value of the freeholder's interest in the specified premises in a case where the increase is attributable to any such leasehold interest with a negative value as is mentioned in paragraph 14(2).

Freeholder's share of marriage value

4.—(1) The marriage value is the amount referred to in sub-paragraph (2), and the freeholder's share of the marriage value is—
   (a) such proportion of that amount as is determined by agreement between the reversioner and the nominee purchaser or, in default of agreement, as is determined by a leasehold valuation tribunal to be the proportion which in its opinion would have been determined by an agreement made at the valuation date between the parties on a sale on the open market by a willing seller, or
   (b) 50 per cent. of that amount,
whichever is the greater.

(2) The marriage value is any increase in the aggregate value of the freehold and every intermediate leasehold interest in the specified premises, when regarded as being (in consequence of their being acquired by the nominee purchaser) interests under the control of the participating tenants, as compared with the aggregate value of those interests when held by the persons from whom they are to be so acquired, being an increase in value—
   (a) which is attributable to the potential ability of the participating tenants, once those interests have been so acquired, to have new leases granted to them without payment of any premium and without restriction as to length of term, and
   (b) which, if those interests were being sold to the nominee purchaser on the open market by willing sellers, the nominee purchaser would have to agree to share with the sellers in order to reach agreement as to price.

(3) For the purposes of sub-paragraph (2) the value of the freehold or any intermediate leasehold interest in the specified premises when held by the person from whom it is to be acquired by the nominee purchaser and its value when acquired by the nominee purchaser—
   (a) shall be determined on the same basis as the value of the interest is determined for the purposes of paragraph 2(1)(a) or (as the case may be) paragraph 6(1)(b)(i); and
   (b) shall be so determined as at the valuation date.

(4) Accordingly, in so determining the value of an interest when acquired by the nominee purchaser—
   (a) the same assumptions shall be made under paragraph 3(1) (or, as the case may be, under paragraph 3(1) as applied by paragraph 7(1)) as are to be made under that provision in determining the value of the interest when held by the person from whom it is to be acquired by the nominee purchaser; and
   (b) any merger or other circumstances affecting the interest on its acquisition by the nominee purchaser shall be disregarded.

Compensation for loss resulting from enfranchisement

5.—(1) Where the freeholder will suffer any loss or damage to which this paragraph applies, there shall be payable to him such amount as is reasonable to compensate him for that loss or damage.

(2) This paragraph applies to—
   (a) any diminution in value of any interest of the freeholder in other property resulting from the acquisition of his interest in the specified premises; and
   (b) any other loss or damage which results therefrom to the extent that it is referable to his ownership of any interest in other property.

(3) Without prejudice to the generality of paragraph (b) of sub-paragraph (2), the kinds of loss falling within that paragraph include loss of development value in relation to the specified premises to the extent that it is referable as mentioned in that paragraph.

(4) In sub-paragraph (3) "development value", in relation to the specified premises, means any increase in the value of the freeholder's interest in the premises which is attributable to the possibility of demolishing, reconstructing, or carrying out substantial works of construction on, the whole or a substantial part of the premises.

(5) Where the freeholder will suffer loss or damage to which this paragraph applies, then in determining the amount of compensation payable to him under this paragraph, it shall not be material that—
   (a) the loss or damage could to any extent be avoided or reduced by the grant to him, in accordance with section 36 and Schedule 9, of a lease granted in pursuance of Part III of that Schedule, and

(b) he is not requiring the nominee purchaser to grant any such lease.

PART III

INTERMEDIATE LEASEHOLD INTERESTS

Price payable for intermediate leasehold interests

6.—(1) Where the nominee purchaser is to acquire one or more intermediate leasehold interests—
   (a) a separate price shall be payable for each of those interests, and
   (b) (subject to the provisions of this paragraph) that price shall be the aggregate of—
         (i) the value of the interest as determined in accordance with paragraph 7, and
         (ii) any amount of compensation payable to the owner of that interest in accordance with paragraph 8.
(2) Where in the case of any intermediate leasehold interest the amount arrived at in accordance with sub-paragraph (1)(b) is a negative amount, the price payable by the nominee purchaser for the interest shall be nil.

Value of intermediate leasehold interests

7.—(1) Subject to sub-paragraph (2), paragraph 3 shall apply for determining the value of any intermediate leasehold interest for the purposes of paragraph 6(1)(b)(i) with such modifications as are appropriate to relate that paragraph to a sale of the interest in question subject (where applicable) to any leases intermediate between that interest and any lease held by a qualifying tenant of a flat contained in the specified premises.
(2) The value of an intermediate leasehold interest which is the interest of the tenant under a minor intermediate lease shall be calculated by applying the formula set out in sub-paragraph (7) instead of in accordance with sub-paragraph (1).
(3) "A minor intermediate lease" means a lease complying with the following requirements, namely—
   (a) it must have an expectation of possession of not more than one month, and
   (b) the profit rent in respect of the lease must be not more than £5 per year;
and, in the case of a lease which is in immediate reversion on two or more leases, those requirements must be complied with in connection with each of the sub-leases.
(4) Where a minor intermediate lease is in immediate reversion on two or more leases—
   (a) the formula set out in sub-paragraph (7) shall be applied in relation to each of those sub-leases (and sub-paragraphs (5) and (6) shall also so apply); and
   (b) the value of the interest of the tenant under the minor intermediate lease shall accordingly be the aggregate of the amounts calculated by so applying the formula.
(5) "Profit rent" means an amount equal to that of the rent payable under the lease on which the minor intermediate lease is in immediate reversion, less that of the rent payable under the minor intermediate lease.
(6) Where the minor intermediate lease or that on which it is in immediate reversion comprises property other than a flat held by a qualifying tenant, then in sub-paragraph (5) the reference to the rent payable under it means so much of that rent as is apportioned to any such flat.
(7) The formula is—

$$P = £\ \frac{R}{Y} - \frac{R}{Y(1 + Y)^n}$$

where—
   P = the price payable;
   R = the profit rent;
   Y = the yield (expressed as a decimal fraction) from 2½ per cent. Consolidated Stock;
   n = the period, expressed in years (taking any part of a year as a whole year), of the remainder of the term of the minor intermediate lease as at the valuation date.
(8) In calculating the yield from 2½ per cent. Consolidated Stock, the price of that stock shall be taken to be the middle market price at the close of business on the last trading day in the week before the valuation date.
(9) For the purposes of this paragraph the expectation of possession carried by a lease in relation to a lease ("the sub-lease") on which it is in immediate reversion is the expectation of possession which it carries at the valuation date after the sub-lease, on the basis that—
   (a) (subject to sub-paragraph (10)) where the sub-lease is a lease held by a qualifying tenant

28–259

of a flat contained in the specified premises, it terminates at the valuation date if its term date fell before then, or else it terminates on its term date; and

(b) in any other case, the sub-lease terminates on its term date.

(10) In a case where before the relevant date for the purposes of this Chapter the landlord of any such qualifying tenant as is mentioned in sub-paragraph (9)(a) had given notice to quit terminating the tenant's sub-lease on a date earlier than that date, the date specified in the notice to quit shall be substituted for the date specified in that provision.

Compensation for loss on acquisition of interest

8. Sub-paragraphs (1) to (4) of paragraph 5 shall apply in relation to the owner of any intermediate threshold interest as they apply in relation to the freeholder.

Owners of intermediate interests entitled to part of marriage value

9.—(1) This paragraph applies where—

(a) the price payable for the freehold of the specified premises includes an amount in respect of the freeholder's share of the marriage value, and

(b) the nominee purchaser is to acquire any intermediate leasehold interests.

(2) The amount payable to the freeholder in respect of his share of the marriage value shall be divided between the freeholder and the owners of the intermediate leasehold interests in proportion to the value of their respective interests in the specified premises (as determined for the purposes of paragraph 2(1)(a) or paragraph 6(1)(b)(i), as the case may be).

(3) Where the owner of an intermediate leasehold interest is entitled in accordance with sub-paragraph (2) to any par of the amount payable to the freeholder in respect of the freeholder's share of the marriage value, the amount to which he is so entitled shall be payable to him by the freeholder.

PART IV

OTHER INTERESTS TO BE ACQUIRED

Price payable for other interests

10.—(1) Where the nominee purchase is to acquire any freehold interest in pursuance of section 1(2)(a) or (4) or section 21(4), then (subject to sub-paragraph (3) below) the price payable for that interest shall be the aggregate of—

(a) the value of the interest as determined in accordance with paragraph 11,

(b) any share of the marriage value to which the owner of the interest is entitled under paragraph 12, and

(c) any amount of compensation payable to the owner of the interest in accordance with paragraph 13.

(2) Where the nominee purchaser is to acquire any leasehold interest by virtue of section 2(1) other than an intermediate leasehold interest, or he is to acquire any leasehold interest in pursuance of section 21(4), then (subject to sub-paragraph (3) below) the price payable for that interest shall be the aggregate of—

(a) the value of the interest as is determined in accordance with paragraph 11, and

(b) any amount of compensation payable to the owner of the interest in accordance with paragraph 13.

(3) Where in the case of any interest the amount arrived at in accordance with sub-paragraphs (1) or (2) is a negative amount, the price payable by the nominee purchaser for the interest shall be nil.

Value of other interests

11.—(1) In the case of any such freehold interest as is mentioned in paragraph 10(1), paragraph 3 shall apply for determining the value of the interest with such modifications as are appropriate to relate it to a sale of the interest subject (where applicable) to any leases intermediate between that interest and any lease held by a qualifying tenant of a flat contained in the specified premises.

(2) In the case of any such leasehold interest as is mentioned in paragraph 10(2), then—

(a) (unless paragraph (b) below applies) paragraph 3 shall apply as mentioned in sub-paragraph (1) above;

(b) if it is the interest of the tenant under a minor intermediate lease within the meaning of paragraph 7, sub-paragraphs (2) to (10) of that paragraph shall apply with such modifications as are appropriate for determining the value of the interest.

(3) In its application in accordance with sub-paragraph (1) or (2) above, paragraph 3(6) shall have effect as if the reference to paragraph 14(2) were a reference to paragraph 18(2).

Marriage value

12.—(1) Where any such freehold interest as is mentioned in paragraph 10(1) is an interest in any such property as is mentioned in section 1(3)(a)—

(a) sub-paragraphs (2) to (4) of paragraph 4 shall apply with such modifications as are appropriate for determining the marriage value in connection with the acquisition by the nominee purchaser of that interest, and

(b) sub-paragraph (1) of that paragraph shall apply with such modifications as are appropriate for determining the share of the marriage value to which the owner of that interest is entitled.

(2) Where—

(a) the owner of any such freehold interest is entitled to any share of the marriage value in respect of any such property, and

(b) the nominee purchaser is to acquire any leasehold interests in that property superior to any lease held by a participating tenant,

the amount payable to the owner of the freehold interest in respect of his share of the marriage value in respect of that property shall be divided between the owner of that interest and the owners of the leasehold interests in proportion to the value of their respective interests in that property (as determined for the purposes of paragraph 10(1) or (2), as the case may be).

(3) Where the owner of any such leasehold interest ("the intermediate landlord") is entitled in accordance with sub-paragraph (2) to any part of the amount payable to the owner of any freehold interest in respect of his share of the marriage value in respect of any property, the amount to which the intermediate landlord is so entitled shall be payable to him by the owner of that freehold interest.

Compensation for loss on acquisition of interest

13. Sub-paragraphs (1) to (4) of paragraph 5 shall apply in relation to the owner of any such freehold or leasehold interest as is mentioned in paragraph 10(1) or (2) and to the acquisition of that interest as they apply in relation to the freeholder and to the acquisition of his interest in the specified premises (and accordingly any reference in those provisions of paragraph 5 to the specified premises shall be read for this purpose as a reference to the property in which any such freehold or leasehold interest subsists).

PART V

VALUATION ETC. OF INTERESTS IN SPECIFIED PREMISES WITH NEGATIVE VALUES

Valuation of freehold and intermediate leasehold interests

14.—(1) Where—

(a) the value of the freeholder's interest in the specified premises (as determined in accordance with paragraph 3), or

(b) the value of any intermediate leasehold interest (as determined in accordance with paragraph 7),

is a negative amount, the value of the interest for the relevant purposes shall be nil.

(2) Where sub-paragraph (1) applies to any intermediate leasehold interest whose value is a negative amount ("the negative interest"), then for the relevant purposes any interests in the specified premises superior to the negative interest and having a positive value shall be reduced in value—

(a) beginning with the interest which is immediately superior to the negative interest and continuing (if necessary) with any such other superior interests in order of proximity to the negative interest;

(b) until the aggregate amount of the reduction is equal to the negative amount in question; and

(c) without reducing the value of any interest to less than nil.

(3) In a case where sub-paragraph (1) applies to two or more intermediate leasehold interests whose values are negative amounts, sub-paragraph (2) shall apply separately in relation to each of those interests—

(a) beginning with the interest which is inferior to every other of those interests and then in order of proximity to that interest; and

(b) with any reduction in the value of any interest for the relevant purposes by virtue of any prior application of sub-paragraph (2) being taken into account.

(4) For the purposes of sub-paragraph (2) an interest has a positive value if (apart from that sub-paragraph) its value for the relevant purposes is a positive amount.

(5) In this Part of this Schedule "the relevant purposes"—

(a) as respects the freeholder's interest in the specified premises, means the purposes of paragraph 2(1)(a); and

(b) as respects any intermediate leasehold interest, means the purposes of paragraph 6(1)(b)(i).

Calculation of marriage value

15.—(1) Where (as determined in accordance with paragraph 4(3) and (4)) the value of any interest—

(a) when held by the person from whom it is to be acquired by the nominee purchaser, or

(b) when acquired by the nominee purchaser,

is a negative amount, then for the purposes of paragraph 4(2) the value of the interest when so held or acquired shall be nil.

(2) Where sub-paragraph (1) above applies to any intermediate leasehold interest whose value when held or acquired as mentioned in paragraph (a) or (b) of that sub-paragraph is a negative amount, paragraph 14(2) to (4) shall apply for determining for the purposes of paragraph 4(2) the value when so held or acquired of other interests in the specified premises, as if—

(a) any reference to paragraph 14(1) were a reference to sub-paragraph (1) above; and

(b) any reference to the relevant purposes were, as respects any interest, a reference to the purposes of paragraph 4(2) as it applies to the interest when so held or acquired.

(3) References in paragraph 16 or 17 to paragraph 14(2) or (3) do not extend to that provision as it applies in accordance with sub-paragraph (2) above.

Apportionment of marriage value

16.—(1) Where paragraph 14(1) applies to an interest, the value of the interest for the purposes of paragraph 9(2) shall be nil, unless sub-paragraph (2) below applies.

(2) In a case where paragraph 14(1) applies to the freeholder's interest in the specified premises and to every intermediate leasehold interest—

(a) sub-paragraph (1) above shall not apply for the purposes of paragraph 9(2); and

(b) any division falling to be made on the proportional basis referred to in paragraph 9(2) shall be so made in such a way as to secure that the greater the negativity of an interest's value the smaller the share in respect of the interest.

(3) In a case where—

(a) paragraph 14(2) operates to reduce the value of any such superior interest as is there mentioned ("the superior interest"), and

(b) after the operation of that provision there remains any interest whose value for the relevant purposes is a positive amount,

the value of the superior interest for the purposes of paragraph 9(2) shall be the value which (in accordance with paragraph 14(2)) it has for the relevant purposes.

(4) In a case where—

(a) paragraph 14(2) operates to reduce the value of any such superior interest as is there mentioned ("the superior interest"), but

(b) after the operation of that provision there remains no such interest as is mentioned in sub-paragraph (3)(b) above,

the value of the superior interest for the purposes of paragraph 9(2) shall be the value which it has for the relevant purposes apart from paragraph 14(2).

Adjustment of compensation

17.—(1) Where—

(a) paragraph 14(2) operates to reduce the value of any such superior interest as is there mentioned ("the superior interest"), and

(b) apart from this paragraph any amount of compensation is payable under paragraph 8 to the owner of any relevant inferior interest in respect of that interest,

there shall be payable to the owner of the superior interest so much of the amount of compensation as is equal to the amount of the reduction or, if less than that amount, the whole of the amount of compensation.

(2) Where—

(a) paragraph 14(2) operates to reduce the value of two or more such superior interests as are there mentioned ("the superior interests"), and

(b) apart from this paragraph any amount of compensation is payable under paragraph 8 to the owner of any relevant inferior interest in respect of that interest, sub-paragraph (1) shall apply in the first instance as if the reference to the owner of superior interest were to the owner of such of the superior interests as is furthest from the negative interest, and then, as respects any remaining amount of compensation, as if that reference were to the owner of such of the superior interests as is next furthest from the negative interest, and so on.

(3) In sub-paragraph (1) or (2) "relevant inferior interest", in relation to any interest whose value is reduced as mentioned in that sub-paragraph ("the superior interest"), means—

(a) the negative interest on account of which any such reduction is made, or

(b) any other interest intermediate between that negative interest and the superior interest;

but sub-paragraph (1) shall apply in the first instance in relation to any amount of compensation payable to the owner of that negative interest, and then, for the purpose of offsetting (so far as possible) any reduction remaining to be offset in accordance with sub-paragraph (1) or (2), in relation to any amount of compensation payable to the owner of the interest immediately superior to that negative interest, and so on in order of proximity to it.

(4) To the extent that an amount of compensation is payable to the owner of any interest by virtue of this paragraph—

(a) paragraph 2(1)(c) or 6(1)(b)(ii) shall have effect as if it were an amount of compensation payable to him, as owner of that interest, in accordance with paragraph 5 or 8, as the case may be; and

(b) the person who would otherwise have been entitled to it in accordance with paragraph 8 shall accordingly not be so entitled.

(5) In a case where paragraph 14(2) applies separately in relation to two or more negative interests in accordance with paragraph 14(3), the preceding provisions of this paragraph shall similarly apply separately in relation to the reductions made on account of each of those interests, and shall so apply—

(a) according to the order determined by paragraph 14(3)(a); and

(b) with there being taken into account any reduction in the amount of compensation payable to any person under paragraph 8 which results from the prior application of the preceding provisions of this paragraph.

PART VI

VALUATION ETC. OF OTHER INTERESTS WITH NEGATIVE VALUES

Valuation of freehold and leasehold interests

18.—(1) Where—

(a) the value of any freehold interest (as determined in accordance with paragraph 11(1)), or

(b) the value of any leasehold interest (as determined in accordance with paragraph 11(2)),

is a negative amount, the value of the interest for the relevant purposes shall be nil.

(2) Where, in the case of any property, sub-paragraph (1) applies to any leasehold interest in the property whose value is a negative amount ("the negative interest"), then for the relevant purposes any interests in the property superior to the negative interest and having a positive value shall, if they are interests which are to be acquired by the nominee purchaser, be reduced in value—

(a) beginning with the interest which is nearest to the negative interest and continuing (if necessary) with any such other superior interests in order of proximity to the negative interest;

(b) until the aggregate amount of the reduction is equal to the negative amount in question; and

(c) without reducing the value of any interest to less than nil.

(3) In a case where sub-paragraph (1) applies to two or more leasehold interests in any property whose values are negative amounts, sub-paragraph (2) shall apply separately in relation to each of those interests—

(a) beginning with the interest which is inferior to every other of those interests and then in order of proximity to that interest; and

(b) with any reduction in the value of any interest for the relevant purposes by virtue of any prior application of sub-paragraph (2) being taken into account.

(4) For the purposes of sub-paragraph (2) an interest has a positive value if (apart from that sub-paragraph) its value for the relevant purposes is a positive amount.

(5) In this Part of this Schedule "the relevant purposes"—

(a) as respects any freehold interest, means the purposes of paragraph 10(1)(a); and

(b) as respects any leasehold interest, means the purposes of paragraph 10(2)(a).

Calculation of marriage value

19.—(1) Where (as determined in accordance with paragraph 14(3) and (4)) the value of any interest—

(a) when held by the person from whom it is to be acquired by the nominee purchaser, or

(b) when acquired by the nominee purchaser,

is a negative amount, then for the purposes of paragraph 4(2) the value of the interest when so held or acquired shall be nil.

(2) Where, in the case of any property, sub-paragraph (1) above applies to any leasehold interest in the property whose value when held or acquired as mentioned in paragraph (a) or (b) of that sub-paragraph is a negative amount, paragraph 18(2) to (4) shall apply for determining for the purposes of paragraph 4(2) the value when so held or acquired of other interests in the property, as if—

(a) any reference to paragraph 18(1) were a reference to sub-paragraph (1) above; and

(b) any reference to the relevant purposes were, as respects any interest, a reference to the purposes of paragraph 4(2) as it applies to the interest when so held or acquired.

(3) In this paragraph any reference to any provision of paragraph 4 is a reference to that provision as it applies in accordance with paragraph 12(1).

(4) References in paragraph 20 and 21 to paragraph 18(2) or (3) do not extend to that provision as it applies in accordance with sub-paragraph (2) above.

Apportionment of marriage value

20.—(1) Where paragraph 18(1) applies to any interest in any property to which paragraph 12(1) applies, the value of the interest for the purposes of paragraph 12(2) shall be nil, unless sub-paragraph (2) below applies.

(2) Where, in the case of any property, paragraph 18(1) applies to every interest which is to be acquired by the nominee purchaser—

(a) sub-paragraph (1) above shall not apply for the purposes of paragraph 12(2); and

(b) any division falling to be made on the proportional basis referred to in paragraph 12(2) shall be so made in such a way as to secure that the greater the negativity of an interest's value the smaller the share in respect of the interest.

(3) Where in the case of any property—

(a) paragraph 18(2) operates to reduce the value of any such superior interest as is there mentioned ("the superior interest"), and

(b) after the operation of that provision there remains any interest which is to be acquired by the nominee purchaser and whose value for the relevant purposes is a positive amount,

the value of the superior interest for the purposes of paragraph 12(2) shall be the value which (in accordance with paragraph 18(2)) it has for the relevant purposes.

(4) Where in the case of any property—

(a) paragraph 18(2) operates to reduce the value of any such superior interest as is there mentioned ("the superior interest"), but

(b) after the operation of that provision there remains no such interest as is mentioned in sub-paragraph (3)(b) above.

the value of the superior interest for the purposes of paragraph 12(2) shall be the value which it has for the relevant purposes apart from paragraph 18(2).

Adjustment of compensation

21.—(1) Where in the case of any property—

(a) paragraph 18(2) operates to reduce the value of any such superior interest as is there mentioned ("the superior interest"), and

(b) apart from this paragraph any amount of compensation is payable by virtue of paragraph 13 to the owner of any relevant inferior interest in respect of that interest,

there shall be payable to the owner of the superior interest so much of the mount of compensation as is equal to the amount of the reduction or, if less than that amount, the whole of the amount or compensation.

(2) Where in the case of any property—

(a) paragraph 18(2) operates to reduce the value of two or more such superior interests as are there mentioned ("the superior interests"), and

(b) apart from this paragraph any amount of compensation is payable by virtue of paragraph 13 to the owner of any relevant inferior interest in respect of that interest,

sub-paragraph (1) shall apply in the first instance as if the reference to the owner of the superior interest were to the owner of such of the superior interests as is furthest from the negative interest, and then, as respects any remaining amount of compensation, as if that reference were to the owner of such of the superior interests as is next furthest from the negative interest, and so on.

(3) In sub-paragraph (1) or (2) "relevant inferior interest", in relation to any interest whose value is reduced as mentioned in that sub-paragraph ("the superior interest"), means—

(a) the negative interest on account of which any such reduction is made or

(b) any other interest in the property in question which is to be acquired by the nominee purchaser and is intermediate between that negative interest and the superior interest;

but sub-paragraph (1) shall apply in the first instance in relation to any amount of compensation payable to the owner of that negative interest, and then, for the purpose of offsetting (so far as possible) any reduction remaining to be offset in accordance with sub-paragraph (1) or (2), in relation to any amount of compensation payable to the owner of such interest falling within paragraph (b) above as is nearest to that negative interest, and so on in order of proximity to it.

(4) To the extent that an amount of compensation is payable to the owner of any interest by virtue of this paragraph—

(a) paragraph 10(1)(c) or (as the case may be) paragraph 10(2)(b) shall have effect as if it were an amount of compensation payable to him, as owner of that interest, in accordance with paragraph 13; and

(b) the person who would otherwise have been entitled to it in accordance with paragraph 13 shall accordingly not be so entitled.

(5) In a case where paragraph 18(2) applies separately in relation to two or more negative interests in accordance with paragraph 18(3), the preceding provisions of this paragraph shall similarly apply separately in relation to the reductions made on account of each of those interests, and shall so apply—

(a) according to the order determined by paragraph 18(3)(a); and

(b) with there being taken into account any reduction in the amount of compensation payable to any person by virtue of paragraph 13 which results from the prior application of the preceding provisions of this paragraph.

GENERAL NOTE

There are three main elements in calculating the price payable by a nominee purchaser in a case of collective enfranchisement and Sched. 5 deals with the ascertainment of these elements.

Para. 1

"The valuation date" is clearly an essential concept. It is established by the date when an agreement as to the enfranchisement is entered into or when the terms of the acquisition are decided by a leasehold valuation tribunal under s.24. There may be some gain in accelerating or retarding agreement dependent on the market prevailing.

Para. 3(2)

This paragraph makes it clear that the tribunal may make other assumptions but it gives no clue what they are.

Para. 4

The marriage value element of the price of enfranchisement is potentially very important. It is based on the assumption that the purchased interests together are worth more than they are separately. The "marriage value" to be taken is limited to values satisfying both two conditions in para. 4(2)(a) and (b). That is values arising out of the potential for reletting to the existing tenants which would have been agreed between willing seller and buyer.

Para. 7

For a "minor intermediate lease" the formula in para. 7 is aimed at producing a price. Assume a minor intermediate lease with a term of two years to run and a profit rent of £5 p.a.

$$P = \frac{5}{.05} - \frac{5}{.05(1.05)^2}$$

$$= 100 - \frac{5}{.055125}$$

$$= 100 - 90.70$$

$$= £9.30p$$

This calculation illustrates correctly that the sums payable for a minor intermediate lease will be very small. Even if the term to run were 40 years the result is still a small price. The expression $Y(1+Y)^n$ becomes $.05(1.05)^{40}$ which is 0.352. The price payable becomes £85.80p.

Para. 7(9)
This paragraph should read and must mean "the expectation of possession after the sub lease which it carries at the valuation date". The valuation procedure could be as follows, example, valuation of Freehold in Attlee Court purchased by 80 of the 100 tenants forming a nominee company. Twenty of the remainder are long leases at £5 with 40 years to run. The remaining 20 are 19 Rent Act 1977 tenancies and one assured shorthold under the Housing Act 1988.

Step 1
Value the freehold on the para. 2 assumptions. Clearly the repairing obligations under the Landlord and Tenant Act 1985, s.11 is important. If the 20 short tenancies are in substantial disrepair then this may have a very significant effect.

Step 2
Value the intermediate leaseholds before acquisition.

Step 3
Value "the aggregate value of the freehold and intermediate leaseholds" after acquisition. But the value must exceed the result of Step 1 and Step 2 only by the factors mentioned in para. 4(2)(a) and (b).

Step 4
The marriage value is calculated by adding the result of Step 1 and Step 2 and deducting this from the result of Step 3. The value of the freehold is the Return (R) on all the leases but a small amount for the value. The following example showing how the Act operates was prepared by Martin Angel, Esq., a surveyor with Allsop & Co., 27 Soho Square, London W1: "Consider the example of a freehold block of 20 flats, each of which are held leasehold with terms of 30 years unexpired, each paying a fixed ground rent of £100 p.a. and each having a leasehold value of £130,000. The freeholder's interest would comprise the right to receive 20 × £100 p.a. until the leases end in 30 years' time, followed by the right to receive market rents. Let us assume this has a total value to him of, say, £200,000. Let us also assume that, with an extended lease (say, 999 years at a peppercorn rent, and with a share in the freehold), each of the flats would have a vacant possession value of £250,000. Under the Bill, I believe the formulae would work as shown in Table A.

Table A

(1) Value of freeholder's interest =   £200,000

(2) Marriage value

Proposed merged interest =	20 × £250,000 =	£5,000,000
Less existing leasehold values =	20 × £130,000 =	£2,600,000
Less existing freehold value		£200,000
Marriage value =		£2,200,000"

Assume 50 per cent. of the marriage value is to be payable to the freeholder   £1,100,000

Assuming that there is no compensation payable as a result of diminution in value of any interest of the freeholder in any other property, the price to be paid is   £1,300,000"

An example by Mr. Angel of valuation of an extended lease purchase is shown in the note on Sched. 13.

Section 34   SCHEDULE 7

CONVEYANCE TO NOMINEE PURCHASER ON ENFRANCHISEMENT

Interpretation

1. In this Schedule—
(a) "the relevant premises" means, in relation to such a conveyance as is mentioned in section 34(1), the premises of which the freehold is to be conveyed by means of the conveyance;
(b) "the freeholder", in relation to any such conveyance, means the person whose freehold interest in the relevant premises is to be conveyed by means of the conveyance;

(c) "other property" means property of which the freehold is not to be acquired by the nominee purchaser under this Chapter; and

(d) "the appropriate time" means the time when the freehold of the relevant premises is to be conveyed to the nominee purchaser.

General

2.—(1) The conveyance shall not exclude or restrict the general words implied in conveyance under section 62 of the Law of Property Act 1925, or the all-estate clause implied under section 63 of that Act, unless—

(a) the exclusion or restriction is made for the purpose of preserving or recognising any existing interest of the freeholder in tenant's incumbrances or any existing right or interest of any other person, or

(b) the nominee purchaser consents to the exclusion or restriction.

(2) The freeholder shall not be bound—

(a) to convey to the nominee purchaser any better title than that which he has or could require to be vested in him, or

(b) to enter into any covenant for title other than such covenant as under section 76(1)(F) of the Law Property Act 1925 is implied in the case of a person conveying, and expressed to convey, as trustee or mortgagee.

(3) In this paragraph "tenant's incumbrances" includes any interest directly or indirectly derived out of a lease, and any imcumbrance on a lease or any such interest (whether or not the same matter is an incumbrance also on any interest reversionary on the lease); and "incumbrances" has the same meaning as it has for the purposes of section 34 of this Act.

Rights of support, passage of water etc.

3.—(1) This paragraph applies to rights of any of the following descriptions, namely—

(a) rights of support for a building or part of a building;

(b) rights to the access of light and air to a building or part of a building;

(c) rights to the passage of water or of gas or other piped fuel, or to the drainage or disposal of water, sewage, smoke or fumes, or to the use or maintenance of pipes or other installations for such passage, drainage or disposal;

(d) rights to the use or maintenance of cables or other installations for the supply of electricity, for the telephone or for the receipt directly or by landline of visual or other wireless transmissions;

and the provisions required to be included in the conveyance by virtue of sub-paragraph (2) are accordingly provisions relating to any such rights.

(2) The conveyance shall include provisions having the effect of—

(a) granting with the relevant premises (so far as the freeholder is capable of granting them)—

(i) all such easements and rights over other property as are necessary to secure as nearly as may be for the benefit of the relevant premises the same rights as exist for the benefit of those premises immediately before the appropriate time, and

(ii) such further easements and rights (if any) as are necessary for the reasonable enjoyment of the relevant premises; and

(b) making the relevant premises subject to the following easements and rights (so far as they are capable of existing in law), namely—

(i) all easements and rights for the benefit of other property to which the relevant premises are subject immediately before the appropriate time, and

(ii) such further easements and rights (if any) as are necessary for the reasonable enjoyment of other property, being property in which the freeholder has an interest at the relevant date.

Rights of way

4. Any such conveyance shall include—

(a) such provisions (if any) as the nominee purchaser may require for the purpose of securing to him and the persons deriving title under him rights of way over other property, so far as the freeholder is capable of granting them, being rights of way that are necessary for the reasonable enjoyment of the relevant premises; and

(b) such provisions (if any) as the freeholder may require for the purpose of making the relevant premises subject to rights of way necessary for the reasonable enjoyment of other property, being property in which he is to retain an interest after the acquisition of the relevant premises.

Restrictive covenants

5.—(1) As regards restrictive covenants, the conveyance shall include—

(a) such provisions (if any) as the freeholder may require to secure that the nominee purchaser is bound by, or to indemnify the freeholder against breaches of, restrictive covenants which—

(i) affect the relevant premises otherwise than by virtue of any lease subject to which the relevant premises are to be acquired or any agreement collateral to any such lease, and

(ii) are immediately before the appropriate time enforceable for the benefit of other property; and

(b) such provisions (if any) as the freeholder or the nominee purchaser may require to secure the continuance (with suitable adaptations) of restrictions arising by virtue of any such lease or collateral agreement as is mentioned in paragraph (a)(i), being either—

(i) restrictions affecting the relevant premises which are capable of benefiting other property and (if enforceable only by the freeholder) are such as materially to enhance the value of the other property, or

(ii) restrictions affecting other property which are such as materially to enhance the value of the relevant premises; and

(c) such further restrictions as the freeholder may require to restrict the use of the relevant premises in a way which—

(i) will not interfere with the reasonable enjoyment of those premises as they have been enjoyed during the currency of the leases subject to which they are to be acquired, but

(ii) will materially enhance the value of other property in which the freeholder has an interest at the relevant date.

(2) In this paragraph "restrictive covenant" means a covenant or agreement restrictive of the user of any land or building.

GENERAL NOTE

Para. 2

These provisions are taken (with some re-arrangement of order) from various parts of the Leasehold Reform Act 1967 and will presumably be given the same interpretation by the courts. Paragraph 2(1) derives from s.10(1) and s.8 of the Leasehold Reform Act 1967. Its effect may be to turn permissive rights enjoyed by the tenants into easements, see, for example, *Wright* v. *MacAdam* [1949] 2 K.B. 744. Section 62 operates without the rights implied or the section being mentioned in the conveyance. Both the reversioner and the nominee purchaser may, however, prefer the rights which are to be enjoyed by the nominee purchaser to be expressly set out in the conveyance. Section 62 does not operate in favour of the grantor and accordingly the reversioner will require any rights it needs over the land conveyed to be expressly set out. Paragraph 2(2) derives also from s.10(1) of the Leasehold Reform Act 1967—there has been no case-law at all reported on s.10. Paragraph 2(3)—this definition derives from s.8(2) of the Leasehold Reform Act 1967.

Para. 3

This paragraph derives from s.10(2) of the Leasehold Reform Act 1967. There is no reported case-law on the relevant parts of s.10(2).

Para. 4

This paragraph, with small changes, derives from s.10(3) of the Leasehold Reform Act 1967.

Para. 5

This paragraph derives from s.10(4) of the Leasehold Reform Act 1967. It entitles the freeholder to the usual form of indemnity against covenants for breach of which the freeholder remains liable. Paragraph (1)(c) should be noted which entitles the freeholder to new restrictive covenants which will benefit its other property.

Section 35   SCHEDULE 8

DISCHARGE OF MORTGAGES ETC.: SUPPLEMENTARY PROVISIONS

Construction

1. In this Schedule—

"the consideration payable" means the consideration payable for the acquisition of the relevant interest;

"the landlord" means the person from whom the relevant interest is being acquired;

"the relevant interest" means any such interest as is mentioned in paragraph 2(1).

Duty of nominee purchaser to redeem mortgages

2.—(1) Where in accordance with section 35(1) a conveyance will operate to discharge any interest from a mortgage to secure the payment of money, it shall be the duty of the nominee purchaser to apply the consideration payable in the first instance, in or towards the redemption of any such mortgage (and, if there are more than one, then according to their priorities).

(2) If any amount payable in accordance with sub-paragraph (1) to the person entitled to the benefit of a mortgage is not so paid, nor paid into court in accordance with paragraph 4, the relevant interest shall remain subject to the mortgage as regards the amount in question, and to that extent section 35(1) shall not apply.

(3) Subject to sub-paragraph (4), sub-paragraph (1) shall not apply to a debenture holders' charge, that is to say, a charge (whether a floating charge or not) in favour of the holders of a series of debentures issued by a company or other body of persons, or in favour of trustees for such debenture holders; and any such charge shall be disregarded in determining priorities for the purposes of sub-paragraph (1).

(4) Sub-paragraph (3) shall not have effect in relation to a charge in favour of trustees for debenture holders which, at the date of the conveyance by virtue of which the relevant interest is acquired by the nominee purchaser, is (as regards that interest) a specific and not a floating charge.

Determination of amounts due in respect of mortgages

3.—(1) For the purpose of determining the amount payable in respect of any mortgage under paragraph 2(1)—

(a) a person entitled to the benefit of a mortgage to which that provision applies shall not be permitted to exercise any right to consolidate that mortgage with a separate mortgage on other property; and

(b) if the landlord or any participating tenant is himself entitled to the benefit of a mortgage to which that provision applies, it shall rank for payment as it would if another person were entitled to it, and the nominee purchaser shall be entitled to retain the appropriate amount in respect of any such mortgage of a participating tenant.

(2) For the purpose of discharging any interest from a mortgage to which paragraph 2(1) applies, a person may be required to accept three months or any longer notice of the intention to pay the whole or part of the principal secured by the mortgage, together with interest to the date of payment, notwithstanding that the terms of the security make other provision or no provision as to the time and manner of payment; but he shall be entitled, if he so requires, to receive such additional payment as is reasonable in the circumstances—

(a) in respect of the costs of re-investment or other incidental costs and expenses; and

(b) in respect of any reduction in the rate of interest obtainable on re-investment.

Payments into court

4.—(1) Where under section 35(1) any interest is to be discharged from a mortgage and, in accordance with paragraph 2(1), a person is or may be entitled in respect of the mortgage to receive the whole or part of the consideration payable, then if—

(a) for any reason difficulty arises in ascertaining how much is payable in respect of the mortgage, or

(b) for any reason mentioned in sub-paragraph (2) below difficulty arises in making a payment in respect of the mortgage,

the nominee purchaser may pay into court on account of the consideration payable the amount, if known, of the payment to be made in respect of the mortgage or, if that amount is not known, the whole of that consideration or such lesser amount as the nominee purchaser thinks right in order to provide for that payment.

(2) Payment may be made into court in accordance with sub-paragraph (1)(b) where the difficulty arises for any of the following reasons, namely—

(a) because a person who is or may be entitled to receive payment cannot be found or his identity cannot be ascertained;

(b) because any such person refuses or fails to make out a title, or to accept payment and give a proper discharge, or to take any steps reasonably required of him to enable the sum payable to be ascertained and paid; or

(c) because a tender of the sum payable cannot, by reason of complications in the title to it or the want of two or more trustees or for other reasons, be effected, or not without incurring or involving unreasonable cost or delay.

(3) Without prejudice to sub-paragraph (1)(a), the whole or part of the consideration payable shall be paid into court by the nominee purchaser if, before execution of the conveyance referred to in paragraph 2(1), notice is given to him—

(a) that the landlord, or a person entitled to the benefit of a mortgage on the relevant interest, requires him to do so for the purpose of protecting the rights of persons so entitled, or for reasons related to the bankruptcy or winding up of the landlord, or

(b) that steps have been taken to enforce any mortgage on the relevant interest by the bringing of proceedings in any court, or by the appointment of a receiver, or otherwise;

and where payment into court is to be made by reason only of a notice under this sub-paragraph, and the notice is given with reference to proceedings in a court specified in the notice other than a county court, payment shall be made into the court so specified.

Savings

5.—(1) Where any interest is discharged by section 35(1) from a mortgage (without the obligations secured by the mortgage being satisfied by the receipt of the whole or part of the consideration payable), the discharge of that interest from the mortgage shall not prejudice any right or remedy for the enforcement of those obligations against other property comprised in the same or any other security, nor prejudice any personal liability as principal or otherwise of the landlord or any other person.

(2) Nothing in this Schedule or section 35 shall be construed as preventing a person from joining in the conveyance referred to in paragraph 2(1) for the purpose of discharging the relevant interest from any mortgage without payment or for a lesser payment than that to which he would otherwise be entitled; and, if he does so, the persons to whom the consideration payable ought to be paid shall be determined accordingly.

GENERAL NOTE

This is an important provision so far as regards practical conveyancing in collective enfranchisement cases. Where there is an outstanding mortgage on the interests being purchased then the purchase money is first applied towards redeeming that mortgage. It will be apparent in the case of a first mortgage that the deeds are held by the mortgagee. The nominee purchaser will search in the Land Charge Registry in unregistered land to discover the mortgages. The nominee purchaser is more under a duty to use the purchase money in discharge of these mortgages (para. 2). Caution is necessary. Written redemption statements should be obtained. The money should be paid directly to the mortgagee. If it is suggested that it be paid to the freeholder against an undertaking to discharge such a mortgage it is suggested that it be ascertained that the freeholder is duly appointed as an agent of the mortgagee to receive the mortgage money (see *Wong (Edward) Finance Co.* v. *Johnson Stokes & Master* [1984] A.C. 1296).

Para. 2

There is a problem with para. 2(2). An amount may not be paid because the nominee purchaser is unaware of the mortgage because it is not registered. In registered land a purchaser once registered would be free of the mortgage (s.20(1) of the Land Registration Act 1925) and in unregistered land on completion the purchaser would take free of the unregistered mortgage on satisfying s.4 of the Land Charges Act 1972. Paragraph 2(2) seems to suggest that the mortgage will remain on the property purchased and makes no mention of these other provisions. It will be noted that s.31(5) provides for the nominee purchaser always to be treated as a purchaser for money or money's worth. Is this not intended to ensure the purchase is free of unregistered incumbrances? This problem is compounded by paras. 2(3) and 2(4) which provide in effect for floating charges which have crystallized to fall within para. 2(1). A nominee purchaser will know of such debentures in registered land only if registered in the Land Registry. This suggests that a company search will be necessary in respect of all purchases under Chap. I.

Section 36

SCHEDULE 9

GRANT OF LEASES BACK TO FORMER FREEHOLDER

PART I

GENERAL

1.—(1) In this Schedule—

"the appropriate time" means the time when the freehold of the specified premises is acquired by the nominee purchaser;

"the demised premises", in relation to a lease granted or to be granted in pursuance of Part II or III of this Schedule, means—

(a) the flat or other unit demised or to be demised under the lease, or

(b) in the case of such a lease under which two or more units are demised, not or all of those units or (if the context so permits) any of them;

"the freeholder" means the person who owns the freehold of the specified premises immediately before the appropriate time;

"housing association" has the meaning given by section 1(1) of the Housing Associations Act 1985;

"intermediate landlord", in relation to a flat or other unit let to a tenant, means a person who holds a leasehold interest in the flat or other unit which is superior to that held by the tenant's immediate landlord;

"other property" means property other than the demised premises.

(2) In this Schedule any reference to a flat or other unit, in the context of the grant of a lease of it, includes any yard, garden, garage, outhouses and appurtenances belonging to or usually enjoyed with it and let with it immediately before the appropriate time.

PART II

MANDATORY LEASEBACK

Flats etc. let under secure tenancies

2.—(1) This paragraph applies where immediately before the appropriate time any flat contained in the specified premises is let under a secure tenancy and either—

(a) the freeholder is the tenant's immediate landlord, or

(b) the freeholder is a public sector landlord and every intermediate landlord of the flat (as well as the immediate landlord under the secure tenancy) is also a public sector landlord.

(2) Sub-paragraph (1)(b) has effect whether any such intermediate landlord, or the immediate landlord under the secure tenancy, is or is not a qualifying tenant of the flat.

(3) Where this paragraph applies, the nominee purchase shall grant to the freeholder a lease of the flat in accordance with section 36 and paragraph 4 below.

(4) In this paragraph any reference to a flat includes a reference to a unit (other than a flat) which is used as a dwelling.

Flats etc. let by housing associations under tenancies other than secure tenancies

3.—(1) This paragraph applies where immediately before the appropriate time any flat contained in the specified premises is let by a housing association under a tenancy other than a secure tenancy and—

(a) the housing association is the freeholder, and

(b) the tenant is not a qualifying tenant of the flat.

(2) Where this paragraph applies, the nominee purchase shall grant to the freeholder (that is to say, the housing association) a lease of the flat in accordance with section 36 and paragraph 4 below.

(3) In this paragraph any reference to a flat includes a reference to a unit (other than a flat) which is used as a dwelling.

Provisions as to terms of lease

4.—(1) Any lease granted to the freeholder in pursuance of paragraph 2 or 3, and any agreement collateral to it, shall conform with the provisions of Part IV of this Schedule except to the extent that any departure from those provisions is agreed to by the nominee purchaser and the freeholder with the approval of a leasehold valuation tribunal.

(2) A leasehold valuation tribunal shall not approve any such departure from those provisions unless it appears to the tribunal that it is reasonable in the circumstances.

(3) In determining whether any such departure is reasonable in the circumstances, the tribunal shall have particular regard to the interests of the tenant under the secure tenancy referred to in paragraph 2(1) or (as the case may be) under the housing association tenancy referred to in paragraph 3(1).

(4) Subject to the preceding provisions of this paragraph, any such lease or agreement as is mentioned in sub-paragraph (1) may include such terms as are reasonable in the circumstances.

PART III

RIGHT OF FREEHOLDER TO REQUIRE LEASEBACK OF CERTAIN UNITS

Flats without qualifying tenants and other units

5.—(1) Subject to sub-paragraph (3), this paragraph applies to any unit contained in the specified premises which is not immediately before the appropriate time a flat let to a person who is a qualifying tenant of it.

(2) Where this paragraph applies, the nominee purchaser shall, if the freeholder by notice requires him to do so, grant to the freeholder a lease of the unit in accordance with section 36 and paragraph 7 below.

(3) This paragraph does not apply to a flat or other unit to which paragraph 2 or 3 applies.

Flat etc. occupied by resident landlord

6.—(1) This paragraph applies where immediately before the appropriate time—
(a) the specified premises are premises with a resident landlord; and
(b) the freeholder is the person by virtue of whose occupation of a flat or other unit contained in those premises they are premises with a resident landlord, and
(c) the freeholder is a qualifying tenant of that flat or other unit ("the relevant unit").

(2) Where this paragraph applies—
(a) the nominee purchaser shall, if the freeholder by notice required him to do so, grant to him a lease of the relevant unit in accordance with section 36 and paragraph 7 below; and
(b) any lease of that unit held by the freeholder immediately before the appropriate time shall be deemed to have been surrendered by him on the grant of the lease referred to in paragraph (a).

(3) Sections 5, 7 and 8 shall apply for the purpose of determining whether, for the purposes of sub-paragraph (1)(c) above, the freeholder is a qualifying tenant of a unit other than a flat as they apply for the purpose of determining whether a person is a qualifying tenant of a flat.

Provisions as to terms of lease

7.—(1) Any lease granted to the freeholder in pursuance of paragraph 5 or 6, and any agreement collateral to it, shall conform with the provisions of Part IV of this Schedule except to the extent that any departure from those provisions—
(a) is agreed to by the nominee purchaser and the freeholder; or
(b) is directed by a leasehold valuation tribunal on an application made by either of those persons.

(2) A leasehold valuation tribunal shall not direct any such departure from those provisions unless it appears to the tribunal that it is reasonable in the circumstances.

(3) In determining whether any such departure is reasonable in the circumstances, the tribunal shall have particular regard to the interests of any person who will be the tenant of the flat or other unit in question under a lease inferior to the lease to be granted to the freeholder.

(4) Subject to the preceding provisions of this paragraph, any such lease or agreement as is mentioned in sub-paragraph (1) may include such terms as are reasonable in the circumstances.

PART IV

TERMS OF LEASE GRANTED TO FREEHOLDER

Duration of lease and rent

8. The lease shall be a lease granted for a term of 999 years at a peppercorn rent.

General rights to be granted

9. The lease shall not exclude or restrict the general words implied under section 62 of the Law of Property Act 1925, unless the exclusion or restriction is made for the purpose of preserving or recognising an existing right or interest of any person.

Rights of support, passage of water etc.

10.—(1) This paragraph applies to rights of any of the following descriptions, namely—
(a) rights of support for a building or part of a building;
(b) rights to the access of light and air to a building or part of a building;
(c) rights to the passage of water or of gas or other piped fuel, or to the drainage or disposal

of water, sewage, smoke or fumes, or to the use or maintenance of pipes or other installations for such passage, drainage or disposal; and

(d) rights to the use or maintenance of cables or other installations for the supply of electricity, for the telephone or for the receipt directly or by landline of visual or other wireless transmissions;

and the provisions required to be included in the lease by virtue of sub-paragraph (2) are accordingly provisions relating to any such rights.

(2) The lease shall include provision having the effect of—

(a) granting with the demised premises (so far as the lessor is capable of granting them)—
  (i) all such easements and rights over other property as are necessary to secure as nearly as may be for the benefit of the demised premises the same rights as exist for the benefit of those premises immediately before the appropriate time, and
  (ii) such further easements and rights (if any) as are necessary for the reasonable enjoyment of the demised premises; and

(b) making the demised premises subject to the following easements and rights (so far as they are capable of existing in law), namely—
  (i) all easements and rights for the benefit of other property to which the demised premises are subject immediately before the appropriate time, and
  (ii) such further easements and rights (if any) as are necessary for the reasonable enjoyment of other property, being property in which the lessor acquires an interest at the appropriate time.

Rights of way

11. The lease shall include—

(a) such provisions (if any) as the lessee may require for the purpose of securing to him, and persons deriving title under him, rights of way over other property (so far as the lessor is capable of granting them), being rights of way that are necessary for the reasonable enjoyment of the demised premises; and

(b) such provisions (if any) as the lessor may require for the purpose of make the demised premises subject to rights of way necessary for the reasonable enjoyment of other property, being property in which the lessor acquires an interest at the appropriate time.

Common use of premises and facilities

12. The lease shall include, so far as the lessor is capable of granting them, the like rights to use in common with others any premises, facilities or services as are enjoyed immediately before the appropriate time by any tenant of the demised premises.

Covenants affecting demised premises

13. The lease shall include such provisions (if any) as the lessor may required to secure that the lessee is bound by, or to indemnify the lessor against breaches of, restrictive covenants (that is to say, covenants or agreements restrictive of the use of any land or premises) affecting the demised premises immediately before the appropriate time and enforceable for the benefit of other property.

Covenants by lessor

14.—(1) The lease shall include covenants by the lessor—

(a) to keep in repair the structure and exterior of the demised premises and of the specified premises (including drains, gutters and external pipes) and to make good any defect affecting that structure;

(b) to keep in repair any other property over or in respect of which the lessee has rights by virtue of this Schedule;

(c) to ensure, so far as practicable, that the services which are to be provided by the lessor and to which the lessee is entitled (whether alone or in common with others) are maintained at a reasonable level, and to keep in repair any installation connected with the provision of any of those services.

(2) The lease shall include a covenant requiring the lessor—

(a) to insure the specified premises for their full reinstatement value against destruction or damage by fire, tempest, flood or any other cause against the risk of which it is the normal practice to insure;

(b) to rebuild or reinstate the demised premises or the specified premises in the case of any such destruction or damage.

Covenants by lessee

15. The lease shall include a covenant by the lessee to ensure that the interior of the demised premises is kept in good repair (including decorative repair).

Contributions by lessee

16.—(1) The lease may require the lessee to bear a reasonable part of the costs incurred by the lessor in discharging or insuring against the obligations imposed by the covenants required by paragraph 14(1) or in discharging the obligation imposed by the covenant required by paragraph 14(2)(a).

(2) Where a covenant required by paragraph 14(1) or (2)(a) has been modified to any extent in accordance with paragraph 4 or 7, the reference in sub-paragraph (1) above to the obligations or (as the case may be) the obligation imposed by that covenant shall be read as a reference to the obligations or obligation imposed by that covenant as so modified.

Assignment and sub-letting of premises

17.—(1) Except where the demised premises consist of or include any unit let or intended for letting on a business lease, the lease shall not include any provision prohibiting or restricting the assignment of the lease or the sub-letting of the whole or part of the demised premises.

(2) Where the demised premises consist of or include any such unit as is mentioned in sub-paragraph (1), the lease shall contain a prohibition against—

(a) assigning or sub-letting the whole or part of any such unit, or

(b) altering the user of any such unit,

without the prior written consent of the lessor (such consent not to be unreasonably withheld).

Restriction on terminating lease

18. The lease shall not include any provision for the lease to be terminated otherwise than by forfeiture on breach of any term of the lease by the lessee.

GENERAL NOTE
This deals with the cases where there will be a leaseback to the freeholder. Part II of the Schedule deals with the mandatory leasebacks where flat(s) are subject to secure tenancies under the Housing Act 1985 and the other conditions of s.3 are satisfied. Part III deals with leasebacks of property not let to qualifying tenants. The terms of the lease will be dealt with by Pt. IV in the case of both Pt. II and Pt. III leases.

Para. 4
This applies to leasebacks of secure tenancies and housing association flats. It should be noted that the parties are free to vary the lease as much as they choose. No variance from the lease is permitted without the approval of a leasehold valuation tribunal. It is not entirely clear what the effect of a lease not conforming with Pt. IV and not approved by a leasehold valuation tribunal will be. There is no penalty or effect of non-compliance stated.

Para. 7
This contains a similar provision to para. 4 dealing with variance of the terms of a lease under a "Pt. III leaseback". The words of the Schedule seem clear that the lease "shall" conform with Pt. IV unless the procedure under paras. 4 or 7 as the case may be is followed. It is suggested, therefore, that a lease non-conforming with Pt. IV cannot be enforced by the court to that effect unless the correct procedure has been followed. Thus, suppose a lease is agreed permitting forfeiture on the grounds of insolvency. This does not conform with para. 18 which permits forfeiture only after breach. No forfeiture on the grounds of insolvency will be permitted by the court unless the paras. 4 or 7 procedure has been followed and the leasehold valuation tribunal's consent or direction obtained. In drafting a lease which departs from Pt. IV it is, therefore, desirable to recite the relevant approval or direction of the leasehold valuation tribunal and retain a copy order with the title.

Paras. 9–11 and 14
See notes on Sched. 6 which these provisions follow.

Para. 18
This does not permit forfeiture on the grounds of insolvency.

ACQUISITION OF INTERESTS FROM LOCAL AUTHORITIES ETC.

Disapplication of provisions relating to disposals by local authorities etc.

1.—(1) It is hereby declared that nothing in any of the provisions specified in sub-paragraph (2) (which impose requirements as to consent or consultation or other restrictions in relation to disposals falling within those provisions) applies to any disposal of a freehold or leasehold interest in any premises which is made in pursuance of this Chapter.

(2) The provisions referred to in sub-paragraph (1) are—

(a) sections 32 and 43 of the Housing Act 1985 (disposals of land by local authorities) and section 133 of the Housing Act 1988 (certain subsequent disposals);

(b) section 9(1) and (1A) of the Housing Associations Act 1985 (disposals by registered and unregistered housing associations);

(c) section 79(1) and (2) of the Housing Act 1988 (disposals by housing action trusts) and section 81 of that Act (certain subsequent disposals); and

(d) section 105(1) of that Act (disposals subsequent to change of landlord of secure tenants).

Provisions relating to secure tenants following leaseback

2.—(1) This paragraph applies where a lease is granted to a public sector landlord in pursuance of paragraph 2 of Schedule 9.

(2) Where—

(a) immediately before the appropriate time the public sector landlord was the immediate landlord under a secure tenancy of a flat contained in the demised premises, and

(b) that tenancy continues in force after the grant of the lease referred to in sub-paragraph (1),

the tenant shall be deemed to have continued without interruption as tenant of the landlord under the secure tenancy, despite the disposal of the landlord's interest which immediately preceded the grant of the lease referred to in that sub-paragraph.

(3) Where—

(a) immediately before the appropriate time a person was a successor in relation to a secure tenancy of a flat contained in the demised premises, and

(b) that person is, in connection with the grant of the lease referred to in sub-paragraph (1), granted a new secure tenancy of that flat which is a tenancy for a term certain,

then for the purposes of sections 87 to 90 of the Housing Act 1985 (succession on death of tenant) that person shall also be a successor in relation to the new tenancy.

(4) Where—

(a) immediately before the appropriate time a person was the tenant under a secure tenancy of a flat contained in the demised premises, and

(b) that person is, connected with the grant of the lease referred to in sub-paragraph (1), granted a new secure tenancy of that flat,

then, for the purpose of determining whether either of the conditions referred to in sub-paragraph (5) is satisfied, the new tenancy shall not be regarded as a new letting of the flat but shall instead be regarded as a continuation of the secure tenancy referred to in paragraph (a) above.

(5) Those conditions are—

(a) the condition specified in sub-paragraph (1)(b) of paragraph 5 of Schedule 5 to the Housing Act 1985 (exception to the right to buy in case of letting in connection with employment); and

(b) the condition specified in sub-paragraph (1)(b) of paragraph 11 of that Schedule (exception to the right to buy in case of letting for occupation by person of pensionable age etc.).

(6) In this paragraph—

(a) any reference to a secure tenancy of a flat is a reference to a secure tenancy of a flat whether with or without any yard, garden, garage, outhouses or appurtenances belonging to or usually enjoyed with it; and

(b) any reference to a flat includes a reference to a unit (other than a flat) which is used as a dwelling.

(7) In this paragraph—

(a) "the appropriate time" and "the demised premises" have the same meaning as in Schedule 9; and

(b) "successor" has the same meaning as in section 88 of the Housing Act 1985.

GENERAL NOTE

This schedule deals with a number of issues involving collective enfranchisement and local authorities.

Para. 1

In some cases a local authority may have to dispose of interest pursuant to a collective enfranchisement. This paragraph simply disapplies any legislation which would prevent such a disposal.

Para. 2

Under s.36 and Sched. 9, para. 2, local authorities take a mandatory lease-back of flats held on secure tenancies. This paragraph provides: (a) that the secure tenant is treated as having an uninterrupted tenancy. This benefit is extended to successors of the former tenant who are waiting to take over their tenancy at the time of the lease-back; (b) for the same purpose the new tenancy if the secure tenant is not regarded a new tenancy.

Section 40   SCHEDULE 11

PROCEDURE WHERE COMPETENT LANDLORD IS NOT TENANT'S IMMEDIATE LANDLORD

PART I

PROCEDURE IN RELATION TO TENANT'S NOTICE

Tenant's notice may be given to any of the other landlords

1. The tenant's notice under section 42 shall be regarded as given to the competent landlord for the purposes of subsection (2)(a) of that section if it is given to any of the other landlords instead; and references in this Chapter to the relevant date shall be construed accordingly.

Tenant to give copies of notice

2.—(1) Where the tenant's notice is given to the competent landlord, the tenant shall give a copy of the notice to every person known or believed by him to be one of the other landlords.

(2) Where the tenant's notice is, in accordance with paragraph 1, given to one of the other landlords, the tenant shall give a copy of the notice to every person (apart from the recipient of the notice) known or believed by the tenant to be either the competent landlord or one of the other landlords.

(3) The tenant's notice shall state whether copies are being given in accordance with this paragraph to anyone other than the recipient and, if so, to whom.

Recipient of notice or copy to give further copies

3.—(1) Subject to sub-paragraph (2), a recipient of the tenant's notice or of a copy of it (including a person receiving a copy under this sub-paragraph)—
    (a) shall forthwith give a copy to any person who—
            (i) is known or believed by him to be the competent landlord or one of the other landlords, and
            (ii) is not stated in the recipient's copy of the notice, or known by him, to have received a copy; and
    (b) if he knows who is, or he believes himself to be, the competent landlord, shall—
            (i) give a notice to the tenant stating who is the person thought by him to be the competent landlord, and
            (ii) give a copy of it to that person (if not himself) and to every person known or believed by him to be one of the other landlords.

(2) Sub-paragraph (1) does not apply where the recipient is neither the competent landlord nor one of the other landlords.

(3) Where a person gives any copies of the tenant's notice in accordance with sub-paragraph (1)(a), he shall—
    (a) supplement the statement under paragraph 2(3) by adding any further persons to whom he is giving copies or who are known by him to have received one; and
    (b) notify the tenant of the persons added by him to that statement.

Consequences of failure to comply with paragraph 2 or 3

4.—(1) Where—

(a) the competent landlord or any of the other landlords does not receive a copy of the tenant's notice before the end of the period specified in it in pursuance of section 42(3)(f), but

(b) he was given a notice under section 41 by the tenant and, in response to the notice under that section, notified the tenant of his interest in the tenant's flat,

the tenant's notice shall cease to have effect at the end of that period.

(2) Where—

(a) sub-paragraph (1) does not apply, but

(b) any person fails without reasonable cause to comply with paragraph 2 or 3 above, or is guilty of any unreasonable delay in complying with either of those paragraphs,

he shall be liable for any loss thereby occasioned to the tenant or to the competent landlord or any of the other landlords.

PART II

CONDUCT OF PROCEEDINGS BY COMPETENT LANDLORD ON BEHALF OF OTHER LANDLORDS

Counter-notice to specify other landlords

5. Any counter-notice given to the tenant by the competent landlord must specify the other landlords on whose behalf he is acting.

Acts of competent landlord binding on other landlords

6.—(1) Without prejudice to the generality of section 40(2)—

(a) any notice given under this Chapter by the competent landlord to the tenant,

(b) any agreement for the purposes of this Chapter between that landlord and the tenant, and

(c) any determination of the court or a leasehold valuation tribunal under this Chapter in proceedings between that landlord and the tenant,

shall be binding on the other landlords and on their interests in the property demised by the tenant's lease or any other property; but in the event of dispute the competent landlord or any of the other landlords may apply to the court for directions as to the manner in which the competent landlord should act in the dispute.

(2) Subject to paragraph 7(2), the authority given to the competent landlord by section 40(2) shall extend to receiving on behalf of any other landlord any amount payable to that person by virtue of Schedule 13.

(3) If any of the other landlords cannot be found, or his identity cannot be ascertained, the competent landlord shall apply to the court for directions and the court may make such order as it thinks proper with a view to giving effect to the rights of the tenant and protecting the interests of other persons; but subject to any such directions, the competent landlord shall proceed as in other cases.

(4) The competent landlord, if he acts in good faith and with reasonable care and diligence, shall not be liable to any of the other landlords for any loss or damage caused by any act or omission in the exercise or intended exercise of the authority given to him by section 40(2).

Other landlords acting independently

7.—(1) Notwithstanding any thing in section 40(2), any of the other landlords shall, at any time after the giving by the competent landlord of a counter-notice under section 45 and on giving notice to both the competent landlord and the tenant of his intention to be so represented, be entitled to be separately represented—

(a) in any legal proceedings in which his title to any property comes in question, or

(b) in any legal proceedings relating to the determination of any amount payable to him by virtue of Schedule 13.

(2) Any of the other landlords may also, on giving notice to the competent landlord and the tenant, require that any amount payable to him by virtue of Schedule 13 shall be paid by the tenant to him, or to a person authorised by him to receive it, instead of to the competent landlord; but if, after being given proper notice of the time and method of completion with the tenant, either—

(a) he fails to notify the competent landlord of the arrangements made with the tenant to receive payment, or

(b) having notified the competent landlord of those arrangements, the arrangements are not duly implemented,

the competent landlord shall be authorised to receive the payment for him, and the competent landlord's written receipt for the amount payable shall be a complete discharge to the tenant.

Obligations of other landlords to competent landlord

8.—(1) It shall be the duty of each of the other landlords (subject to paragraph 7) to give the competent landlord all such information and assistance as he may reasonably require; and, if any of the other landlords fails to comply with this sub-paragraph, that landlord shall indemnify the competent landlord against any liability incurred by him in consequence of the failure.

(2) Each of the other landlords shall make such contribution as shall be just to costs and expenses which are properly incurred by the competent landlord in pursuance of section 40(2) but are not recoverable or not recovered from the tenant.

Applications made by other landlords under section 47(1)

9.—(1) The authority given to the competent landlord by section 40(2) shall not extend to the bringing of proceedings under section 47(1) on behalf of any of the other landlords, or preclude any of those landlords from bringing proceedings under that provision on his own behalf as if he were the competent landlord.

(2) In section 45(2)(c) any reference to the competent landlord shall include a reference—
(a) to any of the other landlords, or
(b) to any two or more of the following, namely the competent landlord and the other landlords, acting together;
and in section 47(1) and (2) references to the landlord shall be construed accordingly; but if any of the other landlords intends to make such an application as is mentioned in section 45(2)(c), whether alone or together with any other person or persons, his name shall be stated in the counter-notice.

Deemed surrender and re-grant of leases of other landlords

10.—(1) Where a lease is executed under section 56 or 93(4) or in pursuance of any order made under this Chapter, then (subject to sub-paragraph (3)) that instrument shall have effect for the creation of the tenant's new lease of his flat, and for the operation of the rights and obligations conferred and imposed by it, as if there had been a surrender and re-grant of any subsisting lease intermediate between the interest of the competent landlord and the existing lease; and the covenants and other provisions of that instrument shall be framed and take effect accordingly.

(2) Section 57(2) shall apply to the new lease on the basis that account is to be taken of obligations imposed on any of the other landlords by virtue of that or any superior lease; and section 59(3) shall apply on the basis that the reference there to the tenant's landlord includes the immediate landlord form whom the new lease will be held and all superior landlords, including any superior to the competent landlord.

(3) Where a lease of the tenant's flat superior to the existing lease is vested in the tenant or a trustee for him, the new lease shall include an actual surrender of that superior lease without a re-grant, and it shall accordingly be disregarded for the purposes of the preceding provisions of this paragraph.

Discharge of existing mortgages

11. Where by reason of section 58(2) it is necessary to make any payment to discharge the tenant's flat from a mortgage affecting the interest of any landlord, then if the competent landlord is not the landlord liable or primarily liable in respect of the mortgage, he shall not be required to make that payment otherwise than out of money made available for the purpose by the landlord so liable, and it shall be the duty of that landlord to provide for the mortgage being discharged.

GENERAL NOTE

Para. 1
The tenant's task where the competent landlord for the individual right to an extended lease is not his actual landlord is eased by providing that service of the s.12 notice on any relevant landlord is good service.

Para. 2
The tenant is required in such cases to give a copy of the notice to every known relevant landlord.

Para. 3
The recipients of tenant notices have to give a copy to any relevant landlord known to them who has not received one and inform the tenant whom they believe to be the relevant landlord.

Para. 4

The consequence to the tenant of failing to comply with his obligation to serve notice under paras. 2 and 3 may be that the s.42 notice ceases to have effect. Paragraph 4(2) also permits damages to be obtained for loss suffered by a failure to comply with paras. 2 and 3, but this is only in cases where para. 4(1) does not invalidate the tenant's notice.

Para. 5

The counter-notice must specify other landlords for whom the competent landlord acts.

Para. 6

This allows the competent landlord to bind the other landlords. Note that any landlord can apply to the court for directions if there is a dispute and the competent landlord may do so if another landlord cannot be found or identified.

Para. 7

Any landlord may choose to be represented separately. Notice must be given to the competent landlord and the tenant. No special form is required. This should simply state that notice is given under Sched. 11, para. 7 of the Act that the particular landlord chooses to be separately represented. Similarly, any landlord may give a simple notice requiring its share of the price to be paid to a named person. That landlord must then comply with the completion arrangements or be bound to accept the competent landlord's receipt as a discharge.

Para. 8

The landlords have to co-operate with each other subject to the possibility of an indemnity for loss the other(s) suffer.

Para. 8(2)

This paragraph requires each landlord to pay a "just" share of the cash and will invariably lead to disputes. It will be more satisfactory to agree this in writing out the outset of a transaction.

Section 42   SCHEDULE 12

THE TENANT'S NOTICE: SUPPLEMENTARY PROVISIONS

PART I

EFFECT OF TENANT'S NOTICE ON OTHER NOTICES, FORFEITURES ETC.

Prior notice by tenant terminating lease

1. A notice given by a qualifying tenant of a flat under section 42 shall be of no effect if it is given—
    (a) after the tenant has given notice terminating the lease of the flat (other than a notice that has been superseded by the grant, express or implied, of a new tenancy); or
    (b) during the subsistence of an agreement for the grant to the tenant of a future tenancy of the flat, where the agreement is one to which paragraph 17 of Schedule 10 to the Local Government and Housing Act 1989 applies.

Prior notice by landlord terminating lease

2.—(1) Subject to sub-paragraph (2), a notice given by a qualifying tenant of a flat under section 42 shall be of no effect if it is given more than two months after a landlord's notice terminating the tenant's lease of the flat has been given under section 4 of the Landlord and Tenant Act 1954 or served under paragraph 4(1) of Schedule 10 to the Local Government and Housing Act 1989 (whether or not the notice has effect to terminate the lease).

(2) Sub-paragraph (1) does not apply where the landlord gives his written consent to a notice being given under section 42 after the end of those two months.

(3) Where in the case of a qualifying tenant of a flat who gives a notice under section 42—
    (a) any such landlord's notice is given or served as mentioned in sub-paragraph (1), but
    (b) that notice was not given or served more than two months before the date on which the notice under section 42 is given to the landlord,
the landlord's notice shall cease to have effect on that date.

(4) If—
    (a) any such landlord's notice ceases to have effect by virtue of sub-paragraph (3), but
    (b) the claim made by the tenant by the giving of his notice under section 42 is not effective,

then sub-paragraph (5) shall apply to any landlord's notice terminating the tenant's lease of the flat which—
  (i) is given under section 4 of the Landlord and Tenant Act 1954 or served under paragraph 4(1) of Schedule 10 to the Local Government and Housing Act 1989, and
  (ii) is so given or served within one month after the expiry of the period of currency of that claim.
  (5) Where this sub-paragraph applies to a landlord's notice, the earliest date which may be specified in the notice as the date of termination shall be—
  (a) in the case of a notice given under section 4 of that Act of 1954—
        (i) the date of termination specified in the previous notice, or
        (ii) the date of expiry of the period of three months beginning with the date of the giving of the new notice,
    whichever is the later; or
  (b) in the case of a notice served under paragraph 4(1) of Schedule 10 to that Act of 1989—
        (i) the date of termination specified in the previous notice, or
        (ii) the date of expiry of the period of four months beginning with the date of service of the new notice,
    whichever is the later.
  (6) Where—
  (a) by virtue of sub-paragraph (5) a landlord's notice specifies as the date of termination of a lease a date earlier than six months after the date of the giving of the notice, and
  (b) the notice proposes a statutory tenancy,
section 7(2) of the Landlord and Tenant Act 1954 shall apply in relation to the notice with the substitution, for references to the period of two months ending with the date of termination specified in the notice and the beginning of that period, of references to the period of three months beginning with the date of the giving of the notice and the end of that period.

Orders for possession and pending proceedings for forfeiture etc.

  3.—(1) A notice given by a qualifying tenant of a flat under section 42 shall be of no effect if at the time when it is given he is obliged to give up possession of his flat in pursuance of an order of a court or will be so obliged at a date specified in such an order.
  (2) Except with the leave of the court, a qualifying tenant of a flat shall not give a notice under section 42 at a time when any proceedings are pending to enforce a right of re-entry or forfeiture terminating his lease of the flat.
  (3) Leave shall only be granted under sub-paragraph (2) if the court is satisfied that the tenant does not wish to give such a notice solely or mainly for the purpose of avoiding the consequences of the breach of the terms of his lease in respect of which proceedings are pending.
  (4) If—
  (a) leave is so granted, and
  (b) the tenant by such a notice makes a claim to acquire a new lease of his flat,
the tenant's lease shall be deemed for the purposes of the claim to be a subsisting lease despite the existence of those proceedings and any order made afterwards in those proceedings; and, if the claim is effective, the court in which those proceedings were brought may set aside or vary any such order to such extent and on such terms as appear to that court to be appropriate.

Notice terminating lease given by tenant or landlord during currency of claim

  4. Where by a notice given under section 42 a tenant makes a claim to acquire a new lease of a flat, any notice terminating the tenant's lease of the flat, whether it is—
  (a) a notice given by the tenant, or
  (b) a landlord's notice given under section 4 of the Landlord and Tenant Act 1954 or served under paragraph 4(1) of Schedule 10 to the Local Government and Housing Act 1989,
shall be of no effect if it is given or served during the currency of the claim.

Tenant's notice operates to prevent termination of lease

  5.—(1) Where by a notice under section 42 a tenant makes a claim to acquire a new lease of a flat, then during the currency of the claim and for three months thereafter the lease of the flat shall not terminate—
  (a) by effluxion of time, or
  (b) in pursuance of a notice to quit given by the immediate landlord of the tenant, or
  (c) by the termination of a superior lease;
but if the claim is not effective, and but for this sub-paragraph the lease would have so terminated before the end of those three months, the lease shall so terminate at the end of those three months.

(2) Sub-paragraph (1) shall not be taken to prevent an earlier termination of the lease in any manner not mentioned in that sub-paragraph, and shall not affect—

  (a) the power under section 146(4) of the Law of Property Act 1925 (relief against forfeiture of leases) to grant a tenant relief against the termination of a superior lease, or

  (b) any right of the tenant to relief under section 16(2) of the Landlord and Tenant Act 1954 (relief where landlord proceeding to enforce covenants) or under paragraph 9 of Schedule 5 to that Act (relief in proceedings brought by superior landlord).

Restriction on proceedings to enforce right of re-entry or forfeiture

6. Where by a notice under section 42 a tenant makes a claim to acquire a new lease of a flat, then during the currency of the claim—

  (a) no proceedings to enforce any right of re-entry or forfeiture terminating the lease of the flat shall be brought in any court without the leave of that court, and

  (b) leave shall only be granted if the court is satisfied that the notice was given solely or mainly for the purpose of avoiding the consequences of the breach of the terms of the tenant's lease in respect of which proceedings are proposed to be brought;

but where leave is granted, the notice shall cease to have effect.

Effect of notice under section 16(2) of Landlord and Tenant Act 1954 on tenant's notice

7.—(1) A tenant who, in proceedings to enforce a right of re-entry or forfeiture or a right to damages in respect of a failure to comply with any terms of his lease, applies for relief under section 16 of the Landlord and Tenant Act 1954 is not thereby precluded from making a claim to acquire a new lease under this Chapter; but if he gives notice under section 16(2) of that Act (under which the tenant is relieved from any order for recovery of possession or for payment of damages, but the tenancy is cut short), any notice given by him under section 42 with respect to property comprised in his lease shall be of no effect or, if already given, shall cease to have effect.

(2) Sub-paragraph (1) shall apply in relation to proceedings relating to a superior tenancy with the substitution for the references to section 16 and to section 16(2) of the Landlord and Tenant Act 1954 of references to paragraph 9 and to paragraph 9(2) of Schedule 5 to that Act.

Interpretation

8.—(1) For the purposes of this Part of this Schedule—

  (a) references to a notice under section 42 include, in so far as the context permits, references to a notice purporting to be giving under that section (whether by a qualifying tenant or not), and references to the tenant by whom a notice is given shall be construed accordingly;

  (b) references to a claim being effective are references to a new lease being acquired in pursuance of the claim; and

  (c) references to the currency of a claim are—

    (i) where the claim is made by a valid notice under section 42, references to the period during which the notice continues in force in accordance with subsection (8) of that section, or

    (ii) where the claim is made by a notice which is not a valid notice under section 42, references to the period beginning with the giving of the notice and ending with the time when the notice is set aside by the court or is withdrawn or when it would (if valid) cease to have effect or be deemed to have been withdrawn.

(2) For the purposes of sub-paragraph (1)(c) the date when a notice is set aside, or would (if valid) cease to have effect, in consequence of an order of a court shall be taken to be the date when the order becomes final.

(3) The references in this Schedule—

  (a) to section 16 of the Landlord and Tenant Act 1954 and subsection (2) of that section, and

  (b) to paragraph 9 of Schedule 5 to that Act and sub-paragraph (2) of that paragraph,

include references to those provisions as they apply in relation to Schedule 10 to the Local Government and Housing Act 1989 (security of tenure on ending of long residential tenancies).

PART II

OTHER PROVISIONS

9.—(1) The tenant's notice shall not be invalidated by any inaccuracy in any of the particulars required by section 42(3) or by any misdescription of any of the property to which the claim extends.

(2) Where the tenant's notice—

(a) specifies any property which he is not entitled to have demised to him under a new lease granted in pursuance of this Chapter, or

(b) fails to specify any property which he is entitled to have so demised to him,

the notice may, with the leave of the court and on such terms as the court may think fit, be amended so as to exclude or include the property in question.

GENERAL NOTE

Para. 1(a)

The right to an extended lease is lost once the tenant serves a notice to quit unless another tenancy is granted.

Para. 1(b)

This is a potential trap for the tenant. Schedule 10 to the Local Government and Housing Act 1989 replaced the scheme for security of tenure for long leases at a low rent under Landlord and Tenant Act 1954, Pt. I. Paragraph 1 of Sched. 10 provides that if the parties agree a new tenancy not at a low rent before the term date of the long tenancy then the Sched. 10 provisions do not apply. Once such an agreement has been made the right to an individual extended lease is lost.

Para. 2

The landlord's procedure to terminate a long residential tenancy by notice is rarely used. Under s.4 of the 1954 Act the notices are contained in Landlord and Tenant (Notices) Regulations 1957 (S.I. 1957 No. 1157). There appear to be no prescribed forms under Sched. 10, para. 4.

Para. 4

Once a tenant has served a s.42 notice (including a purported s.42 notice—para. 8) then the landlord cannot terminate a long tenancy by notice under s.4 of the Landlord and Tenant Act 1954 or para. 4, of Sched. 10 to the Local Government and Housing Act 1989.

Para. 5

This has to be read in the context of s.7(5). Leases continued under Landlord and Tenant Act 1954, Pt. I or Sched. 10 to the Local Government and Housing Act 1989 are qualifying long leases. These Acts provide that such leases do not expire by effluxion of time (s.3 of the 1954 Act and Sched. 10, para. 3 of the 1989 Act). If the lease is not one continued under these Acts then the tenant must make a claim first learning the currency of the lease. This will arise, for example, if the tenancy is not within the rateable value limits for the 1954 Act (s.2 of that Act; and s.4 of the Rent Act 1977) or the same rateable value limits applied to Sched. 10 tenancies (except those granted on or after April 1, 1990) which have the substitute formula contained in para. 2A of Schedule 10 to the 1989 Act.

Para. 9

This is an important provision where issues arise as to whether a tenant's notice has actually been served. It is wide-sweeping in its effect. Taken with para. 8(1)(a) it means that anything purporting to be a tenant's notice will be a tenant's notice however woefully drafted.

Section 56 SCHEDULE 13

PREMIUM AND OTHER AMOUNTS PAYABLE BY TENANT ON GRANT OF NEW LEASE

PART I

GENERAL

1. In this Schedule—

"intermediate leasehold interest" means the interest of any person falling within section 40(4)(c), to the extent that it is an interest in the tenant's flat subsisting immediately before the grant of the new lease;

"the valuation date" means the date when all of the terms of acquisition (apart from those relating to the premium and any other amounts payable by virtue of this Schedule in connection with the grant of the new lease) have been determined either by agreement or by a leasehold valuation tribunal under this Chapter.

PART II

PREMIUM PAYABLE IN RESPECT OF GRANT OF NEW LEASE

Premium payable by tenant

2. The premium payable by the tenant in respect of the grant of the new lease shall be the aggregate of—
  (a) the diminution in value of the landlord's interest in the tenant's flat as determined in accordance with paragraph 3,
  (b) the landlord's share of the marriage value as determined in accordance with paragraph 4, and
  (c) any amount of compensation payable to the landlord under paragraph 5.

Diminution in value of landlord's interest

3.—(1) The diminution in value of the landlord's interest is the difference between—
  (a) the value of the landlord's interest in the tenant's flat prior to the grant of the new lease; and
  (b) the value of his interest in the flat once the new lease is granted.
  (2) Subject to the provisions of this paragraph, the value of any such interest of the landlord as is mentioned in sub-paragraph (1)(a) or (b) is the amount which at the valuation date that interest might be expected to realise if sold on the open market by a willing seller (with the tenant not buying or seeking to buy) on the following assumptions—
  (a) on the assumption that the vendor is selling for an estate in fee simple or (as the case may be) such other interest as is held by the landlord, subject to the relevant lease and any intermediate leasehold interests;
  (b) on the assumption that Chapter I and this Chapter confer no right to acquire any interest in any premises containing the tenant's flat or to acquire any new lease;
  (c) on the assumption that any increase in the value of the flat which is attributable to an improvement carried out at his own expense by the tenant or by any predecessor in title is to be disregarded; and
  (d) on the assumption that (subject to paragraph (b)) the vendor is selling with and subject to the rights and burdens with and subject to which the relevant lease has effect or (as the case may be) is to be granted.
  (3) In sub-paragraph (2) "the relevant lease" means either the tenant's existing lease or the new lease, depending on whether the valuation is for the purposes of paragraph (a) or paragraph (b) of sub-paragraph (1).
  (4) It is hereby declared that the fact that sub-paragraph (2) requires assumptions to be made as to the matters specified in paragraphs (a) to (d) of that sub-paragraph does not preclude the making of assumptions as to other matters where those assumptions are appropriate for determining the amount which at the valuation date any such interest of the landlord as is mentioned in sub-paragraph (1)(a) or (b) might be expected to realise if sold as mentioned in sub-paragraph (2).
  (5) In determining any such amount there shall be made such deduction (if any) in respect of any defect in title as on a sale of that interest on the open market might be expected to be allowed between a willing seller and a willing buyer.
  (6) The value of any such interest of the landlord as is mentioned in sub-paragraph (1)(a) or (b) shall not be increased by reason of—
  (a) any transaction which—
       (i) is entered into on or after the date of the passing of this Act (otherwise than in pursuance of a contract entered into before that date), and
       (ii) involves the creation or transfer of an interest superior to (whether or not preceding) any interest held by the tenant; or
  (b) any alteration on or after that date of the terms on which any such superior interest is held.

Landlord's share of marriage value

4.—(1) The marriage value is the amount referred to in sub-paragraph (2), and the landlord's share of the marriage value is—
  (a) such proportion of that amount as is determined by agreement between the landlord and the tenant or, in default of agreement, as is determined by a leasehold valuation tribunal to be the proportion which in its opinion would have been determined by an agreement made at the valuation date between the parties on a sale on the open market by a willing seller, or

(b) 50 per cent, of that amount,
whichever is the greater.

(2) The marriage value is the difference between the following amounts, namely—

(a) the aggregate of—

 (i) the value of the interest of the tenant under his existing lease,

 (ii) the value of the landlord's interest in the tenant's flat prior to the grant of the new lease, and

 (iii) the values prior to the grant of that lease of all intermediate leasehold interest (if any); and

(b) the aggregate of—

 (i) the value of the interest to be held by the tenant under the new lease,

 (ii) the value of the landlord's interest in the tenant's flat once the new lease is granted, and

 (iii) the values of all intermediate leasehold interests (if any) once that lease is granted.

(3) For the purposes of sub-paragraph (2)—

(a) the value of any interest of the tenant shall be determined as at the valuation date;

(b) the value of any such interest of the landlord as is mentioned in paragraph (a) or paragraph (b) of that sub-paragraph is the amount determined for the purposes of paragraph 3(1)(a) or paragraph 3(1)(b) (as the case may be); and

(c) the value of any intermediate leasehold interest shall be determined in accordance with paragraph 8, and shall be so determined as at the valuation date.

Compensation for loss arising out of grant of new lease

5.—(1) Where the landlord will suffer any loss or damage to which this paragraph applies, there shall be payable to him such amount as is reasonable to compensate him for that loss or damage.

(2) This paragraph applies to—

(a) any diminution in value of any interest of the landlord in any property other than the tenant's flat which results from the grant to the tenant of the new lease; and

(b) any other loss or damage which results therefrom to the extent that it is referable to the landlord's ownership of any such interest.

(3) Without prejudice to the generality of paragraph (b) of sub-paragraph (2), the kinds of loss falling within that paragraph include loss of development value in relation to the tenant's flat to the extent that it is referable as mentioned in that paragraph.

(4) In sub-paragraph (3) "development value", in relation to the tenant's flat, means any increase in the value of the landlord's interest in the flat which is attributable to the possibility of demolishing, reconstructing, or carrying out substantial works of construction affecting, the flat (whether together with any other premises or otherwise).

PART III

AMOUNTS PAYABLE TO OWNERS OF INTERMEDIATE LEASEHOLD INTERESTS

Amount payable to owner of intermediate interest

6. In connection with the grant of the new lease to the tenant there shall be payable by the tenant to the owner of any intermediate leasehold interest an amount which is the aggregate of—

(a) the diminution in value of that interest as determined in accordance with paragraph 7; and

(b) any amount of compensation payable to him under paragraph 9.

Diminution in value of intermediate interest

7.—(1) The diminution in value of any intermediate leasehold interest is the difference between—

(a) the value of that interest prior to the grant of the new lease; and

(b) the value of that interest once the new lease is granted.

(2) Each of those values shall be determined, as at the valuation date, in accordance with paragraph 8.

Value of intermediate interests

8.—(1) Subject to sub-paragraph (2), paragraph 3(2) to (6) shall apply for determining the value of any intermediate leasehold interest for the purposes of any provision of this Schedule with such modifications as are appropriate to relate those provisions of paragraph 3 to a sale of the interest in question subject to the tenant's lease for the time being and to any leases intermediate between the interest in question and that lease.

(2) The value of an intermediate leasehold interest which is the interest of the tenant under a minor intermediate lease shall be calculated by applying the formula set out in sub-paragraph (6) instead of in accordance with sub-paragraph (1).

(3) "A minor intermediate lease" means a lease complying with the following requirements, namely—

(a) it must have an expectation of possession of not more than one month, and

(b) the profit rent in respect of the lease must be not more than £5 per year.

(4) "Profit rent" means an amount equal to that of the rent payable under the lease on which the minor intermediate lease is in immediate reversion, less that of the rent payable under the minor intermediate lease.

(5) Where the minor intermediate lease or that on which it is in immediate reversion comprises property other than the tenant's flat, then in sub-paragraph (4) the reference to the rent payable under it means so much of that rent as is apportioned to that flat.

(6) The formula is—

$$P = £\frac{R}{Y} - \frac{R}{Y(1 + Y)^n}$$

where—

  P = the price payable;

  R = the profit rent;

  Y = the yield (expressed as a decimal fraction) from 2½ per cent. Consolidated Stock;

  n = the period, expressed in years (taking any part of a year as a whole year), of the remainder of the term of the minor intermediate lease as at the valuation date.

(7) In calculating the yield from 2½ per cent. Consolidated Stock, the price of that stock shall be taken to be the middle market price at the close of business on the last trading day in the week before the valuation date.

(8) For the purposes of this paragraph the expectation of possession carried by a lease is the expectation which it carries at the valuation date of possession after the tenant's lease, on the basis that—

(a) (subject to sub-paragraph (9)) the tenant's lease terminates at the valuation date if its term date fell before then, or else it terminates on its term date; and

(b) any other lease terminates on its term date.

(9) In a case where before the relevant date for the purposes of this Chapter the immediate landlord of the tenant had given notice to quit terminating the tenant's lease on a date earlier than that date, the date specified in the notice to quit shall be substituted for the date specified in sub-paragraph (8)(a) above.

Compensation for loss arising out of grant of new lease

9. Paragraph 5 shall apply in relation to the owner of any intermediate leasehold interest as it applies in relation to the landlord.

Owners of intermediate interests entitled to part of marriage value

10.—(1) This paragraph applies in a case where—

(a) the premium payable by the tenant in respect of the grant of the new lease includes an amount in respect of the landlord's share of the marriage value, and

(b) there are any intermediate leasehold interests.

(2) The amount payable to the landlord in respect of his share of the marriage value shall be divided between the landlord and the owners of any such intermediate interests in proportion to the amounts by which the values of their respective interests in the flat will be diminished in consequence of the grant of the new lease.

(3) For the purposes of sub-paragraph (2)—

(a) the amount by which the value of the landlord's interest in the flat will be so diminished is the diminution in value of that interest as determined for the purposes of paragraph 2(a); and

(b) the amount by which the value of any intermediate leasehold interest will be so diminished is the diminution in value of that interest as determined for the purposes of paragraph 6(a).

(4) Where the owner of any intermediate leasehold interest is entitled in accordance with sub-paragraph (2) to any part of the amount payable to the landlord in respect of the landlord's share of the marriage value, the amount to which he is so entitled shall be payable to him by the landlord.

GENERAL NOTE

The principles of valuation on the grant of a new lease are very similar to those under Sched. 6 on enfranchisement and the notes on that schedule may be referred to.

Para. 3

This provides the main apparent difference between a Sched. 6 valuation and a Sched. 13 valuation. In Sched. 6 the valuer looks at the open market value of the freehold. In Sched. 13 at the diminution in value of the landlord's interest in the reversion in respect of which the extended lease is granted. But, then that diminution is valued by valuing the interest (that is the reversion) on an open market basis and the exercise becomes very much the same, and *ceteris paribus* the same assumptions are made.

The following example was prepared by Martin Angel Esq., a surveyor with Allsop & Co., 27 Soho Square, London W1: "Consider the example of a freehold block of 20 flats, each of which are held leasehold with terms of 30 years unexpired, each paying a fixed ground rent of £100 p.a. and each having a leasehold value of £130,000. The freeholder's interest would comprise the right to receive 20 × £100 p.a. until the leases end in 30 years' time, followed by the right to receive market rents. Let us assume this has a total value to him of, say, £200,000. Let us also assume that, with an extended lease (say, 999 years at a peppercorn rent, and with a share in the freehold), each of the flats would have a vacant possession value of £250,000. Consider (Table B) what would be payable on the assumption that the flat was one where the lessee is seeking a lease extension.

Table B

(1) Diminution in freeholder's interest in the subject flat			
Present value		£10,000	
Value after lease extension of 90 years (total 120 years) at peppercorn ground rent is nominal, say		£100	£9,900
(2) Landlord's share of the marriage value			
Proposed extended leasehold value		£249,000	
Existing leasehold value	£130,000		
Existing freehold interest in the flat	£10,000		
		£140,000	
Marriage value		£109,000	
Assume 50% of the marriage value is to be payable to the freeholder			£54,500
			£64,400"

An example by Mr. Angel of the price payable on a freehold enfranchisement is shown in the note on Sched. 6.

Section 61   SCHEDULE 14

PROVISIONS SUPPLEMENTARY TO SECTION 61

1.—(1) This Schedule has effect where a tenant of a flat is entitled to be paid compensation under section 61, or would be so entitled on the landlord obtaining an order for possession, or where an application for such an order is dismissed or withdrawn.

(2) In this Schedule—

"application for possession" means a landlord's application under section 61;

"the new lease" has the same meaning as in that section; and

"order for possession" means an order made under that section;

and (except in the case of the reference in paragraph 5(1)(b) to the flat as a dwelling) references to the flat held by the tenant under the new lease shall be construed in accordance with subsection (5) of that section.

2.—(1) Where an order for possession is made—

(a) the new lease shall determine, and

(b) the compensation payable to the tenant by virtue of the order shall become payable,

on such date as may, when the amount of compensation has been determined either by agreement between the landlord and the tenant or by a leasehold valuation tribunal, be fixed by order of the court made on the application of either the landlord or the tenant.

(2) Where the application for possession was made by virtue of section 61(2)(a), then—

(a) (unless paragraph (b) below applies) an order of the court under this paragraph shall not fix a date earlier than the term date of the lease in relation to which the right to acquire a new lease was exercised;

(b) in a case where section 61(2)(a) applies in accordance with section 61(3), an order of the court under this paragraph shall not fix a date earlier than the term date of the lease in relation to which that right was first exercised.

(3) In fixing the date referred to in sub-paragraph (1) the court shall have regard to the conduct of the parties and to the extent to which the landlord has made reasonable preparations for proceeding with the redevelopment (including the obtaining of, or preparations relating to the obtaining of, any requisite permission or consent, whether from any authority whose permission or consent is required under any enactment or from the owner of an interest in any property).

(4) The court may by order direct that the whole or part of the compensation payable to the tenant shall be paid into court, if the court thinks it expedient to do so for the purpose of ensuring that the sum paid is available for meeting any mortgage on the tenant's interest in the flat in question, or for the purpose of division, or for any other purpose.

3.—(1) On the termination of a lease under an order for possession there shall terminate also any immediate or derivative sub-lease, and the tenant shall be bound to give up possession of the flat in question to the landlord except in so far as he is precluded from doing so by the rights of other persons to retain possession under or by virtue of any enactment.

(2) Where a sub-lease of property comprised in the lease has been created after the date of the application for possession, no person shall in respect of that sub-lease be entitled under any of the following provisions (which relate to retaining possession on the termination of a superior tenancy), namely—

(a) subsection (2) of section 137 of the Rent Act 1977, or any enactment (including subsection (5) of that section) applying or extending it,

(b) subsection (2) of section 9 of the Rent (Agriculture) Act 1976 as extended by subsection (5) of that section, or

(c) section 18(1) of the Housing Act 1988,

to retain possession of that property after the termination of the lease under the order for possession.

(3) In exercising its jurisdiction under section 61 [of] this Schedule the court shall assume that the landlord, having obtained an order for possession, will not be precluded from obtaining possession by the right of any person to retain possession by virtue of—

(a) Part VII of the Rent Act 1977 or any enactment applying or extending that Part of that Act,

(b) the Rent (Agriculture) Act 1976, or

(c) Part I of the Housing Act 1988,

or otherwise.

(4) A person in occupation of any property under a sub-lease liable to terminate under sub-paragraph (1) may, with the leave of the court, appear and be heard on any application for possession or any application under paragraph 2.

4. Where an order has been made by a county court under paragraph 2, that court or another county court shall have jurisdiction to hear and determine any proceedings brought by virtue of the order to recover possession of the property or to recover the compensation.

5.—(1) The amount payable to a tenant, by virtue of an order for possession, by way of compensation for loss of his flat shall be the amount which at the valuation date the new lease, if sold on the open market by a willing seller, might be expected to realise on the following assumptions—

(a) on the assumption that Chapter I and this Chapter confer no right to acquire any interest in any premises containing the tenant's flat or to acquire any new lease;

(b) on the assumption that the vendor is selling—

(i) subject to the rights of any person who will on the termination of the lease be entitled to retain possession as against the landlord, but otherwise with vacant possession, and

(ii) subject to any restriction that would be required (in addition to any imposed by the terms of the lease) to limit the uses of the flat to those to which it has been put since the commencement of the lease and to preclude the erection of any new dwelling or any other building not ancillary to the flat as a dwelling; and

(c) on the assumption that (subject to paragraphs (a) and (b)) the vendor is selling with and subject to the rights an burdens with and subject to which the flat will be held by the landlord on the termination of the lease.

(2) It is hereby declared that the fact that sub-paragraph (1) requires assumptions to be made as to the matters specified in paragraphs (a) to (c) of that sub-paragraph does not preclude the making of assumptions as to other matters where those assumptions are appropriate for determining the amount which at the valuation date the new lease might be expected to realise if sold as mentioned in that sub-paragraph.

(3) In determining any such amount there shall be made such deduction (if any) in respect of any defect in title as on a sale of that interest on the open market might be expected to be allowed between a willing seller and a willing buyer.

(4) In this paragraph "the valuation date" means the date when the amount of the compensation payable to the tenant is determined as mentioned in paragraph 2(1).

6.—(1) Part I of the Landlord and Tenant Act 1927 (compensation for improvements on termination of business tenancies) shall not apply on the termination of the new lease or any sub-lease in accordance with this Schedule; and a request for a new tenancy under section 26 of the Landlord and Tenant Act 1954 in respect of the new lease or any sub-lease shall be of no effect if made after the application for possession, or, if already made, shall cease to have effect on the making of that application.

(2) Where a sub-lease terminating with the new lease in accordance with paragraph 3 is one to which Part II of the Landlord and Tenant Act 1954 applies, the compensation payable to the tenant shall be divided between him and the sub-tenant in such proportions as may be just, regard being had to their respective interests in the flat in question and to any loss arising from the termination of those interests and not incurred by imprudence.

(3) Where the amount of the compensation payable to the tenant is agreed between him and the landlord without the consent of a sub-tenant entitled under sub-paragraph (2) to a share in the compensation, and is shown by the sub-tenant to be less than might reasonably have been obtained by the tenant, the sub-tenant shall be entitled under sub-paragraph (2) to recover from the tenant such increased share as may be just.

7.—(1) The landlord shall not be concerned with the application of the amount payable to the tenant by way of compensation under an order for possession, but (subject to any statutory requirements as to payment of capital money arising under a settlement or a disposition on trust for sale and to any order under paragraph 2(4) for payment into court) the written receipt of the tenant shall be a complete discharge for the amount payable.

(2) The landlord shall be entitled to deduct from the amount so payable to the tenant—

(a) the amount of any sum recoverable as rent in respect of the flat up to the termination of the new lease; and

(b) the amount of any other sums due and payable by the tenant to the landlord under or in respect of the lease or any agreement collateral thereto.

8.—(1) Where a landlord makes an application for possession, and it is made to appear to the court that in relation to matters arising out of that application (including the giving up of possession of the flat or the payment of compensation) the landlord or the tenant has been guilty of any unreasonable delay or default, the court may—

(a) by order revoke or vary, and direct repayment of sums paid under, any provision made by a previous order as to payment of the costs of proceedings taken in the court on or with reference to the application; or

(b) where costs have not been awarded, award costs.

(2) Where an application for possession is dismissed or withdrawn, and it is made to appear to the court—

(a) that the application was not made in good faith, or

(b) that the landlord had attempted in any material respect to support by misrepresentation or the concealment of material facts a request to the tenant to deliver up possession without an application for possession,

the court may order that no further application for possession of the flat made by the landlord shall be entertained if it is made within the period of five years beginning with the date of the order.

9. Where—

(a) the new lease is held on trust for sale, and

(b) compensation is paid by the landlord on the termination of the new lease (whether the payment is made in pursuance of an order for possession or in pursuance of an agreement made in conformity with paragraph 5 above without an application having been made under section 61),

the sum received shall be dealt with as if it were proceeds of sale arising under the trust.

10. Where—

(a) the tenant under the new lease is a university or college to which the Universities and College Estates Act 1925 applies, and

(b) compensation is paid as mentioned in paragraph 9(b) above,

the sum received shall be dealt with as if it were an amount payable by way of consideration on a sale effected under that Act.

11. Where—

(a) the tenant under the new lease is a capitular body within the meaning of the Cathedrals Measure 1963 and the lease comprises property which forms part of the endowment of a cathedral church, and

(b) compensation is paid as mentioned in paragraph 9(b) above,

the sum received shall be treated as part of that endowment.

12.—(1) Where—

(a) the tenant under the new lease is a diocesan board of finance and the lease comprises diocesan glebe land, and

(b) compensation is paid as mentioned in paragraph 9(b) above,

the sum received shall be paid to the Church Commissioners to be applied for purposes for which the proceeds of any disposition of property by agreement would be applicable under any enactment or Measure authorising such a disposition or disposing of the proceeds of such a disposition.

(2) In this paragraph "diocesan board of finance" and "diocesan glebe land" have the same meaning as in the Endowments and Glebe Measure 1976.

GENERAL NOTE

This schedule deals with the consequences which follows from the landlord's right to terminate a lease for development purposes under s.61.

Para. 2

Tenants may well be able to use these provisions to obtain deferment of possession where the landlord's plans are clearly not yet advanced (see para. 2(3)). Paragraph 2(4) is very important to mortgagees who will be anxious for the court to use its discretion to order the tenants' compensation to be paid into court.

Para. 3

When the tenant loses possession under s.61 obviously all sub-leases also fall regardless of other statutory regimes protecting sub-tenants. Those sub-tenants are entitled to appear in a s.61 application for possession.

Para. 5

This is the nub of a s.61 application. Compensation is awarded as if the tenant had no rights under this Act but subject to existing protected sub-leases *and* on the assumption that its use was (as is) not with the benefit of whatever lucrative planning permission the landlord has obtained. This altogether makes for a depressed level of compensation. Mortgagees who lend on long leases must be aware of this possibility in valuing the security.

Para. 7

This is also very important for mortgagees. The compensation is paid directly to the tenant subject to the possibly large deductions under para. 7(2). Unless the money is ordered to be paid into court under para. 2(4) the mortgagee is substantially at risk.

Para. 8

Applications and proceedings under s.61 (as under other parts of this procedurally tortuous Act) may be used tactically. The costs consequence—para. 8(1) must be carefully noted by those adjoining the parties. Equally punitive are the provisions in para. 8(2) for applications made not in good faith or "dishonestly". The five-year ban on applications may have a disastrous financial effect and this provision should be explicitly drawn to the attention of landlords embarking on a s.61 application.

Section 66   SCHEDULE 15

SECTION 9 OF THE LEASEHOLD REFORM ACT 1967, AS AMENDED

Purchase price and costs of enfranchisement, and tenant's right to withdraw

9.—(1) Subject to subsection (2) below, the price payable for a house and premises on a conveyance under section 8 above shall be the amount which at the relevant time the house and premises, if sold in the open market by a willing seller (with the tenant and members of his family who reside in the house not buying or seeking to buy), might be expected to realise on the following assumptions:—

(a) on the assumption that the vendor was selling for an estate in fee simple, subject to the tenancy but on the assumption that this Part of this Act conferred no right to acquire the freehold, and if the tenancy has not been extended under this Part of this Act, on the assumption that (subject to the landlord's rights under section 17 below) it was to be so extended;

(b) on the assumption that (subject to paragraph (a) above) the vendor was selling subject, in respect of rentcharges to which section 11(2) below applies, to the same annual charge as the conveyance to the tenant is to be subject to, but the purchaser would otherwise be effectively exonerated until the termination of the tenancy from any liability or charge in respect of tenant's incumbrances; and

(c) on the assumption that (subject to paragraphs (a) and (b) above) the vendor was selling with and subject to the rights and burdens with and subject to which the conveyance to the tenant is to be made, and in particular with and subject to such permanent or extended rights and burdens as are to be created in order to give effect to section 10 below.

The reference in this subsection to members of the tenant's family shall be construed in accordance with section 7(7) of this Act.

(1A) Notwithstanding the foregoing subsection, the price payable for a house and premises,—

(i) the rateable value of which was above £1,000 in Greater London and £500 elsewhere on 31st March 1990, or,

(ii) which had no rateable value on that date and R exceeded £16,333 under the formula in section 1(1)(a) above (and section 1(7) above shall apply to that amount as it applies to the amount referred to in subsection (1)(a)(ii) of that section)

shall be the amount which at the relevant time the house and premises, if sold in the open market by a willing seller, might be expected to realise on the following assumptions:—

(a) on the assumption that the vendor was selling for an estate in fee simple, subject to the tenancy, but on the assumption that this Part of this Act conferred no right to acquire the freehold or an extended lease and, where the tenancy has been extended under this Part of this Act, that the tenancy will terminate on the original term date;

(b) on the assumption that at the end of the tenancy the tenant has the right to remain in possession of the house and premises—

(i) if the tenancy is such a tenancy as is mentioned in subsection (2) or subsection (3) of section 186 of the Local Government and Housing Act 1989, or is a tenancy which is a long tenancy at a low rent for the purposes of Part I of the Landlord and Tenant Act 1954 in respect of which the landlord is not able to serve a notice under section 4 of that Act specifying a date of termination earlier than 15th January 1999, under the provisions of Schedule 10 to the Local Government and Housing Act 1989; and

(ii) in any other case under the provisions of Part I of the Landlord and Tenant Act 1954;

(c) on the assumption that the tenant has no liability to carry out any repairs, maintenance or redecorations under the terms of the tenancy or Part I of the Landlord and Tenant Act 1954;

(d) on the assumption that the price be diminished by the extent to which the value of the house and premises has been increased by any improvement carried out by the tenant or his predecessors in title at their own expense;

(e) on the assumption that (subject to paragraph (a) above) the vendor was selling subject, in respect of rentcharges to which section 11(2) below applies, to the same annual charge as the conveyance to the tenant is to be subject to, but the purchaser would otherwise be effectively exonerated until the termination of the tenancy from any liability or charge in respect of tenant's incumbrances; and

(f) on the assumption that (subject to paragraphs (a) and (b) above) the vendor was selling with and subject to the rights and burdens with and subject to which the conveyance to the tenant is to be made, and in particular with and subject to such permanent or extended rights and burdens as are to be created in order to give effect to section 10 below.

(1B) For the purpose of determining whether the rateable value of the house and premises is above £1000 in Greater London, or £500 elsewhere, the rateable value shall be adjusted to take into account any tenant's improvements in accordance with Schedule 8 to the Housing Act 1974.

(1C) Notwithstanding subsection (1) above, the price payable for a house and premises where the right to acquire the freehold arises by virtue of any one or more of the provisions of sections 1A and 1B above shall be determined in accordance with subsection (1A) above; but in any such case—

    (a) if in determining the price so payable there falls to be taken into account any marriage value arising by virtue of the coalescence of the freehold and leasehold interests, the share of the marriage value to which the tenant is to be regarded as being entitled shall not exceed one-half of it; and

    (b) section 9A below has effect for determining whether any additional amount is payable by way of compensation under that section;

and in a case where the provision (or one of the provisions) by virtue of which the right to acquire the freehold arises [in] section 1A(1) above, subsection (1A) above shall apply with the omission of the assumption set out in paragraph (b) of that subsection.

(2) The price payable for the house and premises shall be subject to such deduction (if any) in respect of any defect in the title to be conveyed to the tenant as on a sale in the open market might be expected to be allowed between a willing seller and a willing buyer.

(3) On ascertaining the amount payable, or likely to be payable, as the price for a house and premises in accordance with this section (but not more than one month after the amount payable has been determined by agreement or otherwise), the tenant may give written notice to the landlord that he is unable or unwilling to acquire the house and premises at the price he must pay; and thereupon—

    (a) the notice under section 8 above of his desire to have the freehold shall cease to have effect, and he shall be liable to make such compensation as may be just to the landlord in respect of the interference (if any) by the notice with the exercise by the landlord of his power to dispose of or deal with the house and premises or any neighbouring property; and

    (b) any further notice given under that section with respect to the house or any part of it (with or without other property) shall be void if given within the following three years.

(4) Where a person gives notice of his desire to have the freehold of a house and premises under this Part of this Act, then unless the notice lapses under any provision of this Act excluding his liability, there shall be borne by him (so far as they are incurred in pursuance of the notice) the reasonable costs of or incidental to any of the following matters:—

    (a) any investigation by the landlord of that person's right to acquire the freehold;

    (b) any conveyance or assurance of the house and premises or any part thereof or of any outstanding estate or interest therein;

    (c) deducing, evidencing and verifying the title to the house and premises or any estate or interest therein;

    (d) making out and furnishing such abstracts and copies as the person giving the notice may require;

    (e) any valuation of the house and premises;

but so that this subsection shall not apply to any costs if on a sale made voluntarily a stipulation that they were to be borne by the purchaser would be void.

(5) The landlord's lien (as vendor) on the house and premises for the price payable shall extend—

    (a) to any sums payable by way of rent or recoverable as rent in respect of the house and premises up to the date of the conveyance; and

    (b) to any sums for which the tenant is liable under subsection (4) above; and

    (c) to any other sums due and payable by him to the landlord under or in respect of the tenancy or any agreement collateral thereto.

GENERAL NOTE
The annotations on Chap. III deal with this Schedule.

SCHEDULE 16

SCHEDULE INSERTED AFTER SCHEDULE 6 TO THE HOUSING ACT 1985

SCHEDULE 6A

REDEMPTION OF LANDLORD'S SHARE

Obligation to redeem landlord's share in certain circumstances

1.—(1) The conveyance or grant shall contain a covenant binding on the secure tenant and his successors in title to make to the landlord, immediately after—

(a) the making of a relevant disposal which is not an excluded disposal, or

(b) the expiry of the period of one year beginning with a relevant death,

(whichever first occurs), a final payment, that is to say, a payment of the amount required to redeem the landlord's share.

(2) A disposal is an excluded disposal for the purposes of this paragraph if—

(a) it is a further conveyance of the freehold or an assignment of the lease and the person or each of the persons to whom it is made is, or is the spouse of, the person or one of the persons by whom it is made;

(b) it is a vesting in a person taking under a will or intestacy; or

(c) it is a disposal in pursuance of an order under section 24 of the Matrimonial Causes Act 1973 (property adjustment orders in connection with matrimonial proceedings) or section 2 of the Inheritance (Provision for Family and Dependants) Act 1975 (orders as to financial provision to be made from estate),

and (in any case) an interest to which this paragraph applies subsists immediately after the disposal.

(3) In this paragraph "relevant death" means the death of a person who immediately before his death was the person or, as the case may be, the last remaining person entitled to an interest to which this paragraph applies.

(4) A beneficial interest in the dwelling-house is an interest to which this paragraph applies if the person entitled to it is—

(a) the secure tenant or, as the case may be, one of the secure tenants, or

(b) a qualifying person.

Right to redeem landlord's share at any time

2.—(1) The conveyance or grant shall include provision entitling the secure tenant and his successors in title to make a final payment at any time.

(2) The right shall be exercisable by written notice served on the landlord claiming to make a final payment.

(3) The notice may be withdrawn at any time by written notice served on the landlord.

(4) If the final payment is not tendered to the landlord before the end of the period of three months beginning with the time when the value of the dwelling-house is agreed or determined in accordance with paragraph 8, the notice claiming to make a final payment shall be deemed to have been withdrawn.

Value of landlord's share and amount of final payment

3. The value of the landlord's share shall be determined by the formula—

$$VS = \frac{V \times S}{100}$$

and the amount required to redeem that share shall be determined by the formula—

$$R = VS - D$$

where—

    VS = the value of the landlord's share;

     V = the value of the dwelling-house (agreed or determined in accordance with paragraph 8);

     S = the landlord's share expressed as a percentage;

     R = the amount required to redeem the landlord's share;

     D = the amount of the final discount (if any) which is applicable under paragraphs 4 and 5.

Final discount

4.—(1) Where a final payment is made by, or by two or more persons who include—
(a) the secure tenant or, as the case may be, one of the secure tenants, or
(b) a qualifying person,
the person or persons making the payment are entitled, subject to the following provisions of this paragraph and paragraph 5, to a final discount equal to 20 per cent. of the value of the landlord's share.

(2) Sub-paragraph (1) shall not apply if the final payment is made after the end of the protection period, that is to say, the period of two years beginning with the time when there ceases to be an interest to which this sub-paragraph applies.

(3) A beneficial interest in the dwelling-house is an interest to which sub-paragraph (2) applies if the person entitled to it is—
(a) the secure tenant or, as the case may be, one of the secure tenants, or
(b) a qualifying spouse.

(4) The Secretary of State may by order made with the consent of the Treasury provide that the percentage discount shall be such percentage as may be specified in the order.

(5) An order under this paragraph—
(a) may make different provision with respect to different cases or descriptions of case, including different provision for different areas,
(b) may contain such incidental, supplementary or transitional provisions as appear to the Secretary of State necessary or expedient, and
(c) shall be made by statutory instrument and shall not be made unless a draft of the order has been laid before and approved by resolution of each House of Parliament.

Restrictions on and deductions from final discount

5.—(1) Except where the Secretary of State so determines, a final discount shall not reduce the total purchase price, that is to say, the aggregate of the initial payment, the final payment and any interim payments, below the amount which would be applicable under section 131(1) in respect of the dwelling-house if the relevant time were the time when the value of the dwelling-house is agreed or determined.

(2) The total discount, that is to say, the aggregate of the initial discount, the final discount and any interim discounts, shall not in any case reduce the total purchase price by more than the sum prescribed for the purposes of section 131(2) at the time when the value of the dwelling-house is agreed or determined.

(3) If a final payment is made after the end of the first twelve months of the protection period, there shall be deducted from any final discount given by paragraph 4 and the preceding provisions of this paragraph an amount equal to 50 per cent. of that discount.

(4) There shall be deducted from any final discount given by paragraph 4 and the preceding provisions of this paragraph an amount equal to any previous discount qualifying or, the aggregate of any previous discounts qualifying, under the provisions of section 130.

(5) A determination under this paragraph may make different provision for different cases or descriptions of case, including different provision for different areas.

Right to make interim payment at any time

6.—(1) The conveyance or grant shall include provision entitling the secure tenant and his successors in title at any time to make to the landlord an interim payment, that is to say, a payment which—
(a) is less than the amount required to redeem the landlord's share; but
(b) is not less than 10 per cent. of the value of the dwelling-house (agreed or determined in accordance with paragraph 8).

(2) The right shall be exercisable by written notice served on the landlord, claiming to make an interim payment and stating the amount of the interim payment proposed to be made.

(3) The notice may be withdrawn at any time by written notice served on the landlord.

(4) If the interim payment is not tendered to the landlord before the end of the period of three months beginning with the time when the value of the dwelling-house is agreed or determined in accordance with paragraph 8, the notice claiming to make an interim payment shall be deemed to have been withdrawn.

Landlord's reduced share and interim discount

7. The landlord's share after the making of an interim payment shall be determined by the formula—

$$S = \frac{R - IP}{R} \times PS$$

the amount of the interim discount shall be determined by the formula—

$$ID = \frac{PS \times V}{100} - \frac{S \times V}{100} - IP$$

and the the amount of any previous discount which will be recovered by virtue of the making of an interim payment shall be determined by the formula—

$$RD = \frac{IP}{R} \times PD$$

where—

    S = the landlord's share expressed as a percentage;

    R = the amount which would have been required to redeem the landlord's share immediately before the interim payment was made;

    IP = the amount of the interim payment;

    PS = the landlord's share immediately before the interim payment was made also expressed as a percentage;

    ID = the amount of the interim discount;

    V = the value of the dwelling-house (agreed or determined in accordance with paragraph 8);

    RD = the amount of any previous discount which will be recovered by virtue of the making of the interim payment;

    PD = the amount of any previous discount which would be recovered if the tenant were making the final payment.

Value of dwelling-house

8.—(1) For the purposes of the final payment or any interim payment, the value of a dwelling-house is the amount which for those purposes—

(a) is agreed at any time between the parties, or

(b) in default of such agreement, is determined at any time by an independent valuer,

as the amount which, in accordance with this paragraph, is to be taken as its value at that time.

(2) Subject to sub-paragraph (6), that value shall be taken to be the price which the interest of the secure tenant in the dwelling-house would realise if sold on the open market by a willing vendor—

(a) on the assumption that the liabilities mentioned in sub-paragraph (3) would be discharged by the vendor, and

(b) disregarding the matters specified in sub-paragraph (4).

(3) The liabilities referred to in sub-paragraph (2)(a) are—

(a) any mortgages of the interest of the secure tenant,

(b) the liability under the covenant required by paragraph 1, and

(c) any liability under the covenant required by section 155(3) (repayment of discount on early disposal).

(4) The matters to be disregarded in pursuance of sub-paragraph (2)(b) are—

(a) any interests or rights created over the dwelling-house by the secure tenant,

(b) any improvements made by the secure tenant or any of the persons mentioned in section 127(4) (certain predecessors as secure tenant), and

(c) any failure by the secure tenant or any of those persons—

    (i) where the dwelling-house is a house, to keep the dwelling-house in good repair (including decorative repair);

    (ii) where the dwelling-house is a flat, to keep the interior of the dwelling-house in such repair.

(5) Sub-paragraph (6) applies where, at the time when the value of the dwelling-house is agreed or determined, the dwelling-house—

(a) has been destroyed or damaged by fire, tempest, flood or any other cause against the risk of which it is normal practice to insure, and

(b) has not been fully rebuilt or reinstated.

(6) That value shall be taken to include the value of such of the following as are applicable, namely—

(a) any sums paid or falling to be paid to the secure tenant under a relevant policy in so far as they exceed the cost of any rebuilding or reinstatement which has been carried out;

(b) any rights of the secure tenant under the covenant implied by paragraph 14(3) of Schedule 6 (covenant to rebuild or reinstate); and

(c) any rights of the secure tenant under the covenant implied by paragraph 15(4) of that Schedule (covenant to use best endeavours to secure rebuilding or reinstatement).

(7) In sub-paragraph (6) "relevant policy" means a policy insuring the secure tenant against the risk of fire, tempest or flood or any other risk against which it is normal practice to insure.

(8) References in this paragraph to the secure tenant include references to his successors in title.

Costs of independent valuation

9. The conveyance or grant shall include provision requiring any sums falling to be paid to an independent valuer (whether by way of fees or expenses or otherwise) to be paid by the secure tenant or his successors in title.

No charges to be made by landlord

10. A provision of the conveyance or grant is void in so far as it purports to enable the landlord to charge the tenant or his successors in title a sum in respect of or in connection with he making of a final or interim payment.

Other covenants and provisions

11. Subject to the provisions of this Schedule, the conveyance or grant may include such covenants and provisions as are reasonable in the circumstances.

Interpretation

12.—(1) In this Schedule—
"independent valuer" means an independent valuer appointed in pursuance of provisions in that behalf contained in the conveyance or grant;
"protection period" has the meaning given by paragraph 4(2);
"qualifying person" means a qualifying spouse or a qualifying resident.

(2) A person is a qualifying spouse for the purposes of this Schedule if—
(a) he is entitled to a beneficial interest in the dwelling-house immediately after the time when there ceases to be an interest to which this paragraph applies;
(b) he is occupying the dwelling-house as his only or principal home immediately before that time; and
(c) he is the spouse or surviving spouse of the person who immediately before that time was entitled to the interest to which this paragraph applies or, as the case may be, the last remaining such interest, or is the surviving spouse of a person who immediately before his death was entitled to such an interest;
and any reference in this paragraph to the spouse or surviving spouse of a person includes a reference to a former spouse or surviving former spouse of that person.

(3) A person is a qualifying resident for the purposes of this Schedule if—
(a) he is entitled to a beneficial interest in the dwelling-house immediately after the time when there ceases to be an interest to which this paragraph applies;
(b) he is occupying the dwelling-house as his only or principal home immediately before that time;
(c) he has resided throughout the period of twelve months ending with that time—
(i) with the person who immediately before that time was entitled to the interest to which this paragraph applies or, as the case may be, the last remaining such interest, or
(ii) with two or more persons in succession each of whom was throughout the period of residence with him entitled to such an interest; and
(d) he is not a qualifying spouse.

(4) A beneficial interest in the dwelling-house is an interest to which this paragraph applies if the person entitled to it is the secure tenant or, as the case may be, one of the secure tenants.

(5) References in this Schedule to the secure tenant are references to the secure tenant or tenants to whom the conveyance or grant is made and references to the secure tenant or, as the case may be, one of the secure tenants shall be construed accordingly.

(6) References in this Schedule to the secure tenant's successors in title do not include references to any person entitled to a legal charge having priority to the mortgage required by section 151B (mortgage for securing redemption of landlord's share) or any person whose title derives from such a charge.

GENERAL NOTE
It is not anticipated that the right to purchase on rent to mortgage terms will be very much exercised. A straightforward exercise of the right to buy with the aid of public sector finance will

probably remain the popular route. This schedule deals with the redemption of the landlord's share where the right to buy on rent to mortgage terms has been exercised.

Para. 1
This contains a trap which must be pointed out to any person buying on rent to mortgage terms. The landlord's share must be redeemed within one year of the tenant's death.

Para. 2
This deals with the tenant's right to redeem the landlord's share at any time. Essentially the value of the landlord's share is the value of the landlord's share at the time of redemption calculated in accordance with para. 8 and discounted (by 20 per cent.) under para. 4.

Para. 6
The tenant may redeem the landlord's share in part at any time.

Section 158(2)   SCHEDULE 17

CONSTITUTION OF THE AGENCY

Membership

1.—(1) The Agency shall consist of such number of members (being not less than six) as the Secretary of State may from time to time appoint.

(2) The Secretary of State shall appoint one of the members to be chairman and may, if he thinks fit, appoint another of them to be deputy chairman.

(3) Subject to the provisions of this paragraph, a member of the Agency shall hold and vacate office in accordance with the terms of his appointment.

(4) A person who ceases to be a member of the Agency shall be eligible for reappointment.

(5) A member of the Agency may resign his office by notice in writing to the Secretary of State.

(6) The Secretary of State may remove a member of the Agency from office if he is satisfied that he—
(a) is unable or unfit to carry out the functions of a member;
(b) has not complied with the terms of his appointment; or
(c) has become bankrupt or made an arrangement with his creditors.

(7) A person shall cease to be chairman or deputy chairman of the Agency—
(a) if he resigns as such by notice in writing to the Secretary of State; or
(b) if he ceases to be a member of the Agency.

Remuneration, pensions etc.

2.—(1) The Agency shall pay to its members such remuneration, and such allowances, as the Secretary of State may determine.

(2) The Agency may—
(a) pay such pensions, allowances or gratuities to or in respect of any persons who have been or are its members as the Secretary of State may determine;
(b) make such payments as the Secretary of State may determine towards provision for the payment of pensions, allowances or gratuities to or in respect of any such persons.

(3) If, when a person ceases to be a member of the Agency, the Secretary of State determines that there are special circumstances which make it right that he should receive compensation, the Agency shall pay to him a sum by way of compensation of such amount as the Secretary of State may determine.

(4) The approval of the Treasury shall be required for any determination of the Secretary of State under this paragraph.

Staff

3.—(1) There shall be a chief executive of the Agency who shall be responsible to the Agency for the general exercise of the Agency's functions.

(2) The chief executive shall be appointed by the Agency but no person shall be appointed as chief executive unless the Secretary of State has consented to the appointment.

(3) The Agency may appoint such other number of staff as the Secretary of State may approve.

(4) The terms and conditions of appointment of any person appointed by the Agency under this paragraph shall be determined by the Agency with the consent of the Secretary of State.

(5) The Agency shall pay to members of its staff such remuneration, and such allowances, as it may, with the consent of the Secretary of State, determine.

(6) The Agency may—

(a) pay such pensions, allowances or gratuities to or in respect of any persons who have been or are members of its staff;

(b) make such payments towards provision for the payment of pensions, allowances or gratuities to or in respect of any such persons,

as it may, with the consent of the Secretary of State, determine.

(7) Any reference in sub-paragraph (6) to pensions, allowances or gratuities to or in respect of any such persons as are mentioned in that sub-paragraph includes a reference to payments by way of compensation to or in respect of any members of the Agency's staff who suffer loss of office or employment or loss or diminution of emoluments.

(8) The approval of the Treasury shall be required for the giving of any consent under sub-paragraph (4), (5) or (6).

Delegation of powers

4. Anything authorised or required to be done by the Agency under this Part—

(a) may be done by any member of the Agency, or of its staff, who has been authorised for the purpose, whether generally or specially, by the Agency; or

(b) may be done by any committee or sub-committee of the Agency which has been so authorised.

Proceedings

5.—(1) Subject to the following provisions of this Schedule, the Agency may regulate both its own procedure (including quorum) and that of any committee or sub-committee.

(2) The Secretary of State may give directions as to the exercise by the Agency of its power under sub-paragraph (1) to regulate procedure; and directions under this sub-paragraph may be of a general or particular nature and may be varied or revoked by subsequent directions.

(3) The validity of any proceedings of the Agency or of any committee or sub-committee of the Agency shall not be affected—

(a) by a vacancy amongst the members of the Agency, committee or sub-committee;

(b) by a defect in the appointment of a member of the Agency, committee or sub-committee; or

(c) by a contravention of directions under sub-paragraph (2) or of paragraph 6.

(4) With the consent of the Secretary of State, persons who are not members of the Agency may be appointed as members of a committee or sub-committee of the Agency, but any such committee or sub-committee may not consist entirely of persons who are neither members of the Agency nor members of its staff.

(5) The Agency may pay to any person who is a member of a committee or sub-committee but who is not a member of the Agency such remuneration, and such allowances, as the Secretary of State may, with the approval of the Treasury, determine.

Members' interests

6.—(1) A member of the Agency or of any committee or sub-committee who is directly or indirectly interested in any matter brought up for consideration at a meeting of the Agency or of the committee or sub-committee shall disclose the nature of his interest to the meeting.

(2) Where the matter in respect of which such a disclosure is made is a contract or agreement of any description, the member shall not take part in any deliberation or decision of the Agency, committee or sub-committee with respect to the matter.

(3) Where the matter in respect of which such a disclosure is made is one other than a contract or agreement, the member may take part in any deliberation or decision of the Agency, committee or sub-committee with respect to the matter unless the rest of the members decide that the interest disclosed might prejudicially affect the member's consideration of the matter.

Application of seal and proof of instruments

7.—(1) The application of the seal of the Agency shall be authenticated by the signature of any member of the Agency, or of its staff, who has been authorised by the Agency, whether generally or specially, for the purpose.

(2) Every document purporting to be an instrument issued by the Agency and to be duly sealed with the seal of the Agency or to be signed on behalf of the Agency shall be received in evidence and, unless the contrary is shown, shall be deemed to be an instrument so issued.

House of Commons disqualification

8. In Schedule 1 to the House of Commons Disqualification Act 1975 (bodies of which all

members are disqualified for membership of the House of Commons), in Part II there shall be inserted, at the appropriate place, the following entry—

"The Urban Regeneration Agency.";

and the like insertion shall be made in Part II of Schedule 1 to the Northern Ireland Assembly Disqualification Act 1975.

Section 158(2)   SCHEDULE 18

FINANCES OF THE AGENCY

Financial year

1. The financial years of the Agency shall be as follows—
(a) the period beginning with the commencement of this Schedule and ending with the next following 31st March; and
(b) each successive period of twelve months;

and references in this Schedule to a financial year shall be construed accordingly.

Financial duties

2.—(1) After consultation with the Agency, the Secretary of State may, with the approval of the Treasury, determine the financial duties of the Agency; and different determinations may be made in relation to different functions of the Agency.

(2) The Secretary of State shall give the Agency notice of every determination, and a determination may—
(a) relate to a period beginning before the date on which it is made;
(b) contain incidental or supplementary provisions; and
(c) be varied or revoked by a subsequent determination.

Government grants

3.—(1) The Secretary of State may, out of moneys provided by Parliament and with the approval of the Treasury, pay to the Agency, in respect of the exercise of its functions and in respect of its administrative expenses, such sums as he may, with the approval of the Treasury, determine.

(2) The payment may be made on such terms as the Secretary of State may, with the approval of the Treasury, determine.

Borrowing

4.—(1) The Agency may borrow temporarily, by way of overdraft or otherwise, such sums as it may require for meeting its obligations and exercising its functions—
(a) in sterling from the Secretary of State; or
(b) with the consent of the Secretary of State, or in accordance with any general authority given by the Secretary of State, either in sterling or in a currency other than sterling from a person other than the Secretary of State.

(2) The Agency may borrow otherwise than by way of temporary loan such sums as it may require—
(a) in sterling from the Secretary of State; or
(b) with the consent of the Secretary of State, in a currency other than sterling from a person other than the Secretary of State.

(3) The Secretary of State may lend to the Agency any sums it has power to borrow from him under sub-paragraph (1) or (2).

(4) The Treasury may issue to the Secretary of State out of the National Loans Fund any sums necessary to enable him to make loans under sub-paragraph (3).

(5) Loans made under sub-paragraph (3) shall be repaid to the Secretary of State at such times and by such methods, and interest on the loans shall be paid to him at such times and at such rates, as he may determine.

(6) All sums received by the Secretary of State under sub-paragraph (5) shall be paid into the National Loans Fund.

(7) The approval of the Treasury shall be required for the giving of any consent or authority under sub-paragraph (1) or (2), the making of any loan under sub-paragraph (3) or the making of any determination under sub-paragraph (5).

Guarantees

5.—(1) The Treasury may guarantee, in such manner and on such conditions as they think fit, the repayment of the principal of, and the payment of interest on, any sums which the Agency borrows from a person other than the Secretary of State.

(2) Immediately after a guarantee is given under this paragraph, the Treasury shall lay a statement of the guarantee before each House of Parliament; and, where any sum is issued for fulfilling a guarantee so given, the Treasury shall lay before each House of Parliament a statement relating to that sum, as soon as possible after the end of each financial year—

(a) beginning with that in which the sum is issued; and

(b) ending with that in which all liability in respect of the principal of the sum and in respect of interest on it is finally discharged.

(3) Any sums required by the Treasury for fulfilling a guarantee under this paragraph shall be charged on an issued out of the Consolidated Fund.

(4) If any sums are issued in fulfilment of a guarantee given under this paragraph, the Agency shall make to the Treasury, at such times and in such manner as the Treasury may from time to time direct, payments of such amounts as the Treasury so direct in or towards repayment of the sums so issued and payments of interest, at such rates as the Treasury so direct, on what is outstanding for the time being in respect of sums so issued.

(5) Any sums received by the Treasury in pursuance of sub-paragraph (4) shall be paid into the Consolidated Fund.

Surplus funds

6.—(1) This paragraph applies where it appears to the Secretary of State, after consultation with the Treasury and the Agency, that the Agency has a surplus, whether on capital or on revenue account, after making allowance by way of transfer to reserve or otherwise for its future requirements.

(2) The Agency shall, if the Secretary of State with the approval of the Treasury and after consultation with the Agency so directs, pay to the Secretary of State such sum not exceeding the amount of the surplus as may be specified in the direction.

(3) Any sum received by the Secretary of State under this paragraph shall, subject to sub-paragraph (5), be paid into the Consolidated Fund.

(4) The whole or part of any payment made to the Secretary of State by the Agency under sub-paragraph (2) shall, if the Secretary of State with the approval of the Treasury so determines, be treated as made—

(a) by way of repayment of such part of the principal of loans under paragraph 4(3); and

(b) in respect of the repayments due at such times,

as may be so determined.

(5) Any sum treated under sub-paragraph (4) as a repayment of a loan shall be paid by the Secretary of State into the National Loans Fund.

Financial limits

7.—(1) The aggregate amount at any time of borrowed sums shall not exceed £200 million or such greater sum not exceeding £300 million as the Secretary of State may by order made by statutory instrument specify.

(2) In sub-paragraph (1) "borrowed sums" means sums borrowed by the Agency under paragraph 4 minus repayments made or treated as made in respect of those sums.

(3) No order shall be made under sub-paragraph (1) unless a draft of the order has been laid before and approved by resolution of the House of Commons.

Grants and loans: accounts

8.—(1) The Secretary of State shall prepare in respect of each financial year an account—

(a) of the sums issued to him under paragraph 4(4) and the sums received by him under paragraph 4(5) and of the disposal by him of those sums; and

(b) of the sums paid into the Consolidated Fund or National Loans Fund under paragraph 6.

(2) The Secretary of State shall send the account to the Comptroller and Auditor General before the end of the month of November next following the end of that year.

(3) The Comptroller and Auditor General shall examine, certify and report on the account and lay copies of it and of his report before each House of Parliament.

(4) The form of the account and the manner of preparing it shall be such as the Treasury may direct.

Accounts

9.—(1) The Agency shall keep proper accounts and other records in relation to them.

(2) The accounts and records shall show, in respect of the financial year to which they relate, a true and fair view of the Agency's activities.

(3) The Agency shall prepare in respect of each financial year a statement of accounts complying with any requirement which the Secretary of State has, with the approval of the Treasury, notified in writing to the Agency relating to—

    (a) the information to be contained in the statement;

    (b) the manner in which the information is to be presented; and

    (c) the methods and principles according to which the statement is to be prepared.

(4) Subject to any requirement notified to the Agency under sub-paragraph (3), in preparing any statement of accounts in accordance with that sub-paragraph the Agency shall follow, with respect to each of the matters specified in paragraphs (a) to (c) of that sub-paragraph, such course as may for the time being be approved by the Secretary of State with the consent of the Treasury.

Audit

10.—(1) The Agency's accounts and statements of accounts shall be audited by an auditor to be appointed annually by the Secretary of State.

(2) A person shall not be qualified for appointment under sub-paragraph (1) unless—

    (a) he is eligible for appointment as a company auditor under Part II of the Companies Act 1989 (eligibility for appointment as company auditor); and

    (b) if the Agency were a body to which section 384 of the Companies Act 1985 (duty to appoint auditors) applies, he would not be ineligible for appointment as company auditor of the Agency by virtue of section 27 of the Companies Act 1989 (ineligibility on ground of lack of independence).

Transmission to Secretary of State

11. As soon as the accounts and statement of accounts of the Agency for any financial year have been audited, it shall send to the Secretary of State a copy of the statement, together with a copy of any report made by the auditor on the statement or on the accounts.

Reports

12.—(1) As soon as possible after the end of each financial year, the Agency—

    (a) shall make to the Secretary of State a report dealing generally with its operations during the year; and

    (b) shall include in the report a copy of its audited statement of accounts for that year and such information as the Secretary of State may specify.

(2) The Secretary of State shall lay a copy of the report before each House of Parliament.

Information

13. Without prejudice to paragraph 12, the Agency shall provide the Secretary of State with such information relating to its activities as he may require, and for that purpose—

    (a) shall permit any person authorised by the Secretary of State to inspect and make copies of the accounts, books, documents or papers of the Agency; and

    (b) shall afford such explanation of them as that person or the Secretary of State may reasonably require.

Section 161(4)   SCHEDULE 19

VESTING OF LAND IN THE AGENCY: MODIFICATIONS OF ENACTMENTS

Land Compensation Act 1961 (c.33)

1. The Land Compensation Act 1961 shall have effect in relation to orders under section 161(1) of this Act with the modifications specified in paragraphs 2 to 5.

2. References to the date of service of a notice to treat shall be treated as references to the date on which an order under section 161(1) of this Act comes into force.

3. Section 17(2) (certification of appropriate alternative development) shall be treated as if for the words "the authority proposing to acquire the interest have served a notice to treat in respect thereof, or an agreement has been made for the sale thereof to that authority" there were substituted the words "an order under section 161 of the Leasehold Reform, Housing and Urban Development Act 1993 vesting the land in which the interest subsists in the Urban Regeneration Agency has come into force, or an agreement has been made for the sale of the interest to the Agency".

4. Section 22(2) (interpretation of Part III) shall be treated as if at the end of paragraph (c) there were added the words "or

        (ca) where an order has been made under section 161(1) of the Leasehold Reform,

Housing and Urban Development Act 1993 vesting the land in which the interest subsists in the Urban Regeneration Agency".

5. Any reference to a notice to treat in section 39(2) (interpretation) shall be treated as a reference to an order under section 161(1) of this Act.

Compulsory Purchase (Vesting Declarations) Act 1981 (c.66)

6. In section 15 of the Compulsory Purchase (Vesting Declarations) Act 1981 (application to orders under section 141 of Local Government, Planning and Land Act 1980) after the words "vesting declaration)" there shall be inserted the words "or under subsection (1) of section 161 of the Leasehold Reform, Housing and Urban Development Act 1993 (subsection (4) of which makes similar provision)"

7.—(1) In Schedule 2 to that Act (vesting of land in urban development corporation), in paragraph 1 after the words "similar provision)" there shall be inserted the words "or under subsection (1) of section 161 of the Leasehold Reform, Housing and Urban Development Act 1993 (subsection (4) of which contains similar provision)".

(2) In paragraph 3(a) of that Schedule for the words "or, as the case may be, the housing action trust" there shall be substituted the words "the housing action trust or the Urban Regeneration Agency (as the case may be)".

GENERAL NOTE

For the purposes of compensation where land is vested in the Agency under s.161, the provisions of the Land Compensation Act 1961 apply, which deal with land compulsorily acquired, subject to certain exceptions.

Para. 2

The date of service of notice to treat fixes the date for calculation of compensation in compulsory purchase. For land vested under s.161 the equivalent date is the date of the vesting order made under s.161(1).

Para. 3

A certificate of appropriate alternative development indicates the kind of development which is to be assumed for the purposes of compensation on a compulsory purchase order. This paragraph provides that the making of an order under the Act shall be treated as being substituted for the service of a notice to treat for certain purposes relating to applications for certificates of appropriate alternative development.

Para. 4

Section 22(2) of the 1961 Act sets out certain circumstances where an interest in land is taken to be an interest proposed to be acquired by a compulsory purchase order authority. These are extended to include where an order under s.161 of this Act has been made.

Paras. 6 and 7

The Compulsory Purchase (Vesting Declarations) Act 1981 creates the power for acquiring authorities to vest land in themselves once a compulsory purchase order has come into operation by means of a vesting declaration. Section 15 of the 1981 Act provided that orders under s.161 of the 1980 Act had the same effect as a vesting declaration subject to certain qualifications in Sched. 2 to the 1981 Act. Paragraph 6 extends that provision to orders under s.161 of this Act. Paragraph 7 makes consequential extensions to the qualifications in Sched. 2 to the 1981 Act.

Section 169   SCHEDULE 20

THE AGENCY: LAND

PART I

MODIFICATIONS OF ACQUISITION OF LAND ACT 1981

1. The Acquisition of Land Act 1981 (in this Part of this Schedule referred to as "the 1981 Act") shall have effect in relation to the compulsory acquisition of land under this Part of this Act with the modifications specified in paragraph 2 and 3.

2.—(1) Where a compulsory purchase order authorising the acquisition of and land is submitted to the Secretary of State in accordance with section 2(2) of the 1981 Act (procedure for authorisation), then if the Secretary of State—

(a) is satisfied that the order ought to be confirmed so far as it relates to part of the land comprised in it, but

(b) has not for the time being determined whether it ought to be confirmed so far as it relates to any other such land,

he may confirm the order so far as it relates to the land mentioned in paragraph (a), and give directions postponing the consideration of the order, so far as it relates to any other land specified in the directions, until such time as may be so specified.

(2) Where the Secretary of State gives directions under sub-paragraph (1), the notices required by section 15 of the 1981 Act (notices after confirmation of order) to be published and served shall include a statement of the effect of the directions.

3. The reference in section 17(3) of the 1981 Act (local authority and statutory undertakers' land) to statutory undertakers includes a reference to the Agency.

PART II

LAND: SUPPLEMENTARY

Extinguishment of rights over land

4.—(1) Subject to this paragraph, on an order under section 161(1) of this Act coming into force or the completion by the Agency of a compulsory acquisition of land under this Part of this Act—

(a) all private rights of way of laying down, erecting, continuing or maintaining any apparatus on, under or over the land shall be extinguished; and

(b) any such apparatus shall vest in the Agency.

(2) Sub-paragraph (1) does not apply—

(a) to any right vested in, or apparatus belonging to, statutory undertakers for the purposes of carrying on their undertaking; or

(b) to any right conferred by or in accordance with the telecommunications code on the operator of a telecommunications code system or to any telecommunications apparatus kept installed for the purposes of any such system.

(3) In respect of any right or apparatus not falling within sub-paragraph (2), sub-paragraph (1) shall have effect subject to—

(a) any direction given by the Secretary of State before the coming into force of the order or by the Agency before the completion of the acquisition (as the case may be) that sub-paragraph (1) shall not apply to any right or apparatus specified in the direction, and

(b) any agreement which may be made (whether before or after the coming into force of the order or completion of the acquisition) between the Secretary of State or the Agency and the person in or to whom the right or apparatus in question is vested or belongs.

(4) Any person who suffers loss by the extinguishment of a right or the vesting of any apparatus under this paragraph shall be entitled to compensation from the Agency.

(5) Any compensation payable under this paragraph shall be determined in accordance with the Land Compensation Act 1961.

Power to override easements

5.—(1) The erection, construction, carrying out, or maintenance of any building or work on land which has been vested in or acquired by the Agency under this Part of this Act, whether done by the Agency or by any other person, is authorised by virtue of this paragraph if it is done in accordance with planning permission, notwithstanding that it involves—

(a) interference with an interest or right to which this paragraph applies; or

(b) a breach of a restriction as to the user of land arising by virtue of a contract.

(2) Nothing in sub-paragraph (1) shall authorise interference with any right of way or right of laying down, erecting, continuing or maintaining apparatus on, under or over land, being—

(a) a right vested in or belonging to statutory undertakers for the purpose of the carrying on of their undertaking; or

(b) a right conferred by or in accordance with the telecommunications code on the operator of a telecommunications code system.

(3) This paragraph applies to the following interests and rights, that is to say, any easement, liberty, privilege, right or advantage annexed to land an adversely affecting other land, including any natural right to support.

(4) In respect of any interference or breach in pursuance of sub-paragraph (1), compensation shall be payable under section 7 or 10 of the Compulsory Purchase Act 1965, to be assessed in the same manner and subject to the same rules as in the case of other compensation under those sections in respect of injurious affection where the compensation is to be estimated in connec-

tion with a purchase by the Agency or the injury arises from the execution of works on land acquired by the Agency.

(5) Where a person other than the Agency—

(a) is liable to pay compensation of virtue of sub-paragraph (4); and

(b) fails to discharge that liability,

the liability shall (subject to sub-paragraph (6)) be enforceable against the Agency.

(6) Nothing in sub-paragraph (5) shall be construed as affecting any agreement between the Agency and any other person for indemnifying the Agency against any liability under that sub-paragraph.

(7) Nothing in this paragraph shall be construed as authorising any act or omission on the part of any person which is actionable at the suit of any person on any grounds other than such an interference or breach as is mentioned in sub-paragraph (1).

(8) Nothing in this paragraph shall be construed as authorising any act or omission on the part of the Agency or any body corporate in contravention of any limitation imposed by law on its capacity by virtue of its constitution.

Consecrated land and burial grounds

6.—(1) Any consecrated land, whether including a building or not, which has been vested in or acquired by the Agency under this Part of this Act may (subject to the following provisions of this paragraph) be used by the Agency, or by any other person, in any manner in accordance with planning permission, notwithstanding any obligation or restriction imposed under ecclesiastical law or otherwise in respect of consecrated land.

(2) Sub-paragraph (1) does not apply to land which consists or forms part of a burial ground.

(3) Any use of consecrated land authorised by sub-paragraph (1), and the use of any land, not being consecrated land, vested or acquired as mentioned in that sub-paragraph which at the time of vesting or acquisition included a church or other building used or formerly used for religious worship or the site thereof, shall be subject to compliance with the prescribed requirements with respect to—

(a) the removal and reinterment of any human remains; and

(b) the disposal of monuments,

and, in the case of consecrated land, shall be subject to such provisions as may be prescribed for prohibiting or restricting the use of the land, either absolutely or until the prescribed consent has been obtained, so long as any church or other building used or formerly used for religious worship, or any part thereof, remains on the land.

(4) Any regulations made for the purposes of sub-paragraph (3)—

(a) shall contain such provisions as appear to the Secretary of State to be requisite for securing that any use of land which is subject to compliance with the regulations shall, as nearly as may be, be subject to the like control as is imposed by law in the case of a similar use authorised by an enactment not contained in this Act or by a Measure, or as it would be proper to impose on a disposal of the land in question otherwise than in pursuance of an enactment or Measure;

(b) shall contain requirements relating to the disposal of any such land as is mentioned in sub-paragraph (3) such as appear to the Secretary of State requisite for securing that the provisions of that sub-paragraph shall be complied with in relation to the use of the land; and

(c) may contain such incidental and consequential provisions (including provision as to the closing of registers) as appear to the Secretary of State to be expedient for the purposes of the regulations.

(5) Any land consisting of a burial ground which has been vested in or acquired by the Agency under this Part of this Act may be used by the Agency in any manner in accordance with planning permission, notwithstanding anything in any enactment relating to burial grounds or any obligation or restriction imposed under ecclesiastical law or otherwise in respect of burial grounds.

(6) Sub-paragraphs (5) shall not have effect in respect of any land which has been used for the burial of the dead until the prescribed requirements with respect to the removal and reinterment of human remains and the disposal of monuments in or upon the land have been complied with.

(7) Provision shall be made by any regulations made for the purposes of sub-paragraphs (3) and (6)—

(a) for requiring the persons in whom the land is vested to publish notice of their intention to carry out the removal and reinterment of any human remains or the disposal of any monuments;

(b) for enabling the personal representatives or relatives of any deceased person themselves to undertake the removal and reinterment of the remains of the deceased and the disposal of any monument commemorating the deceased, and for requiring the persons in whom the land is vested to defray the expenses of such removal, reinterment and disposal, not exceeding such amount as may be prescribed;

(c) for requiring compliance with such reasonable conditions (if any) as may be imposed, in the case of consecrated land, by the bishop of the diocese, with respect to the manner of removal and the place and manner of reinterment of any human remains and the disposal of any monuments; and

(d) for requiring compliance with any directions given in any case by the Secretary of State with respect to the removal and reinterment of any human remains.

(8) Subject to the provisions of any such regulations as are referred to in sub-paragraph (7), no faculty shall be required—

(a) for the removal and reinterment in accordance with the regulations of any human remains; or

(b) for the removal or disposal of any monuments;

and the provisions of section 25 of the Burial Act 1857 (which prohibits the removal of human remains without the licence of the Secretary of State except in certain cases) shall not apply to a removal carried out in accordance with the regulations.

(9) Any power conferred by this paragraph to use land in a manner therein mentioned shall be construed as a power so to use the land, whether or not it involves—

(a) the erection, construction or carrying out of any building or work; or

(b) the maintenance of any building or work.

(10) Nothing in this paragraph shall be construed as authorising any act or omission on the part of any person which is actionable at the suit of any person on any grounds other than contravention of any such obligation, restriction or enactment as is mentioned in sub-paragraph (1) or (5).

(11) Sub-paragraph (8) of paragraph 5 shall apply in relation to this paragraph as it applies in relation to that.

(12) In this paragraph—

"burial ground" includes any churchyard, cemetery or other ground, whether consecrated or not, which has at any time been set apart for the purposes of interment; and

"monument" includes a tombstone or other memorial.

(13) In this paragraph "prescribed" means prescribed by regulations made by the Secretary of State.

(14) The power to make regulations under this paragraph shall be exercisable by statutory instrument which shall be subject to annulment in pursuance of a resolution of either House of Parliament.

Open spaces

7.—(1) Any land being, or forming part of, a common, open space or fuel or field garden allotment, which has been vested in or acquired by the Agency under this Part of this Act may be used by the Agency, or by any other person, in any manner in accordance with planning permission, notwithstanding anything in any enactment—

(a) relating to land of that kind; or

(b) by which the land is specially regulated.

(2) Nothing in this paragraph shall be construed as authorising any act or omission on the part of any person which is actionable at the suit of any person on any grounds other than contravention of any such enactment as is mentioned in sub-paragraph (1).

(3) Sub-paragraph (8) of paragraph 5 shall apply in relation to this paragraph as it applies in relation to that.

Displacement of persons

8. If the Secretary of State certifies that possession of a house which—

(a) has been vested in or acquired by the Agency under this Part of this Act; and

(b) is for the time being held by the Agency for the purposes of its objects,

is immediately required for those purposes, nothing in the Rent (Agriculture) Act 1976, the Rent Act 1977 or the Housing Act 1988 shall prevent the Agency from obtaining possession of the house.

Extinguishment of public rights of way

9.—(1) Where any land—

(a) has been vested in or acquired by the Agency under this Part of this Act; and

(b) is for the time being held by the Agency for the purposes of its objects,

the Secretary of State may by order extinguish any public right of way over the land.

(2) Where the Secretary of State proposes to make an order under this paragraph, he shall—
(a) publish in such manner as appears to him to be requisite a notice—
    (i) stating the effect of the order, and
    (ii) specifying the time (not being less than 28 days from the publication of the notice) within which, and the manner in which, objections to the proposal may be made; and
(b) serve a like notice—
    (i) on the local planning authority in whose area the land is situated; and
    (ii) on the relevant highway authority.
(3) In sub-paragraph (2) "the relevant highway authority" means any authority which is a highway authority in relation to the right of way proposed to be extinguished by the order under this paragraph.
(4) Where an objection to a proposal to make an order under this paragraph is duly made and is not withdrawn, the provisions of paragraph 10 shall have effect in relation to the proposal.
(5) For the purposes of this paragraph an objection to such a proposal shall not be treated as duly made unless—
(a) it is made within the time and in the manner specified in the notice required by this paragraph; and
(b) a statement in writing of the grounds of the objection is comprised in or submitted with the objection.
10.—(1) In this paragraph any reference to making a final decision, in relation to an order, is a reference to deciding whether to make the order or what modification, if any, ought to be made.
(2) Unless the Secretary of State decides apart from the objection not to make the order, or decides to make a modification which is agreed to by the objector as meeting the objection, the Secretary of State—
(a) shall, before making a final decision, consider the grounds of the objection as set out in the statement comprised in or submitted with the objection; and
(b) may, if he thinks fit, require the objector to submit within a specified period a further statement in writing as to any of the matters to which the objection relates.
(3) In so far as the Secretary of State, after considering the grounds of the objection as set out in the original statement and in any such further statement, is satisfied that the objection relates to a matter which can be dealt with in the assessment of compensation, he may treat the objection as irrelevant for the purpose of making a final decision.
(4) In any case where—
(a) after considering the grounds of the objection as set out in the original statement and in any such further statement, the Secretary of State is satisfied that, for the purpose of making a final decision, he is sufficiently informed as to the matters to which the objection relates; or
(b) a further statement has been required but is not submitted within the specified period, the Secretary of State may make a final decision without further investigation as to the matters to which the objection relates.
(5) Subject to sub-paragraphs (3) and (4), the Secretary of State, before making a final decision, shall afford to the objector an opportunity of appearing before, and being heard by, a person appointed for the purpose by the Secretary of State; and if the objector avails himself of that opportunity, the Secretary of State shall afford an opportunity of appearing and being heard on the same occasion—
(a) to the Agency; and
(b) to any other persons to whom it appears to the Secretary of State to be expedient to afford such an opportunity.
(6) Notwithstanding anything in the preceding provisions of this paragraph, if it appears to the Secretary of State that the matters to which the objection relates are such as to require investigation by public local inquiry before he makes a final decision, he shall cause such an inquiry to be held; and where he determines to cause such an inquiry to be held, any of the requirements of those provisions to which effect has not been given at the time of that determination shall be dispensed with.

Telegraphic lines

11.—(1) Where an order under paragraph 9 extinguishing a public right of way is made and at the time of the publication of the notice required by sub-paragraph (2) of that paragraph any telecommunication apparatus was kept installed for the purposes of a telecommunications code system under, in, on, over, along or across the land over which the right of way subsisted—
(a) the power of the operator of the system to remove the apparatus shall, notwithstanding the making of the order, be exercisable at any time not later than the end of the period of

three months from the date on which the right of way is extinguished and shall be exercisable in respect of the whole or any part of the apparatus after the end of that period if before the end of that period the operator of the system has given notice to the Agency of his intention to remove the apparatus or that part of it, as the case may be;

(b) the operator of the system may by notice given in that behalf to the Agency not later than the end of the said period of three months abandon the telecommunication apparatus or any part of it;

(c) subject to paragraph (b), the operator of the system shall be deemed at the end of that period to have abandoned any part of the apparatus which he has then neither removed nor given notice of his intention to remove;

(d) the operator of the system shall be entitled to recover from the Agency the expense of providing, in substitution for the apparatus and any other telecommunication apparatus connected with it which is rendered useless in consequence of the removal or abandonment of the first-mentioned apparatus, any telecommunication apparatus in such other place as the operator may require; and

(e) where under the preceding provisions of this sub-paragraph the operator of the system has abandoned the whole or any part of any telecommunication apparatus, that apparatus or that part of it shall vest in the Agency and shall be deemed, with its abandonment, to cease to be kept installed for the purposes of a telecommunications code system.

(2) As soon as practicable after the making of an order under paragraph 9 extinguishing a public right of way in circumstances in which sub-paragraph (1) applies in relation to the operator of any telecommunications code system, the Secretary of State shall give notice to the operator of the making of the order.

Statutory undertakers

12.—(1) Where any land has been vested in or acquired by the Agency under this Part of this Act and—

(a) there subsists over that land a right vested in or belonging to statutory undertakers for the purpose of the carrying on of their undertaking, being a right of way or a right of laying down, erecting, continuing or maintaining apparatus on, under or over that land, or

(b) there is on, under or over the land apparatus vested in or belonging to statutory undertakers for the purpose of the carrying on of their undertaking,

the Agency may serve on the statutory undertakers a notice stating that, at the end of the period of 28 days from the date of service of the notice or such longer period as may be specified therein, the right will be extinguished or requiring that, before the end of that period, the apparatus shall be removed.

(2) The statutory undertakers on whom a notice is served under sub-paragraph (1) may, before the end of the period of 28 days from the service of the notice, serve a counter-notice on the Agency stating that they object to all or any provisions of the notice and specifying the grounds of their objection.

(3) If no counter-notice is served under sub-paragraph (2)—

(a) any right to which the notice relates shall be extinguished at the end of the period specified in that behalf in the notice; and

(b) if, at the end of the period so specified in relation to any apparatus, any requirement of the notice as to the removal of the apparatus has not been complied with, the Agency may remove the apparatus and dispose of it in any way it may think fit.

(4) If a counter-notice is served under sub-paragraph (2) on the Agency, it may either withdraw the notice (without prejudice to the service of a further notice) or apply to the Secretary of State and the appropriate Minister for an order under this paragraph embodying the provisions of the notice with or without modification.

(5) Where by virtue of this paragraph any right vested in or belonging to statutory undertakers is extinguished, or any requirement is imposed on statutory undertakers, those undertakers shall be entitled to compensation from the Agency.

(6) Sections 280 and 282 of the Town and Country Planning Act 1990 (measure of compensation to statutory undertakers) shall apply to compensation under sub-paragraph (5) as they apply to compensation under section 279(4) of that Act.

(7) Except in a case where paragraph 11 applies—

(a) the reference in paragraph (a) of sub-paragraph (1) to a right vested in or belonging to statutory undertakers for the purpose of the carrying on of their undertaking shall include a reference to a right conferred by or in accordance with the telecommunications code on the operator of a telecommunications code system; and

(b) the reference in paragraph (b) of that sub-paragraph to apparatus vested in or belonging to statutory undertakers for the purpose of the carrying on of their undertaking shall include a reference to telecommunication apparatus kept installed for the purposes of any such system.

(8) Where paragraph (a) or (b) of sub-paragraph (1) has effect as mentioned in sub-paragraph (7), in the rest of this paragraph and in paragraph 13—

(a) any reference to statutory undertakers shall have effect as a reference to the operator of any such system as is referred to in sub-paragraph (7); and

(b) any reference to the appropriate Minister shall have effect as a reference to the Secretary of State for Trade and Industry.

13.—(1) Before making an order under paragraph 12 the Secretary of State and the appropriate Minister—

(a) shall afford to the statutory undertakers on whom notice was served under paragraph 12(1) an opportunity of objecting to the application for the order; and

(b) if any objection is made, shall consider the objection and afford to those statutory undertakers and to the Agency an opportunity of appearing before and being heard by a person appointed by the Secretary of State and the appropriate Minister for the purpose;

and the Secretary of State and the appropriate Minister may then, if they think fit, make the order in accordance with the application either with or without modification.

(2) Where an order is made under paragraph 12—

(a) any right to which the order relates shall be extinguished at the end of the period specified in that behalf in the order; and

(b) if, at the end of the period so specified in relation to any apparatus, any requirement of the order as to the removal of the apparatus has not been complied with, the Agency may remove the apparatus and dispose of it in any way it may think fit.

14.—(1) Subject to this paragraph, where any land has been vested in or acquired by the Agency under this Part of this Act and—

(a) there is on, under or over the land apparatus vested in or belonging to statutory undertakers, and

(b) the undertakers claim that development to be carried out on the land is such as to require, on technical or other grounds connected with the carrying on of their undertaking, the removal or re-siting of the apparatus affected by the development.

the undertakers may serve on the Agency a notice claiming the right to enter on the land and carry out such works for the removal or re-siting of the apparatus or any part of it as may be specified in the notice.

(2) Where, after the land has been vested or acquired as mentioned in sub-paragraph (1), development of the land is begun to be carried out, no notice under this paragraph shall be served later than 21 days after the beginning of the development.

(3) Where a notice is served under this paragraph the Agency may, before the end of the period of 28 days from the date of service, serve on the statutory undertakers a counter-notice stating that its objects to all or any of the provisions of the notice and specifying the grounds of its objection.

(4) If no counter-notice is served under sub-paragraph (3), the statutory undertakers shall, after the end of the said period of 28 days, have the rights claimed in their notice.

(5) If a counter-notice is served under sub-paragraph (3), the statutory undertakers who served the notice under this paragraph may either withdraw it or apply to the Secretary of State and the appropriate Minister for an order under this paragraph conferring on the undertakers—

(a) the rights claimed in the notice; or

(b) such modified rights as the Secretary of State and the appropriate Minister think it expedient to confer on them.

(6) Where by virtue of this paragraph or an order made by the Secretary of State and the appropriate Minister under it, statutory undertakers have the right to execute works for the removal or re-siting of apparatus, they may arrange with the Agency for the works to be carried out by the Agency, under the superintendence of the undertakers, instead of by the undertakers themselves.

(7) Where works are carried out for the removal or re-siting of statutory undertakers' apparatus, being works which the undertakers have the right to carry out by virtue of this paragraph or an order made by the Secretary of State and the appropriate Minister under it, the undertakers shall be entitled to compensation from the Agency.

(8) Sections 280 and 282 of the Town and Country Planning Act 1990 (measure of compensation to statutory undertakers) shall apply to compensation under sub-paragraph (7) as they apply to compensation under section 279(4) of that Act.

(9) In sub-paragraph (1)(a), the reference to apparatus vested in or belonging to statutory undertakers shall include a reference to telecommunication apparatus kept installed for the purposes of a telecommunications code system.

(10) Where sub-paragraph (1)(a) has effect as mentioned in sub-paragraph (9), in the rest of this paragraph—

(a) any reference to statutory undertakers shall have effect as a reference to the operator of any such system as is referred to in sub-paragraph (9); and

(b) any reference to the appropriate Minister shall have effect as a reference to the Secretary of State for Trade and Industry.

15.—(1) The powers conferred by this paragraph shall be exercisable where, on a representation made by statutory undertakers, it appears to the Secretary of State and the appropriate Minister to be expedient that the powers and duties of those undertakers should be extended or modified, in order—

(a) to secure the provision of services which would not otherwise be provided, or which would not otherwise be satisfactorily provided, in relation to relevant land; or

(b) to facilitate an adjustment of the carrying on of the undertaking necessitated by any of the acts and events mentioned in sub-paragraph (2).

(2) The said acts and events are—

(a) the vesting in or acquisition by the Agency under this Part of this Act of any land in which an interest was held, or which was used, for the purpose of the carrying on of the undertaking of the statutory undertakers in question; and

(b) the extinguishment of a right or the imposition of any requirements by virtue of paragraph 12.

(3) The powers conferred by this paragraph shall also be exercisable where, on a representation made by the Agency, it appears to the Secretary of State and the appropriate Minister to be expedient that the powers and duties of statutory undertakers should be extended or modified, in order to secure the provision of new services, or the extension of existing services, in relation to relevant land.

(4) Where the powers conferred by this paragraph are exercisable, the Secretary of State and the appropriate Minister may, if they think fit, by order provide for such extension or modification of the powers and duties of the statutory undertakers as appears to them to be requisite in order to secure—

(a) the provision of the services in question, as mentioned in sub-paragraph (1)(a) or sub-paragraph (3); or

(b) the adjustment in question, as mentioned in sub-paragraph (1)(b),

as the case may be.

(5) Without prejudice to the generality of sub-paragraph (4), an order under this paragraph may make provision—

(a) for empowering the statutory undertakers to acquire (whether compulsorily or by agreement) any land specified in the order, and to erect or construct any buildings or works so specified;

(b) for applying, in relation to the acquisition of any such land or the construction of any such works, enactments relating to the acquisition of land and the construction of works;

(c) where it has been represented that the making of the order is expedient for the purposes mentioned in sub-paragraph (1)(a) or (3), for giving effect to such financial arrangements between the Agency and the statutory undertakers as they may agree, or as, in default of agreement, may be determined to be equitable in such manner and by such tribunal as may be specified in the order; and

(d) for such incidental and supplemental matters as appear to the Secretary of State and the appropriate Minister to be expedient for the purposes of the order.

(6) In this paragraph "relevant land" means land in respect of which any of the functions of the Agency under this Part of this Act are being or have been exercised.

16.—(1) As soon as may be after making such a representation as is mentioned in sub-paragraph (1) or (3) of paragraph 15—

(a) the statutory undertakers, in a case falling within sub-paragraph (1), or

(b) the Agency, in a case falling within sub-paragraph (3),

shall publish, in such form and manner as may be directed by the Secretary of State and the appropriate Minister, a notice giving such particulars as may be so directed of the matters to which the representation relates, and specifying the time within which, and the manner in which, objections to the making of an order on the representation may be made, and shall also, if it is so directed by the Secretary of State and the appropriate Minister, serve a like notice on such persons, or persons of such classes, as may be so directed.

(2) Orders under paragraph 15 shall be subject to special parliamentary procedure.

17.—(1) Where, on a representation made by statutory undertakers, the appropriate Minister is satisfied that the fulfilment of any obligations incurred by those undertakers in connection with the carrying out of their undertaking has been rendered impracticable by an act or event to which this sub-paragraph applies, the appropriate Minister may, if he thinks fit, by order direct that the statutory undertakers shall be relieved of the fulfilment of that obligation, either absolutely or to such extent as may be specified in the order.

(2) Sub-paragraph (1) applies to the following acts and events—

(a) the vesting in or acquisition by the Agency under this 1 Part of this Act of any land in which an interest was held, or which was used, for the purpose of the carrying on of the undertaking of the statutory undertakers; and

(b) the extinguishment of a right or the imposition of any requirement by virtue of paragraph 12.

(3) As soon as may be after making a representation to the appropriate Minister under sub-paragraph (1), the statutory undertakers shall, as may be directed by the appropriate Minister, do either or both of the following, that is to say—

(a) publish (in such form and manner as may be so directed) a notice—
  (i) giving such particulars as may be so directed of the matters to which the representation relates; and
  (ii) specifying the time within which, and the manner in which, objection to the making of an order on the representation may be made; and
(b) serve a like notice on such persons, or persons of such classes, as may be so directed.

(4) If any objection to the making of an order under this paragraph is duly made and is not withdrawn before the order is made, the order shall be subject to special parliamentary procedure.

(5) Immediately after an order is made under this paragraph by the appropriate Minister, he shall publish a notice stating that the order has been made and naming a place where a copy of it may be seen at all reasonable hours, and shall serve a like notice—

(a) on any person who duly made an objection to the order and has sent to the appropriate Minister a request in writing to serve him with the notice required by this sub-paragraph, specifying an address for service; and
(b) on such other persons (if any) as the appropriate Minister thinks fit.

(6) Subject to the following provisions of this paragraph, an order under this paragraph shall become operative on the date on which the notice required by sub-paragraph (5) is first published.

(7) When in accordance with sub-paragraph (4) the order is subject to special parliamentary procedure, sub-paragraph (6) shall not apply

(8) If any person aggrieved by an order under this paragraph wishes to question the validity of the order on the ground—

(a) that it is not within the powers conferred by this paragraph, or
(b) that any requirement of this paragraph has not been complied with in relation to the order,

he may, within six weeks from the date on which the notice required by sub-paragraph (5) is first published, make an application to the High Court under this paragraph.

(9) On any application under sub-paragraph (8) the High Court—

(a) may by interim order wholly or in part suspend the operation of the order, either generally or in so far as it affects any property of the applicant, until the final determination of the proceedings; and
(b) if satisfied—
  (i) that the order is wholly or to any extent outside the powers conferred by this paragraph; or
  (ii) that the interests of the applicant have been substantially prejudiced by the failure to comply with any requirement of this paragraph,
  may wholly or in part quash the order, either generally or in so far as it affects any property of the applicant.

(10) Subject to sub-paragraph (8), the validity of an order under this paragraph shall not be questioned in any legal proceedings whatsoever, either before or after the order has been made.

18.—(1) For the purposes of paragraphs 15 and 17, an objection to the making of an order thereunder shall not be treated as duly made unless—

(a) the objection is made within the time and in the manner specified in the notice required by paragraph 16 or 17 (as the case may be); and
(b) a statement in writing of the grounds of the objection is comprised in or submitted with the objection.

(2) Where an objection to the making of such an order is duly made in accordance with sub-paragraph (1) and is not withdrawn, the following provisions of this paragraph shall have effect in relation thereto; but, in the application of those provisions to an order under paragraph 15, any reference to the appropriate Minister shall be construed as a reference to the Secretary of State and the appropriate Minister.

(3) Unless the appropriate Minister decides apart from the objection not to make the order, or decides to make a modification which is agreed to by the objector as meeting the objection, the appropriate Minister, before making a final decision—

(a) shall consider the grounds of the objection as set out in the statement; and
(b) may, if he thinks fit, require the objector to submit within a specified period a further statement in writing as to any of the matters to which the objection relates.

(4) In so far as the appropriate Minister after considering the grounds of the objection as set out in the original statement and in any such further statement, is satisfied that the objection

relates to a matter which can be dealt with in the assessment of compensation, the appropriate Minister may treat the objection as irrelevant for the purpose of making a final decision.

(5) In any case where—

(a) after considering the grounds of the objection as set out in the original statement and in any such further statement, the appropriate Minister is satisfied that, for the purpose of making a final decision, he is sufficiently informed as to the matters to which the objection relates; or

(b) a further statement has been required but is not submitted within the specified period,

the appropriate Minister may make a final decision without further investigation as to the matters to which the objection relates.

(6) Subject to sub-paragraphs (4) and (5), the appropriate Minister, before making a final decision, shall afford to the objector an opportunity of appearing before, and being heard by, a person appointed for the purpose by the appropriate Minister; and if the objector avails himself of that opportunity, the appropriate Minister shall afford an opportunity of appearing and being heard on the same occasion—

(a) to the person (being the Agency or the statutory undertakers) on whose representation the order is proposed to be made; and

(b) to any other persons to whom it appears to the appropriate Minister to be expedient to afford such an opportunity.

(7) Notwithstanding anything in the preceding provisions of this paragraph, if it appears to the appropriate Minister that the matters to which the objection relates are such as to require investigation by public local inquiry before he makes a final decision, he shall cause such an inquiry to be held; and where he determines to cause such an inquiry to be held, any of the requirements of those provisions to which effect has not been given at the time of that determination shall be dispensed with.

(8) In this paragraph any reference to making a final decision, in relation to an order, is a reference to deciding whether to make the order or what modification (if any) ought to be made.

Interpretation

19.—(1) Any expression used in this Part of this Schedule to which a meaning is assigned by paragraph 1 of Schedule 4 to the Telecommunications Act 1984 has that meaning in this Part.

(2) In this Part of this Schedule "statutory undertakers" means persons who are or are deemed to be statutory undertakers for the purposes of any provision of Part XI of the Town and Country Planning Act 1990; and "statutory undertaking" shall be construed in accordance with section 262 of that Act (meaning of "statutory undertaker").

(3) In this Part of this Schedule "the appropriate Minister" shall be construed as if contained in Part XI the Town and Country Planning Act 1990; and any reference to the Secretary of State and the appropriate Minister shall be similarly construed.

PART III

ACQUISITION OF RIGHTS

20.—(1) The Compulsory Purchase Act 1965 (in this Part of this Schedule referred to as "the 1965 Act") shall have effect with the modifications necessary to make it apply to the compulsory acquisition of rights by virtue of section 162(2) of this Act as it applies to the compulsory purchase of land so that, in appropriate contexts, references in the 1965 Act to land are read as referring, or as including references, to the rights or to land over which the rights are or are to be exercisable, according to the requirements of the particular context.

(2) Without prejudice to the generality of sub-paragraph (1), in relation to the acquisition of rights by virtue of section 162(2) of this Act—

(a) Part I of the 1965 Act (which relates to compulsory purchases under the Acquisition of Land Act 1981) shall have effect with the modifications specified in paragraphs 21 to 23; and

(b) the enactments relating to compensation for the compulsory purchase of land shall apply with the necessary modifications as they apply to such compensation.

21. For section 7 of the 1965 Act (which relates to compensation) there shall be substituted the following section—

"7.—(1) In assessing the compensation to be paid by the acquiring authority under this Act regard shall be had not only to the extent, if any, to which the value of the land over which the right is purchased is depreciated by the purchase but also to the damage, if any, to be sustained by the owner of the land by reason of injurious affection of other land of the owner by the exercise of the right.

(2) The modifications subject to which subsection (1) of section 44 of the Land Compensation Act 1973 (compensation for injurious affectation) is to have effect, as

applied by subsection (2) of that section to compensation for injurious affection under this section, are that for the words 'land is acquired or taken' there shall be substituted the words 'a right over land is acquired' and for the words 'acquired or taken from him' there shall be substituted the words 'over which the right is exercisable'."

22. For section 8 of the 1965 Act (which relates to cases in which a vendor cannot be required to sell part only of a building or garden) there shall be substituted the following section—

"8.—(1) Where in consequence of the service on a person in pursuance of section 5 of this Act of a notice to treat in respect of a right over land consisting of a house, building or manufactory or of a park or garden belonging to a house ('the relevant land')—

(a) a question of disputed compensation in respect of the purchase of the right would apart from this section fall to be determined by the Lands Tribunal ('the Tribunal'); and

(b) before the Tribunal has determined that question the person satisfies the Tribunal that he has an interest which he is able and willing to sell in the whole of the relevant land and—

(i) where that land consists of a house, building or manufactory, that the right cannot be purchased without material detriment to that land, or

(ii) where that land consists of such a park or garden, that the right cannot be purchased without seriously affecting the amenity or convenience of the house to which that land belongs,

the compulsory purchase order to which the notice to treat relates shall, in relation to that person, cease to authorise the purchase of the right and be deemed to authorise the purchase of that person's interest in the whole of the relevant land including, where the land consists of such a park or garden, the house to which it belongs, and the notice shall be deemed to have been served in respect of that interest on such date as the Tribunal directs.

(2) Any question as to the extent of the land in which a compulsory purchase order is deemed to authorise the purchase of an interest by virtue of the preceding subsection shall be determined by the Tribunal.

(3) Where in consequence of a determination of the Tribunal that it is satisfied as mentioned in subsection (1) of this section a compulsory purchase order is deemed by virtue of that subsection to authorise the purchase of an interest in land, the acquiring authority may, at any time within the period of six weeks beginning with the date of the determination, withdraw the notice to treat in consequence of which the determination was made; but nothing in this subsection prejudices any other power of the authority to withdraw the notice.

(4) The modifications subject to which subsection (1) of section 58 of the Land Compensation Act 1973 (determination of material detriment) is to have effect, as applied by subsection (2) of that section to the duty of the Tribunal in determining whether it is satisfied as mentioned in subsection (1) of this section, are that—

(a) at the beginning of paragraphs (a) and (b) there shall be inserted the words 'a right over';

(b) for the word 'severance' there shall be substituted the words 'right on the whole of the house, building or manufactory or of the house and the park or garden'; and

(c) for the words 'part proposed' and 'part is' there shall be substituted respectively the words 'right proposed' and 'right is'."

23.—(1) The following provisions of the 1965 Act (which state the effect of a deed poll executed in various circumstances where there is no conveyance by persons with interests in the land), namely—

(a) section 9(4) (failure of owners to convey);

(b) paragraph 10(3) of Schedule 1 (owners under incapacity);

(c) paragraph 2(3) of Schedule 2 (absent and untraced owners); and

(d) paragraphs 2(3) and 7(2) of Schedule 4 (common land),

shall be so modified as to secure that, as against persons with interests in the land which are expressed to be overridden by the deed, the right which is to be acquired compulsorily is vested absolutely in the acquiring authority.

(2) Section 11 of the 1965 Act (powers of entry) shall be so modified as to secure that, as from the date on which the acquiring authority has served notice to treat in respect of any right, it has power, exercisable in the like circumstances and subject to the like conditions, to enter for the purpose of exercising that right (which shall be deemed for this purpose to have been created on the date of service of the notice); and sections 12 (penalty for unauthorised entry) and 13 (entry on sheriff's warrant in the event of obstruction) of the 1965 Act shall be modified correspondingly.

(3) Section 20 of the 1965 Act (compensation for short-term tenants) shall apply with the modifications necessary to secure that persons with such interests as are mentioned in that

section are compensated in a manner corresponding to that in which they would be compensated on a compulsory purchase of the interests but taking into account only the extent (if any) of such interference with such interests as is actually caused, or likely to be caused, by the exercise of the right in question.

(4) Section 22 of the 1965 Act (protection of acquiring authority's possession of land where by inadvertence an interest in the land has not been purchased) shall be so modified as to enable the acquiring authority, in circumstances corresponding to those referred to in that section, to continue to be entitled to exercise the right in question, subject to compliance with that section as respects compensation.

GENERAL NOTE

Para. 3
Section 17 of the Acquisition of Land Act 1981 protects local authorities and statutory undertakers' land from compulsory acquisition without special parliamentary procedure except where land is being acquired by the authorities listed in s.17(3) of that Act. The Agency is added to this list.

Para. 4
This paragraph gives the Agency the right to vest in itself rights and apparatus within land subject to an order under s.161, except the rights and apparatus of statutory undertakers or telecommunications operators' rights or apparatus but only in each case where these are used for the operational part of their undertaking. Rights and apparatus not so used can therefore still be vested under an order.

Para. 5
This paragraph authorises the overriding of easements and rights and of contractual restrictions on user, provided again that the operational rights of statutory undertakers and telecommunications operators may not be overridden. In each case there is a right of compensation under the Compulsory Purchase Act 1965, ss.7 and 10 of which deal with compensation for injurious affection. Regard is had therefore, not only to the value of the land vested in the Agency, but also to the damage sustained by the owner of the right by virtue of its severance or by injurious affection arising out of the vesting (see paras. 20 to 23 post).

Para. 6
Subject to any regulations which may be made under the paragraph, the Agency may use any consecrated land or land including a church or building, for any purpose for which planning permission has been given without the need for a faculty, or other proceedings under ecclesiastical law. Such use shall nonetheless be subject to the prescribed requirements for removal and reinstatement of human remains and the disposal of monuments. Burial grounds may be similarly used, but only where the appropriate requirements in respect of removal and reinterment of human remains and disposal of monuments have been observed. Where the prescribed regulations are followed no faculty shall be required, nor any licence to remove remains under s.25 of the Burial Act 1857.

Para. 8
Where so certified by the Secretary of State the Agency has absolute power to secure possession of the tenancy of a house subject to the qualifications in this paragraph.

Para. 9
This paragraph creates an extensive power to extinguish public rights of way. The Secretary of State can make an extinguishment order, subject to allowing an objector to be heard before an Inspector appointed by the Secretary of State where he does not consider he is sufficiently informed as to the matters to which the objection relates or that the objection is not relevant to his decision. There does not appear to be any formal mechanism whereby the Agency may bring to the attention of the Secretary of State any public right of way which it desires to have extinguished.

Para. 11
Where public rights of way are extinguished, there is an obvious requirement to deal with services contained within them. Paragraph 11 deals with operators of telecommunications systems and gives them the right to remove apparatus within three months of extinguishment (or later, provided they gave notice within that period) or to abandon it if they give notice within the period. If they do not remove or give notice of intention to remove within the period they

will be deemed to have abandoned the equipment and it will vest in the Agency. They will however be entitled in broad terms to recover the costs of providing a substitute system.

Para. 12
This paragraph creates powers to serve notice extinguishing rights of statutory undertakers or requiring them to remove apparatus similar to the powers of urban development corporations under Sched. 28 to the 1980 Act. The statutory undertakers have a right to serve a counter-notice, but if they do not do so the provisions of the Agency's notice will take effect. If a counter-notice is served, determination of the issues will lie with the Secretary of State or the appropriate minister who will invite objection, and will give the statutory undertakers the right to have their objections heard by an Inspector.

Para. 14
This paragraph creates a reciprocal power for statutory undertakers to serve notice claiming the right to enter on vested land to remove or re-site equipment where development to be carried out on the land so requires. This again parallels the powers of statutory undertakers in relation to urban development corporation land under Sched. 28 to the 1980 Act and is subject to similar counter-notice provisions to those in para. 12.

Para. 15
This paragraph provides for the extension or modification of statutory undertakers' powers in vested land by special Parliamentary procedure where rights are extinguished or made subject to any requirements by virtue of para. 12, or where it appears expedient in order to supply new services or extend existing ones. It includes empowering the acquisition of land or construction of buildings or works for these purposes. These powers are created in order to ensure adequate provision of services to land which is or has been Agency land, and to prevent interruption of the provision of services by virtue of the operation of para. 12. The powers are to be exercised by the Secretary of State and the relevant minister on a representation made by the Agency or the statutory undertakers provided that in each case the appropriate notices have been published under para. 16.

Para. 17
This paragraph allows the relevant minister to absolve statutory undertakers from their statutory obligations where the performance of them has been made impracticable either by the vesting of land in the Agency or the operation of para. 12. Again this is subject to statutory publicity and a right of objection, and, in addition, an order relieving statutory undertakers of their obligation may be challenged as to its validity, by a person aggrieved, in the High Court, within six weeks of publication of the notice that it has been made. For "person aggrieved" see *Times Investment* v. *Secretary of State for the Environment and London Borough of Tower Hamlets* [1990] 3 P.L.R. 111. For the extent of the grounds of challenge in relation to a similarly formulated provision in the planning legislation, see Lord Denning M.R. in *Ashbridge Investments* v. *Minister of Housing and Local Government* [1965] 1 W.L.R. 1320. The right of challenge in sub-para. (8) is the only means of judicial challenge to an order under this paragraph, and such an order may not therefore be challenged other than on the grounds in that sub-paragraph.

Para. 19
"Statutory undertaking" for the purposes of s.262 of the Town and Country Planning Act 1990 is construed in accordance with subs. (1) of that section which defines "statutory undertakers" as being persons authorised "to carry on any railway, light railway, tramway, road transport, water transport, canal, inland navigation, dock, harbour, pier, or lighthouse undertaking, or any undertaking for the supply of hydraulic power and a relevant airport operator". It should be noted though that the term "statutory undertaker" is more widely defined in the remainder of that section and in addition is deemed elsewhere within Pt. XI of that Act to extend to other undertakings, for example the British Coal Corporation, and telecommunications operators. The position is similar for the definition of "the appropriate minister" and the 1990 Act will therefore need to be consulted for clarification on each occasion that the phrase occurs in this Schedule. Part III of the Schedule makes important provision for substitution of s.7 of the Compulsory Purchase Act 1965 so as to allow for the compensation in relation to severance or injurious affection to extend to the acquisition of rights as well as the acquisition of land, for the purposes of the present Act. This involves consequential substitution in s.44 of the Land Compensation Act 1973, but means that compensation rights accrue in relation to acquisition of rights, including statutory undertakers and others.

Para. 22

This paragraph makes a similar substitution in s.8 of the 1965 Act. That section provided that no one should be required to sell only part of a property if he was willing or able to sell the whole and chose to do so, unless the Lands Tribunal determined that such compulsory acquisition could take place without harm to the whole. It further made provision as to how to arrive at a value for compensation where part was taken. The substituted s.8 allows the owner of a right secured with a notice to treat similarly to offer the whole of his interest, where a question of disputed compensation has fallen before the Lands Tribunal. In such circumstances the notice to treat will be deemed to extend to the whole of the interest from such date as the tribunal directs and the acquiring authority will have six weeks from the notice of the direction to withdraw the notice to treat if it chooses to do so. This also involves consequential substitutions in s.58 of the Land Compensation Act 1973, which deals with the basis on which the Lands Tribunal should make its determination under s.8 of the 1965 Act, so as to extend the provisions of s.58 to cover acquisition of rights.

Para. 23(1)

This paragraph extends various provisions of the 1965 Act which allows for the acquiring authority to acquire the legal estate in land by deed poll so as to apply them also to acquisition of rights in similar circumstances. The balance of the paragraph merely ensures that 1965 Act rights relating to land in compulsory acquisition are similarly extended to rights acquired by the Agency.

Section 187(1)   SCHEDULE 21

MINOR AND CONSEQUENTIAL AMENDMENTS

Land Registration Act 1925 (c. 21)

1. In section 49(1) of the Land Registration Act 1925 (rules to provide for notices of other rights, interests and claims), there shall be added at the end—

"(k) orders made under section 26(1) or 50(1) of the Leasehold Reform, Housing and Urban Development Act 1993 which in the case of unregistered land may be protected by registration under the Land Charges Act 1972 and which, notwithstanding section 59 of this Act, it may be deemed expedient to protect by notice instead of by caution."

Landlord and Tenant Act 1954 (c. 56)

2. In subsection (1) of section 60 of the Landlord and Tenant Act 1954 (special provisions as to premises provided by English Industrial Estates Corporation etc.), for the words "the English Industrial Estates Corporation" there shall be substituted the words "the Urban Regeneration Agency".

Parliamentary Commissioner Act 1967 (c. 13)

3.—(1) In Schedule 2 to the Parliamentary Commissioner Act 1967 (departments etc. subject to investigation), after the entry "Urban development corporations." there shall be inserted the following entry—

"Urban Regeneration Agency."

(2) After Note 10 of that Schedule there shall be inserted the following Note—

"11. In the case of the Urban Regeneration Agency no investigation under this Act shall be conducted in respect of any action in connection with functions in relation to town and country planning."

Leasehold Reform Act 1967 (c. 88)

4. In subsection (1A) of section 21 of the Leasehold Reform Act 1967 (jurisdiction of leasehold valuation tribunals), for the words from "be" onwards there shall be substituted the words "comply with any requirements imposed by regulations under subsection (4A)(a) or (b) below".

Land Compensation Act 1973 (c. 26)

5. After section 12 of the Land Compensation Act 1973 (tenants entitled to enfranchisement or extension under Leasehold Reform Act 1967) there shall be inserted the following section—

"Tenants participating in collective enfranchisement, or entitled to individual lease extension, under Part I of Leasehold Reform, Housing and Urban Development Act 1993

12A.—(1) A tenancy to which subsection (2) or (3) below applies ("a qualifying tenancy") shall be treated as an owner's interest as defined in section 2(4) above whether or not the unexpired term on the date of service of the notice of claim is of the length there specified.

(2) This subsection applies to a tenancy if the tenant, on the relevant date—
  (a) is in respect of the tenancy a qualifying tenant for the purposes of Chapter I of Part I of the 1993 Act (collective enfranchisement); and
  (b) by virtue of the tenancy, either—
        (i) is a participating tenant in relation to a claim to exercise the right to collective enfranchisement under that Chapter; or
        (ii) is one of the participating tenants on whose behalf the acquisition by the nominee purchaser has been made in pursuance of such a claim.

(3) This subsection applies to a tenancy if the tenant, on the relevant date and in respect of the tenancy, is a qualifying tenant for the purposes of Chapter II of Part I of the 1993 Act (individual right to acquire new lease) who—
  (a) has on or before that date given notice under section 42 of that Act (notice by qualifying tenant of claim to exercise right); and
  (b) has not acquired a new lease before that date.

(4) If no claim is made in respect of a qualifying tenancy before the claimant has ceased to be entitled to it in consequence of a lease being granted to him by the nominee purchaser or, as the case may be, under Chapter II of Part I of the 1993 Act, the claimant may make a claim in respect of the qualifying tenancy as if he were still entitled to it.

(5) No claim shall be made by virtue of subsection (4) above after the claimant has ceased to be entitled to the lease referred to in that subsection, but such a claim may be made before the first claim day if it is made before the claimant has disposed of that lease and after he has made a contract for disposing of it.

(6) Compensation shall not be payable before the first claim day on any claim made by virtue of subsection (5) above.

(7) Any notice of a claim made by virtue of this section shall contain, in addition to the matters mentioned in section 3 above, a statement that it is made in respect of a qualifying tenancy as defined in this section and, if made by virtue of subsection (4) or (5) above, sufficient particulars to show that it falls within that subsection.

(8) In relation to a claim made by virtue of subsection (4) above, section 4(4)(a) above shall have effect as if the reference to the date of service of notice of the claim were a reference to the relevant date.

(9) In this section—
  (a) "the 1993 Act" means the Leasehold Reform, Housing and Urban Development Act 1993; and
  (b) "participating tenant", "nominee purchaser" and "the acquisition by the nominee purchaser" shall be construed in accordance with sections 14, 15 and 38(2) of that Act respectively."

Local Government Act 1974 (c. 7)

6.—(1) In subsection (1) of section 25 of the Local Government Act 1974 (authorities subject to investigation), after paragraph (be) there shall be inserted the following paragraph—
  "(bf) the Urban Regeneration Agency;".

(2) In subsection (7) of section 26 of that Act (matters subject to investigation) after paragraph (b) there shall be inserted the following paragraph—
  "(ba) where the complaint relates to the Urban Regeneration Agency, any designated area within the meaning of Part III of the Leasehold Reform, Housing and Urban Development Act 1993;".

(3) In Schedule 5 to that Act (matters not subject to investigation) after paragraph 7 there shall be inserted the following paragraph—
  "8. Action taken by the Urban Regeneration Agency which is not action in connection with functions in relation to town and country planning."

Rent Act 1977 (c. 42)

7. In subsection (1)(b) of section 74 of the Rent Act 1977 (regulations), for the words from "by rent officers" onwards there shall be substituted the words—
  "(i) by rent officers under this Act; and
  (ii) by rent assessment committees whether under this Act or otherwise; and".

Derelict Land Act 1982 (c. 42)

8. In subsection (5) of section 1 of the Derelict Land Act 1982 (powers of Secretary of State), in the definition of "the prescribed percentage", for paragraphs (b) and (c) there shall be substituted the following paragraph—

"(b) in any other case, 80 per cent. or such other percentage as may be prescribed by order made by the Secretary of State with the consent of the Treasury."

National Heritage Act 1983 (c. 47)

9. After subsection (2A) of section 33 of the National Heritage Act 1983 (general functions of the Historic Buildings and Monuments Commission for England) there shall be inserted the following subsection—

"(2B) In relation to England, the Commission may make, or join in the making of, applications under section 73(1) of the Leasehold Reform, Housing and Urban Development Act 1993, and may exercise, or participate in the exercise of, any rights or powers conferred by a scheme approved under section 70 of that Act."

Housing Act 1985 (c. 68)

10. In subsection (3) of section 101 of the Housing Act 1985 (rent not to be increased on account of tenant's improvements), for paragraph (a) there shall be substituted the following paragraph—

"(a) a person in whom the tenancy was vested, or to whom the tenancy was disposed of, under section 89 (succession to periodic tenancy) or section 90 (devolution of term certain) on the death of the tenant or in the course of the administration of his estate;".

11. In subsection (2) of section 130 of that Act (reduction of discount where previous discount given), after paragraph (aa) there shall be inserted the following paragraph—

"(a) in pursuance of the provision required by paragraphs 3 to 5 or paragraph 7 of Schedule 6A (redemption of landlord's share), or".

12. For subsection (3) of section 140 of that Act (landlord's first notice to complete) there shall be substituted the following subsection—

"(3) A notice under this section shall not be served earlier than twelve months after—

(a) the service of the landlord's notice under section 125 (notice of purchase price and other matters), or

(b) where a notice has been served under section 146 (landlord's notice admitting or denying right to acquire on rent to mortgage terms), the service of that notice."

13.—(1) Immediately before section 153A of that Act (tenant's notices of delay) there shall be inserted the following italic cross heading—

"Tenant's sanction for landlord's delays".

(2) In subsection (1) of that section—

(a) in paragraph (e), for the words "right to be granted a shared ownership lease" there shall be substituted the words "right to acquire on rent to mortgage terms"; and

(b) for the words "any of the cases in paragraphs (a) to (d)" there shall be substituted the words "either of the cases in paragraphs (a) and (b)".

(3) In subsection (3) of that section—

(a) for the words "right to be granted a shared ownership lease" there shall be substituted the words "right to acquire on rent to mortgage terms";

(b) for the words "any of the cases in paragraphs (a) to (d)" there shall be substituted the words "either of the cases in paragraphs (a) and (b)"; and

(c) for the words "section 125, section 146 or section 147" there shall be substituted the words "or section 125".

14.—(1) In subsection (1) of section 153B of that Act (payments of rent attributable to purchase price etc.), for the words "right to be granted a shared ownership lease" there shall be substituted the words "right to acquire on rent to mortgage terms".

(2) In subsection (2) of that section, for the words "any of paragraphs (c) to (e)" there shall be substituted the words "paragraph (d) or (e)".

(3) In subsection (3) of that section, for the words "the tenant's initial contribution for the grant of a shared ownership lease" there shall be substituted the words "the tenant's initial payment".

15. In subsection (2) of section 158 of that Act (consideration for reconveyance or surrender under section 157), after paragraph (a) there shall be inserted the following paragraph—

"(aa) any covenant required by paragraph 1 of Schedule 6A (obligation to redeem landlord's share where conveyance or grant executed in pursuance of right to acquire on rent to mortgage terms), and".

16.—(1) In subsection (1) of section 164 of that Act (Secretary of State's general power to intervene), for the words "right to be granted a shared ownership lease" there shall be substituted the words "right to acquire on rent to mortgage terms".

(2) In subsection (4) of that section, for the words "the right to a mortgage or the right to be granted a shared ownership lease" there shall be substituted the words "or the right to acquire on rent to mortgage terms".

(3) In subsection (5) of that section, for the words "the right to a mortgage and the right to be granted a shared ownership lease" there shall be substituted the words "and the right to acquire on rent to mortgage terms".

17. In subsection (1) of section 167 of that Act (power to give directions as to covenants and conditions), after paragraph (b) there shall be inserted the words "or

(c) in the case of conveyances or grants executed in pursuance of the right to acquire on rent to mortgage terms, the conveyances or grants would not conform with Schedule 6A,".

18. In subsection (2) of section 170 of that Act (power to give assistance in connection with legal proceedings), for the words "right to be granted a shared ownership lease" there shall be substituted the words "right to acquire on rent to mortgage terms".

19. In subsection (2) of section 171C of that Act (modifications of Part V in relation to preserved right), for the words "right to be granted a shared ownership lease" there shall be substituted the words "right to acquire on rent to mortgage terms".

20.—(1) In subsection (2) of section 177 of that Act (errors and omissions in notices), for the words "right to be granted a shared ownership lease" there shall be substituted the words "right to acquire on rent to mortgage terms".

(2) In subsection (3) of that section, for the entries relating to section 147 and paragraph 1(3) of Schedule 8 there shall be substituted the following entry—

"section 146 (landlord's notice admitting or denying right to acquire on rent to mortgage terms)."

21. For section 178 of that Act there shall be substituted the following section—

"**Costs**
178. An agreement between the landlord and a tenant claiming to exercise—
(a) the right to buy,
(b) the right to acquire on rent to mortgage terms, or
(c) any such right as is mentioned in paragraph 2(1) or 6(1) of Schedule 6A (redemption of landlord's share: right to make final or interim payment),
is void in so far as it purports to oblige the tenant to bear any part of the costs incurred by the landlord in connection with the tenant's exercise of that right."

22. In subsection (1) of section 179 of that Act (provisions restricting right to buy etc. of no effect), for the words "right to be granted a shared ownership lease" there shall be substituted the words "right to acquire on rent to mortgage terms".

23. In subsection (1) of section 181 of that Act (jurisdiction of county court), for the words "a shared ownership lease granted in pursuance of this Part" there shall be substituted the words "a conveyance or grant executed in pursuance of the right to acquire on rent to mortgage terms".

24.—(1) In subsection (2) of section 184 of that Act (land let with or used for purposes of dwelling-house), for the words "right to be granted a shared ownership lease" there shall be substituted the words "right to acquire on rent to mortgage terms".

(2) In subsection (3) of that section, for the words "right to be granted a shared ownership lease" there shall be substituted the words "right to acquire on rent to mortgage terms".

25. In section 188 of that Act (index of defined expressions: Part V), at the appropriate places in alphabetical order there shall be inserted the following entries—

"district valuer — section 622"
"final payment — paragraph 1 of Schedule 6A"
"initial payment and interim payment — section 143B and paragraph 6 of Schedule 6A"
"landlord's share — section 148 and paragraph 7 of Schedule 6A"
"minimum initial payment and maximum initial payment — section 143B"

"prescribed	section 614"
"right to acquire on rent to mortgage terms	section 143".

Landlord and Tenant Act 1987 (c. 31)

26. In subsection (2) of section 4 of the Landlord and Tenant Act 1987 (relevant disposals), after paragraph (d) there shall be inserted the following paragraph—

"(da) a disposal of any freehold or leasehold interest in pursuance of Chapter I of Part I of the Leasehold Reform, Housing and Urban Development Act 1993;".

27. In subsection (2) of section 13 of that Act (determination by rent assessment committees of questions relating to purchase notices), for the words from "be" to "particulars," there shall be substituted the words "comply with such requirements (if any) as to the form of, or the particulars to be contained in, any such application".

Town and Country Planning Act 1990 (c. 8)

28. In subsection (5)(a) of section 1 of the Town and Country Planning Act 1990 (subsections (1) to (4) of that section have effect subject to sections 5 to 8), for "8" there shall be substituted "8A".

29. After section 8 of that Act (local planning authority in housing action area) there shall be inserted the following section—

"The Urban Regeneration Agency

8A.—(1) Where a designation order under section 170 of the Leasehold Reform, Housing and Urban Development Act 1993 (power to make designation orders) makes such provision as is mentioned in subsection (1) of section 171 of that Act (Agency as local planning authority), the Urban Regeneration Agency shall be the local planning authority for such area as may be specified in the order in place of any authority who would otherwise be the local planning authority for that area for such purposes and in relation to such kinds of development as may be so specified.

(2) Where such an order makes such provision as is mentioned in subsection (3)(a) of section 171 of that Act, the Urban Regeneration Agency shall have the functions specified in the order for such area as may be so specified in place of any authority (except the Secretary of State) who would otherwise have them in that area."

Planning (Listed Buildings and Conservation Areas) Act 1990 (c. 9)

30.—(1) In subsection (1) of section 72 of the Planning (Listed Buildings and Conservation Areas) Act 1990 (general duty as respects conservation areas in exercise of planning functions), for the words "powers under" there shall be substituted the words "functions under or by virtue of".

(2) In subsection (2) of that section there shall be added at the end "and sections 70 and 73 of the Leasehold Reform, Housing and Urban Development Act 1993".

31. In paragraphs 2 and 4 of Schedule 4 to that Act (further provisions as to exercise of functions by different authorities), for the words "and 8" there shall be substituted the words "8 and 8A".

Planning (Hazardous Substances) Act 1990 (c. 10)

32. After subsection (5) of section 3 of the Planning (Hazardous Substances) Act 1990 (hazardous substances authorities in certain special cases) there shall be inserted the following subsection—

"(5A) If the land is in an area for which the Urban Regeneration Agency is the local planning authority in relation to all kinds of development, the Agency shall be the hazardous substances authority for the land unless subsection (1) or (2) applies."

Section 187(2)   SCHEDULE 22

REPEALS

Chapter	Short title	Extent of repeal
9 & 10 Eliz. 2. c. 33.	The Land Compensation Act 1961.	In section 23(3), the word "or" at the end of paragraph (b).

Chapter	Short title	Extent of repeal
1975 c. 24.	The House of Commons Disqualification Act 1975.	In Schedule 1, in Part II, the entry relating to the English Industrial Estates Corporation.
1975 c. 25.	The Northern Ireland Assembly Disqualification Act 1975.	In Schedule 1, in Part II, the entry beginning "The Industrial Estates Corporations".
1980 c. 51.	The Housing Act 1980.	In section 141, "3,". In Schedule 21, paragraph 3.
1980 c. 65.	The Local Government, Planning and Land Act 1980.	Section 99A(2). Section 165(3).
1981 c. 13.	The English Industrial Estates Corporation Act 1981.	The whole Act.
1982 c. 52.	The Industrial Development Act 1982.	In section 15(1), paragraph (d) and the word "and" immediately preceding it. In Part II of Schedule 2, paragraph 17.
1983 c. 29.	The Miscellaneous Financial Provisions Act 1983.	In Schedule 2, the entry relating to the English Industrial Estates Corporation Act 1981.
1985 c. 25.	The Industrial Development Act 1985.	Sections 1 to 4. Section 6(2).
1985 c. 68.	The Housing Act 1985.	Section 27C. Section 124(3). Section 128(6). Sections 132 to 135. In section 137, in subsection (1), the words "or the right to a mortgage" and, in subsection (2), paragraph (b). In section 138(1), the words "and to the amount to be left outstanding or advanced on the security of the dwelling-house". Section 139(3). In section 140(5), the words "and to the amount to be left outstanding or advanced on the security of the dwelling-house". Section 142. In section 153A(1), paragraphs (c) and (d). In section 153B(1), paragraph (c). Section 164(6). Section 166(6). In section 169(3), paragraph (b) and the word "and" immediately preceding that paragraph. In section 171C(2), paragraph (b). In section 171H, in subsection (1), the words "or the right to a mortgage" and, in subsection (2), paragraph (b). In section 177, in subsection (2)(b) the words "or the Corporation" and in subsection (3), the entries relating to section 135 and paragraph 5 of Schedule 9. In section 180, the words "the Corporation" and "Corporation". In section 181(1), the words "and paragraph 11 of Schedule 8". In section 182(1), the words "or the right to a mortgage". In section 187, the definition of "total share".

Chapter	Short title	Extent of repeal
		In section 188, the entries beginning "additional share and additional contribution", "effective discount", "full mortgage", "initial share and initial contribution", "prescribed percentage", "right to be granted a shared ownership lease", "right to further advances", "right to a mortgage" and "total share".
		In Schedule 6, in paragraphs 16B(4) and 16C(4), paragraph (c) and the word "and" immediately preceding that paragraph.
		Schedules 7 to 9.
1985 c. 71.	The Housing (Consequential Provisions) Act 1985.	In section 6(3), "12".
1986 c. 63.	The Housing and Planning Act 1986.	In Schedule 2, paragraph 12.
		In Schedule 5, paragraph 5.
1987 c. 26.	The Housing (Scotland) Act 1987.	In section 17, in subsection (1), the words "and exercised by".
		In section 61, in subsection (10)(b), sub-paragraphs (i) and (ii).
		In section 62, in subsection (3)(b), the words "continuous" and "immediately".
1987 c. 31.	The Landlord and Tenant Act 1987.	Section 25(3).
		In section 29(2), the words from "and (c)" onwards.
1988 c. 50.	The Housing Act 1988.	Section 41(1).
		In section 69(2), the words from "on grounds" onwards.
		In section 79(2)(b), the words "in accordance with section 84 below".
		In Schedule 9, paragraph 12(2).
1989 c. 42.	The Local Government and Housing Act 1989.	In section 80(1), the words from "and for any year" onwards.
		Section 164.
		In Schedule 11, paragraph 51.
1990 c. 11.	The Planning (Consequential Provisions) Act 1990.	In Schedule 2, paragraph 47.

APPENDICES

APPENDIX 1: Leasehold Reform (Collective Enfranchisement and Lease Renewal) Regulations 1993 (S.I. 1993 No. 2407)

APPENDIX 2: Rent Assessment Committee (England and Wales) (Leasehold Valuation Tribunal) Regulations 1993 (S.I. 1993 No. 2408)

APPENDIX 3: Leasehold Reform (Notices) (Amendment) Regulations 1993 (S.I. 1993 No. 2409)

APPENDIX 4: Housing (Tenant Management Organisations) Regulations [1994] (Draft Regulations)

APPENDIX 5: Draft Guidance on the Urban Regeneration Agency (DOE/1993)

APPENDIX 6: Leasehold Reform, Housing and Urban Development Act 1993 (Commencement and Transitional Provisions No. 1) Order 1993 (S.I. 1993 No. 2134)

APPENDIX 1

LANDLORD AND TENANT, ENGLAND AND WALES

THE LEASEHOLD REFORM (COLLECTIVE ENFRANCHISEMENT AND LEASE RENEWAL) REGULATIONS 1993

(S.I. 1993 No. 2407)

Made - - - - -	*30th September 1993*
Laid before Parliament - - -	*11th October 1993*
Coming into force - - - -	*1st November 1993*

The Secretary of State, as respects England, and the Secretary of State for Wales, as respects Wales, in exercise of the powers conferred on them by sections 98 and 100(1) of the Leasehold Reform, Housing and Urban Development Act 1993 (c. 28) and all other powers enabling them in that behalf, hereby make the following Regulations—

Citation, commencement and interpretation

1.—(1) These Regulations may be cited as the Leasehold Reform (Collective Enfranchisement and Lease Renewal) Regulations 1993 and shall come into force on 1st November 1993.

(2) In these Regulations references to sections and Schedules without more are references to sections of and Schedules to the Leasehold Reform, Housing and Urban Development Act 1993.

Procedure for collective enfranchisement

2. In a transaction undertaken to give effect to an initial notice the nominee purchaser, the reversioner and any relevant landlord shall, unless they otherwise agree, be bound by Schedule 1 to these Regulations.

Procedure for lease renewal

3. In a transaction undertaken to give effect to a tenant's notice, the landlord and the tenant shall, unless they otherwise agree, be bound by Schedule 2 to these Regulations.

Notices

4. Any notice, statement, answer or document required or authorised to be given under these Regulations—
(a) shall be in writing, and
(b) may be sent by post.

Signed by authority of the Secretary of State

G. S. K. Young
Minister of State,
Department of the Environment

30th September 1993

John Redwood
Secretary of State for Wales

30th September 1993

SCHEDULE 1

COLLECTIVE ENFRANCHISEMENT

Interpretation

1. In this Schedule—
"counter-notice" means a notice given under section 21, and "further counter-notice" means a notice required by or by virtue of section 22(3) or section 23(5) or (6);
"qualifying tenant" shall be construed in accordance with section 5;
"the relevant date" has the meaning given by section 1(8);
"terms of acquisition" has the meaning given by section 24(8).

Evidence that residence condition satisfied

2.—(1) The reversioner may require the nominee purchaser to give him evidence of the occupation on which a qualifying tenant who is claimed in the initial notice to satisfy the residence condition relies, by giving him notice within the period of twenty-one days beginning with the relevant date.

(2) The nominee purchaser shall comply with any such requirement by giving a statutory declaration made by that qualifying tenant to the reversioner within the period of twenty-one days beginning with the date the notice is given.

Delivery of proof of title

3.—(1) Sub-paragraph (2) applies where the reversioner has given a counter-notice complying with section 21(2)(a) (admitting the right to collective enfranchisement) or a further counter-notice, or, if no such counter-notice or further counter-notice is given, the nominee purchaser has applied to the court for an order under section 25(1) (applications where reversioner fails to give counter-notice or further counter-notice).

(2) Subject to paragraph 5, the nominee purchaser may require the reversioner to deduce title to the interests proposed to be acquired in accordance with section 13(3)(a) and (c)(i) (matters specified in the initial notice) and to any interest in relation to which the reversioner has made proposals in accordance with section 21(3)(b) and (c) (matters specified in counter-notice), or to any less extensive interest which it has been agreed or determined by a leasehold valuation tribunal will be acquired, by giving him notice.

(3) The reversioner shall comply with any such requirement by giving the nominee purchaser—
(a) in the case of an interest registered in the register of title kept at Her Majesty's Land Registry, all particulars and information which have to be given or may be required to be given on a sale of registered land pursuant to section 110 of the Land Registration Act 1925 (c. 21) (provisions as between vendor and purchaser), and
(b) in the case of any other interest, an epitome of title,
within the period of twenty-eight days beginning with the date the notice is given.

Requisitions

4.—(1) Subject to paragraph 5, the nominee purchaser shall give to the reversioner a statement of any objections to or requisitions on the proof of title within the period of fourteen days beginning with the date the proof is given (whether or not within the time required).

(2) The reversioner shall give to the nominee purchaser an answer to any statement of objections or requisitions within the period of fourteen days beginning with the date the statement is given.

(3) The nominee purchaser shall give to the reversioner a further statement of any objections to or comments on the answer within the period of seven days beginning with the date the answer is given.

(4) Any objection or requisition not included in any statement given within the period referred to in sub-paragraph (1) shall be deemed waived, and any matter which could have been raised in a statement so given shall be deemed not to be a defect in title for the purposes of paragraph 3(3) of Schedule 6 and as it is applied by paragraph 7(1) and by paragraph 11(1) of that Schedule (effect of defect in title on valuation of interest to be acquired).

(5) Any objection not included in any further statement given within the period specified in sub-paragraph (3) shall be deemed waived and any matter which could have been raised in a further statement so given shall be deemed not to be a defect in title for the purposes of paragraph 3(3) of Schedule 6 and as it is applied as described in sub-paragraph (4).

(6) If no further statement is given within the time specified in sub-paragraph (3), the reversioner's answer shall be considered satisfactory.

Relevant landlords acting independently

5.—(1) Sub-paragraph (2) applies where—
(a) a relevant landlord has given notice in accordance with paragraph 7(1)(a) of Schedule 1 (relevant landlord's entitlement to act independently of the reversioner) of his intention to deal directly with the nominee purchaser in connection with deducing, evidencing or verifying his title, or
(b) the nominee purchaser has given notice in accordance with paragraph 7(2) of Schedule 1 (nominee purchaser's entitlement to require a relevant landlord to deal directly with him) to a relevant landlord.
(2) Any notice, statement or further statement given—
(a) under paragraph 3 requiring proof of that relevant landlord's title, or
(b) under paragraph 4 raising requisitions, or making objections to or comments on that relevant landlord's title,
shall be given to him and not to the reversioner, and he will be under a duty to comply with any such notice or respond to any such statement instead of the reversioner.

Preparation of contract

6.—(1) The reversioner shall prepare the draft contract and give it to the nominee purchaser within the period of twenty-one days beginning with the date the terms of acquisition are agreed or determined by a leasehold valuation tribunal.
(2) The nominee purchaser shall give to the reversioner a statement of any proposals for amending the draft contract within the period of fourteen days beginning with the date the draft contract is given.
(3) If no statement is given by the nominee purchaser within the time specified in sub-paragraph (2) he shall be deemed to have approved the draft.
(4) The reversioner shall give to the nominee purchaser an answer, giving any objections to or comments on the proposals in the statement, within the period of fourteen days beginning with the date the statement is given.
(5) If no answer is given by the reversioner within the time specified in sub-paragraph (4), he shall be deemed to have agreed to the nominee purchaser's proposals for amendments to the draft contract.

Payment of deposit

7.—(1) The reversioner may require the nominee purchaser to pay a deposit on exchange of contracts in pursuance of the initial notice.
(2) The amount of the deposit required shall be £500, or 10 per cent. of the purchase price agreed or determined by a leasehold valuation tribunal to be payable for the interests to be acquired, whichever is the greater.
(3) The nominee purchaser shall pay the deposit so required to the reversioner's solicitor or licensed conveyancer as stakeholder.

Cancellation of land charges etc.

8. Where the initial notice has been registered as a land charge or a notice or caution has been registered in respect of it under section 97(1), and either it is withdrawn, deemed to have been withdrawn or otherwise ceases to have effect, the nominee purchaser shall at the request of the reversioner without delay take all steps necessary to procure cancellation of the registration.

Regulation 3   SCHEDULE 2

LEASE RENEWAL

Interpretation

1. In this Schedule—
"counter-notice" means a notice given under section 45, and "further counter-notice" means a notice required by or by virtue of section 46(4) or section 47(4) or (5);
"flat" shall be construed in accordance with section 62(2);
"the landlord" has the meaning given by section 40(1);
"lease" means a lease granted to give effect to a tenant's notice;
"the relevant date" has the meaning given by section 39(8);
"tenant" means a tenant who has given a tenant's notice;
"terms of acquisition" has the meaning given by section 48(7).

Payment of deposit

2.—(1) The landlord may give to the tenant a notice requiring him to pay a deposit on account of the premium payable for the lease at any time when the tenant's notice continues in force under section 42(8).

(2) The amount of the deposit shall be £250, or 10 per cent. of the amount proposed in the tenant's notice as payable on the grant of the lease in accordance with Schedule 13 (premium and other amounts payable by tenant on grant of new lease), whichever is the greater.

(3) The tenant shall pay the deposit so required to the landlord's solicitor or licensed conveyancer as stakeholder within the period of fourteen days beginning with the date the notice is given.

Return of deposit

3.—(1) Subject to sub-paragraph (3), the tenant may give to the landlord a notice requiring him to procure the return of the deposit to the tenant at any time after the tenant's notice is withdrawn, deemed to have been withdrawn or otherwise ceases to have effect.

(2) The landlord shall comply with any such requirement within the period of fourteen days beginning with the date the notice is given.

(3) The landlord shall be entitled to have deducted from the deposit any amount due to him from the tenant in accordance with section 60 (tenant's liability for landlord's costs).

Evidence of tenant's right to a lease

4.—(1) The landlord may require the tenant to—
(a) deduce title to his tenance, and
(b) give evidence by statutory declaration of the occupation on which he relies in the tenant's notice
by giving him notice within the period of twenty-one days beginning with the relevant date.

(2) The tenant shall comply with any such requirement within the period of twenty-one days beginning with the date the notice is given.

Delivery of proof of title

5.—(1) Sub-paragraph (2) applies where the landlord has given a counter-notice complying with section 45(2)(a) (admitting the right to a new lease) or a further counter-notice, or, if no such counter-notice or further counter-notice is given, the tenant has applied to the court for an order under section 49(1) (applications where landlord fails to give counter-notice or further counter-notice).

(2) The tenant may require the landlord to deduce title to his interest in the flat to which the tenant's notice relates by giving him notice.

(3) The landlord shall comply with any such requirement by giving the tenant:—
(a) in the case of an interest registered in the register of title kept at Her Majesty's Land Registry, all particulars and information which have to be given or may be required to be given on a sale of registered land pursuant to section 110 of the Land Registration Act 1925 (c. 21) (provisions as between vendor and purchaser), and
(b) subject to sub-paragraph (4), in the case of any other interest, an epitome of title,
within the period of twenty-eight days beginning with the date the notice is given.

(4) In a case where the landlord is not the freeholder, and the title to the freehold or any leasehold reversion to the landlord's title (if any) is not registered at Her Majesty's Land Registry, the landlord shall use his best endeavours to obtain an epitome of that title and shall also give it to the tenant.

Requisitions

6.—(1) The tenant shall give to the landlord a statement of any objections to or requisitions on the proof of title within the period of fourteen days beginning with the date the proof is given (whether or not within the time required).

(2) The landlord shall give to the tenant an answer to any statement of objections or requisitions within the period of fourteen days beginning with the date the statement is given.

(3) The tenant shall give to the landlord a further statement of any objections to or comments on the answer within the period of seven days beginning with the date the answer is given.

(4) Any objection or requisition not included in any statement given within the period referred to in sub-paragraph (1) shall be deemed waived, and any matter which could have been raised in a statement so given shall be deemed not to be a defect in title for the purposes of

paragraph 3(5) of Schedule 13 and as it is applied by paragraph 8(1) of that Schedule (effect of defect in title on calculation of diminution in value to landlord's interest or any intermediate leasehold interest).

(5) Any objection not included in any further statement given within the period specified in sub-paragraph (3) shall be deemed waived and any matter which could have been raised in a further statement so given shall be deemed not to form a defect in the title for the purposes of paragraph 3(5) of Schedule 13 and as it is applied as described in sub-paragraph (4).

(6) If no further statement is given within the time specified in sub-paragraph (3), the landlord's answer shall be considered satisfactory.

Preparation of lease

7.—(1) The landlord shall prepare a draft lease and give it to the tenant within the period of fourteen days beginning with the date the terms of acquisition are agreed or determined by a leasehold valuation tribunal.

(2) The tenant shall give to the landlord a statement of any proposals for amending the draft lease within the period of fourteen days beginning with the date the draft lease is given.

(3) If no statement is given by the tenant within the time specified in sub-paragraph (2), he shall be deemed to have approved the draft lease.

(4) The landlord shall give to the tenant an answer giving any objections to or comments on the proposals in the statement within the period of fourteen days beginning with the date the statement is given.

(5) If no answer is given by the landlord within the time specified in sub-paragraph (4), he shall be deemed to have approved the amendments to the draft lease proposed by the tenant.

(6) The landlord shall prepare the lease and as many counterparts as he may reasonably require and shall give the counterpart or counterparts to the tenant for execution a reasonable time before the completion date.

(7) The tenant shall give the counterpart or counterparts of the lease, duly executed, to the landlord and the landlord shall give the lease, duly executed, to the tenant, on the completion date or as soon as possible afterwards.

Completion

8.—(1) Subject to sub-paragraph (2), after the draft lease is approved or deemed to have been approved, either the landlord or the tenant may give the other notice requiring him to complete the grant of the lease on the first working day after the expiration of twenty-one days beginning with the date the notice is given.

(2) Sub-paragraph (1) shall not apply if the date for completion would fall after the expiry of the appropriate period specified for the purposes of section 48 or 49 (applications where terms in dispute or failure to enter into new lease, and applications where landlord fails to give counter-notice or further counter-notice), and in that event the date for completion shall be such day as the landlord and tenant agree in writing or the court orders under section 48(3) or 49(4) (order of the court on failure to enter into new lease).

(3) The landlord shall by notice inform any other landlord who has given notice in accordance with paragraph 7(2) of Schedule 11 (other landlords acting independently) of the date for completion as soon as possible after notice has been given in accordance with sub-paragraph (1) or the date for completion agreed or ordered by the court in accordance with sub-paragraph (2).

(4) Completion shall take place at the office of the landlord's solicitor or licensed conveyancer.

Cancellation of land charges etc.

9. Where a tenant's notice has been registered under section 97(1) as a land charge or a notice or caution has been registered in respect of it, and it is withdrawn, deemed to have been withdrawn or otherwise ceases to have effect, the tenant shall at the request of the landlord without delay take all steps necessary to procure cancellation of the registration.

APPENDIX 2

LANDLORD AND TENANT, ENGLAND AND WALES

THE RENT ASSESSMENT COMMITTEE (ENGLAND AND WALES) (LEASEHOLD VALUATION TRIBUNAL) REGULATIONS 1993

(S.I. 1993 No. 2408)

Made - - - - -	*30th September 1993*
Laid before Parliament - - -	*11th October 1993*
Coming into force - - -	*1st November 1993*

The Secretary of State for the Environment, as respects England, and the Secretary of State for Wales, as respects Wales, in exercise of the powers conferred upon them by section 21(4A) of the Leasehold Reform Act 1967 (c. 88; section 21(4A) was inserted by para. 8 of Sched. 2 to the Housing Act 1980 (c. 51)), section 74(1) of the Rent Act 1977 (c. 42; section 74(1) is extended by s.91(5)(a) of the Leasehold Reform, Housing and Urban Development Act 1993 (c. 28), and amended by para. 7 of Sched. 21 to that Act), sections 13(2) and 31(5) of the Landlord and Tenant Act 1987 (c. 31; section 13(2) is amended by para. 27 of Sched. 21 to the Leasehold Reform, Housing and Urban Development Act 1993), and sections 75(4), 88(5) and 91(6) of the Leasehold Reform, Housing and Urban Development Act 1993 and of all other powers enabling them in that behalf, and after consultation with the Council on Tribunals (*see* s.8 of the Tribunals and Inquiries Act 1992 (c. 53)) hereby make the following Regulations:

Citation and commencement

1. These Regulations may be cited as the Rent Assessment Committee (England and Wales) (Leasehold Valuation Tribunal) Regulations 1993 and shall come into force on 1st November 1993.

Interpretation

2. In these Regulations—
"application" means an application to a tribunal under section 21(1) (jurisdiction of leasehold valuation tribunals) of the Leasehold Reform Act 1967, or under section 13 (determination by leasehold valuation tribunals of questions relating to purchase notices) or section 31 (determination by leasehold valuation tribunals of terms where acquisition order) of the Landlord and Tenant Act 1987, or under or by virtue of Part I of the 1993 Act (collective enfranchisement and grant of new lease) and includes, except where the contrary is indicated, a scheme application (section 21 was amended by para. 8 of Sched. 22 to the Housing Act 1980 (c. 51));
"party" includes (as regards a scheme application) two or more landlords or a representative body under section 71 (applications by two or more landlords or by representative body) of the 1993 Act, and the relevant authority for the purposes of section 73 (applications by certain public bodies) of that Act;
"person making representations" means such a person as is mentioned in section 70(6) of the 1993 Act;
"scheme application" means an application under Chapter IV of Part I of the 1993 Act, or under section 19 of the Leasehold Reform Act 1967 (retention of management powers for general benefit of neighbourhood) as it has effect by virtue of section 75 (variation of existing schemes) of the 1993 Act;

"the 1993 Act" means the Leasehold Reform, Housing and Urban Development Act 1993; and

"tribunal" means a leasehold valuation tribunal.

Applications

3.—(1) The particulars to be included in an application, except a scheme application, are those specified in Schedule 1 to these Regulations.

(2) The particulars to be included in a scheme application are those specified in Schedule 2 to these Regulations.

4. On receipt of an application the tribunal shall send a copy of it and of each of the documents which accompanied it to each person named in it as a respondent.

Hearings

5.—(1) A hearing shall be on the date and at the time and place appointed by the tribunal.

(2) The tribunal shall give notice of the appointed date, time and place to the parties not less than 21 days (or such shorter period as the parties may agree) before the appointed date, and the tribunal shall send a copy of the notice—

(a) to any other person who has indicated to the tribunal an intention to appear at the hearing; and

(b) in the case of a scheme application, to any person making representations.

(3) The notice shall contain a statement that an appeal to the Lands Tribunal may only be made by a person who appeared before the tribunal in proceedings to which he was a party (*see*, in relation to the meaning of "party" for this purpose, s.91(10)(b) of the Leasehold Reform, Housing and Urban Development Act 1993).

(4) The tribunal may, where they consider it appropriate, arrange that an application shall be heard together with one or more other applications.

(5) A hearing shall be in public unless, for special reasons, the tribunal decide that a hearing or part of a hearing should be held in private.

6. At a hearing—

(a) the tribunal shall determine the procedure (subject to these Regulations), and the order in which the persons appearing before them are to be heard;

(b) a person appearing before the tribunal may do so either in person or by a representative authorised by him, whether or not that representative is of counsel or a solicitor; and

(c) a person appearing before the tribunal may give evidence on his own behalf, call witnesses, and cross-examine any witnesses called by any other person appearing.

Non-appearance

7. If a party or person mentioned in regulation 5(2) does not appear at a hearing, the tribunal may proceed with the hearing if they are satisfied that notice has been given to that party or person in accordance with these Regulations.

Adjournment

8.—(1) The tribunal may postpone or adjourn a hearing at their discretion either of their own motion, or at the request of the parties or of one or more of the persons appearing before them, but they shall not do so at the request of one party or person except where they consider it reasonable to do so having regard to the grounds for the request, the time at which the request is made and the convenience of the other persons appearing before them.

(2) The tribunal shall give reasonable notice of any postponed or adjourned hearing to the persons appearing before them.

Documents

9.—(1) Before the date of a hearing, the tribunal shall take all reasonable steps to ensure that each of the parties and persons making representations is given—

(a) a copy of, or sufficient extracts from or particulars of, any document relevant to the proceedings which has been received from a party or person making representations (other than a document already in the possession of that party or one of which he has previously been supplied with a copy); and

(b) a copy of any document which embodies the results of any enquiries made by or for the tribunal for the purposes of the proceedings.

(2) At a hearing, if a person appearing before the tribunal does not have in his possession a relevant document or a copy of, or sufficient extracts from or particulars of, a relevant document, then unless—

(a) that person consents to the continuation of the hearing; or

(b) the tribunal consider that that person has a sufficient opportunity to deal with the document without an adjournment of the hearing,

the tribunal shall adjourn the hearing for a period which they consider will give that person a sufficient opportunity to deal with the document.

Inspections

10.—(1) The tribunal may (subject to any necessary consent being obtained) inspect the house, premises or area which are the subject of the proceedings.

(2) An inspection may be made before, during or after the close of a hearing, as the tribunal may decide, and the tribunal shall give the persons appearing before them an opportunity to attend.

(3) Notice of an inspection shall be given as if it were notice of a hearing, but the requirements for notice may be dispensed with or relaxed with the consent of the persons appearing before the tribunal or if the tribunal are satisfied that such persons have received sufficient notice.

(4) Where an inspection is made after the close of a hearing, the tribunal shall, if they consider it expedient to do so on account of any matter arising from the inspection, reopen the hearing; and if the hearing is to be reopened regulation 5(2) shall apply as it applied to the original hearing, except that its requirements may be dispensed with or relaxed with the consent of the parties and persons mentioned in regulation 5(2) or if the tribunal are satisfied that such parties and persons have received sufficient notice.

(5) This regulation shall apply, so far as is reasonable and practicable, to any comparable house, premises or area to which the attention of the tribunal is directed.

Decisions

11.—(1) The decision of the tribunal shall be recorded in a document signed by the chairman of the tribunal (or, in the event of his absence or incapacity, by another member of the tribunal) which shall contain the reasons for the decision.

(2) The chairman (or, in the event of his absence or incapacity, another member of the tribunal) shall have power, by certificate under his hand, to correct any clerical mistakes in the document or any errors arising in it from an accidental slip or omission.

(3) A copy of the document and of any such correction shall be sent by the tribunal to each party and person making representations.

Attendance by member of Council on Tribunals

12. Nothing in these Regulations shall prevent a member of the Council on Tribunals in that capacity from attending any hearing or inspection or from being present during the tribunal's deliberations as to their decision; but a member of the Council on Tribunals may not take part in such deliberations.

Information required by tribunal

13.—(1) Where a tribunal require information to be given under paragraph 7 of Schedule 22 to the Housing Act 1980, the notice shall contain a statement to the effect that any person who fails without reasonable cause to comply with the notice is liable on summary conviction to a fine not exceeding level 3 on the standard scale.

(2) Paragraph (1) above shall not apply in the case of a notice addressed to an appropriate authority in relation to a Crown interest (*see*, as to the definition of "appropriate authority", s.94(11) of the Leasehold Reform, Housing and Urban Development Act 1993).

Notices

14. Where any notice or other document is required under these Regulations to be given or sent by the tribunal, it shall be sufficient compliance with these Regulations if the notice or other document is sent by pre-paid post or by facsimile transmission addressed to the person for whom it is intended at his usual or last known address or (if a person has appointed an agent to act on his behalf) to his agent at the address of the agent supplied to the tribunal.

Amendments

15.—(1) Regulation 2(2) of the Rent Assessment Committees (England and Wales) Regulations 1971 (S.I. 1971 No. 1065; relevant amending instruments are S.I. 1980 No. 1699 and S.I. 1987 No. 2178) is amended by the addition, at the end of the definition of "committee", of the words—

"or by section 75, 88 or 91 (jurisdiction of leasehold valuation tribunals) of the Leasehold Reform, Housing and Urban Development Act 1993".

(2) The Rent Assessment Committee (England and Wales) (Leasehold Valuation Tribunal) (Amendment) Regulations 1987 (S.I. 1987 No. 2178), and the Rent Assessment Committee (England and Wales) (Leasehold Valuation Tribunal) (Amendment) Regulations 1988 (S.I. 1988 No. 484), are each amended by the omission of the following—

(a) in article 2, the definition of "the 1981 Regulations";
(b) article 4; and
(c) the Schedule.

Revocation

16. The Rent Assessment Committee (England and Wales) (Leasehold Valuation Tribunal) Regulations 1981 (S.I. 1981 No. 271; relevant amending instruments are S.I. 1987 No. 2178 and S.I. 1988 No. 484) are hereby revoked.

Signed by authority of the Secretary of State

G. S. K. Young
Minister of State,
30th September 1993   Department of the Environment

John Redwood
30th September 1993   Secretary of State for Wales

PARTICULARS TO BE INCLUDED IN APPLICATIONS

1. The address of the property which is the subject of the application.

2. A statement of the purpose of the application, identifying the relevant statutory provision.

3. The name and address of the applicant.

4. The name, address and profession of the applicant's representative, if any.

5. Whether the applicant is the reversioner or other freeholder or landlord, nominated person, nominee purchaser, or tenant; or, if none of the former, the capacity in which the applicant makes the application.

6. The name and address of the respondent and whether the respondent is the reversioner or other freeholder or landlord, nominated person, nominee purchaser or tenant; or, if none of the former, the capacity of the respondent.

7. If the respondent is not the freeholder, the name and address of the freeholder.

8. The name and address of any intermediate landlord, which the applicant knows or could reasonably obtain.

9. The name and address of any person having a mortgage or other charge over an interest in the property held by the freeholder or other landlord, which the applicant knows or could reasonably obtain.

10. Copies of—

(a) any lease;

(b) any notice served by any party;

(c) any application to court or court order; and

(d) any other document

which are relevant to the application and which the applicant has or could reasonably obtain.

11. Any terms which have already been determined or agreed between the parties, including a copy of any draft conveyance or lease.

12. Any terms which are in dispute.

13. If an amount or price is in dispute, the amount or price which the applicant considers to be appropriate.

14. If the application is for determination of the amount of compensation payable under section 17 or 18 of the Leasehold Reform Act 1967, details of the circumstances under which the claim for compensation arises.

15. If the application includes an application for determination of the amount of a sub-tenant's share of compensation under section 21(2) of the Leasehold Reform Act 1967, the name and address of the sub-tenant, and a copy of any agreement for a sub-tenancy.

16. If the application is made under section 13 of the Landlord and Tenant Act 1987, the date on which the landlord acquired the property, and the terms of acquisition, including the sums paid.

17. If the application is made under the Landlord and Tenant Act 1987 or under the 1993 Act, a map or plan showing the property and any appurtenant property which is relevant to the application.

18. If the application is for apportionment of an amount under section 91(2)(e) of the 1993 Act, the circumstances by which the need for apportionment arises, and the apportionment which the applicant considers to be appropriate.

19. If the application relates to the grant of leases back to a former freeholder under Schedule 9 to the 1993 Act, the name and address of any secure tenant, tenant under housing association tenancy, or sub-tenant to whose interests the tribunal is required to have particular regard.

20. The date of the application.

PARTICULARS TO BE INCLUDED IN SCHEME APPLICATIONS

1. A statement of the purpose of the scheme application, identifying the relevant statutory provision.

2. The name and address of the applicant.

3. The name, address and profession of the applicant's representative, if any.

4. Where the applicant is not a natural person, whether the applicant is a representative body within the meaning of that expression in section 71(3) of the 1993 Act, or a relevant authority within the meaning of that expression in section 73(5) of that Act.

5. In the case of an application under section 70 of the 1993 Act, a copy of any advertisement or other document showing compliance with the requirements of subsection (4) of that section.

6. A description of the area for which the scheme is proposed, including identification of the area by a map or plan.

7. The proposed provisions of the scheme.

8. Where any modification is proposed relating to the extent of the area of an existing scheme, or approval is sought for variation of an existing scheme, a description of the proposed modification, including identification by a map or plan of the area to which the modification or variation relates, and of any part of an area proposed to be excluded or (as the case may be) included.

9. Where any modification to the provisions of the scheme is proposed by the applicant (as to which see section 70(7) of the 1993 Act), a description of the proposed modification, including where relevant identification by a map or plan of the area to which the modification relates.

10. In the case of an application under section 70 of the 1993 Act, a copy of any consent given by the Secretary of State under section 72(1) of that Act.

11. The date of the application.

APPENDIX 3

LANDLORD AND TENANT, ENGLAND AND WALES

THE LEASEHOLD REFORM (NOTICES) (AMENDMENT) REGULA-TIONS 1993

(S.I. 1993 No. 2409)

Made - - - - -	*30th September 1993*
Laid before Parliament - - -	*11th October 1993*
Coming into force - - -	*1st November 1993*

The Secretary of State for the Environment, as respects England, and the Secretary of State for Wales, as respects Wales, in exercise of the powers conferred by section 66 of the Landlord and Tenant Act 1954 (c. 56) as applied by section 22(5) of the Leasehold Reform Act 1967 (c. 88) and now vested in them (S.I. 1974 No. 1896) and of all other powers enabling them in that behalf, hereby make the following Regulations:—

Citation and commencement

1. These Regulations may be cited as the Leasehold Reform (Notices) (Amendment) Regulations 1993 and shall come into force on 1st November 1993.

Amendments

2.—(1) The Appendix to the Leasehold Reform (Notices) Regulations 1967 (S.I. 1967 No. 1768, to which there is an amendment not relevant to these Regulations) is amended in accordance with the following provisions of this regulation.

(2) In Form 1 (notice of leaseholder's claim)—

(a) for paragraphs 3 and 4 of the Schedule substitute—

"Note 7.   3. *Particulars of the tenancy of the house and premises sufficient to identify the instrument creating the tenancy and to show that the tenancy is and has at the material times been a long tenancy or treated as a long tenancy.*

Note 7A.   4. *Particulars of the tenancy of the house and premises sufficient to show that the tenancy is and has at the material times been a tenancy at a low rent or treated as a tenancy at a low rent.*";

(b) after paragraph 6 insert—

"Note 7B.   6A. *Additional particulars sufficient to show that the value of the house and premises does not exceed the applicable financial limit specified in section 1(1)(a)(i) or (ii), (5) or (6) of the Act. (These are not required where the right to have the freehold is claimed in reliance on any one or more of the provisions in section 1A or 1B of the Act.)*

Note 7C.   6B. *Additional particulars sufficient to show whether the house and premises are to be valued in accordance with section 9(1) or section 9(1A) of the Act. (These are not required where the right to have the freehold is claimed in reliance on any one or more of the provisions in section 1A or 1B of the Act.)*"; and

(c) at the end of Note 7 insert—

"In addition to the provisions of section 3 of the Act, section 174(a) of the Housing Act 1985 provides for certain tenancies granted pursuant to the right to buy to be treated as long tenancies. Section 1B of the Act also provides for certain tenancies terminable on death or marriage to be long tenancies for the limited right described in Note 7B.

7A. In addition to the provisions of section 4 of the Act, section 174(b) of the Housing Act 1985 provides for certain shared ownership leases granted pursuant to the right to buy to be treated as tenancies at a low rent. Section 1A(2) of the Act also provides for certain tenancies to be treated as tenancies at a low rent for the limited right described in Note 7B.

7B. A claimant who relies on any one or more of the provisions in section 1A or 1B of the Act has the right to have the freehold at a price determined in accordance with section 9(1C) of the Act, but not the right to have an extended lease. Section 1A(1) applies to a tenancy of a house and premises the value of which exceeds the applicable financial limit. (Sections 1A(2) and 1B are described in Notes 7A and 7 respectively.)

7C. If section 175 of the Housing Act 1985 (leases granted pursuant to the right to buy etc.) applies to a tenancy, the price payable for the house and premises is not determined in accordance with section 9(1).".

(3) In Form 3 (notice of leaseholder's claim under section 28(1)(b)(ii))—

(a) for paragraphs 3 and 4 of the Schedule substitute—

"Note 5.   3. *Particulars of the tenancy of the house and premises sufficient to identify the instrument creating the tenancy and to show that the tenancy is and has at the material times been a long tenancy, or treated as a long tenancy.*

Note 5A.   4. *Particulars of the tenancy of the house and premises sufficient to show that the tenancy is and has at the material times been a tenancy at a low rent, or treated as a tenancy at a low rent.*";

(b) after paragraph 6 of the Schedule insert—

"Note 5B.   6A. *Additional particulars sufficient to show that the value of the house and premises does not exceed the applicable financial limit specified in section 1(1)(a)(i) or (ii), (5) or (6) of the Act. (These are not required where the right to acquire the freehold is claimed in reliance on any one or more of the provisions in section 1A or 1B of the Act.)*

Note 5C.   6B. *Additional particulars sufficient to show whether the house and premises are to be valued in accordance with section 9(1) or section 9(1A) of the Act. (These are not required where the right to acquire the freehold is claimed in reliance on any one or more of the provisions in section 1A or 1B of the Act.)*"; and

(c) at the end of Note 5 insert—

"In addition to the provisions of section 3 of the Act, section 174(a) of the Housing Act 1985 provides for certain tenancies granted pursuant to the right to buy to be treated as long tenancies. Section 1B of the Act also provides for certain tenancies terminable on death or marriage to be long tenancies for the limited right described in Note 5B.

5A. In addition to the provisions of section 4 of the Act, section 174(b) of the Housing Act 1985 provides for certain shared ownership leases granted pursuant to the right to buy to be treated as tenancies at a low rent. Section 1A(2) of the Act also provides for certain tenancies to be treated as tenancies at a low rent for the limited right described in Note 5B.

5B. A claimant who relies on any one or more of the provisions in section 1A or 1B of the Act has the right to have the freehold at a price determined in accordance with section 9(1C) of the Act, but not the right to have an extended lease. Section 1A(1) applies to a tenancy of a house and premises the value of which exceeds the applicable financial limit. (Sections 1A(2) and 1B are described in Notes 5A and 5 respectively.)

5C. If section 175 of the Housing Act 1985 (leases granted pursuant to the right to buy etc.) applies to a tenancy, the price payable for the house and premises is not determined in accordance with section 9(1).".

Transitional

4. These Regulations shall not apply in a case where a notice under section 8 or 14 of the Leasehold Reform Act 1967 (c. 88) (tenant's notice of desire to have the freehold or an extended lease) was given before these Regulations come into force.

Signed by authority of the Secretary of State

G. S. K. Young
Minister of State,
30th September 1993   Department of the Environment

John Redwood
30th September 1993   Secretary of State for Wales

APPENDIX 4

HOUSING, ENGLAND AND WALES

THE HOUSING (TENANT MANAGEMENT ORGANISATIONS) REGULATIONS

The Secretary of State for the Environment, in respect of England, and the Secretary of State for Wales, in respect of Wales, in exercise of the powers conferred on them by sections 27(3), (7) and 27AB of the Housing Act 1985 (1985 c. 68; s.27(3) was amended by s.129(1) of the Leasehold Reform, Housing and Urban Development Act 1993 and ss.27(7) and 27AB were added by ss.129(3) and 132 of that Act, respectively) and of all other powers enabling them in that behalf, hereby make the following Regulations—

Citation, commencement and interpretation

1.—(1) These Regulations may be cited as the Housing (Tenant Management Organisations) Regulations 1994 and shall come into force on 1st April 1994.

(2) In these Regulations—

"approved person" means a member of a panel approved for the purpose of conducting feasibility studies under these Regulations by the Secretary of State;

"full feasibility study" means, in relation to a particular proposal for a management agreement, a study carried out by an approved person to determine—

(a) whether it is reasonable to proceed with the agreement; and

(b) if so, the terms on which the agreement should be entered into;

"initial feasibility study" means, in relation to a particular proposal for a management agreement, a study carried out by an approved person to determine whether it is reasonable to proceed with a full feasibility study;

"proposal notice" means a notice served by a tenant management organisation on a local housing authority which complies with regulation 2 (and, in relation to a particular proposal for a management agreement, references to a proposal notice refer to the notice containing that proposal).

(3) For the purpose of these Regulations, two management agreements overlap when and to the extent that they contain provisions which relate to the exercise of the same management functions in relation to the same houses and land; and "overlapping provisions" shall be construed accordingly.

Proposal notice

2.—(1) Subject to paragraph (2), a notice served by a tenant management organisation on a local housing authority complies with this regulation if it contains a proposal that the local housing authority should enter into a management agreement with the tenant management organisation in relation to such of the authority's houses, not being less than 10, as are identified in the notice and none of those houses are—

(a) outside of the organisation's area (as specified in its constitution in accordance with regulation 9);

(b) outside of the authority's area;

(c) identified in an existing notice which complies with this regulation and which has been served on the authority and not withdrawn; or

(d) already included in a management agreement with a tenant management organisation.

(2) A local housing authority may decline to accept a notice (a "further notice") served on them by a tenant management organisation proposing a management agreement if that further notice contains a similar proposal to the proposal contained in a previous proposal notice which has been withdrawn within the two year period ending on the date on which the further notice is received, and where an authority decline to accept a further notice in accordance with this paragraph that notice shall not be treated as complying with this regulation.

(3) For the purpose of paragraph (2), a further notice contains a similar proposal to a previous proposal notice if at least half of the houses identified in it were also identified in the previous proposal notice.

(4) Where an authority decline to accept a notice in accordance with paragraph (2) they shall notify the tenant management organisation concerned that they have not accepted the notice.

Local authority support following proposal notice

3.—(1) A tenant management organisation which has served a proposal notice on a local housing authority may, at any time after the service of the notice, request the authority to provide or finance the provision of such office accommodation and facilities, and such training, as the organisation reasonably requires at the time of the request for the purpose of pursuing the management agreement proposed in the notice.

(2) A request under paragraph (1) shall be in writing and shall specify the provision which the tenant management organisation considers it reasonably requires at that time for that purpose.

(3) On receipt of a request under paragraph (1), the authority shall—
  (a) determine the provision which they consider the organisation reasonably requires at that time for that purpose; and
  (b) notify the organisation of their determination within 28 days of receipt of the request.

(4) Subject to paragraph (8), the authority shall provide support in accordance with the determination notified under paragraph (3)(b).

(5) If a tenant management organisation is dissatisfied with an authority's determination under paragraph (3) it may, within 28 days of being notified of the determination, refer the request to an arbitrator.

(6) A tenant management organisation which refers a request to an arbitrator under paragraph (5) shall, at the same time, give notice of that referral to the local housing authority.

(7) Where a request is referred to an arbitrator under paragraph (5), the arbitrator shall—
  (a) determine the provision which he considers the organisation reasonably requires for the purpose of pursuing the proposal at the time of the request; and
  (b) notify the local authority and the organisation of his determination within 28 days of the request being referred to him.

(8) Where a request has been referred to an arbitrator under paragraph (5), the local housing authority shall provide support in accordance with the determination notified under paragraph (7)(b).

(9) Where a proposal notice is withdrawn any requirement on an authority to make provision under this regulation shall cease.

Procedure following proposal notice

4.—(1) A local housing authority shall, within three months of being served with a proposal notice, appoint an approved person to carry out an initial feasibility study.

(2) The approved person shall, within nine months of his appointment, send a report of the study to the Secretary of State, the authority and the

tenant management organisation, which shall include his conclusion as to whether or not it is reasonable to proceed with a full feasibility study.

(3) Where the approved person concludes that it is not reasonable to proceed with a full feasibility study, the proposal notice shall be deemed to have been withdrawn.

(4) Where the approved person concludes that it is reasonable to proceed with a full feasibility study, the authority shall, within one month of receiving the approved person's report—

  (a) notify the tenants of each house identified in the proposal notice of the proposal;

  (b) arrange for a ballot or poll to be carried out within that period of those tenants with a view to establishing their opinions about the proposal.

(5) If it appears from a ballot or poll carried out in accordance with paragraph (4)(b) that a majority of the tenants who, on that ballot or poll, express an opinion about the proposal are opposed to it, the authority shall—

  (a) notify the tenant management organisation accordingly; and

  (b) the proposal notice shall be deemed to have been withdrawn.

(6) If it does not appear as mentioned in paragraph (5), the authority shall, within three months of the ballot or poll being carried out, appoint an approved person to carry out a full feasibility study.

(7) The approved person shall, within two years of his appointment, send a report of the full feasibility study to the Secretary of State, the authority and the tenant management organisation, which shall include his conclusion as to whether it is reasonable to proceed with the proposed management agreement and, if so, on what terms the agreement should be entered into.

(8) The terms of a management agreement set out in a report submitted under paragraph (7) shall be in such form as may be approved by the Secretary of State for the purpose of this regulation.

(9) Where the approved person concludes that it is not reasonable to proceed with the proposed agreement, and this conclusion is not referred to an arbitrator under regulation 5, the proposal notice shall be deemed to have been withdrawn.

(10) Where the approved person concludes that it is reasonable to proceed with the proposed agreement, and neither this conclusion nor his conclusion as to the terms to be included in the agreement are referred to an arbitrator under regulation 5, the authority shall, within one month of receiving the approved person's report submitted under paragraph (7)—

  (a) serve a notice on the tenants of each house identified in the proposal notice—

      (i) summarising the terms of the proposed agreement set out in the approved person's report; and

      (ii) containing the address of a place within the locality of the identified houses at which a copy of that report, containing those terms, may be inspected;

  (b) arrange for a ballot or poll to be carried out within the period for complying with this paragraph of those tenants with a view to establishing their opinion about the proposal to enter into a management agreement on those terms.

(11) If it does not appear from a ballot or poll carried out in accordance with paragraph (10)(b) that a majority of the tenants are in favour of the proposal the proposal notice shall be deemed to have been withdrawn.

(12) Subject to paragraph (13), if it does appear as mentioned in paragraph (11), the authority shall, within three months of the ballot or poll, enter into a management agreement with the tenant management organisation on the terms made available for inspection pursuant to paragraph (10)(a)(ii), or on those terms subject to such modifications as may be agreed to by the tenant management organisation (provided that the agreement as

so modified is in such form as may be approved by the Secretary of State for the purpose of this regulation).

(13) An authority shall not enter into a management agreement under paragraph (12) until the tenant management organisation becomes registered if it has not already done so; and where the organisation is not registered on the expiry of the three month period mentioned in that paragraph the proposal notice shall be deemed to have been withdrawn.

Determination of disputes under regulation 4

5.—(1) Subject to paragraph (6), where an approved person submits a report under regulation 4(7), the local housing authority or the tenant management organisation may refer any of the conclusions set out in the report with which they disagree to an arbitrator.

(2) Where the approved person's conclusion as to whether it is reasonable to proceed with the proposed management agreement is referred to an arbitrator, the arbitrator shall decide whether it is reasonable to so proceed and notify the local housing authority and the tenant management organisation of his decision within 28 days of the matter being referred to him.

(3) Where the arbitrator decides that it is not reasonable to proceed with the agreement, the proposal notice shall be deemed to have been withdrawn.

(4) Where the arbitrator decides that it is reasonable to proceed with the agreement and this decision accords with the approved person's conclusion—

(a) if the approved person's conclusion as to the terms on which the agreement should be entered into has not been referred to the arbitrator, the authority shall comply with paragraphs (a) and (b) of regulation 4(10) within one month of being notified of the arbitrator's decision;

(b) if that conclusion has been so referred, the arbitrator shall comply with paragraph (7).

(5) Where the arbitrator decides that it is reasonable to proceed with the agreement and that decision does not accord with the approved person's conclusion, the matter shall be referred back to the approved person, who shall, within three months of the matter being referred back to him, resubmit his report under regulation 4(7), which report shall be in accordance with the decision of the arbitrator.

(6) Where a report is resubmitted in accordance with paragraph (5), the approved person's conclusion in the resubmitted report as to whether it is reasonable to proceed with the agreement shall not be referred to an arbitrator.

(7) Where the approved person's conclusion as to the terms on which the agreement should be entered into is referred to an arbitrator, the arbitrator shall, within 28 days of the matter being referred to him (or, where he has given notice under paragraph (2) of his decision that it is reasonable to proceed with the agreement and paragraph (4)(b) applies, within 28 days of that notice)—

(a) determine the terms on which the agreement should be entered into (which shall be in such form as may be approved by the Secretary of State for the purpose of this regulation); and

(b) notify the local housing authority and the tenant management organisation of his determination, setting out those terms in his notification.

(8) Where an authority is notified of a determination under paragraph (7) they shall comply with paragraphs (a) and (b) of regulation 4(10) within one month of being so notified; and, for the purpose of such compliance, the reference in paragraph (a) of that regulation to the terms of the agreement as

set out in the approved person's report and to that report shall be construed as a reference to the terms of the agreement as set out in the determination notified under paragraph (7) of this regulation and to that determination.

Withdrawal of proposal notice

6.—(1) A tenant management organisation may withdraw a proposal notice served by it at any time.

(2) Where a proposal notice is withdrawn no further action shall be taken in relation to that notice under these regulations.

Guidance by Secretary of State

7. Any person exercising functions under these Regulations shall act in accordance with any guidance given by the Secretary of State.

Management agreements with tenant management organisations and other management agreements

8.—(1) A management agreement (other than an agreement with a tenant management organisation) shall contain a provision (a "break clause") enabling the local authority to determine it to the extent that it overlaps with any subsequent management agreement entered into with a tenant management organisation.

(2) A break clause contained in a management agreement in accordance with paragraph (1) shall provide that the local authority may exercise it at different times in relation to different overlapping provisions and that it shall determine the provisions in relation to which it is exercised within three months of it being exercised.

(3) Where a tenant management organisation serves a proposal notice on a local housing authority, that authority shall not enter into a management agreement with any other person in relation to the houses identified in the notice unless—

(a) the notice is withdrawn; or

(b) any management agreement entered into in relation to the notice is terminated.

(4) This paragraph applies where a local housing authority enter into a management agreement with a tenant management organisation in pursuance of these regulations and at the time of entering into that agreement a previous agreement is in operation which overlaps with it (or which subsequently overlaps with it on the variation of either agreement) and which contains provisions which allow the authority to determine the overlapping provisions (whether by determining the whole of the previous agreement or otherwise).

(5) Subject to paragraph (6), where paragraph (4) applies the local housing authority shall determine the overlapping provisions in the previous agreement (whether by determining the whole of that agreement or otherwise) as soon as possible after the two agreements overlap.

(6) Where paragraph (4) applies, if the tenant management organisation agrees in writing, the local housing authority may postpone the determination of the overlapping provisions (or some of them, if the previous agreement allows the authority to determine the provisions at different times) until such time as may be agreed.

(7) Nothing in this regulation requires an agreement (or any part of an agreement) to be determined otherwise than in accordance with provisions contained in that agreement.

Tenant management organisation

9. For the purpose of the definition of "tenant management organisation" in section 27AB(8) of the Housing Act 1985, the conditions which a body must satisfy to be a tenant management organisation are that its constitution—

(a) specifies an area as being the area of the organisation in relation to which it may serve a proposal notice;

(b) conforms to a model constitution approved by the Secretary of State for the purpose of this regulation.

Local housing authority participation in tenant management organisations

10. A local housing authority may, if invited to do so by the organisation concerned, nominate one or more persons to be directors or other officers of any tenant management organisation with whom the authority have entered into, or propose to enter into, a management agreement.

Transitional provisions

11.—(1) This regulation applies where a study or a ballot or poll has been carried out or is being carried out immediately before the date on which these Regulations come into force (the "commencement date") in anticipation of a local housing authority entering into a management agreement with a tenant management organisation in relation to houses within the area of the authority and the organisation.

(2) Where this regulation applies the tenant management organisation shall be treated as having served a proposal notice on the local housing authority in relation to those houses.

(3) Where a study has been carried out or is being carried out immediately before the commencement date, which, if it had been carried out or were being carried out by an approved person for the purpose of regulation 4(2) would comply (or substantially comply) with the requirement in that regulation to carry out an initial feasibility study (a "pre commencement initial feasibility study"), and none of the following paragraphs of this regulation apply, the study shall be treated, on and after that date, as having been carried out or being carried out by an approved person for the purpose of complying with that requirement and—

(a) if the study has been completed before that date, it shall be treated as having been submitted under regulation 4(2) on the commencement date;

(b) if the study has not been completed before that date, it shall be submitted under that regulation within nine months of that date.

(4) Where a ballot or poll has been carried out or is being carried out immediately before the commencement date following a pre commencement initial feasibility study, which, if it had been carried out or were being carried out for the purpose of regulation 4(4) would comply (or substantially comply) with the requirement in that regulation to carry out a ballot or poll, and none of the following paragraphs of this regulation apply, the ballot or poll shall be treated, on and after that date, as having been carried out or being carried out for the purpose of complying with that requirement (the preceding paragraphs of regulation 4 having been complied with) and—

(a) if the ballot or poll has been completed before that date, it shall be treated as having been completed on the commencement date for the purpose of regulation 4;

(b) if the ballot or poll has not been completed before that date, it shall be completed within one month of that date.

(5) Where a study has been carried out or is being carried out immediately before the commencement date, which, if it had been carried out or were being carried out by an approved person for the purpose of regulation 4(7) would comply (or substantially comply) with the requirement in that regulation to carry out a full feasibility study (a "pre commencement full

feasibility study"), and none of the following paragraphs of this regulation apply, the study shall be treated, on and after that date, as having been carried out or being carried out by an approved person for the purpose of complying with that requirement (the preceding paragraphs of regulation 4 having been complied with) and—

  (a) if the study has been completed before that date, it shall be treated as having been submitted under regulation 4(7) on the commencement date;

  (b) if the study has not been completed before that date, it shall be submitted under that regulation within two years of that date.

(6) Where a ballot or poll has been carried out or is being carried out immediately before the commencement date following a pre commencement full feasibility study, which, if it had been carried out or were being carried out for the purpose of regulation 4(10) would comply (or substantially comply) with the requirement in that regulation to carry out a ballot or poll, the ballot or poll shall be treated, on and after that date, as having been carried out or being carried out for the purpose of complying with that requirement (the preceding paragraphs of regulation 4 having been complied with) and—

  (a) if the ballot or poll has been completed before that date, it shall be treated as having been completed on the commencement date for the purpose of regulation 4;

  (b) if the ballot or poll has not been completed before that date, it shall be completed within one month of that date.

Secretary of State for the Environment
Secretary of State for Wales

APPENDIX 5

URBAN REGENERATION AGENCY
DRAFT GUIDANCE (DOE/1993)

1. The statutory objects of the Agency are set out in section 159 of the Leasehold Reform, Housing and Urban Development Act 1993 ("the Act"). Section 167 requires the Agency to have regard to guidance given by the Secretary of State in deciding:
  (a) which land is suitable for regeneration or development; and
  (b) which of its functions it is to exercise for securing the regeneration or development of any particular land and how it is to exercise those functions.
This document constitutes such guidance.

Objective

2. In pursuing its statutory objects the Agency should focus on:
  the promotion of the regeneration of areas of need through the reclamation, development or redevelopment of land and buildings.
Areas of need are defined in paragraphs 8 to 9 below.

3. The Agency should seek to achieve this objective in a manner which provides the best value for the taxpayer's money and which satisfies the requirements of financial propriety and accountability to Parliament.

4. The Agency, whilst concentrating on the regeneration and development of land, should seek to operate within a broader regeneration strategy which aims to tackle the problems of an area in the round. It should therefore ensure that its programmes address the need for land for a variety of purposes, including housing, industrial and commercial premises, the attraction of inward investment, infrastructure, leisure, recreation and green space. The Act states that its objects are to be achieved in particular by the following means:
  (a) by securing that land and buildings are brought into effective use;
  (b) by developing, or encouraging the development of, existing and new industry and commerce;
  (c) by creating an attractive and safe environment;
  (d) by facilitating the provision of housing and providing, or facilitating the provision of social and recreational facilities.
The Agency should therefore develop close links with the private sector, local authorities, the voluntary sector, including amenity groups, and bodies responsible for other aspects of regeneration.

The culture of the Agency

5. The Agency's preferred mode of operation should be to act wherever possible as an enabling body, achieving its objective by helping others, particularly the private sector, to regenerate land and buildings. To that end it may assemble, plan and service sites and provide the vision, energy and, where necessary, financial support which will encourage others to proceed with projects which meet its objectives. Where such facilitation mechanisms are insufficient in themselves to produce the desired result, the Agency may as a last resort carry out direct development, having first satisfied itself that to do so will not displace or disadvantage private sector development or investment in the area and that it cannot achieve its aim through other means. Whilst the Agency should always have regard to value for money, any assets created by direct development should generally be sold at the earliest opportunity.

6. The Agency should develop particularly close links with local authorities and should as far as possible discuss its plans with them. It must always operate within the planning framework and should involve local people as much as possible in its activities. How the Agency achieves this will be for it to decide.

7. The Agency must be seen to be fair and financially prudent in all that it undertakes. It should abide by the six principles of public service set out in the Citizen's Charter.

Areas of need

8. In deciding which land is suitable for regeneration the Agency should pay particular attention to the following types of need:

(a) Areas of urban deprivation or areas of localised high unemployment where bringing vacant, unused and derelict land into use can contribute significantly to regeneration;

(b) Derelict land in both urban and rural areas which should be reclaimed for health and safety reasons or because it is blighting the area.

9. The Agency should take account of Government initiatives such as the Black Country Limestone programme. It should focus its activities on the Urban Priority and Assisted Areas, but it should also take account of Government priorities and commitments outside the areas of need such as the present work of DLG in rural areas, including the National Forest; English Estates' programmes outside Assisted Areas, such as its work in Chatham; and the East Thames Corridor. The precise balance between these priorities and between rural and urban land reclamation will be for the Agency to suggest to the Department and to discuss during the formulation of its corporate plan.

The Rural Development Commission

10. The URA should avoid duplicating the activities of the Rural Development Commission, particularly in the RDC's priority areas. In areas such as the coalfields, where both bodies have been given a specific remit to provide assistance, close liaison will be necessary. The Agency can also continue to act as an agent for the RDC.

Urban Development Corporations

11. The Agency should not normally undertake work within an Urban Development Area. It should, however, take account of the activities of the Urban Development Corporations where this is appropriate.

The selection of projects

12. As soon as possible after the issue of this guidance the Agency should publish its own guide to the private sector, local authorities and other bodies describing how it intends to formulate its programmes. This should be designed to encourage the early development of schemes which meet its priorities.

13. The scope and detail of the guide will be a matter for the Agency but they should probably include an indication of the geographical areas and types of project which it is most interested in promoting and an outline of the appraisal method and criteria. It is for the Agency to decide how to invite bids for its help.

14. As well as reacting to bids the Agency should develop a proactive approach to the regeneration of strategic sites. Where it has identified projects that it would like to see undertaken or areas that should be regenerated, it should invite public, private and voluntary organisations to submit competitive preliminary proposals for their involvement in these schemes.

Performance Indicators

15. The Agency should have clear outputs in mind for all its schemes and output measurement should be built into project appraisal and management. It should set its own targets in consultation with the department, where they will be approved and monitored through the corporate plan process.

Land acquisition and disposal

16. The Agency should acquire land only where this is necessary to achieve the objectives in its corporate plan. It should have a clear purpose for all land that it intends to acquire and unless there are exceptional circumstances it should have identified an exit route before it takes possession. All purchases should be at no more than the market price. The Agency should work by agreement wherever possible and only use its CPO powers where absolutely necessary.

17. Although the Agency may well be operating in a rising market for land it needs to take full account of the cost and risk of building up large holdings for which there is no immediately foreseeable use. It should therefore aim to dispose of its complete interest in land at the earliest date consistent with the achievement of its objectives and value for money. Asset sales should be at best market price unless the consent of the Department has been obtained.

Environmental Implications

18. The Agency should always take account of the environmental implications of its activities. It should carry out environmental assessments of major projects. Its projects and in particular its financial assistance should always reflect the polluter pays principle. It should not therefore use public resources to clear up contamination if the polluter can be identified and has the resources to undertake appropriate remedial action. Likewise the terms on which the Agency acquires land from, or enters into joint ventures with, owners of polluted land should reflect the polluter pays principle.

19. The Agency should be alert to heritage and conservation issues, liaising where necessary with bodies involved in this work.

Public Rights of Way

20. The Agency should take into account the effects of its activities on public access to land and buildings. It should request extinguishment of a public right of way across land which it has acquired only when it is convinced that this is necessary. It should endeavour to provide satisfactory replacement rights of way wherever possible.

When designation may be necessary

21. Areas where the URA will have development control powers and/or some highway powers will be designated by the Secretary of State, either at the request of the Agency or on his own initiative. The boundaries of these areas will be published and all major landowners within them informed before the final boundary is fixed in an order placed before Parliament. This would be a major step for the area concerned and would therefore require proper prior consultation.

22. The URA should seek designation only where the dereliction and underuse is so widespread that no other method is appropriate or where other approaches have failed.

23. Where the URA does take over development control and/or highway powers in a designated area it should operate within the framework of existing good practice and guidance. When determining planning applications submitted to it within a designated area, or deeming itself planning permission for its own developments, the Agency is statutorily required to have regard to the provisions of the development plan and any other material considerations. The Agency should observe existing local authority targets for handling planning applications and should make all planning meetings open to the public, subject to the constraints of commercial confidentiality. Where the Agency intends to require a highway authority to adopt a road within a designated area it should first ensure that the road meets the authority's standards.

24. Further guidance on the operation of the URA within designated areas will be issued if and when the first designation order is in preparation.

Monitoring and appraisal by the Department

25. Ministers will answer to Parliament for the general policy and direction of the URA. The management of individual projects will be for the Agency. Ministers' chief mechanism for assuring themselves on matters of policy and monitoring more routine functions will be the annual corporate planning process.

26. The Agency should maintain close contact with the Department at all times, giving as much early warning as possible of major issues of policy or of any matters that will require consent. The Department should be alerted to all novel or contentious issues as soon as they arise. The Department will occasionally need to seek information from the Agency to answer Parliamentary Questions, Ministerial correspondence etc.

27. The Agency's formal contact with the Department will be with the sponsor division. It should, however, also maintain close contact with the Department's regional offices and should discuss with them the local implications of its corporate plan before submitting it to the Department. DOE regional offices will coordinate the views of other Departments' regional offices on the plan.

APPENDIX 6

HOUSING, ENGLAND AND WALES
LANDLORD AND TENANT, ENGLAND AND WALES
URBAN DEVELOPMENT

THE LEASEHOLD REFORM, HOUSING AND URBAN DEVELOPMENT ACT 1993 (COMMENCEMENT AND TRANSITIONAL PROVISIONS NO. 1) ORDER 1993

(S.I. 1993 No. 2134 (C. 41))

Made -   -   -   -   -   -   *1st September 1993*

The Secretary of State, in exercise of the powers conferred on him by section 188(2) and (3) of the Leasehold Reform, Housing and Urban Development Act 1993 (c. 28) and all other powers enabling him in that behalf, hereby makes the following Order—

Citation

1. This Order may be cited as the Leasehold Reform, Housing and Urban Development Act 1993 (Commencement and Transitional Provisions No. 1) Order 1993.

Interpretation

2. In this Order—
"the first commencement date" means the 2nd September 1993;
"the second commencement date" means the 11th October 1993;
"the third commencement date" means the 1st November 1993;
"the 1967 Act" means the Leasehold Reform Act 1967 (c. 88);
"the 1985 Act" means the Housing Act 1985 (c. 68);
"the 1987 Act" means the Landlord and Tenant Act 1987 (c. 31); and
"the 1993 Act" means the Leasehold Reform, Housing and Urban Development Act 1993 and references to sections and Schedules without more are references to sections of and Schedules to that Act.

Commencement

3. The following provisions of the 1993 Act shall come into force on the first commencement date—
section 26(9),
so much of sections 75, 88, 91, 99 and 108 as confers on the Secretary of State a power to make orders, regulations or declarations,
section 98,
section 100,
section 187(1) in so far as it relates to paragraphs 4, 7 and 27 of Schedule 21, and
section 187(2) in so far as it relates to the repeals in Schedule 22 of section 41(1) of the Housing Act 1988 (c. 50) and paragraph 51 in Schedule 11 to the Local Government and Housing Act 1989 (c. 42).

4. The following provisions of the 1993 Act shall come into force on the second commencement date—
(a) section 123,
sections 128 and 129,
section 131,
section 174,

section 176,
section 179,
section 180 except in so far as it relates to the insertion of section 165A(2) in the Local Government, Planning and Land Act (1980) (c. 65),
section 182,
section 187(1) in so far as it relates to paragraph 10 of Schedule 21,
section 187(2) in so far as it relates to the repeals in Schedule 22 in the Local Government, Planning and Land Act 1980 and in section 69(2) of the Housing Act 1988; and

(b) subject to the transitional provisions and savings in Schedule 1 to this Order,—
sections 104 to 107,
section 108 in so far as it is not in force,
sections 109 to 120,
sections 124 and 125,
section 130,
sections 133 and 134,
section 178,
section 187(1) in so far as it relates to paragraphs 11 to 25 of Schedule 21,
section 187(2) in so far as it relates to the repeals in Schedule 22 specified in Schedule 2 to this Order, and
Schedule 16.

5. The following provisions of the 1993 Act shall come into force on the third commencement date—
(a) sections 1 to 25,
section 26 in so far as it is not in force,
sections 27 to 62,
sections 63 to 66,
sections 69 to 74,
section 75 in so far as it is not in force,
sections 76 to 84,
section 87,
section 88 in so far as it is not in force,
sections 89 and 90,
section 91 in so far as it is not in force,
sections 92 to 97,
section 99 in so far as it is not in force,
sections 101 to 103,
section 187(1) in so far as it relates to paragraphs 1, 9, 26 and 30 of Schedule 21,
section 187(2) in so far as it relates to the repeals in Schedule 22 in the Housing Act 1980 (c. 51) and the Housing (Consequential Provisions) Act 1985 (c. 71),
Schedules 1 to 15; and

(b) subject to the transitional provisions and savings in Schedule 1 to this Order,—
sections 67 and 68,
sections 85 and 86,
section 187(1) in so far as it relates to paragraph 5 of Schedule 21, and
section 187(2) in so far as it relates to the repeals in Schedule 22 in the 1987 Act.

Signed by authority of
the Secretary of State

David Curry
Minister of State,
1st September 1993 Department of the Environment

SCHEDULE 1

TRANSITIONAL PROVISIONS AND SAVINGS

1. The amendments made by sections 67 and 68 (amendments to the 1967 Act) do not have effect in a case where the right to acquire the freehold of a house and premises arises other than by virtue of any one or more of the provisions of sections 1A and 1B of the 1967 Act in relation to a lease created after the third commencement date pursuant to a contract entered into before that date.

2. The amendments made by—
section 85 (amendments to Part III of the 1987 Act), and
section 187(2) in so far as it relates to the repeals in Schedule 22 in the 1987 Act
do not have effect in a case where a notice under section 27 of the 1987 Act (tenants' preliminary notice) was served before the third commencement date.

3. The amendment made by section 86 (amendment to Part IV of the 1987 Act) does not have effect in a case where an application under section 35(1) of the 1987 Act was made before the third commencement date.

4.—(1) The amendments made by—
sections 104 and 105,
sections 107 to 120,
section 187(1) in so far as it relates to paragraphs 11 to 25 of Schedule 21, and
section 187(2) in so far as it relates to the repeals in the 1985 Act, the Housing and Planning Act 1986 (c. 63) and in the Local Government and Housing Act 1989 (c. 42) specified in Schedule 2 to this Order
(amendments to Part V of the 1985 Act: the right to buy) do not have effect—
  (a) in a case where a notice under section 122 of the 1985 Act (tenant's notice claiming to exercise the right to buy) is served before the second commencement date; and
  (b) in relation to the operation of Part V of the 1985 Act as applied by the Local Government Reorganisation (Preservation of Right to Buy) Order 1986 (S.I. 1986 No. 2092).

(2) For the purpose of paragraph (1)(a), no account shall be taken of any steps taken under section 177 of the 1985 Act (errors and omissions in notices).

(3) The amendments made by section 106 (exceptions to the right to buy) do not have effect in relation to the operation of Part V of the 1985 Act as applied by the Order mentioned in paragraph (1)(b).

5. The amendments made by—
sections 124 and 125 to Part III of the Housing Act 1988 (c. 50) (housing action trusts), and
section 187(2) in so far as it relates to the repeal in the Housing Act 1988 specified in Schedule 2 to this Order
do not have effect in relation to a proposed disposal in a case where a notice under section 84(2) of that Act was served before the second commencement date.

6. The substitution, by section 130, of section 27A of the 1985 Act shall have effect, in a case where a local housing authority who propose to enter into a management agreement have taken steps before the second commencement date to comply with the requirements of section 27A(1) and (2) of the 1985 Act in the form in which it was in force immediately before the second commencement date, so as to enable the authority to take into account the steps already taken when determining what arrangements they consider appropriate for the purpose of section 27A(1) as substituted.

7. The substitutions made by sections 133 and 134 (priority of charges securing repayment of discount) do not have effect in relation to the order of priority between a charge taking effect by virtue of section 36 of the 1985 Act or paragraph 2 of Schedule 2 to the Housing Associations Act 1985 (c. 69) (as the case may be) and any advance made before the second commencement date.

8. The substitution, by section 178, of section 157 of the Local Government, Planning and Land Act 1980 (c. 65) does not have effect in a case where a notice under subsection (1) of that section was served before the second commencement date.

9.—(1) The amendment made by section 187(1) in so far as it relates to paragraph 5 of Schedule 21 (amendment to Part I of the Land Compensation Act 1973 (c. 26) does not have effect in a case where the relevant date is before the third commencement date.

(2) In sub-paragraph (1) "relevant date" has the same meaning as in section 2 of the Land Compensation Act 1973.

10. Section 187(2) in so far as it relates to the repeals of sections 142 and 153B(1)(c) of the 1985 Act and in paragraphs 16B(4) and 16C(4) of Schedule 16 to that Act does not have effect in relation to provisions in Part V of the 1985 Act relating to the preserved right to buy in a case where a person has the preserved right to buy (as defined in section 171A of that Act) before the second commencement date.

SCHEDULE 2

REPEALS

Repeals coming into force on the second commencement date subject to the transitional provisions and savings in Schedule 1

Chapter	Short title	Extent of repeal
1985 c.68	The Housing Act 1985	Section 124(3). Section 128(6). Sections 132 to 135. In section 137, in sub-section (1), the words "or the right to a mortgage" and, in sub-section (2), paragraph (b). In section 138(1), the words "and to the amount to be left outstanding or advanced on the security of the dwelling-house". Section 139(3). In section 140(5), the words "and to the amount to be left outstanding or advanced on the security of the dwelling-house". Section 142. In section 153A(1), paragraphs (c) and (d). In section 153B(1), paragraph (c). Section 164(6). Section 166(6). In section 169(3), paragraph (b) and the word "and" immediately preceding that paragraph. In section 171C(2), paragraph (b). In section 171H, in subsection (1), the words "or the right to a mortgage" and, in subsection (2), paragraph (b). In section 177, in subsection (2)(b) the words "or the Corporation" and in sub-section (3), the entries relating to section 135 and paragraph 5 of Schedule 9. In section 180, the words "the Corporation" and "Corporation". In section 181(1), the words "and paragraph 11 of Schedule 8". In section 182(1), the words "or the right to a mortgage". In section 187, the definition of "total share". In section 188, the entries beginning "additional share and additional contribution", "effective discount", "full mortgage", "initial share and initial contribution", "prescribed percentage", "right to be granted a shared ownership lease", "right to further advances", "right to a mortgage" and "total share". In Schedule 6, in paragraphs 16B(4) and 16C(4), paragraph (c) and the word "and" immediately preceding that paragraph. Schedules 7 to 9.
1986 c.63	The Housing and Planning Act 1986	In Schedule 5, paragraph 5.

Chapter	Short title	Extent of repeal
1988 c.50	The Housing Act 1988	In section 79(2)(b), the words "in accordance with section 84 below".
1989 c.42	The Local Government and Housing Act 1989	Section 164.

INDEX